MAR CARIBE

OCÉANO ATLÁNTICO

Maracaibo
Barranquilla
Caracas
PANAMÁ
GUYANA
VENEZUELA
Georgetown
Medellín
Paramaribo
Panamá
Río Orinoco
Cayena
Bogotá
SURINAME
GUYANA FRANCESA
Cali
COLOMBIA
Quito
Ecuador
ECUADOR
Río Amazonas
Belém
Guayaquil
Manaus
PERÚ
BRASIL
Recife
Cuzco
Lima
La Paz
Brasília
Arequipa
BOLIVIA
Sucre
Antofagasta
PARAGUAY
Río de Janeiro
Trópico de Capricornio
CHILE
San Miguel de Tucumán
Asunción
São Paulo
OCÉANO PACÍFICO
La Serena
Córdoba
Rosario
OCÉANO ATLÁNTICO
Valparaíso
URUGUAY
Santiago
ARGENTINA
Montevideo
Concepción
Buenos Aires
Río de la Plata
Bahía Blanca
Puerto Montt
Bariloche
Chiloé
N

Islas Malvinas

AMÉRICA DEL SUR

Estrecho de Magallanes

Punta Arenas
Tierra del Fuego

0	1500 kilómetros
0	1000 millas

Cabo de Hornos

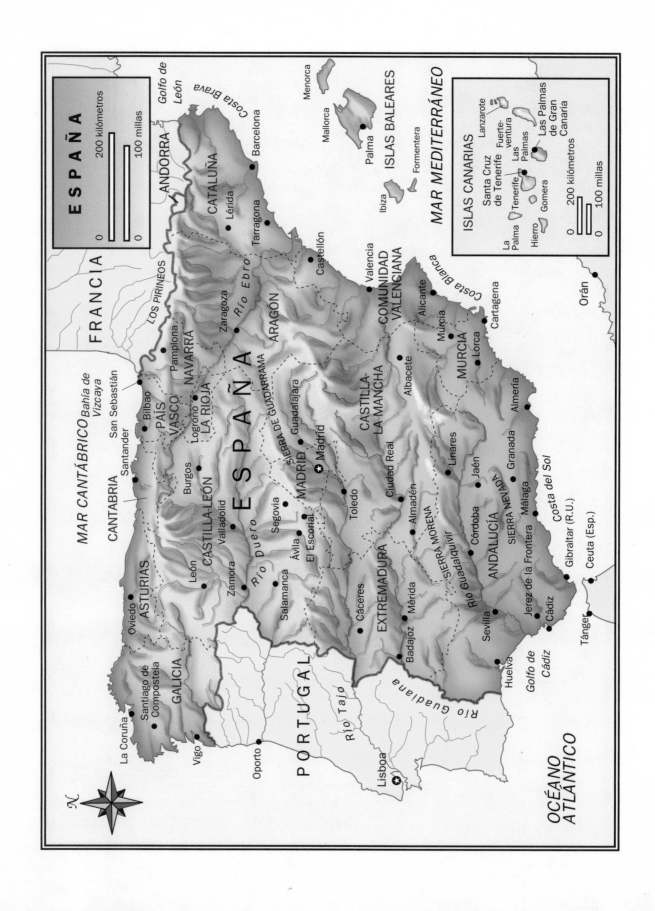

¿Qué tal?

AN INTRODUCTORY COURSE

Sixth Edition

Thalia Dorwick

Ana María Pérez-Gironés
Wesleyan University

Marty Knorre

William R. Glass

Hildebrando Villarreal
California State University, Los Angeles

Contributing Writers:

Manuel Cortés-Castañeda
Eastern Kentucky University

Hope Doyle D'Ambrosio
American University

Becky S. Jaimes
Austin Community College

Talía Loaiza
Austin Community College

McGraw
Hill

Boston   Burr Ridge, IL   Dubuque, IA   Madison, WI   New York   San Francisco   St. Louis
Bangkok   Bogotá   Caracas   Kuala Lumpur   Lisbon   London   Madrid   Mexico City
Milan   Montreal   New Delhi   Santiago   Seoul   Singapore   Sydney   Taipei   Toronto

McGraw-Hill Higher Education

A Division of The **McGraw-Hill** Companies

This is an  book.

¿Qué tal?
An Introductory Course

Published by McGraw-Hill, an imprint of The McGraw-Hill Companies, Inc., 1221 Avenue of the Americas, New York, NY 10020. Copyright © 2003, 1999, 1995, 1991, 1987, 1983 by The McGraw-Hill Companies, Inc. All rights reserved. No part of this publication may be reproduced or distributed in any form or by any means, or stored in a database or retrieval system, without the prior written consent of The McGraw-Hill Companies, Inc., including, but not limited to, in any network or other electronic storage or transmission, or broadcast for distance learning.

This book is printed on acid-free paper.

4 5 6 7 8 9 0 VNH VNH 0 9 8 7 6 5 4 3

ISBN 0-07-249641-X (Student's Edition)
ISBN 0-07-253517-2 (Instructor's Edition)

Vice President and Editor-in-chief: *Thalia Dorwick*
Publisher: *William R. Glass*
Sponsoring editor: *Christa Harris*
Director of development: *Scott Tinetti*
Executive marketing manager: *Nick Agnew*
Senior production editor: *David M. Staloch*
Senior production supervisor: *Richard DeVitto*
Senior supplements producer: *Louis Swaim*
Interior and cover designer: *Violeta Díaz*
Photo researcher: *Alexandra Ambrose*
Art editor: *Robin Mouat*
Editorial Assistant: *Jennifer Chow*
Compositor: *TechBooks*
Typeface: *10/12 Palatino*
Printer and binder: *Von Hoffmann Press*

Cover image: *Detail from a mosaic mural at the San Antonio Convention Center by Carlos Mérida, commissioned for the 1967 Hemisfair. Copyright © Estate of Carlos Mérida/SOMAAP, México/VAGA, New York, NY. Photograph by David Walden, San Antonio, TX.*

Because this page cannot accommodate all the copyright notices, credits are listed after the index and constitute an extension of the copyright page.

LIBRARY OF CONGRESS CATALOGING-IN-PUBLICATION DATA

¿Qué tal? An Introductory Course / Thalia Dorwick . . . [et al.]—6th ed.
    p. cm
Includes index.
English and Spanish.
Includes index.
ISBN 0-07-249641-X
1. Spanish language—Textbooks for foreign speakers—English. I. Dorwick, Thalia , 1944–

PC4129.E5 Q4 2002
468.2'421—dc21

2002016696

http://www.mhhe.com

Contents

Contents

"... to help students develop proficiency in the four language skills essential to truly communicative language learning..."

from the preface to *¿Qué tal?*, first edition, 1983

Welcome to the sixth edition of *¿Qué tal? An Introductory Course.* It has been twenty years since the publication of the first edition, and the coauthors are grateful to the instructors and students who have responded so positively to the goals and approach of *¿Qué tal?*

In those twenty years, much has changed and much has remained constant in *¿Qué tal? ¿Qué tal?* has remained true to the goals of the first edition, as cited above. The approach, however, has evolved and kept pace with technological advances and our increasing knowledge of how languages are learned. The ancillary package for the first edition of *¿Qué tal?* was excellent for its time but seems small in comparison to the plethora of materials available to instructors and students today. Particularly noteworthy are the wide variety of new technologies that enhance language learning in ways not yet dreamed of twenty years ago.

In addition to these new technologies, instructors will find in the sixth edition those features that they have come to know and trust over the years. These features include:

- the popular, four-part chapter structure that facilitates lesson planning and organization
- grammar, vocabulary, and culture that work together as interactive units
- an abundance of practice materials, ranging from form-focused to communicative
- an emphasis on the meaningful use of Spanish
- a positive portrayal of Hispanic cultures around the world
- supplementary materials carefully coordinated with the core text and that actually 'work' with it

Here are some of the exciting, new features of the sixth edition:

- new text-integrated **En contexto** video segments that focus on high-frequency functional situations such as purchasing train tickets and visiting a pharmacy
- a new **Cultura en contexto** cultural feature that highlights a cultural topic illustrated in the text-integrated video segments
- **Notas culturales** and **En los Estados Unidos y el Canadá** cultural readings have been thoroughly revised and updated to reflect current student interests
- new chapter-culminating communicative activities (**A conversar**) that underscore the four-skills development featured in **Paso 4: Un paso más**
- a completely revised interactive Student CD-ROM that provides outstanding practice and review of vocabulary and grammar, interactive listening and speaking practice, and cultural video and activities.
- a new self-scoring, self-grading Electronic Workbook/ Laboratory Manual that offers students and instructors an enhanced, interactive alternative to the traditional Workbook/Laboratory Manual
- a new Online Learning Center that offers a wide variety of practice and study materials, including flashcards, self-quizzes, Internet cultural activities, crossword puzzles, and much more

Please turn the page for a fully illustrated Guided Tour of the sixth edition of *¿Qué tal?*

The sixth edition of *¿Qué tal?* features a uniquely clear and user-friendly organization. Each of its eighteen regular chapters is divided into four **pasos**, highlighted with color tabs for easy reference, with a cultural feature in the middle. Thus, each regular chapter has the following structure:

> **Paso 1: Vocabulario**
> **Paso 2: Gramática**
> **Enfoque cultural**
> **Paso 3: Gramática**
> **Paso 4: Un paso más**

Paso 1: Vocabulario

This section presents and practices the chapter's thematic vocabulary. The lexical lists in these sections are read on the Listening Comprehension Audio CD and are signaled by a headphone icon. Each new lexical list is followed by a **Conversación** section that practices the new vocabulary in context.

Pasos 2 and 3: Gramática

These sections present one to two grammar points each. Each grammar point is introduced by a minidialogue, a cartoon or drawing, realia, or a brief reading that presents the grammar topic in context. Grammar explanations, in English, appear in the left-hand column of the two-column design; paradigms and sample sentences appear in the right-hand column. Each grammar presentation is followed by a series of contextualized exercises and activities that progress from more controlled (**Práctica**) to more open-ended (**Conversación**).

Paso 4: Un paso más

This section integrates the vocabulary and grammar from the first three **pasos** in a rich and stimulating selection of skill-building activities: **Videoteca: En contexto** (video comprehension and discussion questions); **A leer** (readings and pre-reading strategies); **A escribir** (brief writing assignments based on the chapter theme); and **A conversar** (chapter-culminating communicative activities). The **A leer** and **A escribir** sections are found in odd-numbered chapters; **A conversar** activities are found in even-numbered chapters.

Enfoque cultural

The cultures of the Spanish-speaking world are an integral part of every section of *¿Qué tal?*, but they take central stage in the **Enfoque cultural** section of each chapter. Located between **Pasos 2** and **3**, **Enfoque cultural** brings to life the richness and variety of Spanish-speaking cultures in a single, at-a-glance presentation. Each **Enfoque cultural** section focuses on a distinct country or region and includes interesting facts about people, places, and events in that geographical area. A video icon refers to corresponding cultural footage on the Video Program.

Also featured on this page is a unique Internet icon, which directs students to visit the *¿Qué tal?* website. Among other things, the *¿Qué tal?* website contains links to authentic web pages from the Spanish-speaking world that provide more information about the people, places, and events featured in the **Enfoque cultural** sections.

Additional features

- **Un poco de todo** activities, found in **Paso 3: Gramática**, combine and review grammar presented in the chapter as well as important grammar from previous chapters. Major topics that are continuously spiraled in this section include **ser** and **estar**, preterite and imperfect, gender and gender agreement, and indicative and subjunctive.

- **Nota cultural** features highlight an aspect of Hispanic cultures throughout the world.

- **En los Estados Unidos y el Canadá** are brief sections that focus on U.S. and Canadian Hispanics and institutions. Key words and phrases are highlighted in these sections in order to facilitate comprehension.

- **Nota comunicativa** sections provide additional information about communication in Spanish.

- **Vocabulario útil** boxes give additional vocabulary that may be necessary to work through a chapter's activities.

- **Cultura en contexto** sidebars in the **Videoteca: En contexto** section highlight a cultural point illustrated in the **En contexto** video segment.

For more information on these and other features of *¿Qué tal?*, please visit the text-specific website at **www.mhhe.com/quetal**.

The Video

The Video Program that accompanies the sixth edition of *¿Qué tal?* offers a variety of video materials for use both in and out of class. There are three components to the Video Program, which comprise almost three hours of video material:

- **Minidramas** situational episodes: The **Minidramas**, linked by theme to each chapter of the textbook, follow the story of three different groups of people. The minidramas were filmed on location in Mexico, Spain, and Ecuador.

- **En contexto** functional vignettes: These vignettes, integrated directly into the textbook in **Paso 4** of every chapter, illustrate high-frequency functional language exchanges such as purchasing train tickets, bargaining for handcrafted items, shopping for produce, and visiting a post office. The **En contexto** vignettes were filmed on location in Peru, Mexico, and Costa Rica.

- **Enfoque cultural** segments: The **Enfoque cultural** segments provide cultural overview footage for every Spanish-speaking country and are integrated with the **Enfoque cultural** sections of the textbook.

Instructors will find all three of these video components, available on the Video Program, organized by chapter for easy access. Additionally, the Video Program is available to students on the Video on CD, packaged free with every new copy of the textbook, making the video materials completely accessible to students at all times and providing additional flexibility to the instructor.

The **Videoteca: En contexto** section of each chapter's **Paso 4: Un paso más** includes comprehension and discussion questions along with additional activities appropriate for use in the classroom. Additional activities are available in the Instructor's Manual and Resource Kit.

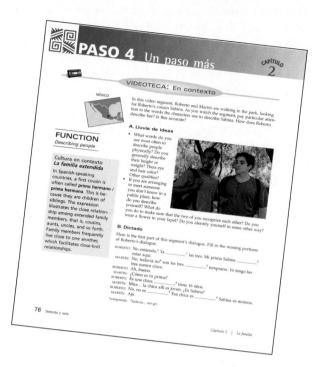

Here are some of the people and places featured in the Video Program:

Manuel and Lola, a couple from Seville, celebrate their anniversary.

Mariela, a computer lab director from San José, Costa Rica, purchases vegetables from her local greengrocer.

Juan Carlos, a student in Lima, Peru, purchases medication at a Lima pharmacy.

Roberto, a young man from Mexico City, asks a passerby for directions.

Elisa and her son José Miguel, who live in Quito, Ecuador, help a passing motorist find a mechanic.

Diego, a student from California, meets Antonio, a student in Mexico City, on the campus of the **Universidad Nacional Autónoma de México**.

The Online Learning Center Website

The new Online Learning Center (OLC) Website brings the Spanish-speaking world directly into students' lives and their language-learning experience through a myriad of resources and activities. Resources for students include vocabulary and grammar activities for each chapter, Internet cultural links and activities, and vocabulary flashcards. For instructors, the OLC provides grammar PowerPoint slides, online transparencies, additional **A leer**, **A escribir**, and **A conversar** activities, and links to professional organizations and other resources. The *¿Qué tal?* OLC can be accessed at **www.mhhe.com/quetal**.

The CD-ROM

Available in multiplatform format, the CD-ROM continues the emphasis on the meaningful use of Spanish that characterizes the student text. Correlated with the textbook by chapter, the CD-ROM offers multiple opportunities for learners to review and practice vocabulary and grammar in a meaningful, interactive format. A video segment in each lesson invites learners to "participate" in a dialogue with a native speaker of Spanish and further practice the language functions presented in the **En contexto** video. In addition, learners continue their development of reading, writing, listening, and speaking skills through interaction with textual passages and other engaging content. Cultural themes introduced in the textbook are further discussed in the CD-ROM, and a link from the CD-ROM takes the user directly to the *¿Qué tal?* Online Learning Center Website. The inclusion of additional learning resources, including the McGraw-Hill Electronic Language Tutor program, a "talking" glossary of terms, and verb reference charts, makes the *¿Qué tal?* CD-ROM a unique multimedia learning tool for the student of Spanish.

¿QUÉ TAL?: A SHORTER COURSE

As with all previous editions of *¿Qué tal?*, the sixth edition is based on the highly successful *Puntos de partida* first-year Spanish text. Responding to the wishes of many instructors across the country, *¿Qué tal?* retains the methodology and functionality of the *Puntos* program but in a shorter version, which can be ideal for classes meeting three or fewer times per week.

In order to create *¿Qué tal?* from *Puntos,* the coauthors reduced the amount of activities and exercises in the *Puntos* main text and supplements as well as the actual number of grammar points presented in *Puntos*. Additional points are subsumed within related structures or within other parts of the text (Instructor's Edition annotations, **Nota comunicativa** features, and so on).

The *Puntos* grammar points that were modified or removed for the sixth edition of *¿Qué tal?* are:

- Asking Yes/No Questions
- Relative Pronouns
- **Hace… que** + *present* and *preterite*
- Summary of the Subjunctive
- Stressed Possessives
- Hypothetical Situations

With one to three grammar points per chapter, we feel *¿Qué tal?* to be a very manageable book for you and your students. Above all, we believe *¿Qué tal?* to be a *flexible* program, one that can be adapted to suit different teaching and learning styles.

SUPPLEMENTARY MATERIALS FOR THE SIXTH EDITION

The supplements listed here may accompany the sixth edition of *¿Qué tal?* Please contact your local McGraw-Hill Higher Education representative for details concerning policies, prices, and availability, as some restrictions may apply.

Workbook / Laboratory Manual and *Audio Program,* by Alice Arana (formerly of Fullerton College), Oswaldo Arana (formerly of California State University, Fullerton), and María Sabló-Yates. The two volumes of the Workbook / Laboratory Manual provide a wealth of activities, both aural and written, that reinforce chapter content. Audio Program CDs are free to adopting institutions and are also available for student purchase upon request. An Audioscript is also available.

The *Electronic Workbook / Laboratory Manual*, Vols. 1 and 2 provide an enhanced alternative to the print *Workbook / Laboratory Manual*. Available for student purchase, these enhanced versions offer even more practice than the print *Workbook / Laboratory Manual,* in an electronic environment that offers immediate feedback, self-grading activities, and activ-

ity tracking for instructors. The laboratory portion includes the entire Audio Program on the same CD-ROM.

The *Instructor's Manual and Resource Kit* offers an extensive introduction to teaching techniques, general guidelines for instructors, suggestions for lesson planning in semester and quarter schedules, and additional pre- and post-viewing activities for the video. Also included are a wide variety of interactive and communicative games for practicing vocabulary and grammar.

The *Testing Program* reflects the revisions in the student text for the sixth edition. It also includes sections for testing reading and listening comprehension, as well as tests for oral proficiency and sections designed to test cultural material presented in the program.

Packaged with every new student text is a free *Listening Comprehension Audio CD* that provides additional vocabulary practice for the **Paso 1: Vocabulario** sections of the text. This audio supplement was designed to meet the needs of individual students and can be used to review and practice vocabulary as well as to practice pronunciation.

Packaged with every new student text is a free ***Video on CD*** that provides students with the complete Video Program for *¿Qué tal?* It also includes a transcript of all video segments. Comprehension activities for the video segments are available on the *¿Qué tal?* Online Learning Center Website.

A set of ***Overhead Transparencies***, most in full color, contains drawings from the text and supplementary drawings for use with vocabulary and grammar presentation. An electronic online version of the Transparencies is available to instructors on the *¿Qué tal?* Online Learning Center Website.

The ***McGraw-Hill Electronic Language Tutor (MHELT)***, available in both PC and Macintosh formats, offers most of the more controlled exercises from the student text as well as some supplementary mechanical practice. A parsing tool provides students with guided feedback while they complete the exercises and keeps track of their work.

A ***training/orientation manual*** for use with teaching assistants, by James F. Lee (Indiana University), offers practical advice for beginning language instructors and language coordinators.

Also available for use with *¿Qué tal?* is a software program called ***Spanish Partner***, developed by Monica Morley and Karl Fisher (Vanderbilt University). This user-friendly program helps students master first-year vocabulary and grammar topics. Available for student purchase, Spanish Partner also offers clear feedback that helps students learn from their errors.

The ***Destinos Video Modules*** are also available for use with the sixth edition of *¿Qué tal?*. Containing footage from the popular "Destinos" telecourse series, as well as from original footage shot on location, the modules offer high-quality video segments that enhance learning of vocabulary, functional language, situational language, and culture.

A ***Practical Guide to Language Learning***, by H. Douglas Brown (San Francisco State University), provides beginning foreign-language students with a general introduction to the language-learning process. This guide is free to adopting institutions, and it can also be made available for student purchase.

Ultralingua en español, a Spanish-English bilingual dictionary on CD-ROM, is available for student purchase. This dual-platform CD-ROM contains 180,000 words and expressions, a special wild-card search function, an extensive hyperlinked grammar reference, and other valuable reference tools.

The ***¡A leer! Easy Reader Series*** features two short readers, ***Cocina y comidas hispanas***, on regional Hispanic cuisines; and ***Mundos de fantasía***, which contains fairy tales and legends. These readers can be used as early as the second semester.

The ***El mundo hispano*** reader features five major regions of the Hispanic world as well as a section on Hispanics in the United States.

ACKNOWLEDGMENTS

The suggestions, advice, and work of the following friends and colleagues are gratefully acknowledged by the authors of the sixth edition.

- Dr. Bill VanPatten (University of Illinois, Chicago), whose creativity has been an inspiration to us for a number of editions and from whom we have learned so very much about language teaching and how students learn.

- María Sabló-Yates, whose extensive research provides the basis for many of the **Enfoque cultural** sections.

- Dr. Manuel Cortés-Castañeda (Eastern Kentucky University), whose engaging and creative **A conversar** activities provide wonderful chapter-culminating communicative tasks and projects.

- Dr. Hope Doyle D'Ambrosio (American University), whose new **Cultura en contexto** cultural notes enrich the video-viewing experience for students and provide excellent topics for in-class discussion.

- Becky S. Jaimes and Talía Loaiza (both of Austin Community College), whose extensively revised and completely new **Notas culturales** offer students a series of outstanding cultural readings on a wide range of high-interest topics.

- Dr. A. Raymond Elliott (University of Texas, Arlington) whose contributions to the Instructor's Edition and Instructor's Manual and Resource Kit have served to make those supplements even more invaluable teaching resources.

- Laura Chastain (El Salvador), whose invaluable contributions to the text range from language usage to suggestions for realia.

- Ruth Ordás and Dr. Theodore V. Higgs, whose contributions to previous editions are still evident in the sixth edition.

In addition, the publishers wish to acknowledge the suggestions received from the following instructors and professional friends across the country. The appearance of their names in this list does not necessarily constitute their endorsement of the text or its methodology.

Joseph M. Amable
Cañada College
Geraldine Ameriks
University of Notre Dame
Catherine L. Angell
Austin Community College
Louise C. Barbaro-Medrano
Western Illinois University
Sandra Livingston Barboza
Trident Technical College
Julia Caballero
Duke University
Cecelia J. Cavanaugh
Chestnut Hill College
William David Cooper
Shasta College
Pilar del Carmen Tirado
State University of New York at Plattsburgh
Guillermina Elissondo
Worchester State College
Angélica Fernández
Front Range Community College

Janet D. Foley
Eastern Kentucky University
Frank Gangler
Dawson Community College
John G. Gladstein
Hanover College
Ying Han
Savannah State University
Lora Hittle
Western Wyoming Community College
Danielle Holden
Oakton Community College
Lisa Huempfner
Illinois State University
Susan M. Keener
Forsyth Technical Community College
Constance Kihyet
Saddleback College
Ellen Leeder
Barry University

Domenico Maceri
Allan Hancock College
Lourdes Manyé
Furman University
Bryan C. McBride
Eastern Arizona College
David Michels
Cardinal Stritch College
Constance Montross
Clark University
Judith Némethy
New York University
MacGregor O'Brien
Frostburg State University
Kathy A. Ogle
Pacific Lutheran University
Dale Edward Omundson
Anoka Ramsey Community College
Sue Pechter
Illinois Institute of Technology
Amanda R. Plumlee
LaGrange College

Rhea Rehark-Griffith
West Hills College
Karen L. Robinson
University of Nebraska at Omaha
Regina F. Roebuck
University of California, Santa Barbara
Karen Rose
Collin County Community College
Lynne C. Rushing
Collin County Community College
Jack Shreve
Allegheny Community College
Marguerite Solari
Oakton College
Amy E. Zink
Indiana University Southeast
Begoña Zubiri
Thomas More College

Within McGraw-Hill, we would like to acknowledge the contributions of the following: Linda Toy, Diane Renda, and the McGraw-Hill production group, especially Violeta Díaz for her work on the design of the sixth edition, David Staloch for his invaluable assistance as Production Editor, Rich DeVitto and Louis Swaim for their work on various aspects of production, Alexandra Ambrose for her contributions as Photo Researcher, and Robin Mouat for her work as Art Editor. We would also like to thank Jennifer Chow and Fionnuala McEvoy for their invaluable editorial assistance. Special thanks are due to Eirik Børve, who originally brought some of us together, and to Nick Agnew, Rachel Amparo, and the McGraw-Hill marketing and sales staff for their constant support and efforts. Our thanks also go to Scott Tinetti, our Director of Development, and Christa Harris, our Sponsoring Editor, for their guidance and their contributions to the development of this edition. Finally, we would like to thank the development editor, Dr. Pennie Nichols-Alem, for her patient and knowledgeable editorial talents that are seen in the textbook and other parts of the *¿Qué tal?* package.

The only reasons for publishing a new textbook or to revise an existing one are to help the profession evolve in meaningful ways and to make the task of daily classroom instruction easier and more enjoyable for experienced instructors and teaching assistants alike. Foreign language teaching has changed in important ways in the twenty years since the publication of the first edition of *¿Qué tal?* We are delighted to have been—and to continue to be—one of the agents of that evolution. And we are grateful to McGraw-Hill for its continuing creative support for our ideas.

¿Qué tal?

AN INTRODUCTORY COURSE

Sixth Edition

Primeros pasos

¿Qué tal? means *Hi, how are you doing?* in Spanish. This textbook, called *¿Qué tal?*, will help you to begin learning Spanish and to become more familiar with the many people here and abroad who use it.

With *¿Qué tal?*, you will begin to learn Spanish and to communicate with Spanish speakers in this country and in Spanish-speaking countries. To speak a language involves much more than just learning its grammar and vocabulary; to know a language is to know the people who speak it. For this reason, *¿Qué tal?* will provide you with cultural information to help you understand and appreciate the traditions and values of Spanish-speaking people all over the world.

Are you ready for the adventure of learning Spanish? **Pues, ¡adelante!** (*Well, let's go!*)

¡Hola! ¿Qué tal? San Antonio, Texas ▶

Saludos° y expresiones de cortesía *Greetings*

1. Sevilla, España

2. Quito, Ecuador

3. La Ciudad de México, México

Here are some words, phrases, and expressions that will enable you to meet and greet others appropriately in Spanish.

1.
MANOLO: ¡Hola, Maricarmen!
MARICARMEN: ¿Qué tal, Manolo? ¿Cómo estás?
MANOLO: Muy bien. ¿Y tú?
MARICARMEN: Regular. Nos vemos, ¿eh?
MANOLO: Hasta mañana.

2.
ELISA VELASCO: Buenas tardes, señor Gómez.
MARTÍN GÓMEZ: Muy buenas, señora Velasco. ¿Cómo está?
ELISA VELASCO: Bien, gracias. ¿Y usted?
MARTÍN GÓMEZ: Muy bien, gracias. Hasta luego.
ELISA VELASCO: Adiós.

¿Qué tal?, **¿Cómo estás?**, and **¿Y tú?** are expressions used in informal situations with people you know well, on a first-name basis.

¿Cómo está? and **¿Y usted?** are used to address someone with whom you have a formal relationship.

3.
LUPE: Buenos días, profesor.
PROFESOR: Buenos días. ¿Cómo te llamas?
LUPE: Me llamo Lupe Carrasco.
PROFESOR: Mucho gusto, Lupe.
LUPE: Igualmente.

¿Cómo se llama usted? is used in formal situations. **¿Cómo te llamas?** is used in informal situations—for example, with other students. The phrases **mucho gusto** and **igualmente** are used by both men and women when meeting for the first time. In response to **mucho gusto**, a woman can also say **encantada**; a man can say **encantado**.

---

1. MANOLO: Hi, Maricarmen! MARICARMEN: How's it going, Manolo? How are you? MANOLO: Very well. And you? MARICARMEN: OK. See you around, OK? MANOLO: See you tomorrow.
2. ELISA VELASCO: Good afternoon, Mr. Gómez. MARTÍN GÓMEZ: Afternoon, Mrs. Velasco. How are you? ELISA VELASCO: Fine, thank you. And you? MARTÍN GÓMEZ: Very well, thanks. See you later. ELISA VELASCO: Bye.
3. LUPE: Good morning, professor. PROFESSOR: Good morning. What's your name? LUPE: My name is Lupe Carrasco. PROFESSOR: Nice to meet you, Lupe. LUPE: Likewise.

NOTA COMUNICATIVA

Otros saludos y expresiones de cortesía

buenos días	good morning (*used until the midday meal*)
buenas tardes	good afternoon (*used until the evening meal*)
buenas noches	good evening; good night (*used after the evening meal*)
señor (Sr.)	Mr., sir
señora (Sra.)	Mrs., ma'am
señorita (Srta.)	Miss (**¡OJO!*** *There is no Spanish equivalent for Ms. Use* **Sra.** *or* **Srta.** *as appropriate.*)
gracias	thanks, thank you
muchas gracias	thank you very much
de nada, no hay de qué	you're welcome
por favor	please (*also used to get someone's attention*)
perdón	pardon me, excuse me (*to ask forgiveness or to get someone's attention*)
con permiso	pardon me, excuse me (*to request permission to pass by or through a group of people*)

Conversación

A. Cortesía. How many different ways can you respond to the following greetings and phrases?

1. Buenas tardes.
2. Adiós.
3. ¿Qué tal?
4. Hola.
5. ¿Cómo está?
6. Buenas noches.
7. Muchas gracias.
8. Hasta mañana.
9. ¿Cómo se llama usted?
10. Mucho gusto.

B. Situaciones. If the following persons met or passed each other at the times given, what might they say to each other? Role-play the situations with a classmate.

1. Mr. Santana and Miss Pérez, at 5:00 P.M.
2. Mrs. Ortega and Pablo, at 10:00 A.M.
3. Ms. Hernández and Olivia, at 11:00 P.M.
4. you and a classmate, just before your Spanish class

Watch out!, Careful!* **¡OJO! will be used throughout *¿Qué tal?* to alert you to pay special attention to the item that follows.

C. Más (*More*) **situaciones.** Are these people saying **por favor, con permiso,** or **perdón**?

D. Entrevista (*Interview*)**.** Turn to a person sitting next to you and do the following.

- Greet him or her appropriately, that is, with informal forms.
- Find out his or her name.
- Ask how he or she is.
- Conclude the exchange.

Now have a similar conversation with your instructor, using the appropriate formal forms.

El alfabeto español

There are twenty-eight letters in the Spanish alphabet (**el alfabeto**)—two more than in the English alphabet. The two additional letters are the **ñ** and **rr** (considered one letter even though it is a two-letter group). The letters **k** and **w** appear only in words borrowed from other languages.

Until recently, the **Real Academia Española** (*Royal Spanish Academy*), which establishes many of the guidelines for the use of Spanish throughout the world, considered the **ch** (**che**) and **ll** (**elle**) to be separate letters of the Spanish alphabet. In *¿Qué tal?*, you will not see them listed as separate letters. However, the **ch** and **ll** *do* maintain a distinct pronunciation.*

Listen carefully as your instructor pronounces the names listed with the letters of the alphabet.

---

*The **ch** is pronounced with the same sound as in English *cherry* or *chair*, as in **nachos** or **muchacho**. The **ll** is pronounced as a type of *y* sound. Spanish examples of this sound that you may already know are **tortilla** and **Sevilla**.

Letters	Names of Letters	Examples		
a	a	Antonio	Ana	(la) Argentina
b	be	Benito	Blanca	Bolivia
c	ce	Carlos	Cecilia	Cáceres
d	de	Domingo	Dolores	Durango
e	e	Eduardo	Elena	(el) Ecuador
f	efe	Felipe	Francisca	Florida
g	ge	Gerardo	Gloria	Guatemala
h	hache	Héctor	Hortensia	Honduras
i	i	Ignacio	Inés	Ibiza
j	jota	José	Juana	Jalisco
k	ca (ka)	(Karl)	(Kati)	(Kansas)
l	ele	Luis	Lola	Lima
m	eme	Manuel	María	México
n	ene	Nicolás	Nati	Nicaragua
ñ	eñe	Íñigo	Begoña	España
o	o	Octavio	Olivia	Oviedo
p	pe	Pablo	Pilar	Panamá
q	cu	Enrique	Raquel	Quito
r	ere	Álvaro	Clara	(el) Perú
rr	erre or ere doble	Rafael	Rosa	Monterrey
s	ese	Salvador	Sara	San Juan
t	te	Tomás	Teresa	Toledo
u	u	Agustín	Lucía	(el) Uruguay
v	ve or uve	Víctor	Victoria	Venezuela
w	doble ve, ve doble, or uve doble	Oswaldo	(Wilma)	(Washington)
x	equis	Xavier	Ximena	Extremadura
y	i griega	Pelayo	Yolanda	(el) Paraguay
z	ceta (zeta)	Gonzalo	Esperanza	Zaragoza

Práctica

A. **¡Pronuncie!** The letters and combinations of letters listed on the following page represent the Spanish sounds that are the most different from English. You will practice the pronunciation of some of these letters in upcoming chapters of *¿Qué tal?* For the moment, pay particular attention to their pronunciation when you see them. Can you match the Spanish letters with their equivalent pronunciation?

EXAMPLES/SPELLING

PRONUNCIATION

1. mucho: **ch**
2. Geraldo: **ge** (also: **gi**)
   Jiménez: **j**
3. hola: **h**
4. gusto: **gu** (also: **ga, go**)
5. me llamo: **ll**
6. señor: **ñ**
7. profesora: **r**
8. Ramón: **r** (to start a word)
   Monterrey: **rr**
9. nos vemos: **v**

a. like the *g* in English *garden*
b. similar to *tt* of *butter* when pronounced very quickly
c. like *ch* in English *cheese*
d. like Spanish **b**
e. similar to a "strong" English *h*
f. like *y* in English *yes* or like the *li* sound in *million*
g. a trilled sound, several Spanish **r**'s in a row
h. similar to the *ny* sound in *canyon*
i. never pronounced

B. Deletreo (*Spelling*)

Paso (*Step*) **1.** Pronounce these U.S. place names in Spanish. Then spell aloud the names in Spanish. All of them are of Hispanic origin: **Toledo, Los Ángeles, Texas, Montana, Colorado, El Paso, Florida, Las Vegas, Amarillo, San Francisco.**

Paso 2. Spell your own name aloud in Spanish, and listen as your classmates spell their names. Try to remember as many of their names as you can.

MODELO: Me llamo María: **M** (eme) **a** (a) **r** (ere) **í** (i acentuada) **a** (a).

Los cognados

Many Spanish and English words are similar or identical in form and meaning. These related words are called *cognates* (**los cognados**). Spanish and English share so many cognates because a number of words in both languages are derived from the same Latin root words—and also because Spanish and English are "language neighbors," especially in the southwestern United States. Each language has borrowed words from the other and adapted them to its own sound system.

Many cognates are used in **Primeros pasos**. Don't try to memorize all of them—just get used to the sound of them in Spanish.

Here are some Spanish adjectives that are cognates of English words. These adjectives can be used to describe either a man or a woman.

Cognados
leader → **el líder**
el lagarto (*the lizard*) →
alligator

adjectives = words used to describe people, places, and things

arrogante	importante	pesimista
cruel	independiente	realista
eficiente	inteligente	rebelde
egoísta	interesante	responsable
elegante	liberal	sentimental
emocional	materialista	terrible
flexible	optimista	valiente
idealista	paciente	vulnerable

The following adjectives change form. Use the **-o** ending when describing a man, the **-a** ending when describing a woman.

extrovertido/a	religioso/a	serio/a
generoso/a	reservado/a	sincero/a
impulsivo/a	romántico/a	tímido/a

¿Cómo es usted?°

¿Cómo... What are you like?

You can use these forms of the verb **ser** (*to be*) to describe yourself and others.

(yo)	**soy**	I am
(tú)	**eres**	you (*familiar*) are
(usted)	**es**	you (*formal*) are
(él, ella)	**es**	he/she is

—¿Cómo es usted?
—Bueno…° Yo soy moderna, urbana, sofisticada…

Well . . .

Conversación

A. Descripciones

Paso 1. With a classmate, describe the famous Hispanic people in these photos, using cognate adjectives (see page 6 and above). **¡OJO!** Remember that some adjectives can end in **-o** or **-a**, such as **romántico/a, serio/a, tímido/a.** Use the **-o** ending when describing a male and the **-a** ending when describing a female.

MODELOS: ESTUDIANTE 1: ¿Cómo es Ricky Martin?
ESTUDIANTE 2: (Ricky Martin) Es importante, romántico y serio.

ESTUDIANTE 1: ¿Cómo es Cameron Díaz?
ESTUDIANTE 2: (Cameron Díaz) Es elegante y extrovertida.

1. Ricky Martin es cantante (*a singer*).

2. Sammy Sosa es beisbolista con los Chicago Cubs.

3. Cameron Díaz es actriz.

4. Jennifer López es cantante y actriz.

Paso 2. Now describe yourself to your classmate.

MODELO: Yo soy muy sentimental y sincero/a. Yo no soy pesimista.

B. Reacciones

Paso 1. Use the following adjectives, or any others you know, to create one sentence about a classmate. You can begin with **Creo que...** (*I think that . . .*). Your classmate will listen to your sentences, then tell you if you are right.

Adjetivos: eficiente, emocional, generoso/a, inteligente, impulsivo/a, liberal, sincero/a

MODELO: ESTUDIANTE 1: Alicia, (creo que) eres generosa.
ESTUDIANTE 2: Sí, soy generosa. (Sí, soy muy generosa.) (No, no soy generosa.)

Paso 2. Now find out what kind of person your instructor is, using the same adjectives. Use the appropriate formal forms.

MODELO: **¿Es usted** optimista (generoso/a...)?

Spanish in the United States and in the World

Although no one knows exactly how many languages are spoken around the world, linguists estimate that there are between 3,000 and 6,000. Spanish, with over 410 million native speakers, is among the top five languages. It is the primary language spoken in Spain, in Mexico, in all of South America (except Brazil and the Guianas), in most of Central America, in Cuba, in Puerto Rico, and in the Dominican Republic—in twenty countries in all. It is also spoken by a great number of people in the United States and Canada.

Like all languages spoken by large numbers of people, modern Spanish varies from region to region. The Spanish of Madrid is different from that spoken in Mexico City, Buenos Aires, or Los Angeles, just as the English of London differs from that of Chicago or Toronto. Although these differences are most noticeable in pronunciation ("accent"), they are also found in vocabulary and special expressions used in different geographical areas. In Great Britain one hears the word *lift,* but the same apparatus is called an *elevator* in the United States. What is called an **autobús** (*bus*) in Spain may be called a **guagua** in the Caribbean. Although such differences are noticeable, they result only rarely in misunderstandings among native speakers, since the majority of structures and vocabulary are common to the many varieties of each language.

You don't need to go abroad to encounter people who speak Spanish on a daily basis. The Spanish language and people of Hispanic descent have been an integral part of U.S. and Canadian life for centuries. In fact, the United States is now the fifth largest Spanish-speaking country in the world!

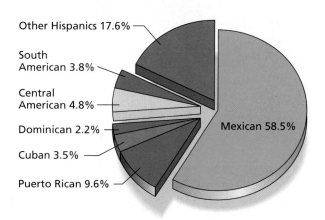

Comparing origins of U.S. Hispanic population
Total population based on U.S. census, 2000 estimates* 35.3 million

- Other Hispanics 17.6%
- South American 3.8%
- Central American 4.8%
- Dominican 2.2%
- Cuban 3.5%
- Puerto Rican 9.6%
- Mexican 58.5%

* Source: Census Bureau. The Hispanic Population: Information from the 2000 Census.

Who are the over 35 million people of Hispanic descent living in the United States today? For one thing, not all Hispanics are similar. They are characterized by great diversity, the result of their ancestors or their country of origin, socioeconomic and professional factors, and, of course, individual talents and aspirations.

There is also great regional diversity among U.S. Hispanics. Many people of Mexican descent inhabit the southwestern part of the United States, including populations as far north as Colorado. Large groups of Puerto Ricans can be found in New York, while Florida is host to a large Cuban and Central American population. More recent immigrants include Nicaraguans and Salvadorans, who have established large communities in many U.S. cities, among them San Francisco and Los Angeles.

Although not all people of Hispanic origin speak Spanish, many are in fact bilingual and bicultural. This dual cultural identity is being increasingly recognized by the media and business community. Many major U.S. cities have one or more Spanish-language newspapers as well as television and radio stations. A wide variety of businesses are owned and operated by Hispanics, and major corporations in the food, clothing, entertainment, and service fields appeal to Hispanic clients . . . in both English and Spanish!

As you will discover in subsequent chapters of *¿Qué tal?*, the Spanish language and people of Hispanic descent have been and will continue to be an integral part of the fabric of this country. Take special note of **En los Estados Unidos y el Canadá...**, a routinely occurring section of *¿Qué tal?* that profiles Hispanics in these two countries.

Mural de la Pequeña Habana, el barrio cubano de Miami

Más cognados

ªSu... (*Here is*) *Your dinner* (literally, *little piece of lettuce*).

Although some English and Spanish cognate nouns are spelled identically (*idea, general, gas, animal, motor*), most will differ slightly in spelling: *position*/**posición,** *secret*/**secreto,** *student*/**estudiante,** *rose*/**rosa,** *lottery*/**lotería,** *opportunity*/**oportunidad,** *exam*/**examen.**

The following exercises will give you more practice in recognizing and pronouncing cognates. Remember: Don't try to learn all of these words. Just get used to the way they sound.

> **noun** = person, place, or thing

Práctica

A. **Categorías.** Pronounce each of the following cognates and give its English equivalent. You will also recognize the meaning of most of the categories (**Naciones, Personas...**). Based on the words listed in the group, can you guess the meaning of the categories indicated with a gloss symbol (°)?

> **Naciones:** el Japón, Italia, Francia, España, el Brasil, China, el Canadá, Rusia
>
> **Personas:** líder, profesor, actriz, pintor, político, estudiante
>
> **Lugares:**° restaurante, café, museo, garaje, bar, banco, hotel, oficina, océano, parque
>
> **Conceptos:** libertad, dignidad, declaración, cooperación, comunismo
>
> **Cosas:**° teléfono, fotografía, sofá, televisión, radio, bomba, novela, diccionario, dólar, lámpara, yate
>
> **Animales:** león, cebra, chimpancé, tigre, hipopótamo
>
> **Comidas y bebidas:**° hamburguesa, cóctel, patata, café, limón, banana
>
> **Deportes:**° béisbol, tenis, vólibol, fútbol americano
>
> **Instrumentos musicales:** guitarra, piano, flauta, clarinete, trompeta, violín

OJO

In **Práctica B**, note that Spanish has two different ways to express *a* (*an*): **un** and **una.** All nouns are either masculine (*m.*) or feminine (*f.*) in Spanish. **Un** is used with masculine nouns, **una** with feminine nouns. You will learn more about this aspect of Spanish in **Capítulo 1.**

SEGUNDO PASO

OJO   Don't try to learn the gender of nouns now. You do not have to know the gender of nouns to do **Práctica B**.

B. ¿Qué es esto? (*What is this?*) Being able to tell what something is or to identify the group to which it belongs is a useful conversation strategy. Begin to practice this strategy by pronouncing these cognates and identifying the category from **Práctica A** to which they belong. Use the following sentences as a guide.

Es **un** lugar (concepto, animal, deporte, instrumento musical).*
Es **una** nación (persona, cosa, comida, bebida).*

MODELO: béisbol → Es un deporte.

1. calculadora	6. actor	11. universidad
2. burro	7. clase	12. fama
3. sándwich	8. limonada	13. terrorista
4. golf	9. elefante	14. acordeón
5. México	10. refrigerador	15. democracia

Conversación

Identificaciones. With a classmate, practice identifying words, using the categories given in **Práctica A**.

MODELO: ESTUDIANTE 1: ¿Qué es un hospital?
ESTUDIANTE 2: Es un lugar.

1. un saxofón	4. un doctor	7. una enchilada
2. un autobús	5. Bolivia	8. una jirafa
3. un rancho	6. una Coca-Cola	9. una turista

Pronunciación

You have probably already noted that there is a very close relationship between the way Spanish is written and the way it is pronounced. This makes it relatively easy to learn the basics of Spanish spelling and pronunciation.

Many Spanish sounds, however, do not have an exact equivalent in English, so you should not trust English to be your guide to Spanish pronunciation. Even words that are spelled the same in both languages are usually pronounced quite differently. It is important to become so familiar with Spanish sounds that you can pronounce them automatically, right from the beginning of your study of the language.

---

*The English equivalent of these sentences is *It is a place (concept, . . .); It is a country (person, . . .)*.

Las vocales (*Vowels*): *a, e, i, o, u*

Unlike English vowels, which can have many different pronunciations or may be silent, Spanish vowels are always pronounced, and they are almost always pronounced in the same way. Spanish vowels are always short and tense. They are never drawn out with a *u* or *i* glide as in English: **lo** + *low;* **de** + *day.*

- **a:** pronounced like the *a* in *father,* but short and tense
- **e:** pronounced like the *e* in *they,* but without the *i* glide
- **i:** pronounced like the *i* in *machine,* but short and tense*
- **o:** pronounced like the *o* in *home,* but without the *u* glide
- **u:** pronounced like the *u* in *rule,* but short and tense

OJO The *uh* sound or schwa (which is how most unstressed vowels are pronounced in English: *canal, waited, atom*) does not exist in Spanish.

A. Sílabas. Pronounce the following Spanish syllables, being careful to pronounce each vowel with a short, tense sound.

1. ma fa la ta pa
2. me fe le te pe
3. mi fi li ti pi
4. mo fo lo to po
5. mu fu lu tu pu
6. mi fe la tu do
7. su mi te so la
8. se tu no ya li

B. Palabras (*Words*). Repeat the following words after your instructor.

1. hasta tal nada mañana natural normal fascinante
2. me qué Pérez Elena rebelde excelente elegante
3. sí señorita permiso terrible imposible tímido Ibiza
4. yo con como noches profesor señor generoso
5. uno usted tú mucho Perú Lupe Úrsula

C. Naciones

Paso 1. Here is part of a rental car ad in Spanish. Say aloud the names of the countries where you can find this company's offices. Can you recognize all of the countries?

Paso 2. Find the following information in the ad.

1. How many cars does the agency have available?
2. How many offices does the agency have?
3. What Spanish word expresses the English word *immediately?*

*The word **y** (*and*) is also pronounced like the letter **i**.

Los números 0–30; *hay*

Canción infantil

Dos y dos son cuatro,
cuatro y dos son seis,
seis y dos son ocho,
y ocho dieciséis.

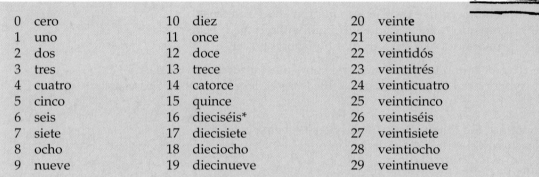

0	cero	10	diez	20	veinte
1	uno	11	once	21	veintiuno
2	dos	12	doce	22	veintidós
3	tres	13	trece	23	veintitrés
4	cuatro	14	catorce	24	veinticuatro
5	cinco	15	quince	25	veinticinco
6	seis	16	dieciséis*	26	veintiséis
7	siete	17	diecisiete	27	veintisiete
8	ocho	18	dieciocho	28	veintiocho
9	nueve	19	diecinueve	29	veintinueve

30 treinta

The number *one* has several forms in Spanish. **Uno** is the form used in counting. **Un** is used before masculine singular nouns, **una** before feminine singular nouns: **un señor, una señora**. Also note that the number **veintiuno** becomes **veintiún** before masculine nouns and **veintiuna** before feminine nouns: **veintiún señores, veintiuna señoras**.

> **OJO**
>
> **uno**, dos, tres,… veinti**uno**, veintidós,…
> *but*
> **un** señor, veinti**ún** señores
> **una** señora, veinti**una** señoras

Use the word **hay** to express both *there is* and *there are* in Spanish. **No hay** means *there is not* and *there are not*. **¿Hay... ?** asks *Is there . . . ?* or *Are there . . . ?*

hay = there is / there are

—¿Cuántos estudiantes **hay** en la clase?
—(**Hay**) Treinta.

How many students are there in the class?
(There are) Thirty.

—¿**Hay** pandas en el zoo? Zoológico
—**Hay** veinte osos, pero **no hay** pandas.

Are there any pandas at the zoo?
There are twenty bears, but there aren't any pandas.

A children's song Two and two are four, four and two are six, six and two are eight, and eight (makes) sixteen.
*The numbers 16 to 19 and 21 to 29 can be written as one word (**dieciséis... veintiuno...**) or as three (**diez y seis... veinte y uno...**).

Práctica

A. Los números. Practique los números según (*according to*) el modelo.

MODELO: 1 señor → Hay un señor.

1. 4 señoras
2. 12 pianos
3. 1 café (*m.*)
4. 21 cafés (*m.*)
5. 14 días
6. 1 clase (*f.*)
7. 21 ideas (*f.*)
8. 11 personas
9. 15 estudiantes
10. 13 teléfonos
11. 28 naciones
12. 5 guitarras
13. 1 león (*m.*)
14. 30 señores
15. 20 oficinas

q with u

B. Problemas de matemáticas. Do the following simple mathematical equations in Spanish. *Note:* + (**y**), − (**menos**), = (**son**).

MODELO: 2 + 2 = 4 → Dos y dos son cuatro.
4 − 2 = 2 → Cuatro menos dos son dos.

1. 2 + 4 = ? 6
2. 8 + 17 = ? 25
3. 11 + 1 = ? 12
4. 3 + 18 = ? 21
5. 9 + 6 = ? 15
6. 5 + 4 = ? 9
7. 1 + 13 = ? 14
8. 15 − 2 = ? 13
9. 9 − 9 = ? 0
10. 13 − 8 = ? 5
11. 14 + 12 = ? 26
12. 23 − 13 = ? 10

Conversación

Preguntas (*Questions*)

1. ¿Cuántos estudiantes hay en la clase de español? ¿Cuántos estudiantes hay en clase hoy (*today*)? ¿Hay tres profesores o un profesor?
2. ¿Cuántos días hay en una semana (*week*)? ¿Hay seis? (No, no hay…) ¿Cuántos días hay en un fin de semana (*weekend*)? Hay cuatro semanas en un mes. ¿Qué significa **mes** en inglés? ¿Cuántos días hay en el mes de febrero? ¿en el mes de junio? ¿Cuántos meses hay en un año?
3. Hay muchos edificios (*many buildings*) en una universidad. En esta (*this*) universidad, ¿hay una cafetería? ¿un teatro? ¿un cine (*movie theater*)? ¿un laboratorio de lenguas (*languages*)? ¿un bar? ¿una clínica? ¿un hospital? ¿un museo? ¿muchos estudiantes? ¿muchos profesores?

unos = some

una ciudad

Gustos° y preferencias

Likes

¿Te gusta el fútbol? →

- Sí, me gusta mucho el fútbol.
- No, no me gusta el fútbol.
- Sí, me gusta, pero me gusta más el fútbol americano.

Do you like soccer? → • Yes, I like soccer very much. • No, I don't like soccer. • Yes, I like soccer, but I like football more.

To indicate that you like something in Spanish, say **Me gusta** _____. To indicate that you don't like something, use **No me gusta** _____. Use the question **¿Te gusta** _____? to ask a classmate if he or she likes something. Use **¿Le gusta** _____? to ask your instructor the same question.

In the following conversations, you will use the word **el** to mean *the* with masculine nouns and the word **la** with feminine nouns. Don't try to memorize which nouns are masculine and which are feminine. Just get used to using the words **el** and **la** before nouns.

You will also be using a number of Spanish verbs in the infinitive form, which always ends in **-r**. Here are some examples: **estudiar** = *to study;* **comer** = *to eat.* Try to guess the meanings of the infinitives used in these activities from context. If someone asks you, for instance, **¿Te gusta** *beber* **Coca-Cola?**, it is a safe guess that **beber** means *to drink.*

En español, **fútbol** = *soccer* y **fútbol americano** = *football.*

> **verb** = a word that describes an action or a state of being

Conversación

A. Gustos y preferencias

Paso 1. Make a list of six things you like and six things you don't like, following the model. If you wish, you may choose items from the **Vocabulario útil** box below. All words are provided with the appropriate definite article.

MODELO: Me gusta *la clase de español.* No me gusta *la clase de matemáticas.*

Vocabulario útil*

el café, el té, la limonada, la cerveza (*beer*)
la música moderna, la música clásica, el rap, la música *country*
la pizza, la pasta, la comida mexicana, la comida de la cafetería
  (*cafeteria food*)
el actor _____, la actriz _____
el/la cantante (*singer*) _____ (**¡OJO!** **cantante** is used for both men
  and women)
el cine (*movies*), el teatro, la ópera, el arte abstracto

Paso 2. Now ask a classmate if he or she shares your likes and dislikes.

MODELO: ¿Te gusta la clase de español? ¿y la clase de matemáticas?

---

*The material in **Vocabulario útil** lists is not active; that is, it is not part of what you need to focus on learning at this point. You may use these words and phrases to complete exercises or to help you converse in Spanish, if you need them.

B. Más (*More*) **gustos y preferencias**

Paso 1. Here are some useful verbs and nouns to talk about what you like. For each item, combine a verb (shaded) with a noun to form a sentence that is true for you. Use context to guess the meaning of verbs you don't know.

MODELO: Me gusta _____. → Me gusta estudiar inglés.

1. beber   café   té   limonada   chocolate
2. comer   pizza   enchiladas   hamburguesas   pasta
3. estudiar   español   matemáticas   historia
             computación   (*computer science*)
4. hablar   español   con mis amigos (*with my friends*)
             por teléfono (*on the phone*)
5. jugar   al tenis   al fútbol   al fútbol americano   al béisbol
             al basquetbol   *el baloncesto (basketball)*
6. tocar   la guitarra   el piano   el violín

Paso 2. Ask a classmate about his or her likes.

MODELO: ¿Te gusta comer enchiladas?

Paso 3. Now ask your professor if he or she likes certain things. **¡OJO!** Remember to address your professor in a formal manner.

MODELO: ¿Le gusta jugar al tenis?

[handwritten margin notes: think in dream with; a Judy le gusta hablar por teléfono]

A LEER

El mundo hispánico (Parte 1)

Estrategia:° Recognizing Interrogative Words and *estar*

Strategy

In the following brief reading, note that the word **está** means *is located;* **está** and other forms of the verb **estar** (*to be*) are used to tell where things are. You will learn more about the uses of **estar** in **Capítulo 5.**

    The reading also contains a series of questions with interrogative words. You are already familiar with **¿cómo?, ¿qué?,** and **¿cuántos?** (and should be able to guess the meaning of **¿cuántas?** easily). The meaning of other interrogatives may not be immediately obvious to you, but the sentences in which the words appear may offer some clues to meaning. You probably do not know the meaning of **¿dónde?** and **¿cuál?,** but you should be able to guess their meaning in the following sentences.

    Cuba está en el Mar Caribe. ¿<u>Dónde</u> está la República Dominicana?
    Managua es la capital de Nicaragua. ¿<u>Cuál</u> es la capital de México?

Note that the reading has been divided into four very short parts. Each part corresponds to a map that offers geographical and population information about the countries of the Spanish-speaking world. Use the statements in the short parts as models to answer the questions.

Las naciones del mundo hispánico

Parte 1 México y Centroamérica

Hay noventa y siete (97) millones de habitantes en México. ¿Cuántos millones de habitantes hay en Guatemala? ¿en El Salvador? ¿en las demás[a] naciones de Centroamérica? ¿En cuántas naciones de Centroamérica se habla español? México es parte de Norteamérica. ¿En cuántas naciones de Norteamérica se habla español? ¿Cuál es la capital de México? ¿de Costa Rica?

Parte 2 El Caribe

Cuba está en el Mar Caribe. ¿Dónde está la República Dominicana? ¿Qué parte de los Estados Unidos está también[b] en el Mar Caribe? ¿Dónde está el Canal de Panamá?

Parte 3 Sudamérica

¿En cuántas naciones de Sudamérica se habla español? ¿Se habla español o portugués en el Brasil? ¿Cuántos millones de habitantes hay en Venezuela? ¿en Chile? ¿en las demás naciones? ¿Cuál es la capital de cada[c] nación?

[a]las… *the other*   [b]*also*   [c]*each*

Parte 4 España

España está en la Península Ibérica. ¿Qué otra nación está también en esa[d] península? ¿Cuántos millones de habitantes hay en España? No se habla español en Portugal. ¿Qué lengua se habla allí[e]? ¿Cuál es la capital de España? ¿Está en el centro de la península?

[d]*that*   [e]*there*

¿Qué hora es?

Es la una.

Son las dos.

Son las cinco.

¿Qué hora es? is used to ask *What time is it?* In telling time, one says *Es* **la una** but *Son* **las dos** (**las tres, las cuatro,** and so on).

Es la una y { **cuarto.**
              quince.

Son las dos y { **media.**
               treinta.

Son las cinco **y diez.**

Son las ocho **y veinticinco.**

Note that from the hour to the half-hour, Spanish, like English, expresses time by adding minutes or a portion of an hour to the hour.

Son las dos **menos** { **cuarto.**
                        quince.

Son las ocho
menos diez.

Son las once
menos veinte.

From the half-hour to the hour, Spanish usually expresses time by subtracting minutes or a part of an hour from the *next* hour.

Son las cuatro de la tarde **en punto.**
¿A qué hora es la clase de español?
Hay una recepción **a las once** de la mañana.

It's exactly 4:00 P.M.
(At) What time is Spanish class?
There is a reception at 11:00 A.M.

O J O Don't confuse **Es/Son la(s)...** with **A la(s)...** The first is used for telling time, the second for telling at what time something happens (at what time class starts, at what time one arrives, and so on).

NOTA COMUNICATIVA

Para expresar° la hora

Para... *To express*

de la mañana	A.M., in the morning
de la tarde	P.M., in the afternoon (*and early evening*)
de la noche	P.M., in the evening
en punto	exactly, on the dot, sharp
¿a qué hora?	(at) what time?
a la una (las dos...)	at 1:00 (2:00 . . .)

Práctica

A. **¡Atención!** Listen as your instructor says a time of day. Find the clock or watch face that corresponds to the time you heard and say its number in Spanish. (Note the sun or the moon that accompanies each clock to indicate whether the time shown is day or night.)

1.   2.   3.   4.

5.   6.   7.   8.

B. **¿Qué hora es?** Express the time in full sentences in Spanish.

1.	1:00 P.M.	5.	3:15	8.	11:45 exactly
2.	6:00 P.M.	6.	6:45	9.	9:10 on the dot
3.	11:00 A.M.	7.	4:15	10.	9:50 sharp
4.	1:30				

Conversación

A. Entrevista

Paso 1.   Ask a classmate at what time the following events or activities take place. He or she will answer according to the cue or will provide the necessary information.

> MODELO: la clase de español (10:00 A.M.) →
> > ESTUDIANTE 1: ¿A qué hora es la clase de español?
> > ESTUDIANTE 2: A las diez de la mañana… ¡en punto!

1.   la clase de francés (1:45 P.M.)
2.   la sesión de laboratorio (3:10 P.M.)
3.   la excursión (8:45 A.M.)
4.   el concierto (7:30 P.M.)

Paso 2.   Now ask what time your partner likes to perform these activities. He or she should provide the necessary information.

> MODELO: cenar (*to have dinner*) →
> > ESTUDIANTE 1: ¿A qué hora te gusta cenar?
> > ESTUDIANTE 2: Me gusta cenar a las ocho de la noche.

1.   almorzar (*to have lunch*)
2.   mirar (*to watch*) la televisión
3.   ir (*to go*) al laboratorio de lenguas
4.   ir al cine
5.   desayunar (*to eat breakfast*)
6.   hacer la tarea (*to do homework*)
7.   salir con amigos (*to go out with friends*)
8.   hacer ejercicio (*to exercise*)

B. Situaciones.
How might the following people greet each other if they met at the indicated time? With a classmate, create a brief dialogue for each situation.

> MODELO: Jorge y María, a las once de la noche →
> > JORGE: Buenas noches, María.
> > MARÍA: Hola, Jorge. ¿Cómo estás?
> > JORGE: Bien, gracias. ¿Y tú?
> > MARÍA: ¡Muy bien!

1.   el profesor Martínez y Gloria, a las diez de la mañana
2.   la Sra. López y la Srta. Luna, a las cuatro y media de la tarde
3.   usted y su (*your*) profesor(a) de español, en la clase de español

eye = hay — there is, there are, is there, are there.
(pronunciation) ✓

Palabras interrogativas

You have already used a number of interrogative words and phrases to get information. Some other useful ones are listed here, along with the ones you already know, and you will learn more in later chapters. Be sure you know the meaning of all these words before you begin the activities in the **Práctica** section.

¿a qué hora?	¿A qué hora es la clase?
¿cómo?	¿Cómo estás? ¿Cómo es Gloria Estefan?
	¿Cómo te llamas?
¿cuál?*	¿Cuál es la capital de Colombia?
¿cuándo?	¿Cuándo es la fiesta?
¿cuánto?	¿Cuánto es?
¿cuántos?, ¿cuántas?	¿Cuántos días hay en una semana?
	¿Cuántas naciones hay en Sudamérica?
¿dónde?	¿Dónde está España?
¿qué?*	¿Qué es un hospital? ¿Qué es esto?
	¿Qué hora es?
¿quién?	¿Quién es el presidente?

Note that in Spanish the voice falls at the end of questions that begin with interrogative words.

¿Qué es un tren?   ¿Cómo estás?

---

*Use **¿qué?** to mean *what?* when you are asking for a definition or an explanation. Use **¿cuál?** to mean *what?* in all other circumstances. See also Grammar Section 28 in **Capítulo 9**.

Práctica

Preguntas y respuestas (*Questions and answers*)

Paso 1. What interrogative words do you associate with the following information?

1. ¡A las tres en punto!
2. En el centro de la península.
3. Soy profesor.
4. Muy bien, gracias.
5. ¡Es muy arrogante!
6. Hay 5 millones (de habitantes).
7. Dos pesos.
8. (La capital) Es Caracas.
9. Es un instrumento musical.
10. Mañana, a las cinco.
11. Son las once.
12. Soy Roberto González.

Paso 2. Now ask the questions that would result in the answers given in **Paso 1**.

Conversación

Más preguntas. What questions are being asked by the indicated persons? More than one answer is possible for some items. Select questions from the following list, or create your own questions.

PREGUNTAS

¿A qué hora es el programa sobre (*about*) México?

¿Cómo estás?

¿Cuál es la capital de Colombia?

¿Cuándo es la fiesta?

¿Cuántas personas hay en la fiesta?

¿Dónde está Buenos Aires?

¿Dónde está el diccionario?

¿Qué es esto?

¿Qué hay en la televisión hoy?

¿Quién es?

A LEER

El mundo hispánico (Parte 2)

Estrategia: Guessing Meaning from Context

You will recognize the meaning of a number of cognates in the following reading about the geography of the Hispanic world. In addition, you should be able to guess the meaning of the underlined words from the context (the words that surround them); they are the names of geographical features. The photo captions will also be helpful. You have learned to recognize the meaning of the word **¿qué?** in questions; in this reading, **que** (with no accent mark) means *that* or *which*.

Note also that a series of headings divides the reading into brief parts. It is always a good idea to scan such headings before starting to read, in order to get a sense of a reading's overall content.

La geografía del mundo hispánico

Introducción

La geografía del mundo hispánico es impresionante y muy variada. En algunas[a] regiones hay de todo.[b]

En las Américas

En la Argentina hay <u>pampas</u> extensas en el sur[c] y la <u>cordillera</u> de los Andes en el oeste. En partes de Venezuela, Colombia y el Ecuador, hay regiones tropicales de densa <u>selva</u>. En el Brasil está el famoso <u>Río</u> Amazonas. En el centro de México y también en El Salvador, Nicaragua y Colombia, hay <u>volcanes</u> activos. A veces[d] producen erupciones catastróficas. El Perú y Bolivia comparten[e] el enorme <u>Lago</u> Titicaca, situado en una <u>meseta</u> entre los dos países.[f]

La cordillera de los Andes, Chile

Una selva tropical en Colombia

[a]*some* [b]*de... a bit of everything* [c]*south* [d]*A... Sometimes* [e]*share* [f]naciones

La isla de Caja de Muertos, Puerto Rico

Una meseta de La Mancha, España

La ciudad de Montevideo, Uruguay

En las naciones del Caribe

Cuba, Puerto Rico y la República Dominicana son tres <u>islas</u> situadas en el <u>Mar</u> Caribe. Las bellas playas[g] del Mar Caribe y de la <u>península</u> de Yucatán son populares entre[h] los turistas de todo el mundo.

En la Península Ibérica

España, que comparte la Península Ibérica con Portugal, también tiene[i] una geografía variada. En el norte están los Pirineos, la <u>cordillera</u> que separa a España del[j] resto de Europa. Madrid, la capital del país, está situada en la <u>meseta</u> central. En las <u>costas</u> del sur y del este hay playas tan bonitas como las de[k] Latinoamérica y del Caribe.

¿Y las <u>ciudades</u>?

Es importante mencionar también la gran[l] diversidad de las ciudades del mundo hispánico. En la Argentina está la gran ciudad de Buenos Aires. Muchos consideran a Buenos Aires «el París» o «la Nueva York» de Sudamérica. En Venezuela está Caracas, y en el Perú está Lima, la capital, y Cuzco, una ciudad antigua de origen indio.

Conclusión

En fin,[m] el mundo hispánico es diverso respecto a la geografía. ¿Y Norteamérica? ▪

[g]bellas... *beautiful beaches* [h]*among* [i]*has* [j]*from the* [k]*tan... as pretty as those of* [l]*great* [m]En... *In short*

Comprensión

Demonstrate your understanding of the words underlined in the reading and other words from the reading by giving an example of a similar geographical feature found in this country or close to it. Then give an example from the Spanish-speaking world.

MODELO: un río → *the Mississippi*, el Río Grande

1. un lago
2. una cordillera
3. un río
4. una isla
5. una playa
6. una costa
7. un mar
8. un volcán
9. una península

VIDEOTECA: En contexto

FUNCTION

Greetings and leave-takings

The **En contexto** segments represent highly functional contexts and language that you are likely to encounter in your interactions with Spanish speakers.

COSTA RICA

The scenes have been filmed in San Jose, Costa Rica; Lima, Peru; and Mexico City, Mexico.

In this chapter's episode, Mariela Castillo, who is moving to a new apartment, meets her neighbors. Pay attention to the greetings and introductions used in the segment.

A. Lluvia de ideas (*Brainstorm*)

This recurring activity will direct your attention to a topic or topics featured in the **En contexto** video segment in order to help you understand it more fully.

- How would you introduce yourself to a new neighbor? What if the neighbor were older than you? What if the neighbor were younger than you?
- How do these greetings differ in English and Spanish?

B. Dictado (*Dictation*)

This recurring activity requires that you complete part of the dialogue in the video in order to help you focus on the specific language used by the video characters.

Fill in the missing portions of the dialogue. (There is an underlined space for each word.)

MARIELA: ¿Cómo te llamás?*
RICARDO: Me llamo Ricardo. ¿Cómo _____¹ _____² usted?
MARIELA: Yo _____³ _____⁴ Mariela Castillo. Mucho _____,⁵ Ricardo.
RICARDO: _____,⁶ Sra. Castillo.
MARIELA: _____⁷ soy señora; soy _____.⁸ Por el momento.ᵃ

ᵃPor... *At this time.*

C. Un diálogo original

Paso 1. In groups of three, re-enact the situation between Mariela, Ricardo, and his mom (**mamá**). Don't forget to say **bienvenido** or **bienvenida** (*welcome*) to the new neighbor!

Paso 2. With a different classmate, role-play a situation similar to the one in the video. Each of you should choose one of the following two roles:

ESTUDIANTE 1: You are a new student moving into a dormitory.
ESTUDIANTE 2: You are a returning student at the dormitory. You want to greet and welcome the new student.

---

*Note that Mariela says **llamás** instead of **llamas**, with the stress on the last syllable of the word. This is known as **voseo**, a common dialectical feature of Spanish in Costa Rica and other Spanish-speaking countries. **Voseo** forms will not be actively taught or practiced in *¿Qué tal?* For now, you just need to know that Mariela is asking the young boy's name.

Cultura en contexto
¿*Usted* o *tú*?

The formal *you* form, **usted** (abbreviated **Ud.**), is more widely employed in Latin America than in Spain. In Spain, the use of **usted** is diminishing in general. In social settings, the use of **tú** is most common among young people even if they don't know each other. In some countries, such as Colombia, Chile, and Peru, **usted** is the pronoun of choice in the same context.

En resumen

VOCABULARIO

Although you have used and heard many words in this preliminary chapter of *¿Qué tal?*, the following words are the ones considered to be active vocabulary. Be sure that you know all of them before beginning **Capítulo 1**.

Saludos y expresiones de cortesía

Buenos días. Buenas tardes. Buenas noches. Hola.
(Muy) Buenas. ¿Qué tal? ¿Cómo está(s)?
Regular. (Muy) Bien.
¿Y tú? ¿Y usted?
Adiós. Hasta mañana. Hasta luego. Nos vemos.

¿Cómo te llamas? ¿Cómo se llama usted?
　Me llamo ———.

señor (Sr.), señora (Sra.), señorita (Srta.)

(Muchas) Gracias.
De nada. No hay de qué.
Por favor. Perdón. Con permiso.
Mucho gusto. Igualmente. Encantado/a.

¿Cómo es usted?

soy, eres, es

Los números

cero, uno, dos, tres, cuatro, cinco, seis, siete,
　ocho, nueve, diez, once, doce, trece, catorce,
　quince, dieciséis, diecisiete, dieciocho,
　diecinueve, veinte, treinta

Gustos y preferencias

¿Te gusta ———? ¿Le gusta ———? Sí, me
gusta ———. No, no me gusta ———.

¿Qué hora es?

es la… , son las… y/menos cuarto (quince), y
　media (treinta), en punto, de la mañana (tarde,
　noche), ¿a qué hora?, a la(s)…

Palabras interrogativas

¿cómo?	how?; what?
¿cuál?	what?, which?
¿cuándo?	when?
¿cuánto/a?	how much?
¿cuántos/as?	how many?
¿dónde?	where?
¿qué?	what?, which?
¿quién?	who?, whom?

Palabras adicionales

sí	yes
no	no
está	is (located)
hay	there is/are
no hay	there is not / are not
hoy	today
mañana	tomorrow
y	and
o	or
a	to; at (*with time*)
de	of; from
en	in; on; at
pero	but
también	also

En la universidad

Hay estudiantes de muchas nacionalidades en las universidades de este país (*this country*), como esta (*this one*) en Boston, Massachusetts. ¿Cómo son los estudiantes en su (*your*) universidad?

VOCABULARIO

- In the classroom
- University subjects

GRAMÁTICA

1 Singular Nouns: Gender and Articles
2 Nouns and Articles: Plural Forms
3 Subject Pronouns; Present Tense of **-ar** Verbs; Negation

CULTURA

- **Enfoque cultural:** Los hispanos en los Estados Unidos
- **Nota cultural:** The Hispanic Educational System
- **En los Estados Unidos y el Canadá:** Jaime Escalante
- **Cultura en contexto:** Expressing *Cool!*

Multimedia

 You will learn about discussing classes and schedules in the **En contexto** video segment.

 Review vocabulary and grammar and practice language skills with the interactive CD-ROM.

Ww. Get connected to the Spanish-speaking world with the *¿Qué tal?* Online Learning Center: **www.mhhe.com/quetal**.

En la clase

¿Qué? Cosas

la ventana
la puerta
el papel
la pizarra
la silla
el escritorio
el libro
el libro de texto
la mochila
el cuaderno
la mesa
el dinero
la calculadora
el lápiz
el bolígrafo
el diccionario

¿Dónde? Lugares en la universidad

la biblioteca	the library
la cafetería	the cafeteria
la clase	the class
el edificio	the building
la librería	the bookstore
la oficina	the office
la residencia	the dormitory

¿Quién? Personas

el bibliotecario	the (male) librarian
la bibliotecaria	the (female) librarian
el compañero de clase	the (male) classmate
la compañera de clase	the (female) classmate
el compañero de cuarto	the (male) roommate
la compañera de cuarto	the (female) roommate
el consejero	the (male) advisor
la consejera	the (female) advisor
el estudiante	the (male) student
la estudiante	the (female) student
el hombre	the man
la mujer	the woman
el profesor	the (male) professor
la profesora	the (female) professor
el secretario	the (male) secretary
la secretaria	the (female) secretary

Conversación

A. ¿Dónde están ahora (*are they now*)**?** Tell where these people are. Then identify the numbered people and things: 1 = **la mesa**, 3 = **el consejero**, and so on. Refer to the drawing and lists on page 30 as much as you need to.

1. Están en _____.   2. Están en _____.   3. Están en _____.   4. Están en _____.

B. Identificaciones. ¿Es hombre o mujer?

MODELO: ¿La consejera? → Es mujer.

1. ¿El profesor?   3. ¿El secretario?   5. ¿La bibliotecaria?
2. ¿La estudiante?   4. ¿El estudiante?   6. ¿El compañero de cuarto?

Las materias

The names for most of these subject areas are cognates. See if you can recognize their meaning without looking at the English equivalent. You should learn in particular the names of subject areas that are of interest to you.

la administración de empresas	business
el arte	art
la computación	computer science
las comunicaciones	communications
la economía	economics
el español	Spanish
la filosofía	philosophy
la física	physics
la historia	history
el inglés	English
la literatura	literature
las matemáticas	mathematics
la química	chemistry
la sicología	psychology
la sociología	sociology

las ciencias	sciences
las humanidades	humanities
las lenguas extranjeras	foreign languages

Universidad Nacional Autónoma de México (UNAM), México, Distrito Federal (D.F.)

Conversación

A. Asociaciones. ¿Con qué materia(s) asocia usted a… ?

1. Louis Pasteur, Marie Curie
2. la doctora Joyce Brothers, B. F. Skinner
3. Barbara Walters, Peter Jennings
4. Aristóteles, Confucio
5. Mark Twain, Toni Morrison
6. Frida Kahlo, Pablo Picasso
7. Microsoft, IBM
8. Isaac Newton, Stephen Hawking

B. ¿Qué te gusta estudiar (*to study*)**?**

Paso 1. Make a list with subjects you like to study and another list with subjects you don't like.

Me gusta estudiar…   No me gusta estudiar…

Paso 2. In pairs, ask and answer questions about what you like and don't like to study.

MODELO: —¿Te gusta estudiar matemáticas?
—No, no me gusta estudiar matemáticas.

NOTA CULTURAL

The Hispanic Educational System

The educational system in Hispanic countries differs considerably from that of this country. Elementary school (**la escuela primaria**) can last five to eight years, depending on the country. After that, secondary school (**la escuela secundaria, el colegio**) may last four to seven years.

Hispanic universities have a long and respected history. At the university (always called **la universidad** and never **el colegio** or **la escuela**), students begin specialized programs (**la carrera**) in areas such as law, medicine, engineering, literature, and so on, immediately upon admission. The courses and standards for these university-level programs are generally established by national ministries of education, and their academic curricula are not very flexible; they usually offer only a few elective courses.

University students in Hispanic countries may be required to take up to eight different subjects in a single academic term. Academic performance is evaluated on a scale of one to ten, with five or six considered passing, depending on the country. In Spain, it is common to have one cumulative test at the end of the term. In other countries like Ecuador, students may have one or two partial tests in addition to a comprehensive final.

Esta estatua de Fray Luis de León está en la Universidad de Salamanca. La Universidad, que (*which*) data del año 1220 (mil doscientos veinte), es una de las más antiguas (*oldest*) de España.

1 Identifying People, Places, and Things • Singular Nouns: Gender and Articles*

En *la clase* del *profesor* Durán: *El primer* día

PROFESOR DURÁN: Aquí está *el programa* del *curso.* Son necesarios *el libro de texto* y *un diccionario.* También hay *una lista* de novelas y libros de poesía.

ESTUDIANTE 1: ¡Es *una lista* infinita!

ESTUDIANTE 2: Sí, y los libros cuestan demasiado.

ESTUDIANTE 1: No, *el problema* no es *el precio* de los libros. ¡Es *el tiempo* para leer los libros!

Escoja (*Choose*) las palabras o frases correctas según el diálogo.

1. La clase del profesor Durán es de (literatura / filosofía).
2. En el curso del profesor Durán (es necesario / no es necesario) leer (*to read*) mucho.
3. En un curso de literatura (es lógico / no es lógico) usar un diccionario.

To name persons, places, things, or ideas, you need to be able to use nouns. In Spanish, all *nouns* (**los sustantivos**) have either masculine or feminine *gender* (**el género**). This is a purely grammatical feature of nouns; it does not mean that Spanish speakers perceive things or ideas as having male or female attributes.

Since the gender of all nouns must be memorized, it is best to learn the definite article along with the noun; that is, learn **el lápiz** rather than just **lápiz**. The definite article will be given with nouns in vocabulary lists in this book.

	Masculine Nouns		**Feminine Nouns**	
Definite Articles	**el** hombre	*the man*	**la** mujer	*the woman*
	el libro	*the book*	**la** mesa	*the table*
Indefinite Articles	**un** hombre	*a (one) man*	**una** mujer	*a (one) woman*
	un libro	*a (one) book*	**una** mesa	*a (one) table*

---

*The grammar sections of *¿Qué tal?* are numbered consecutively throughout the book. If you need to review a particular grammar point, the index will refer you to its page number.

In Professor Durán's class: The first day PROFESSOR DURÁN: Here's the course syllabus. The textbook and a dictionary are required. There is also a list of novels and poetry books. STUDENT 1: It's an immense list! STUDENT 2: Yes, and the books cost too much. STUDENT 1: No, the problem isn't the price of the books. It's the time to read the books!

GENDER

A. Nouns that refer to male beings and most nouns that end in **-o** are *masculine* (**masculino**) in gender.

sustantivos masculinos: hombre, libro

B. Nouns that refer to female beings and most nouns that end in **-a, -ción, -tad,** and **-dad** are *feminine* (**femenino**) in gender.

sustantivos femeninos: mujer, mesa, nación, libertad, universidad

C. Nouns that have other endings and that do not refer to either male or female beings may be masculine or feminine. The gender of these words must be memorized.

el lápiz, la clase, la tarde, la noche

D. Many nouns that refer to persons indicate gender

  1. by changing the last vowel

el compañero ⟶ la compañera
el bibliotecario ⟶ la bibliotecaria

  2. by adding **-a** to the last consonant of the masculine form to make it feminine

un profesor ⟶ una profesora

E. Many other nouns that refer to people have a single form for both masculine and feminine genders. Gender is indicated by an article.

el estudiante (*the male student*) ⟶ **la** estudiante (*the female student*)
el cliente (*the male client*) ⟶ **la** cliente (*the female client*)
el dentista (*the male dentist*) ⟶ **la** dentista (*the female dentist*)

However, a few nouns that end in **-e** also have a feminine form that ends in **-a**.

el presidente ⟶ la presidenta
el dependiente (*the male clerk*) ⟶ la dependienta (*the female clerk*)

OJO

A common exception to the normal rules of gender is the word **el día**, which is masculine in gender. Many words ending in **-ma** are also masculine: **el problema, el programa, el sistema,** and so on. Watch for these exceptions as you continue your study of Spanish.

ARTICLES

A. In English, there is only one *definite article* (**el artículo definido**): *the*. In Spanish, the definite article for masculine singular nouns is **el**; for feminine singular nouns it is **la**.

definite article: *the*
m. sing. → **el**
f. sing. → **la**

B. In English, the singular *indefinite article* (**el artículo indefinido**) is *a* or *an*. In Spanish, the indefinite article, like the definite article, must agree with the gender of the noun: **un** for masculine nouns, **una** for feminine nouns.
Un and **una** can mean *one* as well as *a* or *an*. Context determines meaning.

indefinite article: *a, an*
m. sing. → **un**
f. sing. → **una**

Práctica

A. Artículos

Dé (*Give*) el artículo definido apropiado (**el, la**).

1. escritorio
2. biblioteca
3. bolígrafo
4. mochila
5. hombre
6. diccionario
7. universidad
8. dinero
9. mujer
10. nación
11. bibliotecario
12. calculadora

Ahora (*Now*) dé el artículo indefinido apropiado (**un, una**).

1. día un
2. mañana una
3. problema un
4. lápiz un
5. clase una
6. noche una
7. papel un
8. condición una
9. programa un

B. Escenas de la universidad

Paso 1. Haga una oración con las palabras (*words*) indicadas.

MODELO: estudiante / librería → Hay un estudiante en la librería.

1. un consejero / la oficina
2. una profesora / la clase
3. un lápiz / la mesa
4. un cuaderno / el escritorio
5. un libro / la mochila
6. un bolígrafo / la silla
7. una palabra / el papel
8. una oficina / la residencia
9. un compañero / la biblioteca

Paso 2. Now create new sentences by changing one of the words in each item in **Paso 1**. If you do this with a partner, try to come up with as many variations as possible.

MODELO: Hay un estudiante en *la residencia*. (Hay *una profesora* en la librería.)

Conversación

A. Definiciones. Con un compañero / una compañera, defina estas palabras en español según el modelo.

MODELO: biblioteca / edificio → ESTUDIANTE 1: ¿La biblioteca?
ESTUDIANTE 2: Es un edificio.

Categorías: cosa, edificio, materia, persona

1. cliente / persona
2. bolígrafo / cosa
3. residencia / edificio
4. dependiente / ¿ ?
5. hotel (*m.*) / ¿ ?
6. calculadora / ¿ ?
7. computación / ¿ ?
8. inglés / ¿ ?
9. ¿ ?

B. Asociaciones. Identifique dos cosas y dos personas que usted asocia con los siguientes lugares.

MODELO: la clase → la silla, el libro de texto
el profesor, el estudiante

1. la biblioteca
2. la librería
3. una oficina
4. la residencia

---

2 | ## Identifying People, Places, and Things • Nouns and Articles: Plural Forms

- You can find many nouns in this ad. Can you guess the meaning of most of them?
- Some of the nouns in the ad are plural. Can you tell how to make nouns plural in Spanish, based on these nouns?
- Look for the Spanish equivalent of the following words.

  adults   preparation   financing   course

- **Idioma** is another word for *language,* and it is a false cognate. It never means *idiom.*
- Using the vocabulary in the ad, guess what **en el extranjero** means.

	Singular	Plural	
Nouns Ending in a Vowel	el libro la mesa un libro una mesa	los libros las mesas unos libros unas mesas	*the books* *the tables* *some books* *some tables*
Nouns Ending in a Consonant	la universidad un papel	las universidades unos papeles	*the universities* *some papers*

A. Spanish nouns that end in a vowel form plurals by adding **-s**. Nouns that end in a consonant add **-es**. Nouns that end in the consonant **-z** change the **-z** to **-c** before adding **-es**: lápiz → lápices.

Plurals in Spanish:

- vowel + **s**
- consonant + **es**
- **-z** → **-ces**

B. The definite and indefinite articles also have plural forms: **el → los, la → las, un → unos, una → unas. Unos** and **unas** mean *some, several,* or *a few.*

- **el → los**
- **la → las**
- **un → unos**
- **una → unas**

C. In Spanish, the masculine plural form of a noun is used to refer to a group that includes both males and females.

los amig**os**
the friends (both male and female)

unos extranjer**os**
some foreigners (both male and female)

Práctica

A. **Singular → plural.** Dé la forma plural.

1. la mesa
2. el papel
3. el amigo
4. la oficina
5. un cuaderno
6. un lápiz
7. una universidad
8. un bolígrafo
9. un edificio

B. **Plural → singular.** Dé la forma singular.

1. los profesores
2. las calculadoras
3. las bibliotecarias
4. los estudiantes
5. unos hombres
6. unas tardes
7. unas residencias
8. unas sillas
9. unos escritorios

Conversación

A. Identificaciones. Identifique las personas, las cosas y los lugares.

MODELO: Hay _____ en _____. → Hay unos estudiantes en la clase.

Palabras útiles: la computadora, el experimento, la planta, el teléfono

1. **2.**

B. Semejanzas (*Similarities*) **y diferencias**

Paso 1. ¿Cuáles son las semejanzas y las diferencias entre los dos cuartos? Hay por lo menos (*at least*) seis diferencias.

MODELO: En el dibujo A, hay _____.
En el dibujo B, hay sólo (*only*) _____.
En el escritorio del dibujo A, hay _____.
En el escritorio del dibujo B, hay _____.

Palabras útiles: la cama (*bed*), la computadora, el estante (*bookshelf*), la lámpara, la planta

Ⓐ   Ⓑ

Paso 2. Ahora indique qué hay en su propio (*your own*) cuarto. Use palabras del **Paso 1**.

MODELO: En mi cuarto hay _____. En mi escritorio hay _____.

Enfoque *cultural*

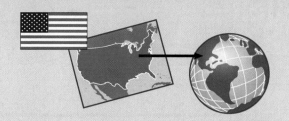

Los hispanos en los Estados Unidos

Datos[a] esenciales

La población hispánica total de los Estados Unidos: más de 35 (treinta y cinco) millones en el año 2000 (dos mil).

Orígenes de la población hispánica en los Estados Unidos:

México: 58,5% (cincuenta y ocho coma cinco por ciento)

Centroamérica, Sudamérica y otros países:[b] 28,4%

Puerto Rico: 9,6%

Cuba: 3,5%

[a]*Facts* [b]*otros... other countries*

¡Fíjese![a]

- En 2001 (dos mil uno) había[b] veintiún hispanos en el Congreso de los Estados Unidos. ¿Cuántos hay ahora?

- De los más de[c] 35 millones de hispanos en los Estados Unidos, la mayoría[d] habla español (mucho o poco).

- Las palabras **hispano** e[e] **hispánico** se refieren al[f] idioma y a la cultura, no a la raza[g] o al grupo étnico.

[a]*Check it out!* [b]*there were* [c]*De... Of the more than* [d]*majority* [e]*y* [f]*se... refer to the* [g]*race*

Conozca a[a]... César Chávez

César Chávez

La contribución de César Chávez (1927–1993 [mil novecientos veintisiete a mil novecientos noventa y tres]) al movimiento de los trabajadores agrícolas[b] es enorme. La educación de Chávez, hijo de campesinos migrantes,[c] sólo llega al séptimo grado.[d]

En 1962 (mil novecientos sesenta y dos), Chávez organiza a los campesinos que cosechan uvas.[e] Como resultado de las huelgas[f] y el boicoteo de las uvas de mesa,[g] los campesinos reciben contratos más favorables para ellos; el United Farm Workers se establece[h] como sindicato[i] oficial.

Hoy en día,[j] la vida,[k] los sacrificios y los ideales de Chávez sirven de[l] inspiración a muchas personas.

[a]*Conozca... Meet* [b]*trabajadores... agricultural workers* [c]*campesinos... migrant farm workers* [d]*llega... goes up to the seventh grade* [e]*cosechan... harvest grapes* [f]*strikes* [g]*uvas... table grapes* [h]*se... is established* [i]*union* [j]*Hoy... Nowadays* [k]*life* [l]*sirven... serve as an*

Capítulo 1 of the video to accompany *¿Qué tal?* contains cultural footage of Hispanics in the United States.

WW. Visit the *¿Qué tal?* website at www.mhhe.com/quetal.

3 **Expressing Actions** • Subject Pronouns; Present Tense of *-ar* Verbs; Negation

Escuchando furtivamente

Escuche lo que Diego le dice a Lupe. Luego imagine la parte de Lupe en la conversación.

DIEGO: *Yo hablo* con mi familia con frecuencia. Por eso *pago* mucho en cuentas de teléfono. ¿Y tú?

LUPE: [...]

DIEGO: *Necesito* dinero para comprar libros. Por eso *enseño* inglés a un estudiante de matemáticas. ¿Y tú?

LUPE: [...]

DIEGO: En mi tiempo libre *escucho* música. También *toco* la guitarra. En las fiestas *bailo* mucho y *tomo* cerveza con mis amigos. Los fines de semana, *busco* libros de antropología en las librerías. ¿Y tú?

LUPE: [...]

Comprensión: ¿Cierto o falso?

1. Diego no habla mucho con su familia.
2. Es estudiante de ciencias.
3. No le gusta la música.
4. Es una persona introvertida y solitaria.
5. Habla francés.

Subject Pronouns			
Singular		**Plural**	
yo	I	**nosotros / nosotras**	we
tú	you (*fam.*)	**vosotros / vosotras**	you (*fam. Sp.*)
usted (Ud.)*	you (*form.*)	**ustedes (Uds.)***	you (*form.*)
él	he	**ellos / ellas**	they
ella	she		

Eavesdropping   *Listen to what Diego is saying to Lupe. Then imagine Lupe's part in the conversation.*
DIEGO: I speak often with my family. That's why I pay a lot in telephone bills. And you? LUPE: [...] DIEGO: I need money to buy books. That's why I teach English to a math student. And you? LUPE: [...] DIEGO: In my spare time I listen to music. I also play the guitar. At parties I dance a lot and drink beer with my friends. On weekends, I look for anthropology books in bookstores. And you? LUPE: [...]
*****Usted** and **ustedes** are frequently abbreviated in writing as **Ud.** or **Vd.**, and **Uds.** or **Vds.**, respectively.

A. Several *subject pronouns* (**los pronombres personales**) have masculine and feminine forms. The masculine plural form is used to refer to a group of males as well as to a group of males and females.

> **pronoun** = a word that takes the place of a noun
> Ted → *he*
> Martha and Ted → *they*

ellos = *they* (all males; males and females)
ellas = *they* (all females)

B. Spanish has different words for *you*. In general, **tú** is used to refer to a close friend or a member of your family, while **usted** is used with people with whom the speaker has a more formal or distant relationship. The situations in which **tú** and **usted** are used also vary among different countries and regions.

tú → close friend, family member
usted (Ud.) → formal or distant relationship

C. In Latin America and in this country, the plural for both **usted** and **tú** is **ustedes**. In Spain, however, **vosotros/vosotras** is the plural of **tú**, while **ustedes** is used as the plural of **usted** exclusively.

Latin America, North America	Spain
tú ⎱ ustedes	tú → vosotros/vosotras
usted (Ud.) ⎰ (Uds.)	usted (Ud.) → ustedes (Uds.)

D. Subject pronouns are not used as frequently in Spanish as they are in English and may usually be omitted. You will learn more about the uses of Spanish subject pronouns in **Capítulo 2.**

VERBS: INFINITIVES AND PERSONAL ENDINGS

A. The *infinitive* (**el infinitivo**) of a verb indicates the action or state of being, with no reference to who or what performs the action or when it is done (present, past, or future). In Spanish all infinitives end in **-ar, -er,** or **-ir**. Infinitives in English are indicated by *to: to* speak, *to* eat, *to* live.

-ar:	hablar	*to speak*
-er:	comer	*to eat*
-ir:	vivir	*to live*

B. To *conjugate* (**conjugar**) a verb means to give the various forms of the verb with their corresponding subjects: *I speak, you speak, she speaks,* and so on. All regular Spanish verbs are conjugated by adding *personal endings* (**las terminaciones personales**) that reflect the subject doing the action. These are added to the *stem* (**la raíz** (root) or **el radical**), which is the infinitive minus the infinitive ending.

hablar → habl-
comer → com-
vivir → viv-

C. The right-hand column shows the personal endings that are added to the stem of all regular **-ar** verbs.

Regular **-ar** verb endings:
o, -as, -a, -amos, -áis, -an

		hablar (*to speak*): habl-			
	Singular			**Plural**	
(yo)	hablo	*I speak*	(nosotros) (nosotras)	hablamos	*we speak*
(tú)	hablas	*you speak*	(vosotros) (vosotras)	habláis	*you speak*
(Ud.) (él) (ella)	habla	*you speak; he/she speaks*	(Uds.) (ellos) (ellas)	hablan	*you/they speak*

Some important **-ar** verbs in this chapter include those on the right.

> **OJO**
>
> Note that in Spanish the meaning of the English word *for* is included in the verbs **buscar** (*to look for*) and **pagar** (*to pay for*); *to* is included in **escuchar** (*to listen to*).

bailar	to dance	**hablar**	to speak; to talk
buscar	to look for	**necesitar**	to need
cantar	to sing	**pagar**	to pay (for)
comprar	to buy	**practicar**	to practice
desear	to want	**regresar**	to return (*to a place*)
enseñar	to teach	**tocar**	to play (*a musical instrument*)
escuchar	to listen (to)	**tomar**	to take; to drink
estudiar	to study	**trabajar**	to work

D. As in English, when two Spanish verbs are used in sequence and there is no change of subject, the second verb is usually in the infinitive form.

Necesito llamar a mi familia.
I need to call my family.

Me gusta bailar.
I like to dance.

E. In both English and Spanish, conjugated verb forms also indicate the *time* or *tense* (**el tiempo**) of the action: *I speak* (present), *I spoke* (past).

Some English equivalents of the present tense forms of Spanish verbs are shown at the right.

hablo		
	I speak	Simple present tense
	I am speaking	Present progressive (indicates an action in progress)
	I will speak	Near future action

NEGATION

In Spanish the word **no** is placed before the conjugated verb to make a negative sentence.

El estudiante **no** habla español.
The student doesn't speak Spanish.

No, **no** necesito dinero.
No, I don't need money.

Práctica

A. Mis compañeros y yo

Paso 1. Read the following statements and tell whether they are true for you and your classmates and for your classroom environment. If any statement is not true for you or your class, make it negative or change it in another way to make it correct.

MODELO: Toco el piano → Sí, toco el piano.
(No, no toco el piano. Toco la guitarra.)

1. Necesito más (*more*) dinero.
2. Trabajo en la biblioteca.
3. Tomo ocho clases este semestre/trimestre (*this term*).
4. En clase, cantamos en francés.
5. Deseamos practicar español.
6. Tomamos Coca-Cola en clase.
7. El profesor / La profesora enseña español.
8. El profesor / La profesora habla el alemán (*German*) muy bien.

Paso 2. Now turn to the person next to you and rephrase each sentence as a question, using **tú** forms of the verbs in all cases. Your partner will indicate whether the sentences are true for him or her.

MODELO: ¿Tocas el piano? → Sí, toco el piano. (No, no toco el piano.)

B. En una fiesta.
The following paragraphs describe a party. Scan the paragraphs first, to get a general sense of their meaning. Then complete the paragraphs with the correct form of the numbered infinitives.

Esta noche[a] hay una fiesta en el apartamento de Marcos y Julio. Todos[b] los estudiantes (cantar[1]) y (bailar[2]). Una persona (tocar[3]) la guitarra y otras personas (escuchar[4]) la música.

    Jaime (buscar[5]) un café. Marta (hablar[6]) con un amigo. María José (desear[7]) enseñarles a todos[c] un baile[d] de Colombia. Todas las estudiantes desean (bailar[8]) con el estudiante mexicano —¡él (bailar[9]) muy bien!

    La fiesta es estupenda, pero todos (necesitar[10]) regresar a casa[e] o a su[f] cuarto temprano.[g] ¡Hay clases mañana!

[a]Esta... *Tonight*   [b]*All*   [c]enseñarles... *to teach everyone*   [d]*dance*   [e]a... *home*   [f]*their*   [g]*early*

Comprensión: ¿Cierto o falso?

1. Marcos es un profesor de español.
2. A Jaime le gusta la cerveza.
3. María José es de Colombia.
4. Los estudiantes desean bailar.

En los Estados Unidos y el Canadá...

Jaime Escalante

Argueably the most famous high school teacher in the United States, Jaime Escalante was born in La Paz, Bolivia, where he was a math and physics teacher for fourteen years. He emigrated to California in 1964 when he was 33. Since he did not speak English, he took menial jobs while he learned the language and went to college to become an accredited teacher. He started teaching in 1974 at Garfield High School, in East Los Angeles, where the students were mostly low-income Latinos. With Escalante's help, their test scores were comparable to those of students in high-income areas of the city. In fact, Escalante's students did so well that the Educational Testing Service thought they had cheated and asked them to retake the test.

Escalante became an overnight celebrity. The 1988 film *Stand and Deliver* (with a Spanish version called *Con ganas de triunfar*) portrays his and his students' efforts. He was later awarded the United States Presidential Medal and the Andrés Bello award by the Organization of American States.

Jaime Escalante

NOTA COMUNICATIVA

The Verb *estar*

Estar is another Spanish **-ar** verb. It means *to be,* and you have already used forms of it to ask how others are feeling or to tell where things are located. Here is the complete conjugation of **estar**. Note that the **yo** form is irregular. The other forms take regular **-ar** endings, and some have a shift in the stress pattern (indicated by the accented **á**).

yo	**estoy**	nosotros/as	**estamos**
tú	**estás**	vosotros/as	**estáis**
Ud., él, ella	**está**	Uds., ellos, ellas	**están**

You will learn the uses of the verb **estar**, along with those of **ser** (the other Spanish verb that means *to be*), gradually, over the next several chapters. For now, just answer the following questions, using forms of **estar**.

1. ¿Cómo está Ud. en este momento (*right now*)?
2. ¿Cómo están sus (*your*) compañeros de clase?
3. ¿Dónde está Ud. en este momento?

Conversación

A. ¿Qué hacen? (*What are they doing?*) Tell where these people are and what they are doing. Note that the definite article is used with titles when you are talking about a person: **el señor, la señora, el profesor, la profesora.**

MODELO: La Sra. Martínez _____. →
La Sra. Martínez está en la oficina. Busca un libro, trabaja…

Frases útiles: hablar por teléfono, preparar la lección, pronunciar las palabras, tomar apuntes (*to take notes*), usar una computadora

1. Estas (*These*) personas están en la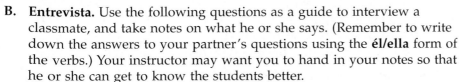
La profesora Gil _____.
Casi (*Almost*) todos los
estudiantes _____.
Unos estudiantes _____.

2. Estas personas están _____.
El Sr. Miranda _____.
La bibliotecaria _____.
El secretario _____.

3. Estas personas _____.
El cliente _____.
La dependienta _____.

B. Entrevista. Use the following questions as a guide to interview a classmate, and take notes on what he or she says. (Remember to write down the answers to your partner's questions using the **él/ella** form of the verbs.) Your instructor may want you to hand in your notes so that he or she can get to know the students better.

MODELO: ESTUDIANTE 1: Karen, ¿estudias filosofía?
ESTUDIANTE 2: No, no estudio filosofía. Estudio música.
ESTUDIANTE 1: (escribe [*writes*]): Karen no estudia filosofía. Estudia música.

1. ¿Estudias mucho o poco (*a lot or a little*)? ¿Dónde estudias, en casa (*at home*) o en la biblioteca? ¿Cuándo estudias, por la mañana (*in the morning*), por la tarde (*afternoon*) o por la noche (*at night*)?
2. ¿Cantas bien o mal (*poorly*)? ¿Tocas un instrumento musical? ¿Cuál es? (el piano, la guitarra, el violín…)
3. ¿Trabajas? ¿Dónde? ¿Cuántas horas a la semana (*per week*) trabajas?
4. ¿Quiénes pagan los libros de texto, tú o los profesores? ¿Qué más (*more*) necesitas pagar? ¿diccionarios? ¿la matrícula (*tuition*)? ¿el alquiler (*rent*)? ¿ ?

UN POCO DE TODO

A. Una carta (*letter*) **a una amiga.** Complete the following paragraphs from Ángela's letter about college to a friend in her hometown. Give the correct form of the words in parentheses, as suggested by the context. When two possibilities are given in parentheses, select the correct word.

Mi amiga Kathy y yo estamos muy contentas. ¡Todo (ser[1]) fantástico! Kathy (tomar[2]) cuatro clases y yo, cinco. (*Nosotras:* Estudiar[3]) mucho. A mí (me/te[4]) gusta ir[a] temprano a la cafetería. A esas horas[b] hay unos donuts riquísimos.[c] (*Yo:* Comprar[5]) un café y dos donuts y (estudiar[6]) unos minutos o media hora, especialmente para[d] (el/la[7]) clase de español.

En la residencia hay (un/una[8]) estudiante de Puerto Rico, Luisa, que vive[e] en el cuarto de enfrente.[f] Con Luisa (*nosotras:* practicar[9]) (el/la[10]) pronunciación. Ella también nos[g] enseña canciones en español. Kathy (cantar[11]) muy mal, pero (bailar[12]) la salsa muy bien… o «chévere», como dice Luisa.[h]

Kathy y yo también (trabajar[13]). Yo trabajo en la biblioteca (por/de[14]) las tardes. Kathy no trabaja en (el/la[15]) universidad, pero su trabajo[i] no (ser[16]) muy diferente. Es (cliente/dependienta[17]) en una librería. ¡Las dos (*nosotras:* estar[18]) con libros todo (el/la[19]) día!

[a]*to go* [b]*A… At that time* [c]*extremely delicious* [d]*for* [e]*que… who lives* [f]*de… in front (of us)*
[g]*us* [h]*como… as Luisa says* [i]*su… her work*

Comprensión: ¿Cierto o falso? Which of these statements do you agree with after reading Ángela's letter? Change incorrect statements to make them true.

1. Ángela toma Español 1 en la universidad.
2. A Ángela no le gusta el español como materia.
3. Ángela no estudia con frecuencia.
4. Todos los amigos de Ángela son de habla inglesa (*English-speaking*).

B. ¿Qué pasa (*What's happening*) **en la fiesta?**

Paso 1. With a classmate, briefly describe what's going on in the following scene.

Paso 2. Now compare the scene with parties *you* go to. You can use the **nosotros** form of verbs to describe what you and your friends do at these parties.

Vocabulario útil: descansar (*to rest*), escuchar, fumar (*to smoke*), mirar una película/la tele (*to watch a movie/TV*), tocar el piano/la guitarra, tomar cerveza/vino/refrescos (*beer/wine/soft drinks*)

VIDEOTECA: En contexto

EL PERÚ

In this video segment, Peruvian student Juan Carlos engages a fellow student in conversation. As you watch the segment, pay particular attention to the information they give. What classes are they taking? What do they like to do on weekends?

FUNCTION
Talking about class schedules

Cultura en contexto
Expressing *Cool!*

As in all languages, slang is widely used in Spanish, and it varies from region to region and generation to generation. As in the video segment, a student from Peru might say **¡Qué bacán!** to express *Cool!* while in Mexico you would probably hear **¡Qué padre!** The expression **¡Qué chévere!** is widely used throughout the Caribbean and in parts of Latin America, and **¡Qué guay!** is common in Spain.

A. Lluvia de ideas

What usually happens when you attend a class for the first time? Do you talk to your fellow students? What do you talk about?

B. Dictado

Here is the second half of this segment's dialogue. Fill in the missing portions of Eduardo's dialogue. (There is an underlined space for each word.)

EDUARDO: …Oye, ¿tomas también la clase de sociología con el profesor Ramón?
JUAN CARLOS: Sí, también tomo esa[a] clase.
EDUARDO: ¿A _____[1] _____[2] es la clase de _____[3]? ¿Es a la una o a la una _____[4] _____[5]?
JUAN CARLOS: Es a la una y media, creo[b]… Sí, a la una y media.
EDUARDO: Este _____[6] es excelente.
JUAN CARLOS: Sí, escucho su[c] música con frecuencia. Me gusta mucho el jazz.
EDUARDO: Ah, ¿sí? Yo _____[7] en el Café Azul. Allí[d] _____[8] _____[9] jazz todos los fines de semana por la noche.
JUAN CARLOS: ¡Qué bacán![e] ¿A qué hora?
EDUARDO: A las _____[10].
JUAN CARLOS: ¡Perfecto! Entonces, este[f] fin de semana escucho jazz en tu[g] café. Oye,[h] ¿qué hora es?
EDUARDO: Son las _____[11] y cinco. ¿Dónde _____[12] _____[13] _____[14]? La clase es a las once.

[a]*that* [b]*I think* [c]*their* [d]*There* [e]*¡Qué… Cool!* [f]*this* [g]*your* [h]*Hey*

C. Un diálogo original

Paso 1. With a classmate, re-enact the situation between Eduardo and Juan Carlos.

Paso 2. With a different classmate, role-play a situation similar to the one in the video. Here are the roles:

ESTUDIANTE 1: You are a student coming into the classroom the first day of classes. You want to start a conversation with a classmate. As you sit down, you let your classmate see a CD (pronounced as the letters **c d** [**ce de**]), which you like a lot.

ESTUDIANTE 2: You are already sitting in class. You are also interested in making a new friend. One of your classmates has a CD of one of your favorite bands.

PASO FINAL

 A LEER

Estrategia: More on Guessing Meaning from Context

As you learned in **El mundo hispánico** (**Primeros pasos**), you can often guess the meaning of unfamiliar words from the context (the words that surround them) and by using your knowledge about the topic in general. Making "educated guesses" about words in this way will be an important part of your reading skills in Spanish.

What is the meaning of the underlined words in these sentences?

1. En una lista alfabetizada, la palabra **grande** aparece <u>antes de</u> **grotesco**.
2. El edificio no es moderno; es <u>viejo</u>.
3. Me gusta estudiar español, pero detesto la biología. En general, <u>odio</u> las ciencias como materia.

Some words are underlined in the following reading (and in the readings in subsequent chapters). Try to guess their meaning from context.

Like the passages in **Primeros pasos** and some others in subsequent chapters, this reading contains section subheadings. Scanning these subheadings in advance will help you make predictions about the reading's content, which will also help to facilitate your overall comprehension. Another useful way to manage longer passages is to read section by section. At this point, don't try to understand every word. Your main objective should be to understand the general content of the passage.

Sobre la lectura... This reading was written by the authors of *¿Qué tal?* for students of Spanish like you. Later on in this text, you will have the chance to read more "authentic" selections.

Las universidades hispánicas

Introducción
En el mundo hispánico —y en los Estados Unidos y el Canadá— hay universidades grandes[a] y pequeñas; públicas, religiosas y privadas; modernas y antiguas. Pero el concepto de «vida[b] universitaria» es diferente.

El campus
Por ejemplo, en los países[c] hispánicos la universidad no es un centro de actividad social. No hay muchas residencias estudiantiles. En general, los estudiantes viven en pensiones[d] o en casas particulares[e] y llegan a la universidad en coche o en autobús. En algunas[f] universidades hay un *campus* similar a los de[g] las universidades de los Estados Unidos y el Canadá. En estos casos se habla[h] de la «ciudad[i] universitaria». Otras universidades ocupan sólo un edificio grande, o posiblemente varios edificios, pero no hay zonas verdes.[j]

Estudiantes de Medicina en Caracas, Venezuela

Los deportes
Otra diferencia es que en la mayoría de las universidades hispánicas los deportes no son muy importantes. Si los estudiantes desean practicar un deporte —el tenis, el fútbol o el béisbol— hay clubes deportivos, pero estos[k] no forman parte de la universidad.

Las diversiones[l]
Como se puede ver,[m] la forma y la organización de la universidad son diferentes en las dos culturas. Pero los estudiantes estudian y se divierten[n] en todas partes.[o] A los estudiantes hispanos —así como[p] a los estadounidenses* y canadienses[q] les gusta mucho toda clase de música: la música moderna —la nacional[r] y la importada (y hay para todos: Madonna, 'N Sync, R.E.M…)— la música clásica y la música con raíces[s] tradicionales. Otras diversiones preferidas por los estudiantes son las discotecas y los cafés. Hay cafés ideales para hablar con los amigos. También hay exposiciones de arte, obras de teatro y películas[t] interesantes.

Conclusión
Los días favoritos de muchos jóvenes[u] hispánicos son los fines de semana. ¿Realmente son muy distintos los estudiantes hispanos? ■

[a]*large* [b]*life* [c]*naciones* [d]*boarding houses* [e]*private* [f]*some* [g]*los… those of* [h]*se… one speaks* [i]*city* [j]*green* [k]*they* (literally *these*) [l]*Las… Entertainment* [m]*Como… As you can see* [n]*se… have a good time* [o]*en… everywhere* [p]*Así… like* [q]*estadounidenses… people from the U.S. and Canada* [r]*la… (music) from their own country* [s]*roots* [t]*movies* [u]*young people*

---

*Although, technically, **norteamericano** refers to all North Americans, the term is sometimes used to refer solely to people from the United States of America. In this book, **estadounidenses** will refer to people of the United States and **norteamericanos** to North Americans.

Comprensión

A. ¿Cierto o falso? Indique si las siguientes oraciones son ciertas o falsas.

1. En los países hispánicos, la mayoría de los estudiantes vive en residencias.
2. En las universidades hispánicas, los deportes ocupan un lugar esencial en el programa de estudios del estudiante.
3. En una universidad hispánica, no hay mucho tiempo para asistir a (*time for attending*) conciertos y exposiciones de arte.
4. No hay mucha diferencia entre (*between*) una universidad hispánica y una universidad norteamericana con respecto al *campus*.
5. La música es una diversión para los estudiantes en todas partes.

B. ¿Qué universidad? Indique si las siguientes oraciones son de un estudiante de la Universidad de Sevilla o de un estudiante de la Universidad de Michigan... ¡o de los dos!

	SEVILLA	MICHIGAN	LOS DOS
1. «Me gusta jugar al Frisbee en el *campus*.»	☐	☐	☐
2. «La casa es muy cómoda (*comfortable*) y tengo derecho a usar la cocina (*I have kitchen privileges*).»	☐	☐	☐
3. «Después de mi clase, ¿qué tal si tomamos un café?»	☐	☐	☐
4. «El sábado (*Saturday*) hay un partido de basquetbol. ¿Deseas ir (*to go*)?»	☐	☐	☐

 ## A ESCRIBIR

In light of what you now know about some differences and similarities between universities in this country and in Hispanic countries, what information do you think would be important to share with a Hispanic student planning on studying at *your* university? In a brief paragraph, describe your university to such a student. Include information such as: **el número de residencias; si la universidad es grande/pequeña, pública/privada; el edificio más grande** (*biggest*); and so on.

Mi universidad...

En resumen

GRAMÁTICA

To review the grammar points presented in this chapter, refer to the indicated grammar presentations. You'll find further practice of these structures in the Workbook/Laboratory Manual, on the CD-ROM, and on the website.

1. Singular Nouns: Gender and Articles

Do you understand the gender of nouns and how to use the articles **el, la, uno,** and **una**?

2. Nouns and Articles: Plural Forms

Do you know how to make nouns plural and use the articles **los, las, unos,** and **unas**?

3. Subject Pronouns; Present Tense of *-ar* Verbs; Negation

You should be able to use subject pronouns, conjugate regular **-ar** verbs in the present tense, and form negative sentences.

VOCABULARIO

Los verbos

bailar	to dance
buscar	to look for
cantar	to sing
comprar	to buy
desear	to want
enseñar	to teach
escuchar	to listen (to)
estar (*irreg.*)	to be
estudiar	to study
hablar	to speak; to talk
hablar por teléfono	to talk on the phone
necesitar	to need
pagar	to pay (for)
practicar	to practice
regresar	to return (*to a place*)
regresar a casa	to go home
tocar	to play (*a musical instrument*)
tomar	to take; to drink
trabajar	to work

Los lugares

el apartamento	apartment
la biblioteca	library
la cafetería	cafeteria
la clase	class
el cuarto	room
el edificio	building
la fiesta	party
la librería	bookstore
la oficina	office
la residencia	dormitory
la universidad	university

Las personas

el/la amigo/a	friend
el/la bibliotecario/a	librarian
el/la cliente	client
el/la compañero/a (de clase)	classmate
el/la compañero/a de cuarto	roommate
el/la consejero/a	advisor

el/la dependiente/a	clerk
el/la estudiante	student
el/la extranjero/a	foreigner
el hombre	man
la mujer	woman
el/la profesor(a)	professor
el/la secretario/a	secretary

Las lenguas (extranjeras)

el alemán	German
el español	Spanish
el francés	French
el inglés	English
el italiano	Italian

Otras materias

la administración de empresas, el arte, las
ciencias, la computación, las comunicaciones, la
economía, la filosofía, la física, la historia, las
humanidades, la literatura, las matemáticas, la
química, la sicología, la sociología

Las cosas

el bolígrafo	pen
la calculadora	calculator
el cuaderno	notebook
el diccionario	dictionary
el dinero	money
el escritorio	desk
el lápiz (pl. lápices)	pencil
el libro (de texto)	(text)book
la mesa	table
la mochila	backpack
el papel	paper
la pizarra	chalkboard
la puerta	door
la silla	chair
la ventana	window

Otros sustantivos

el café	coffee
la cerveza	beer
el día	day
la matrícula	tuition

¿Cuándo?

ahora	now
con frecuencia	frequently
el fin de semana	weekend
por la mañana	in the morning
(tarde, noche)	(afternoon, evening)
tarde/temprano	late/early
todos los días	every day

Pronombres personales

yo, tú, usted (Ud.), él/ella, nosotros/nosotras,
vosotros/vosotras, ustedes (Uds.), ellos/ellas

Palabras adicionales

aquí	here
con	with
en casa	at home
mal	poorly
más	more
mucho	much; a lot
muy	very
poco	little; a little bit
por eso	therefore
sólo	only

CAPÍTULO
2

La familia

Los fines de semana, muchas familias mexicanas pasan la tarde en Xochimilco. **Xochimilco** significa «jardín de flores» (*garden of flowers*) en el idioma de los aztecas.

VOCABULARIO

- Family and relatives
- Adjectives
- Numbers 31–100

GRAMÁTICA

4 Present Tense of **ser**; Summary of Uses
5 Possessive Adjectives (Unstressed)
6 Adjectives: Gender, Number, and Position
7 Present Tense of **-er** and **-ir** Verbs; More about Subject Pronouns

CULTURA

- **Enfoque cultural:** México
- **Nota cultural:** Hispanic Last Names
- **En los Estados Unidos y el Canadá:** Los Sheen, una familia de actores
- **Cultura en contexto:** La familia extendida

Multimedia

 You will learn more about describing other people in the **En contexto** video segment.

 Review vocabulary and grammar and practice language skills with the interactive CD-ROM.

W.W. Get connected to the Spanish-speaking world with the *¿Qué tal?* Online Learning Center: **www.mhhe.com/quetal**.

La familia y los parientes°

relatives

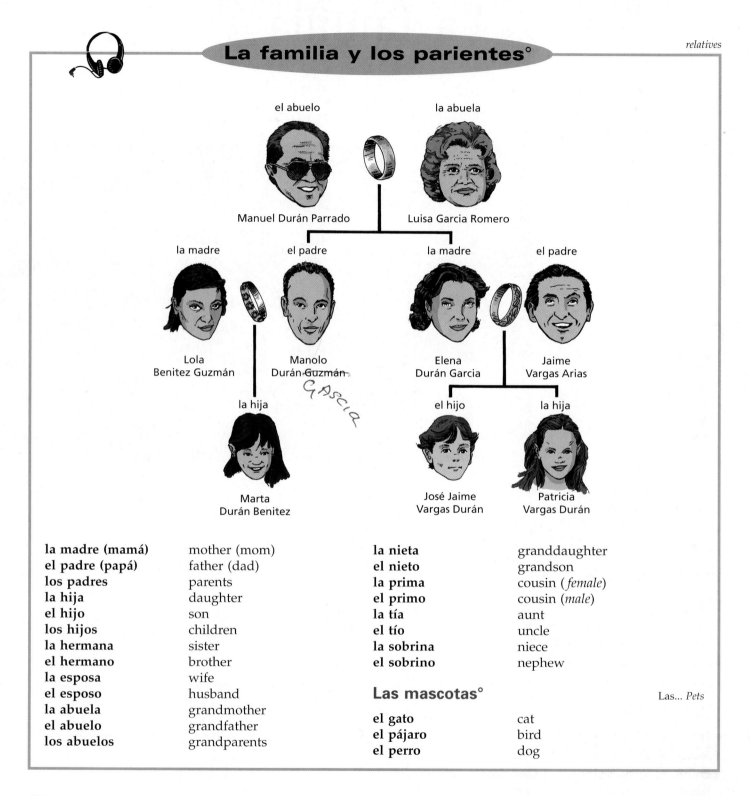

el abuelo — la abuela

Manuel Durán Parrado — Luisa Garcia Romero

la madre — el padre — la madre — el padre

Lola Benitez Guzmán — Manolo Durán Guzmán — Elena Durán Garcia — Jaime Vargas Arias

la hija

Marta Durán Benitez

el hijo — la hija

José Jaime Vargas Durán — Patricia Vargas Durán

la madre (mamá)	mother (mom)	**la nieta**	granddaughter
el padre (papá)	father (dad)	**el nieto**	grandson
los padres	parents	**la prima**	cousin (*female*)
la hija	daughter	**el primo**	cousin (*male*)
el hijo	son	**la tía**	aunt
los hijos	children	**el tío**	uncle
la hermana	sister	**la sobrina**	niece
el hermano	brother	**el sobrino**	nephew
la esposa	wife		
el esposo	husband	**Las mascotas°**	*Las... Pets*
la abuela	grandmother		
el abuelo	grandfather	**el gato**	cat
los abuelos	grandparents	**el pájaro**	bird
		el perro	dog

<table>
<tr><td colspan="2" align="center">**Vocabulario útil**</td></tr>
<tr><td>el padrastro / la madrastra</td><td>stepfather/stepmother</td></tr>
<tr><td>el hijastro / la hijastra</td><td>stepson/stepdaughter</td></tr>
<tr><td>el hermanastro / la hermanastra</td><td>stepbrother/stepsister</td></tr>
<tr><td>el medio hermano / la media hermana</td><td>half-brother/half-sister</td></tr>
<tr><td>el suegro / la suegra</td><td>father-in-law/mother-in-law</td></tr>
<tr><td>el yerno / la nuera</td><td>son-in-law/daughter-in-law</td></tr>
<tr><td>el cuñado / la cuñada</td><td>brother-in-law/sister-in-law</td></tr>
<tr><td>…**(ya) murió**</td><td>… has (already) died</td></tr>
</table>

Conversación

A. ¿Cierto o falso? Look at the drawing of the family tree that appears on page 54. Decide whether each of the following statements is true (**cierto**) or false (**falso**) according to the drawing. Correct the false statements.

1. José Jaime es el hermano de Marta.
2. Luisa es la abuela de Patricia.
3. Marta es la sobrina de Jaime y Elena.
4. Patricia y José Jaime son primos.
5. Elena es la tía de Manolo.
6. Jaime es el sobrino de José Jaime.

B. ¿Quién es?

Paso 1. Complete las oraciones lógicamente.

1. La madre de mi (*my*) padre es mi _____.
2. El hijo de mi tío es mi _____.
3. La hermana de mi padre es mi _____.
4. El esposo de mi abuela es mi _____.

Paso 2. ¿Quiénes son? Siga (*Follow*) el mismo (*same*) modelo.

1. prima   2. sobrino   3. tío   4. abuelo

C. Entrevista. Find out about the family of a classmate using the following dialogue as a guide. Use **tengo** (*I have*) and **tienes** (*you have*), as indicated. Use **¿cuántos?** with male relations and **¿cuántas?** with females.

MODELO: E1:* ¿Cuántos hermanos tienes?
E2: Bueno (*Well*), tengo seis hermanos y una hermana.
E1: ¿Y cuántos primos?
E2: ¡Uf! Tengo un montón (*bunch*). Más de veinte.

---

*From this point on in the text, ESTUDIANTE 1 and ESTUDIANTE 2 will be abbreviated as E1 and E2, respectively.

NOTA CULTURAL

Hispanic Last Names

In many Hispanic countries, people are given two last names (**apellidos**) such as in the case of **Amalia *Lázaro Aguirre***. The first last name (**Lázaro**) is that of Amalia's father; the second (**Aguirre**) is her mother's. This system for assigning last names is characteristic of all parts of the Spanish-speaking world, although it is not widely used by Hispanics living in this country. When Hispanic women marry, they might formally replace their second (maternal) last name with that of their husband's first (paternal) last name.

Adjetivos

guapo   handsome,
           good-looking
bonito   pretty
feo   ugly

grande   pequeño

casado   married
soltero   single

simpático   nice, likeable
antipático   unpleasant

rubio   moreno

joven   nuevo   viejo

corto   short (*in length*)
largo   long

bueno   good
malo   bad

listo   smart, clever
tonto   silly, foolish

trabajador   perezoso

rico   rich
pobre   poor

delgado   thin, slender
gordo   fat

alto   bajo

To describe a masculine singular noun, use **alt*o*, baj*o***, and so on; use **alt*a*, baj*a***, and so on for feminine singular nouns.

Conversación

A. Preguntas. Conteste según los dibujos.

el mono

Einstein

1. Einstein es listo.
   ¿Y el mono (*monkey*)?

Roberto

José

2. Roberto es trabajador.
   ¿Y José?

1.95

1.60

Pepe   Pablo

3. Pepe es bajo.
   ¿Y Pablo?

Satanás

el ángel

Ramón Ramírez

Paco Pereda

el libro

el lápiz

4. El ángel es bueno y simpático. También es guapo. ¿Y el demonio?

5. Ramón Ramírez es casado. También es viejo. ¿Y Paco Pereda?

6. El libro es viejo y corto. ¿Y el lápiz?

B. **¿Cómo es?** Describe a famous personality using as many adjectives as possible so that your classmates can guess who the person is. Use cognate adjectives that you have seen in **Primeros pasos** and **Capítulo 1**.

MODELO: Es un hombre importante; controla una gran compañía de *software*. Es muy trabajador y muy rico. (Bill Gates)

Los números 31–100

Continúe la secuencia:

treinta y uno, treinta y dos…
ochenta y cuatro, ochenta y cinco…

31	treinta y uno	36	treinta y seis	
32	treinta y dos	37	treinta y siete	
33	treinta y tres	38	treinta y ocho	
34	treinta y cuatro	39	treinta y nueve	
35	treinta y cinco	40	cuarenta	

50 cincuenta
60 sesenta
70 setenta
80 ochenta
90 noventa
100 cien, ciento

¿Qué cuenta (*counts*) el perro?

Beginning with 31, Spanish numbers are *not* written in a combined form; **treinta y uno,*** **cuarenta y dos, sesenta y tres**, and so on must be three separate words.

Cien is used before nouns and in counting.

cien casas
noventa y ocho, noventa y nueve, **cien**

a (one) hundred houses
ninety-eight, ninety-nine, one hundred

*Remember that when **uno** is part of a compound number (**treinta y uno, cuarenta y uno**, and so on), it becomes **un** before a masculine noun and **una** before a feminine noun: **cincuenta y una mesas; setenta y un coches**.

Conversación

A. Más problemas de matemáticas. Recuerde: + **y,** − **menos,** = **son.**

1. 30 + 50 = ?
2. 45 + 45 = ?
3. 32 + 58 = ?

4. 77 + 23 = ?
5. 100 − 40 = ?
6. 99 − 39 = ?

7. 84 − 34 = ?
8. 78 − 36 = ?
9. 88 − 28 = ?

NOTA COMUNICATIVA

Expressing Age

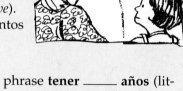

NIETA: ¿Cuántos años tienes, abuela?
ABUELA: Setenta y tres, Nora.
NIETA: ¿Y cuántos años tiene el abuelo?
ABUELA: Setenta y cinco, mi amor (*love*).
Y ahora, dime (*tell me*), ¿cuántos años tienes tú?
NIETA: Tengo tres.

In Spanish, age is expressed with the phrase **tener** _____ **años** (literally, *to have . . . years*). You have now seen all the singular forms of **tener** (*to have*): **tengo, tienes, tiene.**

B. ¡Seamos (*Let's be*) **lógicos!** Complete las oraciones lógicamente.

1. Un hombre que (*who*) tiene noventa años es muy ____.
2. Un niño (*small child*) que tiene sólo un año es muy ____.
3. La persona más vieja (*oldest*) de mi familia es mi ____. Tiene ____ años.
4. La persona más joven de mi familia es mi ____. Tiene ____ años.
5. En mi opinión, es ideal tener ____ años.
6. Cuando una persona tiene ____ años, ya es adulta.
7. Para (*In order to*) tomar cerveza en esta ciudad (*city*), es necesario tener ____ años.
8. Para mí (*For me*), ¡la idea de tener ____ años es inconcebible (*inconceivable*)!

¿Recuerda Ud.?

Before beginning Grammar Section 4, review the forms and uses of **ser** that you have already learned by answering these questions.

1. ¿Es Ud. estudiante o profesor(a)?
2. ¿Cómo es Ud.? ¿Es una persona sentimental? ¿inteligente? ¿paciente? ¿elegante?
3. ¿Qué hora es? ¿A qué hora es la clase de español?
4. ¿Qué es un hospital? ¿Es una persona? ¿una cosa? ¿un edificio?

---

4 ### Expressing *to be* • Present Tense of *ser;* Summary of Uses

Presentaciones

—Hola. Me llamo Manolo Durán.

- *Soy* profesor en la universidad.
- *Soy* alto y moreno.
- *Soy* de Sevilla, España.

—¿Y Lola Benítez, mi esposa? Complete la descripción de ella.

Es _____ (profesión).
Es _____ y _____ (descripción).
Es de _____ (origen).

Málaga,
España
bonita
profesora
delgada

As you know, there are two Spanish verbs that mean *to be:* **ser** and **estar**. They are not interchangeable; the meaning that the speaker wishes to convey determines their use. In this chapter, you will review the uses of **ser** that you already know and learn some new ones. Remember to use **estar** to express location and to ask how someone is feeling. You will learn more about the uses of **estar** in **Capítulo 5**.

A. Here are some basic language functions of **ser**. You have used or seen all of them already in this and previous chapters.

ser (*to be*)			
yo	**soy**	nosotros/as	**somos**
tú	**eres**	vosotros/as	**sois**
Ud. ⎫		Uds. ⎫	
él ⎬	**es**	ellos ⎬	**son**
ella ⎭		ellas ⎭	

- To *identify* people and things
  [Práctica A]

  O J O When you see a note in brackets [**Práctica A**] here, it refers you to that exercise for the grammar point. In this case, Exercise A (page 61) in the next **Práctica** section will allow you to practice this point.

Yo soy **estudiante**.
Alicia y yo somos **amigas**.
La doctora Ramos es **profesora**.
Esto (*This*) es **un libro**.

- To *describe* people and things*

Soy **sentimental**:
I'm sentimental (a sentimental person).

El coche es **muy viejo**.
The car is very old.

- With **de**, to express *origin*
  [Práctica B–C]

Somos **de los Estados Unidos**, pero nuestros padres son **de la Argentina**. ¿**De dónde** es Ud.?
We're from the United States, but our parents are from Argentina. Where are you from?

- To express *generalizations* (only **es**)
  [Conversación B]

Es **importante** estudiar, pero no es **necesario** estudiar todos los días.
It's important to study, but it's not necessary to study every day.

---

*You will practice this language function of **ser** in Grammar Section 6 in this chapter and in subsequent chapters.

B. Here are two basic language functions of **ser** that you have not yet practiced.

- With **de**, to express *possession*

[Práctica D]

> **OJO**
>
> Note that there is no **'s** in Spanish.
>
> The masculine singular article **el** contracts with the preposition **de** to form **del**. No other article contracts with **de**.

Es el perro **de Carla**.
It's Carla's dog.

Son las gatas **de Jorge**.
They're Jorge's (female) cats.

Es la casa **del** profesor.
It's the (male) professor's house.

Es la casa **de la** profesora.
It's the (female) professor's house.

> **OJO**
>
> de + el → del

- With **para**, to tell for whom or what something *is intended*

[Conversación A]

¿Romeo y Julieta? Es **para** la clase de inglés.
Romeo and Juliet? It's for English class.

— ¿**Para** quién son los regalos?
— (Son) **Para** mi nieto.
Who are the presents for?
(They're) For my grandson.

Práctica

A. Los parientes de Manolo. Look back at the family tree on page 54. Then tell whether the following statements are true (**cierto**) or false (**falso**) from Manolo's standpoint. Correct the false statements.

1. Lola y yo somos hermanos.
2. Mi esposa es la prima de Patricia.
3. Manuel y Luisa son mis (*my*) padres.
4. José Jaime es mi sobrino.
5. Mi hermana es la esposa de Jaime.
6. Mi padre no es abuelo todavía (*yet*).
7. Mi familia no es muy grande.

B. Nacionalidades. ¿De dónde son, según los nombres y apellidos?

Países (*Countries*): Francia, México, Italia, los Estados Unidos, Inglaterra (*England*), Alemania (*Germany*)

1. John Doe
2. Karl Lotze
3. Graziana Lazzarino
4. María Gómez
5. Claudette Moreau
6. Timothy Windsor

C. Personas extranjeras. ¿Quiénes son, de dónde son y dónde trabajan ahora?

MODELO: Teresa: actriz / de Madrid / en Cleveland →
Teresa es actriz. Es de Madrid. Ahora trabaja en Cleveland.

1. Carlos Miguel: médico (*doctor*) / de Cuba / en Milwaukee
2. Maripili: profesora / de Burgos / en Miami
3. Mariela: dependienta / de Buenos Aires / en Nueva York
4. Juan: dentista* / de Lima / en Los Ángeles
5. un amigo o pariente suyo (*of yours*) / ¿ ? / ¿ ?

D. ¡Seamos (*Let's be*) **lógicos!** ¿De quién son estas cosas? Con un compañero/una compañera, haga y conteste preguntas (*ask and answer questions*) según el modelo.

MODELO: E1: ¿De quién es el perro?
E2: Es de…

Personas: las estudiantes, la actriz, el niño, la familia con diez hijos, el estudiante extranjero, los señores Schmidt

¿De quién es/son… ?

1. la casa en Beverly Hills
2. la casa en Viena
3. la camioneta (*station wagon*)
4. el perro
5. las fotos de la Argentina
6. las mochilas con todos los libros

NOTA COMUNICATIVA

Explaining Your Reasons

In conversation, it is often necessary to explain a decision, tell why someone did something, and so on. Here are some simple words and phrases that speakers use to offer explanations.

porque because	**para** in order to
—¿Por qué necesitamos un televisor nuevo?	*Why do we need a new TV set?*
—Pues… **para** mirar el partido de fútbol… ¡Es el campeonato!	*Well . . . (in order) to watch the soccer game . . . It's the championship!*
—¿Por qué trabajas tanto?	*Why do you work so much?*
—¡**Porque** necesitamos el dinero!	*Because we need the money!*

Note the differences between **porque** (one word, no accent) and the interrogative **¿por qué?**

---

*A number of professions end in **-ista** in both masculine and feminine forms. The article indicates gender: **el/la dentista, el/la artista**, and so on.

Conversación

A. El regalo ideal. The first column below lists gifts that Diego would like to give to certain members of his family, listed in the second column. For him, money is no object! Decide who receives each gift, and explain your decisions by using the additional information included about the family members.

MODELO: _____ es para _____ →

El dinero es para Carmina, la hermana. Ella desea estudiar en otro (*another*) estado. Por eso necesita el dinero.

REGALOS

1. la calculadora
2. los libros de literatura clásica
3. los discos compactos de Andrés Segovia
4. el televisor
5. el radio
6. el dinero

MIEMBROS DE LA FAMILIA

a. José, el padre: Le gusta escuchar las noticias (*news*).
b. Julián y María, los abuelos: Les gusta mucho la música de guitarra clásica.
c. Carmen, la madre: Le gusta mirar programas cómicos.
d. Joey, el hermano: Le gustan mucho las historias viejas.
e. Carmina, la hermana: Desea estudiar en otro estado.
f. Raulito, el primo: Le gustan las matemáticas.

B. ¿Qué opinas? Exprese opiniones originales, afirmativas o negativas, con estas palabras.

(No) {
Es importante
Es muy práctico
Es necesario
Es tonto (*foolish*)
Es fascinante
Es una lata (*pain, drag*)
Es posible
}

mirar la televisión todos los días
hablar español en la clase
tener muchas mascotas
llegar (*to arrive*) a clase puntualmente
tomar cerveza en clase
hablar con los animales / las plantas
tomar mucho café y fumar cigarrillos
trabajar dieciocho horas al día
tener muchos hermanos
ser amable con todos los miembros de la familia
estar en las fiestas familiares
pasar mucho tiempo con la familia

5   Expressing Possession • Possessive Adjectives (Unstressed)*

La familia de Carlos IV (cuarto)

La familia de Carlos IV, un rey español del siglo XVIII. En el cuadro están *su* esposa, *sus* hijos… ¿y *sus* padres y *sus* abuelos? ¿Quiénes son las personas a la izquierda del rey?

¿Tiene Ud. una foto reciente de *su* familia? ¿Quiénes están en la foto?

La familia de Carlos IV, por Francisco de Goya (español)

You have already seen and used several possessive adjectives in Spanish. Here is the complete set.

	Possessive Adjectives			
my	**mi** libro/mesa **mis** libros/mesas	*our*	nuest**ro** libro nuest**ros** libros	nuest**ra** mesa nuest**ras** mesas
your	**tu** libro/mesa **tus** libros/mesas	*your*	vuest**ro** libro vuest**ros** libros	vuest**ra** mesa vuest**ras** mesas
your, his, } *her, its* }	**su** libro/mesa **sus** libros/mesas	*your,* } *their* }	**su** libro/mesa **sus** libros/mesas	

In Spanish, the ending of a possessive adjective agrees in form with the person or thing possessed, not with the owner or possessor. Note that these possessive adjectives are placed before the noun.

The possessive adjectives **mi(s), tu(s),** and **su(s)** show agreement in number only with the nouns they modify. **Nuestro/a/os/as** and **vuestro/a/os/as,** like all adjectives that end in **-o,** show agreement in both number and gender.

The possessive adjectives **vuestro/a/os/as** are used extensively in Spain, but are not common in Latin America.

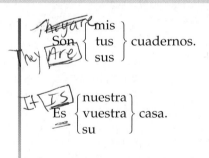

Carlos IV's Family   The family of Carlos IV, an 18th-century Spanish king. In the painting are his wife, his children . . . and his parents and grandparents? Who are the people to the left of the king?

*Another set of possessives are called the *stressed possessive adjectives.* They can be used as nouns. For information on them, see Appendix 2, Using Adjectives as Nouns.

Su(s) can have several different equivalents in English: *your* (*sing.*), *his*, *her*, *its*, *your* (*pl.*), and *their*. Usually its meaning will be clear in context. When context does not make the meaning of **su(s)** clear, **de** and a pronoun are used instead, to indicate the possessor.

el coche ⎫
la casa ⎬ de él (de ella, de Ud., de
los libros ⎪ ellos, de ellas, de Uds.)
las mesas ⎭

¿Son jóvenes los hijos **de él**?
Are his children young?

¿Dónde vive el abuelo **de ellas**?
Where does their grandfather live?

Práctica

A. Posesiones. Which nouns can these possessive adjectives modify without changing form?

1. su: problema   primos   dinero   tías   escritorios   familia
2. tus: perro   idea   hijos   profesoras   abuelo   examen
3. mi: ventana   médicos   cuarto   coche   abuela   gatos
4. sus: animales   oficina   nietas   padre   hermana   abuelo
5. nuestras: guitarra   libro   materias   lápiz   sobrinas   tía
6. nuestro: gustos   consejeros   parientes   puerta   clase   residencia

B. ¿Cómo es la familia de Carlos IV?

Paso 1. Mire la ilustración de Carlos IV y su familia en la página 64. Conteste según el modelo.

MODELO: familia / grande → Su familia es grande.

1. hijo pequeño / guapo
2. esposa / fea
3. retrato (*portrait*) / bueno
4. hijas / solteras
5. familia / importante y rica

Paso 2. Imagine que Ud. es Carlos IV. Cambie las respuestas (*answers*) del 1 al 3.

MODELO: hijo pequeño / guapo → Mi hijo pequeño es guapo.

Conversación

Entrevista. This interview will help you gather more information about the families of your classmates and instructor. Use the questions as a guide to interview your instructor or a classmate (use **tú[s]**) and take notes on what he or she says. Then report the information to the class.

1. ¿Cómo es su familia? ¿Grande? ¿pequeña? ¿Cuántas personas hay?
2. ¿Son simpáticos sus padres? ¿generosos? ¿cariñosos (*caring*)?
3. ¿Cuántos hijos tienen (*have*) sus padres? ¿Cuántos años tienen?
4. ¿Cómo son sus hermanos? ¿Inteligentes? ¿traviesos (*mischievous*)? ¿trabajadores? ¿Estudian o trabajan? ¿Dónde?
5. ¿Tiene Ud. (*Do you have*) esposo/a (compañero/a de cuarto)? ¿Cómo es? ¿Trabaja o estudia?

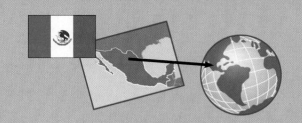

Enfoque *cultural*

México

Datos esenciales

Nombre oficial: Estados Unidos Mexicanos

Capital: la Ciudad de México, o México, Distrito Federal (el D.F.)

Población: 97.000.000 de habitantes

Moneda:[a] el nuevo peso

Idiomas:[b] el español (oficial), el zapoteca, el mixteca, el náhuatl, varios dialectos mayas

[a]*Currency* [b]*Languages*

¡Fíjese!

- México tiene 31 estados y el Distrito Federal.

- La población de México es aproximadamente: 25% indígena, 15% blanca y 60% mestiza (que se refiere a las personas de padres de razas indígena y blanca).

- Los indígenas mexicanos pertenecen a[a] grupos diversos: aztecas, mayas, zapotecas, mixtecas, olmecas y otros. La influencia de estas culturas indígenas contribuye a la diversidad y la riqueza de la cultura mexicana actual.[b]

- La ciudad de México ocupa el lugar del antiguo[c] Lago Texcoco. En el centro del lago estaba[d] Tenochtitlán, la capital del imperio azteca. Tenochtitlán era[e] una de las ciudades más grandes del mundo en el siglo XVI.[f]

- La Universidad Autónoma de México es una de las universidades más antiguas[g] de las Américas: es del año[h] 1551 (mil quinientos cincuenta y uno).

[a]*pertenecen… belong to* [b]*current* [c]*old, ancient* [d]*was* [e]*was* [f]*siglo… 16th century* [g]*más… oldest* [h]*es… it dates from the year*

Conozca a... los grandes muralistas mexicanos

El muralismo es el estilo de pintura[a] que decora las paredes[b] de edificios públicos. Con su obra,[c] los muralistas desean enseñar la historia y la cultura de su país, y con frecuencia sus murales representan sus ideales políticos también.

The Epic of American Civilization es un mural de Orozco. Está en Dartmouth College.

Tres pintores mexicanos —Diego Rivera (1886–1957 [mil ochocientos ochenta y seis a mil novecientos cincuenta y siete]), José Clemente Orozco (1883–1949 [mil ochocientos ochenta y tres a mil novecientos cuarenta y nueve]) y David Alfaro Siqueiros (1898–1974 [mil ochocientos noventa y ocho a mil novecientos setenta y cuatro])— son probablemente los muralistas más famosos de hoy. Hay muchos murales de estos tres grandes muralistas por todo México.

[a]*painting* [b]*walls* [c]*work*

Capítulo 2 of the video to accompany *¿Qué tal?* contains cultural footage of Mexico.

WW. Visit the *¿Qué tal?* website at www.mhhe.com/quetal.

6 **Describing** • Adjectives: Gender, Number, and Position

Un poema sencillo

Amigo
Fiel
Amable
Simpático
¡Lo admiro!

Amiga
Fiel
Amable
Simpática
¡La admiro!

According to their form, which of the adjectives below can be used to describe each person? Which can refer to you?

Marta:
Mario: { fiel   amable   simpática   simpático

Adjectives (**Los adjetivos**) are words used to talk about nouns or pronouns. Adjectives may describe or tell how many there are.

You have been using adjectives to describe people since **Primeros pasos**. In this section, you will learn more about describing the people and things around you.

 adjective = a word used to describe a noun or pronoun

large desk   *few* desks
tall woman   *several* women

ADJECTIVES WITH *ser*

In Spanish, forms of **ser** are used with adjectives that describe basic, inherent qualities or characteristics of the nouns or pronouns they modify.

Tú **eres amable**.
You're nice. (You're a nice person.)

El diccionario **es barato**.
The dictionary is inexpensive.

A simple poem Friend   Loyal   Kind   Nice   I admire him/her!

FORMS OF ADJECTIVES

Spanish adjectives agree in gender and number with the noun or pronoun they modify. Each adjective has more than one form.

A. Adjectives that end in **-o** (**alto**) have four forms, showing gender and number.*

	Masculine	Feminine
Singular	amigo alt**o**	amiga alt**a**
Plural	amigos alt**os**	amigas alt**as**

B. Adjectives that end in **-e** (**inteligente**) or in most consonants (**fiel**) have only two forms, a singular and a plural form. The plural of adjectives is formed in the same way as that of nouns.

[Práctica A–C]

	Masculine	Feminine
Singular	amigo inteligent**e**	amiga inteligent**e**
	amigo fiel	amiga fiel
Plural	amigos inteligent**es**	amigas inteligent**es**
	amigos fiel**es**	amigas fiel**es**

C. Most adjectives of nationality have four forms.

The names of many languages—which are masculine in gender—are the same as the masculine singular form of the corresponding adjective of nationality **el español, el inglés, el alemán, el francés**, and so on.

[Práctica D]

OJO
Note that in Spanish the names of languages and adjectives of nationality are not capitalized, but the names of countries are: **español, española**, but **España**.

	Masculine	Feminine
Singular	el doctor	la doctor**a**
	mexican**o**	mexican**a**
	español	español**a**
	alemán	aleman**a**
	inglés	ingles**a**
Plural	los doctor**es**	las doctor**as**
	mexican**os**	mexican**as**
	español**es**	español**as**
	aleman**es**	aleman**as**
	ingles**es**	ingles**as**

PLACEMENT OF ADJECTIVES

As you have probably noticed, adjectives do not always precede the noun in Spanish as they do in English. Note the following rules for adjective placement.

A. Adjectives of quantity, like numbers, *precede* the noun, as do the interrogatives **¿cuánto/a?** and **¿cuántos/as?**

Hay **muchas** sillas y **dos** escritorios.
There are many chairs and two desks.

¿Cuánto dinero necesitas?
How much money do you need?

---

*Adjectives that end in **-dor, -ón, -án**, and **-ín** also have four forms: **trabajador, trabajador**a, **trabajador**es, **trabajador**as.

OJO   **Otro/a** by itself means *another* or *other*. The indefinite article is never used with **otro/a**.

Busco **otro** coche
I'm looking for another car.

B. Adjectives that describe the qualities of a noun and distinguish it from others generally *follow* the noun. Adjectives of nationality are included in this category.

un perro **bueno**
un dependiente **trabajador**
una joven **delgada** y **morena**
un joven **español**

C. The adjectives **bueno** and **malo** may precede or follow the noun they modify. When they precede a masculine singular noun, they shorten to **buen** and **mal**, respectively.

[Práctica C]

un **buen** perro / un perro **bueno**
una **buena** perra / una perra **buena**
un **mal** día / un día **malo**
una **mala** noche / una noche **mala**

After the noun means that you are emphasizing.

D. The adjective **grande** may also precede or follow the noun. When it precedes a singular noun—masculine or feminine—it shortens to **gran** and means *great* or *impressive*. When it follows the noun, it means *large* or *big*.

[Conversación]

Nueva York es una ciudad **grande**.
New York is a large city.

Nueva York es una **gran** ciudad.
New York is a great (impressive) city.

FORMS OF *this/these*

A. The demonstrative adjective *this/these* has four forms in Spanish.* Learn to recognize them when you see them.

este hijo	*this son*
esta hija	*this daughter*
estos hijos	*these sons*
estas hijas	*these daughters*

B. You have already seen the neuter demonstrative **esto**. It refers to something that is as yet unidentified.

¿Qué es esto?
What is this?

Práctica

A. La familia de José Miguel. For each item, choose the adjectives that can complete the statement logically.

1. El tío Miguel es _____. (trabajador/alto/nueva/grande/fea/amable)
2. Los abuelos son _____. (rubio/antipático/inteligentes/viejos/religiosos/sinceras)
3. Su madre es _____. (rubio/elegante/sentimental/buenas/simpática)
4. Las primas son _____. (solteras/morenas/lógica/bajos/mala)

---

*You will learn all forms of the Spanish demonstrative adjectives (*this, that, these, those*) in Grammar Section 8.

Vocabulario útil

Here are some adjectives to use in this section. You should be able to guess the meaning of some of them.

agresivo/a	¿ ?	**chistoso/a**	amusing	**sensible**	sensitive
amistoso/a	friendly	**comprensivo/a**	understanding	**suficiente**	¿ ?
animado/a	lively	**difícil**	difficult	**tolerante**	¿ ?
atrevido/a	daring	**encantador(a)**	delightful	**travieso/a**	mischievous
cariñoso/a	affectionate	**fácil**	easy		

B. Hablando (*Speaking*) **de la universidad.** Tell what you think about aspects of your university by telling whether you agree (**Estoy de acuerdo.**) or disagree (**No estoy de acuerdo.**) with the statements. If you don't have an opinion, say **No tengo opinión**.

1. Hay suficientes actividades sociales.
2. Los profesores son excelentes.
3. Las residencias son buenas.
4. Hay suficientes gimnasios.
5. Hay suficientes zonas verdes.
6. La cafetería es buena.
7. En la librería, los precios son bajos.
8. Los bibliotecarios son cooperativos.

C. ¡Dolores es igual! Cambie Diego → Dolores.

Diego es un buen estudiante. Es listo y trabajador y estudia mucho. Es estadounidense de origen mexicano, y por eso habla español. Desea ser profesor de antropología. Diego es moreno, guapo y atlético. Le gustan las fiestas grandes y tiene buenos amigos en la universidad. Tiene parientes estadounidenses y mexicanos.

D. Nacionalidades. Tell what nationality the following people could be and where they might live: **Portugal, Alemania, China, Inglaterra, España, Francia, Italia**.

1. Monique habla francés; es _____ y vive (*she lives*) en _____.
2. José habla español; es _____ y vive en _____.
3. Greta y Hans hablan alemán; son _____ y viven en _____.
4. Gilberto habla portugués; es _____ y vive en _____.
5. Gina y Sofía hablan italiano; son _____ y viven en _____.
6. Winston habla inglés; es _____ y vive en _____.
7. Hai (*m.*) y Han (*m.*) hablan chino; son _____ y viven en _____.

Conversación

Asociaciones: With several classmates, how many names can you associate with the following phrases? To introduce your suggestions, you can say **Creo que** (_____ **es un gran hombre**). To express agreement or disagreement, use (**No**) **Estoy de acuerdo.**

1. un mal restaurante
2. un buen programa de televisión
3. una gran mujer, un gran hombre
4. un buen libro, un libro horrible

¿Recuerda Ud.?

The personal endings used with **-ar** verbs share some characteristics of those used with **-er** and **-ir** verbs, which you will learn in the next section. Review the endings of **-ar** verbs by telling which subject pronoun(s) you associate with each of these endings.

1. -amos   2. -as   3. -áis   4. -an   5. -o   6. -a

7

Expressing Actions • Present Tense of *-er* and *-ir* Verbs; More about Subject Pronouns

Diego se presenta.

Hola. Me llamo Diego González. Soy estudiante de UCLA, pero este año *asisto* a la Universidad Nacional Autónoma de México. *Vivo* con mi tía Matilde en la Ciudad de México. *Como* pizza con frecuencia y *bebo* cerveza en las fiestas. Me gusta la ropa de moda; por eso *recibo* varios catálogos. *Leo* muchos libros de antropología para mi especialización. También *escribo* muchas cartas a mi familia. *Creo* que una educación universitaria es muy importante. Por eso estudio y *aprendo* mucho. ¡Pero *comprendo* también que es muy importante estar con los amigos y con la familia!

¿Es Diego un estudiante típico? ¿Cómo es Ud.? Adapte las oraciones de Diego a su conveniencia.

VERBS THAT END IN -er AND -ir

A. The present tense of **-er** and **-ir** verbs is formed by adding personal endings to the stem of the verb (the infinitive minus its **-er/-ir** ending). The personal endings for **-er** and **-ir** verbs are the same except for the first and second person plural.

comer (*to eat*)		vivir (*to live*)	
como	comemos	vivo	vivimos
comes	coméis	vives	vivís
come	comen	vive	viven

Diego introduces himself. Hello. My name is Diego González. I'm a student at UCLA, but this year I attend the Universidad Nacional Autónoma de México. I live with my aunt Matilde in Mexico City. I eat pizza frequently and I drink beer at parties. I like the latest fashions; that's why I receive various catalogues. I read lots of anthropology books for my major. I also write a lot of letters to my family. I think that a university education is very important. That's why I study and learn a lot. But I also understand that it's very important to be with friends and family!

Paso 3 | *Gramática*

B. Some frequently used **-er** and
-ir verbs in this chapter
include those on the right.

[handwritten: If it's believe in V/ add "en"]

[handwritten: Always add the "a"]

-er verbs		-ir verbs	
aprender	to learn	abrir	to open
beber	to drink	asistir (a)	to attend, go to
comer	to eat		(a class, *function*)
comprender	to understand	escribir	to write
creer (en)	to think, believe (in)	recibir	to receive
deber (+ *inf.*)	should, must, ought	vivir	to live
	to (*do something*)		
leer	to read		
vender	to sell		

OJO

Remember that the Spanish present tense has a
number of present tense equivalents in English
and can also be used to express future meaning.

como = *I eat, I am eating, I will eat*

USE AND OMISSION OF SUBJECT PRONOUNS

In English, a verb must have an expressed subject (a noun or pronoun): *she says, the train arrives*. In Spanish,
however, as you have probably noticed, an expressed subject is not required. Verbs are accompanied by a subject
pronoun only for clarification, emphasis, or contrast.

- *Clarification:* When the context does not make the
  subject clear, the subject pronoun is expressed.
  This happens most frequently with third person
  singular and plural verb forms.

Ud./él/ella vende
Uds./ellos/ellas venden

- *Emphasis:* Subject pronouns are used in Spanish
  to emphasize the subject when in English you
  would stress it with your voice.

—¿Quién debe pagar?
—¡**Tú** debes pagar!
Who should pay?
You should pay!

- *Contrast:* Contrast is a special case of emphasis.
  Subject pronouns are used to contrast the actions
  of two individuals or groups.

Ellos leen mucho; **nosotros** leemos poco.
They read a lot; we read little.

Práctica

A. En la clase de español

Paso 1. Read the following statements and tell whether they are true for
your classroom environment. If any statement is not true for you or your
class, make it negative or change it in another way to make it correct.

MODELO: Bebo café en clase. → Sí, bebo café en clase.
(No, no bebo café en clase. Bebo café en casa.)

1. Debo estudiar más para esta clase.
2. Leo todas las partes de las lecciones.
3. Comprendo bien cuando mi profesor(a) habla.
4. Asisto al laboratorio con frecuencia.
5. Debemos abrir más los libros en clase.
6. Escribimos mucho en esta clase.
7. Aprendemos a hablar español en esta clase.*
8. Vendemos nuestros libros al final del año (*year*).

Paso 2. Now turn to the person next to you and rephrase each sentence, using **tú** forms of the verbs. Your partner will indicate whether the sentences are true for him or her.

MODELO: Debes estudiar más para esta clase, ¿verdad (*right*)? →
Sí, debo estudiar más.
(No, no debo estudiar más.)
(No, debo estudiar más para la clase de matemáticas.)

B. Diego habla de su padre. Complete este párrafo con la forma correcta de los verbos entre paréntesis.

Mi padre (vender[1]) coches y trabaja mucho. Mis hermanos y yo (aprender[2]) mucho de papá. Según mi padre, los jóvenes (deber[3]) (asistir[4]) a clase todos los días, porque es su[a] obligación. Papá también (creer[5]) que no es necesario mirar la televisión por la noche. Es más interesante (leer[6]) el periódico[b] o un buen libro. Por eso nosotros (leer[7]) o (escribir[8]) por la noche y no miramos la televisión mucho. Yo admiro mucho a[†] mi papá y (creer[9]) que él (comprender[10]) la importancia de la educación.

[a]*their* [b]*newspaper*

C. Un sábado (*Saturday*) en Sevilla. Using all the cues given, form complete sentences about Manolo's narration about a certain Saturday at home with his family. Make any changes and add words when necessary. When the subject pronoun is in parentheses, do not use it in the sentence.

1. yo / leer / periódico
2. mi hija, Marta / mirar / televisión
3. también / (ella) escribir / composición
4. mi esposa, Lola / abrir / y / leer / cartas
5. ¡hoy / (nosotros) recibir / carta / tío Ricardo!
6. (él) ser de / España / pero / ahora / vivir / México
7. ¡ay! / ser / dos / de / tarde
8. ¡(nosotros) / deber / comer / ahora!

Note: **aprender** + **a** + infinitive = to learn how to (*do something*)
[†]Note the use of **a** here. In this context, the word **a** has no equivalent in English. It is used in Spanish before a direct object that is a specific person. You will learn more about this use of **a** in **Capítulo 6.** Until then, the exercises and activities in *¿Qué tal?* will indicate when to use it.

Conversación

NOTA COMUNICATIVA

Telling How Frequently You Do Things

Use the following words and phrases to tell how often you perform an activity.
Some of them will already be familiar to you.

todos los días, siempre	every day, always	**una vez a la semana**	once a week
con frecuencia	frequently	**casi nunca**	almost never
a veces	at times	**nunca**	never

Hablo con mis amigos **todos los días**. Hablo con mis padres **una vez a la semana**. **Casi nunca** hablo con mis abuelos. Y **nunca** hablo con mis tíos que viven en Italia.

For now, use the expressions **casi nunca** and **nunca** only at the beginning of a sentence. You will learn more about how to use them in Grammar 18.

¿Con qué frecuencia?

Paso 1. How frequently do you do the following things?

		CON FRECUENCIA	A VECES	CASI NUNCA	NUNCA
1.	Asisto al laboratorio de lenguas (o uso los discos compactos).	☐	☐	☐	☐
2.	Recibo cartas.	☐	☐	☐	☐
3.	Escribo poemas.	☐	☐	☐	☐
4.	Leo novelas románticas.	☐	☐	☐	☐
5.	Como en una pizzería.	☐	☐	☐	☐
6.	Recibo y leo catálogos.	☐	☐	☐	☐
7.	Aprendo palabras nuevas en español.	☐	☐	☐	☐
8.	Asisto a todas mis clases.	☐	☐	☐	☐
9.	Compro regalos para los amigos.	☐	☐	☐	☐
10.	Vendo los libros al final del semestre/trimestre.	☐	☐	☐	☐

Paso 2. Now compare your answers with those of a classmate. Then answer the following questions. (*Note:* **los/las dos** = *both* [*of us*]; **ninguno/a** = *neither*)

		YO	MI COMPAÑERO/A	LOS/LAS DOS	NINGUNO/A
1.	¿Quién es muy estudioso/a?	☐	☐	☐	☐
2.	¿Quién come mucha pizza?	☐	☐	☐	☐
3.	¿Quién compra muchas cosas?	☐	☐	☐	☐
4.	¿Quién es muy romántico/a?	☐	☐	☐	☐
5.	¿Quién recibe mucho (*a lot*) por correo (*by mail*)?	☐	☐	☐	☐

En los Estados Unidos y el Canadá...

Los Sheen, una familia de actores

Two generations of Sheens have made names for themselves in film and television. Martin Sheen, the father, was born Ramón Estévez in Dayton, Ohio (1940), to a Spanish father and an Irish mother. Martin explains that he felt he needed to change his Hispanic name in order to successfully pursue an acting career in the 1950s. In his heart, however, he says he is still Ramón. Martin's acting career spans several decades and includes important movies such as *Apocalypse Now.* Most recently, he

Charlie Sheen, Martin Sheen y Emilio Estevez

stars as a U.S. president in the television series "The West Wing," which won several 2001 Emmy awards, including Best Drama Series.

Martin and his wife of more than 40 years, Janet Sheen, have four children—Emilio (1962), Ramón (1963), Carlos (1965), and Renée (1967)—all of whom have pursued acting careers. Emilio, who uses his father's original last name, Estévez, and Carlos, who is known as Charlie Sheen, are the most famous actors of the Sheen children.

UN POCO DE TODO

¿Existe la familia hispánica típica? Complete the following paragraphs about families. Give the correct form of the words in parentheses, as suggested by the context.

Muchas personas (creer[1]) que (todo[2]) las familias (hispánico[3]) son (grande[4]). Pero el concepto de la familia (ser[5]) diferente ahora, sobre todo[a] en las ciudades (grande[6]).

(Ser[7]) cierto que la familia rural (típico[8]) es grande, pero es así[b] en casi (todo[9]) las sociedades rurales del mundo.[c] Muchos hijos (trabajar[10]) la tierra[d] con sus padres. Por eso es bueno y (necesario[11]) tener muchos niños.

Pero en los grandes centros (urbano[12]) las familias con sólo dos o tres hijos (ser[13]) más comunes. Es difícil[e] tener (mucho[14]) hijos en una sociedad (industrializado[15]). Y cuando los padres (trabajar[16]) fuera de[f] casa, ellos (pagar[17]) mucho para cuidar a[g] los niños. Esto pasa especialmente en las familias de la clase media.[h]

Pero es realmente difícil (hablar[18]) de una familia (hispánico[19]) típica. ¿Hay una familia (norteamericano[20]) típica?

[a]sobre... *above all*   [b]es... *that's the way it is*   [c]*world*   [d]*land*   [e]*difficult*   [f]fuera... *outside of the*   [g]cuidar... *care for*   [h]*middle*

Comprensión: ¿Cierto o falso? Corrija las oraciones falsas.

1. Todas las familias hispánicas son iguales.
2. Las familias rurales son grandes en casi todas partes del mundo.
3. Las familias rurales necesitan muchos niños.
4. Por lo general (*Generally*), las familias urbanas son más pequeñas.

PASO 4 Un paso más

VIDEOTECA: En contexto

MÉXICO

In this video segment, Roberto and Martín are walking in the park, looking for Roberto's cousin Sabina. As you watch the segment, pay particular attention to the words the characters use to describe Sabina. How does Roberto describe her? Is this accurate?

FUNCTION
Describing people

Cultura en contexto
La familia extendida

In Spanish-speaking countries, a first cousin is often called **primo hermano / prima hermana**. This is because they are children of siblings. The expression illustrates the close relationship among extended family members, that is, cousins, aunts, uncles, and so forth. Family members frequently live close to one another, which facilitates close-knit relationships.

A. Lluvia de ideas

- What words do you use most often to describe people physically? Do you generally describe their height or weight? Their eye and hair color? Other qualities?
- If you are arranging to meet someone you don't know in a public place, how do you describe yourself? What do

you do to make sure that the two of you recognize each other? Do you wear a flower in your lapel? Do you identify yourself in some other way?

B. Dictado

Here is the first part of this segment's dialogue. Fill in the missing portions of Roberto's dialogue.

ROBERTO: No entiendo.ª Ya _____¹ las tres. Mi prima Sabina _____² estar aquí.

MARTÍN: No, todavía noᵇ son las tres. _____³ temprano. Yo tengo las tres menos cinco.

ROBERTO: Ah, bueno.

MARTÍN: ¿Cómo es tu prima?

ROBERTO: Es una chica _____.⁴ Tiene 16 años.

MARTÍN: Mmm… Mira… la chica allí es joven. ¿Es Sabina?

ROBERTO: No, no es _____.⁵ Esa chica es _____.⁶ Sabina es morena.

MARTÍN: Ajá.

ªcomprendo ᵇtodavía… *not yet*

C. Un diálogo original

Paso 1. With a classmate, reenact the situation between Roberto and Martín.

Paso 2. Then, imagine that you and a different classmate are looking for someone during a crowded party at your school. These are the roles:

E1: You are looking for a friend that you are supposed to meet at the party.
E2: You don't know the person that **Estudiante 1** is looking for. You ask questions about that person's appearance, to help find him or her.

PASO FINAL

A CONVERSAR

La familia y los amigos

Paso 1. Using the verbs and adjectives you have learned, write five sentences describing what your family members and friends do or what they are like.

MODELO: Mi padre trabaja mucho. Mi amigo John es perezoso.

Paso 2. Work with a partner to find out which of your family members and friends do the same thing or fit the same description. Use **¿Quién de tu familia... ?** (*Who in your family . . . ?*) and **¿Cuál de tus amigos... ?** (*Which of your friends . . . ?*) to get the information. If your answer to a question is *no one* or *none*, use **Nadie en mi familia es...** (*No one in my family is . . .*) or **Ninguno de mis amigos es...** (*Not one of my friends is . . .*).

MODELOS: E1: Mi padre trabaja mucho. ¿Quién de tu familia trabaja mucho?
E2: Mi tía Anita trabaja mucho. (OR: Nadie en mi familia trabaja mucho.) Pero mi amigo John es perezoso. ¿Cuál de tus amigos es perezoso?
E1: Mi amiga Raquel es perezosa. (OR: Ninguno de mis amigos es perezoso.)

Paso 3. Ask follow-up questions about information you learned.

MODELO: E1: ¿Dónde trabaja tu tía Anita?
E2: Trabaja en un hospital.

Paso 4. Compare notes with the rest of the class. Talk about your family and friends and what you learned about your partner's family and friends.

MODELO: La tía de Jorge, Anita, trabaja en un hospital. Ella trabaja mucho...

En resumen

GRAMÁTICA

To review the grammar points presented in this chapter, refer to the indicated grammar presentations. You'll find further practice of these structures in the Workbook/Laboratory Manual, on the CD-ROM, and on the website.

4. Present Tense of *ser*; Summary of Uses

Can you conjugate and use the irregular verb **ser** in the present tense?

5. Possessive Adjectives (Unstressed)

You should be able to recognize and use the possessive adjectives **mi, tu, su, nuestro**, and **vuestro**.

6. Adjectives: Gender, Number, and Position

You should know how to modify adjectives such as **alto, inteligente, español**, and **inglés** to agree with the nouns they describe, as well as where to place an adjective.

7. Present Tense of *-er* and *-ir* Verbs; More about Subject Pronouns

Can you conjugate verbs such as **comer** and **escribir** in the present tense? Do you know how to use subject pronouns and when to omit them?

VOCABULARIO

Los verbos

abrir	to open
aprender	to learn
asistir (a)	to attend, go to (*a class, function*)
beber	to drink
comer	to eat
comprender	to understand
creer (en)	to think, believe (in)
deber (+ *inf.*)	should, must, ought to (*do something*)
escribir	to write
leer	to read
llegar	to arrive
mirar	to look at, watch
mirar la televisión	to watch television
recibir	to receive
ser (*irreg.*)	to be
vender	to sell
vivir	to live

La familia y los parientes

el/la abuelo/a	grandfather/grandmother
los abuelos	grandparents
el/la esposo/a	husband/wife
el/la hermano/a	brother/sister
el/la hijo/a	son/daughter
los hijos	children
la madre (mamá)	mother (mom)
el/la nieto/a	grandson/granddaughter
el/la niño/a	small child; boy/girl
el padre (papá)	father (dad)
los padres	parents
el/la primo/a	cousin
el/la sobrino/a	niece/nephew
el/la tío/a	uncle/aunt

Las mascotas

el gato	cat
el pájaro	bird
el perro	dog

Otros sustantivos

la carta	letter
la casa	house, home
la ciudad	city
el coche	car
el estado	state
el/la médico/a	(medical) doctor
el país	country
el periódico	newspaper
el regalo	present, gift
la revista	magazine

Los adjetivos

alto/a	tall
amable	kind; nice
antipático/a	unpleasant
bajo/a	short (*in height*)
bonito/a	pretty
buen, bueno/a	good
casado/a	married
corto/a	short (*in length*)
delgado/a	thin, slender
este/a	this
estos/as	these
feo/a	ugly
fiel	faithful
gordo/a	fat
gran, grande	large, big; great
guapo/a	handsome; good-looking
inteligente	intelligent
joven	young
largo/a	long
listo/a	smart; clever
mal, malo/a	bad
moreno/a	brunet(te)
mucho/a	a lot
muchos/as	many
necesario/a	necessary
nuevo/a	new
otro/a	other, another
pequeño/a	small
perezoso/a	lazy
pobre	poor
posible	possible
rico/a	rich
rubio/a	blond(e)

simpático/a	nice; likeable
soltero/a	single (*not married*)
todo/a	all; every
tonto/a	silly, foolish
trabajador(a)	hardworking
viejo/a	old

Los adjetivos de nacionalidad

alemán/alemana, español(a), francés/francesa, inglés/inglesa, mexicano/a, norteamericano/a

Los adjetivos posesivos

mi(s)	my
tu(s)	your (*fam. sing.*)
nuestro/a(s)	our
vuestro/a(s)	your (*fam. pl. Sp.*)
su(s)	his, hers, its, your (*form. sing.*); their, your (*form. pl.*)

Los números

treinta, cuarenta, cincuenta, sesenta, setenta, ochenta, noventa, cien (ciento)

¿Con qué frecuencia... ?

a veces	sometimes, at times
casi nunca	almost never
con frecuencia	frequently
nunca	never
siempre	always
una vez a la semana	once a week

Palabras adicionales

bueno...	well . . .
¿de dónde es Ud.?	where are you from?
¿de quién?	whose?
del	of the, from the
(no) estoy de acuerdo	I (don't) agree
para	(intended) for; in order to
¿por qué?	why?
porque	because
que	that; who
según	according to
si	if
tener (*irreg.*)... años	to be . . . years old

De compras

 Estas personas van de compras (*are going shopping*) en el Metrocentro, un centro comercial en Managua, Nicaragua.

VOCABULARIO

- Shopping and clothing
- Colors
- Numbers over 100

GRAMÁTICA

[8] Demonstrative Adjectives

[9] **Tener, venir, preferir, querer,** and **poder**; Some Idioms with **tener**

[10] **Ir; ir + a +** Infinitive; The Contraction **al**

CULTURA

- **Enfoque cultural:** Nicaragua
- **Nota cultural:** Clothing in the Hispanic World
- **En los Estados Unidos y el Canadá:** Los hispanos en el mundo de la moda (*fashion*)
- **Cultura en contexto:** Hispanic Currencies

Multimedia

 You will learn more about shopping for clothes in the **En contexto** video segment.

Review vocabulary and grammar and practice language skills with the interactive CD-ROM.

WW. Get connected to the Spanish-speaking world with the *¿Qué tal?* Online Learning Center: **www.mhhe.com/quetal.**

De compras: La ropa°

De... *Shopping: Clothing*

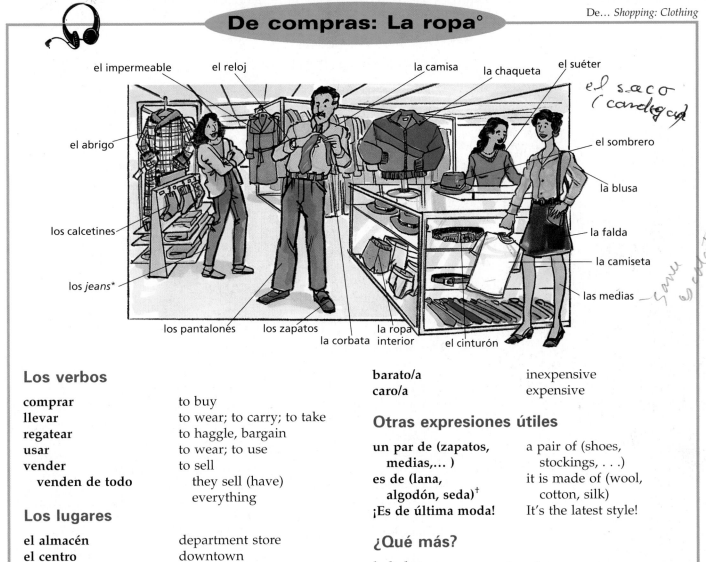

el impermeable · el reloj · la camisa · la chaqueta · el suéter · el saco (cardigan) · el abrigo · el sombrero · la blusa · los calcetines · la falda · la camiseta · los *jeans** · las medias · los pantalones · los zapatos · la corbata · la ropa interior · el cinturón

Los verbos

comprar	to buy
llevar	to wear; to carry; to take
regatear	to haggle, bargain
usar	to wear; to use
vender	to sell
venden de todo	they sell (have) everything

Los lugares

el almacén	department store
el centro	downtown
el centro comercial	shopping mall
el mercado	market(place)
la tienda	shop, store

¿Cuánto cuesta?

la ganga	bargain
el precio	price
el precio fijo	fixed (set) price
las rebajas	sales

barato/a	inexpensive
caro/a	expensive

Otras expresiones útiles

un par de (zapatos, medias,...)	a pair of (shoes, stockings, . . .)
es de (lana, algodón, seda)[†]	it is made of (wool, cotton, silk)
¡Es de última moda!	It's the latest style!

¿Qué más?

la bolsa	purse
las botas	boots
la cartera	wallet
las sandalias	sandals
el traje	suit
el traje de baño	swimsuit
el vestido	dress
los zapatos de tenis	tennis shoes

---

*The influx of North American goods to Latin America and Spain has affected common language. *Jeans* is one example of an English word that is commonly used in Spanish-speaking countries.
[†]Note another use of **ser** + **de**: to tell what material something is made of.

Conversación

A. **La ropa.** ¿Qué ropa llevan estas personas?

1. El Sr. Rivera lleva _____.

2. La Srta. Alonso lleva _____. El perro lleva _____.

3. Sara lleva _____.

4. Alfredo lleva _____. Necesita comprar _____.

B. **Asociaciones.** Complete las oraciones lógicamente.

1. Un _____ es una tienda grande.
2. No es posible _____ cuando hay precios fijos.
3. En la librería, _____ de todo: libros, cuadernos, lápices, cintas (*tapes*). Hay grandes _____ ahora y todo es muy barato.
4. Siempre hay *boutiques* en los _____.
5. El _____ de una ciudad es la parte céntrica.
6. Estos artículos de ropa no son para hombres: _____.
7. Estos artículos de ropa son para hombres y mujeres: _____.
8. La ropa de _____ (*material*) es muy elegante.
9. La ropa de _____ es muy práctica.

Vocabulario útil

Use the preposition **para** followed by an infinitive to express *in order to*.

Para llegar al centro, tomo el autobús número 16.
(*In order*) *To get downtown, I take the number 16 bus.*

C. **¿Qué lleva Ud.?** Para hablar de Ud. y de la ropa, complete estas oraciones lógicamente.

1. Para ir (*go*) a la universidad, me gusta usar _____.
2. Para ir a las fiestas con los amigos, me gusta usar _____.
3. Para pasar un día en la playa (*beach*), me gusta llevar _____.
4. Cuando estoy en casa todo el día, llevo _____.
5. Nunca uso _____.
6. _____ es un artículo de ropa absolutamente necesario.

NOTA CULTURAL

Clothing in the Hispanic World

In Hispanic countries, people tend to dress more formally than do people in this country. As a rule, Hispanics consider neatness and care for one's appearance to be very important.

In the business world, women wear dressy pants, skirts, or dresses, and many wear high-heeled shoes. Men generally dress in trousers, shirts, and ties. Jeans, T-shirts, and tennis shoes are considered inappropriate in traditional business environments. Students at some business schools, like ESAN (**Escuela de administración de negocios**) in Peru, are even required to wear formal business attire to attend classes as if they were already working at a company. Shorts and sweatpants are considered very casual and are reserved almost exclusively for use at home, for a day at the beach, or for sports.

Young adults generally dress casually in social situations, and as in other countries, are often concerned with dressing according to current styles. As a rule, what is considered stylish in this country is also in style in Europe and Latin America.

Ropa diseñada por (*designed by*) la famosa venezolana Carolina Herrera

¿De qué color es?

Here are colors and other helpful phrases you can use to describe clothing and other objects.

amarillo/a	yellow
anaranjado/a	orange
azul	blue
blanco/a	white
gris	gray
morado/a	purple
negro/a	black
pardo/a	brown ~~carmela or café~~
rojo/a	red
rosado/a	pink
verde	green

¿Cuántos colores hay en este cuadro (*painting*) de Gonzalo Endara Crow? ¿Cuáles son?

Después de (After) *la noche*, por Gonzalo Endara Crow (ecuatoriano)

Otras frases útiles

de cuadros	plaid
de lunares	polka-dotted
de rayas	striped

OJO
Note that some colors only have one form for masculine and feminine nouns.

el traje **azul**, la camisa **azul**

Conversación

A. **¿Escaparates idénticos?** These showcase windows are almost alike . . . but not quite! Can you find at least eight differences between them? In Spanish, activities like this one are often called **¡Ojo alerta!** (*Eagle eye!*).

MODELO: En el dibujo A hay _____, pero en el dibujo B hay _____.

A.

B.

B. **¿De qué color es?**

Paso 1. Tell the color of things in your classroom, especially the clothing your classmates are wearing.

MODELO: El bolígrafo de Anita es amarillo. Roberto lleva calcetines azules, una camisa de cuadros morados y azules, *jeans*…

Paso 2. Now describe what someone in the class is wearing, without revealing his or her name. Using your clues, can your classmates guess whom you are describing?

C. **Asociaciones.** ¿Qué colores asocia Ud. con… ?

1. el dinero
2. la una de la mañana
3. una mañana bonita
4. una mañana fea
5. el demonio
6. los Estados Unidos
7. una jirafa
8. un pingüino
9. un limón
10. una naranja
11. un elefante
12. las flores (*flowers*)

Más allá del° número 100

Más... *Beyond the*

Continúe la secuencia:

noventa y nueve, cien, ciento uno,…
mil, dos mil,…
un millón, dos millones,…

100	cien, ciento	500	quinientos/as	1.000*	mil
101	ciento uno/una	600	seiscientos/as	2.000	dos mil
200	doscientos/as	700	setecientos/as	1.000.000	un millón
300	trescientos/as	800	ochocientos/as	2.000.000	dos millones
400	cuatrocientos/as	900	novecientos/as		

- **Ciento** is used in combination with numbers from 1 to 99 to express the numbers 101 through 199: **ciento uno, ciento dos, ciento setenta y nueve**, and so on. **Cien** is used in counting and before numbers greater than 100: **cien mil, cien millones**.
- When the numbers 200 through 900 modify a noun, they must agree in gender: **cuatrocientas niñas, doscientas dos casas**.
- **Mil** means *one thousand* or *a thousand*. It does not have a plural form in counting, but **millón** does. When used with a noun, **millón** (**dos millones**, and so on) must be followed by **de**.

3.000 habitantes	tres mil habitantes
14.000.000 **de** habitantes	catorce millones de habitantes

- Note how years are expressed in Spanish.

1899	mil ochocientos noventa y nueve
2002	dos mil dos

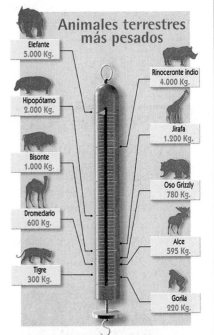

Animales terrestres más pesados

Elefante 5.000 Kg.
Hipopótamo 2.000 Kg.
Bisonte 1.000 Kg.
Dromedario 600 Kg.
Tigre 300 Kg.
Rinoceronte indio 4.000 Kg.
Jirafa 1.200 Kg.
Oso Grizzly 780 Kg.
Alce 595 Kg.
Gorila 220 Kg.

De los animales terrestres, el elefante, con sus 5.000 kilos de peso medio entre todas sus especies, es sin duda el mamífero más pesado. El hipopótamo y el rinoceronte son los siguientes en la lista, y el hombre, ni aparece.

Conversación

A. ¿Cuánto pesan? (*How much do they weigh?*) Mire el gráfico que acompaña (*to accompany*) la presentación del vocabulario. ¿Cuánto pesan los animales en kilos? **¡OJO!** Use el artículo masculino para todos los nombres, menos para (*except for*) los nombres que terminan (*that end*) en **-a**.

B. ¿Cuánto es? Diga los precios.

el dólar (los Estados Unidos, el Canadá, Puerto Rico), el nuevo peso (México), el bolívar (Venezuela), el euro[†] (España), el quetzal (Guatemala)

1.	750 euros	**4.**	670 bolívares	**7.**	836 bolívares
2.	$100	**5.**	$1.000.000	**8.**	101 euros
3.	5.710 quetzales	**6.**	528 nuevos pesos	**9.**	$4.000.000,00

---

[*]In many parts of the Spanish-speaking world, a period in numerals is used where English uses a comma, and a comma is used to indicate the decimal where English uses a period: **$10,45; 65,9%**.
[†]As of January 1, 2002, the **euro** became the official monetary unit of Spain and 11 other European countries.

8 Pointing Out People and Things • Demonstrative Adjectives

Suéteres a buenos precios

VENDEDOR: *Estos* suéteres de aquí cuestan 150 pesos y *ese* suéter en su mano cuesta 250 pesos.

SUSANA: ¿Por qué es más caro *este*?

VENDEDOR: Porque *esos* son de pura lana virgen, de excelente calidad.

SUSANA: ¿Y *aquellos* suéteres de rayas?

VENDEDOR: *Aquellos* cuestan cien pesos solamente; son acrílicos.

¿Quién habla, Susana, Jorge o el vendedor?

1. Me gustan estos suéteres de rayas, y sólo cuestan cien pesos.
2. Señores, miren (*look at*) estos suéteres rojos. Cuestan 150 pesos.
3. Voy a (*I am going*) comprar este suéter. Me gusta la ropa de lana.
4. Este suéter acrílico es más barato que aquel suéter de lana.

	Singular			Plural	
this	este libro	esta mesa	*these*	estos libros	estas mesas
that {	ese libro	esa mesa	*those* {	esos libros	esas mesas
	aquel libro (allí)	aquella mesa (allí)		aquellos libros (allí)	aquellas mesas (allí)

Sweaters at good prices SALESMAN: These sweaters here cost 150 pesos and that sweater in your hand costs 250 pesos. SUSANA: Why is this one more expensive? SALESMAN: Because those are of pure virgin wool, of excellent quality. SUSANA: What about those striped sweaters over there? SALESMAN: Those cost only one hundred; they are acrylic.

OJO est**e** but est**os**, es**e** but es**os** (no **o** in the masculine singular forms)

Demonstrative adjectives (**los adjetivos demostrativos**) are used to point out or indicate a specific noun or nouns. In Spanish, demonstrative adjectives precede the nouns they modify. They also agree in number and gender with the nouns.

est**e** cuadern**o**	*this notebook*
es**a** casa	*that house*
aquell**os** chic**os**	*those boys (over there)*

- There are two ways to say *that/those* in Spanish. Forms of **ese** refer to nouns that are not close to the speaker in space or in time. Forms of **aquel** are used to refer to nouns that are even farther away.

Este niño es mi hijo. **Ese** joven es mi hijo también. Y **aquel** señor allí es mi esposo.
This boy is my son. That young man is also my son. And that man over there is my husband.

- To express English *this one* (*that one*), just drop the noun.

este coche y **ese**
this car and that one

aquella casa y **esta***
that house (over there) and this one

- Use the neuter demonstratives **esto, eso,** and **aquello** to refer to as yet unidentified objects or to a whole idea, concept, or situation.

¿Qué es **esto**?
What is this?

Eso es todo.
That's it. That's all.

¡**Aquello** es terrible!
That's terrible!

use "o" at end when you don't know gender.

Práctica

A. Comparaciones

Paso 1. Restate the sentences, changing forms of **este** to **ese** and adding **también**, following the model.

MODELO: Este abrigo es muy grande. →
Ese abrigo también es muy grande.

1. Esta falda es muy pequeña.
2. Estos pantalones son muy largos.
3. Este libro es muy bueno.
4. Estas corbatas son muy feas.

---

*Some Spanish speakers prefer to use accents on these forms: **este coche y ése, aquella casa y ésta**. However, it is acceptable in modern Spanish, per the **Real Academia Española** in Madrid, to omit the accent on these forms when context makes the meaning clear and no ambiguity is possible. To learn more about these forms, consult Appendix 2, Using Adjectives as Nouns.

Paso 2. Now change the forms of **este** to **aquel**.

MODELO: Este abrigo es muy grande. →
Aquel abrigo también es muy grande.

B. Situaciones. Find an appropriate response for each situation.

Posibilidades: ¡Eso es un desastre!, ¿Qué es esto?, ¡Eso es magnífico!, ¡Eso es terrible!

1. Aquí hay un regalo para Ud.
2. Ocurre un accidente en la cafetería: Ud. tiene tomate en su camisa favorita.
3. No hay clases mañana.
4. La matrícula cuesta más este semestre/trimestre.
5. Ud. tiene una A en su examen de español.

Conversación

Una tarde en un patio mexicano

Paso 1. ¿A qué parte del dibujo se refieren las siguientes oraciones? Habla la mujer de los zapatos verdes.

1. Aquella mujer es de Cuernavaca.
2. Estas plantas son un regalo de un amigo chileno.
3. Ese pájaro habla inglés y español.
4. Aquel joven es un primo de Taxco.

Paso 2. Ahora, con un compañero/una compañera, imagine que Uds. son otras personas en el dibujo e inventen oraciones sobre el dibujo.

9 Expressing Actions and States • *Tener, venir, preferir, querer,* and *poder;* Some Idioms with *tener*

Una gorra para José Miguel, después de mirar en tres tiendas

ELISA: ¿Qué gorra *prefieres*, José Miguel?

JOSÉ MIGUEL: *Prefiero* la gris.

ELISA: ¡Pero ya *tienes* una gris, y es casi idéntica!

JOSÉ MIGUEL: Pues, no *quiero* esas otras gorras. ¿*Podemos* mirar en la tienda anterior otra vez?

ELISA: ¿Otra vez? Bueno, si realmente insistes…

Comprensión: ¿Sí o no?

1. José Miguel quiere comprar una corbata.
2. Él prefiere la gorra azul.
3. No puede decidir entre las gorras.
4. Parece que (*It seems that*) Elisa tiene mucha paciencia.

tener (*to have*)	**venir** (*to come*)	**preferir** (*to prefer*)	**querer** (*to want*)	**poder** (*to be able, can*)
tengo	vengo	prefiero	quiero	puedo
tienes	vienes	prefieres	quieres	puedes
tiene	viene	prefiere	quiere	puede
tenemos	venimos	preferimos	queremos	podemos
tenéis	venís	preferís	queréis	podéis
tienen	vienen	prefieren	quieren	pueden

- The **yo** forms of **tener** and **venir** are irregular.
- In other forms of **tener, venir, preferir,** and **querer,** when the stem vowel **e** is stressed, it becomes **ie.**
- Similarly, the stem vowel **o** in **poder** becomes **ue** when stressed. In vocabulary lists these changes are shown in parentheses after the infinitive: **poder (ue).** You will learn more verbs of this type in Grammar 12.

Irregularities:

tener: yo tengo, tú tienes (e → ie)…
venir: yo vengo, tú vienes (e → ie)…
preferir, querer: (e → ie)
poder: (o → ue)

O J O **Nosotros** and **vosotros** forms for these verbs do not have irregular changes.

A cap for José Miguel, after looking in three stores ELISA: Which cap do you prefer, José Miguel? JOSÉ MIGUEL: I prefer the gray one. ELISA: But you already have a gray one, and it's almost identical! JOSÉ MIGUEL: Well, I don't want those other caps. Can we look in the previous store again? ELISA: Again? Well, if you really insist . . .

SOME IDIOMS WITH *tener*

A. Many ideas expressed in English with the verb *to be* are expressed in Spanish with *idioms* (**los modismos**) using **tener.** You have already used one **tener** idiom: **tener… años.** At the right are some additional ones. Note that they describe a condition or state that a person can experience.

tener miedo (de)	to be afraid (of)
tener prisa	to be in a hurry
(no) tener razón	to be right (wrong)
tener sueño	to be sleepy

> **OJO** Idiomatic expressions are often different from one language to another. For example, in English, *to pull Mary's leg* usually means *to tease her,* not *to grab her leg and pull it.* In Spanish, *to pull Mary's leg* is **tomarle el pelo a Mary** (literally, *to take hold of Mary's hair*).

B. Other **tener** idioms include **tener ganas de** (*to feel like*) and **tener que** (*to have to*). The infinitive is always used after these two idiomatic expressions.

Tengo ganas de **comer.**
I feel like eating.

¿No tiene Ud. que **leer** este capítulo?
Don't you have to read this chapter?

> **OJO** Note that the English translation of one of these examples results in a verb ending in *-ing,* not the infinitive.

NOTA COMUNICATIVA

Using *mucho* and *poco*

In the first chapters of *¿Qué tal?*, you have used the words **mucho** and **poco** as both adjectives and adverbs. *Adverbs* (**Los adverbios**) are words that modify verbs, adjectives, or other adverbs: *quickly, very smart, very quickly.* In Spanish and in English, adverbs are invariable in form. However, in Spanish adjectives agree in number and gender with the word they modify.

> **adverb** = a word that modifies a verb, adjective, or another adverb

ADVERB

Rosario estudia **mucho** hoy.   *Rosario is studying a lot today.*
Julio come **poco.**   *Julio doesn't eat much.*

ADJECTIVE

Rosario tiene **mucha** ropa.   *Rosario has a lot of*
  Sobre todo tiene   *clothes. She especially*
  muchos zapatos.   *has a lot of shoes.*
Julio come **poca** carne.   *Julio doesn't eat much meat.*
  Come **pocos** postres.   *He eats few desserts.*

Práctica

A. ¡Sara tiene mucha tarea (*homework*)!

Paso 1. Haga oraciones con las palabras indicadas. Añada (*Add*) palabras si es necesario.

1. Sara / tener / muchos exámenes
2. (ella) venir / a / universidad / todos los días
3. hoy / trabajar / hasta (*until*) / nueve / de / noche
4. preferir / estudiar / en/ biblioteca
5. querer / leer / más / pero / no poder
6. por eso / regresar / a / casa
7. tener / ganas de / leer / más
8. pero / unos amigos / venir a mirar / televisión
9. Sara / decidir / mirar / televisión / con ellos

She

Paso 2. Now retell the same sequence of events, first as if they had happened to you, using **yo** as the subject of all but sentence number 8, then as if they had happened to you and your roommate, using **nosotros/as**.

B. Situaciones. Expand the situations described in these sentences by using an appropriate idiom with **tener**. There is often more than one possible answer.

MODELO: Tengo un examen mañana. Por eso… → Por eso tengo que estudiar mucho.

1. ¿Cuántos años? ¿Cuarenta? No, yo…
2. Un perro grande y feo vive en esa casa. Por eso yo…
3. ¿Ya son las tres de la mañana? Ah, por eso…
4. No, dos y dos no son cinco. Son cuatro. Tú…
5. Tengo que estar en el centro a las tres. Ya (*Already*) son las tres menos cuarto. Yo…
6. Cuando hay un terremoto (*earthquake*), todos…
7. ¿Los exámenes de la clase de español? ¡Esos son siempre muy fáciles! Yo no…
8. Sí, la capital de la Argentina es Buenos Aires. Tú…

Conversación

A. Estereotipos. Draw some conclusions about Isabel based on the following scene. Think about things that she has, needs to or has to do or buy, likes, and so on. When you have finished, compare your predictions with those of others in the class. Did you all reach the same conclusions?

Palabras útiles: los aretes (*earrings*), el juguete (*toy*), hablar por teléfono, los muebles (*furniture*), el sofá, tener alergia a (*to be allergic to*)

B. **Entrevista: Más preferencias.** With a classmate, explore preferences in a number of areas by asking and answering questions based on the following cues. Form your questions with expressions like these:

¿Prefieres... o ... ?
¿Te gusta más (*infinitive*) o (*infinitive*)?

If you have no preference, express that by saying **No tengo preferencia**. Be prepared to report some of your findings to the class. If you both agree, you will express this by saying **Preferimos...** or **No tenemos preferencia**. If you do not agree, give the preferences of both persons: **Yo prefiero..., pero Cecilia prefiere...**

1. Los animales: ¿los gatos siameses o los persas? ¿los perros pastores alemanes o los perros de lanas (*poodles*)?
2. El color de la ropa informal: ¿el color negro o el blanco? ¿el rojo o el azul?
3. La ropa informal: ¿las camisas de algodón o las de seda? ¿los *jeans* de algodón o los pantalones de lana?
4. La ropa de mujeres: ¿las faldas largas o las minifaldas? ¿los pantalones largos o los pantalones cortos?
5. La ropa de hombres: ¿las camisas de cuadros o las de rayas? ¿las camisas de un solo (*single*) color? ¿chaqueta y pantalón o un traje formal?
6. Las actividades en casa: ¿mirar la televisión o leer una novela? ¿escribir cartas o hablar con unos amigos?

Enfoque *cultural*

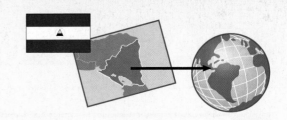

Nicaragua

Datos esenciales

Nombre oficial: República de Nicaragua

Capital: Managua

Población: 4.000.000 de habitantes

Moneda: el córdoba

Idiomas: el español (oficial), el misquito, el sumo*

Nota histórica

Cristóbal Colón llegó[a] a las costas de Nicaragua en 1502, pero la región no fue colonizada[b] hasta[c] 1524.

Nicaragua tiene una historia turbulenta por las luchas[d] entre las fuerzas conservadoras y las fuerzas liberales. La lucha se complicó[e] por la intervención de los Estados Unidos en la política del país. En 1990 terminó[f] una época[g] difícil de dictadura y lucha: hubo[h] una revolución y un movimiento en contra de la revolución. Esta lucha fue entre los sandinistas (revolucionarios marxistas) y los «contras» (antirrevolucionarios).

[a] *arrived* [b] *no... was not colonized* [c] *until* [d] *struggles* [e] *se... was complicated* [f] *ended* [g] *time* [h] *there was*

¡Fíjese!

- En 1856, un norteamericano, William Walker, se declaró[a] presidente de Nicaragua. Dos años después, fue derrotado por[b] los nicaragüenses, liberales y conservadores que se unieron[c] para expulsarlo[d] del país.

Violeta Barrios de Chamorro

- El Lago de Nicaragua es el lago más grande de Centroamérica. Hay más de 300 islas en el lago. En «las Isletas», hay pequeñas comunidades agrícolas[e] y, en algunas,[f] casas de personas ricas.

- Violeta Barrios de Chamorro fue[g] presidenta de Nicaragua de 1990 a 1997. Fue la primera[h] presidenta en Centroamérica. En 2001, Enrique Bolaños Geyer fue elegido[i] presidente.

[a] *se... declared himself* [b] *fue... he was defeated by* [c] *se... joined together* [d] *expel him* [e] *agricultural* [f] *some* [g] *was* [h] *first* [i] *fue... was elected*

Capítulo 3 of the video to accompany *¿Qué tal?* contains cultural footage of Nicaragua.

VWw. Visit the *¿Qué tal?* website at www.mhhe.com/quetal.

*En la costa oeste (*west coast*) de Nicaragua, también se habla un dialecto criollo (*creole*) que está basado en el inglés.

10 **Expressing Destination and Future Actions • *Ir; ir* + *a* + Infinitive; The Contraction *al***

¿Qué *va a* hacer Ud. este fin de semana?

- ¿*Va a ir al* centro?   Sí, *voy a ir al* centro.
- ¿*Va a ir* de compras?   No, no *voy a ir* de compras.
- ¿*Va a* hablar con sus amigos?   Sí, *voy a* hablar con mis amigos.
- ¿*Va a* estudiar español?   ¡Claro que sí!

Si quiere añadir (*add*) otras actividades a la lista, use la frase **También voy a** + *infinitive*.

Ir is the irregular Spanish verb used to express *to go*.

ir (*to go*)	
voy	vamos
vas	vais
va	van

The first person plural of **ir, vamos** (*we go, are going, do go*), is also used to express *let's go*.

Ir + **a** + infinitive is used to describe actions or events in the near future.

Vamos a clase ahora mismo.
Let's go to class right now.

Van a venir a la fiesta esta noche.
They're going to come to the party tonight.

Voy a ir de compras esta tarde.
I'm going to go shopping this afternoon.

THE CONTRACTION *al*

In **Capítulo 2** you learned about the contraction **del** (**de** + **el** → **del**). The only other contraction in Spanish is **al** (**a** + **el** → **al**). **¡OJO!** Both **del** and **al** are obligatory contractions.

a + **el** → **al**

Voy **al** centro comercial.
I'm going to the mall.

Vamos **a la** tienda.
I'm going to the store.

Práctica

A. **¿Adónde van de compras?** Haga oraciones completas usando **ir**. Recuerde: **a** + **el** = **al**.

MODELO: Marta / el centro → Marta *va al* centro.

1. Ud. / una *boutique*
2. Francisco / el almacén Goya

3. Jorge y Carlos / el centro comercial
4. tú / un mercado
5. nosotros / una tienda pequeña
6. yo / ¿ ?

B. ¡Vamos de compras en Sevilla! Describa el día, desde el punto de vista (*from the point of view*) de Lola Benítez. Use **ir** + **a** + el infinitivo.

MODELO: Manolo compra un regalo para su madre. →
Manolo *va a comprar* un regalo para su madre.

1. Llegamos al centro a las diez de la mañana.
2. La niña quiere comer algo (*something*).
3. Compro unos chocolates para Marta.
4. Manolo busca una blusa de seda.
5. No compras esta blusa de rayas, ¿verdad? (*right?*)
6. Buscamos algo más barato ¿no? (*right?, OK?*)
7. ¿Vas de compras mañana también?

Conversación

A. ¿Adónde vas si... ? ¿Cuántas oraciones puede hacer Ud.?

Me gusta
- leer novelas.
- ir de compras —y ¡no regateo!
- buscar gangas y regatear.
- hablar con mis amigos.
- comer en restaurantes elegantes.
- mirar programas de detectives.

Por eso voy a _____.

B. Entrevista: El fin de semana

Paso 1. Interview a classmate about his or her plans for the weekend. Try to personalize the interview by asking additional questions. For example, if your partner is going to read a novel, ask questions like **¿Qué novela?** or **¿Quién es el autor?**

¿Sí o no? ¿Vas a... ?

1. ir de compras
2. leer una novela
3. asistir a un concierto
4. estudiar para un examen
5. ir a una fiesta
6. escribir una carta
7. ir a bailar
8. escribir los ejercicios para la clase de español
9. practicar un deporte (*sport*)
10. mirar mucho la televisión

Paso 2. En general, ¿es muy activo/a su compañero/a? ¿O prefiere la tranquilidad? En el **Paso 1**, los números pares (2, 4, 6,...) son actividades más o menos pasivas o tranquilas. Los números impares (1, 3, 5,...) representan actividades más activas. ¿Cómo es su compañero/a?

En los Estados Unidos y el Canadá...

Los hispanos en el mundo de la moda

Christy Turlington

Christy Turlington is one of many Hispanic celebrities in the U.S. world of fashion. Born in San Francisco, California (1969), to a Salvadoran mother, Turlington has been a household name since the 1990s. During her career as a supermodel, she became an activist for and benefactor of several causes, including breast cancer and animal rights. Furthermore, after being diagnosed with early-stage emphysema and subsequently quitting smoking, Christy became the spokesperson for a government anti-tobacco campaign.

UN POCO DE TODO

Pero, ¿no se puede (*can't one*) **regatear?** Complete the following paragraph with the correct form of the words in parentheses, as suggested by the context. When two possibilities are given in parentheses, select the correct word.

En (los/las[1]) ciudades hispánicas, hay una (grande[2]) variedad de tiendas para (ir[3]) de compras. Hay almacenes, centros comerciales y *boutiques* (elegante[4]), como en (los/las[5]) Estados Unidos, donde los precios son siempre (fijo[6]).

También hay tiendas (pequeño[7]) que venden un solo[a] producto. Por ejemplo,[b] en una zapatería sólo hay zapatos. En español el sufijo **-ería** se usa[c] para (formar[8]) el nombre de la tienda. ¿Dónde (creer[9]) Ud. que venden papel y (otro[10]) artículos de escritorio? ¿A qué tienda (ir[11]) a ir Ud. a comprar fruta?

Si Ud. (poder[12]) pagar el precio que piden,[d] (deber[13]) comprar los recuerdos[e] en (los/las[14]) almacenes o *boutiques*. Pero si (tener[15]) ganas o necesidad de regatear, tiene (de/que[16]) ir a un mercado: un conjunto[f] de tiendas o locales[g] donde el ambiente[h] es más (informal[17]) que[i] en los (grande[18]) almacenes. Ud. no (deber[19]) pagar el primer[j] precio que menciona el vendedor.[k] ¡Casi siempre va (a/de[20]) ser muy alto!

[a]*single* [b]*Por... For example* [c]*se... is used* [d]*they ask for* [e]*souvenirs* [f]*group* [g]*stalls* [h]*atmosphere* [i]*than* [j]*first* [k]*seller*

Comprensión: ¿Cierto o falso? Corrija las oraciones falsas.

1. En el mundo hispánico, todas las tiendas son similares.
2. Uno puede regatear en un almacén hispánico.
3. Es posible comprar limones en una papelería.
4. En un mercado, el vendedor siempre ofrece un precio bajo al principio (*beginning*).

Un paso más PASO 4

VIDEOTECA: En contexto

In this video segment, which takes place in Costa Rica, Mariela bargains with a street vendor for a very special item. As you watch this segment, pay particular attention to the words that the salesperson uses to convince Mariela to buy. Do they both agree on prices? Who "wins"?

COSTA RICA

FUNCTION
Shopping for clothes

A. Lluvia de ideas

- ¿Hay mercados al aire libre en su ciudad? ¿Qué venden? ¿Compra Ud. en ellos con frecuencia?
- En este país, ¿son normales los precios fijos? ¿Hay alguna (*any*) ocasión en que Ud. regatea?

B. Dictado

Here is the first part of this segment's dialogue. Fill in the missing portions of the dialogue.

MARIELA: Buenos días, señora. [...] ¿ _____[1] qué son las chaquetas?
VENDEDORA: Las chaquetas _____[2] de pura _____.[3] Son muy bonitas, ¿_____[4]?
MARIELA: Sí, son bonitas. ¿_____[5] cuestan?
VENDEDORA: _____[6] 5.000 colones. Son, eh... muy buenas chaquetas.
MARIELA: No estoy segura. Es _____.[7]
VENDEDORA: Pero ¡el precio es una _____![8] Son realmente buenas.
MARIELA: Sí, Ud. tiene _____,[9] son chaquetas muy bonitas, pero de todos modos son un _____[10] caras.

C. Un diálogo original

Paso 1. Con un compañero/una compañera, dramatice la escena de Mariela con la vendedora.

Paso 2. Imagine que Ud. y su compañero/a están de compras en casa de una persona que va a mudarse (*move*).

E1: You want to buy some old clothes that are for sale. You want a cheaper price because you want to buy several items.
E2: You are selling household items. You are willing to lower your prices, but not too much. Your items are high-quality.

Cultura en contexto
Hispanic Currencies

Due to emerging political and commercial alliances, some currencies in the Spanish-speaking world are changing.

- While the **colón** continues to be the currency in Costa Rica, the U.S. dollar replaced the **sucre** in Ecuador in 2000 and the **colón** in El Salvador in 2001.

- In January 2002, the **euro** replaced the currencies of 11 of the 14 European Union member states, including the Spanish **peseta**.

PASO FINAL

A LEER

Sobre la lectura… This reading is adapted from an article that appeared in *Quo*, a magazine published in Spain that is comparable to *Vanity Fair, Details,* and other glossy general interest magazines. *Quo* publishes articles about topics ranging from diet and health to fashion to politics.

Estrategia: Using Visuals and Graphics to Predict Content

In **Capítulo 1** you learned that you can use section subheadings to help you better understand a passage. Another useful strategy is to use photographs and other visual clues (charts, drawings, graphic images, and so on) that accompany the reading as tools to help you predict the content of the passage. A successful reader is able to make predictions about content in advance, and then confirms or rejects these predictions while reading.

Before reading the article below, look at the subheadings. What predictions can you make based on the visual presentation of the subheadings?

La psicología de los colores

«Está demostrado[a] que los colores percibidos[b] por la vista[c] <u>provocan</u> una reacción psicológica sobre nuestro estado de ánimo[d]», asegura Carlos Obelleiro, <u>experto</u> en la utilización de color. Y de un buen estado de ánimo depende mucho la salud física. Según expertos en psicología de los colores, cada uno indica una actitud en quien lo lleva puesto.[e]

Rojo
Es el color que produce mayor impacto visual. Actúa como un estimulante psíquico, pero activa la <u>agresividad</u> y si alguien lo lleva puede incomodar a los demás.[f]

Amarillo
Está íntimamente relacionado con la autoestima[g] y <u>estimula</u> la creatividad, pero puede resultar agresivo para gente emocionalmente <u>frágil.</u>

Azul
Favorece la calma y la concentración en trabajos que exigen[h] esfuerzo[i] mental. Tranquiliza, pero puede dar imagen de frialdad.[j] Cuanto más oscuro es[k] más idea da[l] de eficiencia y autoridad.

Verde
Es el color más relajante y suele[m] provocar una sensación de <u>equilibrio</u> y de tranquilidad personal.

Blanco
Aunque[n] es muy higiénico, puede resultar muy severo y dar la impresión de que la persona que lo lleva quiere crear una barrera.[o]

Rosa
Es la más pura expresión de la <u>feminidad</u>. Utilizado en decoración actúa como relajante, pero en exceso causa debilitamiento.[p]

Negro
Es elegante, pero puede resultar amenazador[q] y, como el blanco, crear barreras entre la persona que lo lleva y el resto de la gente.

[a]*Está… It has been shown* [b]*perceived* [c]*sight* [d]*estado… state of mind* [e]*quien… the person who wears it* [f]*incomodar… make others uncomfortable* [g]*self-esteem* [h]*demand* [i]*effort* [j]*coldness* [k]*Cuanto… The darker it is* [l]*it gives* [m]*it tends to* [n]*Although* [o]*crear… to create a barrier* [p]*debilitation, weakness* [q]*threatening*

Violeta

Es el color de la introversión. Puede transmitir la sensación de que quien lo viste[r] quiere estar solo, sin intromisiones.[s]

Gris

Se trata del único color totalmente <u>neutro</u>, con lo que no tiene apenas[t] propiedades psicológicas. A veces puede indicar falta[u] de confianza en uno mismo. ■

[r]quien... *the person who wears it*   [s]sin... *without intrusions*   [t]*hardly any*   [u]*a lack*

Comprensión

A. **¿Qué color?** Identify the color (or colors!) that corresponds to each psychological trait below according to the reading.

   1.   Este color no se asocia con la extroversión, sino lo contrario (*but rather the opposite*).

   2.   A veces este color se asocia con la frigidez.

   3.   Estos dos colores dan la impresión de crear obstáculos.

   4.   Este color provoca reacciones muy agresivas.

   5.   Este color provoca la creatividad.

B. **¿Qué color recomienda Ud.** (*do you recommend*)**?** Which color do you recommend a person wear in order to make the following impressions or provoke the following reactions?

   1.   Una persona desea dar una impresión de control y poder (*power*).
   2.   Una persona quiere expresar su confianza en sí misma (*confidence in him- or herself*).
   3.   Una persona no quiere producir ningún (*any*) impacto.

A ESCRIBIR

Mi ropa favorita. In a brief paragraph, write a description of your favorite article of clothing. You will want to include information such as the material that it is made of, why you like it, and so on. And be sure to identify the color! How do you feel when you wear it? Does the color provoke certain reactions in you, similar to those described in the reading? What reactions? Your instructor can help you with words or constructions that are unfamiliar to you.

En resumen

GRAMÁTICA

To review the grammar points presented in this chapter, refer to the indicated grammar presentations. You'll find further practice of these structures in the Workbook/Laboratory Manual, on the CD-ROM, and on the website.

8. Demonstrative Adjectives

Do you know the forms for **este, ese**, and **aquel**? Do you know the differences in meaning?

9. *Tener, venir, preferir, querer*, and *poder*; Some Idioms with *tener*

You should be able to conjugate the verbs **tener, venir, preferir, querer**, and **poder** in the present tense. Do you know how to use

expressions like **tengo ganas de, tenemos miedo**, and **tienes razón**?

10. *Ir; ir + a +* Infinitive; The Contraction *al*

You should know the forms of **ir** and how to express *going to do* (*something*). You should also know when to use the contraction **al**.

VOCABULARIO

Los verbos

ir (*irreg.*)	to go
ir a + *inf.*	to be going to (*do something*)
ir de compras	to go shopping
llevar	to wear; to carry; to take
poder (ue)	to be able, can
preferir (ie)	to prefer
querer (ie)	to want
regatear	to haggle, bargain
tener (*irreg.*)	to have
usar	to wear; to use
venir (*irreg.*)	to come

Repaso: comprar, vender

La ropa

el abrigo	coat
los aretes	earrings
la blusa	blouse
la bolsa	purse
la bota	boot
los calcetines	socks
la camisa	shirt
la camiseta	T-shirt
la cartera	wallet
la chaqueta	jacket
el cinturón	belt
la corbata	tie
la falda	skirt
el impermeable	raincoat
los *jeans*	jeans
las medias	stockings
los pantalones	pants
el par	pair
el reloj	watch
la ropa interior	underwear
la sandalia	sandal
el sombrero	hat
el suéter	sweater
el traje	suit
el traje de baño	swimsuit
el vestido	dress
el zapato (de tenis)	(tennis) shoe

Los colores

amarillo/a	yellow
anaranjado/a	orange
azul	blue
blanco/a	white
gris	gray
morado/a	purple
negro/a	black
pardo/a	brown
rojo/a	red
rosado/a	pink
verde	green

De compras

de cuadros	plaid
de lunares	polka-dotted
de rayas	striped
de última moda	the latest style
la ganga	bargain
el precio (fijo)	(fixed) price
las rebajas	sales, reductions
¿cuánto cuesta?	how much does it cost?
¿cuánto es?	how much is it?

Los materiales

es de...	it is made of . . .
algodón (*m.*)	cotton
lana	wool
seda	silk

Los lugares

el almacén	department store
el centro	downtown
el centro comercial	shopping mall
el mercado	market(place)
la tienda	shop, store

Otros sustantivos

la cinta	tape
el ejercicio	exercise
el examen	exam, test

Los adjetivos

barato/a	inexpensive
caro/a	expensive
poco/a	little

Los números

doscientos/as, trescientos/as, cuatrocientos/as, quinientos/as, seiscientos/as, setecientos/as, ochocientos/as, novecientos/as, mil, un millón (de)

Repaso: cien(to)

Formas demostrativas

aquel, aquella, aquellos/as	that, those (over there)
ese/a, esos/as	that, those
esto, eso, aquello	this, that, that (over there)

Repaso: este/a, estos/as

Palabras adicionales

¿adónde?	where (to)?
al	to the
algo	something
allí	(over) there
de todo	everything
tener...	
ganas de + *inf.*	to feel like (*doing something*)
miedo (de)	to be afraid (of)
prisa	to be in a hurry
que + *inf.*	to have to (*do something*)
razón	to be right
sueño	to be sleepy
no tener razón	to be wrong
¿no?, ¿verdad?	right?, don't they (you, and so on)?

En casa

Una casa en el campo (*countryside*) de Costa Rica

VOCABULARIO

- Days of the week
- Furniture, rooms, and parts of the house
- Prepositions

GRAMÁTICA

11 **Hacer, oír, poner, salir, traer,** and **ver**
12 Present Tense of Stem-Changing Verbs
13 Reflexive Pronouns

CULTURA

- **Enfoque cultural:** Costa Rica
- **Nota cultural:** Houses in the Hispanic World
- **En los Estados Unidos y el Canadá:** Vicente Wolf
- **Cultura en contexto:** Living with Parents

Multimedia

 You will learn more about searching for an apartment in the **En contexto** video segment.

Review vocabulary and grammar and practice language skills with the interactive CD-ROM.

 Get connected to the Spanish-speaking world with the *¿Qué tal?* Online Learning Center: **www.mhhe.com/ quetal**.

what day is today?

¿Qué día es hoy?

Que fecha es hoy?
what date is today?

fechas

lunes	Monday
martes	Tuesday
miércoles	Wednesday
jueves	Thursday
viernes	Friday
sábado	Saturday
domingo	Sunday
el lunes, el martes…	on Monday, on Tuesday . . .
los lunes, los martes…	on Mondays, on Tuesdays . . .
Hoy (Mañana) es viernes.	Today (Tomorrow) is Friday.
Ayer fue miércoles.	Yesterday was Wednesday.
el fin de semana	(on) the weekend
pasado mañana	the day after tomorrow

agosto

lunes 14 *catorce*	jueves 17
martes 15 *quince*	viernes 18
miércoles 16	sábado 19 domingo 20

el próximo (martes, miércoles,…)	next (Tuesday, Wednesday, . . .)
la semana que viene	next week

en la mañana – in the morning

la próxima semana

OJO
- Except for **el sábado / los sábados** and **el domingo / los domingos**, all the days of the week use the same form for the plural as they do for the singular.
- The definite articles are used to express *on* with the days of the week.
- The days are not capitalized in Spanish.
- In Spanish-speaking countries, the week usually starts with **lunes**.

Conversación

A. Preguntas

1. ¿Qué día es hoy? ¿Qué día es mañana? Si hoy es sábado, ¿qué día es mañana? Si hoy es jueves, ¿qué día es mañana? ¿Qué día fue ayer?
2. ¿Qué días de la semana tenemos clase? ¿Qué días no?
3. ¿Estudia Ud. mucho durante (*during*) el fin de semana? ¿y los domingos por la noche?
4. ¿Qué le gusta hacer (*to do*) los viernes por la tarde? ¿Le gusta salir (*to go out*) con los amigos los sábados por la noche?

B. Mi semana. Indique una cosa que Ud. quiere, puede o tiene que hacer cada (*each*) día de esta semana.

MODELO: El lunes tengo que (puedo, quiero) ir al laboratorio de lenguas.

Palabras útiles: dormir (*to sleep*) hasta muy tarde, jugar (*to play*) al tenis (al golf, al vólibol, al…), ir al cine (*movies*), ir al bar (al parque, al museo, a…)

Los muebles,° los cuartos y otras partes de la casa

Los… *Furniture*

el jardín	yard
la pared	wall
el patio	patio; yard
la piscina	swimming pool
la alfombra	rug
el escritorio	desk
el estante	bookshelf
los platos	dishes; plates
la silla	chair

Note: This is the first group of words you will learn for talking about where you live and the things found in your house or apartment. You will learn additional vocabulary for those topics in **Capítulos 9, 12,** and **14.**

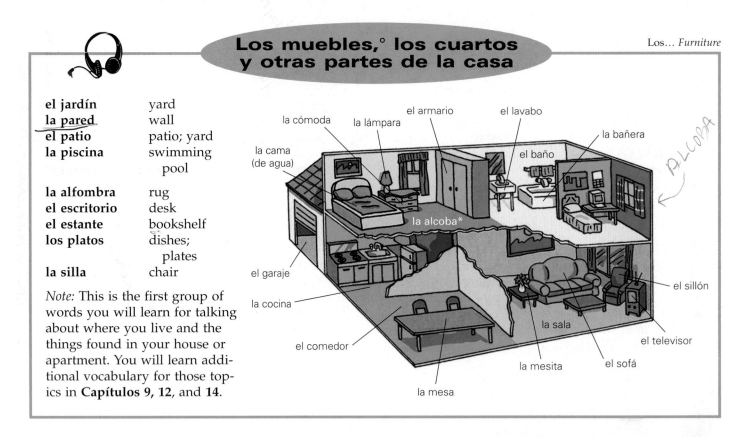

Conversación

A. ¿Qué hay en esta casa? Identifique las partes de esta casa y diga lo que hay en cada cuarto. ¿Qué hay en el patio? ¿Hay una piscina? ¿O solamente hay plantas?

---

*Other frequently used words for *bedroom* include **el dormitorio** and **la habitación.**

B. Asociaciones

Paso 1. ¿Qué muebles o partes de la casa asocia Ud. con las siguientes actividades?

1. estudiar para un examen
2. dormir la siesta (*taking a nap*) por la tarde
3. pasar una noche en casa con la familia
4. celebrar con una comida (*meal*) especial
5. tomar el sol (*sunbathing*)
6. hablar de temas (*topics*) serios con los amigos (padres, hijos)

Paso 2. Ahora compare sus asociaciones con las (*those*) de otros estudiantes. ¿Tienen todos las mismas costumbres (*customs*)?

¿Cuándo? • Preposiciones

Prepositions express relationships in time and space.	The book is *on* the table.
	The homework is *for* tomorrow.

Some common prepositions you have already used include **a, con, de, en, para**, and **por**. Here are some prepositions that express time relationships.	**antes de**	*before*	**durante**	*during*
	después de	*after*	**hasta**	*until*

The infinitive is the only verb form that can follow a preposition.	¿Adónde vas **después de estudiar**? *Where are you going after studying (after you study)?*

Conversación

A. **¿Antes o después?** Complete las oraciones lógicamente, con **antes de** o **después de**.

1. Voy a la clase de español _____ preparar la lección.
2. Por lo general, prefiero estudiar _____ mirar un poco la televisión.
3. Los viernes siempre descanso (*I rest*) _____ salir para una fiesta.
4. Me gusta investigar un tema _____ escribir una composición.
5. Prefiero comer fuera (*to eat out*) _____ ir al cine.
6. Tengo que estudiar mucho _____ tomar un examen.

B. Preguntas

1. ¿Estudia Ud. durante su programa favorito de televisión? ¿Qué más hace (*do you do*) cuando estudia?
2. ¿Habla por teléfono antes o después de estudiar? ¿Dónde habla por teléfono, en la sala o en su cuarto?
3. ¿Hasta qué hora estudia, generalmente? ¿Estudia hasta dormirse (*you fall asleep*)?
4. ¿Lee durante las conferencias (*lectures*) en una clase? ¿Lee la lección antes o después de la explicación (*explanation*) del profesor / de la profesora?
5. ¿Trabaja durante las vacaciones? ¿Cuántas horas? ¿Trabaja por la noche hasta muy tarde?

NOTA CULTURAL

Houses in the Hispanic World

There is no such thing as a typical Hispanic house. Often, the style of housing depends on geographic location. For example, in hot regions, such as southern Spain, many houses are built around a central interior patio. These patios are filled with plants, and some even have a fountain.

The population in Hispanic countries tends to be centered in urban areas. Due to population density in cities, many people live in apartments, like people in larger cities in this country. Here are some more details about Hispanic houses.

Un patio interior en Sevilla, España

- While the Spanish word **hogar** literally means *home,* the word **casa** is often used to mean *home.*

    Voy a casa. *I'm going home.* Estoy en casa. *I'm at home.*

- In Spain, people use the word **piso** or **apartamento** to refer to an apartment; in some Hispanic countries, the word **departamento** is used.
- In big Latin American cities and in more modern homes, a small front yard with ornamental plants and/or small trees is called **un jardín**. Except in rural areas and small towns, a large backyard is uncommon because the lots where houses are built are rather small. If a house has a back area, it is generally referred to as **el patio**. This area, usually paved, adjoins the house and is commonly enclosed by the walls of neighboring buildings.

11 **Expressing Actions** • *Hacer, oír, poner, salir, traer,* and *ver*

Los jóvenes de hoy

«¡Estos muchachos sólo quieren *salir*! No *ponen* sus cosas en orden en su cuarto… Los jóvenes de hoy día no *hacen* nada bien; no son responsables… ¡Hasta quieren *traer* muchachas a su cuarto!»

¿Son estos comentarios típicos de las personas mayores (*adults*) de su país?

¿Cree Ud. que tienen razón?

¿Tienen los jóvenes algunos (*any*) estereotipos sobre (*about*) las personas mayores?

hacer (*to do; to make*)		**oír** (*to hear*)		**poner** (*to put; to place*)		**salir** (*to leave;* *to go out*)		**traer** (*to bring*)		**ver** (*to see*)	
hago	hacemos	oigo	oímos	pongo	ponemos	salgo	salimos	traigo	traemos	veo	vemos
haces	hacéis	oyes	oís	pones	ponéis	sales	salís	traes	traéis	ves	veis
hace	hacen	oye	oyen	pone	ponen	sale	salen	trae	traen	ve	ven

• **hacer**

Some common idioms with **hacer** are **hacer ejercicio** (*to exercise*), **hacer un viaje** (*to take a trip*), and **hacer una pregunta** (*to ask a question*).

¿Por qué no **haces** los ejercicios?
Why aren't you doing the exercises?

Quieren **hacer un viaje** al Perú.
They want to take a trip to Peru.

Los niños siempre **hacen muchas preguntas**.
Children always ask a lot of questions.

• **oír**

The command forms of **oír**—**oye (tú), oiga (Ud.)**, and **oigan (Uds.)**—are used to attract someone's attention in the same way that English uses *Listen!* or *Hey!*

No **oigo** bien por el ruido.
I can't hear well because of the noise.

Oye, Juan, ¿vas a la fiesta?
Hey, Juan, are you going to the party?

¡Oigan! ¡Silencio, por favor!
Listen! Silence, please!

Today's young people These boys only want to go out! They don't put things in order in their rooms . . . Today's young people don't do anything right; they are not responsible people . . . They even want to bring girls to their rooms!

- **poner**

  Many Spanish speakers use **poner** with appliances to express *to turn on*.

  Siempre **pongo** leche y ~~mucho~~ *mucha* azúcar en el café.
  I always put milk and a lot of sugar in my coffee.

  Voy a **poner** el televisor.
  I'm going to turn on the TV.

- **salir**

  Note that **salir** is always followed by **de** to express leaving a place. **Salir con** can mean *to go out with, to date*.

  Use **salir para** to indicate destination.

  Salen de la clase ahora.
  They're leaving class now.

  Salgo con el hermano de Cecilia.
  I'm going out with Cecilia's brother.

  Salimos para la sierra pasado mañana.
  We're leaving for the mountains the day after tomorrow.

- **traer**

  ¿Por qué no **traes** *el* ~~la~~ radio a la cocina?
  Why don't you bring the radio to the kitchen?

- **ver**

  No **veo** bien sin mis lentes de contacto.
  I can't see well without my contact lenses.

Práctica

Cosas rutinarias

Paso 1. ¿Cierto o falso?

1. Hago ejercicio en el gimnasio con frecuencia.
2. Siempre veo la televisión por la noche.
3. Nunca salgo con mis primos por la noche.
4. Siempre hago los ejercicios para la clase de español.
5. Salgo para clase a las ocho de la mañana.
6. Nunca pongo la ropa en la cómoda o en el armario.
7. Siempre traigo todos los libros necesarios a clase.
8. Siempre oigo todo lo que dice (*says*) el profesor / la profesora de español.

Paso 2. Now rephrase each sentence in **Paso 1** as a question and interview a classmate. Use the **tú** form of the verb.

Conversación

A. Consecuencias lógicas. Con un compañero / una compañera, indique una acción lógica para cada situación, usando (*using*) las siguientes frases.

Frases útiles: poner el televisor / el estéreo, oír al profesor / a la profesora,*
salir con/de/para… , hacer un viaje / una pregunta, traer el libro a clase,
ver mi programa favorito.

1. Me gusta esquiar en las montañas. Por eso…
2. En la clase de español usamos este libro todos los días. Por eso…
3. Mis compañeros de cuarto hacen mucho ruido en la sala. Por eso…
4. El televisor no funciona. Por eso no…
5. Hay mucho ruido en la clase. Por eso no…
6. Estoy en la biblioteca y ¡no puedo estudiar más! Por eso…
7. Queremos bailar y necesitamos música. Por eso…
8. No comprendo la lección. Por eso…

B. Preguntas

1. ¿Qué pone Ud. en el armario? ¿en la cómoda? ¿Qué pone en su
   mochila o bolsa todos los días para ir a clase? Generalmente, ¿qué
   más trae a clase?
2. ¿Qué quiere hacer esta noche (*tonight*)? ¿Qué necesita hacer? ¿Qué va
   a hacer? ¿Va a salir con sus amigos (con su familia)? ¿Adónde van?
3. ¿A qué hora sale Ud. de la clase de español? ¿de las otras clases? ¿A
   veces sale tarde de clase? ¿Por qué?
4. ¿Oye Ud. las noticias (*news*) todos los días? ¿Pone Ud. la radio o el
   televisor para oír las noticias? ¿Y para oír música? ¿Qué programa ve
   en la televisión todas las semanas?

¿Recuerda Ud.?

The change in the stem vowels of **querer** and **poder** (**e** and **o**, respectively) follows the same pattern as that of the verbs presented in the
next section. Review the forms of **querer** and **poder** before beginning
that section.

querer: **e** → ¿ ? qu _____ ro   queremos
                      qu _____ res   queréis
                      qu _____ re   qu _____ ren

poder: **o** → ¿ ?   p _____ do   podemos
                      p _____ des   podéis
                      p _____ de   p _____ den

---

*Remember that the word **a** is necessary in front of a human direct object. You will study this
usage of **a** in **Capítulo 6.** For now, you can answer following the pattern of this **frase útil.**

12 Expressing Actions • Present Tense of Stem-Changing Verbs

¡Nunca más!

Volver a = to do it again

ALICIA: ¡No *vuelvo* a comprar en la papelería Franco!
ARMANDO: Yo también *empiezo* a cansarme de esa tienda. Nunca *tienen* los materiales que les *pido*.
ALICIA: ¿No *piensas* que los precios son muy caros? Yo creo que siempre *perdemos* dinero cuando compramos allí.
ARMANDO: Te *entiendo* perfectamente. Los precios son horribles. Como la papelería está tan cerca de la facultad, ¡*piensan* que *pueden* pedir mucho dinero por todo!

Since

¿Quién piensa que...

1. los precios de la papelería son muy caros?
2. la papelería no tiene muchas cosas necesarias?
3. pueden pedir mucho dinero porque la papelería está muy cerca de la facultad?
4. los estudiantes pierden dinero cuando compran en la papelería Franco?

e → ie **pensar (ie)** (*to think*)		o (u) → ue **volver (ue)** (*to return*)		e → i **pedir (i)** (*to ask for; to order*)	
pienso	pensamos	vuelvo	volvemos	pido	pedimos
piensas	pensáis	vuelves	volvéis	pides	pedís
piensa	piensan	vuelve	vuelven	pide	piden

A. You have already learned five *stem-changing verbs* (**los verbos que cambian el radical**): **querer, preferir, tener, venir,** and **poder.** In these verbs the stem vowels **e** and **o** become **ie** and **ue,** respectively, in stressed syllables. The stem vowels are stressed in all present tense forms except **nosotros** and **vosotros.** All three classes of stem-changing verbs follow this regular pattern in the present tense. In vocabulary lists, the stem change will always be shown in parentheses after the infinitive: **volver (ue).**

Stem vowel changes:

e → ie
e → i
o → ue

Nosotros and **vosotros** forms do not have a stem vowel change.

· ·

Never again! ALICIA: I'm not going to shop at Franco's stationery store again! ARMANDO: I'm also beginning to get fed up with that store. They never have the things I ask them for. ALICIA: Don't you think that the prices are very expensive? I think that we always lose money when we buy there. ARMANDO: I understand you perfectly. The prices are awful. Since the stationery store is so close to the campus, they think that they can ask a lot of money for everything!

B. Some stem-changing verbs practiced in this chapter include the following.

e → ie		o (u) → ue		e → i	
cerrar (ie)	*to close*	almorzar (ue)	*to have lunch*	pedir (i)	*to ask for; to order*
empezar (ie)	*to begin*	dormir (ue)	*to sleep*	servir (i)	*to serve*
entender (ie)	*to understand*	jugar (ue)*	*to play* (a game,		
pensar (ie)	*to think*		sport)		
perder (ie)	*to lose; to miss*	volver (ue)	*to return*		
	(a function)		(to a place)		

- When used with an infinitive, **empezar** is followed by **a**.

Uds. **empiezan a hablar** muy bien el español.
You're beginning to speak Spanish very well.

- When used with an infinitive, **volver** is also followed by **a**. The phrase then means *to do (something) again.*

¿Cuándo **vuelves a jugar** al tenis?
When are you going to play tennis again?

- When followed directly by an infinitive, **pensar** means *to intend, plan to.*

The phrase **pensar en** can be used to express *to think about.*

¿Cuándo **piensas contestar** la carta?
When do you intend to answer the letter?

—¿**En** qué **piensas**?
What are you thinking about?

—**Pienso en** la tarea para la clase de física.
I'm thinking about the homework for physics class.

Práctica

A. ¿Dónde están Diego y Antonio? Tell in what part of Antonio's apartment the following things are happening. More than one answer may be possible.

MODELO: Diego y Antonio empiezan la tarea. → Están en la alcoba.

1. Antonio sirve el desayuno (*breakfast*).
2. Antonio cierra la revista y pone el televisor.
3. Los dos almuerzan con un compañero de la universidad.
4. Los dos juegan al ajedrez (*chess*), y Diego pierde.
5. Diego piensa en las cosas que tiene que hacer hoy.

---

*Jugar is the only u → ue stem-changing verb in Spanish. **Jugar** is often followed by **al** when used with the name of a sport: **Juego *al* tenis.** Some Spanish speakers, however, omit the **al**.

6. Antonio vuelve a casa después de las clases.
7. Antonio duerme la siesta.
8. Diego pide una pizza por teléfono.

B. **Una tarde típica en casa.** ¿Cuáles son las actividades de todos? Haga oraciones completas con una palabra o frase de cada grupo. Use sólo los nombres que son apropiados para Ud.

yo	almorzar	descansar, dormir
mi padre/madre	volver	en un sillón cómodo (*comfortable*) / en el patio
mi esposo/a	preferir	toda la tarde
los niños	perder	su pelota (*ball*)
mi amigo/a ____ y yo (no)	pensar	muchos refrescos (*soft drinks*)
el perro/gato	jugar	tarde / temprano a casa
mi compañero/a	pedir	afuera (*outside*)
	dormir	la siesta
	¿ ?	en el patio / en la piscina
		al golf (tenis, vólibol…)
		las películas (*movies*) viejas/recientes
		¿ ?

C. **Hoy queremos comer paella**

Paso 1. Using the following cues as a guide, tell about the visit of Ismael's family to a restaurant that specializes in Hispanic cuisine. Use **ellos** as the subject except where otherwise indicated.

1. familia / de / Ismael / tener ganas / comer / paella
2. volver / a / su / restaurante / favorito
3. pensar / que / paella / de / restaurante / ser / estupendo
4. pedir / paella / para / seis / persona
5. pero / hoy / sólo / servir / menú (*m.*) / mexicano
6. por eso / pedir / tacos / y / guacamole (*m.*)

Paso 2. Now retell the story as if it were your family, using **nosotros** as the subject, except in item 5, where you will use **ellos**.

Conversación

Preguntas

1. ¿A qué hora cierran la biblioteca? ¿A qué hora cierran la cafetería? Y durante la época de los exámenes finales, ¿a qué hora cierran?
2. ¿A qué hora almuerza Ud., por lo general? ¿Dónde le gusta almorzar? ¿Con quién? ¿Dónde piensa Ud. almorzar hoy? ¿mañana?
3. ¿Es Ud. un poco olvidadizo/a? Es decir (*That is*), ¿pierde las cosas con frecuencia? ¿Qué cosa pierde Ud.? ¿El dinero? ¿su cuaderno? ¿su mochila? ¿sus llaves (*keys*)?

Enfoque *cultural*

Costa Rica

Datos esenciales

Nombre oficial: República de Costa Rica

Capital: San José

Población: 3.534.174 de habitantes

Moneda: el colón

Idioma oficial: el español

¡Fíjese!

El ecoturismo es importante para la economía de Costa Rica y para la preservación de la biodiversidad y la belleza[a] natural que existe en el país. El ecoturismo tiene como propósito[b] controlar la entrada[c] de turistas en regiones protegidas[d] y, a la vez,[e] obtener fondos[f] para continuar con la protección de las regiones naturales. Aproximadamente un treinta por ciento (%) del territorio costarricense está cubierto de selvas o bosques.[g] En total, más de un cuarto[h] del territorio del país ha sido destinado[i] para la preservación.

[a]*beauty* [b]*purpose* [c]*entrance* [d]*protected* [e]*a... at the same time* [f]*funds* [g]*está... is covered with jungles or forests* [h]*fourth* [i]*ha... has been set aside*

Conozca a...
Óscar Arias Sánchez

Óscar Arias Sánchez (1941–), presidente de Costa Rica de 1986 a 1990, asistió a[a] la Universidad de Costa Rica, a Boston University y a otras universidades en Inglaterra.[b] En 1987, Arias recibió[c] el Premio Nóbel de la Paz[d] por sus esfuerzos[e] por aliviar las tensiones entre el gobierno

Óscar Arias Sánchez

sandinista de Nicaragua y los Estados Unidos. El acuerdo de paz[f] de Arias se firmó[g] en 1986. Desde 1990, se encarga de[h] la Fundación Arias para la paz y el progreso humano.

[a]*asistió... attended* [b]*England* [c]*received* [d]*Premio... Nobel Peace Prize* [e]*efforts* [f]*acuerdo... peace agreement* [g]*se... was signed* [h]*se... he has been running*

Capítulo 4 of the video to accompany *¿Qué tal?* contains cultural footage of Costa Rica.

Visit the *¿Qué tal?* website at www.mhhe.com/quetal.

13 Expressing -self/selves • Reflexive Pronouns

La rutina diaria de Diego

1.

2.

3.

4.

5.

6.

7.

Me despierto a las siete y media y *me levanto* en seguida (1). Primero, *me ducho* (2) y luego *me cepillo* los dientes (3). *Me peino* (4), *me pongo* la bata (5) y voy al cuarto a *vestirme* (6). Por fin, salgo para mis clases (7). No tomo nada antes de salir para la universidad porque, por lo general, ¡tengo prisa!

¿Cómo es la rutina diaria de Ud.?

1. Yo me levanto a las _____.
2. Me ducho por la (mañana/noche).
3. Me visto en (el baño/mi cuarto).
4. Me peino (antes de/después de) vestirme.
5. Antes de salir para las clases, (tomo/no tomo) el desayuno.

Diego's daily routine I wake up at seven-thirty and I get up right away. First, I take a shower and then I brush my teeth. I comb my hair, I put on my robe, and I go to my room to get dressed. Finally, I leave for my classes. I don't eat or drink anything before leaving for the university because I'm generally in a hurry!

USES OF REFLEXIVE PRONOUNS

bañarse (*to take a bath*)

(yo)	**me** baño	*I take a bath*	(nosotros)	**nos** bañamos	*we take baths*
(tú)	**te** bañas	*you take a bath*	(vosotros)	**os** bañáis	*you take baths*
(Ud.)		*you take a bath*	(Uds.)		*you take baths*
(él)	**se** baña	*he takes a bath*	(ellos)	**se** bañan	*they take baths*
(ella)		*she takes a bath*	(ellas)		*they take baths*

A. The pronoun **se** at the end of an infinitive indicates that the verb is used reflexively. The reflexive pronoun in Spanish reflects the subject doing something to or for himself, herself, or itself. When the verb is conjugated, the reflexive pronoun that corresponds to the subject must be used.

Many English verbs that describe parts of one's daily routine—to get up, to take a bath, and so on—are expressed in Spanish with a reflexive construction.

Reflexive Pronouns

me	myself
te	yourself (*fam., sing.*)
se	himself, herself, itself; yourself (*form. sing.*)
nos	ourselves
os	yourselves (*fam. pl. Sp.*)
se	themselves; yourselves (*form. pl.*)

me baño = I take a bath (bathe myself)

B. Here are some reflexive verbs you will find useful as you talk about daily routines. Note that some of these verbs are also stem-changing.

acostarse (ue)	to go to bed	**levantarse**	to get up; to stand up
afeitarse	to shave		
bañarse	to take a bath	**ponerse**	to put on (*clothing*)
despertarse (ie)	to wake up		
divertirse (ie)	to have a good time, enjoy oneself	**quitarse**	to take off (*clothing*)
		sentarse (ie)	to sit down
dormirse (ue)	to fall asleep	**vestirse (i)**	to get dressed
ducharse	to take a shower		

Note also the verb **llamarse** (*to be called*), which you have been using since **Primeros pasos**.

All of these verbs can also be used nonreflexively, often with a different meaning. Some examples of this appear at the right.

O
J
O

After **ponerse** and **quitarse**, the definite article, not the possessive as in English, is used with articles of clothing.

[Práctica A–B]

Me llamo——. ¿Cómo se llama Ud.?

dormir = to sleep   **dormirse** = to fall asleep
poner = to put, place   **ponerse** = to put on

Se pone **el** abrigo.
He's putting on his coat.

Se quitan **el** sombrero.
They're taking off their hats.

PLACEMENT OF REFLEXIVE PRONOUNS

Reflexive pronouns are placed before a conjugated verb but after the word **no** in a negative sentence: **No** *se* **bañan.** They may either precede the conjugated verb or be attached to an infinitive.

[Práctica B]

Me tengo que levantar temprano.
Tengo que levantar**me** temprano.
I have to get up early.

Práctica

A. Su rutina diaria. ¿Hace Ud. lo mismo (*the same thing*) todos los días? Conteste con **sí** o **no**.

	LOS LUNES		LOS SÁBADOS	
	SÍ	NO	SÍ	NO
1. Me levanto antes de las ocho.	☐	☐	☐	☐
2. Siempre me baño o me ducho.	☐	☐	☐	☐
3. Siempre me afeito.	☐	☐	☐	☐
4. Me pongo un traje / un vestido / una falda.	☐	☐	☐	☐
5. Me quito los zapatos después de llegar a casa.	☐	☐	☐	☐
6. Me acuesto antes de las once de la noche.	☐	☐	☐	☐

B. La rutina diaria

Paso 1. ¿Qué acostumbran hacer Ud. y las otras personas de su casa? Conteste usando las siguientes indicaciones. Use el sujeto pronominal cuando sea (*whenever it is*) necesario.

MODELO: yo / despertarse / a las ¿ ? → Me despierto a las seis de la mañana.

1. yo / levantarse / a las ¿ ?
2. ¿ ? / levantarse / más tarde
3. ¿ ? / ducharse / por la mañana

4. por costumbre / ¿ ? / no bañarse / por la noche
5. yo / vestirse / antes de ¿ ?
6. ¿ ? / vestirse / después de ¿ ?
7. por la noche / ¿ ? / acostarse / temprano
8. yo / acostarse / a las ¿ ?
9. por lo general / ¿ ? / (no) acostarse / más tarde que (*than*) yo

Paso 2. En su casa, ¿quién… ?

1. se levanta primero
2. se acuesta primero
3. no se baña por la mañana
4. se viste antes de tomar el desayuno

En los Estados Unidos y el Canadá...

Vicente Wolf

As a boy in Cuba, designer Vicente Wolf spent hours in architects' studios and at construction sites. The visits he paid to museums in Havana when he was a teenager awakened his love for art. The experience of being a Cuban refugee who moved to Miami at age 14 and was forced to begin a new life in a foreign country also drove him in his determination to succeed.

Wolf never formally studied interior design but rather learned it on the job. When he was 18, he moved from Miami to New York and found

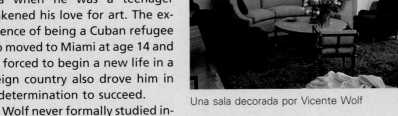
Una sala decorada por Vicente Wolf

work at the Design and Decoration Building in Manhattan. He successfully completed several commissions and then became a business associate of the Spanish designer Robert Patino, a partnership that lasted for sixteen years.

Currently, Wolf runs his own business and lectures at the Parsons School of Design. He believes that it is important for Hispanics to hear about the success that other Hispanic immigrants have had in this country, with the hope that it will instill in them the desire to succeed as he has done.

Conversación

Hábitos. ¿Dónde hace Ud. lo siguiente? Indique el cuarto o la parte de la casa donde Ud. hace cada actividad. Debe indicar también los muebles y otras cosas que usa.

MODELO: estudiar →
Cuando estudio, prefiero estar (por lo general estoy) en la alcoba. Uso el escritorio, una silla, los libros y la computadora.

1. estudiar
2. dormir la siesta
3. quitarse los zapatos
4. bañarse o ducharse
5. despertarse
6. tomar el desayuno
7. sentarse a almorzar
8. vestirse
9. divertirse
10. acostarse

UN POCO DE TODO

De compras y amistades (*friendships*). Complete the following paragraphs with the correct forms of the words in parentheses, as suggested by the context. When two possibilities are given in parentheses, select the correct word. In addition to reviewing vocabulary from previous chapters, these paragraphs ask you to choose between **ser** and **estar** in several situations that you should already know well. You will learn more about **ser** and **estar** in **Capítulo 5**.

(Me/Mi[1]) gusta ir de (comprar/compras[2]) con mi amiga Margarita cuando ella tiene (gangas/ganas[3]) de acompañarme.[a] (Este/Esta[4]) fin de semana, necesito (buscar[5]) unos regalos para los hijos (de el / del[6]) Sr. Suárez. Él (trabajar[7]) con mi madre en el hospital. (Mi[8]) padres (ser/estar[9]) muy buenos amigos de los Suárez, aunque[b] no (ser/estar[10]) siempre de acuerdo con sus opiniones (político[11]). La familia Suárez (venir[12]) a (nuestro[13]) casa con frecuencia.

    Este mes[c] todos los niños de los Suárez (celebrar[14]) su cumpleaños.[d] Por (ese/eso[15]) tengo que (ir[16]) de compras antes (de/en[17]) su visita. La hija mayor,[e] Ana, (ser/estar[18]) una chica muy simpática que (asistir[19]) a la secundaria. (*Yo:* Querer[20]) comprarle[f] un vestido de cuadros o de (rayos/rayas[21]). Ya tiene (tres/trece[22]) años y (empezar[23]) a tener interés en (vestirse[24]) con más elegancia. (Su[25]) hermanos son muy jóvenes todavía —casi siempre (llevar[26]) camisetas y pantalones cortos. Por eso no (*yo:* ir[27]) a comprarles[g] ropa. Creo que (*ellos:* divertirse[28]) más con los juguetes.[h]

    Más tarde, por teléfono

—¿Diga?[i]
—Margarita, ¿eres tú?
—Sí, chica. ¿Qué hay?[j] ¿Cómo (*tú:* ser/estar[29])?
—Muy bien. Oye, ¿qué (hacer[30]) ahora?
—(*Yo:* Leer[31]) una novela para la clase de literatura (inglés[32]). ¿Por qué?
—¿Qué te parece si[k] (*nosotros:* ir[33]) al centro? Hay (mucho[34]) gangas en las tiendas (este[35]) días y tengo que comprar unos regalos.
—¡(Encantado[36])! Voy a (ponerse[37]) el abrigo y (salir[38]) de casa en unos minutos.

[a]*going with me*   [b]*although*   [c]*month*   [d]*birthday*   [e]*oldest*   [f]*to buy her*   [g]*buy them*   [h]*toys*   [i]*Hello?* (on the telephone, Spain)   [j]¿Qué... *What's up?*   [k]¿Qué... *What if . . . ?*

Un paso más **PASO 4**

VIDEOTECA: En contexto

In this video segment, Juan Carlos, the Peruvian student, talks to a real estate agent about an apartment. As you watch the segment, pay particular attention to the questions that the agent asks and to Juan Carlos' answers. What kind of apartment does Juan Carlos want? What rooms would he like?

EL PERÚ

FUNCTION
Searching for an apartment

A. Lluvia de ideas

- ¿Vive Ud. en un apartamento o en una casa? ¿Con quién vive? ¿Le gusta a Ud. su vivienda (*home*)? ¿Por qué?
- ¿Cambia Ud. de vivienda con frecuencia? ¿Qué hace para buscar una nueva vivienda? ¿Usa los servicios de un(a) agente de inmobiliaria (*real estate agent*)?
- ¿Piensa cambiar de vivienda en un futuro próximo (*in the near future*)? ¿Qué tipo de vivienda va a buscar?

B. Dictado

Here is part of this segment's dialogue. Fill in the missing portions of the dialogue.

JUAN CARLOS: Prefiero vivir en un apartamento cerca del[a] centro.
AGENTE: ¿Qué tipo de apartamento _____[1]? Tenemos muchísimos.[b]
JUAN CARLOS: No _____[2] nada grande. Prefiero un _____[3] con un solo dormitorio.
AGENTE: Muy bien. ¿Y qué más quiere?
JUAN CARLOS: Bueno… no necesito mucho. Prefiero un apartamento con _____,[4] una _____[5] en el baño y una _____[6] con lavaplatos.
AGENTE: No hay problema. _____[7] muchísimos _____[8] así.

[a]cerca… *near the*   [b]*lots*

Cultura en contexto
Living with Parents

In both Latin America and Spain, many young people live with their parents until they are ready to settle down and have families of their own. College students who study away from home tend to live with relatives or in apartments shared with nonfamily members. Unlike U.S. and Canadian college students, Hispanic students, particularly women, are less likely to live on their own.

C. Un diálogo original

Paso 1. Con un compañero / una compañera dramatice la escena de Juan Carlos con la agente.

Paso 2. Imagine que Ud. y su compañero/a van a buscar un apartamento juntos/as (*together*). Pero primero (*first*) deben decidir lo que (*what*) necesitan y lo que pueden pagar.

E1: You want at least two bedrooms and no more housemates. You can afford $500/month (**al mes**).

E2: Location is important for you, but you don't have a lot of money (only $400/month). For this reason, you prefer to share (**compartir**) a bedroom or get another housemate.

PASO FINAL

A CONVERSAR

Compartiendo casa°

Compartiendo... *Sharing a house*

Imagine that you and two classmates live in the same house. There's only one bedroom, one living room, and one kitchen. While you all get along, you don't always want to do the same things together. Try to come up with a plan for sharing the house.

Paso 1. Working individually, write three sentences for each room, describing what you do in that room and at what time.

MODELO: la sala → Leo el periódico por la mañana antes de ir a clase (a eso de [*around*] las siete y media). Miro la televisión por la noche, después de hacer la tarea (a eso de las nueve). Me gusta leer una novela antes de dormir (a eso de las once).

Paso 2. Take turns telling what you do and when in the three rooms. If there is a conflict of time or activity, try to reach a compromise.

MODELO: E1: Me ducho por la mañana antes de desayunar, a eso de las seis y media.
E2: Yo también me ducho a eso de las seis y media.
E1: Está bien. Yo puedo ducharme primero, a las seis.

Paso 3. As a group, create schedules for the three rooms. Use a separate sheet of paper to create a schedule for each room similar to the one at the left for Juan, María, and Esteban.

MODELO:

Hora	El baño	La sala	La cocina
6:00	Juan: ducharse	María: leer el periódico	
6:30	María: ducharse		Esteban y Juan: desayunar
7:00			María: desayunar

En resumen

GRAMÁTICA

To review the grammar points presented in this chapter, refer to the indicated grammar presentations. You'll find further practice of these structures in the Workbook/Laboratory Manual, on the CD-ROM, and on the website.

11. *Hacer, oír, poner, salir, traer,* and *ver*

Do you know the forms of the verbs **hacer, oír, poner, salir, traer,** and **ver,** and how to use them?

12. Present Tense of Stem-Changing Verbs

Do you know the forms for verbs like **pensar, volver,** and **pedir**?

13. Reflexive Pronouns

You should be able to talk about your daily routine using reflexive verbs like **levantarse, bañarse,** and **afeitarse.**

VOCABULARIO

Los verbos

almorzar (ue)	to have lunch
cerrar (ie)	to close
contestar	to answer
descansar	to rest
dormir (ue)	to sleep
dormir la siesta	to take a nap
empezar (ie)	to begin
entender (ie)	to understand
hacer (*irreg.*)	to do; to make
hacer ejercicio	to exercise
hacer un viaje	to take a trip
hacer una pregunta	to ask a question
jugar (ue) (al)	to play (*a game, sport*)
oír (*irreg.*)	to hear
pedir (i)	to ask for; to order
pensar (ie)	to think; to intend
perder (ie)	to lose; to miss (*a function*)
poner (*irreg.*)	to put, to place
salir (*irreg.*) (de)	to leave; to go out
servir (i)	to serve
traer (*irreg.*)	to bring
ver (*irreg.*)	to see
volver (ue)	to return (*to a place*)
volver a + *inf.*	to (*do something*) again

Los verbos reflexivos

acostarse (ue)	to go to bed
afeitarse	to shave
bañarse	to take a bath
cepillarse los dientes	to brush one's teeth
despertarse (ie)	to wake up
divertirse (ie)	to have a good time, enjoy oneself
dormirse (ue)	to fall asleep
ducharse	to take a shower
levantarse	to get up; to stand up
llamarse	to be called
peinarse	to comb one's hair
ponerse (*irreg.*)	to put on (*clothing*)
quitarse	to take off (*clothing*)
sentarse (ie)	to sit down
vestirse (i)	to get dressed

Los cuartos y otras partes de una casa

la alcoba	bedroom
el baño	bathroom
la cocina	kitchen
el comedor	dining room
el garaje	garage

el jardín	yard
la pared	wall
el patio	patio; yard
la piscina	swimming pool
la sala	living room

Los muebles y otras cosas de una casa

la alfombra	rug
el armario	closet
la bañera	bathtub
la cama (de agua)	(water) bed
la cómoda	bureau; dresser
el estante	bookshelf
la lámpara	lamp
el lavabo	(bathroom) sink
la mesita	end table
los platos	dishes; plates
el sillón	armchair
el sofá	sofa
el televisor	television set

Repaso: el escritorio, la mesa, la silla

Otros sustantivos

el ajedrez	chess
el cine	movies, movie theater
el desayuno	breakfast
el/la muchacho/a	boy/girl
la película	movie
el ruido	noise
la rutina diaria	daily routine
la tarea	homework

Los adjetivos

cada (*inv.*)	each, every
cómodo/a	comfortable

Preposiciones

antes de	before
después de	after
durante	during
hasta	until
por	during; for
sin	without

¿Cuándo?

ayer fue (miércoles)	yesterday was (Wednesday)
pasado mañana	the day after tomorrow
el próximo (martes)	next (Tuesday)
la semana que viene	next week

Los días de la semana: lunes, martes, miércoles, jueves, viernes, sábado, domingo

Repaso: el fin de semana, hoy, mañana

Palabras adicionales

por fin	finally
por lo general	generally
primero	first

CAPÍTULO 5

Las estaciones, el tiempo y un poco de geografía

► Las nubes de una tormenta se acercan (*approach*) al cementerio de Santiago Sacatepequez en Guatemala. Las familias se reúnen allí el Día de los Muertos.

VOCABULARIO

- Weather expressions
- Months and seasons
- Prepositions of place

GRAMÁTICA

14 Present Progressive: **estar** + **-ndo**
15 Summary of the Uses of **ser** and **estar**
16 Comparisons

CULTURA

- **Enfoque cultural:** Guatemala
- **Nota cultural:** El Niño
- **En los Estados Unidos y el Canadá:** Alfredo Jaar
- **Cultura en contexto:** Belize

Multimedia

You will learn about discussing travel plans in the **En contexto** video segment.

Review vocabulary and grammar and practice language skills with the interactive CD-ROM.

Get connected to the Spanish-speaking world with the *¿Qué tal?* Online Learning Center: **www.mhhe.com/quetal**.

¿Qué tiempo hace hoy?°

¿Qué… *What's the weather like today?*

Hace frío.

Hace calor.

Hace viento.

Hace sol.

Está (muy) nublado.

Llueve.

Nieva.

Hay mucha contaminación.

Hace (mucho) frío (calor, viento, sol). It's (very) cold (hot, windy, sunny).
Hace fresco. It's cool.
Hace (muy) buen/mal tiempo. It's (very) good/bad weather. The weather is (very) good/bad.

Pronunciation hint: Remember that, in most parts of the Spanish-speaking world, **ll** is pronounced exactly like **y: llueve**.

> In Spanish, many weather conditions are expressed with **hace**. The adjective **mucho** is used with the nouns **frío, calor, viento,** and **sol** to express *very*.

Conversación

A. El tiempo y la ropa. Diga qué tiempo hace, según la ropa de cada persona.

1. San Diego: María lleva pantalones cortos y una camiseta.
2. Madison: Juan lleva suéter, pero no lleva chaqueta.
3. Toronto: Roberto lleva suéter y chaqueta.
4. San Miguel de Allende: Ramón lleva impermeable y botas y también tiene paraguas (*umbrella*).
5. Buenos Aires: Todos llevan abrigo, botas y sombrero.

B. Consejos (*Advice*) **para Joaquín.** Joaquín es de Valencia, España. El clima (*climate*) allí es mediterráneo: Hace mucho sol y las temperaturas son moderadas. No hay mucha contaminación.

Paso 1. Joaquín tiene una lista de lugares que desea visitar en los Estados Unidos. Ayúdelo (*Help him*) con información sobre el clima.

1. Seattle, Washington
2. Los Ángeles, California
3. Phoenix, Arizona
4. Nueva Orleans, Louisiana
5. Buffalo, Nueva York

Paso 2. Es obvio que la lista de Joaquín no está completa. ¿Qué otros tres lugares cree Ud. que debe visitar? ¿Qué clima hace allí?

C. El tiempo y las actividades. Haga oraciones completas, indicando una actividad apropiada para cada situación.

cuando llueve	me quedo (*I stay*) en cama/casa
cuando hace buen tiempo	juego al basquetbol/vólibol con mis amigos
cuando hace calor	almuerzo afuera (*outside*) / en el parque
cuando hace frío	me divierto en el parque / en la playa
cuando nieva	(*beach*) con mis amigos
cuando hay mucha contaminación	no salgo de casa
	vuelvo a casa y trabajo o estudio

NOTA COMUNICATIVA

More *tener* Idioms

Several other conditions expressed in Spanish with **tener** idioms—not with *to be*, as in English—include the following.

tener (mucho) calor	to be (very) warm, hot
tener (mucho) frío	to be (very) cold

These expressions are used to describe people or animals only. To be comfortable—neither hot nor cold—is expressed with **estar bien**.

D. ¿Tienen frío o calor? ¿Están bien? Describe the following weather conditions and tell how the people pictured are feeling.

Los meses y las estaciones° del año

seasons

septiembre ⎫
octubre ⎬ el otoño
noviembre ⎭

diciembre ⎫
enero ⎬ el invierno
febrero ⎭

marzo ⎫
abril ⎬ la primavera
mayo ⎭

junio ⎫
julio ⎬ el verano
agosto ⎭

¿Cuál es la fecha de hoy?
(Hoy) Es el primero de abril.
(Hoy) Es el cinco de febrero.

What is today's date?
(Today) It is the first of April.
(Today) It is the fifth of February.

enero							abril						
	1	2	3	4	5	6		1	2	3	4	5	6	7
7	8	9	10	11	12	13	8	9	10	11	12	13	14
14	15	16	17	18	19	20	15	16	17	18	19	20	21
21	22	23	24	25	26	27	22	23	24	25	26	27	28
28	29	30	31				29	30					

febrero / mayo
| | 1 | 2 | 3 | | | 1 | 2 | 3 | 4 | 5 |
4 5 6 7 8 9 10 / 6 7 8 9 10 11 12
11 12 13 14 15 16 17 / 13 14 15 16 17 18 19
18 19 20 21 22 23 24 / 20 21 22 23 24 25 26
25 26 27 28 / 27 28 29 30 31

marzo / junio
1 2 3 / 1 2
4 5 6 7 8 9 10 / 3 4 5 6 7 8 9
11 12 13 14 15 16 17 / 10 11 12 13 14 15 16
18 19 20 21 22 23 24 / 17 18 19 20 21 22 23
25 26 27 28 29 30 31 / 24 25 26 27 28 29 30

- The ordinal number **primero** is used to express the first day of the month. Cardinal numbers (**dos, tres**, and so on) are used for other days.
- The definite article **el** is used before the date. However, when the day of the week is expressed, **el** is omitted: **Hoy es jueves, tres de octubre.**
- As you know, **mil** is used to express the year after 999.

1950 mil novecientos cincuenta   2003 dos mil tres

Conversación

A. El mes de noviembre. Mire este calendario para el mes de noviembre. ¿Qué día de la semana es el 12 (1, 20, 16, 11, 4, 29) de noviembre?

B. Fechas

Paso 1. Exprese estas fechas en español. ¿En qué estación caen (*do they fall*)?

1. March 7
2. August 24
3. December 1
4. June 5
5. 9-19-1997
6. 5-28-1842
7. 1-31-1660
8. 7-4-1776

Paso 2. ¿Cuándo se celebran?

1. el Día de la Raza (*Columbus Day*)
2. el Día del Año Nuevo
3. el Día de los Enamorados (de San Valentín)
4. el Día de la Independencia de los Estados Unidos
5. el Día de los Inocentes (*Fools*), en los Estados Unidos
6. la Navidad (*Christmas*)
7. su cumpleaños (*birthday*)

OJO

Note that the word **se** before a verb changes the verb's meaning slightly. **¿Cuándo se celebran?** = *When are they celebrated?* You will see this construction throughout *¿Qué tal?*

C. **¡Feliz** (*Happy*) **cumpleaños!**

Paso 1. Entreviste a un compañero / una compañera de clase acerca de (*about*) su cumpleaños. Use las siguientes preguntas.

1. ¿Cuál es la fecha de tu cumpleaños?
2. ¿En qué estación es?
3. Generalmente, ¿qué tiempo hace en tu ciudad el día de tu cumpleaños?
4. ¿Cómo celebras tu cumpleaños? (por lo menos tres actividades)
5. ¿Con quién(es) prefieres celebrar tu cumpleaños?

Paso 2. Su profesor(a) o un(a) estudiante va a escribir en la pizarra los nombres de los meses del año. Luego cada estudiante va a escribir la fecha de su cumpleaños en la columna apropiada. ¿En qué mes son la mayoría de los cumpleaños de los estudiantes de la clase? ¿Qué signo del horóscopo tienen?

Los signos: Aries, Tauro, Géminis, Cáncer, Leo, Virgo, Libra, Escorpión, Sagitario, Capricornio, Acuario, Piscis

¿Dónde está? • Las preposiciones

¿Dónde está España? Está *en* la Península Ibérica, *al lado de* Portugal. *Al norte* está Francia, y el continente de Africa está *al sur*. *Al oeste* está el Océano Atlántico y *al este* está el Mar Mediterráneo. La capital de España es Madrid. *Cerca de* la Península Ibérica están las Islas Baleares, que son parte de España. Las Islas Canarias, también parte de España, están *al oeste de* África. Gibraltar está *entre* España y África. No es parte de España. Pertenece (*It belongs*) a Inglaterra.

cerca de	close to	**delante de**	in front of
lejos de	far from	**detrás de**	behind
encima de	on top of	**a la izquierda de**	to the left of
debajo de	below	**a la derecha de**	to the right of
al lado de	alongside of		
entre	between, among		

al este / oeste / norte / sur de   to the east / west / north / south of

In Spanish, the pronouns that serve as objects of prepositions are identical in form to the subject pronouns, except for **mí** and **ti**.

Julio está delante de **mí**.	*Julio is in front of me.*
María está detrás de **ti**.	*María is behind you.*
Me siento a la izquierda de **ella**.	*I sit on her left.*

O J O Note that **mí** has a written accent, but **ti** does not. This is to distinguish the object of a preposition (**mí**) from the possessive adjective (**mi**).

Conversación

A. ¿De qué país se habla?

Paso 1. Escuche la descripción que da (*gives*) su profesor(a) de un país de Sudamérica. ¿Puede Ud. identificar el país?

Paso 2. Ahora describa un país de Sudamérica. Sus compañeros de clase van a identificarlo. Siga el modelo, usando (*using*) todas las frases que sean (*are*) apropiadas.

> MODELO: Este país está al norte/sur/este/oeste de _____.
> También está cerca de _____.
> Pero está lejos de _____. Está entre _____ y _____. ¿Cómo se llama?

Paso 3. Ahora trate de (*try to*) emparejar los nombres de estas capitales de Sudamérica con sus países.

> MODELO: _____ es la capital de _____.

> **Capitales:** Brasilia, Buenos Aires, Bogotá, La Paz, Santiago, Asunción, Quito, Caracas, Montevideo, Lima

B. ¿De dónde es Ud.? Give as much information as you can about the location of your hometown or state, or about the country you are from. You should also tell what the weather is like there.

> MODELO: Soy del pueblo (de la ciudad) de _____. Está cerca de la ciudad de _____. En verano hace _____. En invierno _____. (No) Llueve mucho en primavera.

NOTA CULTURAL

El Niño

Most people have heard of **El Niño**, a weather phenomenon that is often associated with devastating climatic events. But why is it called **El Niño**?

The name **El Niño** dates from the end of the nineteenth century, when Peruvian fishermen noticed the periodic appearance of an abnormally warm ocean current off the coast of Peru. This warm current made its appearance around Christmas time. The name **El Niño** is a reference to the Christ Child, or **El Niño Jesús**, who for Christians also arrived at Christmas. At the time the name only referred to the current. Nowadays, it is used to refer to the meteorological phenomenon as a whole. Torrential rains, flooding, and landslides can occur from the southwestern United States to Peru, whereas in Australia, Indonesia, and southeast Africa, the opposite may happen: severe droughts and the potential for destructive fires.

Destrucción en California causada por (*caused by*) El Niño

14 ¿Qué están haciendo? • Present Progressive: *estar* + *-ndo*

¿Qué están haciendo en Quito, Ecuador?

José Miguel juega al tenis y levanta pesas con frecuencia. Ahora no *está jugando al tenis.* Tampoco *está levantando* pesas. ¿Qué *está haciendo? Está* _____.

Elisa es periodista. Por eso escribe mucho y habla mucho por teléfono. Pero ahora, no *está escribiendo.* Tampoco *está hablando* por teléfono. ¿Qué *está haciendo? Está* _____.

¿Y Ud.? ¿Qué está haciendo Ud. en este momento?

1. ¿Está estudiando en casa? ¿en clase? ¿en la cafetería?
2. ¿Está leyendo? ¿Está mirando la tele al mismo (*same*) tiempo?
3. ¿Está escuchando al profesor / a la profesora?

USES OF THE PROGRESSIVE

In Spanish, you can use special verb forms to describe an action in progress—that is, something actually happening at the time it is being described. These Spanish forms, called **el progresivo**, correspond in form to the English *progressive: I am walking, we are driving, she is studying.* But their use is not identical. Compare the Spanish and English verb forms in the sentences at the right.

In Spanish, the present progressive is used primarily to describe an action that is actually *in progress,* as in the first example. The simple Spanish present is used in other cases where English would use the present progressive: to tell what is going to happen (the second sentence), and to tell what someone is doing over a period of time but not necessarily at this very moment (the third sentence).

1. Ramón **está comiendo** ahora mismo.
   Ramón is eating right now.
2. **Compramos** la casa mañana.
   We're buying the house tomorrow.
3. Adelaida **estudia** química este semestre.
   Adelaida is studying chemistry this semester.

FORMATION OF THE PRESENT PROGRESSIVE

A. The Spanish present progressive is formed with **estar** plus the *present participle* (**el gerundio**), which is formed by adding **-ando** to the stem of **-ar** verbs and **-iendo** to the stem of **-er** and **-ir** verbs.* The present participle never varies; it always ends in **-o**.

tomar → **tomando**	*taking; drinking*
comprender → **comprendiendo**	*understanding*
abrir → **abriendo**	*opening*

O J O Unaccented **i** represents the sound [y] in the participle ending **-iendo: comiendo, viviendo.** Unaccented **i** between two vowels becomes the letter **y: leyendo, oyendo.**

B. The stem vowel in the present participle of **-ir** stem-changing verbs also shows a change. From this point on in *¿Qué tal?* both stem changes for **-ir** verbs will be given with infinitives in vocabulary lists.

preferir (ie, i) → prefiriendo	*preferring*
pedir (i, i) → pidiendo	*asking*
dormir (ue, u) → durmiendo	*sleeping*

USING PRONOUNS WITH THE PRESENT PROGRESSIVE

Reflexive pronouns may be attached to the present participle or precede the conjugated form of **estar**. Note the use of a written accent mark when pronouns are attached to the present participle.

Pablo **se** está bañando.
Pablo está bañándo**se**. } *Pablo is taking a bath.*

Práctica

A. Un sábado típico. Indique lo que Ud. está haciendo a las horas indicadas en un sábado típico. En algunos (*some*) casos hay más de una respuesta (*answer*) posible.

A las ocho de la mañana…

1. estoy durmiendo
2. estoy tomando el desayuno
3. estoy mirando los dibujos animados (*cartoons*) en la tele
4. estoy duchándome
5. estoy trabajando
6. estoy _____

A mediodía (*noon*)…

1. estoy durmiendo
2. estoy almorzando
3. estoy estudiando
4. estoy practicando algún deporte
5. estoy trabajando
6. estoy _____

A las diez de la noche…

1. estoy durmiendo
2. estoy preparándome para salir

*_____

***Ir, poder**, and **venir** have irregular present participles: **yendo, pudiendo, viniendo**. These three verbs, however, are seldom used in the progressive.

3. estoy mirando un programa en la tele
4. estoy bailando en una fiesta o en una discoteca
5. estoy trabajando
6. estoy hablando por teléfono con un amigo / una amiga
7. estoy ＿＿＿

B. Un día especial. Ricardo Guzmán Rama, el tío de Lola Benítez, acaba de llegar (*has just arrived*) de México para visitar a su familia en Sevilla. Por eso, hoy es un día especial. Complete las siguientes oraciones para indicar lo que (*what*) está pasando en este momento en la familia de Lola.

1. Generalmente, Lola está en la universidad toda la mañana. Hoy Lola… (hablar con su tío Ricardo)
2. Casi siempre, Lola va a casa después de sus clases. Hoy Lola y su tío… (tomar un café en la universidad)
3. De lunes a viernes, la hija Marta va al colegio por la tarde. Ahora, a las dos de la tarde ella… (jugar con Ricardo)
4. Generalmente, la familia come a las dos. Hoy todos… (comer a las tres)

En los Estados Unidos y el Canadá...

Alfredo Jaar

Upon arriving in the United States, Chilean artist Alfredo Jaar was surprised to learn that English speakers generally don't think of Canadians, Mexicans, Colombians, and so forth as "Americans." It bothered him that he was perceived as "Hispanic" or "Latin" but not as "American," "This country has co-opted the word *America*," he claimed.

So, Jaar used his artistic talents in an effort to enlighten people in the United States about the true meaning of the word *America*. He created a computerized animation that appeared on a sign board above New York City's Times Square in April 1987. The computer animation depicted a lighted map of the United States with the statement "This is not America" written across it. Slowly the word *America* grew larger and larger until it filled the entire sign. At the same

El arte electrónico de Alfredo Jaar

time, the letter R transformed itself into a map of North and South America. This use of *America* is the meaning used in Spanish, the meaning that Jaar had known.

The message that Jaar was trying to send was that *America* does not belong only to the United States. Another thirty-three nations say that they are a part of America and that their approximately 500 million inhabitants are also Americans.

Jaar was also trying to combat the stereotype that all Hispanics are alike and that all the inhabitants of South America are Hispanics. For one thing, many inhabitants of South America are Brazilians, and thus of Portuguese rather than of Spanish heritage. In addition, there are many indigenous peoples throughout Latin America that have traditions, cultures, and languages that precede Columbus' arrival in this hemisphere.

C. En casa con la familia Duarte

Paso 1. The Duarte family leads a busy life. Each picture sequence shows what the parents, the teenage daughter, and the twins are doing at a particular time of their day. Read the following sentences and tell to which sequence each refers.

MODELO: Se está duchando. Secuencia A.

1. Está levantándose.
2. Está escribiendo cartas.
3. Está vistiéndose.
4. Está preparando la cena (*dinner*).
5. Está leyendo el periódico.

6. Están durmiendo.
7. Está trabajando.
8. Están jugando con el perro.
9. Están comiendo.
10. Está quitándose los zapatos.

A.

B.

C.

Paso 2. Now tell what is happening in each drawing.

MODELO: Secuencia A. Son las seis. Los niños están…

Conversación

Preguntas

1. ¿Pasa Ud. más tiempo leyendo o viendo la televisión? ¿tocando o escuchando música? ¿trabajando o estudiando? ¿estudiando o viajando?
2. ¿Cómo se divierte Ud. más, viendo la tele o bailando en una fiesta? ¿practicando un deporte o leyendo una buena novela? ¿haciendo un *picnic* o preparando una cena elegante en casa? ¿mirando una película en casa o en el cine?

¿Recuerda Ud.?

You have been using forms of **ser** and **estar** since **Primeros pasos**, the preliminary chapter of *¿Qué tal?* The following section will help you consolidate everything you know so far about these two verbs, both of which express *to be* in Spanish. You will learn a bit more about them as well.

Before you begin, think in particular about the following questions: **¿Cómo está Ud.? ¿Cómo es Ud.?** What do these questions tell you about the difference between **ser** and **estar**?

---

15   *¿Ser o estar?* • Summary of the Uses of *ser* and *estar*

Una conversación por larga distancia

Aquí hay un lado de la conversación entre una esposa que *está* en un viaje de negocios y su esposo, que *está* en casa. Habla el esposo. ¿Qué contesta la esposa?

Aló. […[1]] ¿Cómo *estás*, mi amor? […[2]] ¿Dónde *estás* ahora? […[3]] ¿Qué hora *es* allí? […[4]] ¡Huy!, *es* muy tarde. Y el hotel, ¿cómo *es*? […[5]] Oye, ¿qué *estás* haciendo ahora? […[6]] Ay, pobre, lo siento. *Estás* muy ocupada. ¿Con quién *estás* citada mañana? […[7]] ¿Quién *es* el dueño de la compañía? […[8]] Ah, él *es* de Cuba, ¿verdad? […[9]] Bueno, ¿qué tiempo hace allí? […[10]] Muy bien, mi vida. Hasta luego, ¿eh? […[11]] Adiós.

A long-distance conversation Here is one side of a conversation between a wife who is on a business trip and her husband, who is at home. The husband is speaking. What does the wife answer? Hello . . . How are you, dear? . . . Where are you now? . . . What time is it there? . . . Boy it's very late. And how's the hotel? . . . Hey, what are you doing now? . . . You poor thing, I'm sorry. You're very busy. Who are you meeting with tomorrow? . . . Who's the owner of the company? . . . Ah, he's from Cuba, isn't he? . . . Well, what's the weather like? . . . Very well, sweetheart. See you later, OK? . . . Goodbye.

Aquí está el otro lado de la conversación… pero las respuestas no están en orden. Ponga las respuestas en el orden apropiado.

a. _____ Es muy moderno. Me gusta mucho.
b. _____ Sí, pero vive en Nueva York ahora.
c. _____ Son las once y media.
d. _____ Hola, querido (*dear*). ¿Qué tal?
e. _____ Es el Sr. Cortina.
f. _____ Pues, todavía (*still*) tengo que trabajar.
g. _____ Sí, hasta pronto.
h. _____ Estoy en Nueva York.
i. _____ Un poco cansada, pero estoy bien.
j. _____ Pues, hace buen tiempo, pero está un poco nublado.
k. _____ Con un señor de Computec, una nueva compañía de computadoras.

Summary of the Uses of *ser*

• To *identify* people and things	Ella **es doctora**.
• To express *nationality;* with **de** to express *origin*	**Son cubanos. Son de** La Habana.
• With **de** to tell of what *material* something is made	Este bolígrafo **es de plástico**.
• With **para** to tell *for whom something is intended*	El regalo **es para Sara**.
• To tell *time*	**Son las once. Es la una y media.**
• With **de** to express *possession*	**Es de** Carlota.
• With *adjectives* that describe *basic, inherent characteristics*	Ramona **es inteligente**.
• To form many *generalizations*	**Es necesario** llegar temprano **Es importante** estudiar.

Summary of the Uses of *estar*

• To tell *location*	El libro **está en la mesa**.
• To describe *health*	**Estoy** muy **bien**, gracias.
• With *adjectives* that describe *conditions*	**Estoy** muy **ocupada**.
• In a number of *fixed expressions*	**(No) Estoy de acuerdo. Está bien.**
• With *present participles* to form the *progressive tense*	**Estoy estudiando** ahora mismo.

Ser AND *estar* WITH ADJECTIVES

A. **Ser** is used with adjectives that describe the fundamental qualities of a person, place, or thing.

Esa mujer es muy **baja**.
That woman is very short.

Sus calcetines son **morados**.
His socks are purple.

Este sillón es **cómodo**.
This armchair is comfortable.

Sus padres son **cariñosos**.
Their parents are affectionate people.

B. **Estar** is used with adjectives to express conditions or observations that are true at a given moment but that do not describe inherent qualities of the noun. The following adjectives are generally used with **estar**.

abierto/a	open	**limpio/a**	clean
aburrido/a	bored	**loco/a**	crazy
alegre	happy	**nervioso/a**	nervous
cansado/a	tired	**ocupado/a**	busy
cerrado/a	closed	**ordenado/a**	neat
congelado/a	frozen; very cold	**preocupado/a**	worried
contento/a	content, happy	**seguro/a**	sure, certain
desordenado/a	messy	**sucio/a**	dirty
enfermo/a	sick	**triste**	sad
furioso/a	furious, angry		

C. Many adjectives can be used with either **ser** or **estar**, depending on what the speaker intends to communicate. In general, when *to be* implies *looks, feels,* or *appears*, **estar** is used. Compare the following pairs of sentences.

Daniel **es** guapo.
Daniel is handsome. (He is a handsome person.)

Daniel **está** muy guapo esta noche.
Daniel looks very nice (handsome) tonight.

—¿Cómo **es** Amalia?
—**Es** simpática.
What is Amalia like (as a person)?
She's nice.

—Cómo **está** Amalia?
—**Está** enferma todavía.
How is Amalia (feeling)?
She's still sick.

Práctica

A. Las fiestas. Complete the following description with the correct form of **ser** or **estar**, as suggested by the context.

Las fiestas (ser/estar[1]) populares entre los jóvenes de todas partes del mundo. Ofrecen una buena oportunidad para (ser/estar[2]) con los amigos y conocer[a] a nuevas personas. Imagine que Ud. (ser/estar[3]) en una fiesta con unos amigos hispanos en este momento: todos (ser/estar[4]) alegres, comiendo, hablando y bailando… ¡Y (ser/estar[5]) las dos de la mañana!

[a]*to meet*

B. Una tarde horrible. Describa lo que (*what*) pasa hoy por la tarde en esta casa, cambiando por antónimos las palabras indicadas.

1. No hace *buen* tiempo; hace _____.
2. El bebé no está *bien*; está _____.
3. El gato no está *limpio*; está _____.
4. El esposo no está *tranquilo*; está _____ por el bebé.
5. El garaje no está *cerrado*; está _____.
6. Los niños no están *ocupados*; están _____.
7. La esposa no está *contenta*; está _____ por el tiempo.
8. La casa no está *ordenada*; está _____.

Ana   Estela

Conversación

Ana y Estela. Describa este dibujo de un cuarto típico de la residencia. Invente los detalles necesarios. ¿Quiénes son las dos compañeras de cuarto? ¿De dónde son? ¿Cómo son? ¿Dónde están en este momento? ¿Qué hay en el cuarto? ¿En qué condición está el cuarto? ¿Son ordenadas o desordenadas las dos?

Palabras útiles: el cartel (*poster*), la foto

Enfoque cultural

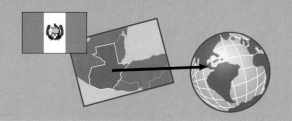

Guatemala

Datos esenciales

Nombre oficial: República de Guatemala

Capital: la Ciudad de Guatemala

Población: 12.007.580 de habitantes

Moneda: el quetzal

Idiomas: el español (oficial), 23 lenguas indígenas (que incluyen el quiché, el cakchiquel y el kekchi)

¡Fíjese!

Más del cincuenta por ciento de los habitantes de Guatemala son descendientes de los antiguos[a] mayas. Esta civilización antigua tenía[b] un sistema de escritura jeroglífica que usaban[c] para documentar su historia, sus costumbres[d] religiosas y su mitología. El calendario maya, base del famoso calendario azteca, era[e] el calendario más exacto de su época. Los mayas también tenían un sistema político y social muy desarrollado.[f] Tikal, en Guatemala, fue[g] una de las ciudades mayas más importantes y también una de las más grandes. Las ruinas de Tikal son muestra[h] de la grandeza de la civilización maya. Hoy día,[i] son un lugar turístico muy visitado.

[a]ancient [b]had [c]they used [d]customs [e]was [f]developed [g]was [h]an example [i]Hoy... Nowadays

Tikal, Guatemala

Conozca a... Rigoberta Menchú

Al período entre los años 1978 y 1985 en Guatemala se le llama[a] con frecuencia «La violencia». Durante este tiempo el ejército guatemalteco[b] empieza una campaña[c] violenta contra la población indígena[d] del norte del país.

Rigoberta Menchú, mujer de la región indígena y de lengua[e] quiché (un grupo étnico de la familia de los mayas) pierde a sus padres y dos hermanos, todos asesinados por el ejército. Menchú describe esta tragedia durante «La violencia» en su famosa autobiografía *Yo, Rigoberta Menchú*.

El trabajo de Menchú a favor de los derechos humanos[f] y del pluralismo étnico de Guatemala le otorgó[g] el Premio Nóbel de la Paz en 1992, exactamente quinientos años después de la llegada[h] de Cristóbal Colón a América.

[a]se... is called [b]ejército... Guatemalan army [c]campaign [d]población... indigenous population [e]language [f]a... on behalf of human rights [g]le... won her [h]arrival

Capítulo 5 of the video to accompany *¿Qué tal?* contains cultural footage of Guatemala.

Visit the *¿Qué tal?* website at www.mhhe.com/quetal.

16 Describing • Comparisons
Dos ciudades

México, D.F. (Distrito Federal)

El barrio de
Santa Cruz,
Sevilla, España

Ricardo hace comparaciones entre la Ciudad de México, o el D.F. (Distrito Federal), y Sevilla.

«De verdad, me gustan las dos ciudades.

- La Ciudad de México es *más* grande *que* Sevilla.
- Tiene *más* edificios altos *que* Sevilla.
- En el D.F. no hace *tanto* calor *como* en Sevilla.

Pero…

- Sevilla es *tan* bonita *como* la Ciudad de México.
- No tiene *tantos* habitantes *como* el D.F.
- Sin embargo, los sevillanos son *tan* simpáticos *como* los mexicanos.

En total, ¡me gusta Sevilla *tanto como* la Ciudad de México!»

Ahora, hable Ud. de su ciudad o pueblo.

Mi ciudad/pueblo…

- (no) es tan grande como Chicago
- es más/menos cosmopolita que Quebec

Me gusta _____ (nombre de mi ciudad/pueblo)

- más que _____ (nombre de otra ciudad)
- menos que _____ (nombre de otra ciudad)
- tanto como _____ (nombre de otra ciudad)

Two Cities Ricardo makes comparisons between Mexico City, or D.F. (Federal District), and Seville. "Really, I like both cities.

- Mexico City is bigger than Seville.
- It has more tall buildings than Seville.
- It is not as hot in Mexico City as it is in Seville.

But…

- Seville is as beautiful as Mexico City.
- It doesn't have as many inhabitants as Mexico City.
- Nevertheless, the people from Seville are as nice as those from Mexico City.

All told, I like Seville as much as Mexico City!"

	Unequal Comparisons	Equal Comparisons
With Adjectives or Adverbs	más/menos _____ que	tan _____ como
With Nouns		tanto/a/os/as _____ como
With Verbs	_____ más/menos que	_____ tanto como

COMPARISON OF ADJECTIVES

EQUAL COMPARISONS

tan + *adjective* + como
(*as*)　　　　　　(*as*)

Enrique es **tan** trabajador **como** Amalia.
Enrique is as hardworking as Amalia.

In English the *comparative* (**el comparativo**) is formed by using the adverbs *more* or *less* (**more** intelligent, **less** important), or by adding -*er* at the end of the adjective (*taller, smarter*).

UNEQUAL COMPARISONS (REGULAR)

más + *adjective* + que
(*more*)　　　　　　(*than*)

Alicia es **más** perezosa **que** Marta.
Alicia is lazier than Marta.

menos + *adjective* + que
(*less*)　　　　　　(*than*)

Julio es **menos** inteligente **que** Jaime.
Julio is less intelligent than Jaime.

UNEQUAL COMPARATIVES WITH IRREGULAR FORMS

bueno/a → mejor

Estos coches son **buenos,** pero esos son **mejores.**
These cars are good, but those are better.

malo/a → peor

Mi lámpara es **peor que** esta.
My lamp is worse than this one.

mayor (*older*)

Mi hermana es **mayor que** yo.
My sister is older than I (am).

menor (*younger*)

Mis primos son **menores que** yo.
My cousins are younger than I (am).

COMPARISON OF NOUNS

EQUAL COMPARISONS

Tanto must agree in gender and number with the noun it modifies.

> tanto/a/os/as + *noun* + como
> (*as much/many*)   (*as*)

Alicia tiene **tantas** bolsas **como** Pati.
Alicia has as many purses as Pati (does).

Pablo tiene **tanto** dinero **como** Sergio.
Pablo has as much money as Sergio (does).

UNEQUAL COMPARISONS

> más/menos + *noun* + que
> (*more/less*)   (*than*)

The preposition **de** is used when the comparison is followed by a number.

> más/menos de + *noun*
> (*more/less than*)

Alicia tiene **más / menos** bolsas **que** Susana.
Alicia has more/fewer purses than Susana (does).

Alicia tiene **más de** cinco bolsas.
Alicia has more than five purses.

[Práctica A–B]

COMPARISON OF VERBS

EQUAL COMPARISONS

Note that **tanto** is invariable is this construction.

> tanto como
> (*as much as*)

Yo estudio **tanto como** mi hermano mayor.
I study as much as my older brother (does).

UNEQUAL COMPARISONS

> más/menos que
> (*more/less than*)

Yo duermo **más que** mi hermano menor.
I sleep more than my younger brother (does).

COMPARISON OF ADVERBS

EQUAL COMPARISONS

> tan + *adverb* + como

Yo juego al tenis **tan** bien **como** mi hermano.
I play tennis as well as my brother (does).

UNEQUAL COMPARISONS

> más/menos + *adverb* + que

Yo como **más** rápido **que** mi padre.
I eat faster than my father (does).

> mejor/peor que

[Práctica C]

Yo juego al tenis **peor que** mi hermana.
I play tennis worse than my sister (does).

Práctica

A. ¿Es Ud. sincero/a? Conteste las preguntas lógicamente.

¿Es Ud... ?

1. tan guapo/a como Antonio Banderas / Jennifer López
2. tan rico como Bill Gates
3. tan fiel como su mejor amigo/a
4. tan inteligente como Einstein
5. tan honesto/a como su padre/madre (novio/a...)

¿Tiene Ud... ?

6. tantos tíos como tías
7. tantos amigos como amigas
8. tanto talento como Carlos Santana
9. tanta sabiduría (*knowledge*) como su profesor(a)

B. Opiniones. Cambie las siguientes oraciones para expresar su opinión personal: **tan _____ como → más/menos _____ que**. Si está de acuerdo con la oración tal como está (*just as it is*), diga (*say*) **Estoy de acuerdo**.

1. Mi casa (apartamento/residencia) es tan grande como la casa del presidente de la universidad.
2. El fútbol (*soccer*) es tan popular como el fútbol americano.
3. Las artes son tan importantes como las ciencias.
4. Los estudios son menos importantes que los deportes.
5. La comida (*food*) de la cafetería es tan buena como la que prepara mi mamá/papá (esposo/a, compañero/a...)
6. Los exámenes de matemáticas son más fáciles (*easier*) que los exámenes de la clase de español.

C. Opiniones personales. Cambie, indicando su opinión personal: **tanto como → más/menos que**, o vice versa. O si es apropiado, diga **Estoy de acuerdo**.

1. Los profesores trabajan más que los estudiantes.
2. Me divierto tanto con mis amigos como con mis parientes.
3. Los niños duermen tanto como los adultos.
4. Aquí llueve más en primavera que en invierno.
5. Necesito el dinero más que la amistad.

Conversación

A. La familia de Amalia y Sancho Jordán

Ramón (24)
Amalia (19)
Sancho (20)
Ramoncito (1)
Lucía (43) Miguel (45) Sarita (25) Laura (75) Javier (80)

Paso 1. Mire la siguiente foto e identifique a los miembros de esta familia. Luego compárelos (*compare them*) con otro pariente. **¡OJO!** Amalia tiene dos hermanos y un sobrino.

> MODELO: Amalia es la hermana de Sancho. Ella es menor que Sancho, pero es más alta que él.

Paso 2. Su familia. Now compare the members of your own family, making ten comparative statements.

> MODELO: Mi hermana Mary es mayor que yo, pero yo soy más alto/a que ella.

Paso 3. Now read your sentences from **Paso 2** to a classmate, who should not take notes on them. Ask him or her questions about your comparisons and see if he or she remembers the details of your family.

> MODELO: ¿Qué miembro de mi familia es mayor que yo?

B. La rutina diaria... en invierno y en verano

Paso 1. ¿Es diferente nuestra rutina diaria en las diferentes estaciones? Complete las siguientes oraciones sobre su rutina.

Palabras útiles: el gimnasio, el parque, afuera

EN INVIERNO...	EN VERANO...
1. me levanto a _____ (hora)	me levanto a _____
2. almuerzo en _____	almuerzo en _____
3. me divierto con mis amigos en _____	me divierto con mis amigos en _____
4. estudio _____ horas todos los días	(no) estudio _____ horas todos los días
5. estoy / me quedo en _____ (lugar) por la noche	estoy / me quedo en _____ por la noche
6. me acuesto a _____	me acuesto a _____

Paso 2. Ahora compare sus actividades en invierno y en verano, según el modelo.

> MODELO: En invierno me levanto más temprano/tarde que en verano.
> (En invierno me levanto a la misma hora que en verano.)
> (En invierno me levanto tan temprano como en verano.)

$$\text{UN POCO DE TODO}$$

A. ¿Qué están haciendo? Diga qué están haciendo las siguientes personas, usando una palabra o frase de cada columna y la forma progresiva. Si Ud. no sabe (*know*) exactamente qué están haciendo esas personas, ¡use su imaginación!

yo	jugar (al)	fútbol/basquetbol
mi mejor amigo/a	dormir(se)	un libro / una novela
mis padres	leer	la radio
los Bills de Buffalo / los Bulls de Chicago	descansar	a los estudiantes / a sus consejeros
el presidente / la presidenta de la universidad	viajar	un informe
el presidente de los Estados Unidos	escuchar	ejercicio físico
el profesor / la profesora de español	trabajar	¿ ?
_____ (un compañero / una compañera de la clase de español que está ausente hoy)	practicar hacer ¿ ?	
mi consejero/a		

B. Dos hemisferios. Complete the following paragraphs with the correct forms of the words in parentheses, as suggested by the context. When two possibilities are given in parentheses, select the correct word.

Hay (mucho[1]) diferencias entre el clima del hemisferio norte y el del hemisferio sur. Cuando (ser/estar[2]) invierno en este país, por ejemplo, (ser/estar[3]) verano en la Argentina, en Bolivia, en Chile… Cuando yo (salir[4]) para la universidad en enero, con frecuencia tengo que (llevar[5]) abrigo y botas. En (los/las[6]) países del hemisferio sur, un estudiante (poder[7]) asistir (a/de[8]) clases en enero llevando sólo pantalones (corto[9]), camiseta y sandalias. En muchas partes de este país, (antes de / durante[10]) las vacaciones en diciembre, casi siempre (hacer[11]) frío y a veces (nevar[12]). En (grande[13]) parte de Sudamérica, al otro lado del ecuador, hace calor y (muy/mucho[14]) sol durante (ese[15]) mes. A veces en enero hay fotos, en los periódicos, de personas que (tomar[16]) el sol y nadan[a] en las playas sudamericanas.

 Tengo un amigo que (ir[17]) a (hacer/tomar[18]) un viaje a Buenos Aires. Él me dice[b] que allí la Navidad[c] (ser/estar[19]) una fiesta de verano y que todos (llevar[20]) ropa como la que[d] llevamos nosotros en julio. Parece[e] increíble, ¿verdad?

[a]*are swimming* [b]*Él… He tells me* [c]*Christmas* [d]*la… that which* [e]*It seems*

Comprensión: ¿Probable o improbable?

1. Los estudiantes argentinos van a la playa en julio.
2. Muchas personas sudamericanas hacen viajes de vacaciones en enero.
3. Hace frío en Santiago (Chile) en diciembre.

VIDEOTECA: En contexto

FUNCTION:

Discussing travel plans

Cultura en contexto
Belize

Belize, formerly known as British Honduras, has many beautiful beaches and coral reefs that attract an increasing number of tourists, particularly those interested in world-class scuba diving. Belize (in Spanish, **Belice**) was once part of Guatemala, though under British occupation at the time. Due to the influence of this British occupation, Belize is the only Central American country whose official language is English.

In this video segment, Roberto visits a travel agent to find out about vacation options. What kind of a vacation would Roberto prefer? What suggestions does the agent make?

MÉXICO

A. Lluvia de ideas

- ¿Le gusta a Ud. hacer viajes? ¿Con quién? ¿Adónde le gusta ir? ¿En qué estación del año prefiere ir?
- Imagine Ud. que una persona quiere visitar su ciudad o su estado. ¿En qué estación debe ir? ¿Qué se puede hacer allí?

B. Dictado

Here is part of this segment's dialogue. Fill in the missing portions of the dialogue.

ROBERTO: ¿Es caro el Caribe?
AGENTE: Depende de la _____.[1] En el invierno, cuesta más. En el _____,[2] cuesta menos.
ROBERTO: Claro. ¿Y qué _____[3] hace en el Caribe durante el verano?
AGENTE: Bueno, julio y _____,[4] por ejemplo, hace _____.[5] Y llueve mucho también. _____[6] casi todos los días.
ROBERTO: ¿Y qué tiempo _____[7] durante el _____?[8]
AGENTE: Hace más fresco, y no llueve _____.[9]
ROBERTO: ¿Tiene alguna otra recomendación?
AGENTE: Hmm… El país de Belice… tiene lugares maravillosos para bucear.[a] Pero no es una _____.[10]
ROBERTO: ¡Belice! ¡Qué buena idea!

[a]*scuba dive*

C. Un diálogo original

Paso 1. Con un compañero/una compañera, dramatice la escena de Roberto con la agente.

Paso 2. Imagine que Ud. y su compañero/a desean hacer un viaje juntos (*together*). Pero primero deben decidir adónde quieren ir.

E1: You like warm weather and exotic places. You don't have money to go to Europe.
E2: You like both eco-tourism (**ecoturismo**) as well as visiting important cities. You'd like to go to Europe, but will consider other options.

(PASO FINAL)

 A LEER

Estrategia: Forming a General Idea about Content

Before starting a reading, it is a good idea to try to form a general sense of the content. The more you know about the reading before you begin to read, the easier it will seem to you. Here are some things you can do to prepare yourself for reading. You have already applied some of these strategies to the readings thus far in *¿Qué tal?*

1. Make sure you understand the title. Think about what it suggests to you and what you already know about the topic. Do the same with any subtitles in the reading.
2. Look at the drawings, photos, or other visual clues that accompany the reading. What do they indicate about the content?
3. Read the comprehension questions before starting to read the selection. They will direct you to the kind of information you should be looking for.

You should be able to determine the general message of the reading if you apply the preceding strategies.

- **The title.** The reading, "**Todos juntos en los trópicos**," contains a key word in the title: **trópicos**. It is a cognate. Can you guess what it means?
- **The art.** The reading is accompanied by a photograph and caption. What additional information do these tell you about the reading?
- **The comprehension questions.** Scan the questions in **Comprensión**. What additional clues do they give you about the content of the passage?

> ***Sobre la lectura…*** This reading is taken from the magazine *Muy interesante*, which generally contains articles about popular science and related topics. Remember that knowing the source of a passage can also help you formulate hypotheses about the reading before you begin to read.

Todos juntos en los trópicos

Los trópicos son las regiones biológicamente más diversas del planeta y cuentan con[a] el triple de especies que en cualquier otra zona. Pero, ¿por qué? Los biólogos no han sido capaces[b] de dar una respuesta unívoca.[c] Es más, las diferentes teorías que se han propuesto[d] tienen todos sus puntos débiles.[e]

En resumen, existen tres razones expuestas para esta riqueza.[f] La primera teoría fue diseñada[g] hace 20 años[h] por Michael Rosenzweigh, de Arizona. Según él, en los trópicos hay más especies, sencillamente[i] porque se cuenta con más espacio geográfico habitable.

[a]cuentan… *tienen* [b]no… *have not been able* [c]respuesta… *unambiguous answer* [d]que… *that have been proposed* [e]puntos… *weak points* [f]expuestas… *given for this wealth* [g]fue… *was outlined* [h]hace… *20 years ago* [i]simply

No hay una teoría única para explicar la exuberancia natural que se produce en los trópicos.

La segunda es de los últimos años 80 y fue diseñada por George Stevens, de Nuevo México: las especies tropicales son esclavas[j] de sus condiciones térmicas;[k] por eso no pueden <u>colonizar</u> nuevos territorios menos cálidos[l] y se concentran como un gueto[m] en el trópico.

La tercera es una teoría histórica y explica que los trópicos fueron[n] las áreas de la Tierra que escaparon al efecto destructor del aumento[o] de las regiones heladas[p] durante las <u>glaciaciones</u>.

Ninguna de las tres ha sido confirmada.[q]

[i]*slaves* [k]*thermal* [l]*hot* [m]*ghetto* [n]*were* [o]*increase* [p]*frozen* [q]*ha... has been confirmed*

Comprensión

A. ¿Se menciona o no? ¿Cuáles de los siguientes temas se mencionan en la lectura?

		SÍ	NO
1.	Información sobre la gente (*people*) indígena de los trópicos.	☐	☐
2.	Teorías que explican (*explain*) la biodiversidad de los trópicos.	☐	☐
3.	Información sobre la deforestación de los trópicos.	☐	☐
4.	Teorías que explican la climatología de los trópicos.	☐	☐

B. Resumen (*Summary*). En inglés, escriba un breve resumen de las tres teorías presentadas en la lectura. Compare su resumen con el de otro estudiante. ¿Cuál de las teorías parece más factible (*feasible*)?

A ESCRIBIR

La biodiversidad local. La lectura comenta la gran biodiversidad de los trópicos, y propone teorías que explican este fenómeno. ¿Cómo es la biodiversidad en la región donde Ud. vive? ¿Hay muchos animales y plantas indígenas? ¿Cuál es la relación entre el clima de la región y la flora y la fauna? Escriba un breve ensayo (*essay*) que comente cómo es el clima donde Ud. vive y qué animales y plantas habitan la zona. (Consulte un diccionario bilingüe si es necesario.)

En resumen

GRAMÁTICA

To review the grammar points presented in this chapter, refer to the indicated grammar presentations. You'll find further practice of these structures in the Workbook/Laboratory Manual, on the CD-ROM, and on the website.

14. Present Progressive: *estar* + *-ndo*

Do you know how to form the present progressive? When is this structure used in Spanish?

15. Summary of the Uses of *ser* and *estar*

You should know whether to use **ser** or **estar** in the following situations: to describe inherent qualities, to describe health and physical conditions, to express time, to form the present progressive.

16. Comparisons

Do you know how to compare things and people?

VOCABULARIO

Los verbos

celebrar	to celebrate
pasar	to spend (*time*); to happen
quedarse	to stay, remain (*in a place*)

¿Qué tiempo hace?

está (muy) nublado	it's (very) cloudy, overcast
hace...	it's . . .
buen/mal tiempo	good/bad weather
calor	hot
fresco	cool
frío	cold
sol	sunny
viento	windy
hay (mucha)	there's (lots of)
contaminación	pollution
llover (ue)	to rain
llueve	it's raining
nevar (ie)	to snow
nieva	it's snowing

Los meses del año

enero, febrero, marzo, abril, mayo, junio, julio, agosto, septiembre, octubre, noviembre, diciembre

Las estaciones del año

la primavera	spring
el verano	summer
el otoño	fall, autumn
el invierno	winter

Los lugares

la capital	capital city
la isla	island
el parque	park
la playa	beach

Otros sustantivos

el clima	climate
el cumpleaños	birthday

la fecha	date (*calendar*)
el/la novio/a	boyfriend/girlfriend
la respuesta	answer

Los adjetivos

abierto/a	open
aburrido/a	bored
alegre	happy
cansado/a	tired
cariñoso/a	affectionate
cerrado/a	closed
congelado/a	frozen; very cold
contento/a	content, happy
desordenado/a	messy
difícil	hard, difficult
enfermo/a	sick
fácil	easy
furioso/a	furious, angry
limpio/a	clean
loco/a	crazy
nervioso/a	nervous
ocupado/a	busy
ordenado/a	neat
preocupado/a	worried
querido/a	dear
seguro/a	sure, certain
sucio/a	dirty
triste	sad

Las comparaciones

más/menos... que	more/less . . . than
tan... como	as . . . as
tanto/a(s)... como	as much/many . . . as
tanto como	as much as
mayor	older
mejor	better; best

| menor | younger |
| peor | worse |

Las preposiciones

a la derecha de	to the right of
a la izquierda de	to the left of
al lado de	alongside of
cerca de	close to
debajo de	below
delante de	in front of
detrás de	behind
encima de	on top of
entre	between, among
lejos de	far from

Los puntos cardinales

el norte, el sur, el este, el oeste

Palabras adicionales

afuera	outdoors
¿Cuál es la fecha de hoy?	What's today's date?
esta noche	tonight
estar (*irreg.*) bien	to be comfortable (*temperature*)
mí (*obj. of prep.*)	me
el primero de	the first of (*month*)
siguiente	following
tener (*irreg.*) (mucho) calor	to be (very) warm, hot
tener (*irreg.*) (mucho) frío	to be (very) cold
ti (*obj. of prep.*)	you
todavía	still

CAPÍTULO 6

¿Qué le gusta comer?

Esta señora compra cebollas (*onions*) en un mercado en Panamá.

VOCABULARIO

- Food and beverages
- **Saber** and **conocer**; Personal **a**

GRAMÁTICA

17 Direct Object Pronouns
18 Indefinite and Negative Words
19 Formal Commands

CULTURA

- **Enfoque cultural:** Panamá
- **Nota cultural:** Foods in the Spanish-Speaking World
- **En los Estados Unidos y el Canadá:** Goya Foods, Inc.
- **Cultura en contexto:** El mercado

Multimedia

 You will learn about shopping for food in the **En contexto** video segment.

Review vocabulary and grammar and practice language skills with the interactive CD-ROM.

 Get connected to the Spanish-speaking world with the *¿Qué tal?* Online Learning Center: **www.mhhe.com/quetal**.

La comida

Las comidas

el desayuno → desayunar
breakfast → to have (eat) breakfast

el almuerzo → almorzar (ue)
lunch → to have (eat) lunch

la cena → cenar
dinner → to have (eat) dinner, supper

los pecos
living Pez=

Otras bebidas

el refresco	soft drink
el té	tea
el vino blanco	white wine

Otras verduras

el champiñón	mushroom
los espárragos	asparagus
los frijoles	beans

---

*The noun **agua** (*water*) is feminine, but the masculine articles are used with it in the singular: *el agua*. This occurs with all feminine nouns that begin with a stressed **a** sound, for example, *el (un)* **ama de casa** (*homemaker*).

Otras frutas

el plantano
el banano

la banana	banana
la naranja	orange

Otras carnes

el bistec	steak
la chuleta (de cerdo)	(pork) chop
la hamburguesa	hamburger
el jamón	ham
el pavo	turkey
la salchicha	sausage; hot dog

Otros pescados y mariscos

el atún	tuna
los camarones	shrimp

la langosta	lobster
el salmón	salmon

Otros postres

el flan	(baked) custard
la galleta	cookie
el helado	ice cream

un de sabor del soda
crema helado

Otras comidas

el arroz	rice
el huevo	egg
el queso	cheese
el sándwich	sandwich
el yogur	yogurt

el emparedado

Conversación

A. **¿Qué quiere tomar?** Match the following descriptions of meals with these categories: **un menú ligero** (*light*) **para una dieta, una comida rápida, una cena elegante, un desayuno estilo norteamericano.**

1. una sopa fría, langosta, espárragos, una ensalada de lechuga y tomate, todo con vino blanco y, para terminar, un pastel
2. jugo de fruta, huevos con jamón, pan tostado y café
3. pollo asado, arroz, arvejas, agua mineral y, para terminar, una manzana
4. una hamburguesa con patatas fritas, un refresco y un helado

B. **Definiciones.** ¿Qué es?

1. un plato de lechuga y tomate
2. una bebida alcohólica blanca o roja
3. un líquido caliente (*hot*) que se toma* con cuchara (*spoon*)
4. una verdura anaranjada
5. la carne típica para la barbacoa en este país
6. una comida muy común en la China y en el Japón
7. la comida favorita de los ratones
8. una verdura frita que se come con las hamburguesas
9. una fruta roja o verde
10. una fruta amarilla de las zonas tropicales

---

*Placing **se** before a verb form can change its English equivalent slightly: **usa** (*he/she/it uses*) → **se usa** (*is used*).

NOTA COMUNICATIVA

More *tener* Idioms

Here are two additional **tener** idioms that you can use to talk about foods and eating.

tener (mucha) hambre	to be (very) hungry
tener (mucha) sed	to be (very) thirsty

C. Consejos (*Advice*) **a la hora de comer.** ¿Qué debe Ud. comer o beber en las siguientes situaciones?

1. Ud. quiere comer algo ligero porque no tiene hambre.
2. Ud. quiere comer algo fuerte (*heavy*) porque tiene mucha hambre.
3. Ud. tiene un poco de sed y quiere tomar algo antes de la comida.
4. Ud. quiere comer algo antes del plato principal.
5. Ud. quiere comer algo después del plato principal.
6. Ud. está a dieta.
7. Ud. está de vacaciones en Maine (o Boston).
8. Después de levantarse, Ud. no está despierto/a (*awake*).

NOTA CULTURAL

Foods of the Spanish-Speaking World

La tortilla española

Often when we think of dishes from the Spanish-speaking world, what comes to mind are rice, beans, spicy **chiles**, corn or flour **tortillas**, and **burritos**. However, that is a misconception.

Corn and flour **tortillas** and **burritos** are unknown in many Spanish-speaking countries. Many Hispanic cuisines are not spicy at all, and if you are in Spain and order **una tortilla**, you will be served a wedge of potato omelette!

The cuisines of Spanish-speaking countries are as diverse as their inhabitants. With the arrival of the Spaniards in the Americas, indigenous cuisines were influenced by European foods that did not exist there before, such as beef and chicken. Likewise, European cuisines were influenced by the introduction of foods from the Americas, such as the tomato, the potato, and chocolate. Later, immigration from countries such as Ireland, Germany, Italy, China, and Japan further influenced American cuisines.*

Las tortillas mexicanas

*Remember that, in this context, *American* refers to all the countries in North, Central, and South America.

¿Qué sabe Ud. y a quién conoce?
Saber and conocer; Personal a

¿Le importa (*Does it matter to you*) mucho la comida? Si son ciertas para Ud. tres de las siguientes oraciones, sí le importa muchísimo (*a lot*).

1. Sé preparar muchos platos diferentes.
2. Conozco al dueño / a la dueña (*owner*) de mi restaurante favorito.
3. Sé el número de teléfono de mi restaurante favorito.
4. Sé cuánto cuesta, aproximadamente, una docena de huevos y un litro de leche.
5. Conozco muchos restaurantes en esta ciudad.

Saber and conocer

Two Spanish verbs express *to know*: **saber** and **conocer**.

saber (*to know*)		conocer (*to know*)	
sé	sabemos	conozco	conocemos
sabes	sabéis	conoces	conocéis
sabe	saben	conoce	conocen

saber
- to know facts or pieces of information

saber + *infinitive*
- to know how to (*do something*)

conocer
- to know or be acquainted (familiar) with a person, place, or thing

- to meet

Ud. **sabe** su número de teléfono, ¿verdad?
You know her phone number, right?

¿**Sabes jugar** al ajedrez?
Do you know how to play chess?

¿**Conoces** a la nueva estudiante francesa?
Do you know the new French student?

Conozco un buen restaurante cerca de aquí.
I know (am familiar with) a good restaurant nearby.

¿Quieres **conocer** al nuevo profesor?
Do you want to meet the new professor?

Personal a

In Spanish, the word **a** immediately precedes the direct object* of a sentence when the direct object refers to a specific person or persons. This **a,** called the **a personal,** has no equivalent in English.[†]

¿Conoces **a** María?
Do you know María?

Llamo **a** mis padres con frecuencia.
I call my parents often.

---

*The *direct object* (**el complemento directo**) is the part of the sentence that indicates to whom or to what the verb is directed or upon whom or what it acts. In the sentence *I saw John,* the direct object is *John.*
[†]The personal **a** is not generally used with **tener: Tengo cuatro hijos.**

O J O	The personal **a** is used before the interrogative words **¿quién?** and **¿quiénes?** when they function as direct objects.	**¿A quién** llamas? *Whom are you calling?*
O J O	The verbs **buscar** (*to look for*), **escuchar** (*to listen to*), **esperar** (*to wait for*), and **mirar** (*to look at*) include the sense of the English prepositions *for, to,* and *at.* These verbs take direct objects in Spanish (not prepositional phrases, as in English).	Busco **mi abrigo.** *I'm looking for my overcoat.* Espero **a mi hijo.** *I'm waiting for my son.*

Conversación

A. ¿Dónde cenamos? Lola y Manolo quieren cenar fuera. Pero, ¿dónde? Complete el diálogo con la forma correcta de **saber** o **conocer.**

LOLA: ¿(Sabes/Conoces[1]) adónde quieres ir a cenar?

MANOLO: No (sé/conozco[2]). ¿Y tú?

LOLA: No. Pero hay un restaurante nuevo en la calle Betis. Creo que se llama Guadalquivir. ¿(Sabes/Conoces[3]) el restaurante?

MANOLO: No, pero (sé/conozco[4]) que tiene mucha fama. Es el restaurante favorito de Virginia. Ella (sabe/conoce[5]) al dueño.

LOLA: ¿(Sabes/Conoces[6]) qué tipo de comida tienen?

MANOLO: No (sé/conozco[7]). Pero podemos llamar a Virginia. ¿(Sabes/Conoces[8]) su teléfono?

LOLA: Está en mi guía telefónica. Y pregúntale[a] a Virginia si ella (sabe/conoce[9]) si aceptan reservas o no.

MANOLO: De acuerdo.[b]

[a]*ask* [b]*De... OK.*

B. Preguntas

1. ¿Qué restaurantes conoce Ud. en esta ciudad? ¿Cuál es su restaurante favorito? ¿Por qué? ¿Qué tipo de comida sirven? ¿Le gusta el ambiente (*atmosphere*)? ¿Come Ud. allí con frecuencia?

2. ¿Conoce Ud. a alguna persona famosa? ¿Quién es? ¿Cómo es? ¿Qué detalles sabe Ud. de la vida de esta persona?

3. ¿Qué platos sabe Ud. preparar? ¿Tacos? ¿enchiladas? ¿pollo frito? ¿hamburguesas? ¿Le gusta cocinar? ¿Cocina con frecuencia?

4. ¿Espera Ud. a alguien para ir a la universidad? ¿Espera a alguien después de la clase? ¿A quién busca cuando necesita ayuda (*help*) con el español? ¿Dónde busca a sus amigos por la noche?

17 **Expressing *what* or *whom*** • Direct Object Pronouns

De compras en el supermercado

Indique cuáles de estas afirmaciones son verdaderas para Ud.

1. la leche
   - ☐ *La* bebo todos los días. Por eso tengo que comprar*la* con frecuencia.
   - ☐ *La* bebo de vez en cuando (*once in a while*). Por eso no *la* compro a menudo (*often*).
   - ☐ Nunca *la* bebo. No necesito comprar*la*.

2. el café
   - ☐ *Lo* bebo todos los días. Por eso tengo que comprar*lo* con frecuencia.
   - ☐ *Lo* bebo de vez en cuando. Por eso no *lo* compro a menudo.
   - ☐ Nunca *lo* bebo. No necesito comprar*lo*.

3. los huevos
   - ☐ *Los* como todos los días. Por eso tengo que comprar*los* con frecuencia.
   - ☐ *Los* como de vez en cuando. Por eso no *los* compro a menudo.
   - ☐ Nunca *los* como. No necesito comprar*los*.

4. las bananas
   - ☐ *Las* como todos los días. Por eso tengo que comprar*las* con frecuencia.
   - ☐ *Las* como de vez en cuando. Por eso no *las* compro a menudo.
   - ☐ Nunca *las* como. No necesito comprar*las*.

Direct Object Pronouns

me	me		**nos**	us
te	you (*fam. sing.*)		**os**	you (*fam. pl.*)
lo*	you (*form. sing.*), him, it (*m.*)		**los**	you (*form. pl.*), them (*m., m. + f.*)
la	you (*form. sing.*), her, it (*f.*)		**las**	you (*form. pl.*), them (*f.*)

A. Like direct object nouns, *direct object pronouns* (**los pronombres del complemento directo**) are the first recipient of the action of the verb. Direct object pronouns are placed before a conjugated verb and after the word **no** when it appears. Third person direct object pronouns are used only when the direct object noun has already been mentioned.

[Práctica A]

¿El libro? Diego no **lo** necesita.
The book? Diego doesn't need it.

¿Dónde están el libro y el periódico? **Los** necesito ahora.
Where are the book and the newspaper? I need them now.

Ellos **me** ayudan.
They're helping me.

B. The direct object pronouns may be attached to an infinitive or a present participle.

[Práctica B]

Las tengo que leer.
Tengo que leer**las**. } *I have to read them.*

Lo estoy comiendo.
Estoy comiéndo**lo**. } *I am eating it.*

C. Note that many verbs commonly used with reflexive pronouns can also be used with direct object nouns and pronouns when the action of the verb is directed at someone other than the subject of the sentence. The meaning of the verb will change slightly.

[Práctica C]

Generalmente me despierto a las ocho. La radio **me** despierta.
I generally wake up at eight. The radio wakes me.

En un restaurante, el camarero **nos** sienta.
In a restaurant, the waiter seats us.

D. Note that the direct object pronoun **lo** can refer to actions, situations, or ideas in general. When used in this way, **lo** expresses English *it* or *that*.

Lo comprende muy bien.
He understands it (that) very well.

No **lo** creo.
I don't believe it (that).

Lo sé.
I know (it).

---

*In Spain and in some other parts of the Spanish-speaking world, **le** is frequently used instead of **lo** for the direct object pronoun *him*. This usage, called **el leísmo**, will not be followed in *¿Qué tal?*

Práctica

A. ¿Qué comen los vegetarianos? Aquí hay una lista de diferentes comidas. ¿Van a formar parte de la dieta de un vegetariano? Conteste según los modelos. Si hay un estudiante vegetariano / una estudiante vegetariana en la clase, pídale que verifique (*ask him or her to verify*) las respuestas de Ud.

MODELOS: el bistec → No lo va a comer.
         la banana → La va a comer.

1. las patatas
2. el arroz
3. las chuletas de cerdo
4. la zanahoria
5. la manzana
6. los camarones
7. el pan
8. los frijoles
9. la ensalada

B. La cena de Lola y Manolo. La siguiente descripción es muy repetitiva. Combine las oraciones, cambiando los nombres de complemento directo por pronombres cuando sea (*whenever it is*) necesario.

MODELO: El camarero (*waiter*) trae un menú. Lola lee el menú. →
         El camarero trae un menú y Lola *lo* lee.

1. El camarero trae una botella de vino tinto. Pone la botella en la mesa.
2. El camarero trae las copas (*glasses*) de vino. Pone las copas en la mesa.
3. Lola quiere la especialidad de la casa. Va a pedir la especialidad de la casa.
4. Manolo prefiere el pescado fresco (*fresh*). Pide el pescado fresco.
5. El camarero trae la comida. Sirve la comida.
6. Manolo necesita otra servilleta (*napkin*). Pide otra servilleta.
7. «¿La cuenta (*bill*)? El dueño está preparando la cuenta para Uds.»
8. Manolo quiere pagar con tarjeta (*card*) de crédito. No trae su tarjeta.
9. Por fin, Lola toma la cuenta. Paga la cuenta.

C. ¿Quién o qué lo hace? Indique a la persona o cosa que hace lo siguiente. Hay más de una respuesta posible.

Palabras útiles: el barbero, los (buenos) amigos, el camarero / la camarera, mi compañero/a, el despertador (*alarm clock*), el doctor / la doctora, el dueño / la dueña, los esposos, mi esposo/a, los estudiantes, mi padre/madre, los padres, los profesores, la radio

1. Por la manana, _____ me despierta.
2. En un restaurante, _____ nos sienta.
3. En una barbería (*barber shop*), _____ nos afeita.
4. En un hospital, _____ nos examina.
5. _____ nos escuchan cuando necesitamos hablar.
6. _____ nos esperan cuando vamos a llegar tarde.
7. Generalmente los niños no se acuestan solos (*by themselves*). _____ los acuesta. _____ también los baña y los viste.
8. En una clase, _____ hacen las preguntas y _____ las contestan.

NOTA COMUNICATIVA

Talking about What You Have Just Done

To talk about what you have *just* done, use the phrase **acabar** + **de** with an infinitive.

Acabo de almorzar con Beto. *I just had lunch with Beto.*
Acabas de celebrar tu *You just celebrated your*
 cumpleaños, ¿verdad? *birthday, didn't you?*

Note that the infinitive follows **de**. As you already know, the infinitive is the only verb form that can follow a preposition in Spanish.

D. **¡Acabo de hacerlo!** Imagine that a friend is pressuring you to do the following things. With a classmate, tell him or her that you just did each one, using either of the forms in the model.

MODELO: E1: ¿Por qué no estudias la lección? →
    E2: Acabo de estudiar*la*. (*La* acabo de estudiar.)

1. ¿Por qué no escribes las composiciones para tus clases?
2. ¿Vas a comprar el periódico hoy?
3. ¿Por qué no pagas los cafés?
4. ¿Vas a preparar la comida para la fiesta?
5. ¿Puedes pedir la cuenta?
6. ¿Tienes hambre? ¿Por qué no comes los tacos que preparé (*I made*)?

Conversación

Una encuesta sobre la comida. Hágales (*Ask*) preguntas a sus compañeros de clase para saber si toman las comidas o bebidas indicadas y con qué frecuencia. Deben explicar también por qué toman o *no* toman cierta cosa.

MODELO: la carne → E1: ¿Comes carne?
      E2: No *la* como casi nunca porque tiene mucho
       colesterol.

Palabras útiles: la cafeína, las calorías, el colesterol, la grasa (*fat*)

Frases útiles: estar a dieta, ser alérgico/a a, ser bueno/a para la salud (*health*), me pone (*it makes me*) nervioso/a, lo/la/los/las detesto

1. la carne	5. las hamburguesas	9. el alcohol
2. los mariscos	6. el pollo	10. el atún
3. el yogur	7. el café	11. los espárragos
4. la pizza	8. los dulces (*sweets; candy*)	12. el hígado (*liver*)

18 Expressing Negation • Indefinite and Negative Words

En la cocina de Diego y Antonio

DIEGO: Quiero comer *algo*, pero *no* hay *nada* de comer en esta casa. Y no tengo ganas de ir de compras. Y además, ¡*no* tengo *ni* un centavo!

ANTONIO: ¡Ay! *Siempre* eres así. Tú *nunca* tienes ganas de ir de compras. Y lo del dinero… ¡esa es otra historia!

¿Quién… ?

1. tiene hambre
2. nunca tiene dinero
3. critica a su amigo
4. no quiere ir de compras

A. Here is a list of the most common indefinite and negative words in Spanish. You have been using many of them since the first chapters of *¿Qué tal?*

algo	something, anything	**nada**	nothing, not anything
alguien	someone, anyone	**nadie**	no one, nobody, not anybody
algún (alguno/a/os/as)	some, any	**ningún (ninguno/a)**	no, none, not any
siempre	always	**nunca, jamás**	never
también	also	**tampoco**	neither, not either

Pronunciation hint: Pronounce the *d* in *nada* and *nadie* as a fricative, that is, like a *th* sound: *na đa, na đie.*

B. Pay particular attention to the following aspects of using negative words.

• When a negative word comes after the main verb, Spanish requires that another negative word—usually **no**—be placed before the verb. When a negative word precedes the verb, **no** is not used.

¿No estudia **nadie**?
¿**Nadie** estudia? } *Isn't anyone studying?*

No estás en clase **nunca**.
Nunca estás en clase. } *You're never in class.*

No quieren cenar aquí **tampoco**.
Tampoco quieren cenar aquí. } *They don't want to have dinner here, either.*

In Diego and Antonio's kitchen DIEGO: I want to eat something, but there's nothing to eat in this house. And I don't feel like going shopping. And furthermore, I don't have a cent! ANTONIO: Ah! You're always like that. You never feel like going shopping. And that bit about the money . . . , that's another story!

- The adjectives **alguno** and **ninguno** shorten to **algún** and **ningún,** respectively, before a masculine singular noun—just as **uno** shortens to **un, bueno** to **buen,** and **malo** to **mal.** The plural forms **ningunos** and **ningunas** are rarely used.

—¿Hay **algunos** recados para mí hoy?
—Lo siento, pero hoy no hay **ningún** recado para Ud.
Are there any messages for me today?
I'm sorry, but there are no messages for you today.
(There is not a single message for you today.)

Práctica

A. **Manolo está de mal humor** (*in a bad mood*)**.** Hoy Manolo tiene una actitud muy negativa. ¿Qué opina Manolo de las afirmaciones de su esposa Lola?

MODELO: LOLA: Tengo algunos estudiantes excelentes este año.
MANOLO: Pues, yo no tengo ningún estudiante excelente este año.

1. Hay muchas clases interesantes en el departamento.
2. Me gusta tomar café con mis estudiantes con frecuencia.
3. Hay algunas personas buenas en la administración.
4. También hay un candidato bueno para el puesto (*position*) de rector.
5. Hay muchas personas inteligentes en la universidad.

B. **¿Qué pasa esta noche en casa?** Tell whether the following statements about what is happening at this house are true (**cierto**) or false (**falso**). Then create as many additional sentences as you can about what is happening, following the model of the sentences.

1. No hay nadie en el baño.
2. En la cocina, alguien está preparando la cena.
3. No hay ninguna persona en el patio.
4. Hay algo en la mesa del comedor.
5. Algunos amigos se están divirtiendo en la sala.
6. Hay algunos platos en la mesa del comedor.
7. No hay ningún niño en la casa.

Conversación

Preguntas

1. ¿Vamos a… ? ¿vivir en la luna (*moon*) algún día? ¿viajar (*to travel*) a otros planetas? ¿vivir allí algún día? ¿establecer contacto con seres (*beings*) de otros planetas algún día?
2. ¿Algunos de los estudiantes de esta universidad son de países extranjeros? ¿De dónde son? ¿Algunos de sus amigos son de habla española (*Spanish-speaking*)? ¿De dónde son?

Enfoque *cultural*

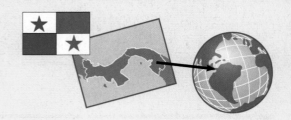

Panamá

Datos esenciales

Nombre oficial: República de Panamá

Capital: Ciudad de Panamá

Población: 2.778.526 de habitantes

Moneda: el balboa (también se usa el dólar estadounidense)

Idioma oficial: el español

Conozca… el Canal de Panamá

El Canal de Panamá, construido a través del[a] istmo entre los dos continentes americanos, comunica los océanos Atlántico y Pacífico. Mide[b] aproximadamente 80 kilómetros (50 millas) de largo, 12,5 metros (41 pies[c]) de ancho[d] y 200 metros (más de 63 pies) de profundidad. Su construcción facilita la comunicación marítima entre las costas este y oeste de los continentes. Antes de la existencia del canal, los barcos tenían que darle la vuelta a[e] América del Sur para ir de una costa a otra. Hoy, el viaje por el Canal de Panamá toma aproximadamente ocho horas, pues[f] es necesario pasar por un número de esclusas.[g]

La idea de construir un canal a través del istmo data de 1534, cuando el emperador español Carlos V (Quinto) la propone. Más tarde, en 1881, el ingeniero francés Fernando de Lesseps también va a sugerir un proyecto similar. Pero

Una esclusa del Canal de Panamá

el canal no se construye hasta el siglo XX, por los Estados Unidos. Esto ocasiona[h] la presencia de los Estados Unidos en la vida de Panamá. Como resultado, hay un uso extendido del inglés en el país, se usa el dólar y ha habido[i] una gran intervención en la política del país.

El canal se inaugura en 1914 y es administrado por los Estados Unidos hasta 1999. Desde el primero de enero del año 2000, la República de Panamá está a cargo de[j] su gran canal.

[a]construido… *built across the* [b]*It measures* [c]*feet* [d]de… *in width* [e]tenían… *had to go around* [f]*because* [g]*canal locks* [h]*brings about* [i]ha… *there has been* [j]a… *in control of*

¡Fíjese!

- **Panamá** es una palabra indígena que significa «tierra de muchos peces[a]».
- La Carretera[b] Panamericana, el sistema de carreteras que va de Alaska al Panamá, se interrumpe[c] en la densa e[d] impenetrable selva[e] panameña de Darién. Para llegar a Sudamérica es necesario tomar un barco[f] hasta Colombia, donde continúa la carretera.

- La Sra. Mireya Moscoso ganó[g] las elecciones presidenciales de 1998. La viuda[h] de otro presidente, doña Mireya es la primera mujer panameña en asumir el cargo.[i]

[a]*fish* [b]*Highway* [c]se… *breaks off, is interrupted* [d]*y* [e]*jungle* [f]*boat* [g]*won* [h]*widow* [i]*post*

Capítulo 6 of the video to accompany *¿Qué tal?* contains cultural footage of Panama.

WW. Visit the *¿Qué tal?* website at www.mhhe.com/quetal.

19 Influencing Others • Formal Commands

Receta para guacamole

El guacamole

Ingredientes:
1 aguacate[a]
1 diente de ajo,[b]
   prensado[c]
1 tomate
jugo de un limón
sal
un poco de cilantro
   fresco[d]

Cómo se prepara
Corte el aguacate y el tomate en trozos[e] pequeños.
Añada el jugo del limón, el ajo, el cilantro y la sal a su
gusto. *Mezcle* bien todos los ingredientes y *sírvalo* con
tortillas fritas de maíz.[f]

En español, los mandatos se usan con frecuencia en
las recetas. Estos verbos se usan en forma de
mandato en esta receta. ¿Puede encontrarlos?

añadir	to add
cortar	to cut
mezclar	to mix
servir (i, i)	to serve

[a]*avocado* [b]*diente… clove of garlic* [c]*crushed* [d]*fresh* [e]*pieces* [f]*corn*

FORMAL COMMAND FORMS

In *¿Qué tal?* you have seen commands throughout the direction lines of
activities: **haga, complete, conteste,** and so on.

   Commands (imperatives) are verb forms used to tell someone to do something. In Spanish, *formal commands* (**los mandatos formales**) are used with
people whom you address as **Ud.** or **Uds.** Here are some of the basic forms.

	hablar	**comer**	**escribir**	**volver**	**decir**
Ud.	hable	coma	escriba	vuelva	diga
Uds.	hablen	coman	escriban	vuelvan	digan
English	*speak*	*eat*	*write*	*come back*	*tell*

A. Almost all formal commands are based on the
yo form of the present tense. Replace the **-o**
with **-e** or **-en** for **-ar** verbs; replace the **-o** with
-a or **-an** for **-er** and **-ir** verbs.

hablo → hable
como → coma
escribo → escriba

B. Formal commands of stem-changing verbs will
show the stem change.

p**ie**nse Ud.
v**ue**lva Ud.
p**i**da Ud.

C. Verbs ending in **-car, -gar**, and **-zar** have a spelling change to preserve the **-c-, -g-**, and **-z-** sounds.

c → qu	buscar: bus**qu**e Ud.
g → gu	pagar: pa**gu**e Ud.
z → c	empezar: empie**c**e Ud.

D. The **Ud./Uds.** commands for verbs that have irregular **yo** forms will reflect the irregularity.

conocer	→ **conozca** Ud.
decir* (*to say, tell*)	→ **diga** Ud.
hacer	→ **haga** Ud.
oír	→ **oiga** Ud.
poner	→ **ponga** Ud.
salir	→ **salga** Ud.
tener	→ **tenga** Ud.
traer	→ **traiga** Ud.
venir	→ **venga** Ud.
ver	→ **vea** Ud.

E. A few verbs have irregular **Ud./Uds.** command forms.

dar* (*to give*)	→ **dé** Ud.
estar	→ **esté** Ud.
ir	→ **vaya** Ud.
saber	→ **sepa** Ud.
ser	→ **sea** Ud.

POSITION OF PRONOUNS WITH FORMAL COMMANDS

- Direct object pronouns and reflexive pronouns must follow affirmative commands and be attached to them. In order to maintain the original stress of the verb form, an accent mark is added to the stressed vowel if the original command has two or more syllables.

Léa**lo** Ud.	*Read it.*
Siénte**se,** por favor.	*Sit down, please.*

- Direct object and reflexive pronouns must precede negative commands.

No lo lea Ud.	*Don't read it.*
No se siente.	*Don't sit down.*

Práctica

A. Profesor(a) por un día. Imagine que Ud. es el profesor / la profesora hoy. ¿Qué mandatos debe dar a la clase?

MODELOS: hablar español → Hablen Uds. español.
hablar inglés → No hablen Uds. inglés.

1. llegar a tiempo
2. leer la lección
3. escribir una composición
4. abrir los libros
5. estar en clase mañana
6. traer los libros a clase
7. estudiar los verbos nuevos
8. ¿ ?

---

*Decir and **dar** are used primarily with indirect objects. Both of these verbs and indirect object pronouns will be formally introduced in **Capítulo 7.**

B. ¡Pobre Sr. Rossi!

Paso 1. El Sr. Rossi no se siente (*feel*) bien. Lea la descripción que él da de algunas de sus actividades.

«*Trabajo* muchísimo[a] —¡me gusta trabajar! En la oficina, *soy* impaciente y *critico* bastante[b] a los otros. En mi vida personal, a veces *soy* un poco impulsivo. *Fumo* bastante y también *bebo* cerveza y otras bebidas alcohólicas, a veces sin moderación… *Almuerzo* y *ceno* fuerte, y casi nunca *desayuno*. Por la noche, con frecuencia *salgo* con los amigos —me gusta ir a las discotecas— y *vuelvo* tarde a casa.»

[a]*a whole lot* [b]*a good deal*

Paso 2. ¿Qué *no* debe hacer el Sr. Rossi para estar mejor? Aconséjele (*Advise him*) sobre lo que (*what*) no debe hacer. Use los verbos indicados o cualquier (*any*) otro, según los modelos.

> MODELOS: Trabajo → Sr. Rossi, no trabaje tanto.
> soy → Sr. Rossi, no sea tan impaciente.

C. Situaciones. El Sr. Rossi quiere adelgazar (*to lose weight*). ¿Debe o no debe comer o beber las siguientes cosas? Con otro/a estudiante, haga y conteste preguntas según los modelos.

> MODELOS: ensalada → E1: ¿Ensalada? postres → E1: ¿Postres?
> E2: Cómala. E2: No los coma.

1. alcohol (*m.*)
2. verduras
3. pan
4. dulces
5. leche
6. hamburguesas con queso
7. frutas
8. refrescos dietéticos
9. pollo
10. carne
11. pizza
12. jugo de fruta

D. ¡Estoy harto de Uds. dos! (*I'm fed up with you two!*) Imagine que Ud. acaba de volver de clase y la casa es un desastre. Está enojado/a y empieza a gritarles (*yell*) mandatos a sus compañeros de casa sobre su apariencia física y sus hábitos.

> MODELO: afeitarse → ¡Aféitense!

1. despertarse más temprano
2. levantarse más temprano
3. bañarse más
4. quitarse esa ropa sucia
5. ponerse ropa limpia
6. vestirse mejor
7. estudiar más
8. no divertirse todas las noches con los amigos
9. ir más a la biblioteca
10. no acostarse tan tarde
11. ayudar con los quehaceres
12. ¿ ?

NOTA COMUNICATIVA

El subjuntivo

Except for the command form, all verb forms that you have learned thus far in *¿Qué tal?* have been part of what is called the *indicative mood* (**el modo indicativo**). In both English and Spanish, the indicative is used to state facts and to ask questions. It objectively expresses most real-world actions or states of being.

Both English and Spanish have another verb system called the *subjunctive mood* (**el modo subjuntivo**). The **Ud./Uds.** command forms that you have just learned are part of the subjunctive system. You will not use the subjunctive actively until it is introduced (in **Capítulo 12**). But from this point on in *¿Qué tal?* you will see the subjunctive used where it is natural to use it. What follows is a brief introduction to the subjunctive that will make it easy for you to recognize it when you see it.

Here are some examples of the forms of the subjunctive. The **Ud./Uds.** forms (identical to the **Ud./Uds.** command forms) are highlighted.

hablar		comer		servir		salir	
hable	hablemos	coma	comamos	sirva	sirvamos	salga	salgamos
hables	habléis	comas	comáis	sirvas	sirváis	salgas	salgáis
hable	hablen	coma	coman	sirva	sirvan	salga	salgan

The subjunctive is used to express more subjective or conceptualized states, in contrast to the indicative, which reports facts, information that is objectively true. Here are just a few of the situations in which the subjunctive is used in Spanish.

- to express what the speaker wants others to do (I want you to . . .)
- to express emotional reactions (I'm glad that . . .)
- to express probability or uncertainty (it's likely that . . .)

E. El cumpleaños de María. Fíjese en (*Notice*) los verbos subrayados (*underlined*). Diga por qué razón están subrayados. (Use la lista de la **Nota comunicativa**.)

En el parque

RAÚL: Como hoy es tu cumpleaños, quiero invitarte a cenar. ¿En qué restaurante quieres que <u>cenemos</u>?

MARÍA: Prefiero que tú me[a] <u>prepares</u> una de tus espléndidas cenas.

RAÚL: ¡Con mucho gusto!

En casa de María

MADRE: (*Hablando por teléfono.*) No, lo siento,[b] pero María no está en casa.

LUISA: ¿Es posible que <u>esté</u> en la biblioteca?

MADRE: No. Sé que ella y Raúl están cenando en casa de él.

LUISA: Ah, sí. Bueno, ¿puede pedirle a ella que <u>llame</u> a Luisa cuando regrese?

MADRE: Sí, cómo no,[c] Luisa. Adiós.

LUISA: Hasta luego.

[a]*for me* [b]*lo… I'm sorry* [c]*cómo… of course*

En los Estados Unidos y el Canadá...*

Necesita Tenerlos

Goya Foods, Inc.

En Norteamérica muchos conocen la marca Goya: hay **frijoles, arroz, condimentos, bebidas, café, productos de coco,**[a] **jugos de frutas tropicales** y muchos productos más que son fundamentales para **las cocinas caribeña, mexicana, centroamericana y sudamericana.**

En los años 30 Prudencio Unanue, **un emigrante vasco** de una región del norte de España, funda[b] la compañía Goya. Unanue y **su esposa puertorriqueña** llegan a Nueva York en 1916 y fundan Unanue Inc. en Manhattan en 1935, una compañía especializada en **importaciones de productos españoles** como **olivas, aceite de oliva**[c] **y sardinas enlatadas.**[d] En 1936 la compañía recibe

el nombre de Goya. Desde 1974 la oficina principal está en Nueva Jersey. Hoy tiene **centros de procesamiento y distribución** en diversos estados, además de Puerto Rico, la República Dominicana y España.

La compañía Goya está todavía en manos de[e] la familia Unanue: los hijos de Prudencio, Joseph y Frank, y seis miembros de **la tercera**[f] **generación.** Goya es la primera compañía propiedad de hispanos representada en el Museo Nacional de Historia Americana del Instituto Smithsonian, en Washington, D.C., donde hay una colección de sus anuncios y envases.[g]

[a]coconut [b]founds [c]aceite... *olive oil* [d]canned [e]está... *still belongs to* [f]third [g]anuncios... *ads and containers*

Conversación

En la oficina del consejero. Imagine that you are a guidance counselor. Students consult you with all kinds of questions, some trivial and some important. Offer advice to them in the form of affirmative or negative commands. How many different commands can you invent for each situation?

1. EVELIA: No me gusta tomar clases por la mañana. Siempre estoy muy cansada durante esas clases y además a esa hora tengo hambre. Pienso constantemente en el almuerzo... y no puedo concentrarme en las explicaciones.
2. FABIÁN: En mi clase de cálculo, ¡no entiendo nada! No puedo hacer los ejercicios y durante la clase tengo miedo de hacer preguntas, porque no quiero parecer (*seem*) tonto.
3. FAUSTO: Fui (*I went*) a México el verano pasado y me gustó (*I liked it*) mucho. Quiero volver a México este verano. Ahora que lo conozco mejor, quiero ir en mi coche y no en autobús como el verano pasado. Desgraciadamente (*Unfortunately*) no tengo dinero para hacer el viaje.

*From this point on in *¿Qué tal?*, the **En los Estados Unidos y el Canadá...** sections will be written in Spanish. Important words will be in boldface type. Scanning those words before you begin to read will help you get the gist of the passage.

UN POCO DE TODO

A. ¿Qué hace Roberto los martes?

Paso 1. Describa la rutina de Roberto, haciendo oraciones según las indicaciones.

1. martes / Roberto / nunca / salir / apartamento / antes de / doce
2. esperar / su amigo Samuel / en / parada (*bus stop*) del autobús
3. (ellos) llegar / universidad / a / una
4. (ellos) buscar / su amiga Ceci / en / cafetería
5. a / dos / todos / tener / clase / de / sicología
6. siempre / (ellos) oír / conferencias (*lectures*) / interesante / y / hacer / alguno / pregunta
7. a / cinco / Samuel y Roberto / volver / esperar / autobús
8. Roberto / preparar / cena / y / luego / mirar / televisión

B. La forma de comer. Complete the following paragraphs with the correct form of the words in parentheses, as suggested by the context. When two possibilities are given, select the correct word.

La forma de comer diferencia a las personas. Aquí habla Pilar Fuentes, una española que (vivir[1]) en California con dos estudiantes (norteamericano[2]).

«Yo creo que las costumbres[a] de mis compañeros son un poco (extraño[3]). Generalmente, (por/para[4]) la mañana, mi compañero Peter (desayunar[5]) dos huevos fritos, y un vaso[b] de leche (frío[6]). También él (preparar[7]) pan tostado sin mantequilla. A la una (almorzar[8]) en la universidad. (Comprar[9]) comida china en uno de (ese[10]) restaurantes pequeños que hay en el *campus*. Por (el/la[11]) tarde, (comer[12]) su cena típica: (un/una[13]) pizza grande y un plato de helado de pistacho con chocolate.

Carol, la otra compañera, es muy diferente. Siempre (ser/estar[14]) a dieta. Además cree que su manera de comer (es/estar[15]) muy natural. (*Ella:* Desayunar[16]) café negro. Para el almuerzo, ella (preparar[17]) un sándwich de pan integral[c] y también (unos/unas[18]) zanahorias y una naranja. Su cena (ser[19]) sencilla:[d] arroz integral y verduras. Parece que ella quiere compensar[e] las calorías de los dulces que (*ella:* comer[20]) para la merienda[f]... »

[a]*customs* [b]*glass* [c]*whole grain* [d]*simple* [e]*make up for* [f]*snack*

Comprensión: ¿Probable o improbable?

1. Pilar cree que la forma de comer de sus compañeros es muy normal.
2. Peter sabe cocinar muy bien.
3. Carol nunca tiene ganas de comer un bistec.
4. Carol es vegetariana.

VIDEOTECA: En contexto

FUNCTION:

Shopping for food

Cultura en contexto
El mercado

En Latinoamérica y España, muchas personas todavía compran verduras, fruta, carne y pescado en los mercados del barrio donde viven. Aunque cada vez más[a] hay grandes supermercados con comidas congeladas[b] y enlatadas,[c] los mercados locales todavía son importantes centros económicos y sociales.

[a]cada... *more and more* [b]*frozen* [c]*canned*

In this video segment, Mariela shops for produce. As you watch the segment, pay particular attention to the information Mariela gives about the meal she's planning. What does the vendor tell her about the produce?

COSTA RICA

A. Lluvia de ideas

- ¿A Ud. le gusta cocinar? ¿Qué sabe preparar? ¿Cuál es su especialidad?
- Cuando hay una ocasión especial, ¿le gusta celebrar en un restaurante o prefiere cocinar algo en casa? ¿Tiene algunas recetas para días importantes?
- ¿Hace Ud. la compra con frecuencia? Por lo general, ¿a qué tiendas va a comprar comida? ¿Compra muchos alimentos precocinados (*precooked foods*)?

B. Dictado.
Aquí está una parte del diálogo entre Mariela y el vendedor, que aparece en la sección de vídeo de este capítulo. Complete el diálogo con las palabras o frases que faltan.

SR. VALDERRAMA: Hola, Srta. Castillo. ¿Qué le doy[a] hoy?

MARIELA: Voy a _____[1] una cena deliciosa. Es la primera vez que los padres de mi novio vienen a _____.[2] ¡Pienso causar una gran impresión!

SR. VALDERRAMA: ¿Qué va a preparar? ¿Tal vez[b] un buen _____[3] frito con _____[4]?

MARIELA: No, a mi novio no le gusta el pescado frito.

SR. VALDERRAMA: ¿Le gustan los _____[5] a su novio?

MARIELA: Sí, le gustan muchísimo.[c]

SR. VALDERRAMA: Entonces, de primer _____,[6] prepare un ceviche de camarones.

[a]le... *can I give you* [b]Tal... *Perhaps* [c]*very much*

C. Un diálogo original

Paso 1. Con un compañero / una compañera dramatice el diálogo entre Mariela y el Sr. Valderrama.

Paso 2. Imagine que Ud. y su compañero/a desean preparar una comida especial para celebrar la visita de sus padres. Hagan un menú y una lista de la comida que deben comprar para hacer la cena.

PASO FINAL

A CONVERSAR

El menú del día

Paso 1. En grupos de tres o cuatro estudiantes, lean el siguiente menú del restaurante El toro bravo. Basándose en el menú, ¿qué tipo de restaurante es? ¿Creen que es un restaurante con un ambiente elegante y caro o un restaurante con un ambiente relajado y precios módicos (*moderate*)? El menú que Uds. leen es el menú del día, es decir, las especialidades del día. En su opinión, ¿qué otras cosas sirven en este restaurante?

Restaurante 'El toro bravo'
Menú del día: €12,60

De entrada:

Ensalada mixta
(lechuga, tomate, zanahoria, cebolla y aceitunas[a] verdes con salsa vinagreta)

Sopa de cebolla con queso fundido[b]

Espárragos con jamón serrano[c]

De plato principal:

Paella de mariscos
(arroz, camarones, almejas,[d] pescado, salchicha)

Pollo asado con patatas al horno

Verduras asadas con cous-cous
(pimiento verde, cebolla, berenjena,[e] broculí, champiñones)

De postre:

Ensalada de frutas
(fresas,[f] melón, manzana, naranja)

Flan

Varios helados

[a]*olives* [b]*melted* [c]*jamón… a type of cured Spanish ham* [d]*clams* [e]*eggplant* [f]*strawberries*

Paso 2.   Ahora, imaginen que Uds. están en el restaurante. Uno/a de Uds. es camarero/a y los demás (*the rest*) son clientes que desean cenar. Antes de improvisar una escena, revisen las expresiones a continuación y piensen en el tipo de personaje que va a representar (un camarero difícil o un camarero simpático, una clienta exigente [*demanding*] o una clienta paciente, etcétera).

Clientes	Camarero/a
¿Qué recomienda (de plato principal / de postre)?	¿Qué les* traigo (hoy / de beber)?
¿Qué hay en (la sopa de cebolla)?	¿Ya saben lo que (*what*) desean tomar?
Quiero (la paella de mariscos), por favor.	¿Y qué quiere de (entrada / plato principal / postre)?
Para mí, (los espárragos), por favor.	¿Y para Ud.?
¿Hay (tomates) en (la ensalada mixta)?	Lo siento mucho, no hay más (flan) hoy.
Por favor, preparen (los espárragos) sin (jamón).	Le(s)* recomiendo (la sopa de cebolla).
	La especialidad de la casa es (la paella).
	Lo siento, no podemos preparar (los espárragos) sin (jamón).
	Muy bien, le* preparamos (los espárragos) sin (jamón).

Paso 3.   Improvisen una escena entre los clientes y el camarero / la camarera. La escena debe incluir saludos, preguntas y respuestas sobre los platos, recomendaciones y sugerencias, el orden. Después de practicar la escena, represéntenla para la clase.

---

*Le and **les** are *indirect object pronouns*. Their equivalents in English are *you* (*sing.*) and *you* (*pl.*), respectively. You will learn more about indirect object pronouns in **Capítulo 7**. For now, you can just use them in the phrases indicated.

En resumen

GRAMÁTICA

To review the grammar points presented in this chapter, refer to the indicated grammar presentations. You'll find further practice of these structures in the Workbook/Laboratory Manual, on the CD-ROM, and on the website.

17. Direct Object Pronouns

Do you know how to avoid repetition by using direct object pronouns?

18. Indefinite and Negative Words

Do you know how to use the double negative in Spanish?

19. Formal Commands

You should know how to use commands to order in restaurants and to have someone do something for you.

VOCABULARIO

Los verbos

acabar de + *inf.*	to have just (*done something*)
ayudar	to help
cenar	to have (eat) dinner
cocinar	to cook
conocer	to know, be acquainted with
desayunar	to have (eat) breakfast
esperar	to wait (for); to expect
invitar	to invite
llamar	to call
preguntar	to ask a question
preparar	to prepare
saber (*irreg.*)	to know
saber + *inf.*	to know how to (*do something*)

Repaso: almorzar (ue)

La comida

el arroz	rice
las arvejas	peas
el atún	tuna
el bistec	steak

los camarones	shrimp
la carne	meat
los cereales	cereal
el champiñón	mushroom
la chuleta (de cerdo)	(pork) chop
los dulces	sweets; candy
los espárragos	asparagus
el flan	(baked) custard
los frijoles	beans
la galleta	cookie
el helado	ice cream
el huevo	egg
el jamón	ham
la langosta	lobster
la lechuga	lettuce
la mantequilla	butter
la manzana	apple
los mariscos	shellfish
la naranja	orange
el pan	bread
el pan tostado	toast
el pastel	cake; pie
la patata (frita)	(French fried) potato
el pavo	turkey
el pescado	fish
el pollo (asado)	(roast) chicken

el postre	dessert
el queso	cheese
la salchicha	sausage; hot dog
la sopa	soup
las verduras	vegetables
la zanahoria	carrot

Las bebidas

el agua (mineral)	(mineral) water
el jugo (de fruta)	(fruit) juice
la leche	milk
el refresco	soft drink
el té	tea
el vino (blanco, tinto)	(white, red) wine

Repaso: el café, la cerveza

Los cognados

la banana, la ensalada, la fruta, la hamburguesa, el salmón, el sándwich, el tomate, el yogur

Las comidas

el almuerzo	lunch
la cena	dinner, supper

Repaso: el desayuno

En un restaurante

el/la camarero/a	waiter/waitress
la cuenta	check, bill
el menú	menu
el plato	dish; course

Otros sustantivos

el consejo	(piece of) advice
el detalle	detail
el/la dueño/a	owner
la tarjeta de crédito	credit card

Los adjetivos

fresco/a	fresh
frito/a	fried
fuerte	heavy (*meal, food*); strong
ligero/a	light, not heavy
rápido/a	fast

Palabras indefinidas y negativas

alguien	someone, anyone
algún (alguno/a/os/as)	some, any
jamás	never
nada	nothing, not anything
nadie	no one, nobody, not anybody
ningún (ninguno/a)	no, none, not any
tampoco	neither, not either

Repaso: algo, nunca, siempre, también

Palabras adicionales

tener (*irreg.*) **(mucha) hambre**	to be (very) hungry
tener (*irreg.*) **(mucha) sed**	to be (very) thirsty

CAPÍTULO 7

De vacaciones

Muchas personas visitan las fascinantes ruinas mayas de Copán cuando van de vacaciones en Honduras. ▶

VOCABULARIO

• Vacation and travel

GRAMÁTICA

20 Indirect Object Pronouns; **Dar** and **decir**
21 **Gustar**
22 Preterite of Regular Verbs and of **dar, hacer, ir,** and **ser**

CULTURA

• **Enfoque cultural:** Honduras y El Salvador
• **Nota cultural:** Vacaciones en el mundo hispánico
• **En los Estados Unidos y el Canadá:** Ellen Ochoa, una viajera espacial
• **Cultura en contexto:** El AVE

Multimedia

 You will learn about purchasing a train ticket in the **En contexto** video segment.

 Review vocabulary and grammar and practice language skills with the interactive CD-ROM.

WW. Get connected to the Spanish-speaking world with the *¿Qué tal?* Online Learning Center: **www.mhhe.com/quetal**.

¡Buen... *Have a good trip!*

¡Buen viaje!°

Ir en avión

el aeropuerto	airport
el/la asistente de vuelo	flight attendant
la sala de espera	waiting room
la sección de (no) fumar	(non)smoking section
el vuelo	flight

Ir en tren/autobús/barco

el barco	boat, ship
la cabina	cabin (*in a ship*)
la estación	station
de autobuses	bus
del tren	train
el maletero	porter
el puerto	port

De viaje

la agencia de viajes	travel agency
el/la agente de viajes	travel agent
el asiento	seat
el billete/el boleto/ el pasaje*	ticket
de ida	one way
de ida y vuelta	round-trip
la demora	delay
el equipaje	baggage, luggage
la llegada	arrival
el/la pasajero/a	passenger
la salida	departure
bajar (de)	to get down (from, off of)
estar atrasado/a	to be late
facturar el equipaje	to check one's bags
guardar (un puesto)	to save (a place)

hacer (*irreg.*) cola	to stand in line
hacer (*irreg.*) escalas/paradas	to make stops
hacer (*irreg.*) la(s) maleta(s)	to pack one's suitcase(s)
hacer (*irreg.*) un viaje	to take a trip
ir (*irreg.*) / estar (*irreg.*) de vacaciones	to go/be on vacation
sacar fotos	to take photos
subir (a)	to go up; to get on (*a vehicle*)
viajar	to travel

De vacaciones

hacer (*irreg.*) *camping*	to go camping
nadar	to swim
tomar el sol	to sunbathe
la camioneta	station wagon
el camping	campground
el mar	sea
las montañas	mountains
el océano	ocean
la playa	beach
la tienda (de campaña)	tent

---

*Throughout Spanish America, **el boleto** is the word used for a *ticket for travel*. **El billete** is commonly used in Spain. **El pasaje** is used throughout the Spanish-speaking world. The words **la entrada** and **la localidad** are used to refer to tickets for movies, plays, or similar functions.

Conversación

A. **Un viaje en avión.** Imagine que Ud. va a hacer un viaje en avión. El vuelo sale a las siete de la mañana. Usando los números del 1 al 9, indique en qué orden van a pasar las siguientes cosas.

a. _____ Subo al avión.

b. _____ Voy a la sala de espera.

c. _____ Hago cola para comprar el boleto de ida y vuelta y facturar el equipaje.

d. _____ Llego al aeropuerto a tiempo (*on time*) y bajo del taxi.

e. _____ Por fin se anuncia la salida del vuelo.

f. _____ Estoy atrasado/a. Salgo para el aeropuerto en taxi.

g. _____ La asistente me indica el asiento.

h. _____ Pido asiento en la sección de no fumar.

i. _____ Hay demora. Por eso todos tenemos que esperar el vuelo allí antes de subir al avión.

B. **En el aeropuerto.** ¿Cuántas cosas y acciones puede Ud. identificar o describir en este dibujo?

NOTA CULTURAL

Vacaciones en el mundo hispánico

Cuando los habitantes de países hispanohablantes **van de vacaciones**, ¿adónde van? Si quieren **viajar al extranjero**, generalmente viajan a Europa o a los Estados Unidos. Entre **los destinos**[a] **preferidos** de los Estados Unidos están California, Nueva York, Texas y Florida.

   Las playas nacionales e internacionales son una atracción común para las vacaciones también. Como a todo el mundo, a los hispanos les gusta disfrutar del[b] **sol**, del **clima tropical** y de las **playas**. Todos los países latinoamericanos que se encuentran en el Caribe ofrecen playas hermosas[c] y actividades como **bucear**[d] y **montar en tabla de vela**.[e]

De noche en South Beach, Miami

   Esquiar es otra actividad popular para las vacaciones. Durante junio, julio y agosto, los meses del invierno en el hemisferio sur, **las montañas** de Chile y la Argentina son destinos muy populares.

[a]*destinations*   [b]disfrutar de = *to enjoy*   [c]*beautiful*   [d]*scuba diving; snorkling*   [e]montar... *windsurfing*

C. Preguntas

1. Por lo general, ¿cuándo toma Ud. sus vacaciones? ¿En invierno? ¿en verano? En las vacaciones, ¿le gusta viajar o prefiere no salir de su ciudad? ¿Le gusta ir de vacaciones con su familia? ¿Prefiere ir solo/a (*alone*), con un amigo/una amiga o con un grupo de personas?

2. De los medios de transporte en **¡Buen viaje!** (página 174), ¿cuáles conoce Ud. por experiencia? De estos medios de transporte, ¿cuál es el más rápido? ¿el más económico? ¿Cuáles hacen más escalas o hacen paradas con más frecuencia? ¿Cómo prefiere Ud. viajar?

NOTA COMUNICATIVA

Other Uses of *se* (For Recognition)

It is likely that you have often seen and heard the phrase shown in the photo that accompanies this box: **Se habla español.** (*Spanish is spoken [here]*). Here are some additional examples of this use of **se** with Spanish verbs. Note how the meaning of the verb changes slightly.

Se venden billetes aquí.	*Tickets are sold here.*
Aquí no **se fuma**.	*You don't (One doesn't) smoke here. Smoking is forbidden here.*

Be alert to this use of **se** when you see it, because it will occur with some frequency in readings and in direction lines in *¿Qué tal?* The activities in this text will not require you to use this grammar point on your own, however.

Nueva York

D. ¿Dónde se hace esto? Indique el lugar (o los lugares) donde se hacen las siguientes actividades.

Lugares: en casa, en la agencia de viajes, en el aeropuerto, en el avión, en la playa

1. Se factura el equipaje.
2. Se hacen las maletas.
3. Se compran los pasajes.
4. Se hace una reservación.
5. Se espera en la sala de espera.
6. Se pide un cóctel.
7. Se mira una película.
8. Se nada y se toma el sol.

20 Expressing *to whom* or *for whom* • Indirect Object Pronouns; *Dar* and *decir*

Prueba: ¿Cómo son sus relaciones con otros?

¿Con qué frecuencia hace Ud. las siguientes actividades, con mucha frecuencia, a veces o nunca?

dinero = 17 = 10

1. *Les* escribo mensajes electrónicos (*e-mail*) a mis amigos.
2. *Les* escribo cartas a mis padres (hijos).
3. *Les* doy (*I give*) consejos a mis amigos.
4. *Les* doy consejos a mis padres (hijos).
5. *Les* digo (*I tell*) la verdad a mis amigos.
6. *Les* digo la verdad a mis padres (hijos).
7. *Les* pido dinero a mis amigos.
8. *Les* pido dinero a mis padres (hijos).

La siguiente parte de la prueba le va a mostrar (*show*) si hay reciprocidad en sus relaciones con sus amigos y con sus padres (hijos). Conteste con: **con mucha frecuencia, a veces** o **nunca.**

NA los escriben para me.

1. Mis amigos me escriben mensajes electrónicos.
2. Mis padres (hijos) me escriben cartas.
3. Mis amigos me dan consejos. *advice*
4. Mis padres (hijos) me dan consejos. *para mi.*
5. Mis amigos me dicen sus problemas. *(los)*
6. Mis padres (hijos) me dicen sus problemas.
7. Mis amigos me piden dinero.
8. Mis padres (hijos) me piden dinero.

Pedir dinero a = to ask for the money

¿Qué le dicen a Ud. sus respuestas? ¿Cómo son sus relaciones con otros?

2. Mis padres me las escriben a mí.
3. Mis amigos me los dan a mi.

INDIRECT OBJECT PRONOUNS

4. Ellos me los dan a mí.
5.

me	to/for me	**nos**	to/for us
te	to/for you (*fam. sing.*)	**os**	to/for you (*fam. pl.*)
le	to/for you (*form. sing.*), him, her, it	**les**	to/for you (*form. pl.*), them

OJO Note that indirect object pronouns have the same form as direct object pronouns, except in the third person: **le, les**.

5. Ellos me los dicen a mí.
6. Ellos me los dicen a mí.

A. Indirect object nouns and pronouns are the second recipient of the action of the verb. They usually answer the questions *to whom?* or *for whom?* in relation to the verb. The word *to* is frequently omitted in English.

Indicate the direct and indirect objects in the following sentences.

1. I'm giving her the present tomorrow.
2. Could you tell me the answer now?
3. El profesor nos va a hacer algunas preguntas.
4. ¿No me compras una revista ahora?

B. Like direct object pronouns, *indirect object pronouns* (**los pronombres del complemento indirecto**) are placed immediately before a conjugated verb. They may also be attached to an infinitive or a present participle.

No, no **te** presto el coche.
No, I won't lend you the car.

Voy a guardar**te** el asiento.
Te voy a guardar el asiento.
I'll save your seat for you.

Le estoy escribiendo una carta **a Marisol**.
Estoy escribiéndo**le** una carta **a Marisol**.
I'm writing Marisol a letter.

C. Since **le** and **les** have several different equivalents, their meaning is often clarified or emphasized with the preposition **a** followed by a pronoun (object of a preposition).

Voy a mandar**le** un telegrama **a Ud. (a él, a ella)**.
I'm going to send you (him, her) a telegram.

Les hago una comida **a Uds. (a ellos, a ellas)**.
I'm making you (them) a meal.

D. It is common for a Spanish sentence to contain both the indirect object noun and the indirect object pronoun, especially with third person forms.

Vamos a decir**le** la verdad **a Juan**.
Let's tell Juan the truth.

¿**Les** guardo los asientos **a Jorge y Marta**?
Shall I save the seats for Jorge and Marta?

[handwritten: Because in the 3rd person you need clarification]

E. As with direct object pronouns, indirect object pronouns are attached to the affirmative command form and precede the negative command form.

Sírva**nos** un café, por favor.
Serve us some coffee, please.

No me dé su número de teléfono ahora.
Don't give me your phone number now.

F. Here are some verbs frequently used with indirect objects.

[handwritten: require to pronoun]

dar (*irreg.*)	to give	**pedir (i, i)**	to ask for
decir (*irreg.*)	to say; to tell	**preguntar**	to ask (*a question*)
escribir	to write	**prestar**	to lend
explicar	to explain	**prometer**	to promise
hablar	to speak	**recomendar (ie)**	to recommend
mandar	to send	**regalar**	to give (*as a gift*)
ofrecer (ofrezco)	to offer	**servir (i, i)**	to serve

[handwritten: prestar a = to lend / prestar de = to borrow]

Dar AND decir

dar (to give)		decir (to say; to tell)	
doy	damos	digo	decimos
das	dais	dices	decís
da	dan	dice	dicen

- **Dar** and **decir** are almost always used with indirect object pronouns in Spanish.

¿Cuándo **me das** el dinero?
When will you give me the money?

¿Por qué no **le dice** Ud. la verdad, señor?
Why don't you tell him/her the truth, sir?

OJO

In Spanish it is necessary to distinguish between the verbs **dar** (*to give*) and **regalar** (*to give as a gift*). Also, do not confuse **decir** (*to say* or *to tell*) with **hablar** (*to speak*).

- **Dar** and **decir** also have irregular formal command forms. There is a written accent on **dé** to distinguish it from the preposition **de**.

Formal commands of **dar** and **decir**:

dar → **dé, den**
decir → **diga, digan**

Práctica

A. De vuelta a Honduras

Paso 1. Your friends the Padillas, from Honduras, need help arranging for and getting on their flight back home. Explain how you will help them, using the cues as a guide.

MODELO: confirmar el vuelo → Les confirmo el vuelo.

1. llamar un taxi
2. bajar (*to carry down*) las maletas
3. guardar el equipaje
4. facturar el equipaje
5. guardar el puesto en la cola
6. guardar el asiento en la sala de espera
7. comprar una revista
8. por fin decir adiós

Paso 2. Now explain the same sequence of actions as if you were talking about your friend Guillermo: *Le confirmo el vuelo*.

Paso 3. Finally, tell your friend Marisol how you will help her: *Te confirmo el vuelo*.

B. ¿Qué hacen estas personas? Complete las siguientes oraciones con un verbo lógico y un pronombre de complemento indirecto.

MODELO: El vicepresidente ___*le ofrece*___ consejos al presidente.

Verbos posibles: dar, ofrecer, prestar, prometer, servir

1. Romeo _____ flores a Julieta.
2. Snoopy _____ besos (*kisses*) a Lucy… ¡Y a ella no le gusta!
3. Eva _____ una manzana a Adán.
4. Ann Landers _____ consejos a sus lectores (*readers*).
5. Los bancos _____ dinero a las personas que quieren comprar una casa.
6. Los asistentes de vuelo _____ bebidas a los pasajeros.
7. George Washington _____ a su padre decir la verdad.

C. ¿Qué va a pasar? Dé varias respuestas.

Palabras útiles: medicinas, Santa Claus, tarjetas navideñas (*Christmas cards*), flores, juguetes (*toys*)

1. Su amiga Elena está en el hospital con un ataque de apendicitis. Todos le mandan… Le escriben… Las enfermeras (*nurses*) le dan… De comer, le sirven…
2. Es Navidad. Los niños les prometen a sus padres… Les piden… También le escriben… Le piden… Los padres les mandan… a sus amigos. Les regalan…
3. Hay una demora y el avión no despega (*takes off*) a tiempo. Un asistente de vuelo nos sirve… Otra asistente de vuelo nos ofrece… El piloto nos dice…
4. Mi coche no funciona hoy. Mi amigo me presta… Mis padres me preguntan… Luego me dan…
5. Es la última (*last*) semana de clases y hay exámenes finales la próxima semana. En la clase de computación, todos le preguntan al profesor… El profesor les explica a los estudiantes…

D. En un restaurante. Imagine that your four-year-old cousin Benjamín has never eaten in a restaurant before. Explain to him what will happen, filling in the blanks with the appropriate indirect object pronoun.

Primero el camarero _____[1] indica una mesa desocupada.[a] Luego tú _____[2] pides el menú al camarero. También _____[3] haces preguntas sobre los platos y las especialidades de la casa y _____[4] dices tus preferencias. El camarero _____[5] trae la comida. Por fin tu papá _____[6] pide la cuenta al camarero. Si tú quieres pagar, _____[7] pides dinero a tu papá y _____[8] das el dinero al camarero.

[a]*vacant*

Conversación

Entrevista: ¿Quién… ? Whom do you associate with the below actions? Working with a partner, ask and answer questions to find out information about each topic.

MODELO: darle consejos →
    E1: ¿A quién le das consejos?
    E2: Con frecuencia le doy consejos a mi compañero de cuarto. ¡Él los necesita!
    E1: ¿Quién te da consejos a ti?
    E2: Mis abuelos me dan muchos consejos.

1. darle consejos
2. pedirle ayuda con los estudios
3. mandarle flores
4. decirle secretos
5. hacerle favores
6. escribirle tarjetas postales (*postcards*)
7. ofrecerle bebidas

¿Recuerda Ud.?

You have already used forms of **gustar** to express your likes and dislikes (**Primeros pasos**). Review what you know by answering the following questions. Then, changing their form as needed, use them to interview your instructor:

1. ¿Te gusta el café (el vino, el té,…)?
2. ¿Te gusta jugar al béisbol (al golf, al vólibol, al…)?
3. ¿Te gusta viajar en avión (fumar, viajar en tren,…)?
4. ¿Qué te gusta más, estudiar o ir a fiestas (trabajar o descansar, cocinar o comer)?

---

21 Expressing Likes and Dislikes • *Gustar*

Los chilenos viajeros

Según el anuncio, a muchos chilenos les gusta viajar a otros países. Lea el anuncio y luego indique si las oraciones son ciertas o falsas.

1. A los chilenos les gusta viajar sólo en este hemisferio.
2. A los chilenos les gustan mucho las playas.
3. Sólo les gusta viajar en países de habla española.
4. No les gustaría el precio del viaje.

MEDIO MILLON DE CHILENOS
DE VACACIONES 2003 AL EXTRANJERO
Y USTED... NO SE QUEDE SIN VIAJAR
¡ RESERVE AHORA MISMO !
El próximo verano '03, con el bajo valor del dólar, muchas personas desearán viajar, los cupos disponibles se agotarán rapidamente. ¡Asegure sus vacaciones! Elija ahora cualquiera de nuestros fantásticos programas.
MIAMI - ORLANDO - BAHAMAS - MÉXICO - CANCÚN ACAPULCO - IXTAPA - COSTA RICA - RIO - SALVADOR PLAYA TAMBOR - PUNTA CANA - LA HABANA VARADERO - GUATEMALA - SUDÁFRICA
Infórmese sobre nuestro SUPER CRÉDITO PREFERENCIAL
Economy Tour
Santa Magdalena 94, Providencia
☎ 2334429 - 2331774 - 2314252 2328294 - 2318608 - 2334862
Fax: 2334428

Y a Ud., ¿le gusta viajar? ¿Le gustan los viajes en avión? ¿Cuál de estos lugares le gustaría visitar?

CONSTRUCTIONS WITH *gustar*

Spanish	Literal Equivalent	English Phrasing
Me gusta la playa.	The beach is pleasing to me.	*I like the beach.*
No le gustan sus cursos.	His courses are not pleasing to him.	*He doesn't like his courses.*
Nos gusta leer.	Reading is pleasing to us.	*We like to read.*

You have been using the verb **gustar** since the beginning of *¿Qué tal?* to express likes and dislikes. However, **gustar** does not literally mean *to like,* but rather *to be pleasing.*

Me gusta viajar.
Traveling is pleasing to me. (I like traveling.)

A. **Gustar** is always used with an indirect object pronoun: Someone or something is pleasing *to* someone else. The verb must agree with the subject of the sentence—that is, the person or thing that is pleasing.

Me **gusta** la comida mexicana.
Mexican food is pleasing to me. (I like Mexican food.)

Me **gustan** los viajes aventureros.
Adventurous trips are pleasing to me.
    (I like adventurous trips.)

B. A phrase with **a** + a *noun* or *pronoun* is often used for clarification or emphasis. This prepositional phrase usually appears before the indirect object pronoun, but it can also appear after the verb.

CLARIFICATION

¿Le gusta **a Ud.** viajar?
Do you like to travel?

A David no le gustan los aviones.
David doesn't like airplanes.

EMPHASIS

> Note that an infinitive is viewed as a singular subject in Spanish.

A mí me gusta viajar en avión, pero **a mi esposo** le gusta viajar en coche.
*I like to travel by plane, but **my husband** likes to travel by car.*

O J O
> The indirect object pronoun *must* be used with **gustar** even when the prepositional phrase **a** + *noun* or *pronoun* is used.

WOULD LIKE/WOULDN'T LIKE

What one *would* or *would not* like to do is expressed with the form **gustaría*** + *infinitive* and the appropriate indirect objects.

A mí me gustaría viajar a Colombia.
I would like to travel to Colombia.

Nos gustaría hacer *camping* este verano.
We would like to go camping this summer.

---

*This is one of the forms of the conditional of **gustar.** You will study all of the forms of the conditional in Grammar Section 45.

Práctica

A. Gustos y preferencias

Paso 1. Using the models as a guide, tell whether or not you like the following.

> MODELOS: ¿el café? → (No) Me gusta el café.
> ¿los pasteles? → (No) Me gustan los pasteles.

1. ¿el vino?
2. ¿los niños pequeños?
3. ¿la música clásica?
4. ¿Ricky Martin?
5. ¿el invierno?
6. ¿hacer cola?
7. ¿el chocolate?
8. ¿las películas de terror?
9. ¿las clases que empiezan a las ocho de la mañana?
10. ¿cocinar?
11. ¿la gramática?
12. ¿las clases de este semestre/trimestre?
13. ¿los vuelos con muchas escalas?
14. ¿bailar en las discotecas?

Paso 2. Now share your reactions with a classmate. He or she will respond with one of the following reactions. How do your likes and dislikes compare?

> REACCIONES
>
> A mí también.   *So do I.*   Pues a mí, sí.   *Well, I do.*
> A mí tampoco.   *Neither do I.*   Pues a mí, no.   *Well, I don't.*

B. ¿Adónde vamos este verano?

Paso 1. The members of the Soto family all prefer different vacation activities and, of course, would like to go to different places this summer. Imagine that you are one of the Sotos and describe the family's various preferences, following the model.

> MODELO: padre/nadar: ir a la playa →
> A mi padre le gusta nadar. Le gustaría ir a la playa.

1. padre/el oceano: ir a la playa
2. hermanos pequeños/nadar también: ir a la playa
3. hermano Ernesto/hacer *camping*: ir a las montañas
4. abuelos/descansar: quedarse en casa
5. madre/la tranquilidad: visitar un pueblecito (*small town*) en la costa
6. hermana Elena/discotecas: pasar las vacaciones en una ciudad grande
7. mí/¿ ?

Paso 2. Now, remembering what you have learned about the vacation preferences of your imaginary family, answer the following questions.

1. ¿A quién le gustaría ir a Nueva York?
2. ¿A quién le gustaría viajar a Acapulco?
3. ¿Quién no quiere salir de casa?
4. ¿A quién le gustaría ir a Cabo San Lucas?
5. ¿Quién quiere ir a Colorado?

Conversación

A. ¿Conoce bien a sus compañeros de clase? Piense en una persona de la clase que Ud. conoce. En su opinión, ¿a esa persona le gustan o no las siguientes cosas? Apunte: **Sí, le gusta(n)** o **No, no le gusta(n)**. Luego, entreviste a su compañero/a para verificar sus respuestas.

1. la música clásica
2. el color negro
3. viajar en coche
4. la comida mexicana
5. tener clases por la mañana
6. estudiar otras lenguas
7. las películas trágicas
8. las casas viejas

NOTA COMUNICATIVA

More about Expressing Likes and Dislikes

Here are some ways to express intense likes and dislikes.

Me gusta mucho/muchísimo.	*I like it a lot/a whole lot.*
No me gusta (para) nada.	*I don't like it at all.*

To express *love* and *hate* in reference to likes and dislikes, you can use **encantar** and **odiar**.

- **Encantar** is used just like **gustar**.

  Les encanta viajar, ¿verdad?   *You love traveling, right?*

- **Odiar,** on the other hand, functions like a transitive verb (one that can take a direct object).

  Mi madre **odia** viajar sola.   *My mother hates traveling alone.*

To express interest in something, use **interesar**. This verb is also used like **gustar** and **encantar**.

  Me interesa la comida salvadoreña.   *I'm interested in Salvadorian food.*

B. ¿Qué te gusta? ¿Qué odias? Almost every situation has aspects that one likes or dislikes, even hates. Pick at least two of the following situations and tell what you like or don't like about them. Add as many details as you can, using **me gustaría** when possible.

MODELO: en la playa →
Me gusta mucho el agua, pero no me gusta el sol. Por eso no me gusta pasar todo el día en la playa. Me encanta nadar pero odio la arena. Me gustaría más ir a nadar en una piscina.

Situaciones: en un avión, en el coche, en un autobús, en un tren, en una discoteca, en una fiesta, en la biblioteca, en clase, en casa con mis padres/hijos, en casa con mis amigos, en una cafetería, en la playa

Enfoque *cultural*

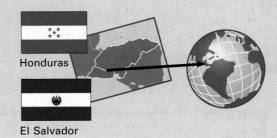

Honduras

El Salvador

Honduras y El Salvador

Datos esenciales

Honduras

- Nombre oficial: República de Honduras
- Capital: Tegucigalpa
- Población: 6.000.000 de habitantes
- Moneda: el lempira
- Idioma oficial: el español

El Salvador

- Nombre oficial: República de El Salvador
- Capital: San Salvador
- Población: 6.000.000 de habitantes
- Moneda: el dólar
- Idioma oficial: el español

¡Fíjese!

- El centro ceremonial maya de Copán, en Honduras, es hoy un parque nacional que contiene una colección de ruinas mayas superadas[a] sólo por las ruinas de Tikal en Guatemala.

- La moneda de Honduras, el lempira, lleva el nombre de un cacique[b] indígena que luchó contra[c] los españoles.

- El nombre indígena de la capital de Honduras, Tegucigalpa, significa «cerros de plata».[d] Honduras recibe su nombre español por la profundidad[e] de sus aguas costeras.[f] El nombre indígena de El Salvador es Cuzcatlán, que significa «tierra de joyas[g] y cosas preciosas».

- Las erupciones del Volcán de Izalco en El Salvador son constantes entre los años 1770 y 1966, por casi dos

[a]*exceeded (in quality)* [b]*chief* [c]*luchó… fought against* [d]*cerros… silver hills* [e]*depth* [f]*coastal* [g]*jewels*

siglos.[h] Este volcán se conoce con el nombre de «el faro[i] del Pacífico», porque está encendido[j] por muchos años y sirve de[k] guía a los navegantes.

[h]*centuries* [i]*lighthouse* [j]*lit up* [k]*sirve de… serves as a*

El Volcán de Izalco, El Salvador

Conozca… al Arzobispo[a] Óscar Arnulfo Romero

El 24 de marzo de 1980 un héroe de El Salvador es asesinado mientras oficia una misa.[b] En vida,[c] el arzobispo Óscar Arnulfo Romero (1917–1980) es la conciencia de su país. Critica a los líderes políticos por su violencia e injusticia, y trabaja para mejorar[d] las condiciones económicas y sociales del país. Por eso, es nominado para el premio Nóbel de la Paz[e] en 1979.

[a]*Archbishop* [b]*oficia… he celebrates a Mass* [c]*life* [d]*improve* [e]*premio… Nobel Peace Prize*

Capítulo 7 of the video to accompany *¿Qué tal?* contains cultural footage about Honduras and El Salvador.

WW. Visit the *¿Qué tal?* website at www.mhhe.com/quétal.

22 **Talking about the Past (1)** • Preterite of Regular Verbs and of *dar, hacer, ir,* and *ser*

Elisa habla de su viaje a Puerto Rico

«Recientemente *fui* a Puerto Rico para escribir un artículo sobre ese país. *Hice* el viaje en avión. El vuelo *fue* largo, pues el avión *hizo* escala en Miami. *Pasé* una semana entera en la isla. *Hablé* con muchas personas de la industria turística y *visité* los lugares más interesantes de Puerto Rico. También *comí* mucha comida típica de la isla. Además, *tomé* el sol en las preciosas playas puertorriqueñas y *nadé* en el mar Caribe. Me *divertí* mucho. ¡Mi viaje *fue* casi como unas vacaciones!»

Comprensión: ¿Cierto o falso?

1. Elisa fue a Puerto Rico para pasar sus vacaciones.
2. El avión hizo escala en los Estados Unidos.
3. Elisa no visitó ningún lugar importante de Puerto Rico.
4. Elisa también pasó tiempo cerca del océano.

In previous chapters of *¿Qué tal?*, you have talked about a number of your activities, but always in the present tense. In this section, you will begin to work with the forms of the preterite, one of the tenses that will allow you to talk about the past. To talk about all aspects of the past in Spanish, you need to know how to use two *simple tenses* (tenses formed without an auxiliary or "helping" verb): the preterite and the imperfect. In this chapter, you will learn the regular forms of the preterite and those of four irregular verbs: **dar, hacer, ir,** and **ser.** In this chapter and in **Capítulos 8, 9, 10,** and **11,** you will learn more about preterite forms and their uses as well as about the imperfect and the ways in which it is used alone and with the preterite.

The *preterite* (**el pretérito**) has several equivalents in English. For example, **hablé** can mean *I spoke* or *I did speak.* The preterite is used to report finished, completed actions or states of being in the past. If the action or state of being is viewed as completed—no matter how long it lasted or took to complete—it will be expressed with the preterite.

Elisa talks about her trip to Puerto Rico. Recently I went to Puerto Rico to write an article about that country. I made the trip by plane. The flight was long because the plane made a stop in Miami. I spent a whole week on the island. I spoke with many people in the tourist industry and I visited the most interesting places in Puerto Rico. I also ate lots of typical food from the island. Furthermore, I sunbathed on the beautiful Puerto Rican beaches and swam in the Caribbean Sea. I had lots of fun. My trip was almost like a vacation!

Paso 2. ¿Quién lo dijo (*said*), Evangelina o Liliana?

1. Mis compañeras no pasaron mucho tiempo en casa hoy.
2. ¡El examen fue desastroso!
3. Estudié mucho hoy.
4. Me gustó mucho el programa de «Oprah» hoy.
5. ¿Saben? Hablé con mis padres hoy y…

Paso 3. Ahora vuelva a contar (*tell*) cómo fue el día de Liliana, pero desde el punto de vista de sus compañeras de cuarto. Luego diga cómo fue el día de Teresa y Evangelina según Liliana.

En los Estados Unidos y el Canadá...

Ellen Ochoa, una viajera espacial

La Dra. Ellen L. Ochoa, de California (1958–), es **la primera mujer hispana astronauta** de los Estados Unidos; trabaja en la NASA desde 1990. Se graduó con un **doctorado**[a] en **ingeniería eléctrica** de la Universidad de Stanford. Pasó más de 700 horas viajando en el espacio, y su próxima misión está programada para el año 2002. Entre[b] sus muchos honores está el de ser[c] miembro de la Comisión Presidencial

Ellen Ochoa

para la Celebración de Mujeres en la Historia Americana.

La Dra. Ochoa no es la única persona hispana en la NASA. Hay otros **cinco astronautas hispanos** en misiones espaciales: el argentino Frank Caldeiro, el costarricense[d] Franklin Chang-Díaz, los españoles Pedro Duque y Michael López-Alegría y el peruano Carlos Noriega.

[a]*Ph.D.* [b]*Among* [c]*el… that of being* [d]*Costa Rican*

Conversación

NOTA COMUNICATIVA

Putting Events in Sequence

You can use the following phrases to put past events into a simple sequence in Spanish. You will learn additional words and phrases of this kind as you learn more about the past tenses.

Primero…	First . . .
Luego… y…	Then . . . and . . .
Después… y…	Afterward . . . and . . .
Finalmente (Por fin)…	Finally . . .

Afeitarse,
se afeitó

A. El sábado por la tarde… The following drawings depict what Julián did last Saturday night. Match the phrases below with the individual drawings in the sequence. Then narrate what Julián did, using verbs in the preterite. Use as many of the words and phrases from the preceding **Nota comunicativa** as possible.

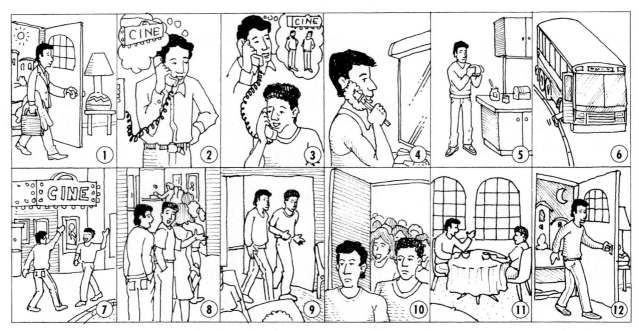

a. _____ hacer cola para comprar las entradas (*tickets*)

b. _____ regresar tarde a casa

c. _____ volver a casa después de trabajar

d. _____ ir a un café a tomar algo

e. _____ llegar al cine al mismo tiempo

f. _____ llamar a un amigo

g. _____ no gustarles la película

h. _____ comer rápidamente

i. _____ ducharse y afeitarse

j. _____ entrar en el cine

k. _____ ir al cine en autobús

l. _____ decidir encontrarse (*to meet up*) en el cine

B. Preguntas

1. ¿Qué le(s) dio Ud. a su mejor amigo/a (su esposo/a, su novio/a, sus hijos) para su cumpleaños el año pasado? ¿Qué le regaló a Ud. esa persona para su cumpleaños? ¿Alguien le mandó a Ud. flores el año pasado? ¿Le mandó Ud. flores a alguien?

2. ¿Dónde y a qué hora comió Ud. ayer? ¿Con quién(es) comió? ¿Le gustaron todos los platos que comió? Si comió fuera, ¿quién pagó?

3. ¿Cuándo decidió Ud. estudiar español? ¿Cuándo lo empezó a estudiar? ¿Va a seguir con el español el semestre/trimestre que viene?

4. ¿Qué hizo Ud. ayer? ¿Adónde fue? ¿Con quién(es)? ¿Ayudó a alguien a hacer algo? ¿Lo/La llamó alguien? ¿Llamó Ud. a alguien?

UN POCO DE TODO

A. Preguntas: La última vez. Conteste las siguientes preguntas. Añada (*Add*) más información si puede.

MODELO: La última vez que Ud. fue a una fiesta, ¿le llevó un regalo al anfitrión (*host*)? →
Sí, le llevé flores / una botella de vino. (No, no le llevé nada.)

La última vez que Ud...

1. hizo un viaje, ¿le mandó una tarjeta postal a un amigo / a una amiga?
2. tomó el autobús / el metro, ¿le ofreció su asiento a una persona mayor?
3. vio a su profesor(a) de español en público, ¿le habló en español?
4. comió en un restaurante, ¿le recomendó un plato a su compañero/a?
5. entró en un edificio, ¿le abrió la puerta a otra persona?

B. Recomendaciones para las vacaciones. Complete the following vacation suggestion with the correct form of the words in parentheses, as suggested by the context. When two possibilities are given in parentheses, select the correct word.

(Les/Los[1]) quiero decir (algo/nada[2]) sobre (el/la[3]) ciudad de Machu Picchu. ¿Ya (lo/la[4]) (saber/conocer[5]) Uds.? (Ser/Estar[6]) situada en los Andes, a unos ochenta kilómetros[a] de la ciudad de Cuzco, Perú. Machu Picchu es conocida[b] como (el/la[7]) ciudad escondida[c] de los incas. Se dice que (ser/estar[8]) una de las manifestaciones (más/tan[9]) importantes de la arquitectura incaica. Era[d] refugio y a la vez[e] ciudad de vacaciones de los reyes[f] (incaico[10]).

Uds. deben (visitarlo/visitarla[11]). (Le/Les[12]) gustaría porque (ser/estar[13]) un sitio inolvidable.[g] Es mejor (ir/van[14]) a Machu Picchu en primavera o verano —son las (mejor[15]) estaciones para visitar este lugar. Pero es necesario (comprar/compran[16]) los boletos con anticipación,[h] porque (mucho[17]) turistas de todos los (país[18]) del mundo visitan este sitio extraordinario. ¡(*Yo:* Saber/Conocer[19]) que a Uds. (los/les[20]) va a gustar el viaje!

[a]ochenta... 50 millas [b]*known* [c]*hidden* [d]*It was* [e]a... *at the same time* [f]*kings* [g]*unforgettable*
[h]con... *ahead of time*

Comprensión: ¿Cierto a falso?   Conteste según la descripción.

1. Machu Picchu está en Chile.
2. Fue un lugar importante en el pasado.
3. Todavía es una atracción turística de gran interés.
4. Sólo los turistas latinoamericanos conocen Machu Picchu.

VIDEOTECA: En contexto

FUNCTION

Purchasing a train ticket

In this video segment, Juan Carlos is talking to a ticket agent about purchasing a train ticket. As you watch the segment, pay particular attention to the words they use to talk about train schedules and about the arrangements that Juan Carlos makes for travel. What is the problem with the train schedule? What finally happens?

EL PERÚ

A. Lluvia de ideas

- Donde Ud. vive, ¿cuál es el medio de transporte más práctico para viajar de una ciudad a otra? En otras áreas del país, ¿se viaja del mismo (*same*) modo? ¿Cómo viajan las personas que no tienen coche?
- ¿Hay una estación de tren en su pueblo o ciudad? ¿Viaja Ud. en tren con frecuencia? ¿Cuándo fue la última vez (*time*)?

B. Dictado.
A continuación está la primera parte del diálogo entre Juan Carlos y la agente de billetes. Complétela con las palabras o frases que faltan (*are missing*).

JUAN CARLOS:	Buenas tardes. Un _____[1] de ida y _____[2] para Tarma, por favor. Sale a las dos y media, ¿verdad?
VENDEDORA DE BILLETES:	Lo siento,[a] pero ese _____[3] está _____[4] hoy. No sale hasta las seis y cuarto.
JUAN CARLOS:	¿Por qué? ¿Qué pasa?
VENDEDORA DE BILLETES:	No estoy segura, pero parece que hay un problema mecánico.
JUAN CARLOS:	Pero, los _____[5] en las otras líneas no _____[6] atrasados, ¿verdad?
VENDEDORA DE BILLETES:	No, los otros trenes deben _____[7] a la hora en punto.

[a]Lo... *I'm sorry*

C. Un diálogo original

Paso 1. Con un compañero / una compañera, dramatice el diálogo entre Juan Carlos y la agente de billetes.

Paso 2. Un viaje a Nueva York

E1: Ud. habla con un(a) agente de viajes porque desea ir a Nueva York. Tiene diez días de vacaciones. No quiere pagar demasiado dinero.

E2: Ud. es el/la agente de viajes. Debe ofrecer más de una opción.

Cultura en contexto
El AVE

El país hispano donde más se viaja en tren es España. Como toda Europa, España tiene un sistema ferroviario bien desarrollado[a] que ofrece una variedad de servicios. El más famoso es el AVE, o «Alta Velocidad[b] Española». Este tren viaja largas distancias con la máxima velocidad de 220 kilómetros (137.5 millas) por hora.

[a]sistema... *well-developed railroad system*
[b]Alta... *High-Speed*

PASO FINAL

A LEER

Estrategia: Identifying the Source of a Passage

If you pick up the *New England Journal of Medicine*, what sort of articles do you expect to find? For whom are they written and for what purpose? Would you anticipate similar articles in *People* magazine?

You can often make useful predictions about an article—its narrative style, its target audience, the author's purpose, and so forth—if you know something about the magazine or journal from which it comes. The article you are about to read was first published in *GeoMundo*, a Spanish-language magazine not unlike *National Geographic*. Knowing this, which of the following topics do you think might be treated in a given issue of this magazine?

1. the Incas and Machu Picchu
2. how to remove coffee stains from silk
3. the search for a great white shark
4. Montreal by night

All but number two might appear in *GeoMundo*. Keeping in mind the source of a reading will often help you to predict its content.

> **Sobre la lectura...** *GeoMundo* is for the reader who is interested in world travel, different cultures and customs, the environment, and similar issues. The following article was taken from a travel section called «**Geoturismo**». This particular section deals with Mexico.

México es mucho más que playas

Además de[a] los populares centros de vacaciones en las costas como Acapulco y Cancún, México tiene otros lugares donde se puede <u>descubrir</u> algo de la historia y la cultura del país. Uno de ellos es la península de Yucatán, donde floreció[b] la gran civilización maya. Allí se puede visitar Palenque, con su <u>imponente pirámide</u> en una exuberante <u>selva</u> tropical. También se puede visitar Uxmal, una clásica ciudad maya, y Chichén Itzá, centro cultural de la región entre los siglos X al XIII. Todos están cerca de excelentes hoteles y restaurantes.

Otra alternativa son las ciudades coloniales de México, cuya[c] elegante arquitectura del siglo XVI <u>refleja</u> su génesis española. Explore estas ciudades:

- San Miguel de Allende, una bulliciosa[d] ciudad donde se han refugiado[e] artistas de todo el mundo
- Guanajuato, sede[f] del prestigioso Festival <u>Cervantino</u> de teatro, con sus serpenteantes calles adoquinadas[g]
- Zacatecas, con sus edificios <u>construidos</u> de <u>granito</u> rosa
- Guadalajara, ciudad donde nació[h] el mariachi

En ninguna de ellas hay dificultad en encontrar[i] un buen lugar para quedarse, pues hay hoteles y pensiones para todos los gustos y bolsillos.[j] ∎

[a]Además... *In addition to* [b]*flourished* [c]*whose* [d]*lively* [e]se... *have taken refuge* [f]*site* [g]serpenteantes ... *winding cobblestoned streets* [h]*was born* [i]*finding* [j]*wallets* (figurative, literally *pockets*)

Guanajuato, México

Comprensión

A. **El título.** Lea otra vez el título del artículo. ¿Por qué se llama así esta lectura? Es decir, ¿qué significa?

1. México tiene más playas que otros países de Latinoamérica.
2. Cuando se habla de las vacaciones en México, muchas personas piensan solamente en las playas mexicanas.
3. Nadie va a las playas mexicanas para pasar sus vacaciones.

B. **¿Adónde les gustaría ir?** A base del (*Based on the*) artículo, identifique un lugar de interés para los siguientes turistas.

1. el profesor Underwood, arqueólogo dedicado al estudio de las culturas indígenas
2. Ana Carbón, guitarrista que tiene interés en la música mexicana
3. Pedro Pérez, pintor y escultor

 A ESCRIBIR

De vacaciones en México. Prepare un reportaje sobre una de las ciudades mencionadas en el artículo. Puede ir a la biblioteca para hacer su investigación. Antes de escribir, haga lo siguiente.

Paso 1. Escoja la ciudad que va a ser el enfoque (*focus*) de su investigación.

Paso 2. Piense en el tipo de información que quiere incluir. Haga una lista de por lo menos (*at least*) tres de los temas que va a investigar (como, por ejemplo, festividades regionales, geografía, platos típicos del lugar, etcétera).

Paso 3. Vaya a la biblioteca o consulte libros de referencia o revistas para hacer su reportaje.

Paso 4. Escriba una breve composición sobre ese lugar.

En resumen

GRAMÁTICA

To review the grammar points presented in this chapter, refer to the indicated grammar presentations. You'll find further practice of these structures in the Workbook/Laboratory Manual, on the CD-ROM, and on the website.

20. Indirect Object Pronouns; *Dar* and *decir*

You should know how to avoid repetition by using indirect object pronouns to express to whom you're telling or giving, or for whom you're doing something.

21. *Gustar*

Do you know how to talk about things you and others like and like to do?

22. Preterite of Regular Verbs and of *dar, hacer, ir*, and *ser*

Do you know how to conjugate regular preterite verbs? Can you use the irregular verbs **dar, hacer, ir,** and **ser** in the preterite as well?

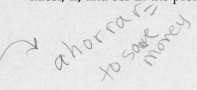

ahorrar= to save money

VOCABULARIO

Los verbos		¡Buen viaje!	
anunciar	to announce	**el aeropuerto**	airport
bajar (de)	to get down (from); to get off (of)	**la agencia de viajes**	travel agency
		el/la agente de viajes	travel agent
contar (ue)	to tell	**el asiento**	seat
dar (*irreg.*)	to give	**el/la asistente de vuelo**	flight attendant
decir (*irreg.*)	to say; to tell	**el autobús**	bus
encantar	to like very much, love	**el avión**	airplane
explicar	to explain	**el barco**	boat, ship
facturar	to check (*baggage*)	**el billete/boleto**	ticket
fumar	to smoke	**de ida**	one-way
guardar	to save (*a place*)	**de ida y vuelta**	round-trip
gustar	to be pleasing	**la cabina**	cabin (*in a ship*)
mandar	to send	**la camioneta**	station wagon
mostrar (ue)	to show	**el** *camping*	campground
nadar	to swim	**la clase turística**	tourist class
odiar	to hate	**la demora**	delay
ofrecer	to offer	**el equipaje**	baggage, luggage
prestar	to lend	**la estación**	station
prometer	to promise	**de autobuses**	bus
recomendar (ie)	to recommend	**del tren**	train
regalar	to give (*as a gift*)	**la foto(grafía)**	photo(graph)
sacar	to take (*photos*)	**la llegada**	arrival
subir (a)	to go up; to get on (*a vehicle*)	**el maletero**	porter
		el mar	sea
viajar	to travel	**la montaña**	mountain

el océano	ocean
el pasaje	passage, ticket
el/la pasajero/a	passenger
la primera clase	first class
el puerto	port
el puesto	place (*in line, etc.*)
la sala de espera	waiting room
la salida	departure
la sección de (no) fumar	(non)smoking section
la tarjeta (postal)	(post)card
la tienda (de campaña)	tent
el tren	train
el vuelo	flight
estar (*irreg.*) de vacaciones	to be on vacation
hacer (*irreg.*) *camping*	to go camping
hacer (*irreg.*) cola	to stand in line
hacer (*irreg.*) escalas/paradas	to make stops
hacer (*irreg.*) la(s) maleta(s)	to pack one's suitcase(s)

ir (*irreg.*) de vacaciones	to go on vacation
tomar el sol	to sunbathe

Repaso: hacer (*irreg.*) un viaje, la playa

Otros sustantivos

la flor	flower
el mundo	world
el/la niño/a	child; boy (girl)

Los adjetivos

atrasado/a (*with* estar)	late
solo/a	alone
último/a	last

Palabras adicionales

a tiempo	on time
de viaje	on a trip
lo que	what, that which
me gustaría…	I would (really) like . . .

Los días festivos

Una celebración navideña ▶
en La Habana, Cuba

VOCABULARIO

- Holidays and celebrations
- Emotions and physical conditions

GRAMÁTICA

23 Irregular Preterites
24 Preterite of Stem-Changing Verbs
25 Double Object Pronouns

CULTURA

- **Enfoque cultural:** Cuba
- **Nota cultural:** Celebraciones
- **En los Estados Unidos y el Canadá:** El día de César Chávez
- **Cultura en contexto:** La música popular

Multimedia

You will learn about returning a purchase in the **En contexto** video segment.

Review vocabulary and grammar and practice language skills with the interactive CD-ROM.

WW. Get connected to the Spanish-speaking world with the *¿Qué tal?* Online Learning Center: **www.mhhe.com/quetal.**

PASO 1 Vocabulario

Los días festivos y las fiestas

La fiesta de cumpleaños

¡FELICITACIONES!

regalar
(to give
[as a gift])

los refrescos

cumplir años
(to have a birthday)

los entremeses

Magda cumple años hoy. Sus amigos le hacen una fiesta de sorpresa y le regalan algo especial.

la sorpresa	surprise	pasarlo bien/mal	to have a good/bad time
celebrar	to celebrate	reunirse (me reúno)	to get together (with)
dar (*irreg.*)/hacer (*irreg.*) una fiesta	to give/have a party	(con)	
		ser (*irreg.*) + en + *place*	to take place at (*place*)
divertirse (ie, i)	to have a good time	—¿Dónde es la fiesta?	*Where is the party?*
faltar	to be absent, lacking	—(Es) En casa de Julio.	(*It's*) *At Julio's house.*
gastar dinero	to spend money		

Vocabulario útil*

el Día de Año Nuevo	New Year's Day
el Día de los Reyes Magos	Day of the Magi (Three Kings)
el Día de San Valentín (de los Enamorados)	Valentine's Day

*The items on this list are not considered active vocabulary for this chapter. Just learn the holidays and celebrations that are relevant to you.

el Día de San Patricio	Saint Patrick's Day
la Pascua (de los hebreos)	Passover
la Pascua (Florida)	Easter
las vacaciones de primavera	spring break
el Cinco de Mayo	Cinco de Mayo (*Mexican awareness celebration in some parts of the U.S.*)
el Día del Canadá	Canada Day (July 1)
el Cuatro de Julio (el Día de la Independencia [estadounidense])	Independence Day (*U.S.*)
el Día de la Raza	Columbus Day (*Hispanic awareness day in some parts of the U.S.*)
el Día de todos los Santos	All Saints' Day (November 1)
el Día de los Muertos	Day of the Dead (November 2)
el Día de Acción de Gracias	Thanksgiving
la Fiesta de las Luces	Hanukkah
la Nochebuena	Christmas Eve
la Navidad	Christmas
la Noche Vieja	New Year's Eve
el cumpleaños	birthday
el día del santo	saint's day (*the saint for whom one is named*)
la quinceañera	young woman's fifteenth birthday party

Conversación

A. Definiciones. ¿Qué palabra o frase corresponde a estas definiciones?

1. el día en que se celebra el nacimiento (*birth*) de Jesús
2. algo que alguien no sabe o no espera
3. algo de comer y algo de beber que se sirve en las fiestas (dos respuestas)
4. el día en que algunos hispanos visitan el cementerio para honrar la memoria de los difuntos (*deceased*)
5. la fiesta en que se celebra el hecho (*fact*) de que una muchacha cumple quince años
6. el día en que todo el mundo (*everybody*) debe llevar ropa verde
7. la noche en que se celebra el final del año
8. palabra que se dice para mostrar una reacción muy favorable, por ejemplo, cuando un amigo cumple años

NOTA CULTURAL

Celebraciones

En la vida de uno hay muchas ocasiones para dar fiestas. Claro que todos los años hay que celebrar **el cumpleaños**. Pero en partes del mundo hispánico se celebra también **el día del santo**. En el calendario religioso católico cada día corresponde al nombre de un santo. Si Ud. se llama Juan, por ejemplo, su santo es San Juan Bautista y el día de su santo es el 24 de junio. En muchas ocasiones este día se celebra igual que el día de su cumpleaños.

Para las señoritas, la fiesta de los quince años, **la quinceañera**, es una de las más importantes, porque desde esa edad a la muchacha se le considera ya[a] mujer.

Una quinceañera mexicana

[a]*already*

B. Hablando de fiestas

Paso 1. ¿Es su opinión de las siguientes fiestas positiva, negativa o neutra?

1. el Cuatro de Julio
2. el Día de Acción de Gracias
3. el Día de San Patricio
4. la Noche Vieja
5. el Día de la Raza
6. el Día de los Enamorados

Paso 2. Ahora compare sus respuestas con las (*those*) de sus compañeros de clase. ¿Coinciden todos en su opinión de algunas fiestas?

Paso 3. Ahora piense en su fiesta favorita. Puede ser una de la lista del **Paso 1** o una del **Vocabulario útil** de las páginas 198–199. Piense en cómo celebra Ud. esa fiesta, para explicárselo (*explain it*) luego a un compañero / una compañera de clase. Debe pensar en lo siguiente:

- los preparativos que Ud. hace de antemano (*beforehand*)
- la ropa especial que lleva
- las comidas o bebidas especiales que compra o prepara
- el lugar donde se celebra
- los adornos especiales que hay

Vocabulario útil			
el árbol	tree	**la fiesta del barrio**	neighborhood (block) party
el corazón	heart		
la corona	wreath	**los fuegos artificiales**	fireworks
el desfile	parade	**el globo**	balloon

Emociones y condiciones

David está contento.
Se ríe.

David **llora** porque **se siente triste.**

David **se pone feliz** otra vez y **sonríe.**

discutir (sobre) (con)	to argue (about) (with)	**portarse bien/mal**	to behave well/poorly
enfermar(se)	to get sick	**quejarse (de)**	to complain (about)
enojar(se) (con)	to get mad (at)	**recordar (ue)**	to remember
llorar	to cry	**reír(se) (i, i) (de)**	to laugh (about)
olvidar(se) de	to forget about	**sentir(se) (ie, i)**	to feel
ponerse + *adj.*	to become, get + *adjective*	**sonreír(se) (i, i)**	to smile

NOTA COMUNICATIVA

Being Emphatic

To emphasize the quality described by an adjective or an adverb, speakers of Spanish often add **-ísimo/a/os/as** to it, adding the idea *extremely* (*exceptionally; very, very; super*) to the quality. You have already used one emphatic form of this type: **Me gusta muchísimo.**

Estos entremeses son
  dificilísimos de preparar.
Durante la época navideña,
  los niños son **buenísimos.**

These hors d'œuvres are very hard to prepare.
At Christmastime, the kids are extremely good.

- If the adjective ends in a consonant, **-ísimo** is added to the singular form: **difícil → dificilísimo** (drop any accents on the word stem).
- If the adjective ends in a vowel, the final vowel is dropped before adding **-ísimo: bueno → buenísimo.**
- Spelling changes occur when the final consonant of an adjective is **c, g,** or **z: riquísimo, larguísimo, felicísimo.**

Conversación

A. Reacciones. ¿Cómo reacciona o cómo se pone Ud. en estas situaciones? Use estos adjetivos o cualquier otro, y también los verbos que describen las reacciones emocionales. No se olvide de usar las formas enfáticas cuando sea (*whenever it is*) apropiado.

serio/a	feliz/triste	avergonzado/a (*embarrassed*)
nervioso/a	furioso/a	contento/a

1. Es Navidad y alguien le hace a Ud. un regalo carísimo.
2. Es su cumpleaños y sus padres/hijos no le regalaron nada.
3. Ud. da una fiesta en su casa pero los invitados no se divierten. Nadie ríe ni sonríe.
4. Hay un examen importante hoy, pero Ud. no estudió anoche.
5. Ud. acaba de terminar un examen difícil/fácil y cree que lo hizo bien/mal.
6. En un examen de química, Ud. no puede recorder una fórmula muy importante.

B. ¿Son buenos todos los días festivos? Los días festivos pueden ser difíciles para muchas personas. Para Ud., ¿son ciertas o falsas las siguientes oraciones? Cambie las oraciones falsas para que sean (*so that they are*) ciertas. Luego compare sus respuestas con las de sus compañeros de clase.

EN LAS FIESTAS DE FAMILIA

1. Toda o casi toda mi familia, incluyendo a mis tíos, primos, abuelos, etcétera, se reúne por lo menos (*at least*) una vez al año.
2. Las fiestas de familia me gustan muchísimo.
3. Hay un pariente que siempre se queja de algo.
4. Uno de mis parientes siempre me hace preguntas indiscretas.
5. Alguien siempre bebe/come demasiado y luego se enferma.
6. A todos les gustan los regalos que reciben.
7. Todos lo pasan bien en las fiestas de familia.

LOS DÍAS FESTIVOS EN GENERAL

8. La Navidad / La Fiesta de las Luces es esencialmente una excusa para gastar dinero.
9. La época de fiestas en noviembre y diciembre es triste y deprimente (*depressing*) para mí.
10. Sólo las personas que practican una religión deben tener vacaciones en los días de fiestas religiosas.
11. Las vacaciones de primavera son para divertirse muchísimo. De hecho (*In fact*), son las mejores vacaciones del año.
12. Debería haber (*There should be*) más días festivos… por lo menos uno al mes.

23 Talking about the Past (2) • Irregular Preterites

La fiesta de la Noche Vieja

Conteste las siguientes preguntas sobre esta fiesta.

1. ¿Quién *estuvo* hablando por teléfono?
2. ¿Quién *dio* la fiesta?
3. ¿Quién no *pudo* ir a la fiesta?
4. ¿Quién *puso* su copa de champán en el televisor?
5. ¿Quién *hizo* mucho ruido?
6. ¿Quiénes *tuvieron* que salir temprano?
7. ¿Quiénes no *quisieron* beber más?
8. ¿Quiénes *vinieron* con sus niñas?
9. ¿Quiénes le *trajeron* un regalo al anfitrión (*host*)?

Y Ud., ¿*estuvo* alguna vez en una fiesta como esta? ¿*Tuvo* que salir temprano o se quedó hasta después de la medianoche (*midnight*)? ¿Le *trajo* algo al anfitrión / a la anfitriona?

- You have already learned the irregular preterite forms of **dar, hacer, ir,** and **ser.** The following verbs are also irregular in the preterite. Note that the first and third person singular endings, which are the only irregular ones, are unstressed, in contrast to the stressed endings of regular preterite forms.

estar	
estuve	estuvimos
estuviste	estuvisteis
estuvo	estuvieron

estar:	**estuv-**	
poder:	**pud-**	**-e**
poner:	**pus-**	-iste
querer:	**quis-**	**-o**
saber:	**sup-**	-imos
tener:	**tuv-**	-isteis
venir:	**vin-**	-ieron

- When the preterite verb stem ends in **-j-,** the **-i-** of the third person plural ending is omitted: **dijeron, trajeron.**

decir:	**dij-**	-e, -iste, -o, -imos, -isteis, **-eron**
traer:	**traj-**	

- The preterite of **hay** (**haber**) is **hubo** (*there was/were*).

Hubo un accidente ayer en el centro.
There was an accident yesterday downtown.

- Several of the following Spanish verbs have an English equivalent in the preterite tense that is different from that of the infinitive.

	Infinitive Meaning	Preterite Meaning
saber	to know (*facts, information*)	to find out
	Ya lo sé. *I already know it.*	Lo **supe** ayer. *I found it out (learned it) yesterday.*
conocer	to know (*be familiar with*) people, places	to meet (*for the first time*)
	Ya la conozco. *I already know her.*	La **conocí** ayer. *I met her yesterday.*
querer	to want	to try
	Quiero hacerlo hoy. *I want to do it today.*	**Quise** hacerlo ayer. *I tried to do it yesterday.*
no querer	not to want	to refuse
	No quiero hacerlo hoy. *I don't want to do it today.*	**No quise** hacerlo anteayer. *I refused to do it the day before yesterday.*
poder	to be able	to succeed (*in doing something*)
	Puedo leerlo. *I can (am able to) read it.*	**Pude** leerlo ayer. *I could (and did) read it yesterday.*
no poder	not to be able, capable	to fail (*in doing something*)
	No puedo leerlo. *I can't (am not able to) read it.*	**No pude** leerlo anteayer. *I couldn't (did not) read it the day before yesterday.*

Práctica

A. La última Noche Vieja. Piense en lo que Ud. hizo la Noche Vieja del año pasado e indique si las siguientes oraciones son ciertas o falsas para Ud.

1. Fui a una fiesta en casa de un amigo / una amiga.
2. Di una fiesta en mi casa.
3. No estuve con mis amigos, sino (*but rather*) con la familia.
4. Quise ir a una fiesta, pero no pude.
5. No pude encontrar (*find*) el lugar de la fiesta.

6. Les dije «¡Feliz Año Nuevo!» a muchas personas.
7. No le dije «¡Feliz Año Nuevo!» a nadie.
8. Conocí a algunas personas nuevas.
9. Tuve que preparar la comida de esa noche.
10. Me puse ropa elegante esa noche.
11. Pude quedarme despierto/a (*awake*) hasta la medianoche.
12. No quise bailar.

B. Una Nochebuena en casa de los Ramírez. Describa lo que pasó en casa de los Ramírez, haciendo el papel (*playing the role*) de uno de los hijos. Haga oraciones en el pretérito según las indicaciones, usando el sujeto pronominal cuando sea necesario.

1. todos / estar / en casa / abuelos / antes de / nueve
2. (nosotros) poner / mucho / regalos / debajo / árbol
3. tíos y primos / venir / con / comida y bebidas
4. yo / tener / que / ayudar / a / preparar / comida
5. haber / cena / especial / para / todos
6. más tarde / alguno / amigos / venir / a / cantar / villancicos (*carols*)
7. niños / ir / a / alcoba / a / diez y / acostarse
8. niños / querer / dormir / pero / no / poder
9. a / medianoche / todos / decir / «¡Feliz Navidad!»
10. al día siguiente / todos / decir / que / fiesta / estar / estupendo

Conversación

A. Un viaje inolvidable. Piense en un viaje inolvidable (malo o bueno) de su vida. Con un compañero / una compañera, haga y conteste las siguientes preguntas sobre sus viajes.

1. ¿Adónde fue de viaje? ¿Con quién(es) fue?
2. ¿Cuánto tiempo estuvo allí? ¿Dónde se alojó (*did you stay*)?
3. ¿Conoció a alguien allí? ¿Le gustó conocer a esa(s) persona(s)?
4. ¿Qué cosas hizo durante el viaje? ¿Qué no pudo hacer?
5. ¿Compró algún recuerdo (*souvenir*)? ¿Para quién?

B. Preguntas

1. ¿En qué mes conoció Ud. al profesor / a la profesora de español? ¿A quién(es) más conoció ese mismo (*same*) día? ¿Tuvo Ud. que hablar español el primer día de clase?
2. El año pasado, ¿dónde pasó Ud. la Nochebuena? ¿el Día de Acción de Gracias? ¿Dónde estuvo durante las vacaciones de primavera? ¿Dónde piensa Ud. estar este año en estas ocasiones?
3. ¿Alguien le dio a Ud. una fiesta de cumpleaños este año? ¿Fue una fiesta sorpresa? ¿Dónde fue? ¿Qué le trajeron sus amigos? ¿Qué le regalaron sus parientes? ¿Alguien le hizo un pastel?

24 Talking about the Past (3) • Preterite of Stem-Changing Verbs

La quinceañera de Lupe Carrasco

Imagine los detalles de la fiesta de Lupe cuando cumplió quince años.

1. Lupe *se vistió* con
   - ☐ un vestido blanco muy elegante.
   - ☐ una camiseta y unos *jeans*.
   - ☐ el vestido de novia^a de su abuela.

2. Cortando el pastel de cumpleaños, Lupe
   - ☐ *empezó* a llorar.
   - ☐ *rió* mucho.
   - ☐ *sonrió* para una foto.

3. Lupe *pidió* un deseo^b al cortar el pastel. Ella
   - ☐ les dijo a todos su deseo.
   - ☐ *prefirió* guardarlo en secreto.

4. En la fiesta *sirvieron*
   - ☐ champán y otras bebidas alcohólicas.
   - ☐ refrescos.
   - ☐ sólo té y café.

5. Todos *se divirtieron* mucho en la fiesta. Los invitados *se despidieron*^c a la(s)_____.

^avestido… *wedding gown* ^b*wish* ^c*se… said good-bye*

Y Ud., ¿recuerda qué hizo cuando cumplió quince años? ¿*Pidió* muchos regalos? ¿*Se divirtió*? ¿Cómo *se sintió*?

A. As you learned in **Capítulo 7**, the **-ar** and **-er** stem-changing verbs have no stem change in the preterite (or in the present participle).

recordar (ue): recordé, re**cor**daste, re**cor**dó, re**cor**damos, recordasteis, re**cor**daron; re**cor**dando

perder (ie): per**dí**, **per**diste, **per**dió, **per**dimos, **per**disteis, **per**dieron; **per**diendo

B. The **-ir** stem-changing verbs do have a stem change in the preterite, but only in the third person singular and plural, where the stem vowels **e** and **o** change to **i** and **u**, respectively. This is the same change that occurs in the present participle of **-ir** stem-changing verbs.

pedir (i, i)		dormir (ue, u)	
pedí	pedimos	dormí	dormimos
pediste	pedisteis	dormiste	dormisteis
pidió	pidieron	durmió	durmieron
pidiendo		durmiendo	

C. Here are some **-ir** stem-changing verbs. You already know or have seen many of them. The reflexive meaning, if different from the nonreflexive meaning, is in parentheses.

OJO

Note the simplification:
ri-ió → rió; ri-ieron → rieron
son-ri-ió → sonrió; son-ri-ieron → sonrieron

conseguir (i, i)	to get, obtain	**pedir (i, i)**	to ask for; to order
conseguir + *inf.*	to succeed in	**preferir (ie, i)**	to prefer
	(*doing something*)	**reír(se) (i, i)**	to laugh
despedirse	to say good-bye (to),	**sentir(se) (ie, i)**	to feel
(i, i) (de)	take leave (of)	**servir (i, i)**	to serve
divertir(se) (ie, i)	to entertain (to have	**sonreír(se) (i, i)**	to smile
	a good time)	**sugerir (ie, i)**	to suggest
dormir(se) (ue, u)	to sleep (to fall asleep)	**vestir(se) (ie, i)**	to dress (to get dressed)
morir(se) (ue, u)	to die		

Práctica

A. **¿Quién lo hizo?** ¿Ocurrieron algunas de estas cosas en clase la semana pasada? Conteste con el nombre de la persona apropiada. Si nadie lo hizo, conteste con **Nadie...**

1. _____ se vistió de una manera muy elegante.
2. _____ se vistió de una manera rara (*strange*).
3. _____ se durmió en clase.
4. _____ se sintió muy contento/a.
5. _____ se divirtió muchísimo, riendo y sonriendo.
6. _____ no sonrió ni siquiera (*not even*) una vez.
7. _____ sugirió tener la clase afuera.
8. _____ prefirió no contestar ninguna pregunta.
9. _____ se rió al oír una noticia (*piece of news*).

B. **Historias breves.** Cuente las siguientes historias breves en el pretérito. Luego continúelas, si puede.

1. **Un día típico:** Rosa (acostarse) temprano y (dormirse) en seguida. (Dormir) bien y (despertarse) temprano. (Vestirse) y (salir) para la universidad. En el autobús (ver) a su amigo José y los dos (sonreír). A las nueve _____.

2. **Dos noches diferentes:** Yo (vestirse), (ir) a una fiesta, (divertirse) mucho y (volver) tarde a casa. Mi compañero de cuarto (decidir) quedarse en casa y (ver) la televisión toda la noche. No (divertirse) nada. (Perder) una fiesta excelente y lo (sentir) mucho. Yo _____.

Conversación

La fiesta de disfraz (*Costume party*). Use the following sentences as a guide for telling about a childhood or more recent costume party, if appropriate.

1. ¿De qué se vistió?
2. ¿Cómo se sintió?
3. ¿Fue de casa en casa?
4. ¿Qué les dijo y qué les pidió a los vecinos (*neighbors*)?
5. ¿Qué le dieron?
6. ¿Se rieron los vecinos cuando lo/la vieron?
7. ¿Consiguió muchos dulces?
8. ¿También asistió a una fiesta?
9. ¿Qué sirvieron en la fiesta?
10. ¿Se divirtió mucho?

Enfoque *cultural*

Cuba

Datos esenciales

Nombre oficial: República de Cuba

Capital: La Habana

Población: 11.000.000 de habitantes

Moneda: el peso cubano

Idioma oficial: el español

¡Fíjese!

- Cuba obtuvo[a] su independencia de España en 1898, tras[b] la guerra de Cuba.[c] Los Estados Unidos ayudó a Cuba en esta guerra.

- Hay una distancia de 145 kilómetros (90 millas) entre Florida y Cuba.

- Después de la revolución socialista cubana en 1959, hubo un éxodo de cubanos a los Estados Unidos. La mayor parte de ellos se estableció en Florida, con la esperanza[d] de volver muy pronto a su isla. Pero empezó el milenio y todavía[e] Fidel Castro, el primer líder de la revolución, gobierna a Cuba.

- El régimen de Castro ha reducido[f] el analfabetismo[g] a menos de 5 por ciento y ha reformado el sistema educativo con resultados admirables. Pero la situación económica del país es difícil. Con la caída[h] de la Unión Soviética, Cuba perdió fondos de apoyo[i] indispensables. El embargo económico de los Estados Unidos afectó las condiciones de vida[j] de los cubanos, pero últimamente se exploran las posibilidades de exportación e importación entre los Estados Unidos y Cuba.

[a]*obtained* [b]*after* [c]*guerra... Spanish-American War* [d]*hope* [e]*still* [f]*ha... has reduced* [g]*illiteracy* [h]*fall* [i]*fondos... economic assistance* [j]*condiciones... living conditions*

Conozca a... Nicolás Guillén

Nicolás Guillén (1902–1989), poeta cubano de origen africano y europeo, es quizás[a] el poeta que mejor refleja la influencia africana en la cultura hispana. El lenguaje, los mitos[b] y las leyendas afrocubanos aparecen en su obra. Sus temas incluyen la injusticia social y una crítica al colonialismo. El siguiente fragmento de un poema de Guillén es representativo de su obra. Después de leerlo, piense: ¿Quiénes son los hombres del poema? ¿Cuál es su condición de vida? ¿Por qué es la sangre[c] «un mar inmenso»?

Nicolás Guillén

[a]*perhaps* [b]*myths* [c]*blood*

Poema con niños

La sangre es un mar inmenso
que baña todas las playas...
sobre sangre van los hombres
navegando[a] en sus barcazas:[b]
reman, que reman,[c] que reman
¡nunca de remar descansan!
Al negro[d] de negra piel
la sangre el cuerpo le baña;
la misma sangre, corriendo,[e]
hierve[f] bajo carne[g] blanca.

[a]*sailing* [b]*boats* [c]*reman... rowing and rowing* [d]persona negra [e]*flowing* [f]*boils* [g]*flesh*

Capítulo 8 of the video to accompany *¿Qué tal?* contains cultural footage about Cuba.

VW. Visit the *¿Qué tal?* website at www.mhhe.com/quetal.

25 Expressing Direct and Indirect Objects Together • Double Object Pronouns

Speech bubbles: ¿ES MUY LINDO!...¿ME LO PRESTAS? — ¡PEATONA!ᵃ

ᵃ*Pedestrian!*

Susanita es una amiga de Mafalda. A veces se porta muy mal y es un poco egocéntrica. ¿Conoce Ud. a personas como Susanita? ¿Le han pasado (*have happened*) las siguientes cosas a Ud.?

	SÍ	NO
1. Una vez le presté un libro a alguien y no me lo devolvió (*returned*).	☐	☐
2. Le pedí una bebida al camarero en un restaurante y no me la trajo.	☐	☐
3. Pedí algunos regalos específicos para mi cumpleaños, pero nadie me los regaló.	☐	☐
4. Les mostré fotos a unas personas, y las doblaron (*they bent them*).	☐	☐

ORDER OF PRONOUNS

When both an indirect and a direct object pronoun are used in a sentence, the indirect object pronoun (**I**) precedes the direct (**D**): **ID**. Note that nothing comes between the two pronouns. The position of double object pronouns with respect to the verb is the same as that of single object pronouns.

—¿Tienes el trofeo?
Do you have the trophy?

—Sí, acaban de dár**melo**.
Yes, they just gave it to me.

—Mamá, ¿está listo el almuerzo?
Mom, is lunch ready?

—**Te lo** preparo ahora mismo.
I'll get it ready for you right now.

Le(s) → se

A. When both the indirect and the direct object pronouns begin with the letter **l**, the indirect object pronoun always changes to **se**. The direct object pronoun does not change.

Le compra unos zapatos.
He's buying her some shoes.

Se los compra.
He's buying them for her.

Les mandamos la blusa.
We'll send you the blouse.

Se la mandamos.
We'll send it to you.

B. Since **se** can stand for **le** (*to/for you* [*sing.*], *him, her*) or **les** (*to/for you* [*pl.*], *them*), it is often necessary to clarify its meaning by using **a** plus the pronoun objects of prepositions.

Se lo escribo (**a Uds., a ellos, a ellas...**).
I'll write it to (*you, them . . .*).

Se las doy (**a Ud., a él, a ella...**).
I'll give them to (*you, him, her . . .*).

Práctica

A. Lo que se oye en casa. ¿A qué se refieren las siguientes oraciones? ¿unas fotos, la sal, unos billetes de avión para Guadalajara, la fiesta, el televisor, los discos compactos de Enrique Iglesias? Fíjese en (*Note*) los pronombres y en el sentido (*meaning*) de la oración.

1. No **lo** prendan (*switch on*). Es mejor que los niños lean o que jueguen.
2. ¿Me **la** pasas? Gracias.
3. Tengo muchas ganas de comprárme**los** todos. Me encanta esa música.
4. ¿Por qué no se **las** mandas a los abuelos? Les van a gustar muchísimo.
5. Tengo que reservárte**los** hoy mismo, porque se va a terminar (*expire*) la oferta especial de Aeroméxico.
6. Yo se **la** organicé a Lupe para su cumpleaños. Antonio y Diego le hicieron un pastel.

B. En el aeropuerto. Cambie los sustantivos a pronombres para evitar (*avoid*) la repetición.

1. ¿La hora de la salida? Acaban de decirnos la hora de la salida.
2. ¿El horario? Sí, léeme el horario, por favor.
3. ¿Los boletos? No, no tiene que darle los boletos aquí.
4. ¿El equipaje? Claro que le guardo el equipaje.
5. ¿Los pasajes? Acabo de comprarte los pasajes.
6. ¿El puesto? No te preocupes. Te puedo guardar el puesto.
7. ¿La clase turística? Sí, les recomiendo la clase turística, señores.
8. ¿La cena? La asistente de vuelo nos va a servir la cena en el avión.

Conversación

A. Regalos especiales. The drawings in **Grupo I** show the presents that a number of people have just received. They were sent by the people in **Grupo II**. Can you match the presents with the sender? Make as many logical guesses as you can. Then compare your matches with those of a partner.

MODELO: ¿Quién le regaló (mandó) a Maritere _____?
¿Quién les regaló (mandó) a Carlos y Juanita _____?
Se lo/la/los/las regaló (mandó) _____.

GRUPO I

GRUPO II

B. ¿Quién le regaló eso?

Paso 1. Haga una lista de los cinco mejores regalos que Ud. ha recibido (*have received*) en su vida. Si no sabe cómo decir algo, pregúnteselo a su profesor(a).

Paso 2. Ahora déle a un compañero / una compañera su lista. Él/Ella le va a preguntar: **¿Quién te regaló _____?** Use pronombres en su respuesta. **¡OJO!** Fíjese en (*Note*) estas formas plurales (**ellos**): **regalaron, dieron, mandaron.**

> MODELO: E1: ¿Quién te regaló los aretes?
> E2: Mis padres me los regalaron.

En los Estados Unidos y el Canadá...

El día de César Chávez

Desde el año 2000, el líder sindical[a] mexicoamericano César Chávez (1927–1993) tiene **un día festivo** en su honor en el estado de **California**. El lunes o el viernes alrededor del[b] 31 de marzo, los colegios y otros organismos[c] pueden cerrar para **honrar**[d] a Chávez y el movimiento en defensa de los **trabajadores agrícolas**[e] que él defendió.

El senador Richard Polanco fue el autor de la legislación que estableció

César Chávez

el día de **César Chávez.** Polanco es un senador demócrata en el senado de California desde 1994 y representa al distrito de Los Ángeles. Desde 2000, Polanco es el Líder de la Mayoría en el Senado.

«[César Chávez] debe ser **honrado** porque su trabajo formó la América en la que hoy vivimos. Su vida nos dio a todos **el coraje**[f] y **la esperanza**[g] de que podemos hacer una diferencia. En su vida, nos enseñó que es importante **llevar una vida moral y responsable.**»

[a]*union* [b]alrededor... *around the* [c]*institutions* [d]*honor* [e]trabajadores... *farm workers* [f]*courage* [g]*hope*

UN POCO DE TODO

Más días festivos. Complete the following paragraphs with the correct form of the words in parentheses, as suggested by the context. When two possibilities are given in parentheses, select the correct word. Use the preterite of the infinitives in italics.

La fiesta de la Virgen de Guadalupe

En (alguno[1]) países hispánicos los días de (varios[2]) santos (ser/estar[3]) fiestas nacionales. El día 12 (de/del[4]) diciembre se (conmemorar[5]) a la santa patrona de México, la Virgen de Guadalupe. (Mucho[6]) mexicoamericanos celebran (este[7]) fiesta también. Se cree que la Virgen María se le (*aparecer*[8]) (a/de[9]) Juan, (un/una[10]) humilde pastor,[a] en el pueblo (a/de[11]) Guadalupe. La Virgen (*dejar*[12])[b] su imagen en un rebozo[c] que todavía se puede (ver[13]) en su Basílica en la Ciudad de México.

[a]*shepherd* [b]*to leave* [c]*shawl*

La fiesta de San Fermín

No (todo[14]) las fiestas hispánicas (ser/estar[15]) religiosas. Esta fiesta de Pamplona (España) lleva (el/la[16]) nombre de un santo y (ser/estar[17]) de origen religioso, pero es esencialmente secular. Durante diez días —entre (el/la[18]) 7 y (el/la[19]) 17 de julio— se interrumpe la rutina diaria (del / de la[20]) ciudad. (Llegar[21]) personas de todas partes de España e inclusive de (otro[22]) países para beber, cantar, bailar... y (pasarlo[23]) bien. Todas las mañanas algunos toros[a] (correr[24]) sueltos[b] por (el/la[25]) calle de la Estafeta, en dirección (al / a la[26]) plaza de toros.[c] (Alguno[27]) personas atrevidas[d] (correr[28]) delante de ellos. No (haber[29]) duda[e] de que (este[30]) demostración de valor[f] (ser/estar[31]) bastante peligrosa.[g] Luego por (el/la[32]) tarde se celebra una corrida[h] en la famosa plaza de toros que (*describir*[33]) Ernest Hemingway en (su[34]) novela *The Sun Also Rises*. En Pamplona todavía (ser/estar[35]) posible (hablar[36]) con personas que (*saber/conocer*[37]) a este famoso escritor estadounidense.

[a]*bulls* [b]*free* [c]*plaza... bullring* [d]*daring* [e]*doubt* [f]*courage* [g]*bastante... quite dangerous*
[h]*bullfight*

Comprensión: ¿Cierto o falso? Corrija las oraciones falsas.

1. Todas las fiestas hispánicas son religiosas.
2. Sólo los mexicanos celebran la fiesta de la Virgen de Guadalupe.
3. La fiesta de San Fermín es esencialmente para los niños.
4. Algunos españoles todavía recuerdan a Hemingway.

Un paso más PASO 4

VIDEOTECA: En contexto

In this video segment, Roberto talks to a store employee about returning a CD. As you watch the segment, pay attention to the way that Roberto talks about events in the past. Listen, too, to the way he and the employee use direct and indirect objects when they speak.

MÉXICO

FUNCTION

Returning a purchase

A. Lluvia de ideas

- ¿Cuáles son los regalos de cumpleaños que a Ud. más le gustan? Antes de comprarle un regalo a Ud., ¿le preguntan sus parientes y sus amigos qué es lo que desea? ¿Cree Ud. que es buena idea preguntarle a alguien lo que desea de regalo o es mejor darle una sorpresa?
- ¿Qué hace Ud. cuando alguien le regala un libro o un disco que ya (*already*) tiene?

B. Dictado

A continuación puede leer parte del diálogo entre Roberto y el dependiente de la tienda de música. Complétela con las palabras o frases que faltan.

ROBERTO: Quisiera[a] devolver _____[1] disco compacto.
DEPENDIENTE: Muy bien, Un momento… ¿Por qué _____[2] devolverlo?
ROBERTO: _____[3] lo tengo.
DEPENDIENTE: ¿Tienes el recibo?
ROBERTO: No, no tengo el recibo. Me _____[4] el disco para mi _____.[5]
DEPENDIENTE: Lo siento,[b] pero en ese caso no _____[6] puedo reembolsar[c] el _____.[7] Necesitas un recibo para un reembolso.

[a]*I would like*   [b]*Lo… I'm sorry*   [c]*refund*

C. Un diálogo original

Con un compañero / una compañera, dramatice la escena entre Roberto y el dependiente en la tienda de música.

E1: Es su cumpleaños y un buen amigo / una buena amiga le da un regalo (por ejemplo, un libro de Isabel Allende, una camiseta de la universidad, unas entradas [*tickets*] para un concierto). Pero otra persona ya le hizo el mismo (*same*) regalo.

E2: Ud. le hizo un regalo a su amigo/a sin saber (*without knowing*) que su amigo/a ya tiene otro igual. Trate de (*Try to*) resolver el problema.

Cultura en contexto
La música popular

Los jóvenes del mundo hispanohablante compran con frecuencia la música popular de los Estados Unidos y el Canadá en discos compactos (CDs). Por otro lado, hay una larga y fuerte tradición musical en las culturas hispanas. Y hay música de todo tipo y un sinfín[a] de excelentes músicos en todos los países hispanohablantes.

[a]un… *an endless number*

PASO FINAL

A CONVERSAR

¿Cómo celebraron los días festivos?

Paso 1. En una hoja de papel aparte, prepare un cuadro como el siguiente. Primero, escoja cuatro de los días festivos de la lista en las páginas 198–199. Luego escríbalos en el cuadro. Deje espacios en blanco para escribir el nombre de una persona y sus respuestas breves a tres preguntas.

MODELO:

día festivo:	el Día de San Patricio	la Noche Vieja	el cumpleaños	el Cinco de Mayo
persona:				
actividades:				

Paso 2. Apunte tres preguntas que Ud. puede hacerles a sus compañeros sobre cómo celebraron los días festivos el año pasado.

MODELO: El año pasado, ¿qué hiciste en la Noche Vieja? ¿Te reuniste con amigos en algún lugar especial? ¿Lo pasaste bien o mal?

Paso 3. Formen parejas para hacer y contestar las tres preguntas sobre el primer día festivo en el cuadro. Después de hacer y contestar esas tres preguntas, formen parejas con otras personas para hacer y contestar las preguntas del siguiente día festivo. En total, van a formar cuatro parejas diferentes para hacer y contestar las preguntas sobre los cuatro días festivos. Escriban los nombres de sus compañeros y sus respuestas debajo del día festivo correspondiente para recorder con quiénes hablaron y qué dijeron.

MODELO: la Noche Vieja →
Felipe: Salió con su novia. Se reunieron con unos amigos en un bar. Lo pasaron muy bien.

Paso 4. Escoja uno de los días festivos y cuéntele a la clase cómo lo celebró la persona que contestó sus preguntas.

En resumen

GRAMÁTICA

To review the grammar points presented in this chapter, refer to the indicated grammar presentations. You'll find further practice of these structures in the Workbook/Laboratory Manual, on the CD-ROM, and on the website.

23. Irregular Preterites

Do you know how to conjugate verbs that are irregular in the preterite? How does the preterite change the meaning of **saber, conocer, querer,** and **poder**?

24. Preterite of Stem-Changing Verbs

You should know the stem-changing patterns in the preterite for **-ir** verbs like **pedir, sentir,** and **dormir.**

25. Double Object Pronouns

Do you know in which order the direct and indirect object pronouns occur when they are used together in Spanish? You should also know where to place the pronouns and when an accent is required on the verb form.

VOCABULARIO

Los verbos

conseguir (i, i)	to get, obtain
conseguir + *inf.*	to succeed in (*doing something*)
despedirse (i, i) (de)	to say good-bye (to), take leave (of)
discutir (sobre) (con)	to argue (about) (with)
encontrar (ue)	to find
enfermarse	to get sick
enojarse (con)	to get angry (at)
gastar	to spend (*money*)
llorar	to cry
morir(se) (ue, u)	to die
olvidarse (de)	to forget (about)
ponerse (*irreg.*) + *adj.*	to become, get + *adjective*
portarse	to behave
quejarse (de)	to complain (about)
reaccionar	to react
recordar (ue)	to remember
reír(se) (i, i)	to laugh
sentirse (ie, i)	to feel
sonreír(se) (i, i)	to smile
sugerir (ie, i)	to suggest

Los días festivos y las fiestas

el anfitrión / la anfitriona	host / hostess
el chiste	joke
el deseo	wish
los entremeses	hors d'œuvres
el/la invitado/a	guest
el pastel de cumpleaños	birthday cake
los refrescos	refreshments
la sorpresa	surprise
cumplir años	to have a birthday
dar (*irreg.*) / hacer (*irreg.*) **una fiesta**	to give/have a party
faltar	to be absent, lacking
pasarlo bien/mal	to have a good/ bad time
reunirse (me reúno) (con)	to get together (with)

Repaso: celebrar, el cumpleaños, el dinero, divertirse (ie, i), regalar

Los sustantivos

la emoción	emotion
el hecho	event
la medianoche	midnight
la noticia	piece of news

Los adjetivos

avergonzado/a	embarrassed
feliz (*pl.* felices)	happy
raro/a	strange

Palabras adicionales

¡felicitaciones!	congratulations!
ser (*irreg.*) en + *place*	to take place in/at (*place*)
ya	already

Algunos días festivos

la Navidad, la Nochebuena, la Noche Vieja, la Pascua (Florida)

El tiempo libre

Esta señorita lo pasa bien ▶ tomando un refresco en Cartagena, Colombia.

VOCABULARIO

- Pastimes, fun activities, and hobbies
- Household chores

GRAMÁTICA

26 Imperfect of Regular and Irregular Verbs
27 Superlatives
28 Summary of Interrogative Words

CULTURA

- **Enfoque cultural:** Colombia
- **Nota cultural:** El fútbol y el béisbol
- **En los Estados Unidos y el Canadá:** La impresionante variedad de la música hispana
- **Cultura en contexto:** El voseo

Multimedia

 You will learn more about making plans in the **En contexto** video segment.

 Review vocabulary and grammar and practice language skills with the interactive CD-ROM.

WW. Get connected to the Spanish-speaking world with the *¿Qué tal?* Online Learning Center: **www.mhhe.com/quetal**.

Pasatiempos, diversiones y aficiones°

Pasatiempos... *Pastimes, fun activities, and hobbies*

correr

tomar el sol

pasear en bicicleta

hacer un *picnic*

montar a caballo

patinar en línea

Los pasatiempos

los ratos libres	spare (free) time
dar (*irreg.*) / hacer (*irreg.*) una fiesta	to give a party
dar (*irreg.*) un paseo	to take a walk
hacer (*irreg.*) *camping*	to go camping
hacer (*irreg.*) planes para + *inf.*	to make plans to (*do something*)
ir (*irreg.*)...	to go . . .
al cine / a ver una película	to the movies / to see a movie
a una discoteca / a un bar	to a disco / to a bar
al teatro / a un concierto	to the theater / to a concert
jugar (ue) a las cartas / al ajedrez	to play cards/chess
visitar un museo	to visit a museum
aburrirse	to get bored
ser (*irreg.*) divertido/a, aburrido/a	to be fun, boring

Los deportes

el ciclismo	bicycling
esquiar (esquío)	to ski
el fútbol	soccer
el fútbol americano	football
nadar	to swim
la natación	swimming
patinar	to skate

Otros deportes: el basquetbol, el béisbol, el golf, el hockey, el tenis, el vólibol

entrenar	to practice, train
ganar	to win
jugar (ue) al + *sport*	to play (*a sport*)
perder (ie)	to lose
practicar	to participate (*in a sport*)
ser aficionado/a (a)	to be a fan (of)

Conversación

A. ¿Cómo pasan estas personas su tiempo libre?

Paso 1. ¿Qué cree Ud. que hacen las siguientes personas para divertirse en un sábado típico? Use su imaginación pero manténgase (*keep yourself*) entre los límites de lo posible.

1. una persona rica que vive en Nueva York
2. un grupo de buenos amigos que trabajan en una fábrica (*factory*) de Detroit
3. un matrimonio joven con poco dinero y dos niños pequeños

Paso 2. ¿Cómo se divierten los jóvenes españoles?

Este recorte (*clipping*) de una revista española indica el tiempo medio (*average*) que los jóvenes españoles dedican a sus aficiones. ¿Puede explicar en español lo que significan los términos **Tomar copas** y **prensa**? ¿A qué tipos de «juegos» cree Ud. que se refiere el recorte?

Paso 3. Indique el número de minutos que Ud. les dedica a estas aficiones cada día. ¿Qué diferencia hay entre Ud. y los jóvenes españoles?

TIEMPO QUE DEDICAN A SUS AFICIONES	
(Media de minutos diarios)	
Ver la televisión	120
Tomar copas	60
Pasear	22
Leer libros	15
Escuchar música	15
Oír la radio	8
Hacer deporte	9
Practicar *hobbies*	8
Leer la prensa	6
«Juegos»	4

NOTA CULTURAL

El fútbol* y el béisbol

Sin duda,[a] el deporte más popular en el mundo hispánico es **el fútbol**. El campeonato mundial de fútbol, conocido como **la Copa Mundial**, es el evento deportivo más popular del mundo. Este **torneo internacional** ocurre cada cuatro años y tiene más **espectadores** que cualquier[b] otro evento deportivo. Por ejemplo, en 1998, 2.4 billones de televidentes miraron el partido final de la Copa Mundial mientras 800 millones miraron el *Super Bowl* de los Estados Unidos. Como es un deporte tan popular, en todas las ciudades hispanas hay muchos **campos**[c] **de fútbol**. Los niños y los adultos van a jugar siempre que pueden.[d]

Un partido de la Copa Mundial entre el Brasil y Honduras

   El béisbol también es muy popular, sobre todo en el Caribe. Hay muchos hispanos en **las ligas profesionales** de los Estados Unidos. Por ejemplo, el gran **jugador** de los Chicago Cubs, Sammy Sosa, es de la República Dominicana. El puertorriqueño Roberto Clemente fue el primer hispano elegido al *Baseball Hall of Fame* en 1973.

[a]*doubt* [b]*any* [c]*fields* [d]siempre... *whenever they can*

Sammy Sosa es de la República Dominicana.

*Remember that **fútbol** is *soccer*, not U.S.-style *football*.

B. ¿Cierto o falso? Corrija (*Correct*) las oraciones falsas según su opinión.

1. Ver una película en vídeo es más aburrido que ir al cine.
2. Lo paso mejor con mi familia que con mis amigos.
3. Las actividades educativas me gustan más que las deportivas.
4. Odio el béisbol tanto como el fútbol.

Trabajando en casa

Algunos aparatos domésticos

Los quehaceres domésticos°

Los… *Household chores*

barrer (el piso)	to sweep (the floor)	**pasar la aspiradora**	to vacuum
dejar (en…)	to leave behind (in [*a place*])	**pintar (las paredes)**	to paint (the walls)
hacer (*irreg.*) **la cama**	to make the bed	**planchar la ropa**	to iron clothing
lavar (las ventanas, los platos, la ropa)	to wash (the windows, the dishes, the clothes)	**poner** (*irreg.*) **la mesa**	to set the table
		quitar la mesa	to clear the table
		sacar la basura	to take out the trash
limpiar la casa (entera)	to clean the (whole) house	**sacudir los muebles**	to dust the furniture

Labels in illustration: el horno de microondas, el congelador, la tostadora, la cafetera, el refrigerador, la estufa, el lavaplatos, la secadora, la aspiradora, la lavadora

Conversación

A. Los quehaceres. ¿En qué cuarto o parte de la casa se hacen las siguientes actividades? Hay más de una respuesta en muchos casos.

1. Se hace la cama en _____.
2. Se saca la basura de _____ y se deja en _____.
3. Se sacuden los muebles de _____.
4. Uno se baña en _____. Pero es mejor que uno bañe al perro en _____.
5. Se barre el piso de _____.
6. Se pasa la aspiradora en _____.
7. Se lava y se seca la ropa en _____. La ropa se plancha en _____.
8. Se usa la cafetera en _____.

NOTA COMUNICATIVA

Talking about Obligation

You already know several ways to express the obligation to carry out particular activities.

Tengo que		*I have to*	
Necesito	barrer el piso.	*I need to*	*sweep the floor.*
Debo		*I should*	

Of the three alternatives, **tener que** + *infinitive* expresses the strongest sense of obligation.

The concept *to be someone's turn or responsibility* (to do something) is expressed in Spanish with the verb **tocar** plus an indirect object.

—**¿A quién le toca** lavar los platos esta noche?

Whose turn is it to wash the dishes tonight?

—**A mí me toca** solamente sacar la basura. Creo que **a papá le toca** lavar los platos.

I only have to take out the garbage. I think it's Dad's turn to wash the dishes.

B. Los fines de semana: ¿Tiempo libre o quehaceres?

Paso 1. Marque las actividades típicas para Ud. durante los fines de semana.

- ☐ barrer el piso
- ☐ lavar la ropa
- ☐ hacer deporte/ejercicio
- ☐ limpiar la casa
- ☐ ir de compras al supermercado
- ☐ ir de compras al centro comercial
- ☐ hacer las tareas y estudiar
- ☐ dar fiestas
- ☐ salir a bailar con amigos
- ☐ ¿ ?

Paso 2. Usando la información del **Paso 1**, describa un fin de semana típico. También incluya información sobre las cosas que *no* hace. Para Ud., ¿cuándo empieza el fin de semana? ¿El viernes? ¿El sábado? Finalmente, apunte las cosas que tiene que hacer este fin de semana.

MODELO: Normalmente, los fines de semana yo descanso y salgo con amigos. El viernes, casi siempre… Pero este fin de semana tengo que limpiar la casa porque mis padres vienen a visitarme. Necesito barrer el piso…

Paso 3. Ahora, hable con un compañero / una compañera para comparar sus fines de semanas típicos y sus planes para el próximo fin de semana. Apunte lo que dice su compañero/a para compartir la información con la clase.

26 Descriptions and Habitual Actions in the Past •
Imperfect of Regular and Irregular Verbs

Los aztecas

«Los aztecas construyeron grandes pirámides para sus dioses. En lo alto de cada pirámide *había* un templo donde *tenían* lugar las ceremonias y *se ofrecían* los sacrificios. Las pirámides *tenían* muchísimos escalones, y *era* necesario subirlos todos para llegar a los templos.

Cerca de muchas pirámides *había* un terreno como el de una cancha de basquetbol. Allí *se celebraban* partidos que *eran* parte de una ceremonia. Los participantes *jugaban* con una pelota de goma dura, que sólo *podían* mover con las caderas y las rodillas… »

Comprensión: ¿Cierto o falso?

1. Los aztecas creían en un solo dios.
2. Las pirámides aztecas tenían una función religiosa.
3. Los aztecas practicaban un deporte similar al basquetbol.

You have already learned to use the *preterite* (**el pretérito**) to express events in the past. The *imperfect* (**el imperfecto**) is the second simple past tense in Spanish. In contrast to the preterite, which is used when you view actions or states of being as finished or completed, the imperfect tense is used when you view past actions or states of being as habitual or as "in progress." The imperfect is also used for describing the past.

The imperfect has several English equivalents. For example, **hablaba**, the first person singular of **hablar**, can mean *I spoke, I was speaking, I used to speak*, or *I would speak* (when *would* implies a repeated action). Most of these English equivalents indicate that the action was still in progress or was habitual, except for *I spoke*, which can correspond to either the preterite or the imperfect.

The Aztecs. "The Aztecs constructed large pyramids for their gods. At the top of each pyramid there was a temple where ceremonies took place and sacrifices were offered. The pyramids had many, many steps, and it was necessary to climb them all in order to get to the temples.

"Close to many pyramids there was an area of land like that of a basketball court. Ceremonial matches were celebrated there. The participants played with a ball made of hard rubber that they could only move with their hips and knees . . ."

FORMS OF THE IMPERFECT

hablar		comer		vivir	
hablaba	hablábamos	comía	comíamos	vivía	vivíamos
hablabas	hablabais	comías	comíais	vivías	vivíais
hablaba	hablaban	comía	comían	vivía	vivían

- Stem-changing verbs do not show a change in the imperfect. The imperfect of **hay** is **había** (*there was, there were, there used to be*).

Pronunciation Hint: The pronunciation of a **b** between vowels, such as in the imperfect ending **-aba**, is pronounced as a fricative [ß] sound.

In the other imperfect forms, it is important not to pronounce the ending **-ía** as a diphthong, but to pronounce the **i** and the **a** in separate syllables (the accent mark over the **í** helps remind you of this).

Imperfect of stem-changing verbs = no change

almorzar (ue) → almorzaba
perder (ie) → perdía
pedir (i, i) → pedía

Imperfect of **hay** = **había**

- Only three verbs are irregular in the imperfect: **ir, ser,** and **ver**.

ir		ser		ver	
iba	íbamos	era	éramos	veía	veíamos
ibas	ibais	eras	erais	veías	veíais
iba	iban	era	eran	veía	veían

USES OF THE IMPERFECT

Note the following uses of the imperfect. If you have a clear sense of when and where the imperfect is used, understanding where the preterite is used will be easier. When talking about the past, the preterite *is* used when the imperfect *isn't*. That is an oversimplification of the uses of these two past tenses, but at the same time it is a general rule of thumb that will help you out at first.

The imperfect has the following uses.

- To describe *repeated habitual actions* in the past

Siempre **nos quedábamos** en aquel hotel.
We always stayed (used to stay, would stay) at that hotel.

Todos los veranos **iban** a la costa.
Every summer they went (used to go, would go) to the coast.

- To describe an *action that was in progress* (*when something else happened*)

Pedía la cena.
She was ordering dinner.

Buscaba el coche.
He was looking for the car.

- To describe two *simultaneous past actions in progress*, with **mientras**

Tú **leías mientras** Juan **escribía** la carta.
You were reading while Juan was writing the letter.

- To describe ongoing *physical, mental,* or *emotional states* in the past

Estaban muy distraídos.
They were very distracted.

La **quería** muchísimo.
He loved her a lot.

- To tell *time* in the past and to *express age* with **tener**

O J O Just as in the present, the singular form of the verb **ser** is used with one o'clock, the plural form from two o'clock on.

Era la una. / **Eran** las dos.
It was one o'clock. / It was two o'clock.

Tenía 18 años.
She was 18 years old.

- To form a *past progressive:* imperfect of **estar** + *present participle**

Note that the simple imperfect—**cenábamos, estudiabas**—could also be used in the example sentences to express the ongoing actions. The use of the progressive emphasizes that the action was actually in progress.

Estábamos cenando a las diez.
We were having dinner at ten.

¿No **estabas estudiando**?
Weren't you studying?

Práctica

A. Mi niñez (*childhood*). Indique si las siguientes oraciones eran ciertas o falsas para Ud. cuando tenía 10 años. Luego, corrija las oraciones falsas.

MODELO: 2. Es falso. Me acostaba a las diez, no a las nueve.

1. Estaba en cuarto (*fourth*) grado.
2. Me acostaba a las nueve todas las noches.
3. Los sábados me levantaba temprano para mirar los dibujos animados.
4. Mis padres me pagaban por los quehaceres que hacía: cortar el césped (*cutting the grass*), lavar los platos…
5. Me gustaba acompañar a mi madre/padre al supermercado.
6. Pegaba (*I hit*) a mi hermano/a con frecuencia.
7. Tocaba un instrumento musical en la orquesta de la escuela.
8. Mis héroes eran personajes de las tiras cómicas (*comic strip characters*) como Superman y Wonder Woman.

---

*A progressive tense can also be formed with the preterite of **estar**: *Estuvieron* **cenando hasta las doce**. The use of the progressive with the preterite of **estar**, however, is relatively infrequent, and it will not be practiced in *¿Qué tal?*

B. Cuando Tina era niña... Describa la vida de Tina cuando era muy joven, haciendo oraciones según las indicaciones.

La vida de Tina era muy diferente cuando tenía 6 años.

1. todos los días / asistir / a / escuela primaria
2. por / mañana / aprender / a / leer / y / escribir / en / pizarra
3. a / diez / beber / leche / y / dormir / un poco
4. ir / a / casa / para / almorzar / y / regresar / a / escuela
5. estudiar / geografía / y / hacer / dibujos
6. jugar / con / compañeros / en / patio / de / escuela
7. camino de (*on the way*) casa / comprar / dulces / y / se los / comer
8. frecuentemente / pasar / por / casa / de / abuelos
9. cenar / con / padres / y / ayudar / a / lavar / platos
10. mirar / tele / un rato / y / acostarse / a / ocho

C. El trabajo de niñera (*baby-sitter*). El trabajo de niñera puede ser muy pesado (*difficult*), pero cuando los niños son traviesos (*mischievous*), también puede ser peligroso (*dangerous*). ¿Qué estaba pasando cuando la niñera perdió por fin la paciencia? Describa todas las acciones que pueda, usando **estaba(n)** + **-ndo**.

Palabras útiles: ladrar (*to bark*), pelear (*to fight*), sonar (ue)* (*to ring; to sound*)

Conversación

¡Qué cambio! Una entrevista. Hágale las siguientes preguntas a un compañero / una compañera de clase. Él/Ella va a pensar en las costumbres que tenía a los 14 años, es decir, cuando estaba en el noveno (*ninth*) o décimo (*tenth*) grado.

1. ¿Qué te gustaba comer? ¿Y ahora?
2. ¿Qué programa de televisión no te perdías (*missed*) nunca? ¿Y ahora?
3. ¿Qué te gustaba leer? ¿Y ahora?
4. ¿Qué hacías los sábados por la noche? ¿Y ahora?
5. ¿Qué deportes te gustaba practicar? ¿Y ahora?
6. ¿Con quién discutías mucho? ¿Y ahora?
7. ¿A quién te gustaba molestar (*annoy*)? ¿Y ahora?

---

*Although **sonar** is a stem-changing verb (**o → ue**), remember that the stem of present participles does not change with these verbs (**sonando**).

¿Recuerda Ud.?

Before you move on to the next Grammar Section, review comparisons, which were introduced in **Capítulo 5**. How would you say the following in Spanish?

1. I work as much as you do.
2. I work more/less than you do.
3. Bill Gates has more money than I have.
4. My housemate has fewer things than I do.
5. I have as many friends as you do.
6. My computer is worse/better than this one.

27 Expressing Extremes • Superlatives

¡El número uno!

Jennifer López

Ricky Martin

¿Está Ud. de acuerdo con las opiniones expresadas en estas oraciones?

1. Jennifer López es la mujer más bella (*beautiful*) del mundo.
2. Enrique Iglesias es el mejor cantante (*singer*) de su familia.
3. Ricky Martin es el puertorriqueño más conocido (*well-known*) hoy día (*nowadays*).

The *superlative* (**el superlativo**) is formed in English by adding *-est* to adjectives or by using expressions such as *the most* and *the least* with the adjective. In Spanish, this concept is expressed in the same way as the comparative but is always accompanied by the definite article. In this construction **mejor** and **peor** tend to precede the noun; other adjectives follow. *In* or *at* is expressed with **de**.

> **O J O** The superlative forms **-ísimo/a/os/as** cannot be used with this type of superlative construction.

el/la/los/las + *noun* + **más/menos** + *adjective* + **de**

David es **el estudiante más inteligente de** la clase.
David is the most intelligent student in the class.

el/la/los/las + **mejor/peor** + *noun* + **de**

Son **los mejores doctores de** aquel hospital.
They are the best doctors at that hospital.

Práctica

A. **¿Está Ud. de acuerdo o no?** Indique si Ud. está de acuerdo o no con las siguientes oraciones. Para cada una que no refleje su opinión, invente otra.

MODELO: 4. No estoy de acuerdo. Creo que el día festivo más divertido del año es el Cuatro de Julio.

1. El descubrimiento (*discovery*) científico más importante del siglo XX fue la vacuna (*vaccine*) contra la poliomielitis.
2. La persona más influyente (*influential*) del mundo es el presidente de los Estados Unidos.
3. El problema más serio del mundo es la deforestación de la región del Amazonas.
4. El día festivo más divertido del año es la Noche Vieja.
5. La mejor novela del mundo es *Don Quijote de la Mancha*.

B. **Superlativos.** Expand the information in these sentences according to the model. Then, if you can, restate each sentence with true information at the beginning.

MODELO: Es una estudiante muy *trabajadora*. (la clase) →
Es la estudiante *más trabajadora de la clase*. →
Carlota es la estudiante más trabajadora de la clase.

1. Es un día festivo muy divertido. (el año)
2. Es una clase muy interesante. (todas mis clases)
3. Es una persona muy inteligente. (todos mis amigos)
4. Es una ciudad muy grande. (los Estados Unidos / el Canadá)
5. Es una montaña muy alta. (el mundo)

Conversación

Entrevista. With another student, ask and answer questions based on the following phrases. Then report your opinions to the class.

1. la persona más guapa del mundo
2. la noticia más seria de esta semana
3. un libro interesantísimo y otro pesadísimo (*very boring*)
4. el mejor restaurante de la ciudad y el peor
5. el cuarto más importante de la casa y el menos importante
6. un plato riquísimo y otro malísimo
7. un programa de televisión interesantísimo y otro pesadísimo
8. un lugar tranquilísimo, otro animadísimo y otro peligrosísimo
9. la canción (*song*) más bonita del año y la más fea
10. la mejor película del año y la peor

Enfoque *cultural*

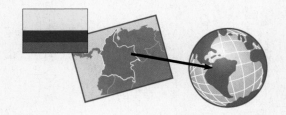

Colombia

Datos esenciales

Nombre oficial: República de Colombia

Capital: Santafé de Bogotá (Bogotá)

Población: 36.000.000 de habitantes

Moneda: el peso

Idioma oficial: el español

Conozca a... Gabriel García Márquez

El escritor latinoamericano más leído en el mundo entero es el colombiano Gabriel García Márquez, ganador[a] del Premio Nóbel de Literatura en 1982. Su novela *Cien años de soledad* se considera una de las novelas más importantes del siglo XX en cualquier lengua. La novela narra la historia de la familia Buendía durante varias generaciones. En ella García Márquez usa una técnica literaria llamada *realismo mágico:* una mezcla[b] de elementos reales y fantásticos en la narración.

Además de ser novelista, García Márquez es un respetado periodista y columnista que escribe para los periódicos más importantes de la lengua castellana.[c]

[a]*recipient*   [b]*combination*   [c]*lengua... Castilian (Spanish) language*

¡Fíjese!

- Colombia obtuvo su independencia de España en 1819, bajo la dirección de Simón Bolívar. Bolívar fue declarado el primer presidente de la independiente República de la Gran Colombia.

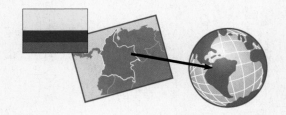

Estatuas de piedra, de San Agustín

- Colombia produce más oro que cualquier[a] otro país sudamericano y tiene los yacimientos[b] de platino más grandes del mundo. Las esmeraldas también son un producto minero importante.

- Aunque el café es reconocido[c] como el producto agrícola principal de exportación de Colombia, en los años noventa lo sobrepasó[d] el petróleo como primer producto de exportación.

- Aproximadamente un 14 por ciento de la población colombiana es de origen africano.

- Las misteriosas estatuas de piedra de San Agustín fueron creadas por una cultura indígena de la cual[e] se sabe muy poco. Se cree que las estatuas son del siglo VI antes de Cristo. Una de las estatuas representa un pájaro con una serpiente en el pico,[f] imagen muy similar a la de una leyenda azteca.

[a]*any*   [b]*deposits*   [c]*recognized*   [d]*surpassed*   [e]*de... of which*   [f]*beak*

Capítulo 9 of the video to accompany *¿Qué tal?* contains cultural footage of Colombia.

Visit the *¿Qué tal?* website at www.mhhe.com/quetal.

28 **Getting Information** • Summary of Interrogative Words

Este es un anuncio de un restaurante de Connecticut.

1. ¿Cómo se llama el restaurante?
2. ¿En qué ciudad de Connecticut está?
3. ¿Cuáles son las especialidades de este restaurante?

¿Cuántas preguntas más puede Ud. hacer sobre este restaurante, basándose en el anuncio?

¿Cómo?	How?	¿Dónde?	Where?
¿Cuándo?	When?	¿De dónde?	From where?
¿A qué hora?	At what time?	¿Adónde?	Where (to)?
¿Qué?	What? Which?	¿Cuánto/a?	How much?
¿Cuál(es)?	What? Which one(s)?	¿Cuántos/as?	How many?
¿Por qué?	Why?	¿Quién(es)?	Who?
		¿De quién(es)?	Whose?

You have been using interrogative words to ask questions and get information since the beginning of *¿Qué tal?* The preceding chart shows all of the interrogatives you have learned so far. Be sure that you know what they mean and how they are used. If you are not certain, the index and end-of-book vocabularies will help you find where they are first introduced. Only the specific uses of **¿qué?** and **¿cuál?** represent new information.

USING *¿qué?* AND *¿cuál?*

• **¿Qué?** asks for a definition or an explanation.

¿Qué es esto?
What is this?

¿Qué quieres?
What do you want?

¿Qué tocas?
What (instrument) do you play?

PASO 3

- **¿Qué?** can be directly followed by a noun.

¿Qué traje necesitas?
What (Which) suit do you need?

¿Qué playa te gusta más?
What (Which) beach do you like most?

¿Qué instrumento musical tocas?
What (Which) musical instrument do you play?

- **¿Cuál(es)?** expresses *what?* or *which?* in all other cases.

¿Cuál es la clase más grande?
What (Which) is the biggest class?

O J O The **¿cuál(es)?** + *noun* structure is not used by most speakers of Spanish: **¿Cuál de los dos libros quieres?** *(Which of the two books do you want?)* BUT **¿Qué libro quieres?** *(Which [What] book do you want?)*

¿Cuáles son tus actrices favoritas?
What (Which) are your favorite actresses?

¿Cuál es la capital del Uruguay?
What is the capital of Uruguay?

¿Cuál es tu teléfono?
What is your phone number?

Práctica

¿Qué o cuál(es)?

1. —¿_____ es esto? —Un lavaplatos.
2. —¿_____ son los Juegos Olímpicos? —Son un conjunto de competiciones deportivas.
3. —¿_____ es el quehacer que más te gusta? —Lavar los platos.
4. —¿_____ bicicleta vas a usar? —La de mi hermana.
5. —¿_____ son los cines más modernos? —Los del centro.
6. —¿_____ vídeo debo sacar? —El nuevo de Robert Rodríguez.
7. —¿_____ es una cafetera? —Es un aparato que se usa para preparar el café.
8. —¿_____ es Rivaldo? —En la foto, es el hombre a la izquierda de la pelota.

Conversación

Datos (*Information*) **personales.** Forme preguntas para averiguar (*find out*) datos de un compañero / una compañera. Puede usar más de una palabra interrogativa para conseguir la información. (Debe usar las formas de **tú**.)

MODELO: su dirección → ¿Cuál es tu dirección? (¿Dónde vives?)

1. su teléfono
2. su dirección
3. su cumpleaños
4. la ciudad en que nació (*you were born*)
5. su número de seguro (*security*) social
6. la persona en que más confía (*you trust*)
7. su tienda favorita
8. la fecha de su próximo examen

En los Estados Unidos y el Canadá...

La impresionante variedad de la música latina

Es difícil hablar de «música latina» porque hay una inmensa **variedad**. La música de España y de toda Latinoamérica cuenta con[a] **diversos orígenes** que luego **se mezclan**.[b] La música de los españoles y portugueses llegó al Nuevo Mundo, pero pronto se mezcló con fuertes **tradiciones indígenas**. Cuando los conquistadores trajeron **esclavos**[c] **africanos** al Nuevo Mundo, estos trajeron consigo[d] sus propias tradiciones musicales, que influyeron en varios tipos de música que hoy consideramos música hispana.

Tito Puente

La salsa es una de las formas musicales hispanas más reconocidas. La salsa es una mezcla de **ritmos afrocaribeños**, y fue creada en Nueva York por músicos hispanos en los años sesenta y setenta del siglo XX. La salsa es muy variada, pero siempre tiene una característica clara: es muy **bailable**. Uno de los nombres más asociados con la salsa es Tito Puente (1923–2000), el famoso **percusionista**. **Carlos Santana** grabó su versión de la composición de Puente, «Oye ¿cómo va?» e introdujo a Puente y un estilo de música hispana no sólo a una nueva generación, sino también al público no hispano.

[a]cuenta... *contains*   [b]se... *are combined*   [c]*slaves*   [d]*with them*

UN POCO DE TODO

Los fines de semana. Complete the following paragraphs with the correct form of the words in parentheses, as suggested by the context. When two possibilities are given in parentheses, select the correct word. *P* and *I* stand for preterite and imperfect, respectively.

Los fines de semana son como las burbujas[a] de oxígeno del calendario. Para muchos, son (los/las[1]) días más especiales. Casi todos los niños (esperar[2]) el sábado y el domingo con ansiedad. Quieren ir (a el / al[3]) parque, o a ver una película o mirar los dibujos animados toda la mañana.

También para los mayores los fines de semana son días diferentes. Hay novios que sólo (poder[4]) verse[b] los sábados y los domingos. (Otro[5]) personas tienen (de/que[6]) hacer visitas o las compras o limpiar la casa. Algunas necesitan (dormir[7]) porque no (dormir: *P*[8]) lo suficiente[c] durante la semana. Hay gente que no (querer[9]) hacer (nada/nunca[10]) y gente que espera hacer todo lo que no (hacer: *P*[11]) durante la semana.

En el mundo moderno, parece[d] que (hay/son[12]) cosas que sólo se pueden hacer los fines de semana, porque (*nosotros:* estar/ser[13]) muy ocupados durante la semana y no podemos hacer (ese[14]) cosas.

¿Qué le (gustar[15]) a Ud. hacer los fines de semana? ¿Qué (preferir: *I*[16]) hacer cuando era más joven?

[a]*bubbles*   [b]*see each other*   [c]*lo... enough*   [d]*it seems*

PASO 4 Un paso más

VIDEOTECA: En contexto

FUNCTION

Making plans with a friend

In this video segment, Mariela and Amalia are trying to make plans for the weekend. As you watch the segment, pay particular attention to the friends' use of language variants that are common in Costa Rica, words such as **tenés, salís, vos,** and **sos.** Can you tell what the traditional Spanish meanings of these words are?

COSTA RICA

A. Lluvia de ideas

- ¿Qué tipo de actividades prefiere Ud. hacer los fines de semana? ¿Con quién las hace? ¿Hay alguna actividad que Ud. haga todos los fines de semana, sin falta (*without fail*)?
- ¿Cómo se entera (*do you find out*) de los eventos en que puede participar? ¿Consulta Ud. algún periódico en particular?

B. Dictado

A continuación está la primera parte del diálogo entre Mariela y Amalia. Complétela con las palabras o frases que faltan.

Cultura en contexto
El voseo

Vos, un pronombre personal como **Ud.** y **tú**, tiene origen en el español antiguo. Su eso se llama **el voseo** y se usa en circunstancias de gran familiaridad social en ciertas partes del mundo hispanohablante. Los costarricenses, en particular, usan **vos** y sus formas verbales en vez de **tú.**

MARIELA: Quiero hacer algo interesante este fin de semana. ¿Vos tenés _____[1] para mañana?

AMALIA: No, no _____[2] planes. Soy muy aburrida, nunca salgo de mi casa. ¿Por qué? ¿Querés hacer algo juntas?

MARIELA: Me encantaría. ¿_____[3] querés hacer?

AMALIA: Mmm… ¿Ir al _____[4]? ¿Hay alguna película _____[5]?

MARIELA: A ver… la verdad es que no. No me interesan para nada estas _____.[6] Pero podemos ir al _____.[7]

C. Un diálogo original

Paso 1. Con un compañero / una compañera, dramatice la escena entre Amalia y Mariela.

Paso 2. Planes para este fin de semana. Dos amigos/as hacen planes para este domingo.

E1: Ud. desea salir el domingo, porque el sábado por la noche le toca trabajar y no va a poder hacer nada interesante. Afortunadamente (*Luckily*), tiene la mañana del lunes libre (*free*) para estudiar o descansar.

E2: Ud. tiene ganas de salir el domingo. El único obstáculo es que tiene bastante tarea y su primera clase es a las 8 de la mañana el lunes.

PASO FINAL

A LEER

Estrategia: Recognizing Derivative Adjectives

In previous chapters you learned to recognize cognates, word endings, and new words that are related to familiar words. In this chapter you will learn about derivative adjectives, a large group of adjectives derived from verbs. These adjectives end in **-ado** or **-ido**. You can often guess their meaning if you know the related verb. For example: **conocer** (*to know*) → **conocido** (*known, famous*); **preparar** (*to prepare*) → **preparado** (*prepared*).

In the following reading there are many **-do** adjectives. Try to guess their meaning from context. You might also notice past participle forms (**-do**) in conjunction with a verb form you don't recognize, such as **ha comentado** (*has commented*). You will study this form, known as the present perfect, in a later chapter of this text. For now, simply learn to recognize it.

> **Sobre la lectura...** Este artículo apareció en la revista *Quo*, una publicación española que trata temas populares, como la tecnología, la salud, las relaciones entre los sexos y los sitios turísticos. La lectura, un fragmento del artículo original, relata el interés creciente (*growing*) en los parques de atracciones (*amusement parks*) en España.

El sitio de mi recreo

La <u>proliferación</u> de <u>parques temáticos</u> y de museos interactivos revela que la concepción del ocio[a] y de vacaciones está cambiando. «Damos una oferta complementaria al sol y la playa. Ahora llegan turistas de toda España, cuando normalmente este no sería[b] un destino turístico», afirma José María Brugués, de Port Aventura, un parque temático en Tarragona.

Ante el éxito[c] de Port Aventura, España intenta ponerse a la altura de[d] mercados como los de los Estados Unidos, Francia o Gran Bretaña. Ya existen más de cincuenta <u>proyectos</u> de parques temáticos en España, entre ellos, en San Martín de la Vega (Madrid) dedicado al cine, un proyecto en el que está involucrada[e] la Warner Brothers.

Julián Rodríguez Luna, consejero delegado del Grupo Parque en España, comenta la popularidad creciente de estas nuevas atracciones. Según él, nuestra sociedad disfruta[f] cada vez más de tiempo libre, y por ello tiende[g] a buscar más <u>opciones</u> de ocio. Los parques, ya sean de atracciones, acuáticos o zoos, son una buena elección. Están configurados para que se puedan disfrutar[h] de una forma <u>participativa</u>, porque fuera del hogar[i] buscamos un ocio activo. Los jóvenes suelen buscar el riesgo[j] y las emociones fuertes, mien-

---

[a]*leisure time*   [b]*no... would not be*   [c]*success*   [d]*ponerse... compete on the same level as*   [e]*involved*   [f]*enjoys*   [g]*tends, is inclined to*   [h]*para... to be enjoyed*   [i]*fuera... outside the home*   [j]*risk*

tras que las familias buscan tranquilidad y pasar un buen rato con los niños.

Aparte de las novedades[k] en parques temáticos y de atracciones, la tecnología también ha llegado[l] a los museos. Al contrario de lo que se podría pensar,[m] los museos de siempre no morirán,[n] aunque muchos de ellos están comenzando a <u>reciclarse</u>. Algunos ya han adaptado varias salas para convertirlas en interactivas. Lo que le interesa al público es tocar y que los museos sean divertidos y lúdicos.[o]

[k]*novelties* [l]*ha... has arrived* [m]*Al... Contrary to what one might believe*
[n]*no... will not die* [o]*entertaining*

Un parque de atracciones en Barcelona, España

Comprensión

A. Selección múltiple. Escoja la respuesta correcta según la lectura.

1. ¿Cómo se explica el número creciente de parques temáticos en España?

   a. El gobierno (*government*) español desea atraer (*attract*) a más turistas internacionales.
   b. A los españoles no les gustan los museos.
   c. La gente tiene más tiempo libre y busca diversiones interactivas.

2. ¿Qué buscan los jóvenes cuando van a los parques?

   a. un sitio romántico
   b. un sitio sin adultos
   c. un sitio que ofrece riesgos

B. Palabras relacionadas. ¿De qué verbos se derivan los siguientes adjetivos?

1. involucrada _____
2. dedicado _____
3. configurados _____
4. divertidos _____

 A ESCRIBIR

Atracciones locales. Para muchas personas, ir a un parque temático es una buena diversión. Pero hay otras atracciones también. ¿Qué atracciones locales hay donde Ud. vive? Imagine que Ud. está en un comité universitario para reclutar (*recruit*) a nuevos estudiantes. A Ud. le toca escribir un ensayo de 250 palabras que describe todas las atracciones que ofrecen la universidad y la ciudad. El título del ensayo es: «Atracciones y diversiones para estudiantes de la Universidad».

En resumen

GRAMÁTICA

To review the grammar points presented in this chapter, refer to the indicated grammar presentations. You'll find further practice of these structures in the Workbook/Laboratory Manual, on the CD-ROM, and on the website.

26. Imperfect of Regular and Irregular Verbs

You should know the imperfect forms of all verbs. What are the three irregular imperfect verbs?

27. Superlatives

Do you know how to express that something is the best or the most?

28. Summary of Interrogative Words

You should know how to form questions and which question words to use in Spanish.

VOCABULARIO

Los verbos

aburrirse	to get bored
dejar (en)	to leave (behind) (in, at)
pegar	to hit
pelear	to fight
sonar (ue)	to ring; to sound

Los pasatiempos, las diversiones y las aficiones

los ratos libres	spare (free) time
dar (*irreg.*) un paseo	to take a walk
hacer (*irreg.*) un picnic	to have a picnic
hacer (*irreg.*) planes para + *inf.*	to make plans to (*do something*)
ir (*irreg.*)...	to go . . .
al cine / a ver una película	to the movies/ to see a movie
a una discoteca / a un bar	to a disco/to a bar
al teatro / a un concierto	to the theater/to a concert

jugar (ue) a las cartas / al ajedrez	to play cards/chess
ser (*irreg.*) divertido/a	to be fun
visitar un museo	to visit a museum

Repaso: dar (*irreg.*) / hacer (*irreg.*) una fiesta, hacer *camping*, jugar (ue) (al), pasarlo bien/mal, ser aburrido/a, tomar el sol

Los deportes

el/la aficionado/a (a)	fan (of)
el ciclismo	bicycling
el fútbol	soccer
el fútbol americano	football
el/la jugador(a)	player
la natación	swimming

Otros deportes: el basquetbol, el béisbol, el golf, el hockey, el tenis, el vólibol

correr	to run; to jog
entrenar	to practice, train
esquiar (esquío)	to ski
ganar	to win
montar a caballo	to ride a horse
pasear en bicicleta	to ride a bicycle

patinar	to skate
patinar en linea	to rollerblade
ser aficionado/a (a)	to be a fan (of)

Repaso: **nadar, perder (ie), practicar**

Algunos aparatos domésticos

la aspiradora	vacuum cleaner
la cafetera	coffeepot
el congelador	freezer
la estufa	stove
el horno de microondas	microwave oven
la lavadora	washing machine
el lavaplatos	dishwasher
el refrigerador	refrigerator
la secadora	clothes dryer
la tostadora	toaster

Algunos quehaceres domésticos

barrer (el piso)	to sweep (the floor)
hacer (*irreg.*) la cama	to make the bed
lavar (las ventanas, los platos, la ropa)	to wash (the windows, the dishes, the clothes)
limpiar la casa (entera)	to clean the (whole) house

pasar la aspiradora	to vacuum
pintar (las paredes)	to paint (the walls)
planchar la ropa	to iron clothing
poner (*irreg.*) la mesa	to set the table
quitar la mesa	to clear the table
sacar la basura	to take out the trash
sacudir los muebles	to dust the furniture

Otros sustantivos

la costumbre	custom, habit
la época	era, time (*period*)
la escuela	school
el grado	grade, year (*in school*)
el/la niñero/a	baby-sitter
la niñez	childhood

Adjetivos

| deportivo/a | sports-loving |
| pesado/a | boring; difficult |

Palabras adicionales

de joven	as a youth
de niño/a	as a child
mientras	while
tocarle a uno	to be someone's turn

CAPÍTULO

10

La salud

VOCABULARIO

- Health and well-being
- At the doctor's office

GRAMÁTICA

29 Using the Preterite and the Imperfect
30 Reciprocal Actions with Reflexive Pronouns

CULTURA

- **Enfoque cultural:** Venezuela
- **Nota cultural:** La medicina en los países hispanos
- **En los Estados Unidos y el Canadá:** Edward James Olmos: Actor y activista de la comunidad
- **Cultura en contexto:** En la farmacia

Multimedia

 You will learn about describing an illness in the **En contexto** video segment.

 Review vocabulary and grammar and practice language skills with the interactive CD-ROM.

W.W. Get connected to the Spanish-speaking world with the *¿Qué tal?* Online Learning Center: **www.mhhe.com/quetal**.

Caminar y pasear en bicicleta son buenas formas de ejercicio (*exercise*). Estas personas pasean por el Museo de los Niños en Caracas, Venezuela.

La salud y el bienestar°

La… *Health and well-being*

El cuerpo humano

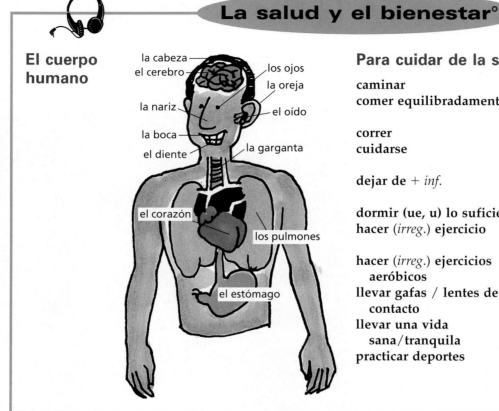

la cabeza
el cerebro
los ojos
la oreja
la nariz
el oído
la boca
el diente
la garganta
el corazón
los pulmones
el estómago

Para cuidar de la salud

caminar	to walk
comer equilibradamente	to eat well-balanced meals
correr	to run; to jog
cuidarse	to take care of oneself
dejar de + *inf.*	to stop (*doing something*)
dormir (ue, u) lo suficiente	to sleep enough
hacer (*irreg.*) **ejercicio**	to exercise; to get exercise
hacer (*irreg.*) **ejercicios aeróbicos**	to do aerobics
llevar gafas / lentes de contacto	to wear glasses / contact lenses
llevar una vida sana/tranquila	to lead a healthy / calm life
practicar deportes	to practice, play sports

Conversación

A. Asociaciones

Paso 1. ¿Qué partes del cuerpo humano asocia Ud. con las siguientes palabras? A veces hay más de una respuesta posible.

1. un ataque **3.** cantar **5.** pensar **7.** el amor **9.** la música
2. comer **4.** las gafas **6.** la digestión **8.** fumar **10.** el perfume

Paso 2. ¿Qué palabras asocia Ud. con las siguientes partes del cuerpo?

1. los ojos **2.** los dientes **3.** la boca **4.** el oído **5.** el estómago

B. Hablando de la salud

Paso 1. ¿Qué significan, para Ud., las siguientes oraciones?

MODELO: Se debe comer equilibradamente. →
Eso quiere decir (*means*) que es necesario comer muchas verduras, que…

Palabras y frases útiles: Eso quiere decir… , Esto significa que… , También…

1. Se debe dormir lo suficiente todas las noches.
2. Hay que hacer ejercicio.
3. Es necesario llevar una vida tranquila.
4. En general, uno debe cuidarse mucho.

Paso 2. ¿Lleva una vida sana? Dígale a un compañero / una compañera cómo vive, usando las frases del **Paso 1** y del **Vocabulario**.

MODELO: Creo que llevo una vida sana porque como equilibradamente: No como muchos dulces, excepto en los días festivos como la Navidad… Además (*Moreover*) duermo por lo menos (*at least*) ocho horas por día.

Paso 3. Ahora cambie su narración para describir lo que hacía de niño/a. ¿Qué hacía y qué *no* hacía Ud.? Debe organizar las ideas lógicamente.

MODELO: De niño, no llevaba una vida muy sana. Comía muchos dulces. También odiaba las frutas y verduras…

En el consultorio°

doctor's office

98,6 grados Fahrenheit

37,0 grados centígrados

el/la enfermero/a	nurse
el/la farmacéutico/a	pharmacist
el/la médico/a	physician
el/la paciente	patient
congestionado/a	congested, stuffed-up
mareado/a	dizzy; nauseated
el antibiótico	antibiotic
el jarabe	(cough) syrup
la pastilla	pill
la receta	prescription
el resfriado	cold
la tos	cough
doler (ue)*	to hurt, ache
enfermarse	to get sick
guardar cama	to stay in bed
internarse (en)	to check in (*to a hospital*)
ponerle (*irreg.*) **una inyección**	to give (someone) a shot

resfriarse	to get/catch a cold
respirar	to breathe
sacar	to extract
sacar la lengua	to stick out one's tongue
sacar una muela	to extract a tooth
tener (*irreg.*) **dolor (de cabeza, estómago, muela)**	to have a (head, stomach, tooth) ache
tener (*irreg.*) **fiebre**	to have a fever
tomar(le) la temperatura	to take someone's temperature
toser	to cough

— Pero ¿cómo quiere que le opere,[a] si no tiene Ud. nada?
— Mejor, doctor. Así la operación le será[b] más fácil…

[a]cómo... *why do you want me to operate on you* [b]*will be*

***Doler** is used like **gustar: Me duel*e* la cabeza. Me duel*en* los ojos.**

Conversación

A. Estudio de palabras. Complete las siguientes oraciones con una palabra de la misma (*same*) familia que la palabra en letras cursivas (*italics*).

1. Si me *resfrío*, tengo ____.
2. La *respiración* ocurre cuando alguien ____.
3. Si me ____, estoy *enfermo/a*. Un(a) ____ me toma la temperatura.
4. Cuando alguien *tose*, se oye una ____.
5. Si me *duele* el estómago, tengo un ____ de estómago.

NOTA CULTURAL

La medicina en los países hispanos

Como regla general, los hispanos **consultan** sobre sus **problemas de salud** no sólo con los médicos sino también[a] con **otros profesionales**. Por ejemplo, ya que[b] muchas medicinas se venden sin receta, se puede pedirle al farmacéutico / a la farmacéutica recomendaciones sobre **medicinas apropiadas** para tratar alguna **enfermedad**. Los farmacéuticos son profesionales con un **entrenamiento** riguroso en la universidad. Están al tanto[c] de los adelantos[d] en **farmacología**. En algunos países, la gente también consulta con los **practicantes** que son profesionales que poseen, por lo menos, tres años de entrenamiento médico y que están facultados[e] para poner inyecciones y aplicar ciertos tratamientos a los pacientes.

En los países hispanos, solamente algunas farmacias están abiertas[f] por la noche y durante los fines de semana. Cada semana diferentes farmacias se alternan para operar en tales[g] horarios. La gente se refiere a ellas como **farmacias de turno** o **de guardia**. Generalmente, los periódicos y los noticieros de radio y televisión locales publican los nombres y las direcciones de las farmacias de turno. Así la gente sabe adónde ir a comprar sus medicinas. En algunas ciudades, las farmacias de turno encienden[h] una luz roja al lado de la entrada para indicar que están atendiendo al público.

[a]sino... *but also* [b]ya... *since* [c]al... *up-to-date* [d]*advances* [e]*authorized* [f]*open* [g]*such* [h]*turn on*

B. Situaciones. Describa Ud. la situación de estas personas. ¿Dónde y con quiénes están? ¿Qué síntomas tienen? ¿Qué van a hacer?

1. Anamari está muy bien de salud. Nunca le duele(n) _____. Nunca tiene _____. Siempre _____. Más tarde, ella va a _____.
2. Martín tiene _____. Debe _____. El dentista va a _____. Después, Martín va a _____.
3. A Inés le duele(n) _____. Tiene _____. El médico y la enfermera van a _____. Luego, Inés tiene que _____.

NOTA COMUNICATIVA

The Good News . . . The Bad News . . .

To describe general qualities or characteristics of something, use **lo** with the masculine singular form of an adjective.

> lo bueno / lo malo   lo más importante
> lo mejor / lo peor lo mismo

This structure has a number of English equivalents, especially in colloquial speech.

> **lo bueno** = the good thing/part/news, what's good

C. Ventajas y desventajas (*Advantages and disadvantages*). Casi todas las cosas tienen un aspecto bueno y otro malo.

Paso 1. ¿Qué es lo bueno y lo malo (o lo peor y lo mejor) de las siguientes situaciones?

1. tener un resfriado
2. ir a una universidad cerca/lejos del hogar familiar (*family home*)
3. tener hijos cuando uno es joven (entre 20 y 25 años)
4. ser muy rico/a
5. ir al consultorio médico / del dentista

Paso 2. Compare sus respuestas con las de sus compañeros. ¿Dijeron algo que Ud. no consideró?

29 Narrating in the Past • Using the Preterite and the Imperfect

En el consultorio de la Dra. Méndez

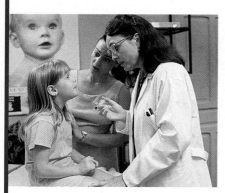

DRA. MÉNDEZ: ¿Cuándo *empezó* a sentirse mal su hija?

LOLA: Ayer por la tarde. *Estaba* congestionada, *tosía* mucho y *se quejaba* de que le *dolían* el cuerpo y la cabeza.

DRA. MÉNDEZ: ¿Y le *notó* algo de fiebre?

LOLA: Sí. Por la noche le *tomé* la temperatura y *tenía* treinta y ocho grados.

DRA. MÉNDEZ: A ver... Tal vez necesito ponerle una inyección...

MARTA: Eh... bueno... ¡Creo que ahora me encuentro un poco mejor!

In the preceding dialogue, locate all of the verbs that do the following.

1. indicate actions (or lack of action)
2. indicate conditions or descriptions

In Dr. Méndez's office DR. MÉNDEZ: When did your daughter begin to feel bad? LOLA: Yesterday afternoon. She was stuffed up, she coughed a lot, and she complained that her body and head were hurting. DR. MÉNDEZ: And did you note any fever? LOLA: Yes. At night I took her temperature and it was thirty-eight degrees. DR. MÉNDEZ: Let's see . . . Perhaps I'll need to give her a shot . . . MARTA: Um . . . well . . . I think I feel a little bit better now! . . .

When speaking about the past in English, you choose different past tense forms to use, depending on the context: *I wrote letters, I was writing letters, I used to write letters*, and so on. Similarly, you can use either the preterite or the imperfect in many Spanish sentences, depending on the meaning you wish to convey. Often the question is: How do you view the action or state of being?

A. Use the preterite to…

- tell about the beginning or the end of a past action

El sábado pasado, el partido de fútbol **empezó** a la una. **Terminó** a las cuatro.
Last Saturday, the soccer game began at one. It ended at four.

Use the imperfect to…

- talk about the habitual nature of an action (something you always did)

Había un partido todos los sábados. Muchas personas **jugaban** todas las semanas.
There was a game every Saturday. Many people played every week.

B. Use the preterite to…

- express an action that is viewed as completed

El partido **duró** tres horas. **Ganaron** Los Lobos, de Villalegre.
The game lasted three hours. The Lobos of Villalegre won.

Use the imperfect to…

- tell what was happening when another action took place and tell about simultaneous events (with **mientras** = *while*)

Yo no vi el final del partido. **Estaba** en la cocina cuando **terminó**.
I didn't see the end of the game. I was in the kitchen when it ended.

Mientras mi amigo **veía** el vídeo, **hablaba** con su novia.
While my friend was watching the video, he was talking with his girlfriend.

C. Use the preterite to…

- express a series of completed actions

Durante el partido, los jugadores **corrieron, saltaron y gritaron**.
During the game, the players ran, jumped, and shouted.

Use the imperfect to…

- give background details of many kinds: time, location, weather, mood, age, physical and mental characteristics

Llovía un poco durante el partido. Todos los jugadores **eran** jóvenes; **tenían** 17 ó 18 años.*
¡Y todos **esperaban** ganar!
It rained a little bit during the game. All the players were young; they were 17 or 18 years old. And all of them hoped to win!

D. Certain words and expressions are frequently associated with the preterite, others with the imperfect.

Some words often associated with the preterite are:

ayer, anteayer, anoche
una vez (*once*), dos veces (*twice*),…
el año pasado, el lunes pasado,…
de repente (*suddenly*)

Some words often associated with the imperfect are:

todos los días, todos los lunes,…
siempre, frecuentemente
mientras
de niño/a, de joven

Some English equivalents also associated with the imperfect are:

was _____ *-ing, were* _____ *-ing* (in English) *used to, would* (when *would* implies *used to* in English)

O J O These words do not *automatically* cue either tense, however. The most important consideration is the meaning that the speaker wishes to convey.

Ayer cenamos temprano.
Yesterday we had dinner early.

Ayer cenábamos cuando Juan llamó.
Yesterday we were having dinner when Juan called.

De niño jugaba al fútbol.
He played soccer as a child.

De niño empezó a jugar al fútbol.
He began to play soccer as a child.

E. Remember that, when used in the preterite, **saber, conocer, querer,** and **poder** have English equivalents different from the infinitives (see **Capítulo 8**). The English equivalents of these verbs in the imperfect do not differ from the infinitive meanings.

*Between digits, the word **o** (*or*) carries an accent to distinguish it from the digit 0.

F. The preterite and the imperfect frequently occur in the same sentence. In the first sentence the imperfect tells what was happening when another action—conveyed by the preterite—broke the continuity of the ongoing activity. In the second sentence, the preterite reports the action that took place because of a condition, described by the imperfect, that was in progress or in existence at that time.

Miguel **estudiaba** cuando **sonó** el teléfono.
Miguel was studying when the phone rang.

Olivia **comió** tanto porque **tenía** mucha hambre.
Olivia ate so much because she was very hungry.

G. The preterite and imperfect are also used together in the presentation of an event. The preterite narrates the action while the imperfect sets the stage, describes the conditions that caused the action, or emphasizes the continuing nature of a particular action.

Práctica

A. En el consultorio. What did your doctor do the last time you had an appointment with him or her? Assume that you had the following conditions and match them with the appropriate procedure.

CONDICIONES: (Yo)…

1. _____ tenía mucho calor y temblaba.
2. _____ me dolía la garganta.
3. _____ tenía un poco de congestión en el pecho (*chest*).
4. _____ creía que estaba anémico/a.
5. _____ no sabía lo que tenía.
6. _____ necesitaba medicinas.
7. _____ sólo necesitaba un chequeo rutinario.

ACCIONES: El médico…

a. me hizo muchas preguntas.
b. me puso una inyección.
c. me tomó la temperatura.
d. me auscultó (*listened to*) los pulmones y el corazón.
e. me analizó la sangre (*blood*).
f. me hizo sacar la lengua.
g. me hizo toser.

B. Pequeñas historias. Complete the brief paragraphs on the following page with the appropriate phrases from the list. Before you begin, it is a good idea to look at the drawing that accompanies each paragraph and to scan through the complete paragraph to get the gist of it, even though you may not understand everything the first time you read it.

1. nos quedamos   nos gustó
    nos quedábamos   nuestra familia decidió
    íbamos   vivíamos

Cuando éramos niños, Jorge y yo _____¹ en la Argentina. Siempre _____² a la playa, a Mar del Plata, para pasar la Navidad. Allí casi siempre _____³ en el Hotel Fénix. Un año, _____⁴ quedarse en otro hotel, el Continental. No _____⁵ tanto como el Fénix y por eso, al año siguiente, _____⁶ en el Fénix otra vez.

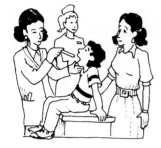

2. examinó   estaba   puso   dio
    intentabaᵃ tomarle   esperaba   llegó   se sintió

El niño tosía mientras que la enfermera _____¹ la temperatura. La madre del niño _____² pacientemente. Por fin _____³ la médica. Le _____⁴ la garganta al niño, le _____⁵ una inyección y le _____⁶ a su madre una receta para un jarabe. La madre todavía _____⁷ muy preocupada, pero inmediatamente después que la médica le habló, _____⁸ más tranquila.

ᵃtried to

C. Rubén y Soledad

Paso 1. Read the following paragraph at least once to familiarize yourself with the sequence of events, and look at the drawing. Then reread the paragraph, giving the proper form of the verbs in parentheses in the preterite or the imperfect, according to the needs of each sentence and the context of the paragraph as a whole.

Rubén (estar¹) estudiando cuando Soledad (entrar²) en el cuarto. Le (preguntar³) a Rubén si (querer⁴) ir al cine con ella. Rubén le (decir⁵) que sí porque se (sentir⁶) un poco aburrido con sus estudios. Los dos (salir⁷) en seguidaᵃ para el cine. (Ver⁸) una película cómica y (reírse⁹) mucho. Luego, como (hacer¹⁰) frío, (entrar¹¹) en su café favorito, El Gato Negro, y (tomar¹²) un chocolate. (Ser¹³) las dos de la mañana cuando por fin (regresar¹⁴) a casa. Soledad (acostarse¹⁵) inmediatamente porque (estar¹⁶) cansada, pero Rubén (empezar¹⁷) a estudiar otra vez.

ᵃen… *right away*

Paso 2. Now answer the following questions based on the paragraph about Rubén and Soledad. **¡OJO!** A question is not always answered in the same tense as that in which it is asked.

1. ¿Qué hacía Rubén cuando Soledad entró?
2. ¿Qué le preguntó Soledad a Rubén?
3. ¿Por qué dijo Rubén que sí?
4. ¿Les gustó la película? ¿Por qué?
5. ¿Qué hicieron cuando llegaron a casa?

Conversación

A. El primer día. Dé Ud. sus impresiones del primer día de su primera clase universitaria. Use estas preguntas como guía.

1. ¿Cuál fue la primera clase? ¿A qué hora era la clase y dónde era?
2. ¿Vino a clase con alguien? ¿Ya tenía su libro de texto o lo compró después?
3. ¿Qué hizo Ud. después de entrar en la sala de clase? ¿Qué hacía el profesor / la profesora?
4. ¿A quién conoció Ud. aquel día? ¿Ya conocía a algunos miembros de la clase? ¿A quiénes?
5. ¿Aprendió Ud. mucho durante la clase? ¿Ya sabía algo de esa materia?
6. ¿Le gustó el profesor / la profesora? ¿Por qué sí o por qué no? ¿Cómo era?
7. ¿Cómo se sentía durante la clase? ¿nervioso/a? ¿aburrido/a? ¿cómodo/a?
8. ¿Les dio tarea el profesor / la profesora? ¿Pudo Ud. hacerla fácilmente?
9. ¿Su primera impresión de la clase y del profesor / de la profesora, ¿fue válida o cambió con el tiempo? ¿Por qué?

B. Unas preguntas sobre el pasado

Paso 1. Con un compañero / una compañera, haga y conteste las siguientes preguntas.

¿Cuántos años tenías cuando... ?

1. aprendiste a pasear en bicicleta
2. hiciste tu primer viaje en avión
3. tuviste tu primera cita
4. empezaste a afeitarte

5. conseguiste tu licencia de manejar (*driver's license*)
6. abriste una cuenta corriente (*checking account*)
7. dejaste de crecer (*grow*)

¿Cuántos años tenías cuando tus padres... ?

8. te dejaron cruzar la calle solo/a
9. te permitieron ir de compras a solas
10. te dejaron acostarte después de las nueve

11. te dejaron quedarte en casa sin niñero/a
12. te permitieron usar la estufa
13. te dejaron ver una película «R»
14. te dejaron conseguir un trabajo

Paso 2. Ahora, en grupos de cuatro, comparen sus respuestas. ¿Son muy diferentes las respuestas que dieron? ¿Quién del grupo tiene los padres más estrictos? ¿los menos estrictos?

Enfoque *cultural*

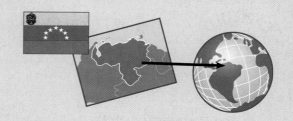

Venezuela

Datos esenciales

Nombre oficial: República de Venezuela

Capital: Caracas

Población: 21.000.000 de habitantes

Moneda: el bolívar

Idiomas: el español (oficial), varios idiomas indígenas

¡Fíjese!

Por su variedad de climas, Venezuela le ofrece al turista atracciones diversas. El clima venezolano varía entre el clima templado de las regiones andinas y el clima tropical de los llanos[a] y la costa. De hecho, el clima es agradable la mayor parte del año. Entre las atracciones turísticas hay lo siguiente:

- las hermosas[b] playas tropicales de la Isla Margarita y la costa caribeña

- la famosa catarata[c] Salto Ángel que, siendo dieciséis veces más alta que las cataratas del Niágara, es considerada la más alta del mundo

- la belleza[d] colonial de Ciudad Bolívar y Coro

- la progresiva y cosmopolita ciudad de Caracas y las majestuosas montañas andinas

[a]*plains*   [b]*beautiful*   [c]*waterfall*   [d]*beauty*

Conozca a... Simón Bolívar

Simón Bolívar (1783–1830) nació en Caracas. La fecha de su cumpleaños, el 24 de julio, es hoy día una fiesta nacional en Venezuela. Bolívar, llamado «el Libertador», ocupa un puesto[a] importante tanto en la historia de Venezuela como en la historia de Colombia, el Perú, el Ecuador y Bolivia por ser el personaje principal en las luchas[b] por la independencia de estos países. Bolívar, influenciado por las ideas de Jean Jacques Rousseau[c] y por la lucha de las colonias estadounidenses contra Inglaterra en el siglo XVIII, soñaba con[d] una América hispánica unida, sueño que nunca vio realizado.[e]

[a]*position*   [b]*struggles*   [c]*French writer and philosopher (1712–1778) whose ideas helped spark the French Revolution*   [d]*soñaba... dreamed about*   [e]*achieved*

Salto Ángel

Capítulo 10 of the video to accompany *¿Qué tal?* contains cultural footage about Venezuela.

Visit the *¿Qué tal?* website at www.mhhe.com/quetal.

30 Expressing *each other* • Reciprocal Actions with Reflexive Pronouns

—¿Tú crees que cada vez que nos encontramos tenemos que *saludarnos dándonos* la mano?[a]

[a]*hand*

1. ¿Dónde *se encuentran* los dos pulpos?
2. ¿Cómo *se saludan* (*do they greet each other*)?
3. *¿Se conocen? ¿Cómo se sabe?*

The plural reflexive pronouns, **nos, os**, and **se**, can be used to express *reciprocal actions* (**las acciones recíprocas**). Reciprocal actions are usually expressed in English with *each other* or *one another*.

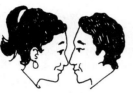

Nos queremos.

Nos queremos.	*We love each other.*
¿Os ayudáis?	*Do you help one another?*
Se miran.	*They're looking at each other.*

Práctica

A. Buenos amigos. Indique las oraciones que describen lo que hacen Ud. y un buen amigo / una buena amiga para mantener su amistad (*friendship*).

1. ☐ Nos vemos con frecuencia.
2. ☐ Nos conocemos muy bien. No hay secretos entre nosotros.
3. ☐ Nos respetamos mucho.
4. ☐ Nos ayudamos con cualquier (*any*) problema.
5. ☐ Nos escribimos cuando no estamos en la misma ciudad.
6. ☐ Nos hablamos por teléfono con frecuencia.
7. ☐ Nos decimos la verdad siempre, sea esta (*be it*) bonita o fea.
8. ☐ Cuando estamos muy ocupados, no importa si no nos hablamos por mucho tiempo.

B. ¿Qué se hacen? Describa las relaciones familiares o sociales en la siguiente página, haciendo oraciones completas con una palabra o frase de cada grupo.

los buenos amigos
los parientes
los esposos
los padres y los niños
los amigos que no viven en
  la misma ciudad
los profesores y los estudiantes
los compañeros de cuarto/casa

(no)

verse con frecuencia
quererse, respetarse
ayudarse (con los problemas
  económicos o los problemas
  personales)
hablarse (todos los días, con
  frecuencia, sinceramente)
llamarse por teléfono (con
  frecuencia), escribirse
mirarse (en la clase, con cariño
  [*affection*])
necesitarse
conocerse bien
saludarse, darse la mano

Conversación

Preguntas

1. ¿Con qué frecuencia se ven Ud. y su novio/a (esposo/a, mejor amigo/a)? ¿Cuánto tiempo hace que se conocen? ¿Con qué frecuencia se dan regalos? ¿se escriben? ¿se telefonean?

2. ¿Con qué frecuencia se ven Ud. y sus abuelos/primos? ¿Por qué se ven Uds. tan poco (tanto)? ¿Cómo se mantienen en contacto? En la sociedad norteamericana, ¿los parientes se ven con frecuencia? En su opinión, ¿es esto común entre los hispanos?

En los Estados Unidos y el Canadá...

Edward James Olmos: Actor y activista de la comunidad

El conocido **actor** de origen mexicano, Edward James Olmos (Los Ángeles, 1947), tiene en su historia profesional papeles inolvidables[a] como el de Jaime Escalante en *Stand and Deliver* (o en la versión en español *Con ganas de triunfar*), y el de policía en la famosa película cultista[b] *Blade Runner*. Además es un reconocido[c] **productor** y fue **director** y **guionista**[d] de la película *American Me*, sobre las pandillas[e] de Los Ángeles. Ha recibido los premios[f] Golden Globe y un Emmy.

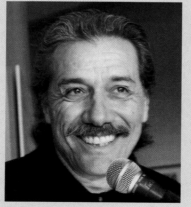

Edward James Olmos

Pero el Sr. Olmos no es sólo un artista sino también un destacado[g] líder de la comunidad latina en los Estados Unidos. Su **trabajo humanitario** y **comunitario** demuestra[h] un profundo compromiso[i] a favor de **la juventud** y **la salud** y contra la violencia de las pandillas y el racismo. Entre los muchos cargos que ha desempeñado[j] están los de embajador[k] de los Estados Unidos en UNICEF, portavoz[l] nacional de la Fundación Juvenil contra la Diabetes, de la Fundación Alerta contra el **SIDA**[m] y del Registro de Votantes, además de ser miembro de varios comités que van desde hospitales para niños al Concejo Nacional de Adopción.

[a]papeles... *unforgettable roles* [b]*cult* [c]*well-known* [d]*scriptwriter* [e]*gangs* [f]*Ha... He has received the awards* [g]*distinguished* [h]*shows*
[i]*commitment* [j]Entre... *Among the many positions he has held* [k]*ambassador* [l]*spokesperson* [m]Fundación... *AIDS Awareness Foundation*

UN POCO DE TODO

A. Lo mejor de estar enfermo

Paso 1. Form complete sentences using the words in the order given. Conjugate the verbs in the preterite or the imperfect and add or change words as needed. Use subject pronouns only when needed.

1. cuando / yo / ser / niño, / pensar / que / lo mejor / de / estar enfermo / ser / guardar cama
2. lo peor / ser / que / con frecuencia / (yo) resfriarse / durante / vacaciones
3. una vez / (yo) ponerme / muy / enfermo / durante / Navidad
4. mi / madre / llamar / a / médico / en / quien / tener / confianza
5. Dr. Matamoros / venir / casa / y / darme / antibiótico / porque / tener / mucho / fiebre
6. ser / cuatro / mañana / cuando / por fin / (yo) empezar / respirar / sin dificultad
7. desgraciadamente (*unfortunately*) / día / de / Navidad / (yo) tener / tomar / jarabe / y / no / gustar / nada / sabor (*taste, m.*)
8. lo bueno / de / este / enfermedad / ser / que / mi / padre / tener / dejar / fumar / mientras / yo / estar / enfermo

Paso 2. Now tell the story again from the point of view of the mother of the sick person. The first sentence is done for you.

> MODELO: **1.** cuando / yo / ser / niño, / pensar / que / lo mejor / de / estar enfermo / ser / guardar cama → Cuando mi hijo era niño, pensaba que lo mejor de estar enfermo era guardar cama.

B. Caperucita Roja

Paso 1. Retell this familiar story, based on the drawings, sentences, and cues that accompany each drawing, using the imperfect or preterite of the verbs in parentheses. Add as many details as you can, using the **Vocabulario útil** box in the margin. Using context, try to guess the meaning of words that are glossed with ¿ ?

Vocabulario útil	
abalanzarse sobre	to pounce on
avisar	to warn
dispararle	to shoot at someone/ something
esconderse	to hide
enterarse de	to find out about
huir (huyó)	to flee
saltar	to jump

1. Érase una vez[a] una niña hermosa que (llamarse[1]) Caperucita Roja. Todos los animales del bosque[b] (ser[2]) sus amigos y Caperucita Roja los (querer[3]) mucho.
2. Un día su mamá le (decir[4]): —Lleva en seguida esta jarrita de miel[c] a casa de tu abuelita. Ten cuidado[d] con el lobo[e] feroz.

①  ②

[a]¿ ? [b]¿ ? [c]jarrita... *jar of honey* [d]Ten... *Be careful* [e]¿ ?

3. En el bosque, el lobo (salir[5]) a hablar con la niña. Le (preguntar[6]): —¿Adónde vas, Caperucita? Esta le (contestar[7]) dulcemente:[f] —Voy a casa de mi abuelita.

4. —Pues, si vas por este sendero,[g] vas a llegar antes, (decir[8]) el malvado[h] lobo. Él (irse[9]) por otro camino más corto.

[f]*sweetly* [g]*path* [h]*¿ ?*

5. El lobo (llegar[10]) primero a la casa de la abuelita y (entrar[11]) silenciosamente. La abuelita (tener[12]) mucho miedo. (*Ella:* Saltar[13]) de la cama y (correr[14]) a esconderse.

6. Caperucita Roja (llegar[15]) por fin a la casa de la abuelita. (*Ella:* Encontrar[16]) a su «abuelita», que (estar[17]) en la cama. Le (decir[18]): —¡Qué dientes tan largos tienes! —¡Son para comerte mejor!— (decir[19]) su «abuelita».

7. Una ardilla[i] del bosque (enterarse[20]) del peligro. Por eso (avisar[21]) a un cazador.[j]

8. El lobo (saltar[22]) de la cama y (abalanzarse[23]) sobre Caperucita. Ella (salir[24]) de la casa corriendo y pidiendo socorro[k] desesperadamente.

[i]*¿ ?* [j]*¿ ?* [k]*help*

9. El cazador (ver[25]) lo que (ocurrir[26]). (*Él:* Dispararle[27]) al lobo y le (hacer[28]) huir.

10. Caperucita (regresar[29]) a la casa de su abuelita. La (abrazar: *ella*[30]) y le (prometer[31]) escuchar siempre los consejos de su mamá.

Paso 2. Hay varias versiones del cuento de Caperucita Roja. La que Ud. acaba de leer termina felizmente, pero otras no. Con otros dos compañeros, vuelvan a contar la historia, empezando por el dibujo número 7. Inventen un diálogo más largo entre Caperucita y el lobo y cambien por completo el final del cuento.

Más vocabulario útil			
atacar	to attack	**matar**	to kill
comérselo/la	to eat something up		

VIDEOTECA: En contexto

In this video segment, Juan Carlos talks to the pharmacist about medication to ease his cold. What cold medications do you prefer? Do you believe that any medication can cure a cold?

A. Lluvia de ideas

- ¿Se enferma Ud. a menudo? ¿De qué se enferma?
- ¿Va Ud. inmediatamente al consultorio médico cuando se siente mal o prefiere esperar a ver si se pone (*you get*) mejor/peor? ¿Por qué?
- En este episodio, el farmacéutico le dice a Juan Carlos que dormir es una de las mejores medicinas. ¿Qué hace Ud. para sentirse mejor?

B. Dictado

A continuación está la primera parte del diálogo entre Juan Carlos y el farmacéutico. Complétela con las palabras o frases que faltan.

FARMACÉUTICO: Buenas tardes, Juan Carlos. ¿_____¹ estás hoy? ¿_____?²

JUAN CARLOS: Pues, me _____³ mucho la _____⁴ y estoy bien _____.⁵

FARMACÉUTICO: ¿Fuiste a ver al _____⁶?

JUAN CARLOS: Tuve una consulta esta mañana.

FARMACÉUTICO: ¿Y qué te dijo?

JUAN CARLOS: Tengo una infección respiratoria. Me dio una _____⁷ para un _____.⁸

C. Un diálogo original

Paso 1. Con un compañero / una compañera, dramatice la escena entre Juan Carlos y el farmacéutico.

Paso 2. Consejos de sus padres. Imagine que Ud. y su compañero son miembros de una familia. Tengan la siguiente conversación.

E1: Ud. está bien resfriado/a. Hable con su mamá/papá u otro pariente para preguntarle lo que debe hacer Ud. para curarse. Por ejemplo, Ud. puede decirles que no sabe si debe ir al médico o no.

E2: Ud. es la mamá / el papá u otro pariente de su compañero/a y le dice lo que debe hacer para cuidarse cuando está enfermo/a. No se olvide de preguntarle por todos los síntomas posibles antes de dar sus consejos (*advice*).

EL PERÚ

FUNCTION

Describing an illness

Cultura en contexto
En la farmacia

En muchas farmacias de Latinoamérica y España los productos están detrás del mostradorᵃ y los clientes tienen que pedírselos al farmacéutico / a la farmacéutica. Inclusoᵇ pastillas como la aspirina no están al alcanceᶜ del cliente.

ᵃ*counter* ᵇ*Even* ᶜ*al... within reach*

PASO FINAL

A CONVERSAR

En la farmacia

Como Ud. leyó en la **Nota cultural** de este capítulo, en muchos países hispanos la gente puede consultar a un farmacéutico / una farmacéutica en vez de ir al médico. La persona enferma describe sus síntomas y el farmacéutico / la farmacéutica o (*either*) le receta un medicamento apropiado o (*or*) le manda a ver al médico.

Paso 1. En una hoja de papel aparte, prepare un cuadro como el siguiente. En su cuadro, escriba los síntomas y los posibles tratamientos para las enfermedades en los espacios en blanco.

enfermedad	una infección de garganta	un resfriado	una migraña
síntomas			
tratamientos			

Paso 2. Con un compañero / una compañera, prepare una escena entre una persona enferma y un farmacéutico / una farmacéutica. Escojan el papel que quieren hacer e improvisen una escena basándose en los cuadros del **Paso 1.** Su escena debe incluir saludos, una descripción de los síntomas, las recomendaciones médicas y una despedida.

> MODELO: E1: Buenos días, Sr. Maldonado.
> E2: Buenos días, Sra. Velázquez. ¿En qué le puedo servir?
> E1: Me siento muy mal hoy. No sé qué me pasa.
> E2: ¿Qué síntomas tiene?…

Paso 3. Cambien papeles e improvisen la escena otra vez.

En resumen

GRAMÁTICA

To review the grammar points presented in this chapter, refer to the indicated grammar presentations. You'll find further practice of these structures in the Workbook/Laboratory Manual, on the CD-ROM, and on the website.

29. Using the Preterite and the Imperfect

Do you know which tense to use to express habitual or repeated actions? Which tense should be used to express the beginning or end of an action?

30. Reciprocal Actions with Reflexive Pronouns

Which reflexive pronouns are used in reciprocal constructions? How can you distinguish a reciprocal from a reflexive action?

VOCABULARIO

Los verbos

encontrarse (ue) (con)	to meet (*someone somewhere*)
saludarse	to greet each other

La salud y el bienestar

caminar	to walk
cuidarse	to take care of oneself
dejar de + *inf.*	to stop (*doing something*)
doler (ue)	to hurt, ache
encontrarse (ue)	to be, feel
examinar	to examine
guardar cama	to stay in bed
hacer (*irreg.*) ejercicios aeróbicos	to do aerobics
internarse (en)	to check in (*to a hospital*)
llevar una vida sana/tranquila	to lead a healthy/calm life
ponerle (*irreg.*) una inyección	to give (someone) a shot, injection
resfriarse (me resfrío)	to get/catch a cold
respirar	to breathe
sacar	to extract
sacar la lengua	to stick out one's tongue
sacar una muela	to extract a tooth

tener (*irreg.*) dolor de	to have a pain in
tomarle la temperatura	to take someone's temperature
toser	to cough

Repaso: comer, correr, dormir (ue, u), enfermarse, hacer (*irreg.*) ejercicio, practicar deportes

Algunas partes del cuerpo humano

la boca	mouth
la cabeza	head
el cerebro	brain
el corazón	heart
el diente	tooth
el estómago	stomach
la garganta	throat
la nariz	nose
el oído	inner ear
el ojo	eye
la oreja	outer ear
los pulmones	lungs
la sangre	blood

Las enfermedades y los tratamientos

el antibiótico	antibiotic
el chequeo	checkup
el consultorio	(medical) office
el dolor (de)	pain, ache (in)

la farmacia	pharmacy
la fiebre	fever
las gafas	glasses
el jarabe	(cough) syrup
los lentes de contacto	contact lenses
la medicina	medicine
el/la paciente	patient
la pastilla	pill
la receta	prescription
el resfriado	cold
la sala de emergencias/ urgencia	emergency room
la salud	health
el síntoma	symptom
la temperatura	temperature
la tos	cough

El personal médico

el/la dentista	dentist
el/la enfermero/a	nurse
el/la farmacéutico/a	pharmacist

Repaso: el/la médico/a

Los sustantivos

la desventaja	disadvantage
la ventaja	advantage

Los adjetivos

congestionado/a	congested
mareado/a	dizzy; nauseated
mismo/a	same

Palabras adicionales

de repente	suddenly
dos veces	twice
equilibradamente	in a balanced way
eso quiere decir...	that means . . .
lo bueno / lo malo	the good thing, news / the bad thing, news
lo suficiente	enough
por lo menos	at least
una vez	once

Presiones de la vida moderna

VOCABULARIO

- Pressures of student life
- Accidents and clumsiness
- How things are done: Adverbs

GRAMÁTICA

31 Another Use of **se**
32 A Summary of the Uses of **por** and **para**

CULTURA

- **Enfoque cultural:** Puerto Rico
- **Nota cultural:** Palabras y frases para momentos difíciles
- **En los Estados Unidos y el Canadá:** Ricky Martin
- **Cultura en contexto:** El bar: Un pasatiempo social

Multimedia

You will learn about asking for and giving directions in the **En contexto** video segment.

Review vocabulary and grammar and practice language skills with the interactive CD-ROM.

WWW. Get connected to the Spanish-speaking world with the *¿Qué tal?* Online Learning Center: **www.mhhe.com/quetal**.

Caminar es buena manera de aliviar (*to relieve*) el estrés. Estas estudiantes caminan en el campus de la Universidad de Puerto Rico en Río Piedras.

Las presiones de la vida estudiantil

Agenda:° del 1 al 7 de febrero   *Appointment calendar*

1° al 7° de febrero

lunes, 1 de febrero
ir a la biblioteca (sacar libros para historia de arte)
informe oral de sociología

martes, 2 de febrero
examen de química

miércoles, 3 de febrero
recoger[a] nuevo permiso de estacionamiento

jueves, 4 de febrero
fecha límite para entregar informe[b] escrito para
historia del arte

viernes, 5 de febrero
prueba[c] de español

sábado, 6 de febrero
hacer llave para apartamento
fiesta de cumpleaños para Rosa

domingo, 7 de febrero

[a]*pick up*   [b]*report*   [c]*test*

acordarse (ue) (de)	to remember
entregar	to turn, hand in
estacionar	to park
llegar a tiempo/tarde	to arrive early/late
pedir (i, i) disculpas	to apologize

Discúlpeme.	Pardon me. / I'm sorry.
¡Lo siento (mucho)!	Pardon me! / I'm (very) sorry!
Perdón.	Pardon me. / I'm sorry.
recoger	to collect; to pick up
sacar	to take out
sacar buenas/malas notas	to get good/bad grades
ser (*irreg.*) flexible	to be flexible
sufrir	to suffer
sufrir (muchas) presiones	to be under (a lot of) pressure

Otros sustantivos

el calendario	calendar
la calificación	grade
el despertador	alarm clock
el estrés	stress
el examen	exam
la fecha límite	deadline
la (falta de) flexibilidad	(lack of) flexibility
el horario	schedule
el informe (oral/escrito)	(oral/written) report
la llave	key
la prueba	quiz; test
la tarjeta de identificación	identification card
el trabajo	job, work; report, (piece of) work
de tiempo completo/parcial	full/part time

Conversación

A. Asociaciones

Paso 1. ¿Qué palabras asocia Ud. con estos verbos? Pueden ser sustantivos, antónimos o sinónimos.

1. estacionar
2. recoger
3. acordarse
4. entregar
5. sacar

Paso 2. ¿Qué palabras y/o situaciones asocia Ud. con los siguientes sustantivos?

1. el calendario
2. el despertador
3. las calificaciones
4. el estrés
5. la fecha límite
6. el horario
7. los informes
8. la llave
9. la tarjeta identificación

B. Situaciones. La lista de la izquierda consta de (*consists of*) preguntas o comentarios hechos por varias personas. La otra incluye las respuestas de otras personas. Decida qué respuesta corresponde a cada comentario. Luego invente un contexto para cada diálogo. ¿Dónde están las personas que hablan? ¿En casa? ¿en una oficina? ¿en clase?

1. —Anoche no me acordé de poner el despertador.
2. —No puede estacionar el coche aquí. No tiene permiso de estacionamiento para esta zona.
3. —¿Sacaste una buena nota en la prueba?
4. —Ramiro no tiene buen aspecto (*doesn't look right*). Creo que algo le causa mucho estrés.
5. —Aquí tiene mi trabajo escrito sobre el Mercado Común.

a. —Pues estoy cansado de buscar estacionamiento por todo el *campus*. Lo voy a dejar aquí.
b. —¿Lo olvidaste otra vez? ¿A qué hora llegaste a la oficina?
c. —Pero la fecha límite era ayer. Es la última vez que acepto un informe suyo (*of yours*) tarde.
d. —Muy buena, pero no la esperaba. No tuve tiempo de estudiar.
e. —Es porque tiene un trabajo de tiempo completo, y también toma tres cursos este semestre.

¡La profesora Martínez se levantó con el pie izquierdo!°

con... *on the wrong side of the bed*

la cabeza
los dedos de la mano
la mano
el brazo

Le duele la cabeza.

la pierna
el pie
los dedos de los pies

Se dio contra el escritorio. Se cayó y se lastimó la pierna.

¡Qué torpe!

«Fue sin querer. Estaba distraída».

Accidentes

caerse	to fall down
darse (*irreg.*) **en/ con/contra**	to hit (a part of one's body)/to run into/bump against
Se dio en el pie.	She bumped her foot.
Se dio con la silla.	She ran into the chair.
Se dio contra la puerta.	She bumped against the door.
doler (ue)	to hurt, ache

equivocarse	to be wrong, make a mistake
hacerse (*irreg.*) **daño**	to hurt oneself
lastimarse	to injure oneself
pegar	to hit, strike
pegarse en/con/ contra	to run, bump into
romper	to break
Fue sin querer.	It was unintentional.
distraído/a	absentminded
torpe	clumsy

Conversación

A. **Posibilidades.** ¿Qué puede Ud. hacer o decir —o qué le puede pasar— en cada situación?

1. A Ud. le duele mucho la cabeza.
2. Ud. le pega a otra persona sin querer.
3. Ud. se olvida del nombre de otra persona.
4. Ud. está muy distraído/a y no mira por dónde camina.
5. Ud. se lastima la mano (el pie).

NOTA CULTURAL

Palabras y frases para momentos difíciles

Hay muchas expresiones para ocasiones de mala suerteᵃ o de presión. Varían mucho de región en región y de país en país. Estas son algunas de las más comunes.

Para expresar dolor, sorpresa o compasión

¡Ay!	*Ah! Ouch!*	¿Qué le vamos a hacer?	*What can you do?*
¡Uy!	*Oops! Oh!*	¡No me digas!	*You're kidding! (You don't say!)*
¡No puede ser!	*That can't be!*		

Para dar ánimoᵇ

¡Venga!	*Come on!*	¡No es para tanto!	*It's not so bad!*
¡Órale! (*Méx.*)	*Come on!*	¡Anímate!	*Cheer up!*

ᵃ*luck* ᵇ*Para… To cheer*

B. Accidentes y tropiezos (*mishaps*)

Paso 1. ¿Le han pasado a Ud. alguna vez las siguientes cosas? Complete las oraciones con información verdadera para Ud. Si nunca le pasó nada de esto, invente una situación que podría haber ocurrido (*could have happened*).

1. Me caí por las escaleras (*stairs*) y _____.
2. No me acordé de hacer la tarea para la clase de _____.
3. Me equivoqué cuando _____.
4. El despertador sonó, pero _____.
5. No pude encontrar _____.
6. Me di con _____ y me lastimé _____.
7. Pasó la fecha límite para entregar un informe y _____.
8. Caminaba un poco distraído/a y _____.

Paso 2. Ahora usando las oraciones del **Paso 1** como guía, pregúntele a un compañero / una compañera cómo le fue ayer. También puede preguntarle si le pasaron desastres adicionales.

MODELO: ¿Te caíste por las escaleras ayer? ¿Te hiciste daño?

Talking about How Things Are Done: Adverbs

- You already know some of the most common Spanish *adverbs* (**los adverbios**). Note that the form of adverbs is invariable.

bien	mucho	pronto	siempre
mal	poco	a tiempo	nunca
mejor	más	tarde	sólo
peor	menos	temprano	muy

- Adverbs that end in *-ly* in English usually end in **-mente** in Spanish. The suffix **-mente** is added to the feminine singular form of adjectives. Adverbs ending in **-mente** have two stresses: one on the adjective stem and the other on **-men**. The stress on the adjective stem is the stronger of the two.

Adjective	Adverb	English
rápido	**rápidamente**	*rapidly*
fácil	**fácilmente**	*easily*
valiente	**valientemente**	*bravely*

- In Spanish, adverbs modifying a verb are placed as close to the verb as possible. When they modify adjectives or adverbs, they are placed directly before them.

Hablan **estupendamente** el español.
They speak Spanish marvelously.

Ese libro es **poco** interesante.*
That book is not very interesting.

Vamos a llegar **muy tarde**.
We're going to arrive very late.

Conversación

A. ¡Seamos (*Let's be*) **lógicos!** Complete estas oraciones lógicamente con adverbios basados en los siguientes adjetivos: **constante, directo, fácil, inmediato, paciente, posible, puntual, rápido, total, tranquilo.**

1. La familia está esperando _____ en la cola.
2. Hay examen mañana y tengo que empezar a estudiar _____.
3. ¿Las enchiladas? Se preparan _____.
4. ¿Qué pasa? Estoy _____ confundido/a (*confused*).
5. Cuando mira la tele, mi hermanito cambia el canal _____.
6. Es necesario que las clases empiecen _____.

B. Entrevista. Con un compañero / una compañera, haga y conteste las siguientes preguntas.

1. ¿Qué haces rápidamente?
2. ¿Qué te toca hacer inmediatamente?
3. ¿Qué hiciste (comiste,...) solamente una vez que te gustó muchísimo?
4. ¿Qué haces tú fácilmente que es difícil para otras personas?

*Note that in Spanish one equivalent of *not very* + *adjective* is **poco** + *adjective*.

Gramática PASO 2

31 Expressing Unplanned or Unexpected Events • Another Use of *se*

Un día fatal

A Diego *se le cayó* la taza de café.

También *se le perdió* la cartera.

A Antonio *se le olvidaron* sus libros y su trabajo cuando fue a clase.

También *se le perdieron* las llaves de su apartamento.

¿Le pasaron a Ud. las mismas cosas —o cosas parecidas (*similar*)— esta semana? Conteste, completando las oraciones.

1. (Se me perdieron / No se me perdieron) las llaves de mi coche/casa.
2. (Se me olvidó / No se me olvidó) una reunión importante.
3. (Se me cayó / No se me cayó) una taza de café.
4. (Se me rompió / No se me rompió) un objeto de mucho valor (*value*) sentimental.

A. Unplanned or unexpected events (*I dropped . . . , We lost . . . , You forgot . . .*) are frequently expressed in Spanish with **se** and a third person form of the verb. In this structure, the occurrence is viewed as happening *to* someone—the unwitting recipient of the action. Thus the victim is indicated by an indirect object pronoun, often clarified by **a** + *noun* or *pronoun*. In such sentences, the subject (the thing that is dropped, broken, forgotten, and so on) usually follows the verb.

Se le olvidaron las llaves.
He forgot the keys. (The keys were forgotten by him.)

(*a* + Noun or Pronoun)	*se*	Indirect Object Pronoun	Verb	Subject
(A mí)	Se	me	cayó	la taza de café.
¿(A ti)	Se	te	perdió	la cartera?
A Antonio	se	le	olvidaron	los apuntes.

The verb agrees with the grammatical subject of the Spanish sentence (**la taza, la cartera, los apuntes**), not with the indirect object pronoun. **No** immediately precedes **se**.

A Antonio *no se* le olvidaron los apuntes.
Antonio didn't forget his notes.

B. Here are some verbs frequently used in this construction.

Note: Although all indirect object pronouns can be used in this construction, this section will focus on the singular of first, second, and third persons (**se me… , se te… , se le…**).

acabar	to finish; to run out of
caer	to fall
olvidar	to forget
perder (ie)	to lose
quedar	to remain, be left
romper	to break

Práctica

A. **¡Qué mala memoria!** Hortensia sufre muchas presiones en su vida. Por eso cuando se fue de vacaciones al Perú, estaba tan distraída que se le olvidó hacer muchas cosas importantes antes de salir. Empareje (*Match*) los lapsos de Hortensia con las consecuencias.

LAPSOS

1. _____ Se le olvidó cerrar la puerta de su casa.
2. _____ Se le olvidó pagar sus cuentas.
3. _____ Se le olvidó pedirle a alguien que cuidara a (*to take care of*) su perro.
4. _____ Se le olvidó cancelar el periódico.
5. _____ Se le olvidó pedirle permiso a su jefa (*boss*).
6. _____ Se le olvidó llevar el pasaporte.
7. _____ Se le olvidó hacer reserva en un hotel.

CONSECUENCIAS

a. Va a perder el trabajo.
b. No la van a dejar entrar en el Perú.
c. Le van a suspender el servicio de la luz (*electricity*) y de gas… ¡y cancelar sus tarjetas de crédito!
d. Alguien le va a robar el televisor.
e. ¡«King» se va a morir!
f. No va a tener dónde alojarse (*to stay*).
g. Todos van a saber que no está en casa.

B. ¡Desastres por todas partes (*everywhere*)!

Paso 1. ¿Es Ud. una persona distraída o torpe? Indique las oraciones que se apliquen (*apply*) a Ud. Puede cambiar algunos de los detalles de las oraciones si es necesario.

1. ☐ Con frecuencia se me caen los libros (los platos,...).
2. ☐ Se me pierden constantemente las llaves (los calcetines,...).
3. ☐ A menudo (*Often*) se me olvida apagar la computadora (la luz,...).
4. ☐ Siempre se me rompen las gafas (las lámparas,...).
5. ☐ De vez en cuando se me quedan los libros (los cuadernos,...) en la clase.
6. ☐ Se me olvida fácilmente mi horario (el teléfono de algún amigo,...).

Paso 2. ¿Es Ud. igual ahora que cuando era más joven? Complete cada oración del **Paso 1** para describir cómo era de niño/a. No se olvide de usar el imperfecto en sus oraciones.

MODELO: De niño/a, (no) se me caían los libros con frecuencia.

Paso 3. Ahora compare sus respuestas con las de un compañero / una compañera. ¿Quién es más distraído/a o torpe ahora? ¿Quién lo era de niño/a?

En los Estados Unidos y el Canadá...

Ricky Martin

Enrique Martín Morales es el puertorriqueño que todo el mundo[a] conoce como **Ricky Martin**. Nació el día de Nochebuena, 1971, en San Juan, Puerto Rico. Desde niño sabía que quería ser artista. En 1984, cuando tenía solamente 12 años, se presentó a un *casting call* para sustituir a un miembro del famoso grupo juvenil **Menudo,** y ¡ganó el puesto! Se quedó con Menudo hasta 1989, y desde entonces no sólo ha sido[b] cantante sino[c] también actor. Desempeñó un papel[d] en una telenovela en México y otro en el programa norteamericano «General Hospital» en 1994.

Ricky Martin

Al talentoso Ricky Martin le gusta todo tipo de música y puede cantar con igual[e] facilidad en inglés como en español. Aunque[f] el español es su lengua materna y siempre cantará[g] en español, le gusta la posibilidad de comunicarse con el público norteamericano también. A finales del siglo XX[h] tuvo un tremendo éxito en los Estados Unidos y en el resto del mundo con su álbum «**Livin' La Vida Loca**» y la canción del mismo nombre. Los hispanos no se sorprendieron; ya lo conocían muy bien.

[a]todo... *everybody* [b]*ha... has he been* [c]*but* [d]Desempeñó... *He played a part* [e]*the same* [f]*Although* [g]*he will sing* [h]*A... At the end of the twentieth century*

Conversación

A. Pablo tuvo un día fatal

Paso 1. Lea la siguiente descripción de lo que le pasó a Pablo ayer. Va a usar los números entre paréntesis en el **Paso 2**.

Pablo no se levantó a las siete, como lo hace generalmente. Se levantó tarde, a las ocho. (1) Se vistió rápidamente y salió de casa descalzo.ᵃ (2) Entró en el garaje pero no pudo abrir la puerta del coche. (3) Por eso tuvo que llegar a la oficina en autobús, pero cuando quiso pagarle al conductor, no tenía dinero. (4) Por eso tuvo que llegar a pie.

Cuando Pablo por fin entró a la oficina, su jefa se ofendió porque Pablo la trató descortésmente. (5) Su primer cliente se enojó porque Pablo no tenía toda la información necesaria para resolver su caso. (6)

Para las diez de la mañana, Pablo tenía muchísima hambre. (7) Por eso fue a la cafetería a comer algo. Se sentó con el vicepresidente de la compañía. Muy pronto esteᵇ se levantó furioso de la mesa. (8) Dijo que su chaqueta estaba arruinada. ¡Pablo ya no podía más! También se levantó y regresó a casa.

ᵃ*barefoot* ᵇ*the latter*

Paso 2. Ahora, con un compañero / una compañera, haga y conteste preguntas para explicar por qué Pablo lo pasó tan mal ayer. La primera persona debe hacer una pregunta. La segunda persona debe contestar, usando las sugerencias en los dibujos. El número uno ya está hecho (*done*).

MODELO: (1) →
E1: ¿Por qué se levantó tarde Pablo?
E2: Porque se le olvidó poner el despertador.

Frases útiles: Se le olvidó/olvidaron… , Se le perdió/perdieron… , Se le cayó/cayeron… , Se le quedó/quedaron…

NOTA COMUNICATIVA

Telling How Long Something Has Been Happening / How Long Ago Something Happened

- In Spanish, the phrase **hace** + *period of time* + **que** + *present tense* is used to express an action that has been going on over a period of time and is still going on.

    —**¿Cuánto tiempo hace que** vives en esta residencia?
    How long have you been living in this dorm?

    —**Dos meses.**
    (For) Two months.

- To say how long *ago* something happened, use the same **hace... que** construction but with the preterite tense instead of the present. Notice also the omission of **que** when the **hace** phrase does not come at the beginning of the sentence.

    Hace tres años **que fui** a Bogotá.
    I went to Bogotá three years ago.

    Fui a Cancún **hace** un mes.
    I went to Cancún a month ago.

B. **¿Quién... ?** ¿Quién hace qué? Haga oraciones completas emparejando (*matching*) las personas con las acciones correspondientes.

MODELO: hace mucho tiempo que / profesor(a) / enseñar español →
Hace mucho tiempo que el profesor / la profesora enseña español.

Hace mucho/poco tiempo que...

Gloria Estefan	hacen programas para niños
Sammy Sosa	canta en español
Antonio Banderas	habla español
los «Teletubbies»	vive en esta ciudad
John Grisham	escribe novelas
el rector / la rectora (*president*)	juega al béisbol
de la universidad	trabaja en esta universidad
el profesor / la profesora	trabaja en Hollywood
de español	¿ ?
un compañero / una compañera	
de clase	

Enfoque *cultural*

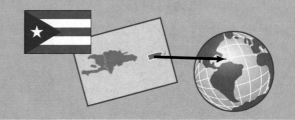

Puerto Rico

Datos esenciales

Nombre oficial: Estado Libre Asociado[a] de Puerto Rico

Capital: San Juan

Población: 4.000.000 de habitantes

Moneda: el dólar estadounidense

Idiomas oficiales: el español y el inglés

[a]Estado… *Free Associated State*

Una calle en el viejo San Juan

¡Fíjese!

- Puerto Rico ha estado relacionado[a] políticamente con los Estados Unidos desde la Guerra hispano-norteamericana de 1898, año en que España perdió las ultimas colonias de su imperio. En 1952, Puerto Rico se convirtió en Estado Libre Asociado. Bajo[b] este sistema de gobierno, los puertorriqueños son ciudadanos[c] estadounidenses. Sin embargo,[d] los que viven en la isla no pueden votar por el presidente de los Estados Unidos y deben servir en el ejército[e] de ese país en caso de guerra.

[a]ha… *has been associated* [b]*Under* [c]*citizens* [d]Sin… *However* [e]*army*

- Otro nombre de Puerto Rico es Borinquen y los puertorriqueños se conocen también como boricuas. Estas palabras originaron en el lenguaje de los indios taínos. Los taínos llegaron a la isla en el siglo[f] XIII pero su cultura casi desapareció con la llegada de los españoles en 1493.

- El Parque Nacional del Yunque, ubicado[g] en una montaña de 1.065 metros de altura que está al noreste de la isla, es pequeño cuando se compara a otros bosques[h] nacionales, pero es el único bosque tropical del sistema de Bosques nacionales de los Estados Unidos.

[f]*century* [g]*located* [h]*forests*

Conozca a... Alonso Ramírez

En 1690 se publica en México la primera novela del Nuevo Mundo, *Infortunios*[a] *de Alonso Ramírez*. Aunque esta obra[b] se atribuyó al mexicano Carlos Sigüenza y Góngora, hoy se cree que el verdadero[c] autor fue el mismo Alonso Ramírez del título. También se cree que la obra no es ficticia, sino autobiográfica: la vida de un puertorriqueño que se cría[d] en la isla, viaja a México y tiene aventuras en muchas partes del Mar Pacífico. Sus aventuras incluyen batallas contra piratas, una estadía[e] en una isla desierta y muchos otros eventos interesantísimos. Es una novela que vale la pena[f] leer.

[a]*Misfortunes* [b]*work* [c]*real* [d]se… *is brought up* [e]*stay* [f]que… *that is worth the trouble*

Capítulo 11 of the video to accompany *¿Qué tal?* contains cultural footage of Puerto Rico.

Visit the *¿Qué tal?* website at www.mhhe.com/quetal.

32 *¿Por o para?* • A Summary of Their Uses

¿Qué se representa?

a. b. c. d.

Empareje cada dibujo con la oración que le corresponde.

1. ＿＿ Le da mil pesos *para* las revistas. 3. ＿＿ Van *por* las montañas.
2. ＿＿ Le da mil pesos *por* las revistas. 4. ＿＿ Van *para* las montañas.

You have been using the prepositions **por** and **para** throughout your study of Spanish. Although most of the information in this section will be a review, you will also learn some new uses of **por** and **para**.

POR

The preposition **por** has the following English equivalents.

• *by, by means of*	Vamos **por** avión (tren, barco,…). *We're going by plane (train, ship, . . .).* Nos hablamos **por** teléfono mañana. *We'll talk by (on the) phone tomorrow.*
• *through, along*	Me gusta pasear **por** el parque y **por** la playa. *I like to stroll through the park and along the beach.*
• *during, in* (time of day)	Trabajo **por** la mañana. *I work in the morning.*
• *because of, due to*	Estoy nervioso **por** la entrevista. *I'm nervous because of the interview.*
• *for = in exchange for*	Piden 1.000 dólares **por** el coche. *They're asking $1,000 for the car.* Gracias **por** todo. *Thanks for everything.*

- *for = for the sake of, on behalf of*

Lo hago **por** ti.
I'm doing it for you (for your sake).

- *for = duration (often omitted)*

Vivieron allí (**por**) un año.
They lived there for a year.

Por is also used in a number of fixed expressions.

por Dios	for heaven's sake
por ejemplo	for example
por eso	that's why
por favor	please
por fin	finally
por lo general	generally, in general
por lo menos	at least
por primera/última vez	for the first/last time
por si acaso	just in case
¡por supuesto!	of course!
por todas partes	everywhere

PARA

Although **para** has many English equivalents, including *for,* it always has the underlying purpose of referring to a goal or destination.

- *in order to* + infinitive

Regresaron pronto **para** estudiar.
They returned soon (in order) to study.

Estudian **para** conseguir un buen trabajo.
They're studying (in order) to get a good job.

- *for = destined for, to be given to*

Todo esto es **para** ti.
All this is for you.

Le di un libro **para** su hijo.
I gave her a book for her son.

- *for = by* (deadline, specified future time)

Para mañana, estudien **por** y **para**.
For tomorrow, study ***por*** *and* ***para***.

La composición es **para** el lunes.
The composition is for Monday.

- *for = toward, in the direction of*

Salió **para** el Ecuador ayer.
She left for Ecuador yesterday.

- *for = to be used for*

OJO Compare the example at the right to **un vaso de agua** = *a glass (full) of water.*

El dinero es **para** la matrícula.
The money is for tuition.

Es un vaso **para** agua.
It's a water glass.

- *for = as compared with others, in relation to others.*

Para mí, el español es fácil.
For me, Spanish is easy.

Para (ser) extranjera, habla muy bien el inglés.
For (being) a foreigner, she speaks English very well.

- *for = in the employ of*

Trabajan **para** el gobierno.
They work for the government.

Práctica

¿Por o para? Complete los siguientes diálogos y oraciones con **por** o **para**.

1. Los Sres. Arana salieron _____ el Perú ayer. Van _____ avión, claro, pero luego piensan viajar en coche _____ todo el país. Van a estar allí _____ dos meses. Va a ser una experiencia extraordinaria _____ toda la familia.
2. Mi prima Graciela quiere estudiar _____ (ser) doctora. _____ eso trabaja _____ un médico _____ la mañana; tiene clases _____ la tarde.
3. —¿ _____ qué están Uds. aquí todavía? Yo pensaba que iban a dar un paseo _____ el parque.
—Íbamos a hacerlo, pero no fuimos _____ la nieve.
4. Este cuadro fue pintado (*was painted*) por Picasso _____ expresar los desastres de la guerra (*war*). _____ muchos críticos de arte, es la obra maestra de este artista.
5. La «Asociación Todo _____ Ellos» trabaja _____ las personas mayores, _____ ayudarlos cuando lo necesitan. ¿Trabaja Ud. _____ alguna asociación de voluntarios? ¿Qué hizo _____ inscribirse (*sign-up*)?

ASOCIACION

T O D O **E L L O S**

POR

Trabajamos por las personas mayores que están solas y con escasos recursos económicos

AYÚDANOS, NO ES POSIBLE SIN TI

Para más información llama al teléfono 907 98 91 15, de 18.00 a 20.00 h. tardes, martes y viernes

CAJAMADRID, SUC. 1028
C/C 6000854579

TODO POR ELLOS es una asociación no gubernamental inscrita en el Registro de Asociaciones del Ministerio del Interior con el número 160.589

Conversación

Entrevista. Hágale preguntas a su profesor(a) para saber la siguiente información.

1. la tarea para mañana y para la semana que viene
2. lo que hay que estudiar para el próximo examen
3. si para él/ella son interesantes o aburridas las ciencias
4. la opinión que tiene de la pronunciación de Uds., para ser principiantes
5. qué debe hacer Ud. para mejorar su pronunciación del español

UN POCO DE TODO

Presiones de la vida moderna. Complete the following paragraphs with the correct form of the words in parentheses—for verbs, the present, preterite, or imperfect—as suggested by the context. When two possibilities are given in parentheses, select the correct word.

Es cierto que (nuestro[1]) generación (disfrutar[2]) de[a] muchas ventajas comparada con las generaciones (anterior[3]). (Por/Para[4]) ejemplo, la medicina (está/es[5]) muy avanzada: Desde hace[b] muchas décadas (*nosotros:* tener[6]) vacunas[c] (muy/mucho[7]) buenas contra enfermedades que antes (ser[8]) mortales. Además, hoy es más fácil (por/para[9]) los amigos y familiares (ser/estar[10]) en contacto, gracias a los avances tecnológicos.

Sin embargo,[d] nuestra vida es también más complicada (que/de[11]) antes. Ahora (ser[12]) necesario trabajar más. (Por/Para[13]) dar una idea de (este/esto[14]), piense en (todo[15]) las madres que tienen un trabajo de tiempo completo y que también (deber[16]) cuidar a sus niños. O piense en las personas que tienen teléfono en el coche (por/para[17]) hacer negocios en la carretera.[e] Por eso, muchas personas (sufrir[18]) de estrés. Y cuando se sufre de estrés, es mucho más posible (ponerse/ponerte[19]) enfermo y tener accidentes.

¿Es toda (este[20]) actividad necesaria? Quizás[f] todos necesitamos (sentarse/sentarnos[21]) a pensar un poco, y (establecer[22]) un poco de calma en nuestra vida. Los avances científicos deben ser una ayuda (por/para[23]) nosotros, no una fuente[g] de más problemas, ¿verdad?

[a]disfrutar... *to enjoy* [b]Desde... *For* [c]*vaccinations* [d]Sin... *Nevertheless* [e]*highway* [f]*Perhaps* [g]*source*

Comprensión. Escoja la respuesta más apropiada.

1. Hoy día nuestra vida es (más/menos) complicada que hace un siglo.
2. (Es posible / No es posible) controlar el estrés.
3. Por los avances tecnológicos y científicos, hoy día es posible estar en (más/menos) contacto con nuestra familia.

VIDEOTECA: En contexto

In this video segment, Roberto gets lost and asks a passerby for directions. As you watch the segment, pay particular attention to the questions that Roberto asks to get directions, and to the man's responses. Where is Roberto trying to go? What landmarks does the man suggest he look for?

MÉXICO

FUNCTION

Asking for and giving directions

A. Lluvia de ideas

- ¿Tiene Ud. un buen sentido de orientación o se pierde con frecuencia? ¿Puede Ud. leer un mapa con facilidad?
- ¿Qué hace Ud. cuando se pierde? ¿Busca la dirección en un mapa? ¿Le pregunta a alguien? ¿Camina hasta encontrar el lugar?

B. Dictado.
A continuación está parte del diálogo entre Roberto y el hombre en la calle. Complétela con las palabras o frases que faltan.

ROBERTO: Esto es imposible… estoy
_____[1] perdido. Esta es la calle
Milagros. _____[2] de venir de la
calle Ibáñez. ¡El bar debe estar
_____[3]! No lo _____.[4]
Eh… Disculpe, señor…

SEÑOR: ¿Sí?

ROBERTO: Perdone la molestia… pero estoy
_____.[5] Busco el bar La copa
alegre. ¿Lo _____[6] Ud.?

SEÑOR: […] Ah, sí. _____[7] el bar. Mire,
es muy fácil llegar. No queda[a]
_____.[8] ¿Ve Ud. el teléfono?

ROBERTO: Sí.

SEÑOR: Esa es la calle Martín Gómez. Doble a la derecha en esa calle.
Luego _____[9] dos cuadras y doble a la _____[10] en la avenida Flores.

[a]No… *It is not located*

> ### Cultura en contexto
> ### *El bar: Un pasatiempo social*
>
> En los países hispanohablantes, es un pasatiempo común ir a un bar para tomar una cerveza, una copa de vino, un refresco o un café. Muchos bares también sirven comida. En España, los bares son famosos por sus tapas, diversos platos de porciones pequeñas. El propósito[a] de reunirse en bares no es emborracharse,[b] sino pasar tiempo con amigos y participar en discusiones y conversaciones interesantes. Es raro ver a una persona tomada[c] en un bar y se considera de muy mala educación[d] emborracharse en público.
>
> [a]*purpose* [b]*to get drunk* [c]*drunk* [d]*se… it is considered very bad manners*

C. Un diálogo original

Paso 1. Con un compañero / una compañera, dramatice la escena entre Roberto y el hombre en la calle.

Paso 2. Perdidos en el *campus*. Imagine que Ud. y un compañero / una compañera son las siguientes personas que tienen una conversación.

E1: Ud. está visitando el *campus* de su universidad por primera vez y ahora está perdido/a. Pare (*Stop*) a una persona en la calle y pregúntele cómo llegar a la biblioteca principal. No se olvide de ser muy amable.

E2: Ud. es una persona que no conoce el *campus* y necesita instrucciones para llegar a la biblioteca.

PASO FINAL

A LEER

Repaso de estrategias: Guessing the Content of a Passage

In previous reading sections, you have learned several different strategies to improve your comprehension of a text. Whenever you can, it's a good idea to utilize as many of these strategies as possible. Of course, this may not always be possible. For example, in the short passages that follow, there is only one visual item that accompanies the text. What else can you rely on to make predictions about the content? One strategy is to identify the source of the passages (see **Sobre la lectura** below). You should also consider the focus of the current chapter. And, of course, the title often reveals a great deal about the content of a passage. Considering all of these sources of information, what do you think these readings will be about?

1. vacation spots in the Spanish-speaking world
2. health-related issues associated with our modern way of life
3. fashion trends in Mexico
4. decorating ideas for your home

If you picked number 2, you were right. The following short passages discuss some of the negative effects that modern life can have on our health.

> **Sobre la lectura...** Esta lectura fue recopilada (*compiled*) de varios ejemplares (*issues*) de la revista española *GeoMundo*. Como Ud. ya sabe (Capítulo 7), el contenido de esta revista es muy similar al de *National Geographic*.

La vida moderna: ¿Saludable o no?

Pasaje 1

La Organización <u>Mundial</u> de la Salud ha determinado[a] que las diez regiones del mundo con mayor <u>incidencia</u> de casos de cáncer en la piel[b] son: Australia, Noruega, Suiza, Dinamarca, Suecia, Escocia, Finlandia, la región francesa de Calvados, Polonia e Italia. En Australia cerca de 40 de cada 100.000 personas <u>desarrollan</u> melanomas malignos, debido[c] principalmente, afirman los especialistas, al origen inglés de su población. La piel de los ingleses evolucionó bajo <u>cielos</u> nublados, pero los descendientes australianos de los ingleses viven bajo los intensos rayos solares subtropicales.

Actualmente la piel <u>bronceada</u> impresiona a la gente ignorante, y el riesgo de sufrir de cáncer en la piel se ha incrementado[d] por la contaminación y la falta de información. Lo mejor: si es Ud. de piel clara, descanse en la playa debajo de una <u>sombrilla</u>.

Pasaje 2

Más del 8 por ciento de 15 millones de europeos que trabajan con ordenadores[e] ocho (o seis) horas del día padecen[f] de males <u>oculares</u> por la «fatiga de la pantalla»[g] y los campos[h] magnéticos y electrostáticos producidos por esas <u>máquinas</u>. Han aparecido[i] en París especialistas médicos del «mal[j] del ordenador» que están trabajando rápidamente para encontrar alivio de este mal sufrido por muchos.

Pasaje 3

¿Son los dolores de cabeza, los vahídos[k] y las náuseas los únicos inconvenientes de la inadecuada ventilación en las cabinas de los aviones? Aparentemente no.

Los asistentes de vuelo y muchos viajeros frecuentes se quejan de que a menudo[l] se enferman de

Esta española puede padecer del «mal del ordenador».

gripe[m] después de los vuelos largos. La pobre calidad del aire también puede complicar la bronquitis, el asma, el enfisema y las alergias de los pasajeros. La baja <u>humedad</u> requerida en los aviones <u>agrava</u> estos problemas secando las membranas mucosas y disminuyendo[n] las defensas contra infecciones.

Lo más inquietante[o] es que la pobre ventilación y los asientos estrechamente apiñados[p] pueden conducir a[q] la transmisión de serias enfermedades.

[a]ha... *has determined* [b]*skin* [c]*due* [d]se... *has increased* [e]*computadoras* [f]*sufren* [g]*screen* [h]*fields* [i]Han... *Have appeared* [j]*sickness* [k]los... *dizziness* [l]a... *often* [m]*flu* [n]*diminishing* [o]*worrisome* [p]estrechamente... *tightly arranged together* [q]conducir... *lead to*

PASO 4

Comprensión

A. ¿A qué pasaje se refiere? A continuación se presentan tres títulos. En su opinión, ¿qué título mejor le corresponde a cada pasaje de la lectura?

a. ——— Las enfermedades de viaje comienzan en el aire.
b. ——— Los peligros del sol
c. ——— Ojos cansados en el lugar de trabajo

B. Problemas. De los siguientes problemas asociados con el sol, el ordenador y el avión, ¿cuáles *no* se mencionan en la lectura? Indique los problemas no mencionados.

EL SOL

1. el cáncer en la piel
2. los problemas oculares
3. la deshidratación

EL ORDENADOR

1. los problemas con los músculos de las manos
2. los problemas oculares
3. los dolores de cabeza

EL AVIÓN

1. las náuseas
2. los problemas respiratorios
3. el insomnio

 A ESCRIBIR

A. Resúmenes breves. Ahora en uno o dos oraciones, resuma (*summarize*) cada uno de los tres pasajes de la lectura. Debe incluir la información más importante de cada uno.

B. El estrés y los estudiantes. Aunque las presiones de la vida moderna nos afectan a todos, sin duda (*doubt*) tienen un impacto tremendo en los estudiantes universitarios. Escríbale una carta al editor del periódico local comentando lo que Ud. cree que es la mayor presión para los estudiantes en su universidad. En la carta, debe identificar la causa de la presión, las consecuencias que tiene y algunas soluciones posibles para combatirla.

Puede comenzar su carta así:

Estimado editor: / Estimada editora: …

En resumen

GRAMÁTICA

To review the grammar points presented in this chapter, refer to the indicated grammar presentations. You'll find further practice of these structures in the Workbook/Laboratory Manual, on the CD-ROM, and on the website.

31. Another Use of *se*

Do you know how to use **se** to express unplanned or unexpected events?

32. A Summary of the Uses of *por* and *para*

Do you know the difference between **por** and **para** and when to use one or the other?

VOCABULARIO

Los verbos

acabar	to finish; to run out of
acordarse (ue) (de)	to remember
caer (*irreg.*)	to fall
caerse	to fall down
entregar	to turn, hand in
equivocarse	to be wrong, make a mistake
estacionar	to park
quedar	to remain, be left
recoger	to collect; to pick up
romper	to break
sacar	to take out; to get
ser (*irreg.*) **flexible**	to be flexible
sufrir	to suffer
(muchas) presiones	to be under (a lot of) pressure

Repaso: caminar, doler (ue), llegar a tiempo/tarde olvidarse de

Accidentes

darse (*irreg.*) **en/ con/contra**	to hit (a part of one's body); to run into, bump against
hacerse (*irreg.*) **daño**	to hurt oneself
lastimarse	to injure oneself
levantarse con el pie izquierdo	to get up on the wrong side of the bed

pedir (i, i) disculpas	to apologize
pegarse en/con/contra	to run/bump into
Discúlpeme.	Pardon me. / I'm sorry.
Fue sin querer.	It was unintentional.
¡Lo siento (mucho)!	Pardon me! / I'm (very) sorry!
¡Qué mala suerte!	What bad luck!

Repaso: perdón

Presiones de la vida estudiantil

la calificación	grade
el estrés	stress
la fecha límite	deadline
la (falta de) flexibilidad	(lack of) flexibility
el horario	schedule
el informe (oral/escrito)	(oral/written) report
la nota	grade
la prueba	quiz; test
la tarjeta de identificación	identification card
el trabajo	job, work; report, (piece of) work
de tiempo completo/parcial	full time/part time

Repaso: el examen

Más partes del cuerpo

el brazo	arm
el dedo (de la mano)	finger
el dedo del pie	toe
la pierna	leg

Repaso: la cabeza

Los adjetivos

distraído/a	absentminded
escrito/a	written
flexible	flexible
torpe	clumsy
universitario/a	(of the) university

Otros sustantivos

el calendario	calendar
el despertador	alarm clock
la llave	key
la luz	light, electricity

Palabras adicionales

hace + *time*	(*time*) ago
hace + *time* + que... + *present*	it's been (*time*) since . . .
por Dios	for heaven's sake
por ejemplo	for example
por lo menos	at least
por primera/ última vez	for the first/last time
por si acaso	just in case
por supuesto	of course
por todas partes	everywhere

Repaso: por eso, por favor, por fin, por lo general, por lo menos

La calidad de la vida

No toda la tecnología es nueva. La tecnología de los incas, quienes construyeron el famoso centro de Machu Picchu, era muy avanzada para su tiempo. ▶

VOCABULARIO

• Things we have, need, and want
• Housing

GRAMÁTICA

33 **Tú** Commands
34 Present Subjunctive: An Introduction
35 Use of the Subjunctive: Influence

CULTURA

• **Enfoque cultural:** el Perú
• **Nota cultural:** Los nombres de los pisos de un edificio
• **En los Estados Unidos y el Canadá:** Las computadoras y la comunidad hispana
• **Cultura en contexto:** El léxico (Las palabras) de la nueva tecnología

Multimedia

You will learn about giving instructions in the **En contexto** video segment.

Review vocabulary and grammar and practice language skills with the interactive CD-ROM.

Get connected to the Spanish-speaking world with the *¿Qué tal?* Online Learning Center: **www.mhhe.com/quetal.**

Tengo... Necesito... Quiero...

el equipo fotográfico
la cámara
el disco compacto
el equipo estereofónico
la computadora / el ordenador
la cámera de vídeo
la videocasetera
el teléfono celular
el walkman
la impresora
la grabadora
el radio (portátil)
el televisor
la cinta
el control remoto

Los vehículos

la bicicleta (de montaña)	(mountain) bike
el carro / el coche (descapotable)	(convertible) car
el monopatín	skateboard
la moto(cicleta)	motorcycle, moped
los patines	roller skates

La electrónica

el contestador automático	answering machine
el correo electrónico	e-mail
el disco duro	hard drive
la impresora	printer
el ordenador (*Spain*)	computer
el ratón	mouse
la red	net
navegar la red	to surf the net
el teléfono (celular, de coche)	(cellular, car) phone

Cognados

el CD-ROM, la computadora, el disco compacto, el disco de computadora, el fax, la memoria, el módem

Verbos útiles

cambiar (de canal, de cuarto, de ropa...)	to change (channels, rooms, clothing . . .)
conseguir (i, i)	to get, obtain
copiar / hacer copia	to copy
fallar	to "crash" (*a computer*)
funcionar	to work, function (*machines*)
grabar	to record, to tape
guardar	to keep, to save (*documents*)

		Para poder gastar	
imprimir	to print		
manejar	to drive; to operate (*a machine*)	**el aumento**	raise
obtener (*irreg.*)	to get, obtain	**el/la jefe/a**	boss
sacar fotos	to take photos	**el sueldo**	salary

Conversación

A. Ud. y los aparatos

Paso 1. ¿Qué se usa en estas situaciones?

1. para mandar inmediatamente copias de documentos no originales
2. para grabar un programa de televisión
3. para cambiar el programa de la tele sin levantarse del sillón
4. para recibir llamadas telefónicas cuando no estamos en casa
5. para escuchar música mientras hacemos ejercicio

Paso 2. Con un compañero / una compañera, piense en cuatro situaciones similares a las del **Paso 1**. La otra persona debe identificar el aparato.

Paso 3. Para Ud., ¿son ciertas o falsas las siguientes oraciones?

1. Soy una persona que tiene habilidad mecánica. Es decir, entiendo cómo funcionan los aparatos.
2. Aprendí con facilidad a usar la computadora.
3. No me puedo imaginar la vida sin los aparatos electrónicos modernos.
4. Me interesa saber qué vehículo maneja una persona, porque el vehículo es una expresión de la personalidad.
5. Una vez me falló la computadora y perdí unos documentos y archivos (*files*) muy importantes.
6. Uso la videocasetera para ver películas, pero no sé grabar.
7. Me gusta navegar la red porque siempre encuentro lo que busco.

B. ¿Qué vehículos... ? ¿Qué vehículo deben tener y usar las siguientes personas?

1. una persona joven no convencional y que vive en Sevilla, una ciudad grande en el sur de España
2. una persona joven que vive en Key West, una isla soleada e informal en el sur de Florida
3. una familia con tres hijos
4. un estudiante de artes liberales que vive en el *campus*
5. unos chicos que viven en Venice Beach, California, y que pasan gran parte de su tiempo libre en la playa y en el *boardwalk*
6. un matrimonio jubilado (*retired*) que vive en Nueva Inglaterra

C. ¿Necesidad o lujo (*luxury*)**?**

Paso 1.   ¿Considera Ud. que las siguientes posesiones son un lujo o una necesidad de la vida moderna? Indique si Ud. tiene este aparato o vehículo. Dé tres cosas más que Ud. considera necesarias en la vida moderna.

> MODELO: un televisor → Para mí, un televisor es una necesidad. Tengo uno. (No tengo uno ahora.)

1. un contestador automático
2. una videocasetera
3. el equipo estereofónico
4. una computadora
5. un coche
6. una bicicleta
7. un *walkman* (una grabadora)
8. el aviso de llamada, la llamada en espera (*call-waiting*)
9. la línea de teléfono
10. el televisor de pantalla (*screen*) grande

Paso 2.   Para terminar, entreviste a un compañero / una compañera para saber si está de acuerdo con Ud. y si tiene las mismas posesiones.

> MODELO: el televisor → E1: ¿El televisor?
> E2: Yo lo considero un lujo y por eso no tengo uno.

La vivienda°

La… *Housing*

La comunidad

el apartamento*	apartment
el barrio / la vecindad	neighborhood
la casa	house
el cuarto	room
el/la dueño/a	owner; landlord, landlady
el/la inquilino/a	tenant; renter
el/la portero/a	building manager, doorperson
la residencia	residence
el/la vecino/a	neighbor

El área

las afueras	outskirts, suburbs
la avenida	avenue
la calle	street

el campo	countryside
la casa (el bloque) de apartamentos	apartment building
el centro	(downtown) shopping area
la dirección	address
la planta	floor
la planta baja	first (ground) floor
el piso	floor (of a building)
el (primer, segundo) piso	(first, second [*Sp*.: second, third]) floor
la vista	view

Los gastos

el alquiler	rent
alquilar	to rent
el gas	gas; heat
la luz (*pl.* luces)	light; electricity

*El **apartamento** is used throughout Latin America and the Caribbean. **El departamento** is used in Mexico, Peru, and other Latin American countries, but **el piso** is the word most commonly used in Spain.

NOTA CULTURAL

Los nombres de los pisos de un edificio

En la mayoría de los dialectos del inglés, las frases *ground floor* y *first floor* tienen el mismo significado. En español, hay dos modos de expresar estos conceptos. Aunque ha habido[a] cambios al lenguaje debido a[b] la influencia norteamericana, **la planta baja** es el equivalente más común de *ground floor*, mientras que **el primer piso** se refiere al *second floor* de los anglohablantes.[c] También en español, el segundo piso se refiere al *third floor*, etcétera.

[a]ha... *there have been*   [b]debido... *due to*   [c]*English speakers*

Conversación

A. A buscar vivienda

Paso 1. Lea los tres anuncios de viviendas en el Perú y conteste las siguientes preguntas.

1. ¿Qué tipo de vivienda se vende en cada anuncio? ¿Son para comprar o alquilar?
2. ¿Cuántos dormitorios tiene cada vivienda?
3. ¿Cree Ud. que estas viviendas son para familias con mucho o poco dinero?

Paso 2. Con un compañero / una compañera, hable sobre el tipo de vivienda que prefiere.

1. Como estudiante universitario/a, ¿prefiere vivir en el *campus* o fuera del *campus*? ¿en una residencia o en una casa o apartamento de alquiler con otras personas?
2. ¿Prefiere Ud. vivir en la planta baja o en los pisos más altos?
3. ¿Prefiere que el alquiler incluya (*include*) todos los gastos o prefiere pagar la luz y el gas por separado?
4. Si pudiera (*If you could*) escoger, ¿qué le gustaría más, tener un apartamento pequeño en un barrio elegante del centro o una casa grande en las afueras?
5. ¿Qué tipo de vecinos le gusta tener?

B. Definiciones. Dé las definiciones de las siguientes palabras.

MODELO: la residencia →
Es un lugar donde viven muchos estudiantes. Por lo general está situada en el *campus* universitario.

Frases útiles: Es una persona que... Es un lugar donde... Es una cosa que...

1. el inquilino	3. el alquiler	5. la vecina	7. la dirección
2. el centro	4. el portero	6. la dueña	8. las afueras

1.

CUZCO

Alquilo casa. Barrio residencial. Semi-amueblada[a] con teléfono. Informes Teléf. Cuzco: 084-226752. Lima: 774153 (horario 2 a 5 p.m.)

2.

DEPARTAMENTOS MONTERRICO

Finos departamentos de 3 dormitorios, 3½ baños, sala de estar,[b] 1 ó 2 cocheras,[c] acabados de primera,[d] verlos todos los días en: Domingo de la Presa 165, espalda cuadra 12 Av. Primavera.

3.

CHACARILLA DEL ESTANQUE

Departamentos exclusivos, diseño especial, 3 dormitorios, comedor de diario, área de servicio, totalmente equipados. Desde $41.500. Buenas facilidades.
**Av. Buena Vista N° 230
(a 2 Cdras. de Velasco Aslete)
Tels. 458107 – 357743**

[a]*Partially furnished*   [b]sala... *living room; sitting room*   [c]1 ó 2... *one- or two-car garage*   [d]acabados... *first-class finishing details*

¿Recuerda Ud.?

In Grammar Section 19 you learned about **Ud.** and **Uds.** commands. Remember that object pronouns (direct, indirect, reflexive) must follow and be attached to affirmative commands; they must precede negative commands.

AFFIRMATIVE: Háblele Ud.   Duérmase.   Dígaselo Ud.
NEGATIVE: No le hable Ud.   No se duerma.   No se lo diga Ud.

¿Cómo se dice en español?

1. Bring me the book. (**Uds.**)
2. Don't give it to her. (**Uds.**)
3. Sit here, please. (**Ud.**)
4. Don't sit in that chair! (**Ud.**)
5. Tell them the truth. (**Uds.**)
6. Tell it to them now! (**Uds.**)
7. Never tell it to her. (**Uds.**)
8. Take care of yourself. (**Ud.**)
9. Lead a healthy life. (**Ud.**)
10. Listen to me. (**Ud.**)

33 Influencing Others • *Tú* Commands

¡Marta, tu cuarto es un desastre!

«¡Marta, qué desordenado está tu cuarto! Por favor, *arréglalo* antes de jugar con tus amigos. *Guarda* la ropa limpia en tu armario, *pon* la ropa sucia en el cesto, *haz* la cama, *recoge* los libros del piso y *ordénalos* en los estantes... Y no *dejes* los zapatos por todas partes... ¡Es muy peligroso!»

¿Quién diría (*would say*) lo siguiente, Marta o Manolo, su padre?

1. No te enojes... Ya voy a arreglarlo todo.
2. Hazlo inmediatamente... ¡antes de salir a jugar!
3. Dime, ¿por qué tengo que hacerlo ahora mismo?
4. La próxima vez, ¡no dejes tu cuarto en tales condiciones!

> *Informal commands* (**los mandatos informales**) are used with persons whom you would address as **tú**.

Marta, your room is a disaster! "Marta, what a messy room you have! Please straighten it up before you go out to play with your friends. Put your clean clothes away in the closet, put your dirty clothes in the hamper, make your bed, pick your books up from the floor and arrange them on the shelves... And don't leave your shoes lying around everywhere... It's very dangerous!"

NEGATIVE *tú* COMMANDS

-*ar* verbs		-*er/-ir* verbs	
No hables.	Don't speak.	**No comas.**	Don't eat.
No cantes.	Don't sing.	**No escribas.**	Don't write.
No juegues.	Don't play.	**No pidas.**	Don't order.

A. Like **Ud.** commands (Grammar Section 19), the negative **tú** commands are expressed using the "opposite vowel": **no hable Ud., no hables (tú).** The pronoun **tú** is used only for emphasis.

No cantes **tú** tan fuerte.
*Don't **you** sing so loudly.*

B. As with negative **Ud.** commands, object pronouns—direct, indirect, and reflexive—precede negative **tú** commands.

No lo mires.
Don't look at him.

No te levantes.
Don't get up.

No les escribas.
Don't write to them.

AFFIRMATIVE *tú* COMMANDS

-*ar* verbs		-*er/-ir* verbs	
Habla.	*Speak.*	**Come.**	*Eat.*
Canta.	*Sing.*	**Escribe.**	*Write.*
Juega.	*Play.*	**Pide.**	*Order.*

A. Unlike the other command forms you have learned, most affirmative **tú** commands have the same form as the third person singular of the present indicative.* Some verbs have irregular affirmative **tú** command forms.

Spelling Hint: One-syllable words, like the affirmative **tú** commands of some verbs (**decir, ir, tener,...**) do not need an accent mark: **di, ve, ten,...** Exceptions to this rule are those forms that could be mistaken for other words, like the command of **ser** (**sé**), which could be mistaken for the pronoun **se.**

decir:	**di**	salir:	**sal**
hacer:	**haz**	ser:	**sé**
ir:	**ve**	tener:	**ten**
poner:	**pon**	venir:	**ven**

Sé puntual pero **ten** cuidado.
Be there on time, but be careful.

---

*As you know, there are two different *moods* in Spanish: the *indicative mood* (the one you have been working with, which is used to state facts and ask questions) and the *subjunctive mood* (which is used to express more subjective actions or states). Beginning with Grammar Section 34, you will learn more about the subjunctive mood.

O
J
O

The affirmative **tú** commands for **ir** and **ver** are identical: **ve.** Context will clarify meaning.

¡**Ve** esa película!
See that movie!

Ve a casa ahora mismo.
Go home right now.

B. As with affirmative **Ud.** commands, object and reflexive pronouns follow affirmative **tú** commands and are attached to them. Accent marks are necessary except when a single pronoun is added to a one-syllable command.

Dile la verdad.
Tell him the truth.

Léela, por favor.
Read it, please.

Póntelos.
Put them on.

Práctica

A. Refranes para todo. Los refranes son frases populares que expresan consejos para todo tipo de situaciones en la vida. Empareje cada refrán en la columna a la izquierda con una explicación a la derecha. Si conoce algún equivalente en inglés, ¡délo!

1. _____ Agua que no has de (vas a) beber, déjala correr.

2. _____ Haz bien y no mires a quién.

3. _____ Dondequiera que fueres (*you go*), haz lo que vieres (*you see*).

4. _____ En martes, ni te cases (*get married*) ni te embarques (*set sail*).

5. _____ Antes de que te cases (*get married*), mira bien lo que haces.

6. _____ A caballo (*horse*) regalado no le mires el diente.

a. Sé una buena persona con todo el mundo, sin excepción.

b. El martes es un día de mala suerte: no hagas nada importante ese día.

c. Aprende las costumbres de otras personas y actúa a su manera cuando estés (*you are*) en su casa o en su país.

d. Da las gracias y no busques los defectos de un regalo.

e. Piensa bien antes de casarte en cómo va a cambiar tu vida.

f. Si no vas a hacer aprecio de alguien, deja a esa persona.

B. Julita, la mal educada

Paso 1. Los Sres. Villarreal no están contentos con el comportamiento de su hija Julita. Continúe los comentarios de ellos con mandatos informales lógicos según cada situación. Siga los modelos.

> MODELOS: *Hablaste* demasiado ayer. → No *hables* tanto hoy, por favor.
> *Dejaste* tu ropa en el suelo anoche. → No la *dejes* allí hoy, por favor.

1. También *dejaste* tus libros en el suelo.
2. ¿Por qué *regresaste* tarde a casa hoy después de las clases?
3. ¿Por qué *vas* al parque todas las tardes?
4. No es bueno que *mires* la televisión constantemente. ¿Y por qué quieres *ver* todos esos programas de detectives?
5. ¿Por qué le *dices* mentiras a tu papá?
6. Siempre *te olvidas* de sacar la basura, que es la única tarea que tienes que hacer.
7. Ay, hija, no te comprendemos. ¡*Eres* tan insolente!

Paso 2. La pobre Julita también escucha muchos mandatos de su maestra en clase. Invente Ud. esos mandatos según las indicaciones.

1. llegar / a / escuela / puntualmente
2. quitarse / abrigo / y / sentarse
3. sacar / libro de matemáticas / y / abrirlo / en / página diez
4. leer / nuevo / palabras / y / aprenderlas / para mañana
5. venir / aquí / a / hablar conmigo / sobre / este / composición

Conversación

A. Situaciones. ¿Qué consejos les daría (*would you give*) a las siguientes personas si fueran (*if they were*) sus amigos? Déles a todos consejos en forma de mandatos informales.

1. A Celia le encanta ir al cine, especialmente los viernes por la noche. Pero a su novio no le gusta salir mucho los viernes. Él siempre está muy cansado después de una larga semana de trabajo. Celia, en cambio (*on the other hand*), tiene mucha energía.
2. Nati tiene 19 años. El próximo año quiere vivir en un apartamento con cuatro amigos. Para ella es una situación ideal: un apartamento económico en un barrio estudiantil y unos buenos amigos (dos de ellos son hombres). Pero los padres de Nati son muy tradicionales y no les va a gustar la situación.
3. Mariana es una *yuppi*. Gana muchísimo dinero pero trabaja demasiado. Nunca tiene tiempo para nada. Duerme poco y bebe muchísimo café para seguir despierta (*awake*). No come bien y jamás hace ejercicio. Acaba de comprarse un teléfono celular para poder trabajar mientras maneja a la oficina.

PASO 2

B. **Entre compañeros de casa.** En su opinión, ¿cuáles son los cinco mandatos que se oyen con más frecuencia en su casa (apartamento, residencia)? Piense no sólo en los mandatos que Ud. escucha sino (*but*) también en los que Ud. les da a los demás (*others*).

Frases útiles: poner la tele, sacar la basura, apagar la computadora, prestarme dinero, contestar el teléfono, no hacer ruido, lavar los platos, ¿ ?

Frase útil: no seas… impaciente, así, pesado/a (*a pain*), precipitado/a (*hasty*), loco/a, impulsivo/a, bobo/a (*dumb*)

34 Expressing Subjective Actions or States •
Present Subjunctive: An Introduction

Una decisión importante

JOSÉ MIGUEL: Quiero comprar una computadora, pero no sé cuál. *No creo que sea* una decisión fácil de tomar.

GUSTAVO: Pues, yo sé bastante de computadoras. Te puedo hacer algunas recomendaciones.

JOSÉ MIGUEL: Bueno, te escucho.

GUSTAVO: Primero, *es buena idea que sepas* para qué quieres una computadora. ¿Quieres navegar por el *Internet*? Entonces, *te sugiero que busques* una computadora con módem y con memoria suficiente para hacerlo. Luego, *quiero que hables* con otras personas que ya manejan computadoras. Y por último, *te aconsejo que vayas* a varias tiendas para comparar precios.

JOSÉ MIGUEL: Bueno, *me alegro de que sepas* tanto de computadoras. ¡Ahora *quiero que vayas* conmigo a las tiendas!

Comprensión: ¿Cierto, falso o no lo dice?

1. José Miguel quiere que Gustavo le compre una computadora.
2. Gustavo le recomienda a José Miguel que aprenda algo sobre computadoras antes de comprarse una.
3. Gustavo no cree que José Miguel tenga suficiente dinero.
4. José Miguel se alegra de que Gustavo esté tan informado sobre computadoras.

An important decision JOSÉ MIGUEL: I want to buy a computer, but I don't know which one. I don't think it's an easy decision to make. GUSTAVO: Well, I know quite a bit about computers. I can give you some recommendations. JOSÉ MIGUEL: OK, I'm listening. GUSTAVO: First, it's a good idea for you to know why you want a computer. Do you want to get on the Internet? Then I suggest that you look for a computer with a modem and enough memory to do it. Then I want you to talk with other people who already work with computers. And finally, I suggest you go to various stores to compare prices. JOSÉ MIGUEL: Well, I'm glad you know so much about computers. Now I want you to go to the stores with me!

PRESENT SUBJUNCTIVE: AN INTRODUCTION

A. Except for command forms, all the verb forms you have learned so far in *¿Qué tal?* are part of the *indicative mood* (**el modo indicativo**). In both English and Spanish, the indicative is used to state facts and to ask questions; it objectively expresses actions or states of being that are considered true by the speaker.

INDICATIVE:

¿Puedes venir a la fiesta?
Can you come to the party?

Prefiero llegar temprano a casa.
I prefer getting home early.

B. Both English and Spanish have another verb system called the *subjunctive mood* (**el modo subjuntivo**). The subjunctive is used to express more subjective or conceptualized actions or states. These include things that the speaker wants to happen or wants others to do, events to which the speaker reacts emotionally, things that are as yet unknown, and so on.

SUBJUNCTIVE:

Espero que **puedas** venir a la fiesta.
I hope (that) you can come to the party.

Prefiero que **llegues** temprano a casa.
I prefer that you be home early.

C. Sentences in English and Spanish may be simple or complex. A simple sentence is one that contains a single verb.

    Complex sentences are comprised of two or more *clauses* (**las cláusulas**). There are two types of clauses: main (independent) clause and subordinate (dependent) clause. *Independent clauses* (**las cláusulas principales**) contain a complete thought and can stand alone. *Dependent clauses* (**las cláusulas subordinadas**) contain an incomplete thought and cannot stand alone. Dependent clauses require an independent clause to form a complete sentence.

    Note in the indicative example above that when there is no change of subject in the sentence, the infinitive is used in the dependent clause.

    However, when the two subjects of a complex sentence are different, the subjunctive is often used in the dependent clause in Spanish. Note that dependent clauses are linked by the conjunction **que**, which is never optional (as it is in English).

Quiero pan.
I want bread.

INDICATIVE

MAIN CLAUSE	SUBORDINATE CLAUSE
Quiero	comprar pan.
I want	*to buy bread.*

SUBJUNCTIVE

MAIN CLAUSE	SUBORDINATE CLAUSE	
Quiere	**que**	compres pan.
She wants	*(for)*	*you to buy bread.*
Espero	**que**	me visites pronto.
I hope	*(that)*	*you visit me soon.*
¿Dudas	**que**	puedan venir?
Do you doubt	*(that)*	*they can come?*

D. Three of the most common uses of the subjunctive are to express influence, emotion, and doubt or denial. These are signaled in the previous examples by the verb forms **quiere, espero,** and **dudas.**

FORMS OF THE PRESENT SUBJUNCTIVE

You already know that many Spanish command forms are part of the subjunctive. The **Ud./Uds.** command forms are shaded in the box that follows. What you have already learned about forming **Ud.** and **Uds.** commands will help you learn the forms of the present subjunctive.

	hablar	comer	escribir	volver	decir
Singular	hable	coma	escriba	vuelva	diga
	hables	comas	escribas	vuelvas	digas
	hable	coma	escriba	vuelva	diga
Plural	hablemos	comamos	escribamos	volvamos	digamos
	habléis	comáis	escribáis	volváis	digáis
	hablen	coman	escriban	vuelvan	digan

A. The personal endings of the present subjunctive are added to the first person singular of the present indicative minus its **-o** ending. **-Ar** verbs add endings with **-e,** and **-er/-ir** verbs add endings with **-a.**

-ar ⟶ -e
-er/-ir ⟶ -a

present tense **yo** stem = present subjunctive stem

B. Verbs ending in **-car, -gar,** and **-zar** have a spelling change in all persons of the present subjunctive, in order to preserve the **-c-, -g-,** and **-z-** sounds.

-car: c ⟶ qu
-gar: g ⟶ gu
-zar: z ⟶ c

buscar: bus**qu**e, bus**qu**es,...
pagar: pa**gu**e, pa**gu**es,...
empezar: empie**c**e, empie**c**es,...

C. Verbs with irregular **yo** forms show the irregularity in all persons of the present subjunctive.

conocer:	**conozca,...**	salir:	**salga,...**
decir:	**diga,...**	tener:	**tenga,...**
hacer:	**haga,...**	traer:	**traiga,...**
oír:	**oiga,...**	venir:	**venga,...**
poner:	**ponga,...**	ver:	**vea,...**

D. A few verbs have irregular present subjunctive forms.

dar:	**dé, des, dé, demos, deis, den**
estar:	**esté,…**
haber (hay):	**haya**
ir:	**vaya,…**
saber:	**sepa,…**
ser:	**sea,…**

E. **-Ar** and **-er** stem-changing verbs follow the stem-changing pattern of the present indicative.

pensar (ie): **pie**nse, **pie**nses, **pie**nse, pensemos, penséis, **pie**nsen

poder (ue): **pue**da, **pue**das, **pue**da, podamos, podáis, **pue**dan

F. **-Ir** stem-changing verbs show a stem change in the four forms that have a change in the present indicative. In addition, however, they show a second stem change in the **nosotros** and **vosotros** forms, similar to the present progressive tense.

**-ir stem-changing verbs
(nosotros and vosotros):**
o → u
e → i

dormir (ue, u): d**ue**rma, d**ue**rmas, d**ue**rma, d**u**rmamos, d**u**rmáis, d**ue**rman

pedir (i, i): p**i**da, p**i**das, p**i**da, p**i**damos, p**i**dáis, p**i**dan

preferir (ie, i): pref**ie**ra, pref**ie**ras, pref**ie**ra, pref**i**ramos, pref**i**ráis, pref**ie**ran

Práctica

Su trabajo actual (*current*). Complete las oraciones de modo (*in such a way*) que se refieran a su situación laboral actual. (Siempre hay más de una respuesta posible.) Si Ud. no trabaja ahora, no importa. ¡Invéntese una respuesta!

1. El jefe / La jefa quiere que ____.
2. También espera que ____.
3. Y duda que ____.
4. Prohíbe (*He/She forbids*) que ____.

5. En el trabajo, es importante que ____.
6. Yo espero que ____.

a. a veces trabajemos los fines de semana
b. todos lleguemos a tiempo
c. hablemos por teléfono con los amigos
d. me den un aumento de sueldo
e. nos paguen más a todos

f. no usemos el fax para asuntos (*matters*) personales
g. me den un trabajo de tiempo completo algún día
h. no perdamos mucho tiempo charlando (*chatting*) con los demás
i. fumemos en la oficina
j. ¿ ?

Conversación

Consejos para comprar y usar la tecnología de multimedia. Complete el siguiente párrafo según su opinión y sus conocimientos (*knowledge*). En el primer espacio en blanco, use el subjuntivo del verbo entre paréntesis. Luego, compare sus respuestas con las de algunos compañeros para ver si están de acuerdo. ¿Quién sabe más del tema en la clase?

Recomiendo que…

> MODELO: _____ (encontrar) _____ para ayudarlo/la a montar (*set up*) la computadora porque… → *encuentre un experto* para ayudarlo/la a montar la computadora porque *es muy difícil*.

1. _____ (ir) a _____ para comprar la computadora porque…
2. _____ (comprar) _____ [marca y modelo de computadora] porque…
3. _____ (mirar) las revistas especializadas, como _____ [nombre de revista] porque…
4. no _____ (pagar) más de $ _____ porque…
5. no _____ (usar) el *software* _____ [marca o tipo] porque…
6. _____ (asegurarse [*to make sure*]) de que la computadora tenga _____ porque…
7. _____ (poner) la computadora en _____ [lugar] porque…

En los Estados Unidos y el Canadá...

Las computadoras y la comunidad hispana

Según un estudio demográfico del año 2000, alrededor del 37 por ciento de las familias hispanas de Los Ángeles, Nueva York, Miami, Chicago y Houston (las cinco ciudades de los Estados Unidos con mayor población hispana) posee[a] una **computadora personal**. Se calcula que hay computadoras en más de un millón y medio de **hogares**[b] hispanos en los Estados Unidos.

El acceso de los hispanos a las computadoras y al Internet es un factor im-portante para su desarrollo[c] personal. Las computadoras y el Internet son herramientas[d] necesarias para **la educación, el trabajo, la comunicación** y sobre todo para **la información**. Casi todos los periódicos principales de los países hispanos se publican ahora en el Internet. A través de las publicaciones ciberespaciales, los hispanos pueden **informarse**. Leen sus noticias en español, y, es más,[e] pueden leer las noticias de su país o ciudad natal. También pueden participar en comunicaciones con **la comunidad hispana** del Internet.

En Chicago, Illinois

[a]*owns* [b]*homes* [c]*development* [d]*tools* [e]*es... furthermore*

Enfoque *cultural*

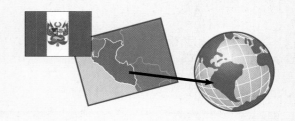

el Perú

Datos esenciales

Nombre oficial: República del Perú

Capital: Lima

Población: 24.000.000 de habitantes

Moneda: el nuevo sol

Idiomas oficiales: el español, el quechua, el aimara

Conozca... *la cultura de los incas*

Cuando los españoles llegaron al Perú en 1532, los incas ya dominaban una gran zona de Sudamérica, desde Colombia hasta Chile, y desde el Pacífico hasta las selvas[a] del este. A partir del siglo XIII[b], muchos otros pueblos indígenas de la inmensa región vivían bajo[c] el dominio de los incas. La capital del imperio era Cuzco.

La palabra *inca* significa *rey* o *príncipe*[d] en quechua, lengua que todavía se habla en el Perú. Bajo su inca, el pueblo tenía un gobierno de poder absoluto y un sistema burocrático y social muy complejo.

Cuzco, Perú

El imperio inca se destacó[e] por la arquitectura, la ingeniería[f] y las técnicas de cultivo. También estableció un sistema de correo y un censo de la población. Tras la conquista[g] de los incas por los españoles Pizarro y Almagro, el Perú y su capital Lima, fundada por Pizarro en 1535, se convierten en un centro fundamental de las colonias españolas en América.

[a]*jungles* [b]*A... Beginning in the thirteenth century* [c]*under* [d]*rey... king or prince* [e]*se... distinguished itself* [f]*engineering* [g]*Tras... After the conquest*

¡Fíjese!

- El Lago Titicaca, que queda entre Bolivia y el Perú, es el lago más grande de Sudamérica y es la ruta de transporte principal entre estos dos países.

- Cientos de años antes de la llegada[a] de los españoles, la agricultura de los indígenas del Perú ya era muy sofisticada. Hace más de 2.000 años, los indígenas ya construían[b] terrazas para sembrar en las faldas[c] de los Andes. Muchas de estas terrazas se usan todavía.

- Uno de los cultivos[d] más importantes de los incas es la papa,[e] que originó en la región cerca del Lago Titicaca.

La papa es una de las pocas plantas que puede subsistir[f] en altitudes de más de 13.000 pies y en regiones frías y áridas.

[a]*arrival* [b]*ya... were already building* [c]*para... so that they could plant on the slopes* [d]*crops* [e]*potato* [f]*survive*

Capítulo 12 of the video to accompany *¿Qué tal?* contains cultural footage of Peru.

W.W. Visit the *¿Qué tal?* website at www.mhhe.com/quetal.

PASO 3 Gramática

35 Expressing Desires and Requests • Use of the Subjunctive: Influence

Escoja la oración que describa cada dibujo.

1. ____

   a. Quiero repasar las formas del subjuntivo.
   b. Quiero que nosotros repasemos juntos las formas del subjuntivo.

1.

2. ____

   a. Insisto en hablar con Jorge.
   b. Insisto en que tú hables con Jorge.

2.

3. ____

   a. Es necesario arreglar esta habitación.
   b. Es necesario que tú arregles esta habitación.

3.

A. So far, you have learned to identify the subjunctive by the features listed at the right.

The subjunctive

- appears in a subordinate (dependent) clause.
- has a different subject from the one in the main (independent) clause.
- is preceded by **que.**

B. In addition, the use of the subjunctive is associated with the presence of a number of concepts or conditions that trigger the use of it in the dependent clause. The concept of influence is one trigger for the subjunctive in a dependent clause. When the speaker wants something to happen, he or she tries to influence the behavior of others, as in these sentences.

    The verb in the main clause is, of course, in the indicative, because it is a fact that the subject of the sentence wants something. The subjunctive occurs in the dependent clause.

MAIN (INDEPENDENT) CLAUSE		SUBORDINATE (DEPENDENT) CLAUSE
Yo **quiero** *I want*	**que**	tú **pagues** la cuenta. *you to pay the bill.*
La profesora **prefiere** *The professor prefers*	**que** *that*	los estudiantes no **lleguen** tarde. *the students don't arrive late.*

C. **Querer** and **preferir** are not the only verbs that can express the main subject's desire to influence what someone else thinks or does. There are many other verbs of influence, some very strong and direct, some very soft and polite.

STRONG	SOFT
insistir en	desear
mandar	pedir (i, i)
permitir (*to permit*)	recomendar (ie)
prohibir (prohíbo)	sugerir (ie, i)

D. An impersonal generalization of influence or volition can also be the main clause that triggers the subjunctive. Some examples of this appear at the right.

Es necesario que…	Es importante que…
Es urgente que…	Es mejor que…

Práctica

A. **En la tienda de aparatos electrónicos.** Imagine que Ud. y un amigo / una amiga están en una tienda de aparatos electrónicos. Ud. quiere comprarse un estéreo pero no sabe cuál; por eso su amigo/a lo/la acompaña. ¿Quién dice las siguientes oraciones, Ud., su amigo/a o el vendedor (*salesperson*)?

1. Prefiero que busques un estéreo en varias tiendas; así puedes comparar precios.
2. Quiero que el estéreo tenga disco compacto con control remoto.
3. Recomiendo que no le digas cuánto dinero quieres gastar.
4. Insisto en que Ud. vea este modelo. ¡Es lo último!
5. Prefiero que me muestre otro modelo más barato.
6. Es mejor que vaya a buscar en otra tienda. No tengo tanto dinero.
7. Quiero que lo sepa: Este estéreo es el mejor de todos.

B. **Expectativas de la educación**

Paso 1. ¿Qué expectativas de la educación tienen los profesores, los estudiantes y los padres de los estudiantes? Forme oraciones según las indicaciones y añada (*add*) palabras cuando sea necesario.

1. todos / profesores / querer / que / estudiantes / llegar / clase / a tiempo
2. profesor(a) de / español / preferir / que / (nosotros) ir / con frecuencia / laboratorio de lenguas
3. profesores / prohibir / que / estudiantes / traer / comida / y / bebida / clase
4. padres / de / estudiantes / desear / que / hijos / asistir a / clases
5. estudiantes / pedir / que / profesores / no dar / mucho / trabajo
6. también / (ellos) querer / que / haber / más vacaciones
7. padres / insistir en / que / hijos / sacar / buenas / notas

Paso 2. Y Ud., ¿qué quiere que hagan los profesores? Invente tres oraciones más para indicar sus deseos.

Conversación

A. Hablan los expertos en tecnología. Imagine que Ud. y sus compañeros de clase son un equipo (*team*) de expertos en problemas relacionados con la tecnología y que juntos (*together*) tienen un programa de radio.

Paso 1. Como miembro del equipo, lea las preguntas que les han mandado (*have sent*) los radioyentes (*radio audience*) por correo electrónico y déles una solución. Es bueno incluir frases como «Le recomiendo/sugiero que... », «Es importante/necesario/urgente que... »

1. Soy una joven de 20 años y soy extremadamente tímida. Por eso no me gusta salir. Prefiero asumir otra personalidad al conectarme en la red. Así estoy feliz por horas. Mi madre dice que esto no es normal y me pide que deje de hacerlo. Ella insiste en que vaya a las discotecas como otros jóvenes de mi edad. ¿Qué piensan Uds.?

2. Mi marido es un hombre muy bueno y trabajador. Tiene un buen trabajo, y es una persona muy respetada en su compañía. El problema es que sólo piensa en *software* y multimedia. Pasa todo su tiempo libre delante de la computadora o leyendo catálogos y revistas sobre computadoras. Yo prefiero que él pase más tiempo conmigo. En realidad (*In fact*), estoy tan aburrida que estoy pensando en dejarlo. ¿Qué recomiendan que haga?

3. Mi jefe quiere que deje de usar mi máquina de escribir (*typewriter*) y empiece a usar una computadora. Pero, no quiero hacerlo: Siempre he hecho bien mi trabajo sin la «caja boba» (*stupid box*). Mi jefe dice que tengo que ponerme al día (*up-to-date*) y me sugiere que tome un curso de computadoras que él promete pagar. Yo no entiendo por qué tengo que cambiar. ¿Me aconsejan (*do you advise*) que hable con un abogado/una abogada (*lawyer*)?

Paso 2. Ahora piense en un problema que se relacione con la tecnología que sea similar a los del **Paso 1**, y escríbalo. El resto de la clase le va a hacer sugerencias de cómo resolverlo.

B. Entrevista

Paso 1. Complete las siguientes oraciones lógicamente... ¡y con sinceridad!

1. Mis padres (hijos, abuelos,...) insisten en que (yo) _____.
2. Mi mejor amigo/a (esposo/a, novio/a,...) desea que (yo) _____.
3. Prefiero que mis amigos _____.
4. No quiero que mis amigos _____.
5. Es urgente que (yo) _____.
6. Es necesario que mi mejor amigo/a (esposo/a, novio/a,...) _____.

Paso 2. Ahora entreviste a un compañero / una compañera para saber cómo él/ella completó las oraciones del **Paso 1**.

MODELO: ¿En qué insisten tus padres?

UN POCO DE TODO

¿Qué quiere o necesita Ud.? Here is a series of answers to that question. Complete them with the correct form of each word in parentheses. When two possibilities are given in parentheses, select the correct word. **¡OJO!** You will use the present indicative, present subjunctive, or preterite of the infinitives. And sometimes, the infinitive itself will be the appropriate form.

1. Deseo que (haber[1]) paz[a] en (mí/mi[2]) país. Y quiero que mi familia (estar[3]) bien. También deseo que no (haber[4]) hambre en el mundo y que los niños no (sufrir[5]). Para (mí/mi[6]), (*yo:* pedir[7]) muy poco.

2. ¡Yo no (saber[8]) por dónde empezar la lista! Necesitamos una casa (tan/más[9]) grande, camas nuevas para los niños (pocos/pequeños[10]), (un/una[11]) televisor… Pero primero tenemos que (comprar[12]) (un/—[13]) otro coche, porque el que[b] tenemos (dejar[14]) de funcionar la semana pasada. ¡Ay!

3. Es necesario que mi jefa me (dar[15]) un aumento de sueldo. Ya trabajo (muchísimo[16]) horas, pero no (*yo:* ganar[17]) lo suficiente. El cheque que recibo cada dos semanas apenas[c] (cubrir[18])[d] los gastos (al/del[19]) apartamento, como (el/la[20]) alquiler, la luz y el gas. Por lo menos la dueña del apartamento es (mucho/muy[21]) simpática y me (gusta/gustan[22]) mucho el barrio donde vivo.

4. ¡Huy! ¡Muchas cosas! Quiero (comprar[23]) (un/una[24]) sofá para la sala, una computadora y equipo estereofónico. Además, me gustaría (comprar[25]) unas pinturas, (un/una[26]) fax…

5. Yo quiero que mi papá me (llevar[27]) al circo. Mi amigo Enrique (ir[28]) la semana pasada y le (gustar[29]) mucho. También necesito (un/una[30]) bici. Y quiero que el bebé que va (a/de[31]) tener mi mamá (ser[32]) un hermanito. Si es una niña, es un rollo,[e] ¡porque no va a (querer[33]) jugar al basquetbol!

[a]*peace*   [b]*el… the one that*   [c]*barely*   [d]*to cover*   [e]*pain*

Comprensión: ¿Cierto o falso?

1. No hay ninguna persona con deseos humanitarios.
2. Es necesario que alguien compre un coche.
3. Una persona quiere que su compañía le pague más.
4. Es completamente necesario que uno de los entrevistados compre unas pinturas y equipo estereofónico.
5. Otro entrevistado quiere que el nuevo bebé de sus padres sea una niña.

FUNCTION
Giving instructions

Cultura en contexto
El léxico (Las palabras) de la nueva tecnología

Tan rápido como se desarro-llan[a] nuevas tecnologías, se inventan nuevas palabras para expresarlas. Hasta ahora, las palabras que se usan en español vienen principalmente del inglés: «el Internet», «el software», «hacer click en» (*to click on*). Este nuevo vocabulario varía de país en país. Por ejemplo, en Latinoamérica, se dice «la computadora» o «el compu-tador». En España se dice «el ordenador».

[a]se... *are developed*

VIDEOTECA: En contexto

In this video segment, Mariela helps a student in the computer laboratory to use e-mail for sending a document. As you watch the segment, pay particular attention to the use of computer-related vocabulary. What do you think **adjuntar documento** means? And what about **dirección electrónica**?

COSTA RICA

A. Lluvia de ideas

- ¿A quién le pide ayuda Ud. cuando tiene problemas con los programas informáticos? Otras personas, ¿le piden ayuda a Ud.?
- ¿Dónde prefiere Ud. hacer las tareas universitarias, en casa o en un laboratorio de computadoras? ¿Por qué?

B. Dictado

A continuación están las instrucciones que Mariela le da al estudiante. Complete la explicación con las palabras o frases que faltan.

ESTUDIANTE: Es que no sé _____[1] bien este programa.
MARIELA: A ver... ¿qué es lo que intenta hacer?
ESTUDIANTE: Quiero _____[2] este documento por correo _____[3] a mi profesor, pero no _____.[4]
MARIELA: Vamos a ver. Con _____[5]...
ESTUDIANTE: ¿Quiere Ud. hacerlo?
MARIELA: No. Prefiero que Ud. lo haga. Así aprende mejor. Bien. Primero, abra su cuenta[a] de _____[6] electrónico. No, es mejor que no abra el _____.[7] Bien. Ahora le sugiero que ponga primero la _____[8] electrónica del profesor en ese espacio. Cuidado,[b] un error tipográfico y no funciona.

[a]*account* [b]*Careful*

C. Un diálogo original

Paso 1. Con un compañero / una compañera, dramatice la escena entre Mariela y el estudiante.

Paso 2. Ayudando a un compañero / una compañera. Imagine que Ud. y un compañero / una compañera tienen una conversación en el laboratorio de computadoras de su universidad.

E1: Ud. es un novato / una novata (*novice*) en eso de computadoras y no sabe llegar al sitio web de su clase de _____ (o no sabe conseguir su correo electrónico). Por eso le pide ayuda a alguien de la clase.

E2: Ud. es «un experto / una experta» en computadoras y ayuda a otro/a estudiante de la clase con los problemas que tiene.

PASO FINAL

A CONVERSAR

Buscando apartamento

Paso 1. Lea los avisos (*ads*) de los apartamentos para alquilar, y escoja el apartamento que Ud. prefiere.

3 dorm. 1 baño.

Cerca del parque y centro comercial. Planta Baja. $900.

1.

Zona residencial excelente. 3 dorm. 2 baños. Garaje gratis. Sala grande. $1000.

2.

¡Cocina para gourmet!

2 dorm. 1 baño. Autobús. Amueblado. Portero. $825.

3.

Paso 2. En grupos de tres, imaginen que necesitan alquilar un apartamento juntos. Indiquen dónde prefieren vivir y por qué. Traten de comenzar sus oraciones con frases como **Prefiero que... , Recomiendo que... , Es mejor que...** o **Es importante que...** Después, cada grupo debe escoger uno de los apartamentos.

MODELO: Recomiendo que alquilemos el apartamento número dos porque tiene una sala grande. También es mejor que haya dos baños.

Paso 3. Cada grupo debe inventar más información sobre el apartamento que escogió. La información puede incluir: dónde está el apartamento, cuánto es el alquiler, si se permiten animales, si está en una casa particular o en una casa de apartamentos, si se incluye la luz en el alquiler, etcétera.

MODELO: El alquiler es setecientos dólares al mes. La luz no está incluida.

Paso 4. Cada grupo debe improvisar una escena entre dos personas que buscan apartamento y el dueño / la dueña que lo alquila, basándose en los avisos y la información que inventaron.

MODELO: E1: ¿Dónde está el apartamento?
E2: Está en el centro, en una zona muy bonita.

En resumen

GRAMÁTICA

To review the grammar points presented in this chapter, refer to the indicated grammar presentations. You'll find further practice of these structures in the Workbook/Laboratory Manual, on the CD-ROM, and on the website.

33. *Tú* Commands

Do you know how to give orders to friends and children in Spanish? How do you tell them what not to do?

34. Present Subjunctive: An Introduction

Do you understand how to form the present subjunctive?

35. Use of the Subjunctive: Influence

You should be able to express that you want or need someone else to do something without giving a direct command.

VOCABULARIO

Los verbos

alegrarse (de)	to be happy (about)
arreglar	to straighten (up); to fix, repair
cambiar (de)	to change
copiar / hacer copia	to copy
dudar	to doubt
esperar	to hope
fallar	to "crash" (*a computer*)
funcionar	to work, function; to run (*machines*)
grabar	to record; to tape
guardar	to keep; to save (*documents*)
haber (*infinitive form* of **hay**)	(*there is, there are*)
imprimir	to print
mandar	to order
manejar	to drive; to operate (*a machine*)
obtener (*irreg.*)	to get, obtain
permitir	to permit, allow
prohibir	to prohibit, forbid

Repaso: conseguir (i, i), sacar fotos

Vehículos

la bicicleta (de montaña)	(mountain) bike
el carro (descapotable)	(convertible) car
el monopatín	skateboard
la moto(cicleta)	motorcycle, moped
los patines	roller skates

Repaso: el coche

La electrónica

el archivo	(computer) file
el canal	channel
el contestador automático	answering machine
el correo electrónico	e-mail
el disco duro	hard drive
el equipo estereofónico/ fotográfico	stereo/photography equipment
la grabadora	tape recorder/ player
la impresora	printer
el ordenador (*Sp.*)	computer
el ratón	mouse
la red	net
navegar la red	to surf the net

el teléfono celular / de coche	cellular/car phone
la videocasetera	video cassette recorder (VCR)

Repaso: la cinta, el televisor

Cognados: la cámara (de vídeo), el CD-ROM, la computadora, el control remoto, el disco compacto, el disco de computadora, el fax, la memoria, el módem, el radio (portátil) / la radio,* el *walkman*

Para poder gastar

el aumento	raise
el/la jefe/a	boss
el sueldo	salary

La vivienda

alquilar	to rent
las afueras	outskirts; suburbs
el alquiler	rent
el área (*but f.*)	area
la avenida	avenue
el barrio	neighborhood
la calle	street

el campo	countryside
el *campus*	(university) campus
la casa (el bloque) de apartamentos	apartment building
la comunidad	community
la dirección	address
el/la dueño/a	landlord, landlady
el gas	gas; heat
el/la inquilino/a	tenant; renter
el piso	floor (of a building)
la planta baja	ground floor
el/la portero/a	building manager; doorman
la vecindad	neighborhood
el/la vecino/a	neighbor
la vista	view

Repaso: el apartamento, la casa, el centro, el cuarto, la luz, la residencia

Otros sustantivos

el gasto	expense
el lujo	luxury

Palabras adicionales

los/las demás	others

---

*El **radio** is the apparatus; **la radio** is the medium.

El arte y la cultura

VOCABULARIO

- The arts
- Ranking things

GRAMÁTICA

36 Use of the Subjunctive: Emotion
37 Use of the Subjunctive: Doubt and Denial

CULTURA

- **Enfoque cultural:** Bolivia y el Ecuador
- **Nota cultural:** Los toros
- **En los Estados Unidos y el Canadá:** Carlos Santana y la Fundación Milagro
- **Cultura en contexto:** El arte y las artesanías

Multimedia

 You will learn about bargaining in the **En contexto** video segment.

Review vocabulary and grammar and practice language skills with the interactive CD-ROM.

 Get connected to the Spanish-speaking world with the *¿Qué tal?* Online Learning Center: **www.mhhe.com/quetal**.

◀ Estos residentes de Quito, Ecuador, miran las obras de arte que se venden en el Parque de la Alameda.

Las artes*

En el teatro

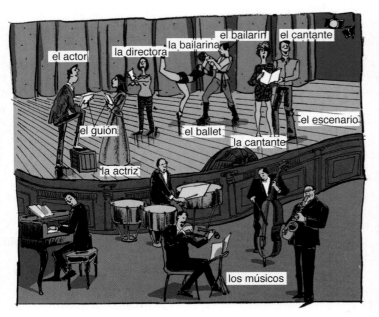

el bailarín
el cantante
la bailarina
la directora
el actor
el guión
el ballet
la cantante
el escenario
la actriz
los músicos

cantar	to sing
crear	to create
dibujar	to draw
escribir	to write
esculpir	to sculpt
pintar	to paint
tejer	to weave

Otras personas

el/la aficionado/a	fan
el/la arquitecto/a	architect
el/la artista	artist
el/la compositor(a)	composer
el/la dramaturgo/a	playwright
el/la escritor(a)	writer
el/la escultor(a)	sculptor
el/la pintor(a)	painter
el/la poeta	poet

La tradición cultural

la artesanía	arts and crafts
la cerámica	pottery, ceramics
las ruinas	ruins
los tejidos	woven goods

La expresión artística

la arquitectura	architecture
el baile / la danza	dance
el cine	film; movies
el drama	drama
la escultura	sculpture
la fotografía	photography
la literatura	literature
la música	music
la ópera	opera
la pintura	painting

Otras palabras útiles

la canción	song
el cuadro / la pintura	painting (*piece of art*) / painting (*piece of art; the art form*)
la obra (de arte)	work (of art)
la obra maestra	masterpiece

*The word **arte** is used with masculine articles and adjectives in the singular and with feminine ones when in the plural.

　　Guillermo es estudiante **del arte moderno**.
　　Me gustan mucho **las artes gráficas**.

Conversación

A. Obras de arte. ¿Qué tipo de arte representan las siguientes obras?

1. la catedral de Notre Dame y la de Santiago de Compostela
2. los murales de Diego Rivera
3. las estatuas griegas y romanas
4. *El lago de los Cisnes* (Swan Lake) y *El amor brujo* (Love, the Magician)
5. *El ciudadano Kane* y *El mago* (Wizard) *de Oz*
6. *La Bohème* y *La Traviata*
7. las ruinas aztecas y mayas
8. *Don Quijote* y *Cien años de soledad*

B. ¿Qué hacen? Forme oraciones completas, emparejando palabras de cada columna. Luego, con dos o tres compañeros, dé nombres de artistas en cada categoría.

la compositora	escribe	novelas y poesía
la actriz	baila	canciones
el director	esculpe	en el ballet
el músico	toca	edificios y casas
el bailarín	interpreta	papeles (*roles*) en la televisión
el dramaturgo	diseña	guiones
la pintora	pinta	con actores
el escritor	mira	obras de teatro
la arquitecta	trabaja	cuadros
	dirige (*directs*)	instrumentos musicales
	compone (*composes*)	

NOTA COMUNICATIVA

Más sobre los gustos y preferencias

Here are additional verbs to talk about what you like and don't like.

- The following two verbs are used like **gustar**.

    aburrir   **Me aburre** el ballet moderno.
                           Modern ballet bores me.

    agradar   Pero **me agrada** el ballet folklórico.
                           But I like folkloric dances.

- This verb functions as a transitive verb (takes a direct object).

    apreciar   **Aprecio** mucho la arquitectura precolombina.
                           I really appreciate pre-Columbian architecture.

C. Preferencias personales

Paso 1. ¿Le gusta el arte? ¿Asiste a funciones culturales de vez en cuando o no asiste a esas funciones nunca? ¡Diga la verdad!

MODELO: asistir a los ballets clásicos →
Me gusta mucho asistir a los ballets clásicos.
(No me agrada para nada asistir a los ballets clásicos.)
(Me aburre asistir a los ballets clásicos. Prefiero ir a la ópera.)

Palabras útiles: gustar, apreciar, preferir, encantar, aburrir, agradar, interesar

1. ir a los museos de arte moderno
2. asistir a funciones teatrales
3. ver obras maestras en los museos grandes
4. escuchar a un(a) guía (*guide*) hablar en un museo
5. ir a conciertos de música clásica
6. asistir a lecturas de poesía en un café

Paso 2. Ahora entreviste a un compañero / una compañera para saber cuáles son sus preferencias con respecto a este tema.

MODELO: E1: ¿Te gusta ir a los museos de arte moderno?
E2: Sí, me gusta muchísimo. Voy siempre que puedo (*whenever I can*).

NOTA CULTURAL

Los toros

El toreo[a] es un espectáculo típicamente hispánico. Viene de una larga tradición histórica. De hecho, no se sabe exactamente cuándo surgió la primera **corrida de toros,**[b] pero hay evidencia histórica de corridas que data desde la Edad Media.

Para sus aficionados, el toreo es **un arte,** y **el torero** necesita mucho más que valor:[c] necesita destreza[d] técnica, gracia y mucha comprensión de **los toros.** Algunos creen que el toreo *no es* un arte, sino un espectáculo cruel y violento que causa la muerte[e] prematura e innecesaria de un animal valiente.

Sea cual sea la opinión que Ud. tiene[f] de las corridas de toros, las corridas son muy simbólicas para los aficionados. El toro es símbolo de fuerza,[g] coraje, bravura, independencia y belleza.[h] Si Ud. visita un país hispánico y tiene ganas de ver una corrida, es aconsejable que les pregunte a algunas personas nativas cuáles son las corridas que debe ver.

Una corrida de toros en Toledo, España

[a]El... *Bullfighting* [b]corrida... *bullfight* [c]*bravery* [d]*skill* [e]*death* [f]Sea... *Whatever your opinion may be* [g]*strength* [h]*beauty*

Ranking Things: Ordinals

primer(o/a)	first	**cuarto/a**	fourth	**sexto/a**	sixth	**noveno/a**	ninth
segundo/a	second	**quinto/a**	fifth	**séptimo/a**	seventh	**décimo/a**	tenth
tercer(o/a)	third			**octavo/a**	eighth		

- Ordinal numbers are adjectives and must agree in number and gender with the nouns they modify. Ordinals usually precede the noun: **la cuarta lección, el octavo ejercicio**.
- Like **bueno**, the ordinals **primero** and **tercero** shorten to **primer** and **tercer**, respectively, before masculine singular nouns: **el primer niño, el tercer mes**.
- Ordinal numbers are frequently abbreviated with superscript letters that show the adjective ending: **las 1ᵃˢ lecciones, el 1ᵉʳ grado, el 5º estudiante**.

Conversación

A. Mis actividades favoritas

Paso 1. Piense en lo que le gusta hacer en su tiempo libre en cuanto a (*regarding*) actividades culturales. Luego ponga en el orden de su preferencia (del 1 al 10) las siguientes actividades.

_____ ir al cine
_____ ir a ver películas extranjeras o clásicas
_____ ir a museos
_____ asistir a conciertos de música clásica/rock
_____ leer poesía
_____ bailar en una discoteca
_____ ver programas de televisión
_____ ver obras teatrales
_____ leer una novela
_____ ¿ ?

Paso 2. Ahora cuéntele a un compañero / una compañera sus cinco actividades favoritas. Use números ordinales.

MODELO: Mi actividad favorita es ir a ver películas clásicas. Mi segunda actividad favorita es…

B. Preguntas

1. ¿Es Ud. estudiante de cuarto año?
2. ¿Es este su segundo semestre/trimestre de español?
3. ¿A qué hora es su primera clase los lunes? ¿y su segunda clase?
4. ¿Vive Ud. en una casa de apartamentos o en una residencia? ¿En qué piso vive? Si vive en una casa, ¿en qué piso está su alcoba?

36 **Expressing Feelings** • Use of the Subjunctive: Emotion

Diego y Lupe escuchan un grupo de mariachis

México, D.F.

DIEGO: Ay, ¡cómo me encanta esta música!

LUPE: *Me alegro de que te guste.*

DIEGO: Y yo *me alegro de que estemos* aquí. ¿Sabes el origen de la palabra **mariachi**?

LUPE: No… ¿Lo sabes tú?

DIEGO: Sí. Viene del siglo diecinueve, cuando los franceses ocuparon México. Ellos contrataban a grupos de músicos para tocar en las bodas. Y como los mexicanos no podían pronunciar bien la palabra francesa *mariage*, pues acabaron por decir **mariachi**. Y de allí viene el nombre de los grupos.

LUPE: ¡Qué fascinante! *Me sorprende que sepas* tantos datos interesantes de nuestra historia.

DIEGO: Pues, todo buen antropólogo debe saber un poco de historia también, ¿no?

Comprensión

1. Lupe se alegra de que _____.
2. Y Diego se alegra de que _____.
3. A Lupe le sorprende que _____.

MAIN (INDEPENDENT) CLAUSE		SUBORDINATE (DEPENDENT) CLAUSE
first subject + *indicative* (expression of emotion)	**que**	second subject + *subjunctive*

A. Expressions of emotion are those in which speakers express their feelings: *I'm glad you're here; It's good that they can come.* Such expressions of emotion are followed by the subjunctive mood in the subordinate (dependent) clause.

Esperamos que Ud. **pueda** asistir.
We hope (that) you'll be able to come.

Tengo miedo de que mi abuelo **esté** muy enfermo.
I'm afraid (that) my grandfather is very ill.

Es una lástima que no **den** aumentos este año.
It's a shame they're not giving raises this year.

....

Diego and Lupe are listening to a mariachi group. DIEGO: Oh, how I love this music! LUPE: I'm glad you like it. DIEGO: And I'm glad we're here. Do you know the origin of the word **mariachi**? LUPE: No . . . Do you? DIEGO: Yes. It comes from the nineteenth century, when the French occupied Mexico. They used to hire musical groups to play at weddings. And because the Mexicans couldn't correctly pronounce the French word *mariage*, they ended up saying **mariachi**. And so that's where the name of the groups comes from. LUPE: How fascinating! I'm surprised you know so much interesting information about our history. DIEGO: Well, all good anthropologists should also know a little bit of history, shouldn't they?

B. Some common expressions of emotion are found in the list at the right.

alegrarse de	to be happy about
esperar	to hope
sentir (ie, i)	to regret; to feel sorry
temer	to fear
tener miedo (de)	to be afraid (of)

Some common expressions of emotion used with indirect object pronouns are in the second list at the right.

me (te, le,...) gusta que	I'm (you're, he's . . .) glad that
me (te, le,...) molesta que	it bothers me (you, him, . . .) that
me (te, le,...) sorprende que	it surprises me (you, him, . . .) that

C. When a new subject is introduced after a generalization of emotion, it is followed by the subjunctive in the subordinate (dependent) clause. Here are some general expressions of emotion.

es extraño	it's strange
es increíble	it's incredible
es mejor/bueno/malo	it's better/good/bad
es ridículo	it's ridiculous
es terrible	it's terrible
es una lástima	it's a shame
es urgente	it's urgent
¡qué extraño!	how strange!
¡qué lástima!	what a shame!

Práctica

A. Opiniones sobre el cine

Paso 1. Indique si las siguientes oraciones son ciertas o falsas para Ud.

1. Me molesta que muchas películas sean tan violentas.
2. Es ridículo que algunos actores ganen tanto dinero.
3. Espero que salgan más actores asiáticos e hispánicos en las películas.
4. Temo que muchas actrices no desempeñen (*play*) papeles inteligentes.
5. Es increíble que gasten millones de dólares en hacer películas.
6. Me sorprende que Julia Roberts sea tan famosa.

Paso 2. Ahora invente oraciones sobre lo que Ud. quiere o no quiere que pase con respecto al cine. Use las oraciones del **Paso 1** como base.

MODELO: **1.** Quiero que las películas sean menos violentas.

NOTA COMUNICATIVA

Expressing Wishes with *ojalá*

¡Ojalá que yo **gane** la lotería algún día!	*I hope I win the lottery some day!*

The word **ojalá** is invariable in form and means *I wish* or *I hope*. It is used with the subjunctive to express wishes or hopes. The use of **que** with it is optional.

¡Ojalá (que) haya paz en el mundo algún día!	*I hope (that) there will be peace in the world some day!*
Ojalá que no **pierdan** tu equipaje.	*I hope (that) they don't lose your luggage.*

Ojalá can also be used alone as an interjection in response to a question.

—¿Te va a ayudar Julio a estudiar para el examen?

—**¡Ojalá!**

B. Una excursión a la ópera. Imagine que Ud. y su amigo/a van a la ópera por primera vez en su vida. Piense en todas las expectativas que Ud. tiene y expréselas usando **ojalá**.

MODELO: las entradas / no costar mucho →
Ojalá que las entradas no cuesten mucho.

1. el escenario / ser / extravagante
2. haber / subtítulos / en inglés
3. el director (*conductor*) / estar / preparado
4. los cantantes / saber / sus papeles
5. nuestros asientos / no estar / lejos del escenario
6. (nosotros) llegar / a tiempo

Conversación

A. Situaciones. Las siguientes personas están pensando en otra persona o en algo que van a hacer. ¿Qué emociones sienten? ¿Qué temen? Conteste las preguntas según los dibujos.

1. Jorge piensa en su amiga Estela. ¿Por qué piensa en ella? ¿Dónde está? ¿Qué siente Jorge? ¿Qué espera? ¿Qué espera Estela? ¿Espera que la visiten los amigos? ¿que le manden algo?
2. Fausto quiere comer fuera esta noche. ¿Quiere que alguien lo acompañe? ¿Dónde espera que cenen? ¿Qué teme Fausto? ¿Qué le parecen (*seem*) los precios del restaurante?
3. ¿Dónde quiere pasar las vacaciones Mariana? ¿Espera que alguien la acompañe? ¿Dónde espera que pasen los días? ¿Qué teme Mariana? ¿Qué espera?

B. ¿Qué le molesta más? The following phrases describe aspects of university life. React to them, using phrases such as: **Me gusta que… , Me molesta que… , Es terrible que… , Es bueno/malo que… , Es una lástima que…**

1. Se pone mucho énfasis en los deportes.
2. Pagamos mucho/poco por la matrícula.
3. Se ofrecen muchos/pocos cursos en mi especialización (*major*).
4. Es necesario estudiar ciencias/lenguas para graduarse.
5. Hay muchos/pocos requisitos (*requirements*) para graduarse.
6. En general, hay muchas/pocas personas en las clases.

Enfoque *cultural*

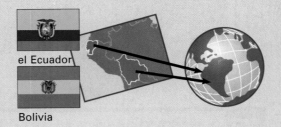

el Ecuador

Bolivia

Bolivia y el Ecuador

Datos esenciales

Bolivia

Nombre oficial: República de Bolivia

Capital: La Paz (sede[a] del gobierno), Sucre (capital constitucional)

Población: 8.000.000 de habitantes

Moneda: el (peso) boliviano

Idiomas oficiales: el español, el quechua, el aimara

el Ecuador

Nombre oficial: República del Ecuador

Capital: Quito

Población: 11.000.000 de habitantes

Moneda: el sucre (el dólar)

Idiomas: el español (oficial), el quechua

[a]*seat*

¡Fíjese!

- Bolivia formó parte del antiguo imperio inca. Aproximadamente, el 55 por ciento de la población boliviana actual es de origen indígena.
- Bolivia fue nombrada[a] en honor a Simón Bolívar, quien luchó por la independencia del país.
- A 12.000 pies de altura, La Paz es la capital más alta del mundo.
- Las Islas Galápagos pertenecen[b] al Ecuador y son de origen volcánico. Fueron descubiertas[c] en 1535, por el español Berlanga. Berlanga las llamó las Islas Encantadas[d] porque las fuertes corrientes[e] marinas confundían a los navegantes[f] como si fuera por[g] acto de magia. Trescientos años más tarde, el biólogo Charles Darwin llegó a las islas. De sus investigaciones de las plantas y animales resultaron sus ideas sobre la evolución y su famoso libro, *El origen de las especies*.

Darwin teorizó que los animales y las plantas cambian y se adaptan a su medio ambiente.[h]

[a]fue... *was named* [b]*belong* [c]Fueron... *They were discovered* [d]*Enchanted* [e]*currents* [f]*sailors* [g]como... *as if by* [h]medio... *environment*

Conozca a...
Oswaldo Guayasamín

Oswaldo Guayasamín (1919–1999) fue un pintor ecuatoriano cuyo[a] arte es un testimonio del sufrimiento[b] humano y de la vida difícil de los indios y los pobres de su país. Guayasamín se inspiró en los símbolos y motivos de los pueblos precolombinos y en el arte colonial del Ecuador.

[a]*whose* [b]*suffering*

Madre y niño, por Oswaldo Guayasamín

Capítulo 13 of the video to accompany *¿Qué tal?* contains cultural footage of Bolivia and Ecuador.

VVW. Visit the *¿Qué tal?* website at www.mhhe.com/quetal.

PASO 3 Gramática

37 Expressing Uncertainty • Use of the Subjunctive: Doubt and Denial

Mire Ud. la siguiente pintura detenidamente (*carefully*) y luego complete las siguientes oraciones de acuerdo con su opinión.

Familia andina, por Héctor Poleo (venezolano)

Vocabulario útil	
la alegría	happiness
la esperanza	hope
el miedo	fear
la tristeza	sadness
los guardias	guardsmen

1. *Es posible que* los miembros de esta familia tengan (miedo/esperanza). Estoy seguro/a de que no tienen (miedo/esperanza).
2. Creo que los colores representan (la alegría / la tristeza). *Dudo que* representen (la alegría / la tristeza).
3. *Es probable que* los guardias estén (enojados/contentos). Estoy seguro/a de que no están (enojados/contentos).

MAIN (INDEPENDENT) CLAUSE		SUBORDINATE (DEPENDENT) CLAUSE
first subject + *indicative* (expression of doubt or denial)	**que**	second subject + *subjunctive*

A. Expressions of doubt and denial are those in which speakers express uncertainty or negation. Such expressions, however strong or weak, are followed by the subjunctive in the dependent clause in Spanish.

No creo que **sean** estudiantes.
I don't believe they're students.

Es imposible que ella **esté** con él.
It's impossible for her to be with him.

B. Some expressions of doubt and denial appear at the right. Not all Spanish expressions of doubt are given here. Remember that any expression of doubt is followed by the subjunctive in the dependent clause.

no creer	*to disbelieve*
dudar	*to doubt*
no estar seguro/a (de)	*to be unsure (of)*
negar (ie)	*to deny*

OJO

Creer and **estar seguro/a** are usually followed by the indicative in affirmative statements because they do not express doubt, denial, or negation. Compare these examples.

Estamos seguros de (Creemos) que el examen **es** hoy.
We're sure (We believe) that the exam is today.

No estamos seguros de (No creemos) que el examen **sea** hoy.
We're not sure (We don't believe) that the exam is today.

C. When a new subject is introduced after a generalization of doubt, the subjunctive is used in the dependent clause. Some generalizations of doubt and denial are included at the right.

OJO

Generalizations that express certainty are not followed by the subjunctive but by the indicative: **Es verdad que cocina bien.**

es posible	it's possible
es imposible	it's impossible
es probable	it's probable (likely)
es improbable	it's improbable (unlikely)
no es cierto	it's not certain
no es seguro	it's not a sure thing
no es verdad	it's not true

Práctica

Opiniones distintas. Imagine que Ud. y un amigo / una amiga están en un museo arqueológico. En este momento están mirando una figura. Desafortunadamente, no hay ningún letrero (*sign*) cerca de Uds. para indicar lo que representa la figura. Haga oraciones completas según las indicaciones. Añada (*Add*) palabras cuando sea necesario.

Habla Ud.:

1. creo / que / ser / figura / de / civilización / maya
2. es cierto / que / figura / estar / hecho (*made*) / de oro
3. es posible / que / representar / dios (*god*) / importante
4. no estoy seguro/a de / que / figura / estar / feliz / o / enojado

Habla su amigo/a:

5. no creo / que / ser / figura / de / civilización / maya
6. creo / que / ser / de / civilización / tolteca
7. estoy seguro/a de / que / estar / hecho / de bronce
8. creo / que / representar / víctima [*m.*] / de / sacrificio humano

Conversación

A. ¿Una ganga? Imagine que Ud. va a un mercado al aire libre. Encuentra algunos objetos de artesanía muy interesantes que parecen ser de origen azteca… ¡y son baratísimos! ¿Cómo reacciona Ud.?

Empiece sus oraciones con estas frases.

1. ¡Es imposible que… !
2. No creo que…
3. Dudo muchísimo que…
4. Estoy seguro/a de que…
5. Es improbable que…

Vocabulario útil

el calendario	calendar
el escudo	shield
la joyería	jewelry
la lanza	spear
la máscara	mask
auténtico/a	authentic
falsificado/a	forged

NOTA COMUNICATIVA

Verbs That Require Prepositions

As you have already learned, when one verb immediately follows another, the second verb is usually the infinitive.

Prefiero *cenar* a las siete.   *I prefer to eat at seven.*

Some Spanish verbs, however, require that a preposition be placed before the second verb (still the infinitive). You have already used many of the important Spanish verbs that have this feature.

• The following verbs require the preposition **a** before an infinitive.

Mis padres me **enseñaron**   *My parents taught me to dance.*
  a bailar.

aprender a	enseñar a	venir a
ayudar a	invitar a	volver (ue) a
empezar (ie) a	ir a	

- These verbs or verb phrases require **de** before an infinitive.

  Siempre **tratamos de llegar**   *We always try to arrive on time.*
     puntualmente.

  acabar de   dejar de   tener ganas de
  acordarse (ue) de   olvidarse de   tratar de

- **Insistir** requires **en** before an infinitive.

  Insisten en venir esta noche.   *They insist on coming over tonight.*

- Two verbs require **que** before an infinitive: **haber que, tener que**.

  Hay que ver el nuevo museo.   *It's necessary to see the new museum.*

B. **¿Qué piensa Ud. del futuro?** Combine una frase de cada columna para formar oraciones que expresen su opinión sobre lo que le puede ocurrir a Ud. en los próximos cinco años. **¡OJO!** No se olvide de usar el subjuntivo en expresiones de duda o negación.

En los próximos años…

(no) creo que…	ir a	ser famoso/a
(no) dudo que…	aprender a	estar casado/a
es (im)posible que…	empezar a	ganar la lotería
(no) estoy seguro/a de que… (yo)	dejar de	pintar cuadros
(no) es cierto que…	tratar de	fumar
	volver a	tener hijos
		terminar mis estudios
		¿ ?

En los Estados Unidos y el Canadá...

Carlos Santana y la Fundación Milagro[a]

El legendario **guitarrista** Carlos Santana, originario de Autlán, México, se hizo **famoso** en el Festival de Woodstock en 1969 con un increíble solo de guitarra. Después de una serie de éxitos[b] en los años 70, entre ellos su inolvidable **interpretación** de «Oye cómo va», creó una nueva sensación en 1999—que le ganó varios *Grammys* en 2000— con su **disco compacto** *Supernatural*, en el que tocó con una variedad de artistas norteamericanos e hispanos para crear una **obra** rica

Carlos Santana

en **estilo** y composición. Santana también es una persona profundamente dedicada a la **comunidad**, especialmente a los niños. Junto con su esposa Deborah, Santana **creó** la Fundación Milagro (*Milagro Foundation*), una organización educativa para niños y jóvenes que **contribuye** dinero a otras organizaciones comunitarias sin fines lucrativos[c] en San Francisco y sus alrededores. El **propósito** es ayudar a la juventud de esa área con programas de salud, educación y arte.

[a]*Miracle* [b]*successes* [c]*sin… non-profit*

UN POCO DE TODO

Guernica, por Pablo Picasso (español)

En el Museo de Arte Moderno Reina (*Queen*) **Sofía.** Imagine que Ud. y su amigo/a están en Madrid con un grupo turístico. Ahora están en el Museo de Arte Moderno Reina Sofía y el guía les habla sobre *Guernica*, el famoso cuadro del pintor español Pablo Picasso. Complete el siguiente diálogo con la forma correcta de los verbos entre paréntesis. Cuando se den dos posibilidades, escoja la palabra correcta.

GUÍA: (Pasar[1]) Uds. por aquí, por favor. También les pido que (dejar[2]) suficiente espacio para todos. Y bien, aquí estamos (delante/ detrás[3]) de *Guernica,* la obra maestra pintada por Picasso. (Ser[4]) obvio que el cuadro (representar[5]) los horrores de la guerra,[a] ¿no? En 1937 Picasso (pintar[6]) este cuadro como reacción al bombardeo[b] (del / de la[7]) ciudad de Guernica durante la Guerra Civil Española. Por razones políticas, (durante / encima de[8]) la dictadura[c] de Franco,[d] el cuadro (fue/estuvo[9]) muchos años en el Museo de Arte Moderno de Nueva York. Pero por deseo expreso del pintor, el cuadro (trasladarse[10])[e] a España después de la muerte de Franco…

UD.: Yo dudo que (este/esto[11]) cuadro (ser[12]) una obra maestra. Creo que no (ser[13]) nada bonito. ¡No hay colores en él!

SU AMIGO/A: Yo no (creer[14]) que todos los cuadros (tener[15]) que (ser[16]) bonitos. Para mí, la falta de color (servir[17]) para expresar el dolor y el desastre… (Por/Para[18]) eso uno (poder[19]) sentir el mensaje de la destrucción de la guerra en la pintura.

[a]*war* [b]*bombing* [c]*dictatorship* [d]Francisco Franco (1892–1975), dictador de España desde 1939 hasta su muerte [e]*to move*

Comprensión. ¿Quién pudo haber dicho (*could have said*) lo siguiente en el diálogo anterior: el guía, Ud. o su amigo/a?

1. Yo prefiero los cuadros en colores.
2. Ahora voy a mostrarles una obra maestra de la pintura española.
3. No me molesta que esta pintura esté pintada en blanco y negro.
4. Quiero que todos me sigan y que se pongan delante del cuadro.

VIDEOTECA: En contexto

EL PERÚ

FUNCTION
Bargaining

Cultura en contexto
El arte y las artesanías

Los países hispanos han brindado al mundo[a] numerosos artistas importantes —tanto pintores como escritores, escultores y músicos. A la vez, los países hispanos son ricos en un arte menos formal: la artesanía, que es el arte folklórico del pueblo.

[a]han... *have given the world*

A. Lluvia de ideas

- ¿Qué tipo de artesanía se elabora (*is crafted*) en su estado o país? ¿Tiene Ud. algo hecho por artesanos locales?
- ¿Es común regatear en su país? ¿En qué tipo de negocio (*business*) se puede regatear? En su opinión, ¿sabe Ud. regatear bien? Dé un ejemplo.

B. Dictado

A continuación aparece un segmento del diálogo entre Juan Carlos y la vendedora de artesanías. Complete la explicación con las palabras o frases que faltan.

VENDEDORA: Todas mis _____[1] son muy buenas. ¿Quiere llevarse esa pieza? Le rebajo el _____[2] un poco, por ser mi _____[3] venta.
JUAN CARLOS: ¿En _____[4] me la deja? [...]
VENDEDORA: A ver... se _____[5] dejo en 60 soles.
JUAN CARLOS: Ajá. [...] ¿Qué precio tiene esta máscara?
VENDEDORA: Bueno, a Ud., nuestro joven viajero, se la dejo en un precio especial. Si me compra la _____[6] y la máscara, sólo le pido 100 soles en total. Fíjese, ¡qué _____[7]!

C. Un diálogo original

Paso 1. Con un compañero / una compañera, dramatice la escena entre Juan Carlos y la vendedora.

Paso 2. Se venden cuadros. Con un compañero / una compañera, dramatice la siguiente situación.

E1: Ud. es un(a) estudiante de cuarto año, a punto de (*just about to*) graduarse. Como va a mudarse muy pronto, desea vender algunas cosas en una venta (*sale*) de garaje. Entre ellas hay tres cuadros que Ud. pintó en su clase de arte. Póngale un precio a cada uno y haga una lista de las características de sus «obras maestras».

E2: Ud. es un(a) estudiante de primer año y quiere decorar su cuarto en la residencia. Piensa comprar algunas cosas en la venta de garaje de otro estudiante. Se interesa especialmente en uno de los cuadros, pero el precio que tiene no le parece bueno.

PASO 4

PASO FINAL

A LEER

Repaso de estrategias: Guessing the Content of a Passage

Look at the photograph that accompanies the reading. Read the title of the passage also. Based on these clues, what do you think the article is going to be about? How do you know? What important information do the photo and the title provide? Remember to always look for these types of visual clues as a useful strategy to facilitate comprehension when reading in a second language (or even in your first language).

> ***Sobre la lectura...*** Esta lectura es la adaptación de un artículo de la revista *GeoMundo.* Ud. ya leyó otro artículo de esta revista en el Capítulo 7. Recuerde que *GeoMundo* es como la revista *National Geographic* y que publica artículos sobre las ciencias, la geografía y otros temas similares.

Museo Virtual de Artes

<u>Aprovechando</u> las ventajas del ciberespacio, se creó el MUVA o Museo Virtual de Artes, sitio dedicado a <u>divulgar</u> el arte uruguayo y latinoamericano. Su directora es la historiadora de arte y curadora Alicia Haber. El sitio es recreativo, educativo y sin fines de lucro.[a]

La idea con que <u>surgió</u> este espacio es la de brindar[b] la sensación de estar en un museo real, pues debido a[c] las limitaciones originadas por la realidad socioeconómica de Uruguay, se ha visto impedida la construcción[d] de un museo nuevo. Cuatro arquitectos diseñaron un edificio con todos los adelantos,[e] la infraestructura técnica y las características edilicias[f] de un museo de primer nivel.[g] Existen innumerables museos en la <u>supercarretera</u> de la información, pero a diferencia de ellos, el MUVA no está construido como las páginas de un catálogo. Se trata de presentar arte uruguayo en el contexto más realista posible y brindarle al visitante la sensación de estar en un verdadero museo. Y no en cualquier museo, sino en

una obra arquitectónica atractiva, cómoda, moderna y eficiente, con escaleras mecánicas, ascensor, sala de acceso con esculturas, varias salas con instalaciones, pisos encerados[h] y hasta un buen sistema de iluminación.

Este museo ya ha recibido[i] 32 premios internacionales desde que entró en línea el 20 de mayo de

Sitio Web del Museo Virtual de Artes

[a]sin... *not-for-profit*   [b]*ofrecer*   [c]*pues... because, due to*   [d]*se... construction . . . has been impossible*   [e]*latest advances (in architecture)*   [f]*for preservation and inspection (of a public trust)*   [g]*class*   [h]*pisos... waxed floors*   [i]*ha... has received*

1997. El más importante es *Best of the Web* (Lo Mejor de la Red), pero también se ha hecho acreedor[j] al *Best Virtual Exhibition* (Mejor Exhibición Virtual del Mundo) entre más de 155 museos en línea. Debido a sus peculiares características, ha sido filmado[k] en CNN Internacional, en la televisión brasileña

y en muchos otros medios uruguayos e internacionales.

Se puede encontrar el MUVA en la dirección **http://www.diarioelpais.com/muva**. ■

[j]*se... it has been deemed worthy of inclusion*   [k]*ha... it has been filmed*

Comprensión

A. Preguntas. Conteste las siguientes preguntas.

1. ¿Qué tipo de museo es el MUVA?
2. ¿En qué país latinoamericano se creó el MUVA?
3. ¿Cuáles son algunos ejemplos del éxito de este museo?
4. ¿Cuál fue el objetivo de los diseñadores del MUVA?

B. Identificación. Identifique las conveniencias que le ofrece el MUVA al visitante, según el artículo.

1. ☐ diversas salas con exhibiciones
2. ☐ un tour guiado
3. ☐ un sistema de iluminación de alta calidad
4. ☐ diferentes maneras de navegar por el museo (ascensores, etcétera)
5. ☐ conversaciones con los artistas

 A ESCRIBIR

La expresión artística. Muchas personas se expresan mediante el arte en sus varias formas. Es decir, el arte no se limita solamente a la pintura y la escultura. El arte puede tomar varias formas: la música, la escritura, el diseño de ropa o muebles, etcétera. ¿Qué «arte» usa Ud. para expresar su personalidad? Escriba un breve ensayo (*essay*) para explicar cómo Ud. se expresa por medio del arte. Ideas para considerar:

- el medio artístico (la música, etcétera)
- cómo el arte expresa sus emociones y personalidad
- si sus preferencias con respecto a la expresión artística están cambiando o si se mantienen estables

Cuando termine su ensayo, entrégueselo a su profesor(a). El profesor / La profesora lo va a presentar al resto de la clase para ver si puede adivinar quién es el autor / la autora.

En resumen

GRAMÁTICA

To review the grammar points presented in this chapter, refer to the indicated grammar presentations. You'll find further practice of these structures in the Workbook/Laboratory Manual, on the CD-ROM, and on the website.

36. Use of the Subjunctive: Emotion

You should know how and when to use the subjunctive in a dependent clause when the main clause of a sentence expresses emotion.

37. Use of the Subjunctive: Doubt and Denial

You should know how and when to use the subjunctive in a dependent clause when the main clause of a sentence expresses doubt or denial.

VOCABULARIO

Los verbos

aburrir	to bore
agradar	to please
apreciar	to appreciate
intentar	to try
negar (ie)	to deny
parecer	to seem
representar	to represent
sentir (ie, i)	to regret; to feel sorry
temer	to fear
tratar de + *inf.*	to try to (*do something*)

Repaso: alegrarse de, creer, dudar, esperar, gustar, tener (*irreg.*) **miedo de**

La expresión artística

la arquitectura	architecture
el arte (*but* **las artes** *pl.*)	art
el baile	dance
el ballet	ballet
la danza	dance
el drama	drama
la escultura	sculpture
la música	music
la ópera	opera
la pintura	painting (*general*)
el teatro	theater

Repaso: el cine, la fotografía, la literatura

crear	to create
desempeñar	to play, perform (*a part*)
dibujar	to draw
esculpir	to sculpt
tejer	to weave

Repaso: cantar, escribir, pintar

Los artistas

el actor / la actriz	actor, actress
el/la aficionado/a	fan
el/la arquitecto/a	architect
el/la artista	artist
el bailarín/la bailarina	dancer
el/la cantante	singer
el/la compositor(a)	composer
el/la director(a)	director
el/la dramaturgo/a	playwright
el/la escritor(a)	writer
el/la escultor(a)	sculptor
el/la músico	musician
el/la pintor(a)	painter
el/la poeta	poet

La tradición cultural

la artesanía	arts and crafts
la cerámica	pottery, ceramics
las ruinas	ruins
los tejidos	woven goods

Otros sustantivos

la canción	song
el cuadro / la pintura	painting (*piece of art*) / painting (*piece of art; the art form*)
el escenario	stage
el/la guía	guide
el guión	script
la obra (de arte)	work (of art)
la obra maestra	masterpiece
el papel	role

Repaso: el museo

Los adjetivos

clásico/a	classic(al)
folklórico/a	folkloric
moderno/a	modern

Los números ordinales

primer(o/a), segundo/a, tercer(o/a), cuarto/a, quinto/a, sexto/a, séptimo/a, octavo/a, noveno/a, décimo/a

Palabras adicionales

es extraño	it's strange
¡qué extraño!	how strange!
es...	it is . . .
cierto	certain
increíble	incredible
preferible	preferable
seguro	a sure thing
urgente	urgent
es una lástima	it's a shame
¡qué lástima!	what a shame!
hay que + *inf.*	it is necessary to (*do something*)
me (te, le,...) molesta	it bothers me (you, him, . . .)
me (te, le,...) sorprende	it surprises me (you, him, . . .)
ojalá (que)	I hope, wish (that)

El medio ambiente

◀ Las cataratas del Iguazú están entre las más grandes del mundo. Se encuentran en la región fronteriza (*border*) entre la Argentina, el Brasil y el Paraguay.

VOCABULARIO

- The environment
- Automobiles

GRAMÁTICA

38 Past Participle Used As an Adjective
39 Perfect Forms: Present Perfect Indicative and Present Perfect Subjunctive

CULTURA

- **Enfoque cultural:** la Argentina
- **Nota cultural:** Programas medioambientales
- **En los Estados Unidos y el Canadá:** Chi Chi Rodríguez
- **Cultura en contexto:** Los verificentros

Multimedia

 You will learn about discussing car trouble in the **En contexto** video segment.

 Review vocabulary and grammar and practice language skills with the interactive CD-ROM.

W.W. Get connected to the Spanish-speaking world with the *¿Qué tal?* Online Learning Center: **www.mhhe.com/quetal**.

El medio ambiente°

medio… *environment*

la contaminación (del aire)

el aire puro

los rascacielos

la fábrica

el árbol

la finca

la agricultora

el campesino

la capa de ozono	ozone layer	**construir***	to build
la energía	energy	**contaminar**	to pollute
eléctrica	electric	**desarrollar**	to develop
eólica	wind	**destruir***	to destroy
hidráulica	hydraulic	**proteger**	to protect
nuclear	nuclear		
solar	solar	## Más vocabulario	
la escasez	lack, shortage	**el aislamiento**	isolation
la falta	lack, absence	**el delito**	crime
el gobierno	government	**el ritmo (acelerado)**	(fast) pace of life
la naturaleza	nature	**de la vida**	
la población	population	**los servicios públicos**	public services
los recursos naturales	natural resources	**el transporte público**	public transportation
		la violencia	violence
acabar	to run out, use up completely	**bello/a**	beautiful
conservar	to save, conserve	**denso/a**	dense

---

*Note the present indicative conjugation of **construir: construyo, construyes, construye, construímos, construís, construyen. Destruir** is conjugated like **construir**.

Conversación

A. Un recurso natural importante

En ECOPETROL tenemos conciencia ambiental y social. Nuestra planeación incluye siempre los estudios de localización e impacto ambiental, buscando no perturbar la naturaleza y la vida de las poblaciones vecinas a nuestras futuras operaciones. En esta planeación el trabajo con la comunidad es indispensable.

Nuestro propósito:
Una mejor convivencia

EMPRESA COLOMBIANA
DE PETROLEOS
ECOPETROL

Paso 1. Lea este anuncio de una empresa (compañía) colombiana y conteste las preguntas.

1. ¿Qué tipo de negocio cree Ud. que es Ecopetrol? ¿Qué produce?
2. ¿Qué asuntos (*matters*) son de mayor interés para esta empresa? ¿El tránsito? ¿la deforestación? ¿las poblaciones humanas? ¿otros asuntos?
3. ¿Le parece que la foto que han elegido (*they have chosen*) para el anuncio es buena para la imagen de la empresa? ¿Por qué?
4. El sustantivo **convivencia** se relaciona con el verbo **vivir** y contiene la preposición **con**. ¿Qué cree Ud. que significa **convivencia**?
5. ¿Sabe Ud. cuáles son algunos de los países que producen lo mismo que Ecopetrol?

Paso 2. Diga a qué tipo de energía corresponde cada descripción.

1. Es la energía más usada en los hogares (*homes*).
2. Según los expertos, es la forma de energía más limpia; es decir, es la que menos contaminación produce.
3. Puede ser la forma de energía más eficiente, pero también la más peligrosa (*dangerous*).
4. Esta energía viene del viento; por eso sólo se puede desarrollar en lugares específicos.
5. Para producir esta forma de energía son necesarios los ríos y las cataratas.

B. Problemas del mundo en que vivimos.
Comente las siguientes opiniones. Puede usar las siguientes expresiones para aclarar (*clarify*) su posición. **¡OJO!** Todas las expresiones requieren el uso del subjuntivo o del infinitivo.

Es / Me parece (*It seems to me*) fundamental / importantísimo / ridículo / ¿ ?
Me opongo a que (*I am against*)…
No creo que…

1. Para conservar energía debemos mantener bajo el termostato en el invierno y elevarlo en el verano.
2. Es mejor calentar las casas con estufas de leña (*wood stoves*) que con gas o electricidad.
3. Se debe crear más parques urbanos, estatales y nacionales.
4. La protección del medio ambiente no debe impedir la explotación de los recursos naturales.

5. Para evitar la contaminación urbana, debemos limitar el uso de los coches y no usarlos algunos días de la semana, como se hace en otros países.

6. El gobierno debe poner multas (*fines*) muy graves a las compañías e individuos que causan la contaminación.

7. El desarrollo de las tecnologías promueve (*promotes*) el ritmo tan acelerado de nuestra vida.

8. Los países desarrollados están destruyendo los recursos naturales de los países más pobres.

C. **¿La ciudad o el campo?** De las siguientes oraciones, ¿cuáles corresponden a la ciudad? ¿al campo?

1. El aire es más puro y hay menos contaminación.
2. La naturaleza es más bella.
3. El ritmo de la vida es más acelerado.
4. Los delitos son más frecuentes.
5. Los servicios financieros y legales son más asequibles (*available*).
6. Hay pocos medios de transporte públicos.
7. La población es menos densa.
8. Hay escasez de viviendas (*housing*).

NOTA CULTURAL

Programas medioambientales

Muchos países del mundo se encuentran en la posición de **equilibrar** la protección del **medio ambiente** con los objetivos del **desarrollo económico**. En muchos casos, **la explotación de recursos naturales** es la mayor fuente de ingreso[a] para la economía de un país. Los gobiernos latinoamericanos están conscientes de la necesidad de **proteger** el medio ambiente y de **conservar** los recursos naturales, y están haciendo lo posible por hacerlo. Los siguientes son algunos de los muchos programas **medioambientales** que se encuentran en los países hispanohablantes.

Madrid, España

• En la Ciudad de México, existe un programa permanente de **restricción vehicular** que se llama **Hoy no circula**.[b] Los coches no deben **circular** un día por semana. El día está determinado por el último número de **la placa**.[c] El propósito de este programa es controlar **la emisión de contaminantes**. Programas semejantes a **Hoy no circula** existen también en otros países como Chile y la Argentina.

• En México, España y otros países existen programas de **separación de basura**. Se depositan materiales distintos en recipientes[d] de colores diferentes, desde **el papel** y **el cartón, el vidrio,**[e] **el metal** y **el plástico,** hasta **la materia orgánica** y **los desechos**[f] **sanitarios.**

[a]fuente... *source of income* [b]Hoy... *Today [these] don't drive.* [c]*license plate* [d]*containers* [e]*glass* [f]*waste*

Los coches

En la gasolinera Gómez

la autopista	freeway	**chocar (con)**	to run into, collide (with)
la calle	street		
el camino	street, road	**doblar**	to turn
la carretera	highway	**estacionar**	to park
la circulación, el tránsito	traffic	**gastar (mucha gasolina)**	to use (a lot of gas)
la esquina	(street) corner	**manejar, conducir**	to drive
la licencia de manejar/conducir	driver's license	**obedecer**	to obey
		parar	to stop
el semáforo	traffic light	**seguir (i, i) (todo derecho)**	to keep on going; to go (straight ahead)
arrancar	to start up (*a car*)		
arreglar	to fix, repair		

Conversación

A. Definiciones

Paso 1. Busque Ud. la definición de las palabras de la columna de la derecha.

1. _____ Se pone en el tanque.
2. _____ Se llenan de aire.
3. _____ Lubrica el motor.
4. _____ Es necesaria para arrancar el motor.
5. _____ Cuando se llega a una esquina, hay que hacer esto o seguir todo derecho.
6. _____ No contiene aire suficiente y por eso es necesario cambiarla.
7. _____ Es un camino público ancho (*wide*) donde los coches circulan rápidamente.
8. _____ Se usan para parar el coche.
9. _____ El policía nos la pide cuando nos para en el camino.
10. _____ Allí se revisan y se arreglan los coches.

a. los frenos (*brakes*)
b. doblar
c. la carretera
d. la batería
e. el taller
f. una llanta desinflada (*flat*)
g. la gasolina
h. las llantas
i. el aceite
j. la licencia

Paso 2. Ahora, siguiendo el modelo de las definiciones anteriores, ¿puede Ud. dar una definición de las siguientes palabras?

1. el semáforo
2. la circulación
3. estacionarse
4. gastar gasolina
5. la gasolinera
6. la autopista

B. Entrevista: Un conductor responsable

Paso 1. Entreviste a un compañero / una compañera de clase para determinar con qué frecuencia hace las siguientes cosas.

1. dejar la licencia en casa cuando va a manejar
2. acelerar (*to speed up*) cuando ve a un policía
3. manejar después de tomar bebidas alcohólicas
4. respetar o exceder el límite de velocidad
5. estacionar el coche donde dice «Prohibido estacionarse»
6. revisar el aceite y la batería
7. seguir todo derecho a toda velocidad cuando no sabe llegar a su destino
8. rebasar (*to pass*) tres carros a la vez (*at the same time*)

Paso 2. Ahora, con el mismo compañero / la misma compañera, hagan una lista de diez cosas que hace —o no hace— un conductor responsable. Pueden usar frases del **Paso 1**, si quieren.

38 Más descripciones • Past Participle Used As an Adjective

Algunos refranes y dichos en español

1. En boca *cerrada* no entran moscas.
2. Estoy tan *aburrido* como una ostra.
3. Cuando está *abierto* el cajón, el más *honrado* es ladrón.

Empareje estas oraciones con el refrán o dicho que explican.

1. Es posible que una persona honrada caiga en la tentación de hacer algo malo si la oportunidad se le presenta.
2. Hay que ser prudente. A veces es mejor no decir nada para evitar (*avoid*) problemas.
3. Las ostras ejemplifican el aburrimiento (*boredom*) porque llevan una vida tranquila… siempre igual.

FORMS OF THE PAST PARTICIPLE

A. The past participle of most English verbs ends in *-ed*: for example, *to walk → walked; to close → closed*. Many English past participles, however, are irregular: *to sing → sung; to write → written*. In Spanish, the *past participle* (**el participio pasado**) is formed by adding **-ado** to the stem of **-ar** verbs, and **-ido** to the stem of **-er** and **-ir** verbs. An accent mark is used on the past participle of **-er/-ir** verbs with stems ending in **-a**, **-e**, or **-o**.

Pronunciation hint: Remember that the Spanish **d** between vowels, as found in past participle endings, is pronounced as the fricative [đ] (see **Pronunciación** in **Capítulo 6** of the Workbook/ Laboratory Manual).

hablar	comer	vivir
hab**lado** (*spoken*)	com**ido** (*eaten*)	viv**ido** (*lived*)

caer → **caído**	oír → **oído**
creer → **creído**	(son)reír → **(son)reído**
leer → **leído**	traer → **traído**

A few Spanish proverbs and sayings 1. Into a closed mouth no flies enter. 2. I am as bored as an oyster. 3. When the (cash) drawer is open, the most honest person is (can become) a thief.

B. The Spanish verbs at the right have irregular past participles.

abrir:	**abierto**	morir:	**muerto**
cubrir	**cubierto**	poner:	**puesto**
(to cover):			
decir:	**dicho**	resolver:	**resuelto**
descubrir:	**descubierto**	romper:	**roto**
escribir:	**escrito**	ver:	**visto**
hacer:	**hecho**	volver:	**vuelto**

THE PAST PARTICIPLE USED AS AN ADJECTIVE

A. In both English and Spanish, the past participle can be used as an adjective to modify a noun. Like other Spanish adjectives, the past participle must agree in number and gender with the noun modified.

Tengo una bolsa **hecha** en El Salvador.
I have a purse made in El Salvador.

El español es una de las lenguas **habladas** en los Estados Unidos y en el Canadá.
Spanish is one of the languages spoken in the United States and in Canada.

B. The past participle is frequently used with **estar** to describe conditions that are the result of a previous action.

La puerta **está abierta**.
The door is open.

Todos los lápices **estaban rotos**.
All the pencils were broken.

OJO

English past participles often have the same form as the past tense: I *closed* the book. The *thief stood behind the* ***closed*** *door.* The Spanish past participle is never identical in form or use to a past tense.

Cerré la puerta. Ahora la puerta está **cerrada**.
I ***closed*** *the door. Now the door is* ***closed***.

Práctica

A. En este momento…

Paso 1. En este momento, ¿son ciertas o falsas las siguientes oraciones con relación a su sala de clase?

Palabras útiles: colgar (ue) (*to hang*), enchufar (*to plug in*), prender (*to turn on* [*lights or an appliance*])

1. La puerta está abierta
2. Las luces están apagadas.
3. Las ventanas están cerradas.
4. Algunos libros están abiertos.
5. Los estudiantes están sentados.
6. Hay algo escrito en la pizarra.
7. Una silla está rota.
8. Hay carteles y anuncios colgados en la pared.
9. Un aparato está enchufado.

Paso 2. Ahora describa el estado de las siguientes cosas en su casa (cuarto, apartamento).

1. las luces
2. la cama
3. el televisor
4. las ventanas
5. la puerta
6. las cortinas (*curtains*)

B. Situaciones. ¿Cual es la situación en este momento? Conteste según el modelo.

MODELO: Natalia les tiene que *escribir* una carta a sus abuelos. →
La carta no está *escrita* todavía.

1. Los Sres. García deben *abrir* la tienda más temprano. ¡Ya son las nueve!
2. El gobernador quiere *cerrar* las fábricas que desperdician (*waste*) los recursos naturales de esta región.
3. Los niños esperan que la tierra se *cubra* de nieve para la Navidad.
4. Delia debe *poner* la mesa. Los invitados llegan a las nueve y ya son las ocho.
5. Claro está que la contaminación va a contribuir a la *destrucción* de la capa de ozono.
6. Es posible que los ingenieros *descubran* el error en la construcción del reactor nuclear.
7. Se debe *resolver* pronto el problema de la escasez de energía.

Conversación

¡Ojo alerta! Hay por lo menos cinco cosas que difieren (*are different*) entre un dibujo y el otro. ¿Puede Ud. encontrarlas? Use participios pasados como adjetivos cuando pueda.

A.

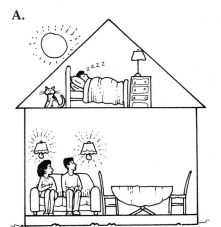

B.

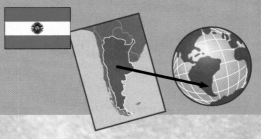

la Argentina

Datos esenciales

Nombre oficial: República Argentina

Capital: Buenos Aires

Población: 37.000.000 de habitantes

Moneda: el peso

Idioma oficial: el español

¡Fíjese!

- La inmigración de europeos en el siglo XIX tuvo un papel decisivo en la formación de la población de la Argentina (así como en la del Uruguay). En 1856 la población argentina era de 1.200.000 de habitantes; para 1930, 10.500.000 de extranjeros entraron en la Argentina por el puerto de Buenos Aires. La mitad[a] estaba formada por italianos, una tercera parte por españoles, y el resto estaba formado principalmente por alemanes y eslavos. Muchos de los que llegaron fueron trabajadores temporales que, más tarde o más temprano, regresaron a Europa. El resto, sin embargo,[b] se estableció permanentemente, porque el gobierno quería estimular la inmigración para poblar la Pampa. Pero muchos, acostumbrados a la vida urbana, se quedaron en Buenos Aires.

- Buenos Aires es una ciudad con una población de más de 10.000.000 de habitantes, lo cual supone[c] el 30 por ciento de la población del país. Es el centro cultural, comercial, industrial y financiero, así como el puerto principal de la Argentina. A las personas de Buenos Aires se les llama «porteños», derivado de «puerto».

[a]La… *Half* [b]sin… *however* [c]lo… *which constitutes*

La Plaza de Mayo data de 1580, año de la fundación de Buenos Aires.

Conozca... el tango

El tango se originó en los barrios pobres de Buenos Aires a finales del siglo XIX. El tango se toca con los instrumentos de los inmigrantes: la guitarra española, el violín italiano y el típico bandoleón, una especie de acordeón alemán.

Los temas del tango muestran una dualidad. Por un lado, representan la agresividad machista,[a] que incluye dramas pasionales y peleas con cuchillos.[b] Por otro, simbolizan la nostalgia, la soledad[c] y el sentimiento de pérdida.[d] El intérprete de tangos más famoso fue el porteño Carlos Gardel (1887–1935).

[a]*male* [b]*peleas… knife fights* [c]*solitude* [d]*loss*

Capítulo 14 of the video to accompany *¿Qué tal?* contains cultural footage of Argentina.

WWW. Visit the *¿Qué tal?* website at www.mhhe.com/quetal.

39 ¿Qué has hecho? • Perfect Forms: Present Perfect Indicative and Present Perfect Subjunctive

Una llanta desinflada

MANOLO: ¡Ay, qué mala suerte!

LOLA: ¿Qué pasa?

MANOLO: Parece que el coche tiene una llanta desinflada. Y como no hay ningún taller por aquí, tengo que cambiarla yo mismo.

LOLA: *¿Has cambiado* una llanta alguna vez?

MANOLO: No. Siempre *he llevado* el coche a un taller cuando hay problemas.

LOLA: Pues, yo nunca *he cambiado* una llanta tampoco. Pero te puedo ayudar, si quieres.

MANOLO: Gracias. ¡Espero que la llanta de recambio no esté desinflada también!

¿Y Ud.? ¿Ha… ?

1. cambiado una llanta desinflada
2. revisado el aceite de su coche
3. arreglado otras cosas del coche
4. tenido un accidente con el coche
5. excedido el límite de velocidad en la autopista

PRESENT PERFECT INDICATIVE

he hablado	*I have spoken*	**hemos** hablado	*we have spoken*
has hablado	*you have spoken*	**habéis** hablado	*you (pl.) have spoken*
ha hablado	*you have spoken, he/she has spoken*	**han** hablado	*you (pl.) / they have spoken*

A flat tire MANOLO: Aw, what bad luck! LOLA: What's wrong? MANOLO: It seems the car has a flat tire. And, as there aren't any repair shops around here, I have to change it myself. LOLA: Have you ever changed a flat tire before? MANOLO: No. I've always taken the car to a repair shop when there are problems. LOLA: Well, I've never changed a tire either. But I can help you, if you want. MANOLO: Thanks. I hope that the spare tire isn't flat too!

A. In English, the present perfect is a compound tense consisting of the present tense form of the verb *to have* plus the past participle: *I have written, you have spoken*, and so on.

In the Spanish *present perfect* (**el presente perfecto**), the past participle is used with present tense forms of **haber**, the equivalent of English *to have* in this construction.

In general, the use of the Spanish present perfect parallels that of the English present perfect.

No **hemos estado** aquí antes.
We haven't been here before.

Me he divertido mucho.
I've had a very good time.

Ya le **han escrito** la carta.
They've already written her the letter.

OJO **Haber**, an auxiliary verb, is not interchangeable with **tener**.

B. The form of the past participle never changes with **haber**, regardless of the gender or number of the subject. The past participle always appears immediately after the appropriate form of **haber** and is never separated from it. Object pronouns and **no** are always placed directly before the form of **haber**.

[Práctica A]

Ella **ha cambiado** una llanta desinflada varias veces.
She's changed a flat tire several times.

Todavía **no le** han revisado el aceite al coche.
They still haven't checked the car's oil.

C. The present perfect form of **hay** is **ha habido** (*there has/have been*).

OJO Remember that **acabar** + **de** + *infinitive*—not the present perfect tense—is used to state that something *has just occurred*.

Ha habido un accidente.
There's been an accident.

Acabo de mandar la carta.
I've just mailed the letter.

PRESENT PERFECT SUBJUNCTIVE

The *present perfect subjunctive* (**el perfecto del subjuntivo**) is formed with the present subjunctive of **haber** plus the past participle. It is used to express *I have spoken* (*written*, and so on) when the subjunctive is required. Although its most frequent equivalent is *I have* plus the past participle, its exact equivalent in English depends on the context in which it occurs.

Note in the model sentences at the right that the English equivalent of the present perfect subjunctive can be expressed as a simple or as a compound tense: *did / have done; came / have come; built / have built*.

[Práctica B]

haya hablado	**hayamos** hablado
hayas hablado	**hayáis** hablado
haya hablado	**hayan** hablado

Es posible que lo **haya hecho**.
It's possible (that) he may have done (he did) it.

Me alegro de que **hayas venido**.
I'm glad (that) you have come (you came).

Es bueno que lo **hayan construido**.
It's good (that) they built (have built) it.

Práctica

A. El coche de Carmina. Carmina acaba de comprarse un coche usado. Su papá es vendedor de autos en Los Ángeles. ¡Así que el coche fue una ganga! Describa lo que le ha pasado a Carmina, según el modelo.

MODELO: ir a la agencia de su padre → Ha ido a la agencia de su padre.

1. pedirle ayuda a su padre
2. hacer preguntas acerca de (*about*) los diferentes coches
3. ver uno bastante barato
4. revisar las llantas
5. conducirlo como prueba

6. regresar a la agencia
7. decidir comprarlo
8. comprarlo
9. volver a casa
10. llevar a sus amigas al cine esa noche

B. ¡No lo creo! ¿Tienen espíritu aventurero sus compañeros de clase? ¿Llevan una vida interesante? ¿O están tan aburridos como una ostra?

Paso 1. De cada par de oraciones, indique la que (*the one that*) expresa su opinión acerca de los estudiantes de esta clase.

Vocabulario útil: el paracaidismo (*skydiving*), escalar (*to climb*), hacer *autostop* (*to hitchhike*)

1. ☐ Creo que alguien en esta clase ha visto las pirámides de Egipto.
   ☐ Es dudoso que alguien haya visto las pirámides de Egipto.
2. ☐ Estoy seguro/a de que por lo menos uno de mis compañeros ha escalado una montaña alta.
   ☐ No creo que nadie haya escalado una montaña alta.
3. ☐ Creo que alguien ha viajado haciendo *autostop*.
   ☐ Dudo que alguien haya hecho *autostop* en un viaje.
4. ☐ Creo que alguien ha practicado el paracaidismo.
   ☐ Es improbable que alguien haya practicado el paracaidismo.
5. ☐ Estoy seguro/a de que alguien ha tomado el metro en Nueva York a medianoche (*midnight*).
   ☐ No creo que nadie haya tomado el metro neoyorquino a medianoche.

Paso 2. Ahora escuche mientras el profesor / la profesora pregunta si alguien ha hecho estas actividades. ¿Tenía Ud. razón en el **Paso 1**?

Conversación

A. Entrevista. Con un compañero / una compañera, haga y conteste preguntas con estos verbos. La persona que contesta debe decir la verdad.

MODELO: visitar México →
E1: ¿Has visitado México?

E2: Sí, he visitado México una vez. / No, no he visitado México nunca. / Sí, he visitado México durante las vacaciones de los últimos años.

1. comer paella
2. estar en Nueva York
3. manejar un Alfa Romeo
4. correr en un maratón
5. abrir hoy tu libro de español
6. escribir un poema
7. actuar en una obra teatral
8. ver un monumento histórico
9. conocer a una persona famosa
10. romperse la pierna alguna vez

B. **Dos dibujos, un punto de vista.** Un español hizo el dibujo de la derecha; un argentino, el de la izquierda. Pero los dos comentan el mismo tema.

Palabras útiles: el arado (*plow*), la deshumanización, la flor, la gente, la mecanización, la mula, el tractor

Paso 1. Conteste estas preguntas sobre el dibujo de la derecha.

1. Describa la ciudad que se ve en el dibujo.
2. ¿Qué ha descubierto la gente? ¿Por qué mira con tanto interés?
3. Para construir esta ciudad, ¿qué han hecho? ¿Qué han destruido?

Paso 2. Conteste estas preguntas sobre el dibujo de la izquierda.

1. ¿Qué se ha comprado el agricultor? ¿Qué ha vendido?
2. ¿Qué es «más moderno», según el otro agricultor?
3. ¿Qué desventaja tiene el tractor?

Paso 3. Ahora explique su reacción personal a estos dos dibujos. ¿Son chistosos (*funny*)? ¿serios?

NOTA COMUNICATIVA

Talking about What You Had Done

Use the past participle with the imperfect form of **haber** (**había, habías,...**) to talk about what you had—or had not—done before a given time in the past. This form is called the past perfect.

Antes de graduarme en la escuela secundaria, no **había estudiado** español.	*Before graduating from high school, I hadn't studied Spanish.*
Antes de 1985, siempre **habíamos vivido** en Kansas.	*Before 1985, we had always lived in Kansas.*

D. Entrevista. Use the cues to interview a classmate about his or her activities before coming to this campus. Begin your questions with **Dime...**

> MODELO: algo / no haber aprendido a hacer antes del año pasado →
> E1: Dime algo que no habías aprendido a hacer antes del año pasado.
> E2: Pues... no había aprendido a nadar. Aprendí a nadar este año en mi clase de natación.

1. algo / no haber aprendido a hacer antes del año pasado
2. una materia / no haber estudiado antes del año pasado
3. el nombre de un deporte / haber practicado mucho
4. algo sobre un viaje / haber hecho varias veces
5. el nombre de un libro importante / no haber leído
6. una decisión / no haber tomado
7. ¿ ?

En los Estados Unidos y el Canadá...

Chi Chi Rodríguez

Juan «Chi Chi» Rodríguez nació en Río Piedras, Puerto Rico, en 1935. Se hizo[a] golfista profesional en 1960 y ha ganado ocho competiciones en la *PGA Tour* y veintidós en la *Senior Tour*. Rodríguez también se hizo popular por su arrolladora[b] personalidad y su fabulosa **precisión técnica** en el golf.

En los años setenta, Bill Hayes, otro golfista profesional y además maestro y agente de un centro de detención juvenil, invitó a Rodríguez a dirigir un pro-

Chi Chi Rodríguez

grama de golf para unos **jóvenes detenidos**.[c] Hayes y Rodríguez decidieron que el campo de golf sería[d] el lugar ideal para ayudar a estos y otros jóvenes en peligro de **fracasar**[e] en la escuela y en la vida. El golf, reconocido como[f] el deporte de las personas que **han tenido éxito**[g] en la vida, requiere **autocontrol, responsabilidad** y **respeto** para los demás. Rodríguez fundó *The Chi Chi Rodríguez Foundation* para los jóvenes del condado[h] de Pinellas, Florida. En la actualidad,[i] hay unos 500 jóvenes entre las edades de 5 y 17 años en el programa.

[a]*Se... He became* [b]*irresistible* [c]*incarcerated* [d]*would be* [e]*en... in danger of failing* [f]*reconocido... recognized as* [g]*tenido... succeeded* [h]*county* [i]*En... Currently*

UN POCO DE TODO

¡Qué descuidado (*careless*) **eres!** Complete the following exchanges with the correct form of the words in parentheses, as suggested by the context. When two possibilities are given in parentheses, select the correct word. Begin with the present indicative. There are also command forms. Use the preterite or the imperfect of infinitives in italics.

En casa

RIGOBERTO: Me parece que debo (llevar / a llevar[1]) el coche (al / a la[2]) taller. Hace varios días que tiene una lucecita encendida.[a]

MARGARITA: (*Tú:* Ser/Estar[3]) muy descuidado con esas cosas. Un día vas a tener una sorpresa desagradable.

RIGOBERTO: Bueno, espero que el mecánico (tener[4]) tiempo (por/para[5]) arreglarlo. Hasta luego.

En el taller

MECÁNICO: Buenos días. ¿Qué desea?

RIGOBERTO: Pues, (mirar: *Ud.*[6]). ¿Ve Ud. (este[7]) luz roja que está encendida? ¿Qué puede ser?

MECÁNICO: Eso es (el/la[8]) aceite. ¿Hace mucho tiempo que no (lo/la[9]) cambia?

RIGOBERTO: La verdad es que no lo (*yo:* recordar[10]).

MECÁNICO: (Dejarme: *Ud.*[11]) revisarlo todo. (Volver: *Ud.*[12]) dentro de (un/una[13]) par de horas.

Más tarde

MECÁNICO: Ud. no (preocuparse[14]) mucho por el auto, ¿verdad? Todos los niveles (estar[15]) muy bajos. También le (*yo:* poner[16]) agua al depósito del limpiaparabrisas[b] y le (*cambiar*[17]) el filtro del aceite.

RIGOBERTO: ¿Eso (ser[18]) todo?

MECÁNICO: El coche casi no (tener[19]) aceite. Sinceramente, si Ud. (seguir[20]) manteniendo el auto así, algún día va a quemar[c] el motor.

RIGOBERTO: No me diga... [d]

MECÁNICO: Y otro consejo. (Cambiar: *Ud.*[21]) pronto las llantas. Hace tiempo que (*perder*[22]) la banda,[e] y eso (ser/estar[23]) peligroso.

[a]lucecita... *little light turned on*   [b]¿ ?   [c]*burn up*   [d]*No... You don't say . . .*   [e]*tread*

Comprensión: ¿Cierto o falso? Corrija las oraciones falsas.

1. Rigoberto se interesa mucho por su coche.
2. Su esposa sabe más de coches que él.
3. El mecánico trata a Rigoberto muy descortésmente.
4. El coche estaba en muy malas condiciones.
5. Rigoberto va a empezar a cuidar su coche.

MÉXICO

VIDEOTECA: En contexto

FUNCTION

Discussing car trouble

SI TRAE NIÑOS CONTROLELOS

In this video segment, Roberto talks to Miguel, his car mechanic, about the problems that he has been having with his car. As you watch the segment, pay particular attention to the problems that Roberto imagines his car has, as opposed to the real problem that Miguel discovers. Do you think Roberto is overreacting?

A. Lluvia de ideas

- ¿Tiene Ud. su propio coche? (Si no tiene uno, refiérase al coche de otra persona al contestar las siguientes preguntas.) ¿Cuándo lo compró? ¿De qué año es el modelo de su coche? ¿Está Ud. contento/a con el coche?
- ¿Sabe Ud. arreglar un coche? ¿Sabe Ud. algo de mecánica en general? ¿Cuáles son los problemas más típicos de un coche?

B. Dictado

A continuación aparece un fragmento del diálogo entre Roberto y Miguel, el mecánico. Complete la explicación con las palabras que faltan.

ROBERTO: ¡Este carro me tiene como loco, Miguel! ¡Es la _____¹ vez que lo arreglas este año!

MIGUEL: Sí, ya lo sé, Roberto. Primero le arreglé los _____²... y _____³ fue la transmisión. ¿Y cómo están los frenos y la transmisión?

ROBERTO: ¡Los frenos y la transmisión están bien! ¡No _____⁴ qué pasa, pero este carro _____⁵ simplemente no quiere _____⁶!

MIGUEL: Cálmate, Roberto. Vamos a ver... _____,⁷ viejo, ¿qué te pasa esta vez? ¿Por qué no arrancas, eh? ¿Qué tienes? ¿Qué necesitas?

ROBERTO: Lo que necesita este carro es ser _____⁸ para convertirlo en lata de aluminio.ᵃ

ᵃlata... *tin can*

C. Un diálogo original

Paso 1. Con un compañero / una compañera, dramatice el diálogo entre Roberto y Miguel.

Paso 2. La compra de un carro. Con un compañero / una compañera, piense en un carro que Uds. podrían (*could*) comprar. Como no tienen mucho dinero, van a comprar un carro de segunda mano. Hagan una lista de todas las cosas que le deben preguntar al dueño antes de hacer la compra.

Cultura en contexto
Los verificentros

En México, como en los Estados Unidos, los coches tienen que pasar por una verificación que determina si el nivelᵃ de contaminantes emitidos por el coche está dentro de los límites aceptables. Esta verificación se hace en lugares designados que se llaman **verificentros**. Como en otros países, esta es una de las medidas gubernamentalesᵇ para controlar la contaminación.

ᵃ*level* ᵇmedidas... *governmental measures*

PASO FINAL

A CONVERSAR

¿Somos buenos o malos conductores?

Paso 1. Con un compañero / una compañera, haga y conteste preguntas basadas en el siguiente cuadro. Utilice el presente perfecto en sus preguntas y respuestas y marque el cuadro según las respuestas de su compañero/a. También añada (*add*) al cuadro otro problema relacionado con los coches.

MODELO: E1: ¿Has superado (*Have you exceeded*) el límite de velocidad recientemente?
E2: Sí, (No, no) he superado el límite de velocidad recientemente.

	sí	no
chocar con otro coche		
superar el límite de velocidad		
pasarse (*to run*) un semáforo en rojo		
desobedecerle a un policía		
¿ ?		

Paso 2. Ahora, entre todos, hablen de sus compañeros/as. En general, ¿son Uds. buenos o malos conductores? Deben marcar la información en un cuadro como el del **Paso 1.** Incluyan los problemas que añadieron al cuadro.

MODELOS: ¿Quiénes han chocado con otro coche recientemente? →
Tom ha chocado con otro coche este mes.

Paso 3. Calculen el porcentaje de personas que contestaron **sí** a cada pregunta del **Paso 1.** Reaccionen a los porcentajes con las siguientes frases. **¡OJO!** Las frases requieren el uso del subjuntivo.

Es bueno / malo que…
Me alegra / No me alegra que…
Me sorprende que / No me sorprende que…

MODELO: Siete de veintiún estudiantes han superado recientemente el límite de velocidad. → El 33% de la clase ha superado recientemente el límite de velocidad.
E1: No me sorprende que el 33% de la clase haya superado el límite de velocidad.

En resumen

GRAMÁTICA

To review the grammar points presented in this chapter, refer to the indicated grammar presentations. You'll find further practice of these structures in the Workbook/Laboratory Manual, on the CD-ROM, and on the website.

38. Past Participle Used As an Adjective

Do you know how to form past participles? You should remember that past participles that are used as adjectives agree with the noun they describe.

39. Perfect Forms: Present Perfect Indicative and Present Perfect Subjunctive

How do you express that you have done something? Do you know how to say that you're happy or sad that someone else did or has done something?

VOCABULARIO

El medio ambiente

acabar	to run out, use up completely
conservar	to save, conserve
construir	to build
contaminar	to pollute
cubrir	to cover
desarrollar	to develop
descubrir	to discover
desperdiciar	to waste
destruir	to destroy
evitar	to avoid
proteger	to protect
reciclar	to recycle
resolver (ue)	to solve, resolve
el aire	air
el bosque	forest
la capa de ozono	ozone layer
la energía	energy
eléctrica	electric
eólica	wind
hidráulica	hydraulic
nuclear	nuclear
solar	solar
la escasez	lack, shortage
la fábrica	factory
la falta	lack, absence

el gobierno	government
la naturaleza	nature
la población	population
los recursos naturales	natural resources

Repaso: la contaminación

¿La ciudad o el campo?

el/la agricultor(a)	farmer
el aislamiento	isolation
el árbol	tree
el/la campesino/a	farm worker; peasant
el delito	crime
la finca	farm
el rascacielos	skyscraper
el ritmo	rhythm, pace
el servicio	service
el transporte	(means of) transportation
la vida	life
la violencia	violence
la vivienda	housing

Hablando de coches

arrancar	to start (a car)
gastar	to use, expend

llenar	to fill (up)
revisar	to check

el aceite	oil
la batería	battery
la estación de gasolina	gas station
los frenos	brakes
la gasolina	gasoline
la gasolinera	gas station
la llanta (desinflada)	(flat) tire
el/la mecánico/a	mechanic
el nivel	level
el parabrisas	windshield
el taller	(repair) shop
el tanque	tank

Repaso: arreglar, limpiar

En el camino

chocar (con)	to run into, collide (with)
conducir	to drive
doblar	to turn
estacionar(se)	to park
obedecer	to obey
parar	to stop
seguir (i, i)	to continue

la autopista	freeway
la calle	street
el camino	street, road
la carretera	highway
la circulación	traffic
el/la conductor(a)	driver
la esquina	(street) corner
la licencia de manejar/conducir	driver's license
el límite de velocidad	speed limit
el/la policía	police officer
el semáforo	traffic signal
el tránsito	traffic
todo derecho	straight ahead

Repaso: manejar

Los adjetivos

acelerado/a	fast, accelerated
bello/a	beautiful
denso/a	dense
público/a	public
puro/a	pure

La vida social y la vida afectiva

◀ Las relaciones sociales son importantes para todo el mundo. Estas personas están sentadas en los bancos de la Plaza de Armas en Punta Arenas, Chile.

VOCABULARIO

- Sentimental relationships
- Stages of life

GRAMÁTICA

40 Subjunctive after Nonexistent and Indefinite Antecedents
41 Subjunctive after Conjunctions of Contingency and Purpose

CULTURA

- **Enfoque cultural:** Chile
- **Nota cultural:** Relaciones en la vida social
- **En los Estados Unidos y el Canadá:** Isabel Allende
- **Cultura en contexto:** Lo social en el mundo de los negocios

Multimedia

 You will learn about making an appointment in the **En contexto** video segment.

Review vocabulary and grammar and practice language skills with the interactive CD-ROM.

 Get connected to the Spanish-speaking world with the *¿Qué tal?* Online Learning Center: **www.mhhe.com/quetal**.

Las relaciones sentimentales

la amistad

la cita

el amor

el noviazgo

la luna de miel

el matrimonio

la boda

el divorcio

Más vocabulario

el/la amigo/a	friend	**amar**	to love
la esposa / la mujer	wife	**casarse (con)**	to marry
el esposo / el marido	husband	**divorciarse (de)**	to get divorced (from)
el/la novio/a	boyfriend/girlfriend;	**enamorarse (de)**	to fall in love (with)
	fiancé(e); groom/bride	**llevarse bien/mal**	to get along well/poorly
la pareja	(married) couple; partner	**(con)**	(with)
		pasar tiempo (con)	to spend time (with)
amistoso/a	friendly	**querer (ie)**	to love
cariñoso/a	affectionate	**romper (con)**	to break up (with)
casado/a*	married	**salir (con)**	to go out (with)
soltero/a*	single, not married	**separarse (de)**	to separate (from)

---

*In **Capítulo 2,** you began to use **ser casado/a**. **Estar casado/a** means *to be married;* **ser casado/a** means *to be a married person.* **Ser soltero/a** is used exclusively to describe an unmarried person.

Conversación

A. Definiciones. Empareje las palabras con sus definiciones. Luego, para cada palabra definida, dé un verbo y el nombre de una persona asociada con esa relación social. Hay más de una respuesta posible en cada caso.

1. _____ el matrimonio
2. _____ el amor
3. _____ el divorcio
4. _____ la boda
5. _____ la amistad

a. Es una relación cariñosa entre dos personas. Se llevan bien y se hablan con frecuencia.

b. Es el posible resultado de un matrimonio, cuando los esposos no se llevan bien.

c. Es una relación sentimental, apasionada, muy especial, entre dos personas. Puede llevar al (*lead to*) matrimonio.

d. Es una ceremonia religiosa o civil en la que (*which*) la novia a veces lleva un vestido blanco.

e. Es una relación legal entre dos personas que viven juntas (*together*) y que a veces tienen hijos.

B. ¡Seamos lógicos! Complete las oraciones lógicamente.

1. Mi abuelo es el _____ de mi abuela.
2. Muchos novios tienen un largo _____ antes de la boda.
3. María y Julio tienen una _____ el viernes para comer en un restaurante. Luego van a bailar.
4. La _____ de Juan y Pati es el domingo a las dos de la tarde, en la iglesia (*church*) de San Martín.
5. En una _____, ¿quién debe pagar o comprar los boletos, el hombre o la mujer?
6. La _____ entre los ex esposos es imposible. No pueden ser amigos.
7. ¡El _____ es ciego (*blind*)!

NOTA CULTURAL

Relaciones en la vida social

Dos palabras españolas que no tienen equivalente exacto en inglés son **amigo** y **novio**. En el diagrama se indica cuándo es apropiado usar estas palabras para describir relaciones sociales en muchas culturas hispánicas y en la norteamericana.

friend	*girlfriend/boyfriend*	*fiancée/fiancé*	*bride/groom*

| amiga/amigo | | novia/novio | |

Como en todas partes del mundo, los enamorados hispanos usan muchos términos de cariño: **mi amor, mi amorcito/a, mi vida, viejo/vieja, querido/querida, cielo, corazón.** Es también frecuente el uso afectuoso de las frases **mi hijo / mi hija** entre esposos y aun[a] entre buenos amigos.

[a]*even*

Etapas de la vida°

Etapas... *Stages of life*

el nacimiento	birth	**nacer**	to be born
la infancia	infancy	**crecer**	to grow
la niñez	childhood	**morir (ue, u)**	to die
la adolescencia	adolescence		
la juventud	youth		
la madurez	middle age		
la vejez	old age		
la muerte	death		

Conversación

A. Etapas de la vida. Relacione las siguientes palabras y frases con las distintas etapas de la vida de una persona. **¡OJO!** Hay más de una posible relación en algunos casos.

1. el amor
2. los nietos
3. los juguetes (*toys*)
4. no poder comer sin ayuda
5. los hijos en la universidad
6. los granos (*pimples*)
7. la universidad
8. la boda

B. Una receta para unas buenas relaciones. En su opinión, ¿cuáles son los ingredientes necesarios para un buen matrimonio o una buena amistad?

Paso 1. Haga una lista de los cinco ingredientes más esenciales. Los ingredientes pueden expresarse con una palabra o una frase.

Paso 2. Compare su lista con las de otros tres estudiantes. ¿Coinciden en la selección de algunos ingredientes? Hablen de todos los ingredientes y hagan una lista de los cinco más importantes.

Paso 3. Ahora comparen los resultados de todos los grupos. ¿Han contestado todos más o menos de la misma manera?

40 ¿Hay alguien que... ? ¿Hay un lugar donde... ? •
Subjunctive after Nonexistent and Indefinite Antecedents

Un buen lunes

Mafalda *tiene un padre que la quiere, la protege y que pasa mucho tiempo* con ella. Por eso, Mafalda ve a su padre como *un hombre que ahora es más guapo* que cuando era joven. Todos los niños *necesitan padres que los quieran, los cuiden y que tengan tiempo* para pasar con ellos.

Comprensión

¿Quién lo dice o piensa, el padre de Mafalda u otro pasajero en el autobús?

1. No hay nadie en este autobús que sea más feliz que yo.
2. Tengo una hija que es una maravilla, ¿verdad?
3. Todos los lunes por la mañana trato de pensar en algo que me haga sonreír en camino al trabajo… pero casi nunca lo puedo hacer.

A. In English and Spanish, statements or questions that give or ask for information about a person, place, or thing often contain two clauses.

Each of the example sentences contains a main clause (*I have a car, Is there a house for sale*). In addition, each sentence also has a subordinate clause (*that gets good mileage, that is closer to the city*) that modifies a noun in the main clause: *car, house*. The noun (or pronoun) modified is called the *antecedent* (**el antecedente**) of the subordinate clause, and the clause itself is called an adjective clause because—like an adjective—it modifies a noun (or pronoun).

I have a **car** *that gets good mileage.*
Is there a **house for sale** *that is closer to the city?*

A good Monday   Mafalda has a father who loves her, protects her, and spends a lot of time with her. That's why Mafalda sees her father as a man who is now more handsome than when he was young. All children need parents who love them, take care of them, and have time to spend with them.

B. Sometimes the antecedent of an adjective clause is something that, in the speaker's mind, does not exist or whose existence is indefinite or uncertain.

In these cases, the subjunctive must be used in the adjective (subordinate) clause in Spanish.

Note in the examples that adjective clauses that describe a place can be introduced with **donde...** as well as with **que...**

NONEXISTENT ANTECEDENT:

There is *nothing* that you can do.

INDEFINITE ANTECEDENT:

We need *a car* that will last us for years. (We don't have one yet.)

EXISTENT ANTECEDENT:

Hay algo aquí que me **interesa.**
There is something here that interests me.

NONEXISTENT ANTECEDENT

No veo nada que me **interese.**
I don't see anything that interests me.

DEFINITE ANTECEDENT:

Hay muchos restaurantes donde **sirven** comida mexicana auténtica.
There are a lot of restaurants where they serve authentic Mexican food.

INDEFINITE ANTECEDENT:

Buscamos un restaurante donde **sirvan** comida salvadoreña auténtica.
We're looking for a restaurant where they serve authentic Salvadoran food.

OJO

The dependent adjective clause structure is often used in questions to find out about someone or something the speaker does not know much about. Note, however, that the indicative is used to answer the question if the antecedent is known to the person who answers.

INDEFINITE ANTECEDENT:

¿Hay algo aquí que te **guste?**
Is there anything here that you like?

DEFINITE ANTECEDENT:

Sí, **hay varias bolsas** que me **gustan.**
Yes, there are several purses that I like.

OJO

The personal **a** is not used with direct object nouns that refer to hypothetical persons.* Compare the use of the indicative and the subjunctive in the sentences at the right.

NONEXISTENT ANTECEDENT:

Busco **un señor** que **sepa** francés.
I'm looking for a man who knows French.

EXISTENT ANTECEDENT:

Busco **al señor** que **sabe** francés.
I'm looking for the man who knows French.

---

*Remember that **alguien** and **nadie** always take the personal **a** when they are used as direct objects: **Busco a alguien que lo sepa. No veo a nadie que sea norteamericano.**

Práctica

A. Hablando de gente que conocemos. En su familia, ¿hay personas que tengan las siguientes características? Indique la oración apropiada en cada par de oraciones.

TENGO UN PARIENTE…	NO TENGO NINGÚN PARIENTE…
1. ☐ que habla alemán.	☐ que hable alemán.
2. ☐ que vive en el extranjero.	☐ que viva en el extranjero.
3. ☐ que es dueño de un restaurante.	☐ que sea dueño de un restaurante.
4. ☐ que sabe tocar el piano.	☐ que sepa tocar el piano.
5. ☐ que es médico/a.	☐ que sea médico/a.
6. ☐ que fuma.	☐ que fume.
7. ☐ que está divorciado/a.	☐ que esté divorciado/a.
8. ☐ que trabaja en la televisión.	☐ que trabaje en la televisión.
9. ☐ ¿ ?	☐ ¿ ?

B. Las preguntas de Carmen

Paso 1. Carmen acaba de llegar aquí de otro estado. Quiere saber algunas cosas sobre la universidad y la ciudad. Haga las preguntas de Carmen según el modelo.

MODELO: restaurantes / sirven comida latinoamericana →
¿Hay restaurantes que sirvan (donde se sirva) comida latinoamericana?

1. librerías / venden libros usados
2. tiendas / se puede comprar revistas de Latinoamérica
3. cafés cerca de la universidad / se reúnen muchos estudiantes
4. apartamentos cerca de la universidad / son buenos y baratos
5. cines / pasan (*they show*) películas en español
6. un gimnasio en la universidad / se juega al ráquetbol
7. parques / la gente corre o da paseos
8. museos / hacen exposiciones de arte latinoamericano

Paso 2. ¿Son ciertas o falsas las siguientes declaraciones?

1. A Carmen no le interesa la cultura hispánica.
2. Carmen es deportista.
3. Es posible que sea estudiante.
4. Este año piensa vivir con unos amigos de sus padres.

Paso 3. Ahora conteste las preguntas de Carmen con información verdadera sobre la ciudad donde Ud. vive y su universidad.

MODELO: ¿Hay restaurantes que sirvan comida latinoamericana? →
No, no hay ningún restaurante que sirva comida latinoamericana. / Sí, hay restaurantes que sirven comida latinoamericana.

Conversación

A. Una encuesta. Las habilidades o características de un grupo de personas pueden ser sorprendentes. ¿Qué sabe Ud. de los compañeros de su clase de español? Pregúnteles a los miembros de la clase si saben hacer lo siguiente o a quién le ocurre lo siguiente. Deben levantar la mano sólo los que puedan contestar afirmativamente. Luego la persona que hizo la pregunta debe hacer un comentario apropiado. Siga el modelo.

MODELO: hablar chino →
En esta clase, ¿hay alguien que hable chino? (*Nadie levanta la mano.*) No hay nadie que hable chino.

1. hablar ruso
2. saber tocar la viola
3. conocer a un actor / una actriz
4. saber preparar comida vietnamita
5. tener el cumpleaños hoy
6. escribir poemas
7. vivir en las afueras
8. ¿ ?

B. Entrevista

Paso 1. Con un compañero / una compañera, haga y conteste las siguientes preguntas.

1. ¿Hay alguien en tu vida que te quiera locamente (*madly*)?
2. ¿Hay algo que te importe más que los estudios universitarios?
3. ¿Con qué tipo de persona te gusta salir?
4. Para el semestre/trimestre que viene, ¿qué clases buscas? ¿una que empiece a las ocho de la mañana?
5. ¿Tienes algún amigo o alguna amiga de la escuela secundaria que esté casado/a? ¿que tenga hijos? ¿que esté divorciado/a?
6. **¡OJO!** Unas preguntas indiscretas: ¿Has conocido recientemente a alguien que te haya gustado mucho? ¿de quien te hayas enamorado? ¿Hay alguna persona de tu familia con quien te lleves muy mal? ¿o muy, muy bien?

Paso 2. Ahora, comparta los detalles interesantes con la clase.

MODELO: Bob dice que no hay nadie en su vida que lo quiera locamente, pero dice que ha conocido a alguien que le ha gustado mucho.

Enfoque *cultural*

Chile

Datos esenciales

Nombre oficial: República de Chile

Capital: Santiago

Población: 15.000.000 de habitantes

Moneda: el peso

Idiomas: el español (oficial), el mapuche, el quechua

Conozca a... Gabriela Mistral

La primera hispanoamericana en ganar el premio Nóbel de Literatura fue Gabriela Mistral (1889–1957). Maestra de escuela, además de poeta, fue una mujer que vivió tristes momentos en su vida (el abandono de su padre, el suicidio de su prometido[a] y su maternidad frustrada) que se ven reflejados en su poesía. El siguiente poema es uno de sus más conocidos.

[a]*fiancé*

Riqueza[a]

Tengo la dicha fiel[b]
y la dicha perdida:
la una como una rosa,
la otra como una espina.[c]
De lo que me robaron
no fui desposeída:[d]
tengo la dicha fiel
y la dicha perdida
y estoy rica de púrpura[e]
y de melancolía.
　¡Ay, qué amada[f]
　　es la rosa
y qué amante[g] es la espina!
Como el noble contorno[h]
de las frutas mellizas[i]
tengo la dicha fiel
y la dicha perdida...

[a]*Wealth* [b]*dicha... constant happiness* [c]*thorn* [d]*no... I was not dispossessed* [e]*purple* [f]*qué... how beloved* [g]*qué... how loving* [h]*contour* [i]*twin*

¡Fíjese!

- El nombre de Chile se deriva de la palabra indígena *chilli* que significa «lugar donde termina la tierra».

- A través del largo y estrecho territorio de Chile, la geografía va de selva[a] a desierto, a fértil valle,[b] a zona de nieves perpetuas en el extremo sur.

- Chile tiene una de las economías más fuertes de Sudamérica. Es el mayor productor de cobre[c] del mundo, y tiene una importante industria vinícola.[d]

[a]*jungle* [b]*valley* [c]*copper* [d]*wine*

Capítulo 15 of the video to accompany *¿Qué tal?* contains cultural footage of Chile.

Visit the *¿Qué tal?* website at www.mhhe.com/quetal.

Un viñedo (*vineyard*) chileno, con los Andes al fondo (*in the background*)

41 **Lo hago para que tú...** • Subjunctive after Conjunctions of Contingency and Purpose

Maneras de amar

¿A qué dibujo corresponde cada una de las siguientes oraciones? ¿Quién las dice?

1. Aquí tienes la tarjeta de crédito, pero úsala sólo *en caso de que haya una emergencia*, ¿eh?
2. Escúchame bien. No vas a salir *antes de que termines* la tarea.
3. Quiero casarme contigo *para que estemos* siempre juntos *y no salgas más* con Raúl.

Comprensión

1. En el primer dibujo, es obvio que el chico _____. Es normal que la madre _____.
2. En el segundo dibujo está claro que la chica _____; por eso el padre se siente _____ (adjetivo).
3. En el tercer dibujo, creo que el chico _____. No estoy seguro/a de que la chica _____. Pienso que esta pareja es muy joven para _____.

A. When one action or condition is related to another—X will happen provided that Y occurs; we'll do Z unless A happens—a relationship of *contingency* is said to exist: one thing is contingent, or depends, on another.

The Spanish *conjunctions* (**las conjunciones**) at the right express relationships of contingency or purpose. The subjunctive always occurs in subordinate clauses introduced by these conjunctions.

a menos que	unless
antes (de) que	before
con tal (de) que	provided (that)
en caso de que	in case
para que	so that

B. Note that these conjunctions introduce subordinate clauses in which the events have not yet materialized; the events are conceptualized, not real-world, events.

Voy **con tal de que** ellos me **acompañen**.
I'm going, provided (that) they go with me.

En caso de que llegue Juan, dile que ya salí.
In case Juan arrives, tell him that I already left.

Ways to love 1. Here you have the credit card, but use it only in case there is an emergency, OK? **2.** Listen to me well. You are not going out until you finish your homework. **3.** I want to marry you so that we are always together and so you don't go out with Raúl any more.

C. When there is no change of subject in the dependent clause, Spanish more frequently uses the prepositions **antes de** and **para**, plus an infinitive, instead of the corresponding conjunctions plus the subjunctive. Compare the sentences at the right.

PREPOSITION: Estoy aquí **para aprender**.
I'm here to (in order to) learn.

CONJUNCTION: Estoy aquí **para que Uds. aprendan**.
I'm here so that you will learn.

PREPOSITION: Voy a comer **antes de salir**.
I'm going to eat before leaving.

CONJUNCTION: Voy a comer **antes de que salgamos**.
I'm going to eat before we leave.

Práctica

A. **¿Es Ud. un buen amigo / una buena amiga?** La amistad es una de las relaciones más importantes de la vida. Indique si las siguientes oraciones son ciertas o falsas para Ud. con respecto a sus amigos. **¡OJO!** No todas las características son buenas. Hay que leer con cuidado.

	C	F
1. Les hago muchos favores a mis amigos, con tal de que ellos después me ayuden a mí.	☐	☐
2. Les ofrezco consejos a mis amigos para que tomen buenas decisiones.	☐	☐
3. Les presto dinero a menos que sepa que no me lo pueden devolver.	☐	☐
4. Les traduzco el menú en los restaurantes mexicanos en caso de que no sepan leer español.	☐	☐
5. Los llevo a casa cuando beben, para que no tengan accidentes de coche.	☐	☐

B. **Julio siempre llega tarde.** Siempre es buena idea llegar un poco temprano al teatro o al cine. Sin embargo, su amigo Julio, quien va al cine con Ud. esta tarde, no quiere salir con un poco de anticipación. Trate de convencerlo de que Uds. deben salir pronto.

JULIO: No entiendo por qué quieres que lleguemos al teatro tan temprano.
UD.: Pues, para que (nosotros)…

Sugerencias: poder estacionar el coche, no perder el principio de la función, poder comprar los boletos, conseguir buenas butacas (*seats*), no tener que hacer cola, comprar palomitas (*popcorn*) antes de que empiece la película, hablar con los amigos

Conversación

A. Situaciones. Con un compañero / una compañera o con un grupo de estudiantes, dé una explicación para las siguientes situaciones. Luego comparen sus explicaciones con las de otro grupo.

1. Los padres trabajan mucho para (que)…
2. Los profesores les dan tarea a los estudiantes para (que)…
3. Los dueños de los equipos deportivos profesionales les pagan mucho a algunos jugadores para (que)…
4. Los padres castigan (*punish*) a los niños para (que)…
5. Las parejas se divorcian para (que)…
6. Los jóvenes forman pandillas (*gangs*) para (que)…

B. Encuesta. Con sus compañeros de clase, comparta información sobre sus planes para el futuro. Usen las frases a la izquierda con una conjunción a la derecha en sus oraciones.

MODELO: Voy a graduarme en diciembre con tal de que salga bien en esta clase.

1. Voy a graduarme en…	a menos que…
2. Este verano voy a…	antes de que…
3. No quiero enamorarme / casarme / divorciarme…	con tal de que…
4. Quiero tener hijos/nietos…	en caso de que…
5. Voy a llevarme bien con…	para que…

En los Estados Unidos y el Canadá...

Isabel Allende

Es posible que la chilena Isabel Allende (1942–) sea **la escritora hispánica más conocida de Norteamérica**. Sobrina del presidente de Chile, Salvador Allende, que fue derrocado[a] violentamente y murió en 1973, Isabel viene de **una familia que tiene un pasado muy interesante**. Este pasado, con su mezcla[b] de lo familiar y lo político, aparece como uno de los elementos más salientes[c] de sus novelas. Estas[d] se caracterizan también por el uso del **«realismo mágico»**, técnica literaria en que elementos fantásticos se entretejen[e] con aspectos de la vida diaria. Su primera novela, *La casa de los espíritus*, apareció en 1982 y fue seguida por otras de igual éxito,[f] entre ellas, *Eva Luna*, *El plan infinito* y *De amor y de sombra*.

Isabel Allende

La vida de Allende no ha sido fácil. Después de los eventos políticos en que murió su tío, tuvo que **abandonar su país** con sus hijos pequeños. Vivió por un tiempo en Venezuela y hoy reside en los Estados Unidos con su **segundo esposo**. **Perdió a su segunda hija**, Paula, después de una larga y trágica enfermedad, cuando esta tenía 28 años. A ella le dedicó un libro en el que[g] cuenta la historia de la familia a la vez que narra los cambios que sufre la escritora a consecuencia del trauma de la enfermedad de su adorada hija. Pero los contratiempos[h] no parecen detener a la incansable Isabel Allende.

Sus libros se consiguen en español y en traducción en los Estados Unidos y el Canadá y son popularísimos.

[a]*overthrown* [b]*mixture* [c]*prominent* [d]*These (novels)* [e]*se… are interwoven* [f]*success* [g]*en… in which* [h]*mishaps, disappointments*

UN POCO DE TODO

La luna de miel. Complete the following dialogues with the correct form of the words in parentheses, as suggested by the context. When two possibilities are given in parentheses, select the correct one. **¡OJO!** You will use indicative, present subjunctive, and command forms. *P* and *I* stand for *preterite* and *imperfect,* respectively. Use the past participle of infinitives in italics.

En el aeropuerto

MUJER: ¡Por fin hemos (*llegar*[1])! ¡Qué vuelo más largo!
MARIDO: Sí. (Soy/Estoy[2]) bastante cansado. Quiero (descansar[3]) un rato antes de que (*nosotros:* salir[4]) a ver la ciudad.
MUJER: Yo (también/tampoco[5]). Vamos a recoger[a] el equipaje. ¡Ojalá que no se nos (ha/haya[6]) perdido!
MARIDO: No (preocuparte[7]). Todo saldrá bien.[b] Vamos.

[a]*pick up* [b]*saldrá... will turn out all right*

En el hotel

MARIDO: Ay, ¡qué desgracia! ¿Qué hemos (*hacer*[8]) nosotros para merecer[a] esto?
MUJER: (Calmarte[9]), mi amor. No pasa (nunca/nada[10]). Si sólo[b] se nos (*P:* perder[11]) una maleta. Y la empleada de la aerolínea nos (*P:* prometer[12]) que (lo/la[13]) vamos a tener para mañana.
MARIDO: Sí, tienes razón. Verdad que hasta (este/esto[14]) momento, todo ha (*salir*[15]) muy bien. ¡Qué boda más (bonito[16]) (*P, nosotros:* tener[17])! (*I:* Haber[18]) muchas más personas de lo que (*I, nosotros:* esperar[19]). Pero creo que todos (*P:* divertirse[20]).
MUJER: Creo que sí. En mi opinión, no hay nadie a quien no le (gustar[21]) una fiesta de bodas...
MARIDO: Bueno, descansemos[c] un poco para que (*nosotros:* poder[22]) disfrutar del[d] resto (del / de la[23]) noche. No quiero que una maleta perdida (aguar[24][e]) la luna de miel.
MUJER: ¡Ni yo (también/tampoco[25])!

[a]*deserve* [b]*Si... Only* [c]*let's rest* [d]*disfrutar... enjoy the* [e]*to spoil*

Comprensión: ¿Cierto, falso o no lo dice?

1. Las dos personas son recién casadas.
2. La fiesta de bodas tuvo lugar en casa de los padres de la mujer.
3. Los esposos perdieron dos maletas.
4. Fueron a Cancún en su luna de miel.
5. La boda fue bonita y muy divertida.

VIDEOTECA: En contexto

In this video segment, Mariela makes an appointment to see the university's career counselor. As you watch the segment, pay attention to the exchange between Mariela and the receptionist and how they decide upon a time that suits both Mariela and the counselor. Does your university or college provide a similar service?

COSTA RICA

A. Lluvia de ideas

- Aparte de (*Aside from*) sus clases, ¿tiene Ud. muchos compromisos sociales y citas? ¿Cómo recuerda Ud. cuándo tiene sus compromisos? ¿Usa una agenda o un calendario?
- ¿Cuándo tiene sus próximas citas? ¿Puede decir con quién las tiene o prefiere que no se sepa?

B. Dictado

A continuación aparece un fragmento del diálogo entre Mariela y la recepcionista de la consejera Valenzuela. Complete la explicación con las palabras o frases que faltan.

RECEPCIONISTA: Buenos días, oficina de la consejera Valenzuela. ¿En qué _____¹ puedo servir?

MARIELA: Muy buenos días. ¿_____² comunica con la consejera Valenzuela, por favor?

RECEPCIONISTA: Disculpe,ᵃ ¿de parte deᵇ _____³? [...] _____⁴ siento pero la consejera está con un _____⁵ en este momento. ¿Quiere dejar un recado?

MARIELA: Bueno, lo que quiero es hacer una _____.⁶

ᵃ*Excuse me.*   ᵇ¿de... *on behalf of*

C. Un diálogo original

Opción 1.   Con un compañero / una compañera, dramatice el diálogo entre Mariela y la recepcionista.

Opción 2.   Una cita para ir a tomar una lección de baile. Imagine que Ud. y su amigo/a han decidido tomar juntos unas lecciones de baile (rumba, merengue, tango, flamenco, etcétera). Tienen que escoger el día y la hora más convenientes para los dos. Si uno/a de Uds. tiene alguna experiencia en este tipo de baile, no se olvide de darle recomendaciones a la persona que no tenga experiencia (decirle, por ejemplo, qué tipo de ropa y zapatos debe llevar).

FUNCTION

Making an appointment

Cultura en contexto
Lo social en el mundo de los negocios

En el mundo hispano, lo social y lo afectivo hacen un papelᵃ muy importante en los negocios. En casi toda interacción, como la búsqueda de trabajo o un acuerdo entre los representantes de dos empresas, lo social tiene mucha importancia. Conocerse en persona y establecer relaciones cordiales es imprescindible para llevar a caboᵇ un acuerdo o una negociación.

ᵃhacen... *play a role*   ᵇes... *is essential for carrying out*

PASO FINAL

A LEER

Estrategia: Using Graphics to Get Information

Sobre la lectura... La lectura, o mejor dicho, el gráfico, a continuación es del periódico *El País*, de España. Es parte de un artículo más largo sobre el divorcio en España. Como Ud. puede ver, el uso de elementos visuales, como este gráfico, sirve para presentar la información de una manera más organizada para el lector.

Reading graphics such as tables and pie charts requires as much concentration as, if not more than, any other reading since a lot of information is often summarized in a compact space. Paying attention to the heading of a section as well as to the categories within the graphic can help you to focus your attention on important parts of the information presented.

The following chart offers a visual snapshot of statistical information pertaining to marriage and divorce in Spain since 1981. As you read and analyze the information in the chart, remember to rely on all of the visual clues that you can to facilitate your comprehension. Maybe you'll be surprised by what you read!

Las separaciones y los divorcios han aumentado el 66% en los últimos diez años

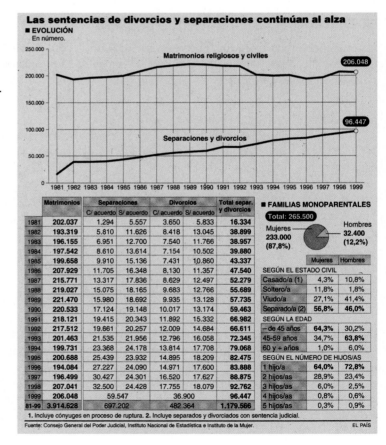

Las sentencias de divorcios y separaciones continúan al alza

■ EVOLUCIÓN
En número.

Matrimonios religiosos y civiles — 206.048

Separaciones y divorcios — 96.447

	Matrimonios	Separaciones		Divorcios		Total separ. y divorcios
		C/ acuerdo	S/ acuerdo	C/ acuerdo	S/ acuerdo	
1981	202.037	1.294	5.557	3.650	5.833	16.334
1982	193.319	5.810	11.626	8.418	13.045	38.899
1983	196.155	6.951	12.700	7.540	11.766	38.957
1984	197.542	8.610	13.614	7.154	10.502	39.880
1985	199.658	9.910	15.136	7.431	10.860	43.337
1986	207.929	11.705	16.348	8.130	11.357	47.540
1987	215.771	13.317	17.836	8.629	12.497	52.279
1988	219.027	15.075	18.165	9.683	12.766	55.689
1989	221.470	15.980	18.692	9.935	13.128	57.735
1990	220.533	17.124	19.148	10.017	13.174	59.463
1991	218.121	19.415	20.343	11.892	15.332	66.982
1992	217.512	19.661	20.257	12.009	14.684	66.611
1993	201.463	21.535	21.956	12.796	16.058	72.345
1994	199.731	23.368	24.178	13.814	17.708	79.068
1995	200.688	25.439	23.932	14.895	18.209	82.475
1996	194.084	27.227	24.090	14.971	17.600	83.888
1997	196.499	30.427	24.301	16.520	17.627	88.875
1998	207.041	32.500	24.428	17.755	18.079	92.762
1999	206.048	59.547		36.900		96.447
81-99	3.914.628	697.202		482.364		1.179.566

1. Incluye cónyuges en proceso de ruptura. 2. Incluye separados y divorciados con sentencia judicial.

Fuente: Consejo General del Poder Judicial, Instituto Nacional de Estadística e Instituto de la Mujer.

EL PAÍS

■ FAMILIAS MONOPARENTALES

Total: 265.500

Mujeres 233.000 (87,8%)

Hombres 32.400 (12,2%)

	Mujeres	Hombres
SEGÚN EL ESTADO CIVIL		
Casado/a (1)	4,3%	10,8%
Soltero/a	11,8%	1,8%
Viudo/a	27,1%	41,4%
Separado/a (2)	56,8%	46,0%
SEGÚN LA EDAD		
– de 45 años	64,3%	30,2%
45-59 años	34,7%	63,8%
60 y + años	1,0%	6,0%
SEGÚN EL NÚMERO DE HIJOS/AS		
1 hijo/a	64,0%	72,8%
2 hijos/as	28,9%	23,4%
3 hijos/as	6,0%	2,5%
4 hijos/as	0,8%	0,6%
5 hijos/as	0,3%	0,9%

Comprensión

A. **¿Qué significa el título?** Utilice el gráfico para determinar el equivalente en inglés de la frase «han aumentado» del título.

☐ have decreased ☐ have increased ☐ have remained unchanged

B. **¿Cierto o falso?** Conteste según el gráfico. Corrija las oraciones falsas.

1. En 1999 hay más divorcios en España que matrimonios.
2. El porcentaje de hogares (*households*) monoparentales encabezados por (*headed by*) madres y padres es igual.

C. **A contestar.** Conteste según el gráfico.

1. ¿En qué año se nota el mayor (*greatest*) número de matrimonios en España?
2. ¿Entre qué años se ve el aumento más profundo en el número total de divorcios y separaciones?

 A ESCRIBIR

Según el gráfico, el número de separaciones y divorcios en España va aumentando constantemente desde 1981, año en que se legalizó el divorcio en dicho (*that*) país. Una consecuencia de este cambio social es el aumento en alternativas fuera del matrimonio. Por ejemplo, muchas personas prefieren convivir (*to live together*) en vez de contraer matrimonio (*getting married*). Esta decisión puede traer ventajas y desventajas.

Paso 1. Imagine que un amigo suyo / una amiga suya (*friend of yours*) le pide consejos respecto al asunto (*about this question*). ¿Qué le va a recomendar? Haga una lista de tres de las ventajas y tres de las desventajas de convivir sin casarse.

Ventajas

1. _____ 2. _____ 3. _____

Desventajas

1. _____ 2. _____ 3. _____

Paso 2. Ahora, escríbale una carta a su amigo/a, presentándole una de las dos perspectivas. Intente formular un buen argumento para persuadirle de que siga sus consejos. Puede empezar su carta así:

Querido/a: _____.

He pensado mucho en tu situación y creo que…

En resumen

GRAMÁTICA

To review the grammar points presented in this chapter, refer to the indicated grammar presentations. You'll find further practice of these structures in the Workbook/Laboratory Manual, on the CD-ROM, and on the website.

40. Subjunctive after Nonexistent and Indefinite Antecedents

You should know how to use the subjunctive in two-clause sentences when the antecedent is nonexistent or indefinite.

41. Subjunctive after Conjunctions of Contingency and Purpose

You should know how and when to use the subjunctive after certain conjunctions of contingency and purpose.

VOCABULARIO

Las relaciones sentimentales

amar	to love
casarse (con)	to marry
divorciarse (de)	to get divorced (from)
enamorarse (de)	to fall in love (with)
llevarse bien/mal (con)	to get along well/poorly (with)
pasar tiempo (con)	to spend time (with)
querer (ie)	to love
romper (con)	to break up (with)
salir (salgo) (con)	to go out (with)
separarse (de)	to separate (from)

la amistad	friendship
el amor	love
la boda	wedding (*ceremony*)
la cita	date
el divorcio	divorce
la luna de miel	honeymoon
el marido	husband
el matrimonio	marriage; married couple
la mujer	wife
el noviazgo	engagement
la pareja	(married) couple; partner

Repaso: el/la amigo/a, el/la esposo/a, el/la novio/a

amistoso/a	friendly

Repaso: cariñoso/a, casado/a, soltero/a

Etapas de la vida

la adolescencia	adolescence
la infancia	infancy
la juventud	youth
la madurez	middle age
la muerte	death
el nacimiento	birth
la vejez	old age

Repaso: la niñez

crecer	to grow
nacer	to be born

Repaso: morir (ue, u)

Otras palabras y expresiones útiles

la gente	people
a primera vista	at first sight
bastante	rather, sufficiently; enough
juntos/as	together
propio/a	own

Conjunciones

a menos que	unless
antes (de) que	before
con tal (de) que	provided (that)
en caso de que	in case
para que	so that

¿Trabajar para vivir o vivir para trabajar?

Estas mujeres profesionales caminan por la Puerta de la Ciudadela en Montevideo, Uruguay.

VOCABULARIO

- Professions and trades
- The working world

GRAMÁTICA

42 Future Verb Forms
43 Subjunctive and Indicative after Conjunctions of Time

CULTURA

- **Enfoque cultural:** el Uruguay y el Paraguay
- **Nota cultural:** Los nombres de las profesiones
- **En los Estados Unidos y el Canadá:** El creciente mercado hispano
- **Cultura en contexto:** Los cajeros automáticos

Multimedia

 You will learn about opening a bank account in the **En contexto** video segment.

 Review vocabulary and grammar and practice language skills with the interactive CD-ROM.

W.w. Get connected to the Spanish-speaking world with the *¿Qué tal?* Online Learning Center: **www.mhhe.com/quetal**.

Profesiones y oficios° *trades*

LUEGO DE PENSARLO MUCHO LLEGUÉ A LA CONCLUSIÓN DE QUE CUANDO SEA GRANDE VOY A SER ESPECIALISTA

¿ESPECIALISTA EN QUÉ, MIGUELITO?

Profesiones

el/la abogado/a	lawyer
el/la bibliotecario/a	librarian
el/la consejero/a	counselor
el/la contador(a)	accountant
el/la enfermero/a	nurse
el hombre / la mujer de negocios	businessperson
el/la ingeniero/a	engineer
el/la maestro/a	schoolteacher
el/la médico/a	doctor
el/la periodista	journalist
el/la trabajador(a) social	social worker
el/la traductor(a)	translator

Oficios

el/la cajero/a	cashier; teller
el/la cocinero/a	cook; chef

el/la comerciante	merchant, shopkeeper
el/la criado/a	servant
el/la dependiente/a	clerk
el/la obrero/a	worker, laborer
el/la peluquero/a	hairstylist
el/la plomero/a	plumber
el soldado / la mujer soldado	soldier
el/la vendedor(a)	salesperson

Cognados

el/la analista de sistemas, el/la dentista, el/la electricista, el/la fotógrafo/a, el/la mecánico/a, el/la profesor(a), el/la programador(a), el/la secretario/a, el/la sicólogo/a, el/la siquiatra, el/la técnico/a, el/la veterinario/a

In the preceding chapters of *¿Qué tal?* you have learned to use a number of the words for professions and trades that are listed here. You will practice all of these words in the following activities. However, you will probably want to learn only those new terms that are particularly important or interesting to you. If the vocabulary needed to describe your career goal is not listed here, look it up in a dictionary or ask your instructor.

Conversación

A. Asociaciones. ¿Qué profesiones u oficios asocia Ud. con estas frases? Consulte la lista de profesiones y oficios y use las siguientes palabras también. Haga asociaciones rápidas. ¡No lo piense demasiado!

1. creativo/rutinario
2. muchos/pocos años de preparación
3. mucho/poco salario
4. mucha/poca responsabilidad
5. mucho/poco prestigio
6. flexibilidad/«de nueve a cinco»
7. mucho/poco tiempo libre
8. peligroso (*dangerous*)/seguro
9. en el pasado, sólo para hombres/mujeres
10. todavía, sólo para hombres/mujeres

actor/actriz
arquitecto/a
asistente de vuelo
barman
camarero/a
carpintero/a
chófer
consejero/a
cura/pastor(a)/ rabino/a

detective
niñero/a
pintor(a)
poeta
policía/mujer policía
político/a
presidente/a
senador(a)

B. ¿Qué preparación se necesita para ser... ? Imagine que Ud. es consejero universitario / consejera universitaria. Explíquele a un estudiante qué cursos debe tomar para prepararse para las siguientes carreras. Consulte la lista de cursos académicos del **Capítulo 1** y use la siguiente lista. Piense también en el tipo de experiencia que debe obtener.

Vocabulario útil	
las comunicaciones	el *marketing*/mercadeo
la contabilidad (*accounting*)	la organización administrativa
el derecho (*law*)	la pedagogía/enseñanza
la gerontología	la retórica (*speech*)
la ingeniería	la sociología

1. traductor(a) en la ONU (Organización de las Naciones Unidas)
2. reportero/a en la televisión, especializado/a en los deportes
3. contador(a) para un grupo de abogados
4. periodista en la redacción (*editorial staff*) de una revista de ecología
5. trabajador(a) social, especializado/a en los problemas de los ancianos
6. maestro/a de primaria, especializado/a en la educación bilingüe

NOTA CULTURAL

Los nombres de las profesiones

En el mundo de habla española hay poco acuerdo sobre las palabras que deben usarse para referirse a las mujeres que ejercen ciertas profesiones. En gran parte, eso se debe al hecho de que, en muchos de estos países, las mujeres acaban de empezar a ejercer esas profesiones; por eso el idioma todavía está cambiando para acomodarse a esa nueva realidad. En la actualidad se emplean, entre otras, las siguientes formas:

- Se usa el artículo **la** con los sustantivos que terminan en **-ista**.

  el dent**ista** → **la** dent**ista**

- En otros casos se usa una forma femenina.

  el médic**o** → **la** médic**a**
  el trabajad**or** → **la** trabajad**ora**

- Se usa la palabra **mujer** con el nombre de la profesión.

  el policía → **la mujer** policía
  el soldado → **la mujer** soldado

Escuche lo que dice la persona con quien Ud. habla para saber las formas que él o ella usa. No se trata de[a] formas correctas o incorrectas, sólo de usos y costumbres locales.

[a]No... *It's not a question of*

¿Qué representan los sombreros que lleva la mujer?

El mundo del trabajo

caerle bien/mal a alguien	to make a good/bad impression on someone
dejar	to quit
llenar	to fill out (*a form*)
renunciar (a)	to resign (from)
el/la aspirante	candidate, applicant
el currículum	resumé
la dirección de personal	personnel office, employment office
el/la director(a) de personal	personnel director
la empresa	corporation, business
el puesto	job, position
la solicitud	application (*form*)

Graduarse

Llenar solicitudes

la directora de personal

la aspirante

escribir a máquina y contestar el teléfono

renunciar al puesto

Una cuestión de dinero

el banco	bank
el cajero automático	automatic teller machine
el cheque	check (*bank*)
la cuenta / la factura	bill
la cuenta corriente	checking account
la cuenta de ahorros	savings account
el efectivo	cash
el préstamo	loan
el presupuesto	budget
el salario / el sueldo	salary
la tarjeta de crédito	credit card
ahorrar	to save (*money*)

cargar (a la cuenta de uno)	to charge (to someone's account)
depositar/sacar	to deposit/withdraw (*money*)
devolver (ue)	to return (*something*)
economizar	to economize
ganar	to earn
pagar a plazos / con cheque	to pay in installments / by check
pagar en efectivo / al contado	to pay in cash
pedir (i, i) prestado/a	to borrow
prestar	to lend

Conversación

A. **En busca de un puesto.** Imagine que Ud. solicitó un puesto recientemente. Usando los números del 1 al 14, indique en qué orden ocurrió lo
siguiente. El número 1 ya está indicado.

a. _____ Se despidió de Ud. cordialmente, di-
ciendo que lo/la iba a llamar en una
semana.

b. _____ Fue a la biblioteca para informarse sobre
la empresa: su historia, dónde tiene su-
cursales (*branches*), etcétera.

c. _____ Ud. llenó la solicitud tan pronto como la
recibió y la mandó, con el currículum, a
la empresa.

d. _____ Por fin, el secretario le dijo que Ud. se
iba a entrevistar con la directora de personal.

e. __1__ En la oficina de empleos de su universidad, Ud. leyó un anuncio para un puesto
en su especialización.

f. _____ Le dijo que le iba a mandar una solicitud
para que la llenara (*you could fill it out*) y
también le pidió que mandara (*you send*)
su currículum.

g. _____ Cuando por fin lo/la llamó la directora,
¡fue para ofrecerle el puesto!

h. _____ Mientras esperaba en la dirección de personal, Ud. estaba nerviosísimo/a.

i. _____ La directora le hizo una serie de preguntas: cuándo se iba a graduar, qué cursos
había tomado, etcétera.

j. _____ Llamó al teléfono que daba el anuncio y
habló con un secretario en la dirección de
personal.

k. _____ La mañana de la entrevista, Ud. se levantó
temprano, se vistió con cuidado y salió
temprano para la empresa para llegar
puntualmente.

l. _____ Al entrar en la oficina de la directora, Ud.
la saludó con cortesía, tratando de caerle
bien desde el principio.

m. _____ También le pidió que hablara (*you speak*)
un poco en español, ya que la empresa
tiene una sucursal en Santiago, Chile.

n. _____ En una semana lo/la llamaron para arreglar una entrevista.

B. Diálogos

Paso 1. Empareje las preguntas de la izquierda con las respuestas de la derecha.

1. _____ ¿Cómo prefiere Ud. pagar?

2. _____ ¿Hay algún problema?

3. _____ Me da su pasaporte, por favor. Necesito verlo para que pueda cobrar (*cash*) su cheque.

4. _____ ¿Quisiera (*Would you like*) usar su tarjeta de crédito?

5. _____ ¿Va a depositar este cheque en su cuenta corriente o en su cuenta de ahorros?

6. _____ ¿Adónde quiere Ud. que mandemos la factura?

a. En la cuenta de ahorros, por favor.

b. Me la manda a la oficina, por favor.

c. No, prefiero pagar al contado.

d. Sí, señorita. Ud. me cobró demasiado por el jarabe.

e. Aquí lo tiene Ud. Me lo va a devolver pronto, ¿verdad?

f. Cárguelo a mi cuenta, por favor.

Paso 2. Ahora invente un contexto posible para cada diálogo. ¿Dónde están las personas que hablan? ¿En un banco? ¿en una tienda? ¿Quiénes son? ¿Clientes? ¿cajeros? ¿dependientes?

C. Situaciones. Describa lo que pasa en los siguientes dibujos. Use las preguntas a continuación como guía.

¿Quiénes son estas personas?
¿Dónde están?
¿Qué van a comprar?
¿Cómo van a pagar?
¿Qué van a hacer después?

1.

2.

3.

4.

42 Talking about the Future • Future Verb Forms

ᵃtareas   ᵇfuturo   ᶜprayers

¿Cómo será su vida dentro de diez años? Conteste sí o no a las primeras cinco oraciones. Complete las últimas dos con información verdadera —¡o por lo menos deseable!

1. Viviré en otra ciudad / otro país.
2. Estaré casado/a.
3. Tendré uno o más hijos (nietos).
4. Seré dueño/a de mi propia casa.
5. Llevaré una vida más tranquila.
6. Trabajaré como _____ (nombre de profesión).
7. Ganaré por lo menos _____ dólares al año.

A. You have already learned to talk about the future in a number of ways. The forms of the present can be used to describe the immediate future, and the **ir** + **a** + *infinitive* construction (Grammar 10) is very common in both spoken and written Spanish. The future can also be expressed, however, with future verb forms.

hablar		comer		vivir	
hablar**é**	hablar**emos**	comer**é**	comer**emos**	vivir**é**	vivir**emos**
hablar**ás**	hablar**éis**	comer**ás**	comer**éis**	vivir**ás**	vivir**éis**
hablar**á**	hablar**án**	comer**á**	comer**án**	vivir**á**	vivir**án**

B. In English, the future is formed with the auxiliary verbs *will* or *shall: I **will/shall** speak*. In Spanish, the *future* (**el futuro**) is a simple verb form (only one word). It is formed by adding future endings to the infinitive. No auxiliary verbs are needed.

Future verb endings:

-é	-emos
-ás	-éis
-á	-án

C. The verbs on the right add the future endings to irregular stems.

decir: diré, dirás, dirá, diremos, diréis, dirán

decir:	**dir-**	
hacer:	**har-**	**-é**
poder:	**podr-**	**-ás**
poner:	**pondr-**	**-á**
querer:	**querr-**	**-emos**
saber:	**sabr-**	**-éis**
salir:	**saldr-**	**-án**
tener:	**tendr-**	
venir:	**vendr-**	

The future of **hay** (**haber**) is **habrá** (*there will be*).*

D. Remember that indicative and subjunctive present tense forms can be used to express the immediate future. Compare the following.

Llegaré a tiempo.
I'll arrive on time.

Llego a las ocho mañana. ¿Vienes a buscarme?
I'll arrive at 8:00 tomorrow. Will you pick me up?

No creo que Pepe **llegue** a tiempo.
I don't think Pepe will arrive on time.

O J O When the English *will* refers not to future time but to the willingness of someone to do something, Spanish uses the verb **querer**, not the future.

¿Quieres cerrar la puerta, por favor?
Will you please close the door?

Práctica

A. Mis compañeros de clase. ¿Cree Ud. que conoce bien a sus compañeros de clase? ¿Sabe lo que les va a pasar en el futuro? Vamos a ver.

Paso 1. Indique si las siguientes oraciones serán ciertas para Ud. algún día.

	SÍ	NO
1. Seré profesor(a) de idiomas.	☐	☐
2. Me casaré (Me divorciaré) dentro de tres años.	☐	☐
3. Me mudaré (*I will move*) a otro país.	☐	☐
4. Compraré un coche deportivo.	☐	☐
5. Tendré una familia muy grande (mucho más grande).	☐	☐
6. Asistiré a una escuela de estudios graduados (*graduate*).	☐	☐
7. Visitaré Latinoamérica.	☐	☐

---

*The future forms of the verb **haber** are used to form the *future perfect tense* (**el futuro perfecto**), which expresses what *will have* occurred at some point in the future.

Para mañana, ya **habré hablado** con Miguel.

By tomorrow, I will have spoken with Miguel.

You will find a more detailed presentation of these forms in Appendix 3, Additional Perfect Forms (Indicative and Subjunctive).

8. Estaré en bancarrota (*bankruptcy*). ☐ ☐
9. Estaré jubilado/a (*retired*). ☐ ☐
10. No tendré que trabajar porque seré rico/a. ☐ ☐

Paso 2. Ahora, para cada oración del **Paso 1**, indique el nombre de una persona de la clase para quien Ud. cree que la oración es cierta. Puede ser un compañero/una compañera de clase o su profesor(a).

Paso 3. Ahora compare sus predicciones con las respuestas de estas personas. ¿Hizo Ud. predicciones correctas?

B. **¿Qué harán?** Imagine que un grupo de amigos está hablando de cómo será su vida en cinco o seis años. Haga oraciones usando el futuro de las frases de abajo. Luego, explique a qué profesión se refiere cada oración.

1. yo
- hablar bien el español
- pasar mucho tiempo en la biblioteca
- escribir artículos sobre la literatura latinoamericana
- dar clases en español

2. tú
- trabajar en una oficina y en la corte
- ganar mucho dinero
- tener muchos clientes
- cobrar por muchas horas de trabajo

3. Felipe
- ver a muchos pacientes
- escuchar muchos problemas
- leer a Freud y a Jung constantemente
- hacerle un sicoanálisis a un paciente

4. Susana y Juanjo
- pasar mucho tiempo sentados
- usar el teclado (*keyboard*) constantemente
- inventar nuevos programas
- mandarles mensajes electrónicos a todos los amigos

C. **Mi amigo Gregorio.** Describa Ud. las siguientes cosas que hará su compañero Gregorio. Luego indique si Ud. hará lo mismo (**Yo también... Yo tampoco...**) u otra cosa.

MODELO: no / gastar / menos / mes →
Gregorio no gastará menos este mes. Yo tampoco gastaré menos. (Yo sí gastaré menos este mes. ¡Tengo que ahorrar!)

1. pagar / tarde / todo / cuentas
2. tratar / adaptarse a / presupuesto
3. volver / hacer / presupuesto / próximo mes
4. no / depositar / nada / en / cuenta de ahorros
5. quejarse / porque / no / tener / suficiente dinero
6. seguir / usando / tarjetas / crédito
7. pedirles / dinero / a / padres
8. buscar / trabajo / de tiempo parcial

Conversación

A. Ventajas y desventajas. What can you do to get extra cash or to save money? Some possibilities are shown in the following drawings. What are the advantages and disadvantages of each suggestion?

MODELO: dejar de tomar tanto café →
Si dejo de tomar tanto café, ahorraré sólo un poco de dinero. Estaré menos nervioso/a, pero creo que será más difícil despertarme por la mañana.

1. pedirles dinero a mis amigos o parientes
2. cometer un robo
3. alquilar unos cuartos de mi casa a otras personas
4. dejar de fumar (beber cerveza, tomar tanto café…)
5. buscar un trabajo de tiempo parcial
6. vender mi disco compacto (coche, televisor…)
7. comprar muchos billetes de lotería

B. El mundo en el año 2500. ¿Cómo será el mundo del futuro? Haga una lista de temas o cosas que Ud. cree que van a ser diferentes en el año 2500. Por ejemplo: el transporte, la comida, la vivienda… Piense también en temas globales: la política, los problemas que presenta la capa de ozono…

Ahora, a base de su lista, haga una serie de predicciones para el futuro.

MODELO: La gente comerá (Nosotros comeremos) comidas sintéticas.

Vocabulario útil

la colonización	el transbordador espacial
la energía nuclear/solar	la vida artificial
el espacio	
los OVNIs (Objetos Volantes	diseñar (*to design*)
No Identificados)	eliminar
el planeta	
la pobreza (*poverty*)	intergaláctico/a
el robot	interplanetario/a
el satélite	sintético/a

NOTA COMUNICATIVA

Expressing Conjecture

Estela, en el aeropuerto

Cecilia, en la carretera

¿Dónde **estará** Cecilia?	*I wonder where Cecilia is. (Where can Cecilia be?)*
¿Qué le **pasará**?	*I wonder what's up with her (what can be wrong)?*
Estará en un lío de tráfico.	*She's probably (must be) in a traffic jam. (I bet she's in a traffic jam.)*

The future can also be used in Spanish to express probability or conjecture about what is happening now. This use of the future is called the *future of probability* (**el futuro de probabilidad**). Note in the preceding examples that the English cues for expressing probability (*probably, I bet, must be, I wonder . . . , Where can . . .*, and so on) are not directly expressed in Spanish. Their sense is conveyed in Spanish by the use of the future form of the verb.

C. Predicciones. ¿Quiénes serán las siguientes personas? ¿Qué estarán haciendo? ¿Dónde estarán? Invente todos los detalles que pueda sobre los siguientes dibujos.

Palabras útiles: el botones (*bellhop*), Cristóbal Colón (*Christopher Columbus*), la propina (*tip*), redondo/a (*round*)

1.

2.

3.

4.

Enfoque *cultural*

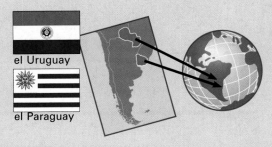

el Uruguay

el Paraguay

el Uruguay y el Paraguay

Datos esenciales

el Uruguay

Nombre oficial: República Oriental del Uruguay

Capital: Montevideo

Población: 3.000.000 de habitantes

Moneda: el peso uruguayo

Idioma oficial: el español

el Paraguay

Nombre oficial: República del Paraguay

Capital: Asunción

Población: 5.000.000 de habitantes

Moneda: el guaraní

Idiomas oficiales: el español y el guaraní

¡Fíjese!

- Aproximadamente el 45 por ciento de la población uruguaya vive en Montevideo.

- Para los uruguayos, la educación primaria, secundaria y universitaria es gratuita.[a] La tasa de alfabetización[b] es de un 96 por ciento, una de las más altas de Latinoamérica.

- El Paraguay es uno de los dos países latinoamericanos sin costa marítima (el otro es Bolivia). Por eso, sus numerosos ríos navegables tienen gran importancia económica para el país.

- La ciudad de Asunción, en el Paraguay, la primera ciudad permanente en la región del Río de la Plata, fue fundada por los españoles en 1537.

- La represa[c] hidroeléctrica de Itaipú, terminada en 1982, es la más grande y potente del mundo. Fue construida en la frontera entre el Paraguay y la Argentina y el Brasil con la ayuda financiera del Brasil, país que recibe la energía eléctrica de la represa.

[a]*free*   [b]*tasa… rate of literacy*   [c]*dam*

Conozca… el guaraní

El Paraguay es el único país latinoamericano que tiene dos lenguas oficiales, una de ellas indígena. El 90 por ciento de la población paraguaya habla guaraní (sólo el 75 por ciento habla español). Hoy hay literatura, música y hasta páginas Web en guaraní.

Guaraní significa **guerrero**[a] en esa lengua, nombre que recuerda las disputas de las diversas etnias guaraníes contra los poderosos incas.

[a]*warrior*

Asunción, el Paraguay

Capítulo 16 of the video to accompany *¿Qué tal?* contains cultural footage about Uruguay and Paraguay.

Visit the *¿Qué tal?* website at www.mhhe.com/quetal.

43 **Expressing Future or Pending Actions** • Subjunctive and Indicative after Conjunctions of Time

Antes de la entrevista

SRA. LÓPEZ: ¿Estás listo para la entrevista?

TOMÁS: Sí. ¿Estoy elegante?

SRA. LÓPEZ: Muy elegante. Recuerda, *cuando llegues a la oficina*, no te olvides de darle la mano a la directora de personal.

TOMÁS: Claro, mamá. No te preocupes.

SRA. LÓPEZ: Y *tan pronto como te sientes*, entrégale el currículum.

TOMÁS: Mamá, se lo daré *después de que ella me lo pida*. Cálmate. Yo soy la persona que va a entrevistarse.

SRA. LÓPEZ: Está bien. Pero llámame *tan pronto como termines* la entrevista.

Comprensión: ¿Cierto o falso?

1. La Sra. López tiene una entrevista hoy.
2. La Sra. López le da consejos a su hijo.
3. Es obvio que Tomás está nervioso.
4. A Tomás le caen bien los consejos de su madre.

A. The subjunctive is often used in Spanish in adverbial clauses, which function like adverbs, telling when the action of the main verb takes place. Such adverbial clauses are introduced by conjunctions (see **Capítulo 15**).

Lo veré **mañana**. (adverb)
I'll see him tomorrow.

Lo veré **cuando venga mañana**. (adverbial clause)
I'll see him when he comes tomorrow.

B. Future events are often expressed in Spanish in two-clause sentences that include conjunctions of time such as those on the right.

antes (de) que	before
cuando	when
después (de) que	after
en cuanto	as soon as
hasta que	until
tan pronto como	as soon as

Before the interview SRA. LÓPEZ: Are you ready for the interview? TOMÁS: Yes. Do I look elegant? SRA. LÓPEZ: Very elegant. Remember, when you get to the office, don't forget to shake hands with the personnel director. TOMÁS: Of course, Mom. Don't worry. SRA. LÓPEZ: And as soon as you sit down, give her the resumé. TOMÁS: Mom, I'll give it to her after she asks for it. Calm down. I'm the one who's going to be interviewed. SRA. LÓPEZ: OK. But call me as soon as you finish the interview.

C. In a subordinate clause after these conjunctions of time, the subjunctive is used to express a future action or state of being—that is, one that is still pending or has not yet occurred from the point of view of the main verb. This use of the subjunctive is very frequent in conversation in phrases such as the examples on the right.

The events in the subordinate clause are imagined—not real-world—events. They haven't happened yet.

Cuando sea grande/mayor…
When I'm older . . .

Cuando tenga tiempo…
When I have the time . . .

Cuando me gradúe…
When I graduate . . .

D. When the present subjunctive is used in this way to express pending actions, the main-clause verb is in the present indicative or future.

PENDING ACTION (SUBJUNCTIVE):

Pagaré las cuentas **en cuanto reciba** mi cheque.
I'll pay the bills as soon as I get my check.

Debo depositar el dinero **tan pronto como** lo **reciba**.
I should deposit money as soon as I get it.

E. However, the indicative (not the present subjunctive) is used after conjunctions of time to describe a habitual action or a completed action in the past. Compare the following.

HABITUAL ACTIONS (INDICATIVE):

Siempre **pago** las cuentas **en cuanto recibo** mi cheque.
I always pay bills as soon as I get my check.

Deposito el dinero **tan pronto como** lo **recibo**.
I deposit money as soon as I receive it.

COMPLETED PAST ACTION (INDICATIVE):

El mes pasado **pagué** las cuentas **en cuanto recibí** mi cheque.
Last month I paid my bills as soon as I got my check.

Deposité el dinero **tan pronto como** lo **recibí**.
I deposited the money as soon as I got it.

OJO The subjunctive is always used with **antes (de) que**. (See **Capítulo 15**.)

Práctica

A. Decisiones económicas. Lea las siguientes oraciones sobre Rigoberto y decida si se trata de una acción habitual o de una acción que no ha pasado todavía. Luego indique la frase que mejor complete la oración.

1. Rigoberto se va a comprar una computadora en cuanto…
   a. el banco le dé el préstamo   **b.** el banco le da el préstamo
2. Siempre usa su tarjeta de crédito cuando…
   a. no tenga efectivo   **b.** no tiene efectivo
3. Cada mes saca el saldo de su cuenta corriente después de que…
   a. reciba el estado de cuentas (*statement*)
   b. recibe el estado de cuentas
4. Piensa abrir una cuenta de ahorros tan pronto como…
   a. consiga un trabajo   **b.** consigue un trabajo
5. No puede pagar sus cuentas este mes hasta que…
   a. su hermano le devuelva el dinero que le prestó
   b. su hermano le devuelve el dinero que le prestó

B. Hablando de dinero: Planes para el futuro. Complete las siguientes oraciones con el presente del subjuntivo de los verbos indicados.

1. Voy a ahorrar más en cuanto… (darme [ellos] un aumento de sueldo [*raise*]; dejar [yo] de gastar tanto)
2. Pagaré todas mis cuentas tan pronto como… (tener el dinero para hacerlo; ser absolutamente necesario)
3. El semestre/trimestre que viene, pagaré la matrícula después de que… (cobrar mi cheque en el banco; mandarme [¿quién?] un cheque)
4. No podré pagar el alquiler hasta que… (sacar dinero de mi cuenta de ahorros; depositar el dinero en mi cuenta corriente)
5. No voy a jubilarme (*retire*) hasta que mis hijos… (terminar sus estudios universitarios; casarse)

C. Algunos momentos en la vida. Las siguientes oraciones describen algunos aspectos de la vida de Mariana en el pasado, en el presente y en el futuro. Lea cada grupo de oraciones para tener una idea general del contexto. Luego dé la forma apropiada de los infinitivos.

1. Hace cuatro años, cuando Mariana (graduarse) en la escuela secundaria, sus padres (darle) un reloj. El año que viene, cuando (graduarse) en la universidad, (darle) un coche.
2. Cuando (ser) niña, Mariana (querer) ser enfermera. Luego, cuando (tener) 18 años, (decidir) que quería estudiar computación. Cuando (terminar) su carrera este año, yo creo que (poder) encontrar un buen trabajo como programadora.
3. Generalmente Mariana no (escribir) cheques hasta que (tener) los fondos en su cuenta corriente. Este mes tiene muchos gastos, pero no (ir) a pagar ninguna cuenta hasta que le (llegar) el cheque de su trabajo de tiempo parcial.

En los Estados Unidos y el Canadá...

El creciente mercado hispano

¿Qué tienen en común Ford, Toyota, Sprint, Dockers, United Health y Toys "Я" Us? Pues que, como muchas compañías norteamericanas, tienen activas **campañas publicitarias** para atraer al **mercado hispano nacional**. Con más de 35 millones de hispanos, según el censo estadounidense del año 2000, los Estados Unidos ocupan **el cuarto puesto**[a] entre las naciones que tienen una población hispano-hablante (se calcula que podría[b] ser **la segunda** o **tercera nación** en los próximos quince años, por delante de España). La población hispana de los Estados Unidos se traduce en[c] un mercado de más de 600.000 millones de dólares.

CNN en español, HBO Latino y People en español se dirigen a[d] la variada comunidad hispana de los Estados Unidos. Muchos programas y publicaciones se originan en Florida, entre ellos Latin Trade, una **revista mensual**[e] de **negocios** y **economía** referente a Norteamérica en relación con todos los países latinos. El ámbito de lectores[f] de Latin Trade incluye a latinos de todo el mundo, un grupo de más de 400 millones de personas.

Desgraciadamente,[g] la importancia numérica de los hispano-americanos, un 12 por ciento de la población de los Estados Unidos, no se ve reflejada[h] en el mundo de **la comunicación**, de **la política** ni de los **negocios**. Es este el gran reto[i] para los hispanos de este país.

[a]position [b]it could [c]se... translates into [d]se... target [e]monthly [f]ámbito... readership [g]Unfortunately [h]no... is not reflected [i]challenge

Conversación

A. **Descripciones.** Describa Ud. los dibujos, completando las oraciones e inventando un contexto para las escenas. Luego describa su propia vida.

1. Pablo va a estudiar hasta que
    _____.

    Esta noche yo voy a estudiar hasta que _____.
    Siempre estudio hasta que _____.
    Anoche estudié hasta que _____.

1.

2. Los Sres. Castro van a cenar tan pronto como _____.

Esta noche voy a cenar tan pronto como _____.
Siempre ceno tan pronto como _____.
Anoche cené tan pronto como _____.

2.

3. Lupe va a viajar al extranjero en cuanto _____.

En cuanto gane la lotería, yo voy a _____.
En cuanto tengo el dinero, siempre _____.
De niño/a, _____ en cuanto tenía el dinero.

3.

B. **Reacciones.** ¿Cómo reaccionará o qué hará cuando ocurran los siguientes acontecimientos? Complete las oraciones con el futuro.

1. Cuando colonicemos otro planeta, _____.
2. Cuando descubran una cura para el cáncer, _____.
3. Cuando haya una mujer presidenta, _____.
4. Cuando me jubile, _____.
5. Cuando yo sea anciano/a, _____.
6. Cuando me gradúe, _____.

UN POCO DE TODO

¿Cómo se ganan la vida (*earn a living*) **los estudiantes?** Complete the following paragraphs with the correct form of the words in parentheses, as suggested by the context. When two possibilities are given in parentheses, select the correct word. Use an adverb derived from the adjectives in italics.

La preocupación por el dinero es (algo/alguien[1]) compartido[a] por los estudiantes en todo el mundo. En (el/la[2]) mayor parte de los países de habla española, (el/la[3]) sistema universitario es gratuito.[b] Sin embargo, hay (de/que[4]) tener dinero para los (gastar/gastos[5]) personales y también para (los/las[6]) cines y otras diversiones.

Aquí, algunos estudiantes hispánicos contestan la pregunta: ¿Cómo (te/se[7]) ganaba Ud. la vida cuando era estudiante?

Una joven de México: A los trece años, (*yo:* empezar[8]) a trabajar en una oficina. Así (*yo:* poder[9]) pagar la colegiatura[c] de mis estudios. (*Yo:* Trabajar[10]) de día y (estudiar[11]) de noche.

Un joven uruguayo: Cuando (*yo:* ser/estar[12]) estudiante, me (ganar[13]) la vida como fotógrafo. (*Yo:* Sacar[14]) fotos de bodas, bautismos, fiestas de cumpleaños. (*Yo:* Trabajar[15]) en cualquier ocasión y en cualquier sitio.

Una mujer española: (*Yo:* Ayudar[16]) a enseñar a párvulos.[d]

Algunos estudiantes (ofrecer[17]) los siguientes comentarios adicionales.

Una joven chilena: Los padres (*normal*[18]) mantienen a sus hijos (*económico*[19]). Pero muchos chicos (trabajar[20]) de todas maneras. Las chicas (cuidar[21]) a niños o (ayudar[22]) en casa y los chicos (trabajar[23]) en talleres. Si los padres tienen dinero, es raro que los hijos (trabajar[24]) hasta que no (terminar[25]) su carrera.[e]

Un joven argentino: En la Argentina, la enseñanza universitaria (ser/estar[26]) gratuita. De todos modos, los estudiantes siempre (necesitar[27]) tener más de un trabajo y los padres los ayudan con (que / lo que[28]) pueden. Muchos estudiantes no (irse[29]) a otras ciudades a (estudiar[30]). (*Ellos:* Vivir[31]) con (su[32]) padres y estudian en (el/la[33]) universidad más cercana.

[a]*shared*   [b]*free*   [c]*fees*   [d]*tots*   [e]*studies*

Comprensión: ¿Cierto o falso?

Corrija las oraciones falsas.

1. El sistema universitario es gratuito en muchos países hispánicos.
2. Los estudiantes hispánicos nunca tienen que trabajar.
3. Generalmente los padres mantienen a sus hijos mientras estos son estudiantes.

VIDEOTECA: En contexto

FUNCTION

Opening a bank account

In this video segment, Juan Carlos opens an account at the bank. As you watch, pay attention to the vocabulary Juan Carlos and the bank employee use for opening an account. Do you have a bank account? Was your experience similar when you went to open it?

EL PERÚ

Cultura en contexto
Los cajeros automáticos

Los cajeros automáticos, disponibles[a] en casi todas los pueblos y las ciudades de Latinoamérica, han facilitado[b] el turismo al ofrecer una manera fácil de conseguir la moneda nacional. Por ejemplo, un turista en el Perú puede sacar dinero de su cuenta personal y recibirlo del cajero automático en soles, la moneda nacional del Perú. De esta manera, ya no es necesario ir a una casa de cambio[c] o a un banco.

[a]*available*   [b]*han... have made easier*
[c]*casa... money exchange office*

A. Lluvia de ideas

- ¿Es Ud. bueno/a para manejar el dinero? ¿Por qué? ¿Sabe Ud. ahorrar o se le va el dinero como agua en las manos?
- ¿Cuántas cuentas tiene Ud.? ¿De qué tipo son? ¿Cuándo las abrió? ¿Por qué razón eligió ese banco?

B. Dictado

A continuación aparece un fragmento del diálogo entre Juan Carlos y el empleado del banco. Complete el diálogo con las palabras o frases que faltan.

EMPLEADO: ¿Y qué tipo de _____[1] quiere Ud. abrir?
JUAN CARLOS: Necesito una cuenta _____[2] y una cuenta de _____.[3] ¿Ganan intereses sus cuentas corrientes?
EMPLEADO: Depende del tipo de cuenta corriente. Si Ud. elige esta cuenta, _____[4] intereses mensualmente, con _____[5] de que mantenga un mínimo de cien soles en la cuenta.
JUAN CARLOS: [...] ¿Tiene este _____[6] cajeros automáticos?
EMPLEADO: Sí, claro. Tenemos un _____[7] automático afuera, y también puede utilizar, sin _____,[8] los cajeros _____[9] de las otras _____[10] del banco.

C. Un diálogo original

Opción 1. Con un compañero / una compañera, dramatice el diálogo entre Juan Carlos y el empleado del banco.

Opción 2. También dramatice la siguiente situación.

E1: Ud. habla con un amigo / una amiga que entiende mucho de finanzas personales. Ud. necesita algún tipo de cuenta, pero no sabe exactamente cuál.

E2: Ud. actúa de consejero de finanzas. Si su amigo/a no le da suficiente información, hágale preguntas para poder darle consejos mejores.

PASO FINAL

A CONVERSAR

Un futuro imaginado

Paso 1. En una hoja de papel aparte, prepare un cuadro como el siguiente. Apunte brevemente sus respuestas en los espacios en blanco. Si el nombre de la profesión que a Ud. le interesa no está en este capítulo, búsquelo en un diccionario. Use su imaginación: ¡el futuro está lleno de posibilidades!

MODELO:

	Mi trabajo	Mi vivienda / El lugar	Mis vacaciones
En cinco años...	cocinera	apartamento/Nueva York	ninguna
En diez años...	dueña de un restaurante elegante	casa/California	una isla en el Caribe
En quince años...			

Paso 2. Con un compañero / una compañera, hable de su futuro. Deben hacer las predicciones indicadas (hasta quince años), pero pueden hablar de un futuro aun más distante si quieren. Utilicen verbos en el futuro en sus preguntas y respuestas.

> MODELO: E1: ¿Qué trabajo tendrás en cinco años?
> E2: Seré cocinera, pero sólo de tiempo parcial. Trabajaré por la noche mientras estudio para la maestría (*Master's*) en negocios. Quiero ser dueña de un restaurante. Será bueno tener experiencia en restaurantes, pero también será importante saber mucho de los negocios. ¿Y tú?
> E1: Me graduaré en dos años, así que en cinco años ya seré trabajador social. Trabajaré con jóvenes delincuentes en Los Ángeles. Muchos de mis familiares son de esa área. ¿Y tú? ¿Dónde vivirás?
> E2: Viviré en un apartamento en Nueva York, cerca de la universidad…

Paso 3. Entre todos, hablen de los planes de sus compañeros. Pueden comparar los planes de sus compañeros con sus propios planes. Usen verbos en el futuro para describir los planes. Deben marcar la información en la pizarra en un cuadro como el del **Paso 1**.

> MODELO: E1: En cinco años, Marsha será cocinera de tiempo parcial. Vivirá en un apartamento en Nueva York, cerca de la universidad donde estudiará para su maestría en negocios. Quiere ser dueña de un restaurante y necesitará la experiencia en restaurantes y la preparación en negocios.

Paso 4. Después de apuntar la información en la pizarra, comparen los planes y las carreras. Traten de hacer algunas generalizaciones sobre la clase, pero hablen también de puntos específicos. ¿Quiénes tendrán las carreras más interesantes? ¿más exigentes (*demanding*)? ¿Quiénes tendrán que pasar más tiempo estudiando y preparándose para su profesión? ¿En qué partes del país (del mundo) vivirá la mayoría de Uds.? ¿Quiénes tendrán las vacaciones más divertidas? ¿originales? Deben expresar sus opiniones y defenderlas si no están de acuerdo.

> MODELO: E1: Marsha tendrá una carrera exigente porque en diez años será dueña de un restaurante. Los restaurantes representan mucho trabajo y Marsha no tendrá mucho tiempo para vacaciones.
> E2: Bill tendrá la carrera más exigente porque será trabajador social y trabajará con jóvenes delincuentes…

En resumen

GRAMÁTICA

To review the grammar points presented in this chapter, refer to the indicated grammar presentations. You'll find further practice of these structures in the Workbook/Laboratory Manual, on the CD-ROM, and on the website.

42. Future Verb Forms

You should know how to form and when to use the future tense, including all irregular forms.

43. Subjunctive and Indicative after Conjunctions of Time

Do you know how to express actions that will take place only after something else takes place? What are the conjunctions that you can use for this?

VOCABULARIO

Los verbos

jubilarse	to retire
mudarse	to move (*residence*)

Profesiones y oficios

el/la abogado/a	lawyer
el/la cajero/a	cashier; teller
el/la cocinero/a	cook; chef
el/la comerciante	merchant, shopkeeper
el/la contador(a)	accountant
el/la criado/a	servant
el hombre / la mujer de negocios	businessperson
el/la ingeniero/a	engineer
el/la maestro/a	schoolteacher
el/la obrero/a	worker, laborer
el/la peluquero/a	hairstylist
el/la periodista	journalist
el/la plomero/a	plumber
el soldado / la mujer soldado	soldier
el/la trabajador(a) social	social worker
el/la traductor(a)	translator
el/la vendedor(a)	salesperson

Cognados: el/la analista de sistemas, el/la electricista, el/la fotógrafo/a, el/la programador(a), el/la sicólogo/a, el/la siquiatra, el/la técnico/a, el/la veterinario/a

Repaso: el/la bibliotecario/a, el/la consejero/a, el/la dentista, el/la dependiente/a, el/la enfermero/a, el/la mecánico/a, el/la médico/a, el/la profesor(a), el/la secretario/a

En busca de un puesto

el/la aspirante	candidate; applicant
el currículum	resumé
la dirección de personal	personnel office, employment office
el/la director(a) de personal	personnel director
la empresa	corporation; business
el/la entrevistador(a)	interviewer
la solicitud	application (*form*)
la sucursal	branch (*office*)

Repaso: el teléfono

caerle bien/mal a alguien	to make a good/bad impression on someone
dejar	to quit
entrevistar	to interview
escribir a máquina	to type
graduarse (en)	to graduate (from)

| llenar | to fill out (*a form*) |
| renunciar (a) | to resign (from) |

Repaso: contestar

Una cuestión de dinero

el aumento de sueldo	raise
el banco	bank
el cajero automático	automatic teller machine
el cheque	check
la cuenta corriente	checking account
la cuenta de ahorros	savings account
el efectivo	cash
la factura	bill
el préstamo	loan
el presupuesto	budget
el salario	salary

Repaso: la cuenta, el sueldo, la tarjeta de crédito

ahorrar	to save (*money*)
cargar	to charge (*to an account*)
cobrar	to cash (*a check*); to charge (*someone for an item or service*)

depositar	to deposit
devolver (ue)	to return (*something*)
economizar	to economize
pedir (i, i) prestado/a	to borrow
sacar	to withdraw, take out
sacar el saldo	to balance a checkbook

Repaso: ganar, pagar, prestar

a plazos	in installments
al contado / en efectivo	in cash
con cheque	by check

Conjunciones

después (de) que	after
en cuanto	as soon as
hasta que	until
tan pronto como	as soon as

Repaso: antes (de) que, cuando

Palabras adicionales

| al principio de | at the beginning of |
| en vez de | instead of |

CAPÍTULO
17

En la actualidad

Antes de las elecciones presidenciales hay mucha propaganda política, como esta en Santo Domingo, la capital de la República Dominicana.

VOCABULARIO

- The news
- Government and civic responsibility

GRAMÁTICA

44 Past Subjunctive

CULTURA

- **Enfoque cultural:** la República Dominicana
- **Nota cultural:** La mayoría de edad en los países hispanos
- **En los Estados Unidos y el Canadá:** Tres hispanos del mundo de la televisión
- **Cultura en contexto:** El periódico

Multimedia

 You will learn about purchasing a newspaper in the **En contexto** video segment.

 Review vocabulary and grammar and practice language skills with the interactive CD-ROM.

WW. Get connected to the Spanish-speaking world with the *¿Qué tal?* Online Learning Center: **www.mhhe.com/quetal**.

Las noticias

el acontecimiento	event
el medio de comunicación	means of communication
la prensa	press; news media
el/la reportero/a	reporter
el/la testigo	witness
el choque	collision
el desastre	disaster
la esperanza	hope
la paz	peace
comunicarse (con)	to communicate (with)
enterarse (de)	to find out, learn (about)
informar	to inform
ofrecer	to offer

Y ahora, el canal 45 les ofrece a Uds. el NOTICIERO 45 con los últimos eventos del mundo...

Nuestro reportero en el Oriente Medio nos informa sobre la guerra: Bombas en el desierto

Huelga de obreros en España

Otro asesinato en la ciudad. Dos testigos cuentan lo que vieron.

Desastre en Centroamérica: erupción de un volcán

Conversación

A. **¿Cómo se entera Ud.?** El público utiliza diferentes medios para enterarse de los acontecimientos locales, nacionales e internacionales. ¿Cómo se entera Ud. de las noticias? Indique con qué frecuencia utiliza los medios en la página 385. Luego, compare sus respuestas con las de sus compañeros. ¿Cuál es el medio preferido?

	TODOS LOS DÍAS	DE 3 A 5 VECES POR SEMANA	CASI NUNCA
1. Leo un periódico local.	☐	☐	☐
2. Leo un periódico nacional.	☐	☐	☐
3. Leo una revista.	☐	☐	☐
4. Leo las noticias en el Internet.	☐	☐	☐
5. Miro el telediario (*newscast*) local.	☐	☐	☐
6. Miro el telediario nacional.	☐	☐	☐
7. Miro CNN.	☐	☐	☐
8. Escucho la radio.	☐	☐	☐

B. Definiciones. ¿Qué palabra se asocia con cada definición?

1. _____ un programa que nos informa de lo que pasa en nuestro mundo
2. _____ la persona que está presente durante un acontecimiento y lo ve todo
3. _____ un medio importantísimo de comunicación
4. _____ la persona que nos informa de las novedades
5. _____ la persona que gobierna un país de una forma absoluta y que no apoya (*supports*) los derechos civiles
6. _____ la persona que emplea la violencia para cambiar el mundo
7. _____ cuando los obreros se niegan a (*refuse*) trabajar
8. _____ la frecuencia en que se transmiten y se reciben los programas de televisión
9. _____ la confrontación armada entre dos o más países

a. el noticiero
b. la guerra
c. el/la terrorista
d. el/la dictador(a) (*dictator*)
e. el canal
f. el/la testigo
g. el/la reportero/a
h. la huelga
i. la prensa

El gobierno y la responsabilidad cívica

[a]un… *not at all*
[b]¡Justo… *That's all I'd need!*

el/la ciudadano/a	citizen	**la ley**	law
el deber	responsibility, obligation	**la política**	politics
los/las demás	others, other people	**el/la político/a**	politician
el derecho	right	**el rey / la reina**	king/queen
la (des)igualdad	(in)equality	**el servicio militar**	military service
la dictadura	dictatorship		
la discriminación	discrimination	**durar**	to last
el ejército	army	**obedecer**	to obey
		votar	to vote

NOTA CULTURAL

La mayoría de edad en los países hispanos

En el mundo hispano los jóvenes se consideran legalmente adultos, es decir, alcanzan[a] **la mayoría de edad**, a los 18 años. Al cumplir los 18 años, los jóvenes hispanos pueden participar en la política y pueden votar. En varios países los hombres de 18 años también tienen la responsabilidad de inscribirse[b] en **el servicio militar**. En Colombia, los jóvenes pueden inscribirse en el servicio militar a los 16 años. La selección de los conscriptos[c] generalmente se hace mediante una lotería. Recientemente, las mujeres mexicanas y argentinas también pueden inscribirse

en el servicio militar, un hecho sin precedentes en Latinoamérica.

A los 18 años, los jóvenes hispanos pueden obtener su **licencia de manejar**. Sin embargo, muchos jóvenes hispanos no esperan hasta los 18 años. A los 16 años solicitan un **permiso especial** para menores de edad para operar un vehículo.

Otro aspecto importante al llegar a la mayoría de edad es el consumo de alcohol. **La edad límite** para tomar bebidas alcohólicas varía entre los 18 y 21 años. En Ecuador, por ejemplo, la edad límite es de 21 años. En algunos países hay menos restricciones sociales sobre el alcohol.

[a]*they reach* [b]de... *of registering* [c]*draftees*

Conversación

A. Asociaciones. ¿Qué cosas, personas o ideas asocia Ud. con las siguientes palabras?

1. el deber
2. el ejército
3. la política
4. la ley
5. la monarquía
6. la dictadura

B. ¡Peligro! (*Jeopardy!*) ¿Cuánto sabe Ud. de la historia y la política? Conteste con la información necesaria y en forma de pregunta.

1. Fue un dictador argentino que tenía una esposa famosa.
2. Se llama Elizabeth y vive en Buckingham Palace.
3. Es una película de Orson Welles, y su protagonista se llama Kane.
4. Fue un presidente estadounidense que se opuso a (*opposed*) la esclavitud de los negros.
5. En algunos países, es un deber de los hombres de cierta edad. Generalmente, tienen que entrar en el ejército por dos años.
6. Es la forma de gobierno que existe en España.
7. Existe cuando muchas personas no tienen los mismos derechos que los demás.
8. Es un deber de los ciudadanos en una democracia.

¿Recuerda Ud.?

In Grammar Section 44, you will learn about and begin to use the forms of the past subjunctive. As you learn this new tense, you will be continually using the past tense forms you have already learned along with the new material, so this section presents many opportunities for review. The following brief exercises will help you get started.

A. To learn the forms of the past subjunctive, you will need to know the forms of the preterite well, especially the third person plural. Regular **-ar** verbs end in **-aron** and regular **-er/-ir** verbs in **-ieron** in the third person plural of the preterite. Stem-changing **-ir** verbs show the second change in the third person: **servir (i, i)** → **sirvieron; dormir (ue, u)** → **durmieron**. Verbs with a stem ending in a vowel change the **i** to **y: leyeron, cayeron, construyeron**. Many common verbs have irregular stems in the preterite: **quisieron, hicieron, dijeron**, and so on. Four common verbs are totally irregular in this tense: **ser/ir** → **fueron, dar** → **dieron, ver** → **vieron**.

Give the third person plural of the preterite for these infinitives.

1.	hablar	11.	destruir
2.	comer	12.	mantener
3.	vivir	13.	traer
4.	jugar	14.	dar
5.	perder	15.	saber
6.	dormir	16.	vestirse
7.	reír	17.	decir
8.	leer	18.	creer
9.	estar	19.	ir
10.	tener	20.	poder

B. The forms of the imperfect are relatively regular. Only three verbs have irregular imperfect forms: **ir, ser,** and **ver**. Give their first person singular and plural forms.

44 ¡No queríamos que fuera así! • Past Subjunctive

¡Qué pena que no nos lleváramos bien!

MARÍA: ¿No recuerdas? ¡Qué mala memoria!

ELISA: Pero, mamá, ¿tú permitías que yo *hablara* así? ¡Qué falta de respeto hacia ti!

MARÍA: Eras muy cabezuda. No había nadie que *pudiera* contigo. ¡Cómo discutíamos! Tú creías que siempre tenías razón. Era imposible que *te equivocaras*. Tampoco querías que te *dijeran* lo que debías hacer.

ELISA: Bueno, por lo menos ahora no soy así. Digo, no tanto…

MARÍA: Sí, pero de todos modos, es necesario que una buena periodista sea un poco terca.

ELISA: Estoy de acuerdo. Es probable que, sin esa cualidad mía, yo no hubiera obtenido ese puesto.

Hace diez años…

1. ¿era difícil que Ud. hablara con sus padres sobre algún tema? ¿Cuál?
2. ¿con quién era imposible que Ud. se pusiera de acuerdo?
3. ¿con quién era imposible que Ud. se comunicara?
4. ¿contra qué orden de sus padres era común que Ud. protestara?

Cuando Ud. era niño/a…

5. ¿era probable que discutiera con alguien en la escuela primaria o en el barrio? ¿Con quién?
6. ¿dónde le prohibían sus padres que jugara?
7. ¿qué era obligatorio que comiera o bebiera?
8. ¿de qué temía que sus padres se enteraran?

Although Spanish has two simple indicative past tenses (preterite and imperfect), it has only one simple subjunctive past tense, the *past subjunctive* (**el imperfecto del subjuntivo**). Generally speaking, this tense is used in the same situations as the present subjunctive but, of course, when talking about past events. The exact English equivalent depends on the context in which it is used.

It's a shame we didn't get along! MARÍA: You don't remember? What a bad memory! ELISA: But Mom, did you allow me to speak in that way? What a lack of respect towards you! MARÍA: You were very stubborn. No one could change your mind. How we used to argue! You thought you were always right. It was impossible that you could ever make a mistake. Nor did you want anyone to tell you what to do. ELISA: Well, at least I'm not like that now. I mean, not as much… MARÍA: Yes, but, in any case, it's necessary for a good journalist to be a little bit stubborn. ELISA: I agree. It's probable that, without that quality of mine, I wouldn't have gotten that job.

FORMS OF THE PAST SUBJUNCTIVE

Past Subjunctive of Regular Verbs*					
hablar:	**hablarǿǿ**	**comer:**	**comierǿǿ**	**vivir:**	**vivierǿǿ**
hablara	habl**áramos**	comiera	comi**éramos**	viviera	vivi**éramos**
hablar**as**	hablar**ais**	comier**as**	comier**ais**	vivier**as**	vivier**ais**
hablara	hablar**an**	comiera	comier**an**	viviera	vivier**an**

A. The past subjunctive endings **-a, -as, -a, -amos, -ais, -an** are identical for **-ar, -er**, and **-ir** verbs. These endings are added to the third person plural of the preterite indicative, minus its **-on** ending. For this reason, the forms of the past subjunctive reflect the irregularities of the preterite.

PAST SUBJUNCTIVE ENDINGS

-ar → -ara
-er, -ir → -iera

B. Stem-changing verbs

-Ar and **-er** verbs: no change

-Ir verbs: all persons of the past subjunctive reflect the vowel change in the third person plural of the preterite.

empezar (ie): empezarǿǿ → **empezara, empezaras,...**
volver (ue): volvierǿǿ → **volviera, volvieras,...**
dormir (ue, u): durmierǿǿ → **durmiera, durmieras,...**
pedir (i, i): pidierǿǿ → **pidiera, pidieras,...**

C. Spelling changes

All persons of the past subjunctive reflect the change from **i** to **y** between two vowels.

i → y (caer, construir, creer, destruir, leer, oír)

creer: creyerǿǿ → **creyera, creyeras, creyera, creyéramos, creyerais, creyeran**

D. Verbs with irregular preterites

dar: dierǿǿ → **diera, dieras, diera, diéramos, dierais, dieran**

decir:	dijerǿǿ → **dijera**	poner:	pusierǿǿ → **pusiera**
estar:	estuvierǿǿ → **estuviera**	querer.	quisierǿǿ → **quisiera**
haber:	hubierǿǿ → **hubiera**	saber:	supierǿǿ → **supiera**
hacer:	hicierǿǿ → **hiciera**	ser:	fuerǿǿ → **fuera**
ir:	fuerǿǿ → **fuera**	tener:	tuvierǿǿ → **tuviera**
poder:	pudierǿǿ → **pudiera**	venir:	vinierǿǿ → **viniera**

---

*An alternative form of the past subjunctive ends in **-se: hablase, hablases, hablase, hablásemos, hablaseis, hablasen**. This form will not be practiced in *¿Qué tal?*

USES OF THE PAST SUBJUNCTIVE

A. The past subjunctive usually has the same applications as the present subjunctive, but it is used for past events. Compare these pairs of sentences.

Quiero que **jueguen** esta tarde.
I want them to play this afternoon.

Quería que **jugaran** por la tarde.
I wanted them to play in the afternoon.

Siente que no **estén** allí esta noche.
He's sorry (that) they aren't there tonight.

Sintió que no **estuvieran** allí anoche.
He was sorry (that) they weren't there last night.

Dudamos que se **equivoquen**.
We doubt that they will make a mistake.

Dudábamos que se **equivocaran**.
We doubted that they would make a mistake.

B. Remember that the subjunctive is used after
(1) expressions of *influence, emotion,* and *doubt;*
(2) *nonexistent* and *indefinite antecedents;* and
(3) *conjunctions* of *contingency and purpose,* as well as those of *time.*

(1) ¿**Era necesario** que **regatearas**?
Was it necessary for you to bargain?

(1) **Sentí** que no **tuvieran** tiempo para ver Granada.
I was sorry that they didn't have time to see Granada.

(2) **No había nadie** que **pudiera** resolverlo.
There wasn't anyone who could (might have been able to) solve it.

(3) Los padres **trabajaron para que** sus hijos **asistieran** a la universidad.
The parents worked so that their children could (might) go to the university.

(3) Anoche, **íbamos** a salir **en cuanto llegara** Felipe.
Last night, we were going to leave as soon as Felipe arrived.

C. The past subjunctive of the verb **querer** is often used to make a request sound more polite.

Quisiéramos hablar con Ud. en seguida.
We would like to speak with you immediately.

Quisiera un café, por favor.
I would like a cup of coffee, please.

Práctica

A. Si pudiera regresar... ¿Le gusta la idea de volver a la escuela secundaria? ¿O prefiere la vida de la universidad?

Paso 1. Lea las siguientes oraciones e indique las que son verdaderas para Ud. Cambie las oraciones falsas para que expresen su propia experiencia.

En la escuela secundaria...

1. ☐ era obligatorio que yo asistiera a todas mis clases.
2. ☐ mis padres insistían en que yo estudiara mucho.
3. ☐ era necesario que yo trabajara para que pudiera asistir a la universidad algún día.
4. ☐ no había ninguna clase que me interesara.
5. ☐ tenía que sacar buenas notas para que mis padres me dieran dinero.
6. ☐ era necesario que volviera a casa a una hora determinada, aun (*even*) en los fines de semana.
7. ☐ mis padres me exigían que limpiara mi cuarto cada semana.
8. ☐ mis padres no permitían que saliera con alguna persona o con los miembros de ciertos grupos.

Paso 2. Ahora considere sus respuestas. ¿Realmente era mejor la vida en la escuela secundaria? ¿Le gustaría regresar a esa época? ¿Por qué sí o por qué no?

B. Y ahora, la niñez

Paso 1. ¿Qué quería Ud. de la vida cuando era niño/a? ¿Y qué querían los demás que Ud. hiciera? Conteste, haciendo oraciones con una frase de cada grupo.

1. Mis padres (no) querían que yo...
2. Mis maestros me pedían que...
3. Yo buscaba amigos que...
4. Me gustaba mucho que nosotros...

ir a la iglesia / al templo con ellos
portarse bien, ser bueno/a
estudiar mucho, hacer la tarea todas las noches, sacar buenas notas
ponerse ropa vieja para jugar, jugar en la calle, pelear con mis amigos
mirar mucho la televisión, leer muchas tiras cómicas, comer muchos dulces
vivir en nuestro barrio, asistir a la misma escuela, tener muchos juguetes, ser aventureros
ir de vacaciones en verano, pasar todos juntos los días feriados, tener un árbol de Navidad muy alto

En los Estados Unidos y el Canadá...

Tres hispanos del mundo de la televisión

Ray Rodríguez, María Hinojosa y Jim Ávila son tres hispanos cuyos[a] nombres se destacan[b] en **el mundo de la televisión** y **los noticieros**. Ray Rodríguez, quien ahora vive en Miami, es contador de profesión y por varios años fue *manager* de Julio Iglesias. En 1992 llegó a ser presidente de Univisión, una **cadena** en español que, según los cálculos, se ve en el 95 por ciento de los hogares hispanos en los Estados Unidos. Junto con Galavisión y Telefutura, la cadena Univisión forma parte de la **compañía de difusión**[c] en español más importante de los Estados Unidos: Univisión Networks. Rodríguez es ahora presidente de esta poderosa[d] empresa.

Una hispana que también se distingue en el mundo de la información es María Hinojosa. Hinojosa nació en

Ray Rodríguez, presidente de Univisión

la Ciudad de México. Estudió en los Estados Unidos, y por varios años trabajó para NPR (*National Public Radio*) en el área de Nueva York. Desde 1997 es **corresponsal**[e] de la CNN (*Cable News Network*), donde se especializa en **cuestiones urbanas**. Es autora de dos libros y ha recibido varios **premios periodísticos**, entre ellos el Premio Rubén Salazar, otorgado[f] por el **Consejo Nacional de la Raza**,[g] una prestigiosa institución de los hispanos estadounidenses.

Jim Ávila tiene una larga y distinguida carrera periodística. Es **reportero** de NBC y reporta **acontecimientos** importantes dentro y fuera de los Estados Unidos. Tiene el récord más alto de reportajes en televisión sobre las minorías. La **Asociación Nacional de Periodistas Hispanos** lo premió[h] en 1999 junto con Hugo Pérez por «*Fire Racism*», una pieza sobre el racismo entre los bomberos[i] de Chicago.

[a]*whose* [b]*se... stand out* [c]*media* [d]*powerful* [e]*correspondent* [f]*awarded* [g]Consejo... *National Council of La Raza* [h]*awarded a prize* [i]*firefighters*

Paso 2. Ahora, conteste las siguientes preguntas. ¿Qué no le gustaba nada cuando era niño/a? ¿Qué quería Ud. que sus padres (sus hermanos) hicieran?

C. El noticiero de las seis. En las noticias los reporteros nos informan de los acontecimientos del día, pero a veces también ofrecen sus propias opiniones.

Paso 1. Lea las siguientes oraciones y cámbielas al pasado. Debe usar el imperfecto del primer verbo en cada oración y luego el imperfecto del subjuntivo en la segunda parte.

1. «Los obreros quieren que les den un aumento de sueldo.»
2. «Es posible que los trabajadores sigan en huelga hasta el verano.»
3. «Es necesario que las víctimas reciban atención médica en la Clínica del Sagrado Corazón.»
4. «Es una lástima que no haya espacio para todos allí.»
5. «Los terroristas piden que los oficiales no los persigan.»

6. «Parece imposible que el gobierno acepte sus demandas.»
7. «Es necesario que el gobierno informe a todos los ciudadanos del desastre.»
8. «Dudo que la paz mundial esté fuera de nuestro alcance (*reach*).»
9. «El presidente y los directores prefieren que la nueva fábrica se construya en México.»
10. «Temo que el número de votantes sea muy bajo en las próximas elecciones.»

Paso 2. Ahora indique si las oraciones representan un hecho o si son una opinión del reportero o de la persona citada (*quoted*).

Conversación

A. **Los consejos se dan gratis** (*free*). Sin duda, varias personas le dieron a Ud. muchos consejos o recomendaciones antes de que Ud. empezara a estudiar en la universidad. ¿Qué le recomendaron las siguientes personas? Indique las oraciones que son apropiadas para Ud. Luego dé por lo menos otro consejo o recomendación más que cada persona o grupo de personas le ofreció a Ud.

1. Mis amigos me recomendaron que viviera en una residencia en vez de en un apartamento.
2. Mis padres me aconsejaron que estudiara mucho.
3. Mi mejor amigo/a me pidió que le escribiera de vez en cuando.
4. Mi consejero/a me recomendó que me especializara en una carrera práctica y útil.

Frases útiles: tomar muchas clases diferentes, hacerme socio/a (*member*) de un(a) *fraternity/sorority*, graduarme dentro de cuatro años, participar en muchas actividades extracurriculares, llamar con frecuencia, evitar el alcohol y las drogas

B. **Preguntas**

1. ¿A qué le tenía miedo Ud. cuando era pequeño/a? ¿Era probable que ocurrieran las cosas que Ud. temía? ¿Temía a veces que sus padres lo/la castigaran (*punish*)? ¿Lo merecía a veces? ¿Era necesario que Ud. siempre los obedeciera? ¿Qué le prohibían a Ud. que hiciera?
2. ¿Qué tipo de clases buscaba Ud. para este semestre/trimestre? ¿Clases que fueran fáciles? ¿interesantes? ¿Las encontró? ¿Han sido las clases tal como Ud. las esperaba? ¿Qué tipo de clases va a buscar para el semestre/trimestre que viene?
3. ¿Qué buscaban los primeros inmigrantes que vinieron a los Estados Unidos? ¿Buscaban un lugar donde pudieran practicar su religión? ¿un lugar donde hubiera abundancia de recursos naturales? ¿menos restricciones? ¿más libertad política y personal? ¿más respeto por los derechos humanos? ¿menos gente? ¿más espacio?

—Verás, quisiera un vaso de agua. Pero no te molestes, porque ya no tengo sed. Sólo quisiera saber si, en el caso de que tuviese otra vez sed, podría (*I could*) venir a pedirte un vaso de agua.

C. Situaciones. El niño del dibujo sabe que está molestando a sus padres cuando los despierta pidiendo ahora un vaso de agua que no quiere pero que podría querer más tarde. Por eso les habla de una forma muy cortés: «quisiera un vaso de agua… quisiera saber… ». ¿Cómo podría Ud. pedir de una forma muy cortés lo que necesita en las siguientes situaciones? ¿Qué diría para conseguirlo?

1. Ud. quiere tener el número de teléfono de un chico / una chica que acaba de conocer. Habla con un amigo de él / una amiga de ella.
2. En un restaurante, el camarero no lo/la atiende como debe. Ud. no quiere perder la paciencia con él, pero quiere la taza de café que le pidió hace diez minutos… y la cuenta.
3. Uds. quieren saber cuándo es el examen final en esta clase y qué va a incluir.
4. Ud. necesita una extensión para el próximo examen de español.
5. Ud. piensa que va a necesitar una extensión para el próximo proyecto.
6. Ud. necesita una carta de recomendación del profesor / de la profesora.
7. Ud. quiere hablar con el rector / la rectora de la universidad para invitarlo/la a cenar en su residencia con motivo de algo especial.

NOTA COMUNICATIVA

I wish I could . . . I wish they would . . .

There are many ways to express wishes in Spanish. As you know, one of the most common is **ojalá (que)** with the subjunctive. The past subjunctive following **ojalá** is one of the most frequent uses of those verb forms.

Ojalá (que) pudiera acompañarlos, pero no es posible.
I wish I could go with you, but it's not possible.
Ojalá inventaran una máquina que hiciera todas las tareas domésticas.
I wish they would invent a machine that would do all the household chores.

D. ¡Ojalá! Complete las oraciones lógicamente.

1. Ojalá que (yo) tuviera _____.
2. Ojalá que pudiera _____.
3. Ojalá inventaran una máquina que _____.
4. Ojalá solucionaran el problema de _____.
5. Ojalá que en esta universidad fuera posible _____.

Enfoque *cultural*

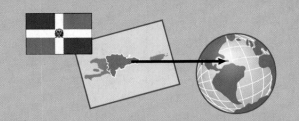

la República Dominicana

Datos esenciales

Nombre oficial: República Dominicana

Capital: Santo Domingo

Población: 8.000.000 de habitantes

Moneda: el peso

Idiomas: el español (oficial), el francés criollo

¡Fíjese!

- Santo Domingo fue fundada en 1496 por Bartólome Colón, hermano de Cristóbal Colón. Esta población en lo que entonces se llamaba la isla de La Española fue la primera colonia europea en el Nuevo Mundo.

- En el siglo XV, bucaneros franceses, que en realidad no eran más que piratas, fundaron la colonia de Sant Domingue en el oeste de la isla. Dentro de poco tiempo, se estableció un sistema de plantaciones basado en la labor de esclavos africanos.

- España le cedió[a] a Francia, en 1697, el tercio occidental[b] de La Española. Por esta razón, este territorio, el actual país de Haití, tiene una cultura y un idioma diferentes a los de la República Dominicana.

- Muchos atletas dominicanos han tenido gran éxito[c] en las Grandes Ligas de los Estados Unidos. Entre los que se han destacado[d] recientemente han sido Sammy Sosa, Juan Marichal y Roberto y Sandy Alomar.

[a]*ceded* [b]*tercio… western third* [c]*han… have been very successful*
[d]*se… have stood out*

Conozca a... Julia Álvarez

Julia Álvarez

Aunque la novelista Julia Álvarez (1950–) nació en la ciudad de Nueva York y ahora es profesora de inglés en Middlebury College en Vermont, pasó su niñez en la República Dominicana. Cuando tenía apenas[a] 10 años, su padre tuvo que exiliarse con la familia después de tratar de derrotar[b] el régimen del dictador Trujillo. Al llegar a la madurez, se destacó como[c] poeta y ganó su primer premio de importancia en 1974, el mismo año en que publicó su primer libro de poesía, *Homecoming*. Pero cuando, en 1991, publicó su primera novela *How the García Girls Lost their Accents* —en verdad, una serie de cuentos entrelazados[d]— recibió atención crítica y pública del mundo entero. Esta obra, como las que la han seguido, refleja su múltiple existencia como mujer, como latina y como americana.

[a]*barely* [b]*defeat* [c]*se… she distinguished herself as a* [d]*linked*

Capítulo 17 of the video to accompany *¿Qué tal?* contains cultural footage of the Dominican Republic.

Visit the *¿Qué tal?* website at www.mhhe.com/quetal.

UN POCO DE TODO

¿Qué lees? Complete the following dialogue with the correct form of the words in parentheses, as suggested by the context. When two possibilities are given in parentheses, select the correct word.

EDUARDO: ¿De quién (ser/estar[1]) esta revista?

LINDA: Es mío.[a] Te (lo/la[2]) puedo prestar si quieres.

EDUARDO: Pues me gustaría que me la (dejar[3]). La he (hojear[4])[b] y me (haber[5]) gustado.

LINDA: Para (yo/mí[6]) también ha sido una sorpresa. No pensaba que (ser/estar[7]) (tan/tanto[8]) buena. Tiene un poco de todo. Aunque yo temía que (resultar[9])[c] superficial, no es así.

EDUARDO: (*Yo: Ser/Estar*[10]) de acuerdo. Trae artículos de política internacional (muy/mucho[11]) interesantes. Quiero terminar de (leer[12]) ese artículo sobre la situación de las antiguas[d] repúblicas soviéticas.

LINDA: (*Tú: Leer*[13]) también el reportaje sobre África. Hace un análisis muy interesante sobre (el/la[14]) relación entre el hambre, la guerra y (el/la[15]) desertización. Pero también habla de la política nacional, de ciencia…

EDUARDO: Sí, y ya (*yo: ver*[16]) que además trae (un/una[17]) reportaje sobre mi actor favorito.

LINDA: (Es/Está[18]) cierto. Trae bastantes comentarios sobre el cine. También puedes (enterarse[19]) de las últimas novedades, tanto sobre libros (que/como[20]) sobre música.

EDUARDO: Y también me imagino[e] que tiene secciones sobre viajes, salud, deportes…

LINDA: Tienes (suerte/razón[21]). Es una buena forma de enterarse de todo lo actual.

[a]*mine* [b]*to look over* [c]*to turn out* [d]*former* [e]*me… I imagine*

Comprensión: ¿Probable o improbable?

1. A Linda le gusta leer más que a Eduardo.
2. La revista de que hablan se publica una vez al año.
3. Es posible que tenga también una sección sobre viajes.

CAPÍTULO
17
Un paso más PASO 4

VIDEOTECA: En contexto

A. Lluvia de ideas

- En su opinión, ¿qué medios de información debe leer una persona que quiere estar bien informada de lo que pasa en el país o en el mundo? ¿Se considera Ud. una persona bien informada? ¿Por qué?
- ¿Está Ud. suscrito/a a alguna revista o algún periódico? ¿Cuáles? Si Ud. compra alguna revista o algún periódico, ¿dónde los compra? ¿Los compra a menudo (*often*)? ¿Qué calidades o valores espera encontrar en una revista o un periódico?
- ¿Sabía Ud. que en los países hispánicos no es tan común como en este país estar suscrito a los periódicos y a las revistas? ¿Qué prefiere Ud., suscribirse a una publicación o comprarla en un quiosco (o puesto de periódicos)? ¿Por qué?

MÉXICO

B. Dictado

A continuación aparece un fragmento del diálogo entre Roberto y la vendedora de periódicos. Complete el diálogo con las palabras o frases que faltan.

DOÑA BEATRIZ: ¡Roberto, hijo! ¿Cómo estás? Estaba muy _____[1] ¿Por qué no _____[2] ayer?

ROBERTO: Doña Beatriz, no debe preocuparse. Me _____[3] tarde ayer y tuve que apurarme[a] para llegar al trabajo.

DOÑA BEATRIZ: Tuve mucho _____[4] ayer. ¿No sabes cuántos _____[5] hay hoy en día?

ROBERTO: Lo _____,[6] doña Beatriz. Fue sin querer. A ver ¿Qué necesito hoy? Un _____[7] liberal, un periódico conservador, una revista internacional, dos revistas _____[8]...

DOÑA BEATRIZ: ¡Cuántas _____[9] y periódicos! ¿Qué pasa, Roberto? ¿Vendes en la otra esquina? ¿Tienes tu propio puesto[b]?

ROBERTO: Es importante _____,[10] doña Beatriz.

[a]*hurry*   [b]*stand*

FUNCTION
Purchasing a newspaper

Cultura en contexto
El periódico

El periodismo tiene una larga tradición en Latinoamérica y España. Varios escritores famosos, entre ellos Gabriel García Márquez, el novelista colombiano y ganador del premio Nóbel de Literatura en 1981, fueron periodistas antes de dedicarse a escribir ficción. En los países hispanos, la gran mayoría de la gente educada lee por lo menos un periódico al día. En las grandes ciudades, algunos periódicos tienen asociaciones políticas y se puede encontrar un periódico para cada filosofía política, desde el más conservador (derechista) hasta el más liberal (izquierdista).

C. Un diálogo original

Opción 1. Con un compañero / una compañera, dramatice el diálogo entre Roberto y doña Beatriz.

Opción 2. ¡Qué desesperación! En esta dramatización uno/a de Uds. hace el papel de una persona que está desesperada por comprar un periódico del extranjero. El otro / La otra es el dueño / la dueña de un quiosco de periódicos.

E1: Ud. tiene un buen amigo que está en un país del Oriente Medio, en un área donde ha estallado (*has broken out*) una guerra. Quiere un periódico de ese país para averiguar (*find out*) más acerca de los acontecimientos. Pero el periódico tiene que ser en inglés o en español, ya que Ud. no sabe leer ni árabe ni hebreo.

E2: Aunque Ud. vende periódicos del extranjero, ninguno de los periódicos del Oriente Medio que tiene es en inglés o en español. Pero Ud. conoce a una reportera árabe en su ciudad que está enterada sobre la guerra. Ud. ofrece comunicarse con ella para que su cliente se pueda informar sobre su amigo.

PASO FINAL

Sobre el autor... Gustavo Pérez Firmat (1949–) nació en La Habana, Cuba, y se crió en Miami, Florida. Su poesía tiene una variedad de temas, entre los que se incluyen las relaciones de familia y la experiencia cubano-americana en los Estados Unidos. Pérez Firmat recibió un doctorado de la Universidad de Michigan y ahora enseña en la Universidad de Columbia. El poema que aquí se presenta, «Cubanita descubanizada», es de una colección que se titula *Bilingual Blues*.

A LEER

Estrategia: Using Language Cues to Understand Poetry

Much of the information you get in a poem is conveyed through the use of particular grammatical forms. These forms may also contribute to a poem's unique mood. For example, a poem written primarily in the imperfect may convey a sense of timelessness or of things recurring in the poet's personal history. The use of the preterite may give you the feeling that the moment was fleeting, perhaps all too fleeting.

As you read the following poem, note the instances of the past subjunctive that you have learned in this chapter. Why do you think the poet chose this form? What or how does it make you feel? Do you think the poem would be different if the poet had chosen a different grammatical form?

Cubanita descubanizada

Cubanita descubanizada
quién te pudiera recubanizar.
Quién supiera devolverte
el ron[a] y la palma,[b]
el alma y el son.[c]

Cubanita descubanizada,
tú que pronuncias todas las eses*
y dices ómnibus[d] y autobús
quién te pudiera
quién te supiera
si te quisieras recubanizar.

[a]*rum*   [b]*palm tree*   [c]*el... the soul and the sound (the **son** is also a popular Cuban dance)*   [d]*synonym for*
autobús *(the author is referring to the rich lexical variety that exists in Cuban Spanish, but that in this*
case signals a departure from its local, rural roots).

Comprensión

A. Definiciones. El autor toma libertades poéticas en su poema e inventa
palabras que sirven para expresar sus ideas. Con un compañero / una
compañera, trate de definir las siguientes palabras inventadas por Pérez
Firmat. Comparen sus definiciones con las de otra persona en la clase.

- descubanizada
- recubanizar

B. Interpretación. ¿Cuál cree Ud. que es el punto de vista del narrador del
poema? ¿Tiene una actitud positiva hacia la vida en el extranjero? ¿Qué
mensaje intenta expresar? ¿Qué elementos de la poesía comunican este
mensaje?

 A ESCRIBIR

El tema de la inmigración es uno que provoca mucha reacción en este país. A
continuación hay dos puntos de vista contrarios. Escoja una de estas postu-
ras y escriba un breve informe en el que presenta y apoya su opinión.

- El bilingüismo y el biculturalismo enriquecen la vida de este país.
- Los inmigrantes a este país deben asimilarse por completo a la lengua, la vida y la cultura.

---

*In general, Cuban Spanish is characterized by a lack of pronunciation of the letter **s** when found
in certain positions within a word.

En resumen

GRAMÁTICA

To review the grammar point presented in this chapter, refer to the indicated grammar presentation. You'll find further practice of this structure in the Workbook/Laboratory Manual, on the CD-ROM, and on the website.

44. Past Subjunctive

You should know the forms of the past subjunctive and when to use it.

VOCABULARIO

Los verbos

apoyar	to support
castigar	to punish
comunicarse (con)	to communicate (with)
durar	to last
enterarse (de)	to find out (about)
gobernar (ie)	to govern, rule
informar	to inform
votar	to vote

Repaso: obedecer, ofrecer

Las últimas novedades

el acontecimiento	event, happening
el asesinato	assassination
el choque	collision
el desastre	disaster
el ejército	army
la esperanza	hope, wish
el evento	event
la guerra	war
la huelga	strike (*labor*)
la libertad	liberty, freedom
el medio de comunicación	means of communication

el noticiero	newscast
la paz (*pl.* paces)	peace
la prensa	press; news media
el/la reportero/a	reporter
el/la terrorista	terrorist
el/la testigo	witness

Repaso: el canal, el/la obrero/a

El gobierno y la responsabilidad cívica

el/la ciudadano/a	citizen
el deber	responsibility, obligation
el derecho	right
la (des)igualdad	(in)equality
el/la dictador(a)	dictator
la dictadura	dictatorship
la discriminación	discrimination
la ley	law
la política	politics
el/la político/a	politician
el rey / la reina	king/queen
el servicio militar	military service

Repaso: los/las demás

CAPÍTULO 18

En el extranjero

Viajar al extranjero nos permite aprender mucho de otras culturas. España es un país de muchas culturas diferentes. Aquí se nota la gran influencia de la cultura árabe en la arquitectura de La Alhambra, en Granada, España.

VOCABULARIO

- Places and things abroad
- On a trip abroad

GRAMÁTICA

45 Conditional Verb Forms

CULTURA

- **Enfoque cultural:** España
- **Nota cultural:** De compras en el extranjero
- **En los Estados Unidos y el Canadá:** Manjares hispanocanadienses
- **Cultura en contexto:** Los paquetes al extranjero

Multimedia

You will learn about mailing letters and packages in the **En contexto** video segment.

Review vocabulary and grammar and practice language skills with the interactive CD-ROM.

Get connected to the Spanish-speaking world with the *¿Qué tal?* Online Learning Center: **www.mhhe.com/quetal**.

Lugares y cosas en el extranjero°

en... *abroad*

Más cosas

el champú	shampoo
el jabon	soap
la pasta dental	toothpaste
el correo	mail
el papel para cartas	stationery

el paquete	package
la revista	magazine
el sobre	envelope
el batido	*drink similar to a milkshake*
una copa / un trago	(*alcoholic*) drink
el pastelito	small pastry

Conversación

A. En el extranjero. Conteste con oraciones completas.

1. ¿Dónde se compra el champú? ¿el jabón?
2. ¿Cuál es la diferencia entre una farmacia de este país y una farmacia en el extranjero?
3. ¿Dónde se puede comprar sellos? (dos lugares)
4. Si se necesitan cigarrillos o fósforos, ¿adónde se va?
5. ¿Qué es un quiosco? ¿Qué cosas se venden allí?
6. ¿Qué venden en una papelería?

NOTA CULTURAL

De compras en el extranjero

Aunque los nombres de muchos lugares y tiendas del mundo hispánico se parecen a los de este país, no siempre son iguales los productos que en ellos se venden. Tomen en cuenta sobre todo las siguientes diferencias.

- En **las farmacias** no venden la variedad de cosas —dulces, tarjetas postales, etcétera— que se venden en las farmacias de los EE.UU.* y el Canadá. Por lo general, sólo se venden medicinas y productos para **la higiene personal** como jabón, pasta dental, champú…
- En **los estancos**, además de productos tabacaleros, se venden **sellos**, así que[a] uno no tiene que ir a una oficina de correos para comprarlos. También se venden **sobres** y **tarjetas postales** en los estancos.
- En **los quioscos** se vende una **gran variedad** de cosas: periódicos, revistas, libros, etcétera, pero también lápices, papel para cartas…

[a]así… *so*

Madrid, España

B. **¿Cierto o falso?** Corrija las oraciones falsas.

1. Se puede comprar batidos y pastelitos en una pastelería.
2. Si yo quisiera tomar una copa, iría (*I would go*) a un quiosco.
3. Se va a un quiosco para mandar paquetes.
4. Es más rápido ir a pie que tomar el metro.
5. Se va a un café a comprar champú.
6. Si yo necesitara pasta dental, iría a la oficina de correos.
7. Se puede comprar fósforos en un estanco.
8. Un batido se hace con vino.

*EE.UU. is one way to abbreviate **Estados Unidos**. E.U. and **USA** are also used.

En un viaje al extranjero

CRUZAR LA FRONTERA

el viajero

DECLARAR LAS COMPRAS

la inspectora
(de aduanas)

REGISTRAR LAS MALETAS

PAGAR LOS DERECHOS / UNA MULTA

viajar al/en el extranjero	to travel abroad	**la habitación**	room (*in a hotel*)
		individual/doble	single/double
la aduana	customs	**con/sin baño/ducha**	with/without bath/shower
los derechos de aduana	customs duty	**el hotel (de lujo)**	(luxury) hotel
la multa	fine, penalty	**el/la huésped(a)**	(*hotel*) guest
la nacionalidad	nationality	**el mozo/botones**	bellhop
el pasaporte	passport	**la pensión**	boardinghouse
		pensión completa	room and full board
		media pensión	room with breakfast and one other meal
El alojamiento°	El... *Lodging*		
alojarse/quedarse	to stay (*in a place*)	**la propina**	tip (*to an employee*)
hacer (*irreg.*)**/confirmar**	to make / to	**la recepción**	front desk
las reservas/	confirm		
reservaciones*	reservations	**completo/a**	full, no vacancy
la criada	maid	**con anticipación**	ahead of time
		desocupado/a	vacant, unoccupied

Conversación

A. En la aduana. ¿Ha viajado Ud. al extranjero? ¿Sabe Ud. cómo portarse al pasar por la aduana? Use el sentido común para explicar cuáles de las siguientes acciones pueden causar problemas en la aduana.

1. ser cortés con el inspector
2. escribir información falsa en el formulario de inmigración
3. no tener el pasaporte (o el visado necesario)
4. declarar todas sus compras
5. llevar gafas oscuras y parecer que está nervioso/a
6. esconder (*hiding*) artículos de contrabando en su equipaje
7. pagar los derechos (o la multa) sin quejarse
8. intentar cruzar la frontera con un pasaporte falsificado
9. tratar de distraer al inspector mientras este (*he*) registra sus maletas

---

*__La reserva__ is used in Spain for a reservation (for accommodations). __La reservación__ is widely used in other parts of the Spanish-speaking world.

B. **¿Quiénes son?** Empareje las personas con la descripción apropiada.

1. el huésped
2. el recepcionista
3. el botones
4. la turista
5. la inspectora de aduanas
6. el viajero

a. la persona que nos ayuda con el equipaje en un hotel
b. la persona que se aloja en un hotel o una pensión
c. una persona que va de un lugar a otro
d. alguien que viaja para ver otros lugares
e. la persona que nos registra las maletas y toma la declaración en la aduana
f. la persona que nos atiende en la recepción de un hotel

C. **Cuando Ud. viaja...**

Paso 1. A continuación hay una lista de acciones que son típicas de los viajeros. ¿Hace Ud. lo mismo cuando viaja? Indique las acciones que son verdaderas para Ud.

1. ☐ Hago una reserva en un hotel (motel) o en una pensión con un mes de anticipación.
2. ☐ Confirmo la reserva antes de salir de viaje.
3. ☐ Voy al banco a conseguir cheques de viajero.
4. ☐ Alquilo un coche.
5. ☐ Me alojo en un hotel de lujo.
6. ☐ Pido que el mozo me suba las maletas.
7. ☐ Llamo al servicio de cuartos en vez de comer en el restaurante.
8. ☐ Le dejo una propina a la criada el último día de mi estancia (*stay*) en la habitación.

D. **Situaciones.** Con un compañero / una compañera, improvise una escena. Hagan los papeles de un viajero / una viajera y del / de la recepcionista de un hotel.

Paso 1. El/La recepcionista le pregunta al viajero / a la viajera, que acaba de llegar:

- si tiene una reserva.
- cuánto tiempo piensa quedarse.
- el tipo de habitación reservada (o deseada).
- la forma de pago.

Paso 2. El/La huésped(a) pide los siguientes servicios:

- el desayuno en su cuarto.
- más toallas (*towels*) / jabón.
- información sobre lugares turísticos de interés.

Paso 3. Por fin, el huésped / la huéspeda pasa por la recepción para pagar la cuenta. Encuentra los siguientes errores en su cuenta.

- Le cobraron (*they charged*) por un desayuno que no tomó.
- Le cobraron por cuatro noches en vez de tres.
- Le cobraron por una llamada a larga distancia que nunca hizo.

45 Expressing What You Would Do • Conditional Verb Forms

La fantasía de la maestra de Mafalda

«¡Ya no aguanto este puesto! Creo que me *gustaría* ser abogada… *Pasaría* todo el día con tipos interesantes… *Ganaría* mucho dinero… *Viajaría* mucho, pues *tendría* clientes en todas partes del país… Me *llamarían* actores, actrices, políticos, hombres y mujeres de negocios para consultar conmigo… También *haría* viajes internacionales para investigar casos en el extranjero… Todo el mundo me *respetaría* y me *escucharía*… »

Y Ud., siendo la maestra / el maestro de Mafalda, ¿cómo sería? Use **no** cuando sea necesario.

- estar contento/a → *Estaría* contento/a.
- ser un tipo / una tipa coherente
- desorientar a los estudiantes
- mirarlos con ojos furiosos
- hacerlos morir de miedo (¡OJO! **har-**)
- ponerles cara de poco sueldo (¡OJO! **pondr-**)
- hacer a los estudiantes llorar de lástima

You have been using the phrase **me gustaría…** for some time to express what you *would like* (to do, say, and so on). **Gustaría** is a conditional verb form, part of a system that will allow you to talk about what you and others would do (say, buy, and so on) in a given situation.

The fantasy of Mafalda's teacher   I can't bear this job anymore! I think I would like to be a lawyer . . . I would spend all day with interesting people . . . I would earn a lot of money . . . I would travel a lot, since I would have clients all over the country . . . Actors, actresses, politicians, businesspeople would call me to consult with me . . . I would also travel internationally to investigate cases abroad . . . Everyone would respect me and listen to me . . .

hablar		comer		vivir	
hablaría	hablaríamos	comería	comeríamos	viviría	viviríamos
hablarías	hablaríais	comerías	comeríais	vivirías	viviríais
hablaría	hablarían	comería	comerían	viviría	vivirían

A. Like the English future, the English conditional is formed with an auxiliary verb: *I **would** speak, I **would** write.* The Spanish *conditional* (**el condicional**), like the Spanish future, is a simple verb form (only one word). It is formed by adding conditional endings to the infinitive. No auxiliary verbs are needed.

CONDITIONAL ENDINGS

-ía, -ías, -ía, -íamos, íais, -ían

B. Verbs that form the future on an irregular stem use the same stem to form the conditional.

The conditional of **hay (haber)** is **habría** (*there would be*).*

decir: diría, dirías, diría, diríamos, diríais, dirían

decir:	**dir-**	
hacer:	**har-**	**-ía**
poder:	**podr-**	**-ías**
poner:	**pondr-**	**-ía**
querer:	**querr-**	**-íamos**
saber:	**sabr-**	**-íais**
salir:	**saldr-**	**-ían**
tener:	**tendr-**	
venir:	**vendr-**	

C. The conditional expresses what you would do in a particular situation, given a particular set of circumstances.

—¿**Hablarías** español en el Brasil?
Would you speak Spanish in Brazil?

—No. **Hablaría** portugués.
No. I would speak Portuguese.

OJO

When *would* implies *used to* in English, Spanish uses the imperfect.

Íbamos a la playa todos los veranos.
We would go (used to go) to the beach every summer.

---

*The conditional forms of the verb **haber** are used to form the *conditional perfect tense* (**el condicional perfecto**), which expresses what *would have* occurred at some point in the past.

Habríamos tenido que buscarla en el aeropuerto.

We would have had to pick her up at the airport.

You will find a more detailed presentation of these forms in Appendix 3, Additional Perfect Forms (Indicative and Subjunctive).

Práctica

A. ¿Qué haría Ud.?

Paso 1. Imagine que hace un viaje a España. Complete las siguientes oraciones de manera que corresponda a la realidad y a lo que a Ud. le gustaría hacer. ¡Es una gran oportunidad de demostrarles a sus compañeros y a su profesor(a) su conocimiento (*knowledge*) sobre la vida y la cultura españolas!

1. Hablaría _____.
2. Comería _____ y bebería _____.
3. Iría a _____ y allí vería _____.
4. No podría irme sin antes visitar _____.
5. Me compraría _____.
6. Me divertiría mucho _____ (¡**OJO!** Se necesita un gerundio: **-iendo** o **-ando**).

Paso 2. Claro que durante un viaje no sólo se hacen actividades culturales. Las oraciones a continuación muestran actividades típicas durante un viaje, pero Ud. debe completarlas con algunos detalles.

1. Yo haría el viaje a España con _____.
2. Tendría que sacar muchas fotos para mostrárselas a _____.
3. Le(s) mandaría tarjetas postales a _____.
4. Querría _____ durante el viaje, pero probablemente no lo haría.
5. Conocería a _____.

Paso 3. Ahora con un compañero / una compañera, haga una lista similar a las del **Paso 1** y el **Paso 2**, pero sobre otro país hispánico.

B. ¿Es posible escapar?

Cuente Ud. la fantasía de esta trabajadora social, dando la forma condicional de los verbos.

Necesito salir de todo esto... Creo que me (gustar[1]) ir a Puerto Rico o a algún otro lugar exótico del Caribe... No (trabajar[2])... (Poder[3]) nadar todos los días... (Tomar[4]) el sol en la playa... (Comer[5]) platos exóticos... (Ver[6]) bellos lugares naturales... El viaje (ser[7]) ideal...

Pero... , tarde o temprano, (tener[8]) que volver a lo de siempre... a los rascacielos de la ciudad... al tráfico... al medio ambiente contaminado... al mundo del trabajo... (Poder[9]) usar mi tarjeta de crédito, como dice el anuncio —pero ¡(tener[10]) que pagar después!

Comprensión: ¿Cierto, falso o no lo dice? Corrija las oraciones falsas.

1. Esta persona trabaja en una ciudad grande.
2. No le interesan los deportes acuáticos.
3. Puede pagar este viaje de sueños (*dreams*) al contado.
4. Tiene un novio con quien quisiera hacer el viaje.

C. ¿Qué harías? Con un compañero / una compañera, haga y conteste las preguntas según el modelo. Pueden cambiar los detalles, si quieren. Para números 9–12, inventen las respuestas.

MODELO: estudiar árabe/japonés →
E1: ¿Estudiarías árabe?
E2: No. Estudiaría japonés.

1. estudiar italiano / chino
2. renunciar un puesto sin avisar / con dos semanas de anticipación
3. hacer un viaje a España / la Argentina
4. salir de casa sin apagar el estéreo / las luces
5. seguir un presupuesto rígido / flexible
6. gastar menos en ropa / libros
7. poner el aire acondicionado en invierno / verano
8. alquilar un coche de lujo / económico
9. dejar de estudiar /¿ ?
10. vivir en otra ciudad /¿ ?
11. ser presidente/a de los Estados Unidos / primer ministro (primera ministra) del Canadá /¿ ?
12. gustarle conocer a una persona famosa /¿ ?

Conversación

A. Entrevista. ¿Cómo será su futuro? ¿Qué hará? ¿Qué haría? Con un compañero / una compañera, haga y conteste las siguientes preguntas.

MODELO:　E1: ¿Dejarás de fumar algún día? →
　　　　　E2: No. No dejaré de fumar nunca. No puedo.
　　　　　　　(Creo que sí. Dejaré de fumar algún día.)

PREGUNTAS CON EL FUTURO

1. ¿Te graduarás en esta universidad (o en otra)?
2. ¿Vivirás en esta ciudad después de graduarte?
3. ¿Buscarás un puesto aquí?
4. ¿Te casarás (¿Te divorciarás) después de graduarte?
5. ¿Cuántos niños (nietos) crees que tendrás algún día?
6. ¿Serás famoso/a algún día?

PREGUNTAS CON EL CONDICIONAL

1. ¿Te casarías con una persona de otro país?
2. ¿Podrías estar contento/a sin la televisión?
3. ¿Serías capaz de (*capable of*) ahorrar el 10 por ciento de tu salario?
4. ¿Te gustaría ayudar a colonizar otro planeta?
5. ¿Podrías vivir sin las tarjetas de crédito?
6. ¿Renunciarías tu trabajo para viajar por el mundo?

NOTA COMUNICATIVA

If I were you, I would . . .

Both English and Spanish use clauses to speculate about likely or unlikely situations. These are called *if* or **si** clauses.

- The present indicative after **si** presents a situation that is likely to occur. It is followed or preceded by a clause in the indicative or by a command.

  LIKELY

  Si **ahorro** suficiente dinero, **iré** de vacaciones a España.　　*If I save enough money, I will go to Spain on vacation.*

- The imperfect subjunctive after **si** introduces an unlikely event. The preceding or following clause includes a verb in the conditional.

  UNLIKELY

  Si **tuviera** dinero suficiente, le **daría** la vuelta al mundo.　　*If I had enough money, I would go around the world.*

B. Circunstancias

Paso 1. ¿Qué hace Ud. si le ocurren estas cosas?

1. Si su primera clase es a las 9:00 de la mañana y Ud. se despierta a las 8:50.
2. Si su mejor amigo/a (novio/a, esposo/a, hijo/a) tiene un resfriado muy fuerte.
3. Si es viernes por la noche y no tiene ningún plan para divertirse esa noche.
4. Si se le pierde la llave de su cuarto/casa.

Paso 2. ¿Qué haría Ud. en estas situaciones?

1. Si le dejaran una herencia (*inheritance*) de dos millones de dólares.
2. Si pudiera hacer lo que quisiera en este momento.
3. Si tuviera un solo (*single*) deseo para todo el mundo.
4. Si pudiera dar la fiesta de sus sueños.

En los Estados Unidos y el Canadá...

Manjares[a] hispanocanadienses

Los que han viajado por la Península Ibérica ya conocen **los sabores**[b] **de los platos españoles y portugueses**. En la capital canadiense, Ottawa, tanto los turistas como los nativos disfrutan de[c] estos mismos platos en dos restaurantes que sirven **auténticas recetas de los países ibéricos**. **El Mesón**, que se encuentra en una casa al estilo victoriano, provee una cocina para satisfacer al cliente más exigente.[d] Desde 1987 José Alves ofrece un **menú de platos típicos regionales** de España y de Portugal que incluye calamares al ajillo, mejillones marineros, vieia a la gallega[e] y tres variedades de paella, el sabroso[f] plato a base de arroz y azafrán. También se ofrece un menú especial para vegetarianos. Para complementar sus platos, El Mesón tiene una impresionante lista de vinos españoles y una selección de los famosos «vinhos verdes»* de Portugal.

Una paella tipo español

Lejos de la vecindad de El Mesón y más cerca del centro de la capital, Ud. puede encontrar un ambiente acogedor[g] y relajado en donde hablar y tomar una copa de vino tinto mientras Alfonso Pérez, del restaurante **Don Alfonso**, le prepara uno de sus famosos platos. Nativo de Galicia, el Sr. Pérez vivió en Venezuela antes de emigrar al Canadá adonde vino primero con el propósito de aprender inglés. Hace más de veinticinco años que los ciudadanos de Ottawa y sus muchos turistas del extranjero disfrutan de los mariscos y los sabrosos platos a la plancha[h] preparados por don Alfonso. Entre muchos, se ofrecen escalopines[i] Tío Pepe, una zarzuela de mariscos y gazpacho andaluz[j].

[a]*Delicacies* [b]*flavors* [c]*disfrutan... enjoy* [d]*demanding* [e]*calamares... squid in garlic sauce, mussels cooked sailor-style, scallops Galician-style* [f]*tasty* [g]*welcoming* [h]*a... grilled* [i]*breaded cutlets* [j]*zarzuela... seafood stew, and a cold vegetable soup from Andalucía*

*Vinho verde (Young wine) is produced in the Minho region of northwest Portugal. Slightly sparkling, it can be either red or white.

Enfoque *cultural*

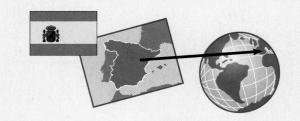

España

Datos esenciales

Nombre oficial: Reino de España

Capital: Madrid

Población: 39.000.000 de habitantes

Moneda: el euro

Idiomas: el español, el catalán, el gallego y el vasco*

Conozca a... Pedro Almodóvar

Las películas del cineasta[a] Pedro Almodóvar (1951–) han tenido y siguen teniendo un éxito enorme dentro y fuera de España, y Almodóvar es el director de cine español más conocido de las últimas décadas. Con temas que satirizan actitudes tradicionales respecto a la familia, la religión, el machismo y la moralidad convencional, sus películas presentan una sociedad española moderna y cambiante.[b]

Muchas de sus películas se pueden conseguir en las bibliotecas públicas y universitarias, así como en los video-clubs de este país: *Mujeres al borde de un ataque de nervios, La ley del deseo, ¿Qué he hecho yo para merecer esto?, ¡Átame!,*[c] *Kika, La flor de mi secreto* y *Todo sobre mi madre,* esta última de 1999 y ganadora del Óscar para la mejor película extranjera.

[a]*director de cine* [b]*changing* [c]*Tie Me Up! Tie Me Down!*

¡Fíjese!

- España es una país donde muchas culturas se han encontrado a través de[a] la historia. Sin embargo fueron los romanos los que marcaron el principio de la historia de la España que hoy conocemos, pues ellos introdujeron el latín a la península durante su dominio (desde el año 200 a.C.[b] hasta la invasión de los visigodos, un pueblo germánico, en el 419 d.C.[c]).

- El latín es la lengua madre del español y también del catalán, el gallego y el portugués. La otra lengua que se habla en la península, el vasco, es una lengua ancestral de origen desconocido: ni siquiera es[d] una lengua indo-europea.

- España no fue siempre un solo país. De hecho,[e] España se unificó en el siglo XV cuando los Reyes Católicos, Isabel y Fernando, monarcas de dos reinos[f] independientes, se casaron. Su campaña[g] de unificación terminó en 1492 con la conquista del reino musulmán[h] de Granada.

- Los árabes vivieron en España durante ocho siglos, hasta su expulsión, junto con los judíos, en el año 1492.

[a]*a... throughout* [b]*a.C.... antes de Cristo* [c]*d.C.... después de Cristo* [d]*ni... it is not even* [e]*De... In fact* [f]*kingdoms* [g]*campaign* [h]*Muslim*

El escudo (*shield*) de Fernando e Isabel

Capítulo 18 of the video to accompany *¿Qué tal?* contains cultural footage of Spain.

Visit the *¿Qué tal?* website at www.mhhe.com/quetal.

*El español es el lenguaje oficial de todo el país; el catalán, el gallego y el vasco también son lenguas oficiales en Cataluña, Galicia y el País Vasco, respectivamente.

UN POCO DE TODO

En busca de alojamiento. Complete the following dialogue with the correct form of the words in parentheses, as suggested by the context. When two possibilities are given in parentheses, select the correct word.

ALFONSO: Yo no (saber/conocer[1]) cómo vamos a encontrar alojamiento. No tenemos (mucho/muy[2]) dinero, y ya (ser/estar[3]) un poco tarde.

ELENA: Y (el/la[4]) equipaje pesa[a] mucho. No podemos (ir[5]) muy lejos.

ALFONSO: (*Tú:* Mirar[6]), en esa oficina parece que dan información.

EMPLEADO: ¿Qué (*Uds.:* desear[7])?

ALFONSO: Pues quisiéramos una habitación (por/para[8]) los dos. Sólo (por/para[9]) esta noche, pues solamente estamos (hacer[10]) escala aquí y mañana (*nosotros:* seguir[11]) con nuestro viaje.

ELENA: (Por/Para[12]) favor, no queremos que (ser/estar[13]) muy cara. Hemos (cambiar[14]) muy poca moneda. Tampoco queremos que (ser/estar[15]) muy lejos.

EMPLEADO: Bien, (*Uds.:* esperar[16]) un momento. Voy a llamar a una pensión (mucho/muy[17]) agradable que no (ser/estar[18]) muy lejos.

Pocos minutos después…

EMPLEADO: Me dicen que (haber[19]) una habitación doble disponible[b].

ALFONSO: ¡Qué bien! ¿Pagamos ahora?

EMPLEADO: No (ser/estar[20]) necesario. Aquí tienen los datos. (Este/Esta[21]) papel sirve como reserva. También (los/les[22]) he anotado el precio. Pero no tarden mucho en (llegar[23]).

ELENA: Muy bien. ¿Podría Ud. indicarnos cómo llegar allí?

EMPLEADO: (*Uds.:* Mirar[24]). Estamos aquí y la pensión (ser/estar[25]) en esta plaza. Se lo marco en (el/la[26]) mapa.

ELENA: ¿Sabe si (ser/estar[27]) incluido el desayuno en el precio?

EMPLEADO: Sí, lo que Uds. (llamar[28]) desayuno continental.

ALFONSO: Y otra cosa. ¿(Ser/Estar[29]) posible dejar parte de nuestro equipaje en la estación? Mañana tenemos (de/que[30]) volver a la estación.

EMPLEADO: Sí. Cuando salgan de la oficina, a mano derecha (*Uds.:* ver[31]) la consigna.[c] Pueden dejar(lo/la[32]) allí.

ALFONSO: Adiós y gracias (por/para[33]) todo.

[a]*weighs* [b]*available* [c]*baggage check*

Comprensión: ¿Quién lo dice?

1. Sí, todavía tenemos una habitación para esta noche.
2. ¡Qué suerte hemos tenido! Una habitación barata y cerca.
3. A ver qué quieren estos dos jóvenes.
4. Sí, señor. El empleado de la estación nos dio este papel como reserva.

PASO 4 Un paso más

VIDEOTECA: En contexto

FUNCTION

Mailing letters and packages

Cultura en contexto
Los paquetes al extranjero

En los países hispanos, como en los Estados Unidos, hay que llenar una declaración de aduanas cuando se envía un paquete al extranjero. En la declaración, hay que describir el contenido del paquete. Después, se indica si se quiere mandar el paquete por correo aéreo o por superficie.[a] El precio del franqueo[b] depende del modo de transporte. Claro, mandar un paquete por vía aérea es más caro que mandarlo por superficie.

[a]*por… by surface (mail)* [b]*postage*

A. Lluvia de ideas

- ¿Para qué tipo de cartas o paquetes usa Ud. el correo? ¿Con cuánta frecuencia?
- ¿Cuánto cuesta actualmente en este país mandar una carta por correo doméstico? ¿y una tarjeta postal al extranjero?

COSTA RICA

B. Dictado

A continuación aparece un fragmento del diálogo entre Mariela y el empleado de la oficina de correos. Complete el diálogo con las palabras o frases que faltan.

MARIELA: Buenos días, señor. Necesito estampillas[a] para tarjetas _____.[1]

EMPLEADO: ¿Son postales para correo doméstico o correo _____[2]?

MARIELA: Esta _____[3] es para correo doméstico. […]

EMPLEADO: Muy bien. ¿Hay algo más?

MARIELA: Sí. Quisiera mandar este _____[4] a Francia. ¿Cuánto cuesta?

EMPLEADO: Eso depende de cómo quiera mandarlo, señorita. Por _____[5] aéreo le cuesta 1.230 colones, pero llega en dos semanas. Si desea mandarlo por barco, le cuesta solamente 780 colones.

MARIELA: […] Es un _____[6] navideño[b] y como todavía nos faltan tres meses para Navidad, por barco está bien.

EMPLEADO: Cómo no, señorita. Por favor, _____[7] aquí el contenido del paquete y el valor. Es para la _____.[8]

[a]*sellos* [b]*Christmas*

C. Un diálogo original

Opción 1. Con un compañero / una compañera, dramatice el diálogo entre Mariela y el empleado de la oficina de correos.

Opción 2. **¿Vale la pena?** (*Is it worthwhile?*) Dos amigos han comprado un regalo de cumpleaños para otro amigo que vive en otro estado. El problema es que el libro que mandan es grande y pesado (*heavy*), y el correo resulta más caro que el libro mismo. Por otro lado, el cumpleaños es pasado mañana (*the day after tomorrow*) y tendrían que mandar el regalo por correo urgente para que llegara a tiempo.

Con un compañero / una compañera, represente una escena entre los amigos y solucionen el problema de cómo mandar el regalo.

PASO FINAL

A CONVERSAR

Improvisación turística

Si Ud. viaja a un país hispanohablante algún día, tendrá la oportunidad de hablar español. Imagine que Ud. es turista en un país hispanohablante. ¿Qué diría en las siguientes situaciones?

Paso 1. Formen grupos de tres o cuatro personas. Escojan una de las siguientes situaciones para improvisar. Lean la situación y escriban en una hoja de papel aparte un esquema (*outline*) de la improvisación.

MODELO: en el aeropuerto → saludarse; pedir los pasaportes; preguntar y contestar por qué vienen a este país…

Lugar	Situación	Personajes
En el aeropuerto	pasar por el control de pasaportes y por la aduana	uno o dos turistas, el/la agente que revisa los pasaportes, el/la agente de aduana
En el hotel	pedir una habitación y pedirle al botones que lleve las maletas a la habitación	uno o dos turistas, el/la recepcionista del hotel, el botones
En la calle	pedirles direcciones a algunas personas	uno o dos turistas, las personas del grupo

Paso 2. Cada miembro del grupo debe escoger un personaje y prepararse para la improvisación, haciendo apuntes sobre las posibles preguntas que necesitará hacer y contestar.

MODELO: agente de aduana → preguntarles si tienen algo que declarar; preguntarles si llevan plantas o productos orgánicos…

Paso 3. Improvisen la escena varias veces, modificándola si es necesario. Luego, presenten su improvisación a la clase.

MODELO: E1: Sus pasaportes, por favor. Gracias. ¿De dónde vienen?
E2: Venimos de los Estados Unidos.
E1: ¿Y por qué vienen a México?
E3: Estamos de vacaciones. Vamos a ir a la playa…

En resumen

GRAMÁTICA

To review the grammar point presented in this chapter, refer to the indicated grammar presentation. You'll find further practice of this structure in the Workbook/Laboratory Manual, on the CD-ROM, and on the website.

45. Conditional Verb Forms

Do you know how to form the conditional tense?
When is the conditional used in Spanish?

VOCABULARIO

Cosas y lugares en el extranjero

el batido	drink similar to a milkshake
el café	café
el champú	shampoo
una copa / un trago	(alcoholic) drink
el correo	mail
la oficina de correos	post office
la estación del metro	subway stop
el estanco	tobacco stand/shop
los fósforos	matches
el jabón	soap
el papel para cartas	stationery
la papelería	stationery store
el paquete	package
la parada del autobús	bus stop
la pasta dental	toothpaste
la pastelería	pastry shop
el pastelito	small pastry
el quiosco	kiosk
el sello	stamp
el sobre	envelope

Repaso: la farmacia, la revista, la tarjeta postal

Ir al extranjero

cruzar	to cross
declarar	to declare
registrar	to search, examine

Repaso: pagar, viajar

la aduana	customs
el cheque de viajero	traveler's check
los derechos (de aduana)	(customs) duty
el extranjero	abroad
el formulario	form (to fill out)
la frontera	border
la inmigración	immigration
el/la inspector(a) (de aduanas)	(customs) inspector
la multa	fine, penalty
el pasaporte	passport
el/la viajero/a	traveler

Repaso: las compras, la maleta, la nacionalidad

El alojamiento

alojarse	to stay (in a place)
confirmar	to confirm
el botones/mozo	bellhop
la criada	maid
la estancia	stay (in a hotel)
la habitación	room (in a hotel)
individual/doble	single/double
con/sin baño/ducha	with(out) bath/shower
el hotel (de lujo)	(luxury) hotel
el/la huésped(a)	(hotel) guest
la pensión	boardinghouse
pensión completa	room and full board
media pensión	room with breakfast and one other meal

la propina	tip (to an employee)	**completo/a**	full, no vacancy
las reservaciones /	reservations	**con anticipación**	ahead of time
las reservas		**desocupado/a**	vacant, unoccupied
recepción	front desk		

Repaso: quedarse

Glossary of Grammatical Terms

ADJECTIVE A word that describes a noun or pronoun.

una casa **grande**
*a **big** house*

Ella es **inteligente.**
*She is **smart.***

Demonstrative adjective An adjective that points out a particular noun.

este chico, **esos** libros, **aquellas** personas
***this** boy, **those** books, **those** people (over there)*

Interrogative adjective An adjective used to form questions.

¿Qué cuaderno?
***Which** notebook?*

¿Cuántos carteles buscas?
***How many** posters are you looking for?*

Possessive adjective (unstressed) An adjective that indicates possession or a special relationship.

sus coches
***their** cars*

mi hermana
***my** sister*

Possessive adjective (stressed) An adjective that more emphatically describes possession.

Es **una** amiga **mía.**
*She's **my** friend / She's a friend **of mine.***

Es **un** coche **suyo.**
*It's **her** car / It's a car **of hers.***

ADVERB A word that describes an adjective, a verb, or another adverb.

Él es **muy** alto.
*He is **very** tall.*

Ella escribe **bien.**
*She writes **well.***

Van **demasiado** rápido.
*They are going **too** quickly.*

ARTICLE A determiner that sets off a noun.

Definite article An article that indicates a specific noun.

el país
***the** country*

la silla
***the** chair*

las mujeres
***the** women*

Indefinite article An article that indicates an unspecified noun.

un chico
***a** boy*

una ciudad
***a** city*

unas zanahorias
***(some)** carrots*

CLAUSE   A construction that contains a subject and a verb.

Main (Independent) clause   A clause that can stand on its own because it expresses a complete thought.

Busco una muchacha.
I'm looking for a girl.

Si yo fuera rica, **me compraría una casa.**
If I were rich, **I would buy a house.**

Subordinate (Dependent) clause   A clause that cannot stand on its own because it does not express a complete thought.

Busco a la muchacha **que juega al tenis.**
I'm looking for the girl **who plays tennis.**

Si yo fuera rico, me compraría una casa.
If I were rich, *I would buy a house.*

COMPARATIVE   The form of adjectives and adverbs used to compare two nouns or actions.

Luis es **menos hablador** que Julián.
*Luis is **less talkative** than Julián.*

Él corre **más rápido** que Julián.
*He runs **faster** than Julián.*

CONJUGATION   The different forms of a verb for a particular tense or mood. This is a present indicative conjugation.

(yo) hablo	(nosotros/as) hablamos
(tú) hablas	(vosotros/as) habláis
(Ud., él/ella) habla	(Uds., ellos/as) hablan

I speak	*we speak*
you (fam. sing.) speak	*you (fam. pl.) speak*
you (form. sing.) speak	*you (pl. fam. & form.) speak*
he/she speaks	*they speak*

CONJUNCTION   An expression that connects words, phrases, or clauses.

Cristóbal **y** Diana
*Cristóbal **and** Diana*

Hace frío, **pero** hace buen tiempo.
*It's cold, **but** it's nice out.*

DIRECT OBJECT   The noun or pronoun that receives the action of a verb.

Veo **la caja.**
*I see **the box.***

La veo.
*I see **it.***

GENDER   A grammatical category of words. In Spanish there are two genders: masculine and feminine. Here are a few examples.

	MASCULINE	FEMININE
ARTICLES AND NOUNS:	**el** disco compacto	**la** cinta
PRONOUNS:	**él**	**ella**
ADJECTIVES:	bonit**o**, list**o**	bonit**a**, list**a**
PAST PARTICIPLES:	El informe está **escrito.**	La composición está **escrita.**

IMPERATIVE   *See* Mood.

IMPERFECT (*IMPERFECTO*)   In Spanish, a verb tense that expresses a past action with no specific beginning or ending.

Nadábamos con frecuencia.
*We **used to swim** often.*

IMPERSONAL CONSTRUCTION   One that contains a third-person singular verb but no specific subject in Spanish. The subject of English impersonal constructions is generally *it.*

Es importante que...
*It **is important** that . . .*

Es necesario que...
*It **is necessary** that . . .*

INDICATIVE   *See* Mood.

INDIRECT OBJECT   The noun or pronoun that indicates for whom or to whom an action is performed. In Spanish, the indirect object pronoun must always be included. The noun that the pronoun stands for may be included for emphasis or clarification.

Marcos **le** da el suéter a **Raquel**. / Marcos **le** da el suéter.
*Marcos gives the sweater **to Raquel**. / Marcos gives **her** the sweater.*

INFINITIVE   The form of a verb introduced in English by *to: to play, to sell, to come*. In Spanish dictionaries, the infinitive form of the verb appears as the main entry.

Luisa va a **comprar** un periódico.
*Luisa is going **to buy** a newspaper.*

MOOD   A set of categories for verbs indicating the attitude of the speaker towards what he or she is saying.

Imperative mood   A verb form expressing a command.

¡**Ten** cuidado!
Be careful!

Indicative mood   A verb form denoting actions or states considered facts.

Voy a la biblioteca.
*I **am going** to the library.*

Subjunctive mood   A verb form, uncommon in English, used primarily in subordinate clauses after expressions of desire, doubt, or emotion. Spanish constructions with the subjunctive have many possible English equivalents.

Quiero que **vayas** inmediatamente.
I want you to go immediately.

NOUN   A word that denotes a person, place, thing, or idea. Proper nouns are capitalized names.

abogado, ciudad, periódico, libertad, Luisa
lawyer, city, newspaper, freedom, Luisa

NUMBER

Cardinal number   A number that expresses an amount.

una silla, **tres** estudiantes
one chair, three students

Ordinal number   A number that indicates position in a series.

la **primera** silla, el **tercer** estudiante
*the **first** chair, the **third** student*

PAST PARTICIPLE   The form of a verb used in compound tenses (*see* Perfect Tenses). Used with forms of *to have* or *to be* in English and with **ser, estar,** or **haber** in Spanish.

comido, terminado, perdido
eaten, finished, lost

PERFECT TENSES   Compound tenses that combine the auxiliary verb **haber** with a past participle.

Present perfect indicative   This form uses a present indicative form of **haber.** The use of the Spanish present perfect generally parallels that of the English present perfect.

No **he viajado** nunca a México.
*I've never **traveled** to Mexico.*

Past perfect indicative   This form uses **haber** in the imperfect tense to talk about something that had or had not been done before a given time in the past.

Antes de 1997, **no había estudiado** español.
*Before 1997, **I hadn't studied** Spanish.*

Present perfect subjunctive   This form uses the present subjunctive of **haber** to express a present perfect action when the subjunctive is required.

¡Ojalá que Marisa **haya llegado** a su destino!
*I hope Marisa **has arrived** at her destination!*

PERSON   The form of a pronoun or verb that indicates the person involved in an action.

	SINGULAR	PLURAL
FIRST PERSON	*I* / yo	*we* / nosotros/as
SECOND PERSON	*you* / tú, Ud.	*you* / vosotros/as, Uds.
THIRD PERSON	*he, she* / él, ella	*they* / ellos, ellas

PREPOSITION   A word or phrase that specifies the relationship of one word (usually a noun or pronoun) to another. The relationship is usually spatial or temporal.

a la escuela
to school

cerca de la biblioteca
near the library

con él
with him

antes de la medianoche
before midnight

PRETERITE (*PRETÉRITO*)   In Spanish, a verb tense that expresses a past action with a specific beginning and ending.

Salí para Roma el jueves.
I left *for Rome on Thursday.*

PRONOUN   A word that refers to a person (*I, you*) or that is used in place of one or more nouns.

Demonstrative pronoun   A pronoun that singles out a particular person or thing.

Aquí están dos libros. **Este** es interesante, pero **ese** es aburrido.
*Here are two books. **This one** is interesting, but **that one** is boring.*

Interrogative pronoun   A pronoun used to ask a question.

¿Quién es él?
Who *is he?*

¿Qué prefieres?
What *do you prefer?*

Object pronoun   A pronoun that replaces a direct object noun or an indirect object noun. Both direct and indirect object pronouns can be used together in the same sentence. However, when the pronoun **le** is used with **lo** or **la,** it changes to **se.**

Veo a **Alejandro. Lo** veo.
*I see **Alejandro.** I see **him.***

Le doy el libro (**a Juana**).
*I give the book **to Juana.***

Se lo doy (**a ella**).
*I give **it** to **her.***

Reflexive pronoun   A pronoun that represents the same person as the subject of the verb.

Me miro en el espejo.
*I look at **myself** in the mirror.*

Relative pronoun   A pronoun that introduces a dependent clause and denotes a noun already mentioned.

El hombre con **quien** hablaba era mi vecino.
*The man with **whom** I was talking was my neighbor.*

Aquí está el bolígrafo **que** buscas.
*Here is the pen (**that**) you are looking for.*

Subject pronoun   A pronoun representing the person or thing performing the action of a verb.

Lucas y Julia juegan al tenis.
Lucas and Julia *are playing tennis.*

Ellos juegan al tenis.
They *are playing tennis.*

SUBJECT The word(s) denoting the person, place, or thing performing an action or existing in a state.	**Sara** trabaja aquí. *Sara works here.* ¡**Buenos Aires** es una ciudad magnífica! *Buenos Aires is a great city!* Mis **libros** y mi **computadora** están allí. *My **books** and my **computer** are over there.*
SUBJUNCTIVE *See* Mood.	
SUPERLATIVE The form of adjectives or adverbs used to compare three or more nouns or actions. In English, the superlative is marked by *most, least,* or *-est.*	Escogí el vestido **más caro.** *I chose **the most expensive** dress.* Ana es la persona **menos habladora** que conozco. *Ana is **the least talkative** person I know.*
TENSE The form of a verb indicating time: present, past, or future.	Raúl **era, es** y siempre **será** mi mejor amigo. *Raúl **was, is,** and always **will be** my best friend.*
VERB A word that reports an action or state.	Ella **llegó.** *She **arrived.*** Ella **estaba** cansada. *She **was** tired.*
Auxiliary verb A verb in conjunction with a participle to convey distinctions of tense and mood. In Spanish, this auxiliary verb is **haber.**	**Han** viajado por todas partes del mundo. *They **have** traveled everywhere in the world.*
Reflexive verb A verb whose subject and object are the same.	Él **se corta** la cara cuando **se afeita.** *He **cuts himself** when he **shaves (himself).***

APPENDIX 2

Using Adjectives as Nouns

Nominalization means using an adjective as a noun. In Spanish, adjectives can be nominalized in a number of ways, all of which involve dropping the noun that accompanies the adjective, then using the adjective in combination with an article or other word. One kind of adjective, the demonstrative, can simply be used alone. In most cases, these usages parallel those of English, although the English equivalent may be phrased differently from the Spanish.

Article + Adjective

Simply omit the noun from an *article + noun + adjective* phrase.

> el **libro** azul → **el azul** (*the blue one*)
> la **hermana** casada → **la casada** (*the married one*)

el **señor** mexicano → **el mexicano** (*the Mexican one*)
los **pantalones** baratos → **los baratos** (*the inexpensive ones*)

You can also drop the first noun in an *article + noun + **de** + noun* phrase.

> la **casa** de Julio → **la de Julio** (*Julio's*)
> los **coches** del Sr. Martínez → **los del Sr. Martínez** (*Mr. Martínez's*)

In both cases, the construction is used to refer to a noun that has already been mentioned. The English equivalent uses *one* or *ones,* or a possessive without the noun.

> —¿Necesitas el libro grande?
> —No. Necesito **el pequeño.**
> —*Do you need the big book?*
> —*No. I need the small one.*

—¿Usamos el coche de Ernesto?
—No. Usemos **el de Ana.**
—*Shall we use Ernesto's car?*
—*No. Let's use Ana's.*

Note that in the preceding examples the noun is mentioned in the first part of the exchange (**libro, coche**) but not in the response or rejoinder.

Note also that a demonstrative can be used to nominalize an adjective: **este rojo** (*this red one*), **esos azules** (*those blue ones*).

Lo + Adjective

As seen in **Capítulo 10, lo** combines with the masculine singular form of an adjective to describe general qualities or characteristics. The English equivalent is expressed with words like *part* or *thing.*

lo mejor   *the best thing* (*part*), *what's best*
lo mismo   *the same thing*
lo cómico *the funny thing* (*part*), *what's funny*

Article + Stressed Possessive Adjective

The stressed possessive adjectives—but not the unstressed possessives—can be used as possessive pronouns: **la maleta suya** → **la suya.** The article and the possessive form agree in gender and number with the noun to which they refer.

Este es mi **banco.** ¿Dónde está **el suyo**?
This is my bank. Where is yours?

Sus **bebidas** están preparadas; **las nuestras,** no.
Their drinks are ready; ours aren't.

No es la **maleta** de Juan; es **la mía.**
It isn't Juan's suitcase; it's mine.

Note that the definite article is frequently omitted after forms of **ser: ¿Esa maleta? Es suya.**

Demonstrative Pronouns

The demonstrative adjective can be used alone, without a noun. An accent mark can be added to the demonstrative pronoun to distinguish it from the demonstrative adjectives (**este, ese, aquel**).

Necesito este diccionario y **ese (ése).**
I need this dictionary and that one.

Estas señoras y **aquellas (aquéllas)** son las hermanas de Sara, ¿no?
These women and those (over there) are Sara's sisters, aren't they?

It is acceptable in modern Spanish, per the **Real Academia Española,** to omit the accent on demonstrative pronouns when context makes the meaning clear and no ambiguity is possible.

APPENDIX 3

Additional Perfect Forms (Indicative and Subjunctive)

Some indicative verb tenses have corresponding perfect forms in the indicative and subjunctive moods. Here is the present tense system.

el presente: yo hablo, como, pongo
el presente perfecto: yo he hablado, comido, puesto
el presente perfecto
  de subjuntivo: yo haya hablado, comido, puesto

Other indicative forms that you have learned also have corresponding perfect indicative and subjunctive forms. Here are the most important ones, along with examples of their use. In each case, the tense or mood is formed with the appropriate form of **haber.**

El pluscuamperfecto del subjuntivo

yo:	hubiera hablado, comido, vivido, *etc.*
tú:	hubieras hablado, comido, vivido, *etc.*
Ud./él/ella:	hubiera hablado, comido, vivido, *etc.*
nosotros:	hubiéramos hablado, comido, vivido, *etc.*
vosotros:	hubierais hablado, comido, vivido, *etc.*
Uds./ellos/ellas:	hubieran hablado, comido, vivido, *etc.*

These forms correspond to **el presente perfecto del indicativo** (**Capítulo 14**). They are most frequently used in **si** clause sentences, along with the conditional perfect. See examples below. (*Si* Clause).

El futuro perfecto

yo:	habré hablado, comido, vivido, *etc.*
tú:	habrás hablado, comido, vivido, *etc.*
Ud./él/ella:	habrá hablado, comido, vivido, *etc.*
nosotros:	habremos hablado, comido, vivido, *etc.*
vosotros:	habréis hablado, comido, vivido, *etc.*
Uds./ellos/ellas:	habrán hablado, comido, vivido, *etc.*

These forms correspond to **el futuro** (**Capítulo 16**) and are most frequently used to tell what *will have already happened* at some point in the future. (In contrast, the future is used to tell what *will happen*.)

Mañana **hablaré** con Miguel.
I'll speak with Miguel tomorrow.

Para las tres, ya **habré hablado** con Miguel.
By 3:00, I'll already have spoken to Miguel.

El año que viene **visitaremos** a los nietos.
We'll visit our grandchildren next year.

Para las Navidades, ya **habremos visitado** a los nietos.
We'll already have visited our grandchildren by Christmas.

El condicional perfecto

yo:	habría hablado, comido, vivido, *etc.*
tú:	habrías hablado, comido, vivido, *etc.*
Ud./él/ella:	habría hablado, comido, vivido, *etc.*
nosotros:	habríamos hablado, comido, vivido, *etc.*
vosotros:	habríais hablado, comido, vivido, *etc.*
Uds./ellos/ellas:	habrían hablado, comido, vivido, *etc.*

These forms correspond to **el condicional** (**Capítulo 18**). They are frequently used to tell what *would have happened* at some point in the past. (In contrast, the conditional tells what one *would do*.)

Yo **hablaría** con Miguel.
I would speak with Miguel (if I were you, at some point in the future).

Yo **habría hablado** con Miguel.
I would have spoken with Miguel (if I had been you, at some point in the past).

Si **Clause: Sentences About the Past**

You have learned (**Capítulo 18**) to use the past subjunctive and conditional to speculate about the present in **si** clause sentences: what *would happen* if a particular event *were* (or *were not*) to occur.

Si **tuviera** el tiempo, **aprendería** francés.
If I had the time, I would learn French (in the present or at some point in the future).

The perfect forms of the past subjunctive and the conditional are used to speculate about the past: what *would have happened* if a particular event *had* (or *had not*) occurred.

En la escuela superior, si **hubiera tenido** el tiempo, **habría aprendido** francés.
In high school, if I had had the time, I would have learned French.

APPENDIX 4

Verbs

A. Regular Verbs: Simple Tenses

Infinitive Present Participle Past Participle	INDICATIVE					SUBJUNCTIVE		IMPERATIVE
	Present	Imperfect	Preterite	Future	Conditional	Present	Imperfect	
hablar hablando hablado	hablo hablas habla hablamos habláis hablan	hablaba hablabas hablaba hablábamos hablabais hablaban	hablé hablaste habló hablamos hablasteis hablaron	hablaré hablarás hablará hablaremos hablaréis hablarán	hablaría hablarías hablaría hablaríamos hablaríais hablarían	hable hables hable hablemos habléis hablen	hablara hablaras hablara habláramos hablarais hablaran	habla tú, no hables hable Ud. hablemos hablen
comer comiendo comido	como comes come comemos coméis comen	comía comías comía comíamos comíais comían	comí comiste comió comimos comisteis comieron	comeré comerás comerá comeremos comeréis comerán	comería comerías comería comeríamos comeríais comerían	coma comas coma comamos comáis coman	comiera comieras comiera comiéramos comierais comieran	come tú, no comas coma Ud. comamos coman
vivir viviendo vivido	vivo vives vive vivimos vivís viven	vivía vivías vivía vivíamos vivíais vivían	viví viviste vivió vivimos vivisteis vivieron	viviré vivirás vivirá viviremos viviréis vivirán	viviría vivirías viviría viviríamos viviríais vivirían	viva vivas viva vivamos viváis vivan	viviera vivieras viviera viviéramos vivierais vivieran	vive tú, no vivas viva Ud. vivamos vivan

B. Regular Verbs: Perfect Tenses

INDICATIVE									
Present Perfect		Past Perfect		Preterite Perfect		Future Perfect		Conditional Perfect	
he has ha hemos habéis han	hablado comido vivido	había habías había habíamos habíais habían	hablado comido vivido	hube hubiste hubo hubimos hubisteis hubieron	hablado comido vivido	habré habrás habrá habremos habréis habrán	hablado comido vivido	habría habrías habría habríamos habríais habrían	hablado comido vivido

SUBJUNCTIVE			
Present Perfect		Past Perfect	
haya hayas haya hayamos hayáis hayan	hablado comido vivido	hubiera hubieras hubiera hubiéramos hubierais hubieran	hablado comido vivido

Infinitive Present Participle Past Participle	Present	Imperfect	Preterite	Future	Conditional	Present	Imperfect	IMPERATIVE
			INDICATIVE			SUBJUNCTIVE		
andar andando andado	ando andas anda andamos andáis andan	andaba andabas andaba andábamos andabais andaban	anduve anduviste anduvo anduvimos anduvisteis anduvieron	andaré andarás andará andaremos andaréis andarán	andaría andarías andaría andaríamos andaríais andarían	ande andes ande andemos andéis anden	anduviera anduvieras anduviera anduviéramos anduvierais anduvieran	anda tú, no andes ande Ud. andemos anden
caer cayendo caído	caigo caes cae caemos caéis caen	caía caías caía caíamos caíais caían	caí caíste cayó caímos caísteis cayeron	caeré caerás caerá caeremos caeréis caerán	caería caerías caería caeríamos caeríais caerían	caiga caigas caiga caigamos caigáis caigan	cayera cayeras cayera cayéramos cayerais cayeran	cae tú, no caigas caiga Ud. caigamos caigan
dar dando dado	doy das da damos dais dan	daba dabas daba dábamos dabais daban	di diste dio dimos disteis dieron	daré darás dará daremos daréis darán	daría darías daría daríamos daríais darían	dé des dé demos deis den	diera dieras diera diéramos dierais dieran	da tú, no des dé Ud. demos den
decir diciendo dicho	digo dices dice decimos decís dicen	decía decías decía decíamos decíais decían	dije dijiste dijo dijimos dijisteis dijeron	diré dirás dirá diremos diréis dirán	diría dirías diría diríamos diríais dirían	diga digas diga digamos digáis digan	dijera dijeras dijera dijéramos dijerais dijeran	di tú, no digas diga Ud. digamos digan
estar estando estado	estoy estás está estamos estáis están	estaba estabas estaba estábamos estabais estaban	estuve estuviste estuvo estuvimos estuvisteis estuvieron	estaré estarás estará estaremos estaréis estarán	estaría estarías estaría estaríamos estaríais estarían	esté estés esté estemos estéis estén	estuviera estuvieras estuviera estuviéramos estuvierais estuviera	está tú, no estés esté Ud. estemos estén
haber habiendo habido	he has ha hemos habéis han	había habías había habíamos habíais habían	hube hubiste hubo hubimos hubisteis hubieron	habré habrás habrá habremos habréis habrán	habría habrías habría habríamos habríais habrían	haya hayas haya hayamos hayáis hayan	hubiera hubieras hubiera hubiéramos hubierais hubieran	
hacer haciendo hecho	hago haces hace hacemos hacéis hacen	hacía hacías hacía hacíamos hacíais hacían	hice hiciste hizo hicimos hicisteis hicieron	haré harás hará haremos haréis harán	haría harías haría haríamos haríais harían	haga hagas haga hagamos hagáis hagan	hiciera hicieras hiciera hiciéramos hicierais hicieran	haz tú, no hagas haga Ud. hagamos hagan

C. Irregular Verbs (continued)

Infinitive Present Participle Past Participle	INDICATIVE Present	Imperfect	Preterite	Future	Conditional	SUBJUNCTIVE Present	Imperfect	IMPERATIVE
ir yendo ido	voy vas va vamos vais van	iba ibas iba íbamos ibais iban	fui fuiste fue fuimos fuisteis fueron	iré irás irá iremos iréis irán	iría irías iría iríamos iríais irían	vaya vayas vaya vayamos vayáis vayan	fuera fueras fuera fuéramos fuerais fueran	ve tú, no vayas vaya Ud. vayamos vayan
oír oyendo oído	oigo oyes oye oímos oís oyen	oía oías oía oíamos oíais oían	oí oíste oyó oímos oísteis oyeron	oiré oirás oirá oiremos oiréis oirán	oiría oirías oiría oiríamos oiríais oirían	oiga oigas oiga oigamos oigáis oigan	oyera oyeras oyera oyéramos oyerais oyeran	oye tú, no oigas oiga Ud. oigamos oigan
poder pudiendo podido	puedo puedes puede podemos podéis pueden	podía podías podía podíamos podíais podían	pude pudiste pudo pudimos pudisteis pudieron	podré podrás podrá podremos podréis podrán	podría podrías podría podríamos podríais podrían	pueda puedas pueda podamos podáis puedan	pudiera pudieras pudiera pudiéramos pudierais pudieran	
poner poniendo puesto	pongo pones pone ponemos ponéis ponen	ponía ponías ponía poníamos poníais ponían	puse pusiste puso pusimos pusisteis pusieron	pondré pondrás pondrá pondremos pondréis pondrán	pondría pondrías pondría pondríamos pondríais pondrían	ponga pongas ponga pongamos pongáis pongan	pusiera pusieras pusiera pusiéramos pusierais pusieran	pon tú, no pongas ponga Ud. pongamos pongan
querer queriendo querido	quiero quieres quiere queremos queréis quieren	quería querías quería queríamos queríais querían	quise quisiste quiso quisimos quisisteis quisieron	querré querrás querrá querremos querréis querrán	querría querrías querría querríamos querríais querrían	quiera quieras quiera queramos queráis quieran	quisiera quisieras quisiera quisiéramos quisierais quisieran	quiere tú, no quieras quiera Ud. queramos quieran
saber sabiendo sabido	sé sabes sabe sabemos sabéis saben	sabía sabías sabía sabíamos sabíais sabían	supe supiste supo supimos supisteis supieron	sabré sabrás sabrá sabremos sabréis sabrán	sabría sabrías sabría sabríamos sabríais sabrían	sepa sepas sepa sepamos sepáis sepan	supiera supieras supiera supiéramos supierais supieran	sabe tú, no sepas sepa Ud. sepamos sepan
salir saliendo salido	salgo sales sale salimos salís salen	salía salías salía salíamos salíais salían	salí saliste salió salimos salisteis salieron	saldré saldrás saldrá saldremos saldréis saldrán	saldría saldrías saldría saldríamos saldríais saldrían	salga salgas salga salgamos salgáis salgan	saliera salieras saliera saliéramos salierais salieran	sal tú, no salgas salga Ud. salgamos salgan
ser siendo sido	soy eres es somos sois son	era eras era éramos erais eran	fui fuiste fue fuimos fuisteis fueron	seré serás será seremos seréis serán	sería serías sería seríamos seríais serían	sea seas sea seamos seáis sean	fuera fueras fuera fuéramos fuerais fueran	sé tú, no seas sea Ud. seamos sean

C. Irregular Verbs (continued)

Infinitive / Present Participle / Past Participle	INDICATIVE					SUBJUNCTIVE		IMPERATIVE
	Present	Imperfect	Preterite	Future	Conditional	Present	Imperfect	
tener teniendo tenido	tengo tienes tiene tenemos tenéis tienen	tenía tenías tenía teníamos teníais tenían	tuve tuviste tuvo tuvimos tuvisteis tuvieron	tendré tendrás tendrá tendremos tendréis tendrán	tendría tendrías tendría tendríamos tendríais tendrían	tenga tengas tenga tengamos tengáis tengan	tuviera tuvieras tuviera tuviéramos tuvierais tuvieran	ten tú, no tengas tenga Ud. tengamos tengan
traer trayendo traído	traigo traes trae traemos traéis traen	traía traías traía traíamos traíais traían	traje trajiste trajo trajimos trajisteis trajeron	traeré traerás traerá traeremos traeréis traerán	traería traerías traería traeríamos traeríais traerían	traiga traigas traiga traigamos traigáis traigan	trajera trajeras trajera trajéramos trajerais trajeran	trae tú, no traigas traiga Ud. traigamos traigan
venir viniendo venido	vengo vienes viene venimos venís vienen	venía venías venía veníamos veníais venían	vine viniste vino vinimos vinisteis vinieron	vendré vendrás vendrá vendremos vendréis vendrán	vendría vendrías vendría vendríamos vendríais vendrían	venga vengas venga vengamos vengáis vengan	viniera vinieras viniera viniéramos vinierais vinieran	ven tú, no vengas venga Ud. vengamos vengan
ver viendo visto	veo ves ve vemos veis ven	veía veías veía veíamos veíais veían	vi viste vio vimos visteis vieron	veré verás verá veremos veréis verán	vería verías vería veríamos veríais verían	vea veas vea veamos veáis vean	viera vieras viera viéramos vierais vieran	ve tú, no veas vea Ud. veamos vean

D. Stem-Changing and Spelling Change Verbs

Infinitive / Present Participle / Past Participle	INDICATIVE					SUBJUNCTIVE		IMPERATIVE
	Present	Imperfect	Preterite	Future	Conditional	Present	Imperfect	
pensar (ie) pensando pensado	pienso piensas piensa pensamos pensáis piensan	pensaba pensabas pensaba pensábamos pensabais pensaban	pensé pensaste pensó pensamos pensasteis pensaron	pensaré pensarás pensará pensaremos pensaréis pensarán	pensaría pensarías pensaría pensaríamos pensaríais pensarían	piense pienses piense pensemos penséis piensen	pensara pensaras pensara pensáramos pensarais pensaran	piensa tú, no pienses piense Ud. pensemos piensen
volver (ue) volviendo vuelto	vuelvo vuelves vuelve volvemos volvéis vuelven	volvía volvías volvía volvíamos volvíais volvían	volví volviste volvió volvimos volvisteis volvieron	volveré volverás volverá volveremos volveréis volverán	volvería volverías volvería volveríamos volveríais volverían	vuelva vuelvas vuelva volvamos volváis vuelvan	volviera volvieras volviera volviéramos volvierais volvieran	vuelve tú, no vuelvas vuelva Ud. volvamos vuelvan

D. Stem-Changing and Spelling Change Verbs (continued)

Infinitive Present Participle Past Participle	INDICATIVE Present	Imperfect	Preterite	Future	Conditional	SUBJUNCTIVE Present	Imperfect	IMPERATIVE
dormir (ue, u) durmiendo dormido	duermo duermes duerme dormimos dormís duermen	dormía dormías dormía dormíamos dormíais dormían	dormí dormiste durmió dormimos dormisteis durmieron	dormiré dormirás dormirá dormiremos dormiréis dormirán	dormiría dormirías dormiría dormiríamos dormiríais dormirían	duerma duermas duerma durmamos durmáis duerman	durmiera durmieras durmiera durmiéramos durmierais durmieran	duerme tú, no duermas duerma Ud. durmamos duerman
sentir (ie, i) sintiendo sentido	siento sientes siente sentimos sentís sienten	sentía sentías sentía sentíamos sentíais sentían	sentí sentiste sintió sentimos sentisteis sintieron	sentiré sentirás sentirá sentiremos sentiréis sentirán	sentiría sentirías sentiría sentiríamos sentiríais sentirían	sienta sientas sienta sintamos sintáis sientan	sintiera sintieras sintiera sintiéramos sintierais sintieran	siente tú, no sientas sienta Ud. sintamos sientan
pedir (i, i) pidiendo pedido	pido pides pide pedimos pedís piden	pedía pedías pedía pedíamos pedíais pedían	pedí pediste pidió pedimos pedisteis pidieron	pediré pedirás pedirá pediremos pediréis pedirán	pediría pedirías pediría pediríamos pediríais pedirían	pida pidas pida pidamos pidáis pidan	pidiera pidieras pidiera pidiéramos pidierais pidieran	pide tú, no pidas pida Ud. pidamos pidan
reír (i, i) riendo reído	río ríes ríe reímos reís ríen	reía reías reía reíamos reíais reían	reí reíste rió reímos reísteis rieron	reiré reirás reirá reiremos reiréis reirán	reiría reirías reiría reiríamos reiríais reirían	ría rías ría riamos riáis rían	riera rieras riera riéramos rierais rieran	ríe tú, no rías ría Ud. riamos rían
seguir (i, i) (g) siguiendo seguido	sigo sigues sigue seguimos seguís siguen	seguía seguías seguía seguíamos seguíais seguían	seguí seguiste siguió seguimos seguisteis siguieron	seguiré seguirás seguirá seguiremos seguiréis seguirán	seguiría seguirías seguiría seguiríamos seguiríais seguirían	siga sigas siga sigamos sigáis sigan	siguiera siguieras siguiera siguiéramos siguierais siguieran	sigue tú, no sigas siga Ud. sigamos sigan
construir (y) construyendo construido	construyo construyes construye construimos construís construyen	construía construías construía construíamos construíais construían	construí construiste construyó construimos construisteis construyeron	construiré construirás construirá construiremos construiréis construirán	construiría construirías construiría construiríamos construiríais construirían	construya construyas construya construyamos construyáis construyan	construyera construyeras construyera construyéramos construyerais construyeran	construye tú, no construyas construya Ud. construyamos construyan
producir (zc) produciendo producido	produzco produces produce producimos producís producen	producía producías producía producíamos producíais producían	produje produjiste produjo produjimos produjisteis produjeron	produciré producirás producirá produciremos produciréis producirán	produciría producirías produciría produciríamos produciríais producirían	produzca produzcas produzca produzcamos produzcáis produzcan	produjera produjeras produjera produjéramos produjerais produjeran	produce tú, no produzcas produzca Ud. produzcamos produzcan

This **Spanish-English Vocabulary** contains all the words that appear in the text, with the following exceptions: (1) most close or identical cognates that do not appear in the chapter vocabulary lists; (2) most conjugated verb forms; (3) diminutives ending in **-ito/a**; (4) absolute superlatives in **-ísimo/a**; and (5) most adverbs ending in **-mente**. Active vocabulary is indicated by the number of the chapter in which a word or given meaning is first listed (P–Preliminar); vocabulary that is glossed in the text is not considered to be active vocabulary and is not numbered. Only meanings that are used in the text are given. The **English-Spanish Vocabulary** is based on the chapter lists of active vocabulary.

The gender of nouns is indicated, except for masculine nouns ending in **-o** and feminine nouns ending in **-a**. Stem changes and spelling changes are indicated for verbs: **dormir (ue, u)**; **llegar (gu)**. Because **ch** and **ll** are no longer considered separate letters, words beginning with **ch** and **ll** are found as they would be found in English. The letter **ñ** follows the letter **n: añadir** follows **anuncio**, for example. The following abbreviations are used:

abbrev.	abbreviation	*inf.*	infinitive	*pl.*	plural
adj.	adjective	*interj.*	interjection	*poss.*	possessive
adv.	adverb	*inv.*	invariable	*p.p.*	past participle
coll.	colloquialism	*i.o.*	indirect object	*P.R.*	Puerto Rico
conj.	conjunction	*irreg.*	irregular	*prep.*	preposition
d.o.	direct object	*L.A.*	Latin America	*pron.*	pronoun
f.	feminine	*m.*	masculine	*refl. pron.*	reflexive pronoun
fam.	familiar	*Mex.*	Mexico	*s.*	singular
fig.	figurative	*n.*	noun	*sl.*	slang
form.	formal	*obj. of a prep.*	object of a preposition	*Sp.*	Spain
gram.	grammatical term	*pers.*	personal	*sub. pron.*	subject pronoun

Spanish-English Vocabulary

A

a to (P); at (*with time*) (P); **a base de** by, based on; **a bordo de** on board; **a consecuencia de** as a result of; **a continuación** following, below; **a diferencia de** unlike; **a esas horas** at that hour; **a finales de** at the end of; **a la(s)...** at (*time*) (P); **a la derecha (de)** to the right (of) (5); **a la izquierda (de)** to the left (of) (5); **a la vez** at the same time; **a menos que** *conj.* unless (15); **a menudo** often; **a partir de** starting from; **a pesar de** in spite of; **a pla-** zos in installments (16); **a primera vista** at first sight (15); **a principios de** at the beginning of; **a punto de** just about to; **¿a qué hora... ?** (at) what time . . . ? (P); **a solas** alone; **a su gusto** to taste (*cooking*); **a tiempo** on time (7); **a través de** through; throughout; across; **a veces** sometimes (2); **a ver** let's see

a. C. (*abbrev. for* **antes de Cristo**) B.C. (*Before Christ*)

abajo below, underneath

abalanzarse (c) sobre to pounce on

abandonar to abandon; to leave

abandono abandonment

abierto/a *p.p.* open(ed) (5)

abogado/a lawyer (16)

abrazar (c) to embrace, hug

abrigo coat (3)

abril *m.* April (5)

abrir (*p.p.* **abierto**) to open (2)

absoluto/a absolute

absorbente absorbing

abstracto/a abstract

abuelo/a grandfather/grandmother (2); **abuelos** *m., pl.* grandparents (2)

abundancia abundance

aburrido/a bored (5); boring

aburrimiento boredom

aburrir to bore (13); **aburrirse** to get bored (9)

acabar to finish (11); to run out, use up completely (14); **acabarse** to run out of (11); **acabar de** + *inf.* to have just (*done something*) (6)

academia: Real Academia Española Royal Spanish Academy

académico/a *adj.* academic

acaso: por si acaso just in case (11)

acceso access

accidente *m.* accident (11)

acción *f.* action; **Día** (*m.*) **de Acción de Gracias** Thanksgiving

aceite *m.* oil (14); **aceite de oliva** olive oil; **filtro de aceite** oil filter

aceituna olive

acelerado/a fast, accelerated (14)

acelerar to accelerate, speed up

acento accent

aceptable acceptable

aceptar to accept

acerca de *prep.* about, concerning

aclarar to clarify

acomodarse (a) to adapt oneself (to)

acompañar to go with; to accompany

acondicionado/a: aire (*m.*) **acondicionado** air conditioning

aconsejable advisable

aconsejar to advise

acontecimiento event, happening (17)

acordarse (ue) (de) to remember (11)

acordeón *m.* accordion

acostar (ue) to put to bed; **acostarse** to go to bed (4)

acostumbrado/a (a) accustomed (to), used (to)

acostumbrar to be accustomed to

acreedor: hacerse (*irreg.*) **acreedor(a)** to be deemed worthy of

acrílico/a acrylic

actitud *f.* attitude

activar to activate

actividad *f.* activity

activo/a active

acto act

actor *m.* actor (13)

actriz *f.* (*pl.* **actrices**) actor, actress (13)

actual *adj.* current, up to date

actualidad *f.* present time

actualmente currently

actuar (actúo) to act

acuario/a Aquarius (*zodiac sign*)

acuático/a *adj.* water

acuerdo agreement; **acuerdo de paz** peace agreement; **de acuerdo** agreed, O.K..; **de acuerdo con** in accordance with; **(no) estoy de acuerdo** I (don't) agree (2); **ponerse** (*irreg.*) **de acuerdo** to reach an agreement

adaptación *f.* adaptation

adaptarse (a) to adapt (to)

adecuado/a appropriate

¡adelante! come in!

adelanto advance

adelgazar (c) to lose weight

además *adv.* moreover; **además de** *prep.* besides

adicional additional (P)

adiós good-bye (P)

adivinar to guess

adjetivo adjective (2); **adjetivo demostrativo** *gram.* demonstrative adjective; **adjetivo posesivo** *gram.* possessive adjective (2)

adjuntar to enclose, attach

administración *f.* administration; **administración de empresas** business administration (1); **administración de negocios** business administration

administrativo/a administrative

admirar to admire

adolescencia adolescence (15)

¿adónde? where (to)? (3)

adopción *f.* adoption

adoquinado/a *adj.* cobblestone

adorado/a adored

adorno ornament, decoration

aduana *s.* customs (18); **agente** (*m., f.*) **de aduana** customs agent; **derechos** (*m. pl.*) **de aduana** customs duty (18); **inspector(a) de aduanas** customs inspector (18)

adulto/a *n., adj.* adult

adverbio adverb

aéreo/a *adj.* air; **correo aéreo** airmail; **por vía aérea** by air; by airmail

aeróbico/a aerobic; **hacer** (*irreg.*) **ejercicios aeróbicos** to do aerobics (10)

aerolínea airline

aeropuerto airport (7)

afectar to affect

afectivo/a emotional

afectuoso/a affectionate

afeitarse to shave (4)

afición *f.* hobby (9)

aficionado/a (a) fan (of) (9); **ser** (*irreg.*) **aficionado/a (a)** to be a fan (of) (9)

afirmación *f.* statement

afirmar to affirm

afirmativo/a affirmative

África Africa

africano/a *adj.* African

afrocaribeño/a *adj.* Afro-Caribbean

afrocubano/a *adj.* Afro-Cuban

afuera *adv.* outside; outdoors (5); **afueras** *n. pl.* outskirts (12); suburbs (12)

agencia agency; **agencia de viajes** travel agency (7)

agenda agenda; date book

agente *m., f.* agent; **agente de aduana** customs agent; **agente de billetes** ticket agent; **agente de inmobiliaria** real estate agent; **agente de pasaportes** passport agent; **agente de viajes** travel agent (7)

agosto August (5)

agradable pleasant

agradar to please (13)

agravar to worsen

agresivo/a aggressive

agrícola *m., f.* agricultural; **trabajador(a) agrícola** agricultural worker

agricultor(a) farmer (14)

agua *f.* (*but* **el agua**) water; **agua mineral** mineral water (6); **cama de agua** water bed (4)

aguacate *m.* avocado

aguar (gü) to spoil (*a party*)

agujero hole

ahí there

ahora now (1); **ahora mismo** right now; at once

ahorrar to save (*money*) (16)

ahorros *m. pl.* savings; **cuenta de ahorros** savings account (16)

aimará *m.* Aymara (*indigenous language*)

aire *m.* aire (14); **aire acondicionado** air conditioning; **al aire libre** outdoors

aislamiento isolation (14)

ajedrez *m.* chess (4); **jugar (ue) (gu) al ajedrez** to play chess (9)

ajo garlic; **diente** (*m.*) **de ajo** garlic clove

al (*contraction of* **al** + **el**) to the (3); **al** + *inf.* upon, while, when + *verb form*; **al aire libre** outdoors; **al borde de** on the verge of; **al contado** in cash (16); **al final de** at the end of; **al fondo** in the background; **al lado de** next to (5); **al otro lado** on the other side; **al principio (de)** at the beginning (of) (16)

alabarse to congratulate oneself

álbum *m.* album

alcance *m.* reach

alcanzar (c) to reach

alce *m.* elk, moose

alcoba bedroom (4)

alcohol *m.* alcohol

alcohólico/a alcoholic

alegrarse (de) to be happy (about) (12)

alegre happy (5)

alegría happiness

alemán *m.* German (*language*) (1)

alemán, alemana *n., adj.* German (2); **pastor alemán** German shepherd (*dog*)

Alemania Germany

alergia allergy

alérgico/a allergic

alerta: ojo alerta be alert, watch out

alfabetización *f.* literacy

alfabetizado/a alphabetized

alfabeto alphabet

alfombra rug (4)

algo something (3)

algodón *m.* cotton (3); **es de algodón** it's made of cotton (3)

alguien someone, anyone (6)

algún, alguno(s)/a(s) some, any (6); **algún día** some day; **alguna vez** once; ever

alimento food

aliviar to relieve

alivio relief

allá over there; **más allá** beyond

allí (over) there (3)

alma *f.* (*but* **el alma**) soul

almacén *m.* department store (3)

almorzar (ue) (c) to have lunch (4)

almuerzo lunch (6)

alojamiento lodging (18)

alojarse to stay (*as a guest*) (18)

alquilar to rent (12)

alquiler *m.* rent (12)

alrededor de *prep.* around; **alrededores** *m. pl.* outskirts, environs

alternarse to alternate

alternativa alternative; choice

altitud *f.* altitude

alto/a tall (2); high

altura height, altitude

aluminio aluminum

amable kind, nice (2)

amado/a *adj.* beloved

amante *adj.* loving

amar to love (15)

amarillo/a yellow (3)

Amazonas *m. s.* Amazon (*river*)

ambiental environmental

ambiente *m.* environment, atmosphere; **medio ambiente** environment (14)

ámbito de lectores readership

amenazador(a) threatening

América America

americano/a *adj.* American; **fútbol** (*m.*) **americano** football (9)

amigo/a friend (1)

amistad *f.* friendship (15)

amistoso/a friendly (15)

amor *m.* love (15)

amueblado furnished; **semi-amueblado/a** partly furnished

analfabetismo illiteracy

análisis *m. s., pl.* analysis

analista (*m., f.*) **de sistemas** systems analyst (16)

analizar (c) to analyze

anaranjado/a *adj.* orange (*color*) (3)

ancho/a wide; **de ancho** in width

anciano/a *n.* old person; *adj.* old

andar (*irreg.*) **en bicicleta** to ride a bicycle

andino/a *adj.* Andean

anémico/a anemic

anfitrión, anfitriona host, hostess (8)

ángel *m.* angel

anglohablante *m., f.* English speaker

animado/a lively; **dibujo animado** (film) cartoon

animarse to cheer up

ánimo: dar (*irreg.*) **ánimo** to cheer, encourage; **estado de ánimo** state of mind

anoche *adv.* last night

anotar to make a note of

ansiedad *f.* anxiety

ante before; **ante todo** first of all

anteayer the day before yesterday

antecedente *m. gram.* antecedent

antemano: de antemano beforehand

anterior previous, preceding

antes *adv.* before; **antes de** *prep.* before (4); **antes de Cristo** Before Christ (B.C.); **antes (de) que** *conj.* before (15)

antibiótico antibiotic (10)

anticipación *f.* anticipation; **con anticipación** ahead of time (18)

anticuado/a antiquated, old-fashioned

antiguo/a old, ancient

antipático/a unpleasant (2)

antónimo antonym

antropología anthropology

anualmente yearly, annually

anunciar to announce (7)

anuncio advertisement; announcement

añadir   to add

año   year (5); **cumplir años**   to have a birthday (8); **Día** (*m.*) **de Año Nuevo**   New Year's Day; **el año pasado**   last year; **Feliz Año Nuevo**   Happy New Year; **Prospero Año Nuevo**   Happy New Year; **tener** (*irreg.*) **... años**   to be . . . years old (2)

apagar (gu)   to turn off (*light*)

aparato   appliance (9); **aparato doméstico**   home appliance (9); **aparato electrónico**   electronic device

aparcamiento   parking

aparcar (qu)   to park

aparecer (zc)   to appear

aparentemente   apparently

apariencia   appearance

apartamento   apartment (1); **casa (bloque** [*m.*]**) de apartamentos**   apartment building (12)

aparte   *adv.* apart; **aparte de**   aside from

apasionado/a   passionate

apellido   last name, surname

apenas   hardly any; barely

apendicitis   *f. s.* appendicitis

aperitivo   appetizer; aperitif

apiñado/a   crammed or packed together

aplazado/a   postponed

aplicar (qu)   to apply

apoyar   to support (17)

apoyo   support; **fondos** (*m. pl.*) **de apoyo**   economic support

apreciar   to appreciate (13)

aprecio: hacer (*irreg.*) **aprecio de**   to appreciate

aprender   to learn (2)

apropiado/a   appropriate

aprovechar   to make use of, take advantage of

aproximadamente   approximately

apuntar   to write down

apunte   *m.* note; **tomar apuntes**   to take notes

apurarse   to hurry

aquel, aquella   *adj., pron.* that (*over there*) (3)

aquél, aquélla   *pron.* that one (*over there*)

aquello   that (*thing*) (*over there*) (3)

aquellos/as   *adj.* those (*over there*) (3)

aquéllos/as   *pron.* those (ones) (*over there*)

aquí   here (1)

árabe   *m.* Arabic (*language*); **árabe** *m., f. n.* Arab; *m., f. adj.* Arabic

Arabia Saudita   Saudi Arabia

árbol   *m.* tree (14)

archivo   (computer) file (12)

ardilla   squirrel

área   *f.* (*but* **el área**)   area (12)

arena   sand

arete   *m.* earring (3)

argentino/a   *n., adj.* Argentinian

argumento   reasoning; argument

árido/a   arid, dry

armado/a   armed

armario   closet (4)

arqueológico/a   archeological

arqueólogo/a   archeologist

arquitecto/a   architect (13)

arquitectónico/a   architectural

arquitectura   architecture (13)

arrancar (qu)   to start (*a motor*) (14)

arreglar   to straighten (up) (12); to fix, repair (12)

arrogante   arrogant

arrollador(a)   overwhelming

arroz   *m.* rice (6)

arruinado/a   ruined

arte   *f.* (*but* **el arte**)   art (1); **obra de arte**   work of art (13)

artesanía   arts and crafts (13)

artesano/a   artisan, craftsperson

artículo   article; **artículo definido** *gram.* definite article

artificial   artificial; **fuegos** (*m. pl.*) **artificiales**   fireworks

artista   *m., f.* artist (13)

artístico/a   artistic (13)

arveja   pea (6)

arzobispo   archbishop

asado/a   roast(ed) (6)

ascensor   *m.* elevator

asco: dar (*irreg.*) **asco**   to make sick

asegurar   to assure; **asegurarse**   to make sure

asequible   available

asesinado/a   assassinated

asesinato   assassination (17)

así   thus, so; **así como**   as well as; like; **así que**   therefore, consequently

asiático/a   *adj.* Asian

asiento   seat (7)

asimilarse   to assimilate

asistente   *m., f.* assistant; **asistente de vuelo**   flight attendant (7)

asistir (a)   to attend, go to (*a function*) (2)

asma   *f.* (*but* **el asma**)   asthma

asociación   *f.* association

asociado/a   associated; **estado libre asociado**   free associated state

asociar   to associate

aspecto   appearance; aspect

aspiradora   vacuum cleaner (9); **pasar la aspiradora**   to vacuum (9)

aspirante   *m., f.* candidate (16); applicant (16)

aspirina   aspirin

astronauta   *m., f.* astronaut

asumir   to assume

asunto   matter, question

atacar (qu)   to attack

ataque   *m.* attack

atar   to tie

atención   *f.* attention

atender (ie)   to attend to; to serve

atlántico: **Océano Atlántico**   Atlantic Ocean

atleta   *m., f.* athlete

atracción   *f.* attraction; **parque** (*m.*) **de atracciones**   amusement park

atractivo/a   attractive

atraer (*like* **traer**)   to attract

atrasado/a: estar (*irreg.*) **atrasado**   to be late (7)

atrevido/a   daring

atribuir (y) (a)   to attribute (to)

atún   *m.* tuna (6)

audición (*f.*) **de reparto**   casting call

aumentar   to increase, raise

aumento   increase; raise (12); **aumento de sueldo**   raise (16)

aun   *adv.* even

aún   *adv.* still, yet

aunque although
auscultar to listen (*medical*)
australiano/a *adj.* Australian
auténtico/a authentic
auto car
autobiografía autobiography
autobiográfico/a autobiographical
autobús *m.* bus (7); **estación** (*f.*) **de autobuses** bus station (7); **ir** (*irreg.*) **en autobús** to go by bus; **parada de autobús** bus stop (18)
autocontrol *m.* self-control
autoestima self-esteem
automático/a: cajero automático automatic teller machine (16); **contestador** (*m.*) **automático** answering machine (12)
automóvil *m.* automobile
automovilístico/a *adj.* automobile
autopista freeway; highway (14)
autor(a) author
autoridad *f.* authority
autostop: hacer (*irreg.*) **autostop** to hitchhike
avance *m.* advance
avanzado/a advanced
ave *m.* bird
avenida avenue (12)
aventura adventure
aventurero/a adventurous
avergonzado/a embarrassed (8)
averiguar (gü) to find out
avestruz *m.* (*pl.* **avestruces**) ostrich
avión *m.* airplane (7); **ir** (*irreg.*) **en avión** to go by plane
avisar to warn
aviso warning
ayer yesterday; **ayer fue (miércoles)** yesterday was (Wednesday) (4)
ayuda help
ayudar to help (6)
azteca *m., f. n., adj.* Aztec
azúcar *m.* sugar
azul blue (3)

B

bacán: ¡qué bacán! *sl.* cool!
bailable danceable
bailar to dance (1)

bailarín, bailarina dancer (13)
baile *m.* dance (13)
bajar to carry down; **bajar (de)** to get down (from) (7); to get off (of) (7)
bajo *prep.* under; **bajo/a** *adj.* short (*height*) (2); low; **planta baja** ground floor (12)
balancear to balance
balboa *unit of currency of Panama*
ballet *m.* ballet (13)
banana banana (6)
bancarrota bankruptcy
banco bank (16)
bandoneón *m.* large concertina (*music*)
bañar to bathe; **bañarse** to take a bath (4)
bañera bathtub (4)
baño bathroom (4); **habitación** (*f.*) **con/sin baño** room with(out) bath (18); **traje** (*m.*) **de baño** swimsuit (3)
bar *m.* bar; **ir** (*irreg.*) **a un bar** to go to a bar (9)
barato/a inexpensive, cheap (3)
barbacoa barbecue
barbería barbershop
barbero barber
barcaza barge, ship
barco boat, ship (7); **ir** (*irreg.*) **en barco** to go by boat
barrer (el piso) to sweep (the floor) (9)
barrera barrier
barrio neighborhood (12); **fiesta de barrio** neighborhood (block) party
basado/a en based on
base *f.* base, foundation; **a base de** by, based on
basquetbol *m.* basketball (9)
bastante *adv.* rather, sufficiently (15); enough (15)
basura trash; **sacar (qu) la basura** to take out the trash (9)
bata robe, bathrobe
batalla battle
batería battery (14)
batido *drink similar to a milkshake* (18)

bautismo baptism
bebé *m.* baby
beber to drink (2)
bebida drink, beverage (6)
béisbol *m.* baseball (9)
beisbolista *m., f.* baseball player
Bélgica Belgium
Belice *m.* Belize
belleza beauty
bello/a beautiful (14)
berenjena eggplant
biblioteca library (1)
bibliotecario/a librarian (1)
bicicleta (de montaña) (mountain) bicycle (12); **montar/andar** (*irreg.*) **en bicicleta** to ride a bicycle; **pasear en bicicleta** to ride a bicycle (9)
biculturalismo biculturalism
bien *adv.* well (P); **caerle** (*irreg.*) **bien a alguien** to make a good impression on someone (16); **estar** (*irreg.*) **bien** to be comfortable (*temperature*) (5); **llevarse bien (con)** to get along well (with) (15); **muy bien** very well, fine (P); **pasarlo bien** to have a good time (8); **salir** (*irreg.*) **bien** to turn out well
bienestar *m.* well-being (10)
bilingüe bilingual
bilingüismo bilingualism
billete *m.* ticket (7); **agente** (*m., f.*) **de billetes** ticket agent; **billete de ida** one-way ticket (7); **billete de ida y vuelta** round-trip ticket (7)
billón trillion
biodiversidad *f.* biodiversity
biología biology
biólogo/a biologist
bisonte *m.* bison
bistec *m.* steak (6)
blanco/a white (3); **vino blanco** white wine (6)
bloque (*m.*) **de apartamentos** apartment building (12)
blusa blouse (3)
bobo/a dumb, stupid
boca mouth (10)
boda wedding (15)
boicoteo boycott, boycotting

boleto ticket (7); **boleto de ida** one-way ticket (7); **boleto de ida y vuelta** round-trip ticket (7)

bolígrafo ballpoint pen (1)

bolívar *m. monetary unit of Venezuela*

boliviano/a *adj.* Bolivian

bolsa purse (3)

bolsillo pocket

bomba light bulb; **la bomba y la plena** *dance and music from the Caribbean*

bombardeo bombardment

bombero/a firefighter

bondadoso/a kind; good-hearted

bonito/a pretty (2)

borde (*m.*)**: al borde de** on the verge of

bordo: a bordo de on board

boricua *m., f. n.* Puerto Rican (*from the indigenous language of Puerto Rico*)

Borinquen *f. indigenous name for Puerto Rico*

bosque *m.* forest (14)

bota boot (3)

botella bottle

botones *m. s., pl.* bellhop (18)

brasileño/a *adj.* Brazilian

bravo/a brave; fierce

bravura bravery; fierceness

brazo arm (11)

breve *adj.* brief

brindar to offer (*a toast*)

bronce *m.* bronze

bronceado/a tanned

bronquitis *f.* bronchitis

bruja witch

brujo magician

bucanero/a buccaneer, pirate

bucear to scuba dive; to snorkel

buen, bueno/a *adj.* good (2); **buen viaje** have a good trip (7); **buenas noches** good evening/night (P); **buenas tardes** good afternoon (P); **buenos días** good morning (P); **de buen gusto** in good taste; **hace buen tiempo** it's good weather (5); **lo bueno** the good thing, news (10); what's good; **muy**

buenas good afternoon/evening (P); **sacar (qu) buenas notas** to get good grades

bueno *interj.* well (2)

bullicioso/a lively

burbuja bubble

burocracia bureaucracy

burocrático/a bureaucratic

burro burro, donkey

busca: en busca de in search of (16)

buscar (qu) to look for (1)

búsqueda search

butaca seat (*in a theater*)

C

caballo horse; **montar a caballo** to ride a horse (9)

cabeza head (10); **dolor** (*m.*) **de cabeza** headache

cabezota *m., f. adj., n.* stubborn

cabezudo/a stubborn

cabina cabin (*on a ship*) (7); **cabina telefónica** telephone booth

cabo: llevar a cabo to carry out

cacique *m.* chief

cada *inv.* each, every (4)

cadena chain

cadera hip (*anatomy*)

caer *irreg.* to fall (11); **caerle bien/mal a alguien** to make a good/bad impression (16); **caerse** to fall down (11)

café *m.* café (18); coffee (1)

cafeína caffeine

cafetera coffeepot (9)

cafetería cafeteria (1)

caída fall

caja box

cajero/a cashier (16); teller (16); **cajero automático** automatic teller machine (16)

cajón *m.* drawer

cakchiquel *m. indigenous language*

calcetín *m.* (*pl.* **calcetines**) sock (3)

calculadora calculator (1)

cálculo calculus; calculation

calendario calendar (11)

calentar (ie) to heat up

calidad *f.* quality

cálido/a hot

caliente hot

calificación *f.* grade (11)

calle *f.* street (12)

calma calm

calmarse to calm down

calor *m.* heat; **hace calor** it's hot (*weather*) (5); **tener** (*irreg.*) **(mucho) calor** to be (very) warm, hot (*feeling*) (5)

caloría calorie

cama (de agua) (water) bed (4); **guardar cama** to stay in bed (10); **hacer** (*irreg.*) **la cama** to make the bed (9)

cámara (de video) (video) camera (12)

camarero/a waiter/waitress (6)

camarón *m.* (*pl.* **camarones**) shrimp (6)

cambiante *adj.* changing

cambiar (de) to change (12)

cambio change; **en cambio** on the other hand

caminar to walk (10)

camino street, road (14); **en camino** on the way

camioneta station wagon (7)

camisa shirt (3)

camiseta T-shirt (3)

campaña campaign; **tienda de campaña** tent (7)

campeonato championship

campesino/a farm worker (14); peasant (14)

camping *m.* campground (7); **hacer** (*irreg.*) *camping* to go camping (7)

campo countryside (12)

campus *m. s.* (university) campus (12)

Canadá *m.* Canada

canadiense *m., f. n.* Canadian

canal *m.* canal; channel (12)

cancelar to cancel

cáncer *m.* cancer

cancha court (*sports*); field (*sports*)

canción *f.* song (13)

candidato/a candidate

cansado/a tired (5)

cansarse to tire, get tired
cantante *m., f.* singer (13)
cantar to sing (1)
capa de ozono ozone layer (14)
capaz (*pl.* **capaces**) able, capable
capital *f.* capital city (5)
capítulo chapter
capricornio Capricorn
cara face
característica *n.* characteristic
caracterizar (c) to characterize
cardinal: punto cardinal cardinal direction (5)
cargar (gu) to charge (*to an account*) (16)
cargo post; charge; **estar** (*irreg.*) **a cargo de** to be in control of, be in charge of
Caribe *m. n.* Caribbean
caribeño/a *adj.* Caribbean
cariño affection
cariñoso/a affectionate (5)
carne *f.* meat (6)
carnet (*m.*) **de conducir/chofer** driver's license
caro/a expensive (3)
carpintero/a carpenter
carrera career; major (*academic*); studies
carretera highway (14)
carro (descapotable) (convertible) car (12)
carta letter (2); **jugar (ue) (gu) a las cartas** to play cards (9); **papel** (*m.*) **para cartas** stationery (18)
cartel *m.* poster
cartera wallet (3)
cartón *m.* cardboard
casa house, home (2); **casa de apartamentos** apartment building (12); **en casa** at home (1); **limpiar la casa (entera)** to clean the (whole) house (9); **regresar a casa** to go home (1)
casado/a married (2)
casarse (con) to marry (15)
cascanueces *m. s., pl.* nutcracker
casi almost; **casi nunca** almost never; hardly ever (2)

caso case; **en caso de que** *conj.* in case (15)
castellano/a Castilian
castigar (gu) to punish (17)
catalán *m.* Catalan (*language spoken in northeastern Spain*)
catálogo catalogue
Cataluña Catalonia (*region of northeastern Spain*)
catarata waterfall
catastrófico/a catastrophic
catedral *f.* cathedral
categoría category
católico/a *n., adj.* Catholic
catorce fourteen (P)
causa cause
causar to cause
cazador(a) hunter
CD-ROM *m.* CD-ROM (12)
cebiche *m. raw fish marinated in lemon juice*
cebolla onion
cebra zebra
ceder to cede
celebración *f.* celebration
celebrar to celebrate (5)
celular: teléfono celular cellular telephone (12)
cementerio cemetery
cena supper, dinner (6)
cenar to have (eat) dinner (6)
censo census
centavo cent
centrico/a central
centro center; downtown (3); **centro comercial** shopping mall (3)
Centroamérica Central America
centroamericano/a *n., adj.* Central American
cepillarse los dientes to brush one's teeth (4)
cerámica pottery, ceramics (13)
cerca de *prep.* close to (5)
cercano/a close, near
cerdo pork; **chuleta de cerdo** pork chop (6)
cereales *m. pl.* cereal (6)
cerebro brain (10)
ceremonia ceremony

cerilla match (*for lighting things*)
cero zero (P)
cerrado/a closed (5)
cerrar (ie) to close (4)
cerro hill
cervantino/a *pertaining to Cervantes*
cerveza beer (1)
césped: cortar el césped to cut the grass
ceta *the letter z*
ceviche *m. raw fish marinated in lemon juice*
champán *m.* champagne
champiñón *m.* mushroom (6)
champú *m.* shampoo (18)
chaqueta jacket (3)
charlar to chat
cheque *m.* (bank) check (16); **cheque de viajero** traveler's check (18); **con cheque** by check (16)
chequeo check-up (10)
¡chévere! *coll.* cool!, great! (*Caribbean*)
chico/a boy/girl
chileno/a *n., adj.* Chilean
chimpancé *m.* chimpanzee
chino *n.* Chinese (*language*)
Chipre *m.* Cyprus
chiste *m.* joke (8)
chistoso/a amusing
chocar (qu) (con) to run into, collide (with) (14)
chocolate *m.* chocolate
chofer *m.* driver, chauffeur; **carnet** (*m.*) **de chofer** driver's license
choque *m.* collision (17)
chuleta (de cerdo) (pork) chop (6)
ciberespacio cyberspace
ciclismo bicycling (9)
ciego/a blind
cielo sky; *fig.* dear
cien, ciento one hundred (2); **por ciento** percent
ciencia science (1)
científico/a *n.* scientific
cierto/a certain (13); true
cigarillo cigarette
cilantro cilantro, fresh coriander
cinco five (P); **Cinco de Mayo** Cinco de Mayo

cincuenta   fifty (2)

cine   *m.* movies (4); movie theater (4);
  ir (*irreg.*) **al cine**   to go to the
  movies (9)

cineasta   *m., f.* film producer,
  film maker

cinta   tape (3)

cinturón   *m.* (*pl.* **cinturones**)   belt (3)

circo   circus

circulación   *f.* traffic (14)

circular   to circulate

circunstancia   circumstance

cisne   *m.* swan

cita   date, appointment (15)

citado/a   quoted

ciudad   *f.* city (2)

ciudadano/a   citizen (17)

ciudadela   citadel

cívico/a   civic (17)

civilización   *f.* civilization

clarinete   *m.* clarinet

claro/a   clear; **claro (que sí)**
  interj. of course

clase   *f.* class (1); **clase turística**
  tourist class (7); **compañero/a de
  clase**   classmate (1); **primera clase**
  first class (7); **sala de clase**   classroom

clásico/a   classic(al) (13)

cláusula   *gram.* clause

cliente   *m., f.* client, customer (1)

clima   *m.* climate (5)

climatología   climatology

clínica   clinic

club   *m.* club

cobrar   to cash (*a check*) (16); to
  charge (*someone for an item or service*)
  (16)

coche   (*m.*) **(descapotable)**   (convertible) car (2); **teléfono de coche**   car
  phone (12)

cochera   one- or two-car garage

cocina   kitchen (4); cuisine

cocinar   to cook (6)

cocinero/a   cook; chef (16)

coctel   *m.* cocktail

cognado   *gram.* cognate (6)

coherente   coherent

coincidir   to coincide

cola   line (*of people*); **hacer** (*irreg.*) **cola**
  to stand in line (7)

colección   *f.* collection

colegio   secondary school

colesterol   *m.* cholesterol

colgar (ue) (gu)   to hang

colombiano/a   *n., adj.* Colombian

colón   *m. monetary unit of Costa Rica*

colonia   colony

colonialismo   colonialism

colonización   *f.* colonization

colonizar (c)   to colonize

color   *m.* color (3)

columna   column

columnista   *m., f.* columnist

combatir   to fight

combinar   to combine

comedor   *m.* dining room (4)

comentar   to comment on

comentario   comment, commentary

comenzar (ie) (c)   to begin

comer   to eat (2); **comérselo**   to eat
  something up

comercial   commercial; **centro
  comercial**   shopping mall (3)

comerciante   *m., f.* merchant,
  shopkeeper (16)

cómico/a   funny; **tira cómica**
  cartoon strip

comida   food (6); meal (6)

comisión   *f.* commission

comité   *m.* committee

como   like; as; **así como**   as well as;
  tal(es) como   such as; **tan... como**
  as . . . as (5); **tan pronto como**   as
  soon as (16); **tanto como**   as much
  as (5); **tanto/a(s)... como**   as
  much/many . . . as (5)

¿cómo?   how? (P); what? (P); **¿cómo es
  usted?**   what are you like? (P);
  ¿cómo está(s)?   how are you? (P);
  **¿cómo te llamas?/¿cómo se llama
  usted?**   what's your name? (P)

cómoda   dresser, bureau (4)

cómodo/a   comfortable (4)

compacto: **disco compacto**   compact
  disk (12)

compañero/a   friend; companion;
  compañero/a de clase   classmate

(1); **compañero/a de cuarto**
  roommate (1)

compañía   company; **compañía de
  difusión**   broadcasting company

comparación   *f.* comparison (5)

comparar   to compare

comparativo   *n. gram.* comparative

compartir   to share

compasión   *f.* compassion

compendio de datos   summary file

compensar   to compensate,
  make up for

competición   *f.* competition

complejo/a   complex

complementario/a   complementary

complemento directo   *gram.* direct
  object pronoun; **complemento
  indirecto**   indirect object pronoun

completar   to complete

completo/a   complete; full, no
  vacancy (18); **de tiempo completo**
  full-time (job) (11); **pensión** (*f.*)
  completa   room and full board
  (18); **por completo**   completely

complicar (qu)   to complicate

componer (*like* **poner**)   to compose

comportamiento   behavior

composición   *f.* composition

compositor(a)   composer (13)

compra: **hacer** (*irreg.*) **la compra**
  to shop

comprar   to buy (1)

compras: **de compras**   shopping (3);
  ir (*irreg.*) **de compras**   to go shopping (3)

comprender   to understand (2)

comprensión   *f.* comprehension

comprensivo/a   *adj.* understanding

compromiso   commitment

computación   *f.* computer science
  (1)

computadora   computer (*L.A.*) (12);
  computadora portátil   laptop
  computer; **disco de computadora**
  computer disk (12)

común   common; **sentido común**
  common sense

comunicación   *f.* communication; *pl.*
  communications (1); **medio de**

comunicación means of communication (17)
comunicar(se) (qu) (con) to communicate (with) (17)
comunicativo/a communicative
comunidad *f.* community (12)
comunismo communism
comunitario/a *adj.* community
con with (1); **con anticipación** ahead of time (18); **con cheque** by check (16); **con cuidado** carefully; **con frecuencia** frequently (1); **con mucho gusto** with pleasure; **con permiso** pardon me, excuse me (P); **con respecto a** with regard/respect to; **con tal (de) que** *conj.* provided (that) (15)
concentración *f.* concentration
concentrarse to concentrate
concepción *f.* conception; idea
concepto concept
conciencia conscience
concierto concert; **ir** (*irreg.*) **a un concierto** to go to a concert (9)
conclusión *f.* conclusion
condado county
condición *f.* condition
condicional *m. gram.* conditional
condimento condiment, spice
conducir *irreg.* to drive (*a vehicle*) (14); **licencia de conducir** driver's license (14)
conductor(a) driver (14)
conectarse (con) to connect (with)
conferencia lecture
conferenciante *m., f.* lecturer
confianza trust; confidence
confiar (confío) to trust
configurado/a configured
confirmar to confirm (18)
confrontación *f.* confrontation
confundido/a confused
confundir to confuse
congelado/a frozen (5); very cold (5)
congelador *m.* freezer (9)
congestión *f.* congestion
congestionado/a congested (10)
congreso congress
conjugar (gu) *gram.* to conjugate

conjunción *f. gram.* conjunction (15)
conjunto group
conmemorar to commemorate
conmigo with me
conocer (zc) to know, be acquainted with (6); to meet
conocido/a well-known
conocimiento knowledge; awareness
conquista conquest
conquistador(a) conqueror
consciente aware, conscious
conscripto draftee
consecuencia consequence; **a consecuencia de** as a result of
conseguir (*like* **seguir**) to get, obtain (8); **conseguir** + *inf.* to succeed in (*doing something*) (8)
consejero/a advisor (1)
consejo (piece of) advice (6); **dar** (*irreg.*) **consejos** to give advice
conservador(a) *n., adj.* conservative
conservar to save, conserve (14)
considerar to consider, think
constante constant
constar de to consist of .
constitucional constitutional
constituir (y) to constitute
construcción *f.* construction
construir (y) to build (14)
consultar to consult
consultorio (medical) office (10)
contabilidad *f.* accounting
contable *m., f.* accountant
contacto contact; **lentes** (*m. pl.*) **de contacto** contact lenses (10)
contado: al contado in cash (16)
contador(a) accountant (16)
contaminación *f.* pollution; **hay (mucha) contaminación** there's (lots of) pollution (5)
contaminante *m.* pollutant, contaminant
contaminar to pollute (14)
contar (ue) to tell (7); to count; **contar con** to count on, depend on
contener (*like* **tener**) to contain
contenido *n.* content(s)
contento/a content, happy (5)

contestador (*m.*) **automático** answering machine (12)
contestar to answer (4)
contexto context
contigo with you (*fam. s.*)
continente *m.* continent
continuación: a continuación following, below
continuar (continúo) to continue
contorno contour
contra against; **darse** (*irreg.*) **contra** to hit/run into
contrabando contraband
contraer (*like* **traer**) to contract
contrario/a opposite, contrary; **al contrario** on the contrary; **lo contrario** the opposite
contratar to contract
contratiempo mishap; disappointment
contrato contract
contribución *f.* contribution
contribuir (y) to contribute
control (*m.*) **remoto** remote control (12)
controlar to control
convencer (z) to convince
convencional conventional
conveniencia convenience
conveniente convenient
conversación *f.* conversation
conversar to converse, talk
convertir (ie, i) to convert, change; **convertirse en** to turn into
convivencia living together, cohabitation
convivir to live together
cooperación *f.* cooperation
cooperativo/a *adj.* cooperative
copa glass; (*alcoholic*) drink (18); **Copa Mundial** World Cup
copia copy; **hacer** (*irreg.*) **copia** to copy (12)
copiar to copy (12)
coraje *m.* courage
corazón *m.* heart (10)
corbata (neck) tie (3)
cordillera mountain range
córdoba *m. monetary unit of Nicaragua*

correcto/a correct
corregir (i, i) (j) to correct
correo mail (18); post office; **correo aéreo** air mail; **correo electrónico** electronic mail, e-mail (12); **oficina de correos** post office (18)
correr to run (9); to jog (9)
corresponder to correspond
correspondiente corresponding
corresponsal *m., f.* correspondent, reporter
corrida (de toros) bullfight
corriente *n.* current; *adj.* current, present; **cuenta corriente** checking account (16)
cortar to cut; **cortar el césped** to cut the grass
corte *f.* court
cortés *m., f.* courteous, polite
cortesía courtesy (P); **saludos y expresiones de cortesía** greetings and expressions of courtesy (P)
cortina curtain
corto/a short (*length*) (2); **pantalones** (*m. pl.*) **cortos** shorts
cosa thing (1)
cosechar to harvest
cosmopólita *m., f.* cosmopolitan
costa coast
costar (ue) to cost
costarricense *m., f. n., adj.* Costa Rican
costo cost
costumbre *f.* custom, habit (9)
creación *f.* creation
crear to create (13)
creatividad *f.* creativity
creativo/a creative
crecer (zc) to grow (15)
creciente *adj.* growing
crédito: tarjeta de crédito credit card (6)
creer (y) (en) to think, believe (in) (2); **creo que sí** I think so; **no creer** to disbelieve
criado/a servant (16); **criada** maid (18)
criarse to be raised, reared
crimen *m.* crime

criollo/a Creole
Cristo: antes de Cristo before Christ (B.C.); **después de Cristo** after Christ; *anno domini* (A.D.)
crítica criticism
criticar (qu) to criticize
crítico/a *n.* critic; *adj.* critical
cruzar (c) to cross (18)
cuaderno notebook (1)
cuadra (city) block
cuadro painting (13); **de cuadros** plaid (3)
¿cuál(es)? what? which? (P); **¿cuál es la fecha de hoy?** what is today's date? (5)
cualidad *f.* quality
cualquier(a) any
cuando when
¿cuándo? when? (P)
¿cuánto/a? how much? (P); **¿cuánto cuesta?** how much does it cost? (3); **¿cuánto es?** how much is it? (3)
cuanto: en cuanto *conj.* as soon as (16); **en cuanto a** regarding
¿cuántos/as? how many? (P)
cuarenta forty (2)
cuarto *n.* room (1); quarter (of an hour) (P); **compañero/a de cuarto** roommate (1); **son las... y/menos cuarto** it's a quarter after/to . . . (*time*) (P)
cuarto/a *adj.* fourth (13)
cuatro four (P)
cuatrocientos/as four hundred (3)
Cuba: Guerra de Cuba Spanish-American War
cubano/a *n., adj.* Cuban
cubierto/a (*p.p. of* **cubrir**) covered
cubrir (*p.p.* **cubierto**) to cover (14)
cuchara spoon
cuchillo knife
cuenta bill, check (6); account; **cuenta corriente** checking account (16); **cuenta de ahorros** savings account (16); **estado de cuentas** (bank) statement
cuento story
cuerpo body (10)

cuesta: ¿cuánto cuesta? how much does it cost? (3)
cuestión *f.* question, matter (16)
cuidado care; **con cuidado** carefully; **¡cuidado!** careful!; **tener** (*irreg.*) **cuidado** to be careful
cuidar(se) to take care of (oneself) (10)
culpa blame
cultista *m., f. adj.* cultivated, learned (*person*)
cultivar to cultivate
cultivo crop
cultura culture
cumpleaños *m. s., pl.* birthday (5); **feliz cumpleaños** happy birthday; **pastel** (*m.*) **de cumpleaños** birthday cake (8)
cumplir años to have a birthday (8)
cuñado/a brother-in-law/sister-in-law
cura *m.* priest; *f.* cure
curador(a) caretaker; curator
curarse to cure oneself
currículum *m.* résumé (16)
curso course
cuyo/a whose

D

danza dance (13)
daño: hacerse (*irreg.*) **daño** to hurt oneself (11)
dar *irreg.* to give (7); **dar ánimo** to cheer, encourage; **dar asco** to make sick; **dar consejos** to give advice; **dar la gana** to feel like (*doing something*); **dar la vuelta** to go around; **dar las gracias** to thank; **dar un paseo** to take a walk (9); **dar una fiesta** to give a party (8); **darse con** to run, bump into (11); **darse en/con/contra** to hit (*a part of one's body*)/run into; **darse la mano** to shake hands
datar (de) to date (from)
dato fact; *pl.* data; **compendio de datos** summary file
dé give (*command for you form.*)
de *prep.* of (P); from (P); **de acuerdo con** in accordance with;

de ancho   in width; de antemano beforehand; de buen/mal gusto good/bad taste; de compras   shopping (3); de cuadros   plaid (3); ¿de dónde es Ud.?   where are you from? (2); de hecho   in fact; de ida one-way (ticket) (7); de ida y vuelta round-trip (ticket) (7); de jóven   as a youth (9); de la mañana/tarde   in the morning/afternoon (P); de la noche   in the evening/at night (P); de lujo   luxury (18); de lunares polka-dotted (3); de modo   in such a way; de nada   you're welcome (P); de niño/a   as a child (9); de nuevo   again; de parte de   on behalf of; ¿de quién... ?   whose? (2); de rayas   striped (3); de repente suddenly (10); de tiempo completo full-time (11); de tiempo parcial part-time (11); de todo   everything (3); de todos modos   anyway; de última moda   the latest style (3); de veras   really; de verdad truly, really; de vez en cuando once in a while; de viaje   on a trip (7)

debajo de   prep. below (5)

deber + inf.   should, must, ought to (do something) (2); deberse a   to be due to

deber   m. responsibility, obligation (17)

debido/a a   because of, due to

débil   weak

debilitamiento   weakness, debilitation

década   decade

decidir   to decide

décimo/a   tenth (13)

decir   irreg. to say (7); to tell (7); es decir   that is to say; eso quiere decir...   that means (10); querer (irreg.) decir   to mean

decisión   f. decision

decisivo/a   decisive

declaración   f. declaration

declarar   to declare (18)

decoración   f. decoration

decorar   to decorate

dedicar (qu)   to dedicate

dedo (de la mano)   finger (11); dedo del pie   toe (11)

defecto   defect

defender   to defend

defensa   defense

definición   f. definition

definido/a: artículo definido   gram. definite article

definir   to define

definitivamente   definitively, decisively

deforestación   f. deforestation

dejar (en)   to leave (behind) (in, at) (9); to quit (16); to leave; dejar de + inf.   to stop (doing something) (10)

del (contraction of de + el)   of the, from the (2)

delante   adv. ahead; delante de   prep. in front of (5)

delegado/a   delegate

deletreo   spelling

delgado/a   thin, slender (2)

delicioso/a   delicious

delincuente   adj. delinquent

delito   crime (14)

demás: los/las demás   the others (12); the rest

demasiado   adv. too, too much; demasiado/a   adj. too much; pl. too many

democracia   democracy

demócrata   m., f. adj. democrat

demonio   devil, demon

demostrativo/a: adjetivo demostrativo   gram. demonstrative adjective (3)

demora   delay (7)

demostración   f. demonstration

demostrar (like mostrar)   to show, demonstrate

denso/a   dense (14)

dental: pasta dental   toothpaste (18)

dentista   m., f. dentist (10)

dentro   adv. in, within, inside; dentro de   prep. inside of

departamento   department; apartment (Sp.)

depender   to depend

dependiente/a   clerk (1)

deporte   sport; practicar (qu) deportes   to practice, play sports

deportista   m., f. sports player

deportivo/a   adj. sports; sports-loving (9)

depositar   to deposit (16)

depósito   deposit; (gas) tank (Sp.)

deprimente   depressing

derecha   n. right; a la derecha (de) to the right (of) (5)

derechista   m., f. adj. right-wing

derecho   n. right (legal) (17); law; derechos (m. pl.) (de aduana) (customs) duty (18); adv. straight; seguir (i, i) (g) todo derecho   to go straight ahead; todo derecho straight ahead (14)

derivarse (de)   to be derived (from)

derrocado/a   overthrown

derrotar   to defeat

desafortunadamente   unfortunately

desagradable   unpleasant

desarrollado/a   developed

desarrollar   to develop (14)

desarrollo   development

desastre   m. disaster (17)

desastroso/a   disastrous

desayunar   to have (eat) breakfast (6)

desayuno   breakfast (4)

descalzo/a   barefoot

descansar   to rest (4)

descapotable: carro descapotable convertible car (12)

descendiente   m., f. n. descendent

desconocido/a   unknown

descortesmente   discourteously

describir (like escribir)   to describe

descripción   f. description

descubanizar (c)   to become less Cuban

descubierto/a (p.p. of descubrir) discovered

descubrimiento   discovery

descubrir (like cubrir)   to discover (14)

descuidado/a   careless

desde *prep.* from; since; **desde hace + *time*** for (*time*); **desde que** *conj.* since

deseable desirable

deseado/a wanted, desired

desear to want, desire (1)

desecho *n.* waste

desempeñar to play (*a role*) (13)

deseo wish (8)

desertización *f.* process of becoming a desert

desesperadamente desperately

desfile *m.* parade

desgracia disgrace

desgraciadamente unfortunately

deshidratación *f.* dehydration

deshonesto/a dishonest

desierto *n.* desert; **desierto/a** *adj.* deserted

designado/a designated

desigualdad *f.* inequality (17)

desinflado/a: llanta desinflada flat tire (14)

desobedecer (zc) to disobey

desocupado/a vacant, unoccupied (18)

desordenado/a messy (5)

desorientar to disorient

despacio *adv.* slowly

despedida good-bye, farewell

despedirse (i, i) (de) to say good-bye (to), take leave (of) (8)

despegar (gu) to take off (*plane*)

desperdiciar to waste (14)

despertador *m.* alarm clock (11)

despertar (ie) (*p.p.* **despierto**) to wake (*someone*); **despertarse** to wake up (4)

despierto/a (*p.p. of* **despertar**) awake

desposeído/a dispossessed

después *adv.* afterward; **después de** *prep.* after (4); **después de Cristo** after Christ; anno domini (A.D.); **después (de) que** *conj.* after (16)

destacado/a renowned, distinguished

destacar (qu) to stand out

destinación *f.* destination

destinar to designate

destino destination; fate, destiny

destreza skill

destrucción *f.* destruction

destructor(a) destructive

destruir (y) to destroy (14)

desventaja disadvantage (10)

detalle *m.* detail (6)

detective *m.* detective

detención *f.* detention

detener (*like* **tener**) to detain

detenidamente carefully

detenido/a arrested, detained

determinar to determine

detestar to hate

detrás de *prep.* behind (5)

devolver (*like* **volver**) to return (*something*) (16)

día *m.* day (1); **algún día** some day; **buenos días** good morning (P); **Día de Acción de Gracias** Thanksgiving; **Día de Año Nuevo** New Year's Day; **Día de la Independencia** Independence Day; **Día de la Raza** Columbus Day; **Día de las Madres** Mother's Day; **Día de los Enamorados (de San Valentín)** Valentine's Day; **Día de los Inocentes** April Fools' Day; **Día de los Muertos/Difuntos** Day of the Dead; **Día de los Padres** Father's Day; **Día de los Reyes Magos** Epiphany; **Día de San Patricio** Saint Patrick's Day; **Día de Todos los Santos** All Saints' Day; **Día del Año Nuevo** New Year's Day; **Día del Canadá** Canada Day; **día del santo** saint's day; **día feriado** holiday; **día festivo** holiday (8); **hoy (en) día** nowadays; **ponerse** (*irreg.*) **al día** to get up-to-date; **todos los días** every day (1)

diabetes *f. s.* diabetes

diagrama *m.* diagram

dialecto dialect

diálogo dialogue

diario/a daily; **rutina diaria** daily routine (4)

dibujar to draw (13)

dibujo drawing; **dibujo animado** (film) cartoon

diccionario dictionary (1)

dice he/she/it says, you (*form.*) say

dicho *n.* saying; **dicho/a** (*p.p. of* **decir**) said

diciembre *m.* December (5)

dictado dictation

dictador(a) dictator (17)

dictadura dictatorship (17)

diecinueve nineteen (P)

dieciocho eighteen (P)

dieciséis sixteen (P)

diecisiete seventeen (P)

diente *m.* tooth (10); **cepillarse los dientes** to brush one's teeth (4); **diente de ajo** garlic clove

dieta diet; **estar** (*irreg.*) **a dieta** to be on a diet

dietético/a *adj.* diet

diez ten (P)

diferencia difference; **a diferencia de** unlike

diferenciar to differentiate

diferente different

diferir (ie, i) to differ

difícil hard, difficult (5)

dificultad *f.* difficulty

difunto/a dead person, deceased; **Día** (*m.*) **de los Difuntos** Day of the Dead

difusión (*f.*): **compañía de difusión** broadcasting company

diga hello (*telephone greeting*) (*Sp.*); **no me diga** *interj.* you don't say

digestión *f.* digestion

dignidad *f.* dignity

Dinamarca Denmark

dinero money (1)

Dios *m.* God; **por Dios** for God's sake (11)

dirección *f.* address (12); **dirección de personal** personnel office, employment office (16)

directo/a direct; **complemento directo** *gram.* direct object

director(a) director (13); **director(a) de personal** personnel director (16)

dirigir (j) to direct

disciplinado/a disciplined

disco disk; **disco compacto** compact disk (12); **disco de computadora** computer disk (12); **disco duro** hard drive (12)

discoteca discotheque; **ir** (*irreg.*) **a una discoteca** to go to a disco (9)

discriminación *f.* discrimination (17)

disculpa: pedir (i, i) disculpas to apologize (11)

discúlpame pardon me, I'm sorry (11)

discutir (sobre) (con) to argue (about) (with) (8)

diseñador(a) designer

diseñar to design

diseño design

disfraz (*m.*): **fiesta de disfraz** costume party

disfrutar (de) to enjoy

disminuir (y) to diminish, lessen

disparar to shoot

disponible available

disputa dispute

distancia distance

distante distant

distinguido/a distinguished

distinto/a different

distraer (*like* **traer**) to distract

distraído/a absentminded (11)

distrito district

diversidad *f.* diversity

diversión *f.* entertainment, amusement (9)

diverso/a diverse; *pl.* various

divertido/a fun; **ser** (*irreg.*) **divertido/a** to be fun (9)

divertir (ie) to entertain; **divertirse** to enjoy oneself, have a good time (4)

divorciado/a divorced

divorciarse (de) to get divorced (from) (15)

divorcio divorce (15)

divulgar (gu) to divulge, disclose

doblar to dub; to bend; to turn (14)

doble double (18); **habitación** (*f.*) **doble** double room (18)

doce twelve (P)

docena dozen

doctor(a) doctor

doctorado doctorate

documentar to document

documento document

dólar *m.* dollar

doler (ue) to hurt, ache (10)

dolor *m.* pain, ache (10); **dolor de cabeza, estómago, muela** headache, stomachache, toothache; **tener** (*irreg.*) **dolor (de)** to have a pain (in) (10)

doméstico/a domestic; **aparato doméstico** home appliance (9); **quehacer** (*m.*) **doméstico** household chore (9); **tarea doméstica** household chore

domingo Sunday (4)

dominicano/a *n., adj.* Dominican

dominio power; control

don *m. title of respect used with a man's first name*

donde where

¿dónde? where? (P); **¿de dónde es Ud.?** where are you from? (2)

dondequiera wherever

doña *f. title of respect used with a woman's first name*

dormir (ue, u) to sleep (4); **dormir la siesta** to take a nap (4); **dormirse** to fall asleep (4)

dormitorio bedroom

dos two (P); **dos veces** twice (10)

doscientos/as two hundred (3)

drama *m.* drama (13)

dramatizar (c) to dramatize

dramaturgo/a playwright (13)

droga drug

dromedario dromedary, camel

dualidad *f.* duality

ducha shower (18); **habitación** (*f.*) **con/sin ducha** room with(out) a shower (18)

ducharse to take a shower (4)

duda doubt; **no hay duda** there is no doubt; **sin duda** without a doubt

dudar to doubt (12)

dudoso/a doubtful

dueño/a landlord/landlady (12); owner (6)

dulce *m.* sweet, candy (6); *adj.* sweet

durante during (4)

durar to last (17)

duro/a hard; **disco duro** hard drive (12)

E

e and (*used instead of* **y** *before words beginning with stressed* **i** *or* **hi**)

ecología ecology

ecológico/a ecological

economía economy (1)

económico/a economical, economic

economizar (c) to economize (16)

ecoturismo ecotourism

ecuatoriano/a *n., adj.* Ecuadorian

edad *f.* age; **edad límite** minimum age; **menor** (*m., f.*) **de edad** minor

edificio building (1)

editor(a) editor

educación *f.* education

educativo/a educational

efectivo cash (16); **en efectivo** in cash (16)

efecto effect

eficiencia efficiency

eficiente efficient

Egipto Egypt

egocéntrico/a egocentric

egoísta *m., f.* selfish

ejemplar *m.* issue (*of a magazine*)

ejemplicar (qu) to exemplify

ejemplo example; **por ejemplo** for example (11)

ejercer (z) to practice (*a profession*)

ejercicio exercise (3); **hacer** (*irreg.*) **ejercicios** to exercise (4); **hacer** (*irreg.*) **ejercicios aeróbicos** to do aerobics (10)

ejército army (17)

el *def. art. m.* the; **el hecho de que** the fact that; **el primero de** first of (*the month*) (5)

él *sub. pron.* he (1); *obj. of a prep.* him

elaborar to make, craft

elección *f.* election

electricidad *f.* electricity

electricista *m., f.* electrician (16)

eléctrico/a electric (14)

electrónica *f. s.* electronics (12); **electrónico/a** *adj.* electronic; **aparato electrónico** electronic device; **correo electrónico** electronic mail (e-mail) (12)

electrostático/a electrostatic

elefante *m.* elephant

elegante elegant

elegido/a elected

elegir (i, i) (j) to elect; to choose

elemento element

elevar to raise

eliminar to eliminate

ella *sub. pron.* she (1); *obj. of a prep.* her

ellos/as *sub. pron.* they (1); *obj. of a prep.* them

embajador(a) ambassador

embargo: sin embargo however, nevertheless

emborracharse to get drunk

embotellamiento traffic jam

emergencia emergency; **sala de emergencias** emergency room (10)

emigrante *m., f.* emigrant

emisión *f.* broadcast; emission

emoción *f.* emotion (8)

emocional emotional

emparejar to match, pair

emperador(a) emperor, empress

empezar (ie) (c) to begin (4)

empleado/a employee

emplear to employ

empleo: oficina de empleos employment office

empresa company; business (16); corporation (16); **administración** (*f.*) **de empresas** business administration (1)

en in (P); on (P); at (P); **en busca de** in search of (16); **en cambio** on the other hand; **en camino** on the way; **en casa** at home (1); **en caso de que** *conj.* in case (15); **en cuanto** as soon as (16); **en cuanto a** regarding; **en efectivo** in cash (16); **en fin** in short; **en general** in general; **en línea** on-line; **en punto** exactly, on the dot (*time*) (P); **en**

realidad in fact; **en seguida** right away; **en vez de** instead of (16)

enamorado/a *n.* person in love; **Día** (*m.*) **de los Enamorados** Valentine's Day

enamorarse (de) to fall in love (with) (15)

encabezado/a por headed by

encantado/a enchanted; pleased to meet you (P)

encantador(a) delightful

encantar to like very much, love (7)

encargarse (gu) de to be in charge of

encender (ie) to light; to turn on (*a light*)

encendido/a turned on (*light*); lit

encerado/a waxed

enchufado/a plugged in

enchufar to plug in

encima de *prep.* on top of (5)

encontrar (ue) to find (8); **encontrarse** to be, feel (10); **encontrarse con** to meet (*someone somewhere*) (10)

encuesta survey, poll

energía energy (14)

enero January (5)

énfasis *m. s.* emphasis

enfático/a emphatic

enfermarse to get sick (8)

enfermedad *f.* sickness, illness (10)

enfermero/a nurse (10)

enfermo/a sick (5)

enfisema *m.* emphysema

enfoque *m.* focus

enfrente *adv.* in front

enlatado/a canned

enojado/a angry

enojar(se) (con) to get angry (at) (8)

enorme huge

enriquecer (zc) to enrich

ensalada salad (6)

ensayo essay

enseñanza teaching

enseñar to teach (1)

entablado: paseo entablado boardwalk

entender (ie) to understand (4)

enterarse (de) to find out (about) (17)

entero/a entire, whole (9); **limpiar la casa entera** to clean the whole house (9)

entonces then

entrada entrance; ticket

entrar to enter

entre between (5); among (5)

entregar (gu) to turn, hand in (11)

entrelazado/a linked

entremeses *m. pl.* hors d'oeuvres (8)

entrenamiento training

entrenar to practice, train (9)

entretejer to interweave

entrevista interview

entrevistado/a interviewee

entrevistador(a) interviewer (16)

entrevistar to interview (16)

envase *m.* container

enviar (envío) to send

eólico/a *adj.* wind (14)

episodio episode

época era, time (*period*) (9)

equilibradamente in a balanced way (10)

equilibrio balance

equipado/a equipped

equipaje *m.* baggage, luggage (7); **facturar el equipaje** to check one's bags (7)

equipo team; equipment; **equipo estereofónico** stereo equipment (12); **equipo fotográfico** photography equipment (12)

equivalente *m. n.* equivalent

equivocarse (qu) to be wrong, make a mistake (11)

eres you (*fam.*) are (P)

error *m.* error, mistake

erupción *f.* eruption

es he/she/it is (P); **¿cómo es usted?** what are you like? (P); **¿cuánto es?** how much is it? (3); **es cierto** it's certain (13); **es de algodón/lana/seda** it's made of cotton/ wool/silk (3); **es extraño** it's strange (13); **es increíble** it's incredible (13); **es la...** it's . . .

o'clock (P); **es preferible** it's preferable (13); **es seguro** it's a sure thing (13); **es un rollo** it's a pain; **es una lástima** it's a shame (13); **es una lata** it's a pain, drag; **es urgente** it's urgent (13); **¿qué hora es?** what time is it? (P)

escala stop; **hacer** (*irreg.*) **escalas** to make stops (7)

escalar to climb

escalera stairs; **escalera mecánica** escalator

escalón *m.* step, stair

escándalo scandal

escapar to escape

escaparate *m.* store (display) window

escasez *f.* (*pl.* **escaseces**) lack, shortage (14)

escena scene

escenario stage (13)

esclavitud *f.* slavery

esclavo/a slave

esclusa canal lock

escoger (j) to choose

esconder to hide

escorpión *m.* Scorpio

escribir (*p.p.* **escrito**) to write (2); **escribir a máquina** to type (16); **máquina de escribir** typewriter; **papel** (*m.*) **de escribir** stationery

escrito/a (*p.p. of* **escribir**) written (11); **informe** (*m.*) **escrito** written report (11)

escritor(a) writer (13)

escritorio desk (1)

escritura writing

escuchar to listen (1)

escudo shield

escuela school (9)

esculpir to sculpt (13)

escultor(a) sculptor (13)

escultura sculpture (13)

ese/a *adj., pron.* that (3)

ése/a *pron.* that one

esencial essential

esfuerzo effort

eslavo/a *n.* Slav

esmeralda emerald

eso *pron. neuter* that (3); **eso quiere decir...** that means (10); **por eso** therefore (1)

esos/as *adj., pron.* those (3)

ésos/as *pron.* those (ones)

espacial *adj.* space; **transbordador** (*m.*) **espacial** space shuttle

espacio *n.* space

espalda back

España Spain

español *n.* Spanish (*language*) (1); **español(a)** *n., adj.* Spanish (2); **Real Academia Española** Royal Spanish Academy

espárragos *m. pl.* asparagus (6)

especial special

especialidad *f.* specialty

especialista *m., f.* specialist

especialización *f.* specialization

especializado/a specialized

especializar (c) to specialize

especie *f.* species

específico/a specific

espectáculo spectacle

espectador(a) spectator

espera: llamada de espera call-waiting; **sala de espera** waiting room (7)

esperanza *n.* hope, wish (17)

esperar to wait (for) (6); to expect (6); to hope (12)

espina thorn

espíritu *m.* spirit

espléndido/a splendid

esposo/a husband/wife (2); spouse

esqueleto skeleton

esquema *m.* outline

esquí: estación (*f.*) **de esquí** ski resort

esquiar (esquío) to ski (9)

esquina (street) corner (14)

esta noche tonight (5)

está he/she/it is (P); **¿cómo está?** how are you? (P); **está (muy) nublado** it's (very) cloudy, overcast (5)

estable *adj.* stable

establecer (zc) to establish

estación *f.* season (5); station (7); **estación de autobúses** bus station (7); **estación de esquí** ski resort;

estación de gasolina gas station (14); **estación del metro** subway stop (18); **estación del tren** train station (7)

estacionamiento parking, parking lot

estacionar(se) to park (11)

estadía *n.* stay

estado state (2); condition; **estado de ánimo** state of mind; **estado de cuentas** (bank) statement; **estado libre asociado** free associated state

Estados Unidos United States

estadounidense *m., f. n., adj.* American (*from the United States*)

estampilla *n.* stamp

están they are, you (*pl.*) are

estancia stay (*in a hotel*) (18)

estanco tobacco stand/shop (18)

estanque *m.* pool, pond

estante *m.* bookshelf (4)

estar *irreg.* to be (1); **¿cómo está(s)?** how are you? (P); **está (muy) nublado** it's (very) cloudy, overcast (5); **estar a cargo de** to be in control of, be in charge of; **estar a dieta** to be on a diet; **estar al tanto** to be up-to-date; **estar atrasado/a** to be late (7); **estar bien** to be comfortable (*temperature*) (5); **estar de acuerdo** to agree; **estar de mal humor** to be in a bad mood; **estar de vacaciones** to be on vacation (7); **(no) estoy de acuerdo** I (don't) agree (2); **sala de estar** living room; sitting room

estas *dem. adj. f.* these

éstas *dem. pron. f.* these (ones)

estatal *adj.* state

estatua statue

este/a *adj.* this (2); **esta noche** tonight (5)

éste/a *pron.* this one

este *m.* east (5)

estéreo stereo

estereofónico/a: equipo estereofónico stereo equipment (12)

estereotipo stereotype

estilo style

estimado/a esteemed, dear (*letter salutation*)

estimulante stimulating

estimular to stimulate

esto *pron. neuter* this (3)

estómago stomach (10); **dolor** (*m.*) **de estómago** stomachache

estos/as *adj., pron.* these (2)

éstos/as *pron.* these (ones)

estoy de acuerdo I agree (2); **no estoy de acuerdo** I don't agree (2)

estrategia strategy

estrecho/a narrow

estrés *m.* stress (11)

estricto/a strict

estudiante *m., f.* student (1)

estudiantil *adj.* student (11)

estudiar to study (1)

estudio study; **estudios graduados** graduate studies

estudioso/a studious

estufa stove (9)

estupendo/a stupendous

etapa stage (15)

étnico/a ethnic

euro euro (*unit of currency for countries in the European Union*)

Europa Europe

europeo/a *n., adj.* European

evento event (17)

evitar to avoid (14)

evolución *f.* evolution

exacto/a exact

examen *m.* test, exam (3)

examinar to examine (10)

exceder to exceed

excelente excellent

excepción *f.* exception

excepto *prep.* except

exceso excess

exclusivo/a exclusive

excursión *f.* excursion

excusa excuse

exhibición *f.* exhibition

exigente *adj.* demanding

exigir (j) to demand

exiliarse to be exiled

existencia existence

existir to exist

éxito success; **tener exito** to be successful

exitoso/a successful

éxodo exodus

exótico/a exotic

expectativa expectation

experiencia experience

experimento experiment

experto/a *n., adj.* expert

explicación *f.* explanation

explicar (qu) to explain (7)

explorar to explore

explotación *f.* exploitation

exportación *f.* export

exposición *f.* exhibition

expresar to express

expresión *f.* expression; **saludos y expresiones de cortesía** greetings and expressions of courtesy (P)

expreso/a precise; clear

expuesto/a (*p.p. of* **exponer**) exposed

expulsar to expel

expulsión *f.* expulsion

extendido/a extended

extenso/a spacious

extranjero *n.* abroad (18); **ir** (*irreg.*) **al extranjero** to go abroad, overseas (18); **extranjero/a** *n.* foreigner (1); *adj.* foreign; **lenguas extranjeras** foreign languages (1)

extraño/a strange (13); **es extraño** it's strange (13); **¡qué extraño!** how strange! (13)

extraordinario/a extraordinary

extravagante extravagant

extremo end, tip

extroversión *f.* extroversion

extrovertido/a extroverted

exuberancia exuberance

exuberante exuberant

F

fábrica factory (14)

fabuloso/a fabulous

fácil easy (5)

facilidad *f.* ease; facility

facilitar to facilitate

factible feasible

factura bill, invoice (16)

facturar to check (*baggage*) (7)

facultad *f.* faculty; campus; department (*of a university*)

facultado/a authorized

falda skirt (3)

fallar to "crash" (*computer*) (12)

falsificado/a forged

falso/a false

falta lack, absence (14); **falta de flexibilidad** lack of flexibility (11); **sin falta** without fail

faltar to be absent, lacking (8)

familia family (2)

familiar *m., f. n.* relative, family member; *adj.* family, *pertaining to the family*

famoso/a famous

fantasía fantasy

fantástico/a fantastic

farmacéutico/a pharmacist (10)

farmacia pharmacy (10)

farmacología pharmacology

faro lighthouse

fascinante fascinating

fatal fateful

fatiga fatigue

favor *m.* favor; **por favor** please (P)

favorecer (zc) to favor

favorito/a favorite

fax *m. s., pl.* fax (12)

febrero February (5)

fecha date (*calendar*) (5); **¿cuál es la fecha de hoy?** what is the date today? (5); **fecha límite** deadline (11)

¡felicitaciones! *f. pl.* congratulations! (8)

feliz (*pl.* **felices**) happy (8); **Feliz Año Nuevo** Happy New Year; **feliz cumpleaños** happy birthday; **Feliz Navidad** Merry Christmas

femenino/a feminine

feminidad *f.* femininity

fenómeno phenomenon

feo/a ugly (2)

feriado/a: día (*m.*) **feriado** holiday

feroz (*pl.* **feroces**) fierce

ferroviario/a *adj.* railroad

fértil fertile

festividad *f.* festivity

festivo/a: día (*m.*) **festivo** holiday (8)

ficción *f.* fiction

ficticio/a fictional
fiebre *f.* fever (10); **tener** (*irreg.*) **fiebre** to have a fever
fiel faithful (2)
fiesta party (1); **dar** (*irreg.*)/**hacer** (*irreg.*) **una fiesta** to give/have a party (8); **fiesta de barrio** neighborhood (block) party; **fiesta de disfraz** costume party; **Fiesta de las Luces** Hanukkah
figura figure
fijarse en to take note of, notice
fijo/a: precio fijo fixed (set) price (3)
filmación *f.* filming
filmar to film
filosofía philosophy (1)
filtro filter; **filtro de aceite** oil filter
fin *m.* end; **en fin** in short; **fin de semana** weekend (1); **por fin** finally, at last (4); **sin fines de lucro** not-for-profit; **sin fines lucrativos** non-profit
final *m.* end; **a finales de** at the end of; **al final de** at the end of; *adj.* final; last
financiación *f.* financing
financiero/a financial
finanza finance
finca farm (14)
Finlandia Finland
fino/a fine, elegant
firmar to sign
física *f. s.* physics (1)
físico/a physical
flan *m.* baked custard (6)
flauta flute
flexibilidad *f.* flexibility (11); **falta de flexibilidad** lack of flexibility (11)
flexible flexible (11); **ser** (*irreg.*) **flexible** to be flexible (11)
flor *f.* flower (7)
florecer (zc) to flourish
flota fleet
folclore *m.* folklore
folklórico/a folkloric (13)
fondo bottom, back; *pl.* funds; **al fondo** in the background; **fondos de apoyo** economic support
fontanero/a plumber (*Sp.*)

forjar to forge
forma form (3); shape
formación *f.* formation
formar to form; **formar parte** to make up
formular to formulate
formulario form (*to fill out*) (18)
fósforo match (*for lighting things*) (18)
foto(grafía) *f.* photo(graph) (7); **sacar (qu) fotos** to take pictures
fotografía photography
fotográfico/a: equipo fotográfico photography equipment (12)
fotógrafo/a photographer (16)
frágil fragile
fragmento fragment
francés *m. n.* French (*language*) (1); **francés, francesa** *n., adj.* French (2)
Francia France
franqueo postage
frase *f.* phrase
frecuencia frequency; **con frecuencia** frequently (1)
frecuente frequent
freno brake (14)
fresco/a fresh (6); cool; **hace fresco** it's cool (*weather*) (5)
frialdad *f.* coldness
frigidez *f.* frigidity
frijol *m.* bean (6)
frío *n.* cold(ness); **hace frío** it's cold (*weather*) (5); **tener** (*irreg.*) **(mucho) frío** to be (very) cold (5); **frío/a** *adj.* cold
frito/a fried (6); **patata frita** French-fried potato (*Sp.*) (6)
frontera *n.* border (18)
fronterizo/a *adj.* border
frustrado/a frustrated
fruta fruit (6); **jugo de fruta** fruit juice (6)
fue: ayer fue yesterday was (4); **fue sin querer** it was unintentional (11)
fuegos artificiales *m. pl.* fireworks
fuente *f.* source
fuera *adv.* outside; **fuera de** *prep.* outside of

fuerte strong (6); heavy (*meal, food*) (6)
fuerza strength; force
fumar to smoke (7); **sección** (*f.*) **de (no) fumar** (no) smoking section (7)
función *f.* function
funcionar to work, function (12); to run (*machine*) (12)
fundación *f.* foundation
fundar to found
furioso/a furious, angry (5)
furtivamente furtively
fútbol *m.* soccer (9); **fútbol americano** football (9)
futuro *n.* future
futuro/a *adj.* future

G

gafas *f. pl.* (eye)glasses (10)
gallego Galician (*language spoken in the northwest of Spain*)
galleta cookie (6)
gana: dar (*irreg.*) **la gana** to feel like; **tener** (*irreg.*) **ganas de** + *inf.* to feel like (*doing something*) (3)
ganador(a) winner
ganar to win (9); to earn
ganga bargain (3)
garaje *m.* garage (4)
garganta throat (10)
gas *m.* gas (12); heat (12)
gasolina gasoline (14); **estación** (*f.*) **de gasolina** gas station (14)
gasolinera gas station (14)
gastar to spend (*money*) (8); to use, expend (14)
gasto expense (12)
gato/a cat (2)
Géminis *m.* Gemini
generación *f.* generation
general general; **en general** in general; **por lo general** generally, in general (4)
generalización *f.* generalization
generoso/a generous
génesis *m.* genesis; beginning(s)
genio/a genius
gente *f. s.* people (15)

geografía geography
geográfico/a geographic
geoturismo geotourism
germánico/a Germanic
gerontología gerontology
gerundio *gram.* gerund
gimnasio gymnasium
glaciación *f.* glaciation
globo balloon
gobernador(a) governor
gobernar (ie) to govern, rule (17)
gobierno government (14)
golf *m.* golf (9)
golfista *m., f.* golfer
goma rubber
gordo/a fat (2)
gorra cap
grabadora tape recorder/player (12)
grabar to record (12); to tape (12)
gracia grace
gracias *f. pl.* thank you (P); **dar**
(*irreg.*) **las gracias** to thank, give
thanks; **Día** (*m.*) **de Acción de**
Gracias Thanksgiving; **muchas**
gracias thank you very much (P)
grado grade, year (*in school*) (9);
degree (*temperature*)
graduado/a: estudios graduados
graduate studies
graduarse (me gradúo) (en) to
graduate (from) (16)
gráfico graph; diagram
gramática grammar
gran, grande large, big (2); great (2);
las grandes ligas the Major Leagues
grandeza greatness
grasa *n.* fat
gratis *adv.* free (*of charge*)
gratuito/a *adj.* free (*of charge*)
grave serious
Grecia Greece
griego/a *adj.* Greek
gripe *f.* flu
gris gray (3)
gritar to yell
grotesco/a grotesque
grupo group
guacamole *m. sauce made from the*
purée of avocados

guagua *coll.* bus (*P.R.*)
guapo/a handsome (2); good-looking
(2)
guaraní *m.* Guarani (*indigenous lan-*
guage from South America)
guardar to keep (12); to save (*a place*)
(7); to save (*documents*) (12); **guardar**
cama to stay in bed (10)
guardia *m.* guard, guardsman; **de**
guardia on duty
guatemalteco/a *adj.* Guatemalan
gubernamental *adj.* governmental
guerra war (17); **Guerra de Cuba**
Spanish-American War; **Segunda**
Guerra Mundial World War II
guerrero/a warrior
gueto ghetto
guía *m., f.* guide (*person*) (13); *f.*
guide (*book*); **guía telefónica** telephone book, directory
guión *m.* script (13)
guionista *m., f.* screenwriter
guitarra guitar
guitarrista *m., f.* guitar player
gustar to be pleasing (7); **¿le**
gusta... ? do you (*form.*) like . . . ?
(P); **no, no me gusta...** no, I don't
like . . . (P); **¿te gusta... ?** do you
(*fam.*) (P); **me gustaría...** I would
like . . . (7); **sí, me gusta...** yes, I
like . . . (P)
gusto taste; like (P); **a su gusto** to
taste (*cooking*); **con mucho gusto**
with pleasure; **de buen/mal gusto**
good/bad taste; **mucho gusto**
pleased to meet you (P)

H

haber *irreg.* (*inf. form of* **hay**) (there
is/are) (12); **no hay remedio**
there's no other way
habitable livable
habitación *f.* room (*in a hotel*) (18);
habitación individual/doble
single/double room (18); **habitación**
con/sin baño/ducha room
with(out) bath/shower (18)
habitante *m., f.* inhabitant
habitar to live (in), inhabit

hábito habit
hablar to speak, to talk (1); **hablar por**
teléfono to talk on the phone (1)
hace + *time* (*time*) ago (11); **hace** +
time + **que...** + *present* it's been
(*time*) since . . . (11)
hacer *irreg.* to do (4); to make (4);
desde hace + *time* for (*time*); **hace**
+ *time* (*time*) ago (11); **hace** + *time*
+ **que...** + *present* it's been (*time*)
since . . . (11); **hace buen/mal**
tiempo it's good/bad weather (5);
hace calor it's hot (5); **hace**
fresco it's cool (*weather*) (5); **hace**
frío it's cold (*weather*) (5); **hace sol**
it's sunny (5); **hace viento** it's
windy (5); **hacer aprecio de** to
appreciate; **hacer autostop** to
hitchhike; **hacer** *camping* to go
camping (7); **hacer cola** to stand in
line (7); **hacer copia** to copy (12);
hacer ejercicio to exercise (4);
hacer ejercicios aeróbicos to do
aerobics (10); **hacer escalas/paradas**
to make stops (7); **hacer la cama** to
make the bed (9); **hacer la compra**
to shop; **hacer las maletas** to pack
one's suitcases (7); **hacer paradas**
to make stops (7); **hacer planes para**
+ *inf.* to make plans to (*do some-*
thing) (9); **hacer un** *picnic* to have
a picnic (9); **hacer un viaje** to take
a trip (4); **hacer una fiesta** to give/
have a party (8); **hacer una pregunta**
to ask a question (4); **hacerse daño**
to hurt oneself (11); **¿qué tiempo**
hace? what's the weather like? (5)
hacia toward
hambre *f.* (*but* **el hambre**) hunger;
tener (*irreg.*) **(mucha) hambre** to
be (very) hungry (6)
hamburguesa hamburger (6)
hasta *prep.* until (4); **hasta luego**
see you later (P); **hasta mañana**
see you tomorrow (P); **hasta pronto**
see you soon; **hasta que** *conj.* until
(16)
hay there is/are (P); **no hay** there
is not/are not (P); **hay (mucha)**

contaminación there's (lots of) pollution (5); **hay que** + *inf.* it is necessary to (*do something*) (13); **no hay de que** you're welcome (P); **no hay remedio** there's no other way

hebreo/a: la Pascua de los hebreos Passover

hecho *n.* fact; event (8); **de hecho** in fact; **el hecho de que** the fact that; **hecho/a** *adj.* (*p.p. of* **hacer**) done; made

helado *n.* ice cream (6); **helado/a** *adj.* frozen

hemisferio hemisphere

hermanastro/a stepbrother/stepsister

hermano/a brother/sister (2); **media hermana** half-sister; **medio hermano** half-brother

hermoso/a beautiful

héroe *m.* hero

hervir (ie) to boil

hidráulico/a hydraulic (14)

hidroeléctrico/a hydroelectric

hígado liver

higiénico/a hygienic

hijastro/a stepson/stepdaughter

hijo/a son/daughter (2); **hijos** *m. pl.* children (2)

hipopótamo hippopotamus

hispánico/a *adj.* Hispanic

hispano/a *n., adj.* Hispanic

Hispanoamérica Latin America

hispanoamericano/a *n.* Latin American

hispanocanadiense *adj.* Hispanic-Canadian

hispanohablante *m., f. n.* Spanish speaker; *adj.* Spanish-speaking

historia history (1); story

historiador(a) historian

histórico/a historic, historical

hockey *m.* hockey (9)

hogar *m.* home

hoja de papel sheet of paper

hojear to look over; to leaf through

hola hello (P)

Holanda Holland

hombre *m.* man (1); **hombre de negocios** businessman (16)

honesto/a honest, sincere

honor *m.* honor

honrar to honor

hora hour; time; **a esas horas** at that hour; **¿a qué hora... ?** (at) what time . . . (P); **¿qué hora es?** what time is it? (P)

horario schedule (11)

horno de microondas microwave oven (9)

horóscopo horoscope

horror *m.* horror

hospital *m.* hospital

hotel *m.* **(de lujo)** (luxury) hotel (18)

hoy today (P); **¿cuál es la fecha de hoy?** what's today's date? (5); **hoy (en) día** nowadays

huelga strike (*labor*) (17)

huésped(a) (hotel) guest (18)

huevo egg (6)

huir (y) to flee

humanidad *f.* humanity; *pl.* humanities (1)

humanitario/a humanitarian

humano/a *adj.* human

humedad *f.* humidity

humilde humble

humor *m.* humor; mood; **estar** (*irreg.*) **de mal humor** to be in a bad mood

¡huy! *interj.* phew!

I

ibérico/a: Península Ibérica Iberian Peninsula

Iberoamérica Latin America, Ibero-America

ida: boleto/billete (*m.*) **de ida** one-way ticket (7); **boleto/billete** (*m.*) **de ida y vuelta** round-trip ticket (7)

idea idea; **lluvia de ideas** brainstorming

idealista *m., f. adj.* idealistic

idéntico/a identical

identificación *f.* identification; **tarjeta de identificación** identification card (11)

identificar (qu) to identify

idioma *m.* language

iglesia church

ignorante ignorant

igual equal; same

igualdad *f.* equality (17)

igualmente likewise, same here (P)

iluminación *f.* lighting

imagen *f.* image

imaginación *f.* imagination

imaginar to imagine

imitar to imitate

impaciente impatient

impacto impact

imparcialmente impartially

impedir (*like* **pedir**) to prevent

imperfecto *gram.* imperfect (*tense*)

imperio empire

impermeable *m.* raincoat (3)

imponente imposing

importación *f.* importation

importado/a imported

importancia importance

importante important

importar to matter; to be important; **importar un pito** to not matter at all

imposible impossible

imprescindible essential

impresión *f.* impression

impresionante impressive

impresora printer (12)

imprimir to print (12)

improbable improbable

improvisación *f.* improvisation

improvisar to improvise

impulsivo/a impulsive

inadecuado/a inadequate

inaugurar to inaugurate

inca *m.* Inca

incaico/a Incan

incansable untiring

incidencia incident

incluir (y) to include

inclusive *adj.* including

incluso *adv.* including

incomodar to make uncomfortable

inconcebible inconceivable

inconveniente *m.* inconvenience

incorrecto/a incorrect

increíble incredible (13); **es increíble** it is incredible (13)

incrementar to increase
indefinido/a: artículo indefinido
  gram. indefinite article
independencia independence; **Día**
  (*m.*) **de Independencia** Independence Day
independiente independent
indicación *f.* indication
indicar (qu) to indicate
indicativo *gram.* indicative
indígena *m., f. n.* native, indigenous
  person; *m., f. adj.* indigenous, native
indio/a *n., adj.* Indian
indirecto/a: complemento indirecto
  gram. indirect object
indiscreto/a indiscreet
individual: habitación (*f.*) **individual**
  single room (18)
individuo *n.* individual; person
indoeuropeo/a *adj.* Indo-European
industria industry
industrializado/a industrialized
inequívoco/a unequivocal
infancia infancy (15)
infantil *adj.* children's
infección *f.* infection
infinitivo *gram.* infinitive
infinito/a infinite
influencia influence
influenciado/a influenced
influir (y) to influence
influyente influential
información *f.* information
informar to inform (17)
informático/a: programa (*m.*) **informá-**
  tico word-processing program
informativo/a informative
informe (oral/escrito) *m.*
  (written/oral) report (11)
infraestructura infrastructure
ingeniería engineering
ingeniero/a engineer (16)
Inglaterra England
inglés *m. n.* English (*language*) (1);
  inglés, inglesa *n.* English person;
  adj. English (2)
ingrediente *m.* ingredient
ingresar en to deposit (*in the bank*)
ingreso income

injusticia injustice
inmediato/a immediate
inmenso/a huge
inmigración *f.* immigration (18)
inmobiliaria: agente (*m., f.*) **de**
  inmobiliaria real estate agent
innecesario/a unnecessary
innumerable innumerable
inocente innocent; **Día** (*m.*) **de los**
  Inocentes April Fools' Day
inolvidable unforgettable
inquietante worrisome
inquilino/a tenant, renter (12)
inscribirse (*p.p.* **inscrito**) to register,
  sign up
insistir to insist; **insistir en** + *inf.*
  to insist on (*doing something*)
insolente insolent
insomnio insomnia
inspector(a) (de aduanas) (customs)
  inspector (18)
inspiración *f.* inspiration
inspirarse en to be inspired by
instalación *f.* facility
instituto institute
instrucción *f.* instruction
instrumento instrument
integral *adj.* whole-grain
inteligente intelligent (2)
intenso/a intense
intentar to try (13)
interacción *f.* interaction
interactivo/a interactive
interés *m.* interest
interesante interesting
interesar to interest
intergaláctico/a intergalactic
interior *adj.* interior, inside; **ropa**
  interior underwear (3)
internacional international
internarse (en) to check into (*a*
  hospital) (10)
Internet *m.* Internet
interplanetario/a interplanetary
interpretación *f.* interpretation
interpretar to interpret
intérprete *m., f.* interpreter
interrogativo/a *adj. gram.*
  interrogative (P)

interrumpir to interrupt
intervención *f.* intervention
íntimamente intimately
introducción *f.* introduction
introducir *irreg.* to introduce
intromisión *f.*: **sin intromisiones**
  without intrusions
introversión *f.* introversion
introvertido/a introverted
invasión *f.* invasion
inventar to invent
investigación *f.* investigation
investigar (gu) to investigate
invierno winter (5)
invitado/a *n.* guest (8)
invitar to invite (6)
involucrado/a involved
inyección *f.* shot, injection; **poner(le)**
  (*irreg.*) **una inyección** to give
  (someone) a shot, injection (10)
ir *irreg.* to go (3); **ir a** + *inf.* to be
  going to (*do something*) (3); **ir a pie**
  to go on foot (walk); **ir a una disco-**
  teca / a un bar to go to a disco/to
  a bar (9); **ir al cine** to go to the
  movies (9); **ir al extranjero** to go
  abroad, overseas (18); **ir al teatro / a**
  un concierto to go to the theater/
  to a concert (9); **ir a ver una pelí-**
  cula to go to see a movie (9); **ir de**
  compras to go shopping (3); **ir de**
  vacaciones to go on vacation (7); **ir**
  en (autobús/avión/barco/tren) to
  go by (bus/airplane/boat/train);
  irse to go away, leave
Irlanda Ireland
irregularidad *f.* irregularity
isla island (5)
Islandia Iceland
istmo isthmus
Italia Italy
italiano *n.* Italian (*language*) (1);
  italiano/a *n., adj.* Italian
izquierda *n.* left-hand side; **a la**
  izquierda (de) to the left (of) (5)
izquierdista *m., f. adj.* left-wing
izquierdo/a: levantarse con el pie
  izquierdo to get up on the wrong
  side of the bed (11)

J

jabón *m.* soap (18)
jamás never, not ever (6)
jamón *m.* ham (6)
Japón *m.* Japan
japonés *m. n.* Japanese (*language*)
jarabe *m.* (cough) syrup (10)
jardín *m.* garden (4)
jarrita jar
jazz *m.* jazz
jeans *m. pl.* jeans (3)
jefe/a boss (12); **jefe/a de redacción** editor-in-chief
jeroglífico/a hieroglyphic
jirafa giraffe
jóven *m., f. n.* youth; **de jóven** as a youth (9); *adj.* young (2)
joyería jewelry store
jubilarse to retire (*from work*) (16)
judío/a *n.* Jew
juego game; **Juegos Olímpicos** Olympic Games
jueves *m. s., pl.* Thursday (4)
jugador(a) player (9)
jugar (ue) (a) to play (*a game, sport*) (4); **jugar a las cartas/al ajedrez** to play cards/chess (9)
jugo (de fruta) (fruit) juice (6)
juguete *m.* toy
julio July (5)
junio June (5)
junto *adv.* together; **juntos/as** *adj.* together (15)
justicia justice
justificar (qu) to justify
justo/a just, fair
juvenil juvenile
juventud *f.* youth (15)

K

kilo kilo(gram)
kilómetro kilometer

L

la *definite article f. s.* the; *d.o. f. s.* it; her; you (*form.*); **la mayor parte** most
labor *f.* labor, work

laboral *adj. pertaining to work or labor*
laboratorio lab, laboratory
lado *n.* side; **al lado de** *prep.* next to; alongside of (5); **al otro lado** on the other side; **por otro lado** on the other hand; **por un lado** on the one hand
ladrar to bark
ladrón, ladrona thief
lagarto lizard
lago lake
lámpara lamp (4)
lana wool (3); **es de lana** it is made of wool (3); **perro de lana** poodle
langosta lobster (6)
lanza spear
lápiz *m.* (*pl.* **lápices**) pencil (1)
lapso lapse
largo/a long (2)
las *definite article f. pl.* the; *d.o. f. pl.* them; you (*form.*); **las demás** the others (12); the rest; **las grandes ligas** the Major Leagues
lástima shame; **es una lástima** it's a shame (13); **¡qué lástima!** what a shame! (13)
lastimarse to injure oneself (11)
lata (tin) can; **es una lata** it's a pain, drag
latín *m.* Latin
latino/a *n., adj.* Latin
Latinoamérica Latin America
latinoamericano/a *n., adj.* Latin American
lavabo (bathroom) sink (4)
lavadora washing machine (9)
lavaplatos *m. s., pl.* dishwasher (9)
lavar to wash (9)
le *i.o. pron.* to/for him/her/you (*form. s.*); **¿le gusta... ?** do you (*form. s.*) like . . . ? (P); **le molesta** it bothers him/her/you (13); **le sorprende** it surprises him/her/you (*form.*) (13)
lección *f.* lesson
leche *f.* milk (6)
lechuga lettuce (6)
lector(a) reader; **ámbito de lectores** readership

lectura *n.* reading
leer (y) to read (2)
legalizar (c) to legalize
legendario/a legendary
legislación *f.* legislation
lejos *adv.* far; **lejos de** *prep.* far from (5)
lempira *monetary unit of Honduras*
lengua language (1); tongue; **lenguas extranjeras** foreign languages (1); **sacar (qu) la lengua** to stick out one's tongue (10)
lenguaje *m.* language
lentes (*m. pl.*) **de contacto** contact lenses (10)
leña: estufa de leña wood stove
les *i.o. pron.* to/for them/you (*pl.*)
letrero sign
levantar to raise; **levantar pesas** to lift weights; **levantarse** to get up (4); to stand up (4); **levantarse con el pie izquierdo** to get up on the wrong side of the bed (11)
léxico lexicon
ley *f.* law (17)
leyenda legend
libertad *f.* freedom, liberty (17)
libertador(a) liberator
Libra Libra
libre free; **al aire libre** outdoors; **estado libre asociado** free associated state; **ratos libres** spare (free) time (9)
librería bookstore (1)
libro (de texto) (text)book (1)
licencia license; **licencia de manejar/conducir** driver's license (14)
líder *m.* leader
liga league; **las grandes ligas** the Major Leagues
ligero/a light, not heavy (6)
limitación *f.* limitation
limitar to limit
límite *m.* limit; **edad** (*f.*) **límite** minimum age; **fecha límite** deadline (11); **límite de velocidad** speed limit (14)
limón *m.* lemon

limonada lemonade

limpiaparabrisas *m. s., pl.* windshield wiper

limpiar to clean; **limpiar la casa (entera)** to clean the (whole) house (9)

limpio/a clean (5)

línea line; **en línea** on-line; **patinar en línea** to rollerblade (9)

lío mess

líquido *n.* liquid

lista list

listo/a ready; smart (2); clever (2)

literatura literature (1)

litro liter

llamada (telephone) call; **llamada en espera** call-waiting

llamar to call (6); **llamarse** to be called (4); **¿cómo se llama usted?** what is your name? (*form.*) (P); **¿cómo te llamas?** what's your name? (*fam.*) (P); **me llamo…** my name is . . . (P)

llanos *m. pl.* plains

llanta (desinflada) (flat) tire (14); **llanta de recambio** spare tire

llave *f.* key (11)

llegada arrival (7)

llegar (gu) to arrive (2); to reach; **llegar a tiempo/tarde** to arrive on time/late (11)

llenar to fill (up) (14); to fill out (16)

lleno/a full

llevar to wear (3); to carry (3); to take (3); **llevar a** to lead to; **llevar a cabo** to carry out; **llevar puesto** to be wearing; **llevar una vida sana/tranquila** to lead a healthy/calm life (10); **llevarse bien/mal (con)** to get along well/poorly (with) (15)

llorar to cry (8)

llover (ue) to rain (5); **llueve** it's raining (5)

lluvia de ideas brainstorm

lo *d.o. m. s.* it; him; you (*form.*); **lo bueno** the good thing, news (10); **lo contrario** the opposite; **lo malo** the bad thing, news (10); **lo que** what, that which (7); **lo siento (mucho)** I'm (very) sorry (11); **lo suficiente** enough (10)

lobo/a wolf

local *m. n.* stall; place; *adj.* local

localización *f.* location

loco/a crazy (5)

lógico/a logical

los *definite article m. pl.* the; *d.o. pron., m. pl.* them; you; **los demás** the others (12); the rest

lotería lottery

lubricar (qu) to lubricate

lucha fight; struggle

luchador(a) fighter

luchar to fight; to struggle

lucrativo/a: sin fines lucrativos non-profit

lucro: sin fines de lucro not-for-profit

luego *adv.* soon; then; **hasta luego** see you later (P); **luego de** *prep.* after

lugar *m.* place (1); **ningún lugar** nowhere; **tener (irreg.) lugar** to take place

lujo luxury (12); **hotel (m.) de lujo** luxury hotel (18)

luna moon; **luna de miel** honeymoon (15)

lunar: de lunares polka-dotted (3)

lunes *m. s., pl.* Monday (4)

Luxemburgo Luxembourg

luz *f.* (*pl.* **luces**) light (11); electricity (11); **Fiesta de las Luces** Hanukkah

M

machismo (male) chauvinism

machista *adj. m., f.* chauvinistic

madera wood

madrastra stepmother

madre *f.* mother (2); **Día (m.) de las Madres** Mother's Day

madurez *f.* maturity; middle age (15)

maestría master's degree

maestro/a teacher (16)

maestro/a: obra maestra masterpiece (13)

magia *n.* magic

mágico/a *adj.* magic, magical

magnético/a magnetic

magnífico/a magnificent

mago wizard; **Día (m.) de los Reyes Magos** Epiphany, Day of the Magi

maíz *m.* corn

majestuoso/a majestic

mal *n.* evil; badness; illness; *adv.* badly; poorly (1); **caerle (irreg.) mal a alguien** to make a bad impression on someone (16); **llevarse mal (con)** to get along poorly (with) (15); **pasarlo mal** to have a bad time (8); **portarse mal** to behave poorly

mal, malo/a *adj.* bad (2); **de mal gusto** in bad taste; **estar (irreg.) de mal humor** to be in a bad mood; **hace mal tiempo** it's bad weather (5); **lo malo** the bad thing, news (10); **¡qué mala suerte!** what bad luck! (11); **sacar (qu) malas notas** to get bad grades

Malasia Malaysia

maleducado/a ill-mannered

maleta suitcase; **hacer (irreg.) la(s) maleta(s)** to pack one's suitcase(s) (7)

maletero porter (7)

malvado/a evil

mamá mom, mother (2)

mambo *dance and music of Cuban origin*

mamífero mammal

mandar to send (7); to order (12)

mandato command

manejar to drive (12); to operate (*a machine*) (12); **licencia de manejar** driver's license (14)

manera manner, way

manifestación *f.* demonstration

mano *f.* hand; **darse (irreg.) la mano** to shake hands; **de segunda mano** second-hand; **dedo de la mano** finger (11); **manos a la obra** let's get to work

mantener (like tener) to maintain, keep

mantequilla butter (6)

manzana apple (6)

mañana morning; *adv.* tomorrow (P); **de la mañana** in the morning (P); **hasta mañana** until tomorrow (P); **pasado mañana** day after tomorrow (4); **por la mañana** in the morning (1)

mapa *m.* map

máquina machine; **escribir a máquina** to type (16); **máquina de escribir** typewriter

mar *m.* sea (7)

maratón *m.* marathon

maravilla wonder, marvel

maravilloso/a wonderful, marvelous

marca brand

marcar (qu) to mark

mareado/a dizzy, nauseated (10)

marido husband (15)

marino/a *adj.* marine, of the sea

mariscos *m. pl.* shellfish (6)

marítimo/a maritime

marketing *m.* marketing

Marruecos *m. s.* Morocco

martes *m. s., pl.* Tuesday (4)

marzo March (5)

mas but, however, although

más *adv.* more (1); **más allá** beyond; **más... que** more than (5)

máscara mask

mascota *n.* pet (2)

masculino/a masculine

matar to kill

matemáticas *f. pl.* mathematics (1)

materia (school) subject (1); matter

material *n. m.* material (3)

materialista *m., f.* materialistic

maternidad *f.* maternity

materno/a maternal

matrícula tuition (1)

matrimonio marriage (15); married couple (15)

máximo/a maximum

maya *m., f. n., adj.* Mayan

mayo May (5); **Cinco de Mayo** Cinco de Mayo (*Mexican awareness celebration*)

mayor *m. n.* elder; *adj.* older (5); greater; **la mayor parte** most

mayoría majority

me *d.o. pron.* me; *i.o. pron.* to/for me; *refl. pron.* myself; **me gustaría...** I would like . . . (7); **me llamo...** my name is . . . (P); **me molesta** I'm annoyed, it bothers me (13); **me sorprende** it surprises me (13); **no, no me gusta...** no, I don't like . . . (P); **sí, me gusta...** yes, I like . . . (P)

mecánica *n. s.* mechanics; **mecánico/a** *n.* mechanic (14); *adj.* mechanical; **escalera mecánica** escalator

medalla medal

media: y media (*time*) (*hour*) thirty, half past (*hour*) (P)

medianoche *f.* midnight (8)

mediante through, by way of

medias *f. pl.* stockings (3)

medicamento medicine (*drug*)

medicina medicine (*subject*) (10)

médico/a (medical) doctor (2); *adj.* medical (10)

medida measure

medio *n.* average; medium; *pl.* means; media; **medio ambiente** environment (14); **medio de comunicación** means of communication (17); **medio/a** *adj.* half; average; middle; **media hermana** half-sister; **media pensión** room with breakfast and one other meal (18); **medio hermano** half-brother

medioambiental environmental

mediodía *m.* noon

mediterraneo/a Mediterranean

mejillón *m.* mussel

mejor better (5); best (5); **mejor que** better than

mejorar to improve

melancolía sadness

melanoma *m.* melanoma

mellizo/a *adj.* twin

membrana membrane

memoria memory (12)

mencionar to mention

menor younger (5); least; **menor de edad** minor

menos less; **a menos que** *conj.* unless (15); **es la / son las... menos cuarto (quince)** it's a quarter (fifteen minutes) to . . . (P); **menos... que** less than (5); **por lo menos** at least (10)

mensaje *m.* message

mensual *adj.* monthly

mentira lie

menú *m.* menu (6)

menudo: a menudo often

mercadeo marketing

mercado market(place) (3)

mercancía merchandise

merecer (zc) to deserve

merengue *m.* music and dance from the Caribbean

merienda (afternoon) snack

mes *m.* month (5)

mesa table (1); **poner** (*irreg.*) **la mesa** to set the table (9); **quitar la mesa** to clear the table (9)

mesita end table (4)

mestizo/a *person descended from two or more different races*

metal *m.* metal

meteorólogo/a meteorologist

metro subway; meter; **estación** (*f.*) **del metro** subway station (18)

metrópolis *f.* city

mexicano/a *n., adj.* Mexican (2)

México Mexico

mexicoamericano/a *n., adj.* Mexican-American

mezcla mixture

mezclar to mix

mi(s) *poss. adj.* my (2)

mí *obj. of prep.* me (5)

microondas: horno de microondas microwave oven (9)

miedo fear; **tener** (*irreg.*) **miedo (de)** to be afraid (of) (3)

miel *f.* honey; **luna de miel** honeymoon (15)

miembro member

mientras while (9); **mientras que** *conj.* while

miércoles *m. s., pl.* Wednesday (4)

migrante *adj.* migrant

mil one thousand (3); **mil millón** one billion

milagro miracle

milenio millennium

militar: servicio militar military service (17)

millón one million (3); **mil millón** one billion

mineral: agua (*f., but* **el agua**) **mineral** mineral water (6)

minero/a *adj.* mining

minidiálogo minidialogue

minifalda miniskirt

mínimo minimum

ministro/a minister; **primer(a) ministro/a** prime minister

minoría minority

minuto *n.* minute (*time*)

mío/a(s) *poss. adj.* my, (of) mine

mirar to look at, watch (2); **mirar la televisión** to watch television (2)

misa mass (*church service*); **oficiar una misa** to celebrate mass

misión *f.* mission

mismo/a self; same (10); **ahora mismo** right now; **lo mismo** the same thing

misquito *indigenous language spoken in Nicaragua*

misterioso/a mysterious

mitad *f.* half

mito myth

mitología mythology

mixteca *m., f. n.* Mixtec (*person*); **mixteca** *n. m.* Mixtec (*language*)

mochila backpack (1)

moda fashion; **de última moda** the latest style (3)

modelo *n.* model

módem *m.* modem (12)

moderado/a moderate

moderno/a modern (13)

módico/a moderate, reasonable

modificar (qu) to modify

modismo idiom

modo way, means; *gram.* mood; **de modo** in such a way; **de todos modos** anyway

molestar to bother, annoy; **me (te, le, ...) molesta** it bothers me (you, him, . . .) (13)

molestia bother, annoyance

momento moment; **por el momento** at this time

monarquía monarchy

moneda currency; coin

monoparental *adj.* single-parent

monopatín *m.* skateboard (12)

monstruo monster

montaña mountain (7); **bicicleta de montaña** mountain bicycle (12)

montar to set up; **montar a caballo** to ride a horse (9); **montar en bicicleta** to ride a bicycle; **montar en tabla de vela** to windsurf

montón *m.* bunch

monumento monument

morado/a purple (3)

moralidad *f.* morality

moreno/a brunet(te) (2)

morir(se) (ue, u) (*p.p.* **muerto**) to die (8)

mosca fly

mostrador *m.* counter

mostrar (ue) to show (7)

motivo motive

moto(cicleta) *f.* motorcycle (12)

motor *m.* motor

movimiento movement

mozo bellhop (18)

muchacho/a boy/girl (4)

mucho *adv.* much (1); a lot (1); **mucho/a** *adj.* a lot (2); *pl.* many (2); **muchas gracias** thank you very much (P); **mucho gusto** nice to meet you (P)

mudarse to move (*residence*) (16)

muebles *m., pl.* furniture (4); **sacudir los muebles** to dust the furniture (9)

muela: dolor (*m.*) **de muela** toothache; **sacar (qu) una muela** to extract a tooth (10)

muerte *f.* death (15)

muerto/a *n.* dead person; **Día** (*m.*) **de los Muertos** Day of the Dead; *adj.* (*p.p. of* **morir**) dead

muestra sample

mujer *f.* woman (1); wife (15); **mujer de negocios** businesswoman (16); **mujer policía** policewoman; **mujer soldado** (female) soldier (16)

multa fine, penalty (18)

mundial *adj.* world; **Copa Mundial** World Cup; **Segunda Guerra Mundial** World War II

mundo *n.* world (7)

muralismo muralism

muralista *m., f.* muralist

músculo muscle

museo museum; **visitar un museo** to visit a museum (9)

música music (13)

músico/a musician (13)

musulmán, mulsulmana *n., adj.* Moslem

mutuo/a mutual

muy very (1); **muy bien** very well (P); **muy buenas** good afternoon/ evening (P)

N

nacer (zc) to be born (15)

nacimiento birth (15)

nación *f.* nation; **Naciones Unidas** United Nations

nacional national

nacionalidad *f.* nationality (2)

nada nothing, not anything (6); **de nada** you're welcome (P)

nadar to swim (7)

nadie no one, not anybody, nobody (6)

nahuatl *m. indigenous language from Central America*

naranja orange (*fruit*) (6)

nariz *f.* (*pl.* **narices**) nose (10)

narración *f.* narration

narrador(a) narrator

narrar to narrate

natación *f.* swimming (9)

nativo/a *adj.* native

natural natural; **recursos** (*m. pl.*) **naturales** natural resources (14)

naturaleza nature (14)

náuseas *f. pl.* nausea

navegable navigable

navegante *m., f.* sailor

navegar (gu) to sail; **navegar la red** to surf the net (12)

Navidad *f.* Christmas (8); **Feliz Navidad** Merry Christmas

navideño/a *adj. pertaining to Christmas*

necesario/a necessary (2)

necesidad *f.* necessity

necesitar to need (1)

negación *f.* negation; denial

negar (ie) (gu) to deny (13)

negativo/a negative (6)

negociación *f.* negotiation

negocio business (*company*); *pl.* business (*general*); **administración** (*f.*) **de negocios** business administration; **hombre** (*m.*)/**mujer** (*f.*) **de negocios** businessperson (16)

negro/a black (3)

neoyorquino/a *adj. of or from New York*

nervio nerve

nervioso/a nervous (5)

neutro/a neutral

nevar (ie) to snow (5); **nieva** it's snowing (5)

ni neither; nor; **ni siquiera** not even

nicaragüense *m., f. n.* Nicaraguan

nieto/a grandson/granddaughter (2); *m. pl.* grandchildren

nieva it's snowing (5)

ningún, ninguno/a no, none, not any (6); neither; **ningún lugar** nowhere

niñero/a babysitter (9)

niñez *f.* childhood (9)

niño/a small child (2); boy/girl (2); **de niño/a** as a child (9)

nivel *m.* level (14)

no no (P); not; **¿no?** right? (3); **no creer** *irreg.* to disbelieve; **no hay de que** you're welcome (P); **no hay duda** there is no doubt; **no me diga** *interj.* you don't say; **no, no me gusta...** no, I don't like . . . (P)

Nóbel: Premio Nóbel Nobel Prize

noche *f.* night; **buenas noches** good evening (P); good night (P); **de la noche** p.m., in the evening (P); **esta noche** tonight (5); **Noche Vieja** New Year's Eve (8); **por la noche** at night (1)

Nochebuena Christmas Eve (8)

nombrar to name

nombre *m.* name

nominado/a nominated

noreste *m.* northeast

norte *m.* north (5)

Norteamérica North America

norteamericano/a *n., adj.* North American (2)

nos *d.o. pron.* us; *i.o. pron.* to/for us; *refl. pron.* ourselves; **nos vemos** see you around (P)

nosotros/as *sub. pron.* we (1); *obj. of a prep.* us

nota note; grade (*in a class*) (11); **sacar (qu) buenas/malas notas** to get good/bad grades

notar to notice

noticia piece of news (8); *pl.* news

noticiero newscast (17)

novato/a *n.* novice

novecientos/as nine hundred (3)

novedades *f. pl.* news (17)

novela novel

novelista *m., f.* novelist

noveno/a ninth (13)

noventa ninety (2)

noviazgo engagement (15)

noviembre *m.* November (5)

novio/a boyfriend/girlfriend (5)

nublado/a cloudy; **está (muy) nublado** it's (very) cloudy, overcast (5)

nuclear nuclear (14)

nuera daughter-in-law

nuestro/a(s) *poss. adj.* our (2); our, of ours

nueve nine (P)

nuevo/a new (2); **de nuevo** again; **Día** (*m.*) **de Año Nuevo** New Year's Day; **Feliz/Próspero Año Nuevo** Happy New Year

numérico/a numerical

número number (P)

numeroso/a numerous

nunca never (2); **casi nunca** almost never (2)

O

o or (P)

obedecer (zc) to obey (14)

objetivo objective

objeto object

obligación *f.* obligation

obligatorio/a obligatory, compulsory

obra work (13); **manos a la obra** let's get to work; **obra de arte** work of art (13); **obra maestra** masterpiece (13)

obrero/a worker, laborer (16)

obstáculo obstacle

obtener (*like* **tener**) to get, obtain (12)

obvio/a obvious

ocasión *f.* occasion

ocasionar to bring about

occidental western

océano ocean (7); **Océano Atlántico** Atlantic Ocean

ochenta eighty (2)

ocho eight (P)

ochocientos/as eight hundred (3)

ocio leisure time

octavo/a *adj.* eighth (13)

octubre *m.* October (5)

ocular *adj. of the eye,* ocular

ocupado/a busy (5)

ocupar to occupy

ocurrir to occur

odiar to hate (7)

odio hatred

oeste *m.* west (5)

ofenderse to be offended

oferta sale; offer

oficial *m. n., adj.* official

oficiar una misa to celebrate mass

oficina office (1); **oficina de correos** post office (18); **oficina de empleos** employment office

oficio trade (16)

ofrecer (zc) to offer (7)

oído inner ear (10)

oír *irreg.* to hear (4)

ojalá (que) I hope, wish (that) (13)
ojear to look over
ojo eye (10); **¡ojo!** watch out!; **ojo alerta** be alert, watch out
olimpiadas Olympics
olímpico: Juegos Olímpicos Olympic Games
oliva olive; **aceite** (*m.*) **de oliva** olive oil
olmeca *m., f. n.* Olmec
olvidar(se) (de) to forget (about) (8)
ómnibus *m.* bus
once eleven (P)
ONU (*abbrev. of* **Organización de las Naciones Unidas**) U.N. (United Nations)
opción *f.* option
ópera opera (13)
operación *f.* operation
operar to operate
opinión *f.* opinion
oponer (*like* **poner**) to oppose
oportunidad *f.* opportunity
optimista *m., f., adj.* optimistic
oración *f.* sentence
orador(a) speaker
oral oral; **informe** (*m.*) **oral** oral report (11)
orden *m.* order; *f.* order, command
ordenado/a neat (5)
ordenador computer (*Sp.*) (12)
oreja outer ear (10)
organismo institution
organización *f.* organization
organizador(a) organizer
organizar (c) to organize
orientación *f.* direction, orientation
oriental eastern
origen *m.* origin
originar to originate
oro gold
orquesta orchestra
os *d.o. pron.* you (*pl. fam.*); *i.o. pron.* to/for you (*pl. fam.*); *refl. pron.* yourselves (*pl. fam.*)
oscuro/a dark
oso/a bear
ostra oyster
otoño autumn, fall (5)

otorgar (gu) to grant
otro/a another, other (2); *pl.* others; **al otro lado** on the other side; **por otro lado** on the other hand
OVNI (*abbrev. of* **objeto volante no identificado**) UFO (unidentified flying object)
oxígeno oxygen
¡oye! hey!
ozono: capa de ozono ozone layer (14)

P

paciencia patience
paciente *m., f. n., adj.* patient (10)
pacífico Pacific (Ocean)
padecer (zc) to suffer
padrastro stepfather
padre *m.* father (2); *pl.* parents (2); **Día** (*m.*) **de los Padres** Father's Day
pagar (gu) to pay (for) (1)
página page; **página** *web* web page
país *m.* country (2)
pájaro bird (2)
palabra word (P)
palma palm tree
palomitas *f. pl.* popcorn
pampa pampa, prairie
pan *m.* bread (6); **pan tostado** toast (6)
panameño/a *adj.* Panamanian
panamericano/a Pan-American
pandilla gang; group of friends
pantalla screen
pantalones *m. pl.* pants (3); **pantalones cortos** shorts
papa potato (*L.A.*)
papá *m.* dad (2)
papel *m.* paper (1); role (13); **hoja de papel** sheet of paper; **papel para cartas** stationery (18)
papelería stationery store (18)
paquete *m.* package (18)
par *m.* pair (3)
para *prep.* (intended) for (2); in order to (2); **para** + *inf.* in order to (*do something*); **para que** *conj.* so that (15)

parabrisas *m. s., pl.* windshield (14)
paracaidismo skydiving
parada stop; **hacer** (*irreg.*) **paradas** to make stops (7); **parada del autobús** bus stop (18)
paraguas *m. s., pl.* umbrella
parar to stop (14)
parcial: de tiempo parcial part-time (11)
pardo/a brown (3)
parecer (zc) to seem (13)
parecido/a similar
pared *f.* wall (4)
pareja (married) couple (15); partner (15)
paréntesis *m. s., pl.* parentheses
pariente *m., f.* relative (2)
parque *m.* park (5); **parque de atracciones** amusement park; **parque temático** theme park
parqueadero parking (lot)
parquear to park
parrado/a standing
párrafo paragraph
parte *f.* part (4); **de parte de** on behalf of; **formar parte** to make up, compose; **la mayor parte** most; **por todas partes** everywhere (11)
participante *m., f.* participant
participar to participate
participativo/a participatory
participio *gram.* participle
particular particular; private
partido game
partir: a partir de starting from
párvulo/a tot (*child*)
pasado *n.* past
pasado/a last; **el año pasado** last year; **pasado mañana** day after tomorrow (4)
pasaje *m.* passage, ticket (7)
pasajero/a passenger (7)
pasaporte *m.* passport (18); **agente** (*m., f.*) **de pasaportes** passport agent
pasar to go by; to pass; to spend (*time*) (5); to happen (5); **pasar la aspiradora** to vacuum (9); **pasarlo bien/mal** to have a good/bad time

(8); **pasar tiempo (con)** to spend time (with) (15)

pasatiempo pastime, hobby (9)

Pascua (Florida) Easter (8); **Pascua de los hebreos** Passover

pasear to take a walk; **pasear en bicicleta** to ride a bicycle (9)

paseo: paseo entablado boardwalk; **dar** (*irreg.*) **un paseo** to take a walk (9)

pasional *adj.* passionate, of passion

paso step

pasta pasta; **pasta dental** toothpaste (18)

pastel *m.* cake (6); pie (6); **pastel de cumpleaños** birthday cake (8)

pastelería pastry shop (18)

pastelito small pastry (18)

pastilla pill (10)

pastor(a) shepherd; **pastor alemán** German shepherd (*dog*)

patata (frita) (French-fried) potato (*Sp.*) (6)

patín, *m.* (*pl.* **patines**) (roller) skate (12)

patinar to skate (9); **patinar en línea** to roller blade (9)

patio patio, yard (4)

patrón: santa patrona patron saint (*f.*)

pavo/a turkey (6)

paz *f.* (*pl.* **paces**) peace (17); **acuerdo de paz** peace agreement

peatón, peatona pedestrian

pecho chest (*part of body*)

pedagogía pedagogy

pedazo piece

pedir (i, i) to ask for (4); to order (*in a restaurant*) (4); **pedir disculpas** to apologize (11); **pedir prestado** to borrow (16)

pegar (gu) to hit (9); **pegarse en/ contra** to run/bump into (11)

peinarse to comb one's hair (4)

pelear to fight (9)

película movie (4); **ir** (*irreg.*) **a ver una película** to go to see a movie (9)

peligro danger; jeopardy

peligroso/a dangerous

pelo hair

pelota ball

peluquero/a hairstylist (16)

pena: valer (*irreg.*) **la pena** to be worth the trouble; **¡qué pena!** what a shame!

pendiente *m.* earring

península peninsula

pensar (ie) (en) to think (about) (4); to intend (4)

pensión *f.* boarding house (18); **media pensión** room with breakfast (18); **pensión completa** room and full board (18)

peor worse (5); worst

pequeño/a small (2)

percibido/a perceived

perder (ie) to lose (4); to miss (*a function, bus, train, etc.*) (4)

pérdida loss

perdón pardon me, excuse me (P); I'm sorry

perezoso/a lazy (2)

perfecto/a perfect

perfume *m.* perfume

periódico newspaper (2)

periodismo journalism

periodista *m., f.* journalist (16)

período period

permanente permanent

permiso permission; permit; **con permiso** pardon me, excuse me (P)

permitir to permit, allow (12)

pero *conj.* but (P)

perro/a dog (2); **perro de lana** poodle

perseguir (*like* **seguir**) to pursue

persiana Venetian blind

persona person (1)

personaje *m.* character (*in literature*)

personal *m. n.* personnel (10); **dirección** (*f.*) **de personal** personnel office (16); **director(a) de personal** personnel director (16); *adj.* personal; **pronombre personal** *m. gram.* subject pronoun (1)

personalidad *f.* personality

perspectiva perspective

persuadir to persuade

pertenecer (zc) (a) to belong (to)

perturbar to disturb

Perú *m.* Peru

peruano/a *n.* Peruvian

pesa: levantar pesas to lift weights

pesado/a heavy; *sl.* boring (9); difficult (9)

pesar to weigh; **a pesar de** in spite of

pescado fish (*cooked*) (6)

peseta *former monetary unit of Spain*

pesimista *m., f.* pessimistic

peso weight; *monetary unit of Mexico*

petróleo oil

petrolero gasoline dealer

pez *m.* (*pl.* **peces**) fish (*live*)

piano piano

picante spicy

picnic: **hacer** (*irreg.*) **un** *picnic* to have a picnic (9)

pico beak

pie *m.* foot; **a pie** on foot; **dedo del pie** toe (11); **levantarse con el pie izquierdo** to get up on the wrong side of the bed (11)

piel *f.* skin

pierna leg (11)

pieza piece

piloto/a pilot

pingüino penguin

pintar (las paredes) to paint (the walls) (9)

pintor(a) painter (13)

pintura *n.* painting (*general*) (13); painting (*piece of art*) (13)

pirámide *f.* pyramid

pirata *m., f.* pirate

Pirineos Pyrenees (*mountains*)

piscina swimming pool (4)

piso floor (12); **barrer el piso** to sweep the floor (9); apartment

pistacho pistachio

pito: importar un pito to not matter at all

pizarra chalkboard (1)

pizzería pizza parlor

placa license plate

placer *m.* pleasure

plan *m.* plan; **hacer** (*irreg.*) **planes para** + *inf.* to make plans to (*do something*) (9)

planchar la ropa to iron clothing (9)

planeación *f.* planning

planeta *m.* planet

planta plant; floor; **planta baja** ground floor (12)

plantación *f.* plantation

plástico *n.* plastic

plata silver (*ore*)

plato plate, dish (4); (*prepared*) dish, course (*of a meal*) (6); **plato principal** main course

playa beach (5)

plaza plaza, square; **plaza de toros** bullring

plazo time, period; **a plazos** in installments (16)

plegaria prayer

plena: bomba y plena *dance and music from the Caribbean*

plomero/a plumber (16)

pluralismo pluralism

población *f.* population (14)

poblar to populate

pobre *m., f. n.* poor person; *adj.* poor (2)

pobreza poverty

poco *n.* a little bit (1); *adv.* little (1); **poco/a** *adj.* little (3)

poder *irreg.* to be able, can (3)

poderoso/a powerful

poema *m.* poem

poesía poetry

poeta *m., f.* poet (13)

poético/a poetic

policía *m., f.* police officer (14); *f.* police (*force*); **mujer** (*f.*) **policía** policewoman

poliomielitis *f.* poliomyelitis

política *f. s.* politics (17); **político/a** *n.* politician (17); *adj.* political

pollo (asado) (roast) chicken (6)

Polonia Poland

poner *irreg.* to put (4); place (4); **poner la mesa** to set the table (9); **ponerle una inyección** to give (someone) a shot, injection (10); **ponerse** to put on (*clothing*) (4); **ponerse** + *adj.* to become, get + *adj.* (8); **ponerse al día** to get up-to-date; **ponerse de acuerdo** to agree, come to an agreement

popularidad *f.* popularity

por *prep.* for (4); during (4); by; through; on; **por ciento** percent; **por completo** completely; **por Dios** for God's sake (11); **por ejemplo** for example (11); **por el momento** at this time; **por eso** therefore (1); **por favor** please (P); **por fin** finally, at last (4); **por la mañana/tarde** in the morning/afternoon (1); **por la noche** in the evening, at night (1); **por lo general** generally (4); **por lo menos** at least (10); **por otro lado** on the other hand; **por primera vez** for the first time (11); **¿por qué?** why? (2); **por si acaso** just in case (11); **por supuesto** of course (11); **por todas partes** everywhere (11); **por última vez** for the last time (11); **por último** finally; **por un lado** on the one hand; **por vía aérea** by air; by airmail

¿por qué? why? (2)

porcentaje *m.* percentage

porción *f.* portion

porque because (2)

portarse to behave (8)

portátil portable (12); **radio portátil** portable radio (12)

portavoz *m.* (*pl.* **portavoces**) spokesperson

porteño/a *person from Buenos Aires*

portero/a building manager (12); doorman (12)

portugués *m.* Portuguese (*language*)

porvenir *m.* future

poseer to possess

posesión *f.* possession

posesivo/a: adjetivo posesivo *gram.* possessive adjective (2)

posibilidad *f.* possibility

posible possible (2)

posición *f.* position

positivo/a positive

postal: tarjeta postal postcard (7)

postre *m.* dessert (6)

postura stance

potente powerful

práctica practice

practicante *m., f.* practitioner; trainee

practicar (qu) to practice (1); to participate in (*a sport*)

práctico/a practical

precedente *m.* precedent

preciado/a valued

precio price (3); **precio fijo** fixed (set) price (3)

precioso/a precious

precipitado/a hasty

precisión *f.* precision

precocinado/a pre-cooked

precolombino/a *adj.* pre-Columbian

predicción *f.* prediction

preferencia preference (P)

preferible preferable (13); **es preferible** it's preferible (13)

preferir (ie, i) to prefer (3)

pregunta question; **hacer** (*irreg.*) **una pregunta** to ask a question (4)

preguntar to ask (*a question*) (6)

preliminar *m., f. adj.* preliminary

prematuro/a premature

premio prize, award

prender to turn on (*a light*)

prensa press (17); news media (17)

preocupación *f.* worry

preocupado/a worried (5)

preocuparse to worry

preparación *f.* preparation (*general*)

preparar to prepare (6)

preparativo preparation (*specific act*)

preposición *f. gram.* preposition (4)

presa capture

presencia presence

presentación *f.* presentation

presentar to present

presente *n. m.* present (*time*); *adj.* present

preservación *f.* preservation

presidencial presidential

presidente/a president

presión *f.* pressure (11); **sufrir (muchas) presiones** to be under (a lot of) pressure (11)

prestado/a: pedir (i, i) prestado to borrow (16)

préstamo loan (16)

prestar to lend (7)

prestigio prestige

prestigioso/a prestigious

presupuesto budget (16)

pretérito *gram.* preterite

primario/a primary

primavera spring (5); **vacaciones** (*f. pl.*) **de primavera** spring break

primer, primero/a first (4); **a primera vista** at first sight (15); **el primero de** first of (*the month*) (5); **por primera vez** for the first time (11); **primer(a) ministro/a** prime minister; **primera clase** first class (7)

primo/a cousin (2)

princesa princess

principal main, principal; **plato principal** main course

príncipe *m.* prince

principiante *m., f.* beginner

principio beginning; **a principios de** at the beginning of; **al principio de** at the beginning of (16)

prisa: tener (*irreg.*) **prisa** to be in a hurry (3)

privado/a private

probabilidad *f.* probability

probable probable

probar (ue) to try; to taste

problema *m.* problem

procesamiento processing

producir *irreg.* to produce

producto product

productor(a) producer

profesión *f.* profession (16)

profesional professional

profesor(a) professor (1)

profundidad *f.* depth

profundo/a deep

programa *m.* program; **programa informático** word-processing program

programador(a) programmer (16)

progresivo/a progressive

progreso progress

prohibir (prohíbo) to prohibit, forbid (12)

proliferación *f.* proliferation

prometer to promise (7)

prometido/a fiancé(e)

promover (ue) to promote

pronombre personal *m. gram.* subject pronoun (1)

pronominal *gram.* pronominal

pronto soon; **hasta pronto** see you soon; **tan pronto como** *conj.* as soon as (16)

pronunciación *f.* pronunciation

pronunciar to pronounce

propiedad *f.* property

propietario/a owner

propina tip (*to a waiter, etc.*) (18)

propio/a *adj.* own (15)

proponer (*like* **poner**) to propose

propósito purpose

próspero/a: Próspero Año Nuevo Happy New Year

protagonista *m., f.* protagonist

protección *f.* protection

proteger (j) to protect (14)

protestar to protest

provocar (qu) to cause, provoke

próximo/a next (4)

proyecto project

prudente cautious

prueba quiz (11); test (11)

psicología psychology

psicológico/a psychological

psíquico/a *adj.* psychic

publicación *f.* publication

publicidad *f.* publicity

publicitario/a *adj.* advertising

público *n.* public; audience; **público/a** *adj.* public (14)

pueblo town; people

puerta door (1)

puerto (sea)port (7)

puertorriqueño/a *n., adj.* Puerto Rican

pues *interj.* well

puesto place (*in line*) (7); job, position (16); stand, stall; **llevar puesto** to be wearing

pulmón *m.* (*pl.* **pulmones**) lung (10)

pulpo octopus

punto point; **a punto de** just about to; **en punto** exactly, on the dot (P); **punto cardinal** cardinal direction (5); **punto de vista** point of view

puntual punctual

puro/a pure (14)

púrpura purple

Q

que that (2), which; who (2)

¿qué? what? (P); which? (P); **¿a qué hora?** at what time? (P); **¿qué hora es?** what time is it? (P); **¿qué tal?** how are you (*doing*)? (P); **¿qué tiempo hace?** what's the weather like? (5)

¡qué... ! what . . . !; **¡qué bacán!** *sl.* how cool!; **¡qué extraño!** how strange! (13); **¡qué lástima!** what a shame! (13); **¡qué mala suerte!** what bad luck! (11); **¡qué pena!** what a shame!

quechua *m.* Quechua, *indigenous language in the Andes region of South America*

quedar to remain, be left (11); to be located; **quedarse** to stay, remain (*in a place*) (5)

quehacer *m.* chore (9); **quehacer doméstico** household chore (9)

quejarse (de) to complain (about) (8)

quemar to burn

querer *irreg.* to want (3); to love (15); **eso quiere decir...** that means . . . (10); **fue sin querer** it was unintentional (11); **querer decir** to mean

querido/a *adj.* dear (5); *n.* dear one, my dear

queso cheese (6)

quetzal *m. monetary unit of Guatemala*

quiché *m.* Quiche, *indigenous language of the Maya*

quien(es) who, whom

¿quién(es)? who?, whom? (P); **¿de quién... ?** whose? (2)

química chemistry (1)

quince fifteen (P)

quinceañera *young woman's fifteenth birthday party*

quinientos/as five hundred (3)

quinto/a fifth (13)

quiosco kiosk (18)

quitar la mesa to clear the table (9); **quitarse** to take off (*clothing*) (4)

quizás perhaps

R

rabino/a rabbi

racismo racism

radical *m. gram.* root, stem

radio *m.* radius (*Sp.*); radio (*apparatus*) (12); *f.* radio (*medium*) (12); **radio portátil** portable radio (12)

radioyentes *m. pl.* radio audience

raíz *f.* (*pl.* **raíces**) root

rancho ranch

rápido/a *adj.* fast (6)

ráquetbol *m.* racquetball

raro/a strange (8)

rascacielos *m. s., pl.* skyscraper (14)

rato while, short time; **ratos libres** spare (free) time (9)

ratón *m.* mouse (12)

raya: de rayas striped (3)

rayo ray

raza race; **Día** (*m.*) **de la Raza** Columbus Day, Hispanic Awareness Day

razón *f.* reason; **no tener** (*irreg.*) **razón** to be wrong (3); **tener** (*irreg.*) **razón** to be right (3)

reacción *f.* reaction

reaccionar to react (8)

real royal; real; **Real Academia Española** Royal Spanish Academy

realidad *f.* reality; **en realidad** in fact

realismo realism

realista *m., f.* realistic

realizar (c) to attain, achieve

rebaja sale, reduction (3)

rebajar to lower

rebasar to pass, exceed

rebelde rebellious

rebozo shawl

recado message

recambio: llanta de recambio spare tire

recepción *f.* front desk (18)

recepcionista *m., f.* front desk clerk

receta prescription (10)

recibir to receive (2)

reciclar to recycle (14)

recién *adv.* recently, newly

reciente recent

recipiente *m.* container

reciprocidad *f.* reciprocity

recíproco/a reciprocal

reclutar to recruit

recoger (j) to collect (11); to pick up (11)

recomendación *f.* recommendation

recomendar (ie) to recommend (7)

reconocer (*like* **conocer**) to recognize

reconocido/a well-known

recopilado/a compiled

récord *m.* record (*sports, etc.*)

recordar (ue) to remember (8)

recorte *m.* clipping

recreativo/a recreational

recreo recreation

rector(a) rector, president (*of a university*)

recubanizar (c) to become more in touch with one's Cuban roots

recuerdo souvenir

recurso resource; **recurso natural** natural resource (14)

red *f.* net (12); **navegar (gu) la red** to surf the net (12)

redacción *f.* editorial staff; **jefe/a de redacción** editor-in-chief

redondo/a round

reducir *irreg.* to reduce

reembolsar to refund

reembolso refund

referencia reference

referente a relating to

referirse (ie, i) (a) to refer (to)

reflejar to reflect

reflexivo/a: verbo reflexivo *gram.* reflexive verb (4)

reformar to reform

refrán *m.* proverb

refresco soft drink (6); refreshment (8)

refrigerador *m.* refrigerator (9)

refugiar to take refuge

refugio refuge

regalar to give (*as a gift*) (7)

regalo present, gift (2)

regatear to haggle, bargain (3)

régimen *m.* regime

región *f.* region

registrar to search, examine (18); to check (*a suitcase*)

registro register

regresar to return (*to a place*) (1); **regresar a casa** to go home (1)

regular *adj.* OK (P)

reina queen (17)

reino kingdom

reír(se) (i, i) (de) to laugh (at) (8)

relación *f.* relationship (15); relation

relacionar to relate, connect; to associate; **relacionarse** to be or become connected

relajado/a relaxed

relajante *n.* relaxant; *adj.* relaxing

relatar to relate, tell

religión *f.* religion

religioso/a religious

rellenar to fill out (*a form*)

reloj *m.* clock; watch (3)

remedio: no hay remedio there's no other way

remoto/a: control (*m.*) **remoto** remote control (12)

rendición *f.* rendition

renunciar (a) to resign (from) (16)

reparto: audición (*f.*) **de reparto** casting call

repasar to review

repaso *n.* review

repente: de repente suddenly (10)

repetición *f.* repetition

repetir (i, i) to repeat

reportaje *m.* report

reportero/a reporter (17)

represa dam

representación *f.* representation

representar to represent (13)

reproducción *f.* reproduction

república republic; **República Dominicana** Dominican Republic

requerir (ie, i) to require

requisito requirement

reserva reservation (18)

reservación *f.* reservation (18)

resfriado cold (*illness*) (10)

resfriarse (me resfrío) to get/catch a cold (10)

residencia residence; dormitory (1)

residencial residential

residente *m., f.* resident

residir to live, reside

resolver (ue) (*p.p.* **resuelto**) to solve, resolve (14)

respectivamente respectively

respecto respect; **con respecto a** with regard/respect to

respetar to respect

respeto respect

respirar to breathe (10)

responsabilidad *f.* responsibility (17)

responsable responsible

respuesta answer (5)

restaurante *m.* restaurant (6)

resto rest

restricción *f.* restriction

resuelto/a (*p.p. of* **resolver**) solved, resolved

resultado result

resultar to turn out

resumen *m.* summary

resumir to summarize

reto challenge

retórica speech

retrato portrait

reunirse (me reúno) (con) to get together (with) (8)

revelar to reveal

revisar to check (14)

revista magazine (2)

revolución *f.* revolution

rey *m.* king (17); **Día** (*m.*) **de los Reyes Magos** Epiphany, Day of the Magi

rico/a rich (2)

ridículo/a ridiculous

riesgo risk

rígido/a rigid

riguroso/a rigorous

rinoceronte *m.* rhinoceros

río river

riqueza wealth

ritmo rhythm, pace (14)

robar to steal

robo theft, robbery

robot *m.* robot

rodilla knee

rojo/a red (3)

rollo: es un rollo it's a pain

romano/a *n., adj.* Roman

romántico/a romantic

romper (*p.p.* **roto**) to break (11); **romper con** to break up with (15)

ron *m.* rum

ropa clothing (3); clothes; **planchar la ropa** to iron clothes (9); **ropa interior** underwear (3)

rosa rose

rosado/a pink (3)

roto/a (*p.p. of* **romper**) broken

rubio/a blond(e) (2)

ruido noise (4)

ruidoso/a noisy

ruina ruin (13)

rumba *music and dance from the Caribbean*

Rusia Russia

ruso Russian (*language*)

ruta route

rutina diaria *n.* daily routine (4)

rutinario/a *adj.* routine

S

sábado Saturday (4)

saber *irreg.* to know (6); **saber** + *inf.* to know how (*to do something*) (6)

sabiduría knowledge

sabor *m.* taste

sacar (qu) to take (*photos*) (7); to extract (10); to take out (11); to get (11); to withdraw, take out (16); **sacar buenas/malas notas** to get good/bad grades; **sacar el saldo** to balance a checkbook (16); **sacar la basura** to take out the trash (9);

sacar la lengua to stick out one's tongue (10); **sacar una muela** to extract a tooth (10)

sacrificio sacrifice

sacudir los muebles to dust the furniture (9)

Sagitario Sagittarius

sagrado/a sacred

sal *f.* salt

sala room; living room (4); **sala de clase** classroom; **sala de emergencias/urgencia** emergency room (10); **sala de espera** waiting room (7)

salario salary (16)

salchicha sausage (6); hot dog (6)

saldo: sacar (qu) el saldo to balance a checkbook (16)

salida departure (7)

salir *irreg.* to leave (4); to go out (4); **salir bien** to turn out well; **salir con** to go out with, date (15)

salmón *m.* salmon (6)

salsa salsa, *music and dance from the Caribbean*

saltar to jump

salud *f.* health (10)

saludable healthy

saludarse to greet (each other) (10)

saludo greeting (P)

salvadoreño/a *adj.* Salvadoran

san, santo/a saint; **Día** (*m.*) **de Todos los Santos** All Saints' Day; **día** (*m.*) **del santo** saint's day; **santo/a patrón/patrona** patron saint

sandalia sandal (3)

sándwich *m.* sandwich (6)

sangre *f.* blood (10)

sanitario/a sanitary

sano/a: llevar una vida sana to lead a healthy life (10)

santo/a holy; **Semana Santa** Holy Week

sardina sardine

satélite *m.* satellite

satirizar (c) to satirize

saxofón *m.* saxophone

se *refl. pron.* herself; himself; itself; yourself (*form.*); themselves; yourselves

sé I know

secadora clothes dryer (9)

secar (qu) to dry

sección *f.* section; **sección de (no) fumar** (no) smoking section (7)

secretario/a secretary (1)

secreto *n.* secret

secuencia sequence

secundario/a secondary

sed *f.* thirst; **tener** (*irreg.*) **(mucha) sed** to be (very) thirsty (6)

seda silk (3); **es de seda** it's made of silk (3)

sede *f.* seat; site

segmento segment

seguida: en seguida right away

seguir (i, i) (g) to continue (14); to follow; **seguir todo derecho** to go straight ahead

según according to (2)

segundo/a *adj.* second (13); **de segunda mano** second hand; **Segunda Guerra Mundial** World War II

seguro/a *adj.* sure, certain (5); **es seguro** it's a sure thing (13); **seguro social** *n.* Social Security

seis six (P)

seiscientos/as six hundred (3)

selección *f.* selection

sello stamp (*postage*) (18)

selva jungle

semáforo traffic signal (14)

semana week; **fin** (*m.*) **de semana** weekend (1); **la semana que viene** next week (4); **Semana Santa** Holy Week; **una vez a la semana** once a week (2)

sembrar (ie) to plant, sow

semejante similar

semejanza similarity

semestre *m.* semester

semi-amueblado/a partly furnished

senado senate

senador(a) senator

sencillo/a simple

sendero path

sensación *f.* sensation

sensible sensitive

sentarse (ie) to sit down (4)

sentido meaning; sense; **sentido común** common sense

sentimiento feeling

sentir (ie, i) to regret (13); to feel sorry (13); **lo siento (mucho)** I'm (very) sorry (11); **sentirse** to feel (8)

señor *m.* man; Mr. (P)

señora *f.* woman; Mrs. (P)

señorita *f.* young woman; Miss (P)

separación *f.* separation

separado: por separado separately

separarse (de) to separate (from) (15)

septiembre *m.* September (5)

séptimo/a seventh (13)

ser *irreg.* to be (2); **fue sin querer** it was unintentional (11); **ser aficionado/a (a)** to be a fan (of) (9); **ser divertido/a** to be fun (9); **ser en** + *place* to take place in/at (*place*) (8); **ser flexible** to be flexible (11)

ser *m.* being

serio/a serious

serpenteante winding

serpiente *f.* snake

servicio service (14); **servicio militar** military service (17)

servilleta (dinner) napkin

servir (i, i) to serve (4)

sesenta sixty (2)

sesión *f.* session

setecientos/as seven hundred (3)

setenta seventy (2)

severo/a severe

sevillano/a *n. person from Seville*

sexo sex

sexto/a sixth (13)

si if (2)

sí yes (P); **sí, me gusta...** yes, I like . . . (P)

siamés *adj.* Siamese

sicoanálisis *m.* psychoanalysis

sicología psychology (1)

sicólogo/a psychologist (16)

SIDA *m.* AIDS

siempre always (2)

siesta nap; **dormir (ue, u) la siesta** to take a nap (4)

siete seven (P)

siglo century

significar (qu) to mean

signo sign

siguiente *adj.* following (5)

sílaba syllable

silencio silence

silla chair (1)

sillón *m.* armchair (4)

simbólico/a symbolic

simbolizar (c) to symbolize

símbolo symbol

simpático/a nice (2); likeable (2)

sin without (4); **sin baño/ducha** without bath/shower (18); **sin duda** without a doubt; **sin embargo** however; **sin falta** without fail; **sin fines de lucro** not-for-profit; **sin fines lucrativos** non-profit; **sin intromisiones** without intrusions

sinceridad *f.* sincerity

sincero/a sincere

sindical *adj.* union, *pertaining to a labor/trade union*

sindicato union (*labor, trade*)

sinfin *m.* endless number

sino but (rather)

sintético/a synthetic

síntoma *m.* symptom (10)

siquiatra *m., f.* psychiatrist (16)

siquiera: ni siquiera not even

sistema *m.* system; **analista** (*m., f.*) **de sistemas** systems analyst (16)

sitio place; site; **sitio** *web* web site

situación *f.* situation

situado/a situated, located

sobre *m.* envelope (18); **sobre** *prep.* on; over; about; **sobre todo** above all

sobrepasar to surpass

sobrino/a nephew/niece (2)

social: seguro social Social Security; **trabajador(a) social** social worker (16)

socialista *m., f. adj.* socialist

sociedad *f.* society

socio/a member

socioeconómico/a socioeconomic

sociología sociology (1)

sociólogo/a sociologist

socorro *n.* help

sofá *m.* sofa (4)

sofisticado/a sophisticated

software *m.* software

sol *m.* sun; *monetary unit of Peru*; **hace sol** it's sunny (5); **tomar el sol** to sunbathe (7)

solamente only

solar solar (14)

solas: a solas alone

soldado soldier (16); **mujer** (*f.*) **soldado** female soldier (16)

soledad *f.* solitude

soler (ue) to be in the habit of

solicitar to ask for

solicitud *f.* application (*form*) (16)

solitario/a solitary

solo/a single; alone (7)

sólo *adv.* only (1)

soltero/a single (*unmarried*) (2)

solución *f.* solution

solucionar to solve

sombra shadow

sombrero hat (3)

sombrilla umbrella

somozista *m., f.* follower of Somoza

son las... it's . . . (*time*) (P)

sonar (ue) to ring (9); to sound (9)

sonreír(se) (i, i) to smile (8)

soñar (ue) (con) to dream (about)

sopa soup (6)

sorprendente surprising

sorprender to surprise; **me (te, le...) sorprende** it surprises me (you, him, . . .) (13)

sorpresa surprise (8)

soviético/a Soviet

soy I am (P)

Sr. (*abbrev. of* **señor**) Mr. (P)

Sra. (*abbrev. of* **señora**) Mrs. (P)

Srta. (*abbrev. of* **señorita**) Miss (P)

su(s) *poss. adj.* his, her, its, your (*form. s.*) (2); their, your (*form. pl.*) (2)

subir (a) to go up (7); to get on (*a vehicle*) (7)

subjuntivo *gram.* subjunctive

subordinado/a subordinate

subrayado/a underlined

subsistir to subsist

subtítulo subtitle

subtropical subtropical

sucio/a dirty (5)

sucre *m. former monetary unit of Ecuador*

sucursal *f.* branch (*office*) (16)

Sudamérica South America

sudamericano/a *n., adj.* South American

Suecia Sweden

suegro/a father-in-law / mother-in-law

sueldo salary (12); **aumento de sueldo** salary raise (16)

suelo floor

suelto/a *adj.* free

sueño sleep; dream; **tener** (*irreg.*) **sueño** to be sleepy (3)

suerte *f.* luck; **¡qué mala suerte!** what bad luck! (11); **tener** (*irreg.*) **suerte** to be lucky

suéter *m.* sweater (3)

suficiente enough; **lo suficiente** enough (10)

sufijo *gram.* suffix

sufrimiento suffering

sufrir to suffer (11); **sufrir (muchas) presiones** to be under (a lot) of pressure (11)

sugerencia suggestion

sugerir (ie, i) to suggest (8)

suicidio suicide

Suiza Switzerland

sujeto subject

sumo *indigenous people of Nicaragua*

superar to overcome

supercarretera superhighway

superficie *f.* surface

superior higher

superlativo *gram.* superlative

supermercado supermarket

suponer (*like* **poner**) to suppose

supuesto: por supuesto of course (11)

sur *m. n.* south (5); *adj.* southern

surgir (j) to spring up, arise

surrealista *m., f. adj.* surrealistic

suscribirse (*p.p.* **suscrito**) to subscribe

suscrito/a (*p.p. of* **suscribirse**) subscribed

suspender to suspend, cut off

sustancioso/a heavy

sustantivo *gram.* noun (1)

sustituir (y) to substitute

suyo(s)/a(s) *poss. adj.* his, (of) his, her, (of) hers, your, (of) yours (*form.*)

T

tabacalero/a *adj.* tobacco, *pertaining to tobacco*

tabaco tobacco

tabla: montar en tabla de vela to windsurf

tailandés, tailandesa *adj.* Thai

taíno *indigenous group of the Caribbean*

tal such (a); just; **con tal (de) que** *conj.* provided (that) (15); **¿qué tal?** how are you (*doing*)? (P); **tal(es) como** such as; **tal vez** perhaps

talento talent

talentoso/a talented

taller *m.* (repair) shop (14)

también also (P)

tamborista *m., f.* drummer

tampoco neither, not either (6)

tan so; as; **tan... como** as . . . as (5); **tan pronto como** *conj.* as soon as (16)

tanque *m.* tank (14)

tanto *adv.* so much; **tanto/a** *adj.* so much; such; *pl.* so many; **estar** (*irreg.*) **al tanto** to be up-to-date; **tanto como** as much as (5); **tantos/as... como** as much / many . . . as (5)

tarde *adv.* late (1); **llegar (gu) tarde** to arrive late (11); **tarde** *f. n.* afternoon; **buenas tardes** good afternoon (P); **de la tarde** p.m., in the afternoon (P); **por la tarde** in the afternoon (1)

tarea homework (4); task; **tarea doméstica** household chore

tarjeta card (7); **tarjeta de crédito** credit card (6); **tarjeta de identificación** identification card (11); **tarjeta postal** postcard (7)

tarta pie
tasa rate
taurino/a *pertaining to bulls*
Tauro Taurus
taxi *m.* taxi
taza cup
te *d.o. pron.* you (*fam. s.*); *i.o. pron.* to/for you (*fam. s.*); *refl. pron.* yourself (*fam. s.*); **¿te gusta... ?** do you (*fam.*) like . . . ? (P)
té *m.* tea (6)
teatral *adj.* theater
teatro *n.* theater (13); **ir** (*irreg.*) **al teatro** to go to the theater (9)
teclado keyboard
técnica technique
técnico/a *n.* technician (16); *adj.* technical
tecnología technology
tecnológico/a technological
tejer to weave (13)
tejidos *pl.* woven goods (13)
telediario newscast
telefonear to telephone
telefónico/a *adj.* telephone; **cabina telefónica** telephone booth; **guía telefónica** telephone book, directory
teléfono telephone; **hablar por teléfono** to talk on the telephone (1); **teléfono celular / de coche** cellular/car phone (12)
telegrama *m.* telegram
telenovela soap opera
televidente *m., f.* television viewer
televisión *f.* television (*medium*); **mirar la televisión** to watch television (2)
televisor *m.* television set (4)
tema *m.* subject, topic; theme
temático/a: parque (*m.*) **temático** theme park
temblar to tremble
temer to fear (13)
temperatura temperature (10); **tomarle la temperatura** to take someone's temperature (10)
templado/a temperate
templo temple
temporal seasonal
temprano *adv.* early (1)

tender (ie) (a) to tend (to), be inclined (to)
tener *irreg.* to have (3); **no tener** (*irreg.*) **razón** to be wrong (3); **ten cuidado** be careful; **tener... años** to be . . . years old (2); **tener (mucho) calor** to be (very) warm, hot (*feeling*) (5); **tener dolor de** to have a pain in (10); **tener éxito** to be successful; **tener fiebre** to have a fever; **tener (mucho) frío** to be (very) cold (5); **tener ganas de** + *inf.* to feel like (*doing something*) (3); **tener (mucha) hambre** to be (very) hungry (6); **tener lugar** to take place; **tener miedo (de)** to be afraid (of) (3); **tener prisa** to be in a hurry (3); **tener que** + *inf.* to have to (*do something*) (3); **tener razón** to be right (3); **tener (mucha) sed** to be very thirsty (6); **tener sueño** to be sleepy (3); **tener suerte** to be lucky
tenis *m.* tennis (9); **zapato de tenis** tennis shoe (3)
tensión *f.* tension
teñir (i, i) to dye
teoría theory
teorizar (c) to theorize
tercer, tercero/a *adj.* third (13)
térmico/a thermal
terminación *f.* ending
terminar to end
término term (*word*)
termostato thermostat
terraza terrace
terremoto earthquake
terreno plot of land
terrestre terrestrial
territorio territory
terror *m.* horror, terror
terrorista *m., f. n.* terrorist (17)
testigo *m., f.* witness (17)
testimonio testimony
texto: libro de texto textbook (1)
ti *obj. of prep.* you (*fam. s.*) (5)
tiempo weather; time; **a tiempo** on time (7); **de tiempo completo/ parcial** full/part-time (11); **hace buen/mal tiempo** it's good/bad weather (5); **llegar (gu) a tiempo**

to arrive on time (11); **pasar tiempo (con)** to spend time (with) (15); **por un tiempo** for a while; **¿qué tiempo hace?** what's the weather like? (5); **tiempo libre** leisure/free time
tienda shop, store (3); **tienda (de campaña)** tent (7)
tierra land; earth
tigre *m.* tiger
tímido/a shy
tinto: vino tinto red wine (6)
tío/a uncle/aunt (2)
típico/a typical
tipo type; **tipo/a** *coll.* guy/girl
tipográfico/a typographical
tira cómica comic strip
titularse to be titled
título title
toalla towel
tocar (qu) to play (*an instrument*) (1); to touch; **tocarle a uno** to be someone's turn (9)
todavía *adv.* still (5)
todo *pron.* all; everything; **ante todo** first of all; **de todo** everything (3); **todo/a(s)** *adj.* all (2); every (2); full; **de todas maneras** anyway; **Día** (*m.*) **de Todos los Santos** All Saints' Day; **por todas partes** everywhere (11); **todo derecho** straight ahead (14); **todos los días** every day (1)
tolerante tolerant
tolteca *m., f. adj.* Toltec
tomado/a *coll.* drunk
tomar to take (1); to drink (1); to eat; **tomar el sol** to sunbathe (7); **tomarle la temperatura** to take someone's temperature (10); **tomar una copa** to have a drink
tomate *m.* tomato (6)
tonto/a silly, foolish (2)
toreo bullfighting
torneo tournament
toro bull; **corrida de toros** bullfight; **plaza de toros** bullring
torpe clumsy (11)
tortilla omelet (*Sp.*); tortilla, *flat corn or flour bread* (*Mex.*)

tos *f.* cough (10)
toser to cough (10)
tostado/a toasted; **pan** (*m.*) **tostado** toast (6)
tostadora toaster (9)
trabajador(a) *n.* worker; **trabajador(a) agrícola** agricultural worker; **trabajador(a) social** social worker (16); *adj.* hard-working (2)
trabajar to work (1)
trabajo work, job (11); report, (piece of) work (11)
trabalenguas *m. s., pl.* tongue-twister
tractor *m.* tractor
tradición *f.* tradition (13)
traducción *f.* translation
traducir *irreg.* to translate
traductor(a) translator (16)
traer *irreg.* to bring (4)
traficar (qu) to traffic
tráfico traffic
tragedia tragedy
trágico/a tragic
trago (*alcoholic*) drink (18)
traje *m.* suit (3); **traje de baño** swimsuit (3)
tranquilidad *f.* tranquility, calm
tranquilizar (c) to tranquilize
tranquilo/a calm; **llevar una vida tranquila** to lead a calm life (10)
transbordador (*m.*) **espacial** space shuttle
tránsito traffic (14)
transmisión *f.* transmission
transmitir to transmit
transporte *m.* (means of) transportation (14)
trasladarse to transfer, move
tratamiento treatment (10)
tratar to treat; **se trata de** it's about; it's a question of; **tratar de** + *inf.* to try (*to do something*) (13)
trauma *m.* trauma
través: a través de through; throughout; across
travieso/a mischievous
trece thirteen (P)
treinta thirty (P); **y treinta** thirty, half past (*time*) (P)

tremendo/a tremendous
tren *m.* train (7); **estación** (*f.*) **de tren** train station (7)
tres three (P)
trescientos/as three hundred (3)
trimestre *m.* trimester
triste sad (5)
tristeza sadness
trofeo trophy
trompeta trumpet
trópico tropics
tropiezo mishap
tu(s) *poss. adj.* your (*fam. s.*) (2)
tú *sub. pron. s.* you (*fam.*) (1); **¿y tú?** and you? (P)
tubería plumbing
turbulento/a turbulent
turista *m., f.* tourist
turístico/a *adj.* tourist; **clase** (*f.*) **turística** tourist class (7)
turno: de turno on duty
tuyo(s)/a(s) *poss. adj.* your, (of) yours (*fam. s.*)

U

u or (*used instead of* **o** *before words beginning with stressed* **o** *or* **ho**)
ubicado/a located
Ud(s). (*abbrev. for* **usted**) you (*form.*) (1)
último/a last (7); **de última moda** the latest style (3); **por última vez** for the last time (11); **por último** finally
un(a) *indef. art.* a, an; **una vez** once (10); **una vez a la semana** once a week (2)
un, uno one (P)
único/a only
unido/a united; close-knit; **Naciones Unidas** United Nations
unificarse (qu) to unify
unión *f.* union
unirse to join together
universidad *f.* university (1)
universitario/a *adj.* (of the) university (11)
unos(as) *indef. art.* some
urbano/a urban
urgencia: sala de urgencia emergency room (10)

urgente urgent (13)
uruguayo/a *adj.* Uruguayan
usar to use (3); to wear (*clothing*) (3)
uso use
usted (Ud.) *sub. pron. s.* you (*form.*) (1); *obj. of prep. s.* you (*form.*); **¿y usted?** and you? (*form.*) (P)
ustedes (Uds.) *sub. pron. pl.* you (*form.*) (1); *obj. of prep. pl.* you (*form.*)
útil useful (15)
utilización *f.* use, utilization
utilizar (c) to use
uva grape
¡uy! *interj.* oops!; oh!

V

vacaciones *f., pl.* vacation; **estar** (*irreg.*) **de vacaciones** to be on vacation (7); **ir** (*irreg.*) **de vacaciones** to go on vacation (7); **vacaciones de primavera** spring break
vacuna vaccine
vahído dizzy spell
Valentín: Día (*m.*) **de San Valentín** Valentine's Day
valer (*irreg.*) **la pena** to be worthwhile
válido/a valid
valiente brave
valor *m.* value; courage, bravery
variar (varío) to vary
variedad *f.* variety
varios/as several
vasco Basque (*language*)
vaso glass
vecindad *f.* neighborhood (12)
vecino/a neighbor (12)
vegetariano/a *n., adj.* vegetarian
vehicular *adj.* vehicular
vehículo vehicle (12)
veinte twenty (P)
veintecinco twenty-five
veinticuatro twenty-four
veintidós twenty-two
veintinueve twenty-nine
veintiocho twenty-eight
veintiséis twenty-six
veintisiete twenty-seven
veintitrés twenty-three
veintiún, veintiuno/a twenty-one

vejez *f.* old age (15)
vela: montar en tabla de vela to windsurf
velocidad *f.* speed; **límite** (*m.*) **de velocidad** speed limit (14)
vendedor(a) salesperson (16)
vender to sell (2)
venezolano/a *adj.* Venezuelan
venir *irreg.* to come (3); **la semana que viene** next week (4); **venga** come on
venta sale
ventaja advantage (10)
ventana window (1)
ventilación *f.* ventilation
ver *irreg.* to see (4); **a ver** let's see; **ir** (*irreg.*) **a ver una película** to go to see a movie (9); **nos vemos** see you around (P)
verano summer (5)
veras: de veras really
verbo *gram.* verb (1)
verdad *f. n.* truth; **¿verdad?** right? (3); okay?; *adj.* true; **de verdad** truly, really
verdadero/a real
verde green (3)
verdura vegetable (6)
verificación *f.* inspection
verificar (qu) to verify
versión *f.* version
vestido dress (3)
vestirse (i, i) to get dressed (4)
veterinario/a veterinarian (16)
vez *f.* (*pl.* **veces**) time; **a veces** sometimes (2); **a la vez** at the same time; **alguna vez** once; **de vez en cuando** once in a while; **dos veces** twice (10); **en vez de** instead of (16); **otra vez** again; **por primera/última vez** for the first/last time (11); **tal vez** perhaps; **una vez** once (10); **una vez a la semana** once a week (2)
vía: por vía aérea by air; by airmail
viajar to travel (7)
viaje *m.* trip; **agencia de viajes** travel agency (7); **agente** (*m., f.*) **de viajes** travel agent (7); **¡buen viaje!**

have a good trip! (7); **de viaje** on a trip (7); **hacer** (*irreg.*) **un viaje** to take a trip (4)
viajero/a *n.* traveler (18); **cheque** (*m.*) **de viajero** traveler's check (18); *adj.* traveling
vicepresidente/a vice-president
víctima *m., f.* victim
vida life (14); **llevar una vida sana/tranquila** to lead a healthy/calm life (10)
vídeo: cámara de vídeo video camera (12)
videocasetera videocassette recorder (VCR) (12)
videoteca video library
vidrio glass
viejo/a old (2); **Noche** (*f.*) **Vieja** New Year's Eve (8)
viento wind; **hace viento** it's windy (5)
viernes *m. s., pl.* Friday (4)
vietnamita *m., f. adj.* Vietnamese
vinícola *m., f. adj. pertaining to wine*
vino (blanco, tinto) (white, red) wine (6)
viñedo vineyard
viola viola
violencia violence (14)
violento/a violent
violín *m.* violin
virgen *f.* virgin
Virgo Virgo
visado visa
visigodo *n.* Visigoth
visita visit
visitante *m., f.* visitor
visitar to visit; **visitar un museo** to visit a museum (9)
vista view (12); sight; **a primera vista** at first sight (15); **punto de vista** point of view
vivienda housing (12)
vivir to live (2)
vocabulario vocabulary
vocal *f.* vowel
volante: objeto volante no identificado (OVNI) unidentified flying object (UFO)

volcán *m.* volcano
volcánico/a volcanic
vólibol *m.* volleyball (9)
voluntario/a volunteer
volver (ue) (*p.p.* **vuelto**) to return (*to a place*) (4); **volver a** + *inf.* to (*do something*) again (4)
vos *pers. pron. s.* you (*substitute for* **tú** *in some areas of Latin America*)
voseo *n. refers to the use of* **vos**
vosotros/as *sub. pron. pl.* you (*fam. Sp.*) (1); *obj. of a prep. pl.* you (*fam. Sp.*)
votante *m., f.* voter
votar to vote (17)
vuelo flight (7); **asistente** (*m., f.*) **de vuelo** flight attendant (7)
vuelta: dar (*irreg.*) **la vuelta** to go around; **billete** (*m.*)**/boleto de ida y vuelta** round-trip ticket (7); **de vuelta** (*to be*) back
vuestro/a(s) *poss. adj.* your (*fam. pl. Sp.*) (2); your, of yours (*fam. pl., Sp.*)

W

walkman *m.* walkman (12)
web: **página** *web* web page; **sitio** *web* website

Y

y and (P); **y cuarto** quarter past (*time*) (P); **y media (treinta)** half past (thirty) (*time*) (P); **¿y tú?** and you? (*fam.*) (P); **¿y usted?** (*form.*) (P)
ya already (8); **ya no** no longer; **ya que** since
yacimiento deposit (*mineral*)
yo *sub. pron.* I (1)
yogur *m.* yogurt (6)

Z

zanahoria carrot (6)
zapatería shoe store
zapato (de tenis) (tennis) shoe (3)
zapoteca *m., f. n.* Zapotec
zona zone, area
zoo *m.* zoo

A

able: to be able **poder** (*irreg.*) (3)
abroad **extranjero** *n.* (18); to go abroad **ir al extranjero** (18)
absence **falta** (14)
absent: to be absent **faltar** (8)
absentminded **distraído/a** (11)
accelerated **acelerado/a** (14)
accident **accidente** *m.* (11)
according to **según** (2)
account **cuenta** (16); checking account **cuenta corriente** (16); savings account **cuenta de ahorros** (16)
accountant **contador(a)** (16)
ache **doler (ue)** *v.* (10); **dolor** *n.m.* (10)
acquainted: to be acquainted with **conocer (zc)** (6)
actor **actor** *m.* (13)
actress **actriz** *f.* (*pl.* **actrices**) (13)
additional **adicional** (P)
address **dirección** *f.* (12)
adjective **adjetivo** *gram.* (2)
administration: business administration **administración** (*f.*) **de empresas** (1)
adolescence **adolescencia** (15)
advantage **ventaja** (10)
advice (piece of) **consejo** (6)
advisor **consejero/a** (1)
aerobic **aeróbico/a** (10); to do aerobics **hacer** (*irreg.*) **ejercicio aeróbico** (10)
affectionate **cariñoso/a** (5)
afraid: to be afraid (of) **tener** (*irreg.*) **miedo (de)** (3)
after *prep.* **después de** (4); *conj.* **después (de) que** (16)
afternoon **tarde** *n. f.* (1); good afternoon **buenas tardes** (P); (a time) in the afternoon **de la tarde** (P); in the afternoon **por la tarde** (1)
again: to (*do something*) again **volver a** + *inf.*
age: old age **vejez** *f.* (15); middle age **madurez** *f.* (15)

agency: travel agency **agencia de viajes** (7)
agent: travel agent **agente** (*m., f.*) **de viajes** (7)
ago (*time*) **hace** + *time* (11)
agree: I agree **estoy de acuerdo** (2)
ahead of time **con anticipación** (18); straight ahead **todo derecho** (14)
air **aire** *m.* (14)
airplane **avión** *m.* (7)
airport **aeropuerto** (7)
alarm clock **despertador** *m.* (11)
all **todo(s)/a(s)** *adj.* (2)
allow **permitir** (12)
almost: almost never **casi nunca** (2)
alone **solo/a** *adj.* (7)
along: to get along well/poorly (with) **llevarse bien/mal (con)** (15)
alongside of **al lado de** (5)
already **ya** (8)
also **también** (P)
always **siempre** (2)
among **entre** *prep.* (5)
amusement **diversión** *f.* (9)
analyst: systems analyst **analista** (*m., f.*) **de sistemas** (16)
and **y** (P)
angry **furioso/a** (5); to get angry (at) **enojarse (con)** (8)
announce **anunciar** (7)
another **otro/a** (2)
answer *v.* **contestar** (4); *n.* **respuesta** (5)
answering machine **contestador** (*m.*) **automático** (12)
antibiotic **antibiótico** (10)
any **algún, alguno/a** (6); not any **ningún (ninguno/a)** (6)
anybody: not anybody **nadie** (6)
anyone **alguien** (6)
anything **algo** (3); not anything **nada** (6)
apartment **apartamento** (1); apartment building **bloque** (*m.*) **de apartamentos** (12); **casa de apartamentos** (12)
apologize **pedir (i, i) disculpas** (11)

apple **manzana** (6)
appliance: home appliance **aparato doméstico** (9)
applicant **aspirante** *m., f.* (16)
application (form) **solicitud** *f.* (16)
appreciate **apreciar** (13)
April **abril** *m.* (5)
architect **arquitecto/a** (13)
architecture **arquitectura** (13)
area **área** *f.* (*but* **el área**) (12)
argue (about) (with) **discutir (sobre) (con)** (8)
arm **brazo** (11)
armchair **sillón** *m.* (4)
army **ejército** (17)
arrival **llegada** (7)
arrive **llegar (gu)** (2); to arrive on time/late **llegar a tiempo/tarde** (11)
art **arte** *f.* (*but* **el arte**) (1); work of art **obra de arte** (13)
article **artículo** (1)
artist **artista** *m., f.* (13)
artistic **artístico/a** (13)
arts and crafts **artesanía** (13)
as . . . as **tan... como** (5); as much/many as **tanto/a... como** (5); as soon as **tan pronto como** *conj.*; **en cuanto** *conj.* (16)
ask: to ask for **pedir (i, i)** (4); to ask a question **hacer** (*irreg.*) **una pregunta** (4); **preguntar** (6)
asleep: to fall asleep **dormirse (ue) (u)** (4)
asparagus **espárragos** *m. pl.* (6)
assassination **asesinato** (17)
at **en** (P); **a** (*with time*) (P); at . . . (hour) **a la(s)...** (P); at home **en casa** (1); at last **por fin** (4); at least **por lo menos** (10); at the beginning of **al principio de** (16); at times **a veces** (2)
attend (*a function*) **asistir (a)** (2)
attendant: flight attendant **asistente** (*m., f.*) **de vuelo** (7)
August **agosto** (5)
aunt **tía** (2)

automatic teller machine **cajero automático** (16)
autumn **otoño** (5)
avenue **avenida** (12)
avoid **evitar** (14)

B

baby-sitter **niñero/a** (9)
backpack **mochila** (1)
bad **mal, malo/a** *adj.* (2); it's bad weather **hace mal tiempo** (5); the bad thing, news **lo malo** (10); to have a bad time **pasarlo mal** (8); what bad luck **qué mala suerte** (11)
baggage **equipaje** *m.* (7)
balance a checkbook **sacar (qu) el saldo** (16)
balanced: in a balanced way **equilibradamente** (10)
ballet **ballet** *m.* (13)
ballpoint pen **bolígrafo** (1)
banana **banana** (6)
bank **banco** (16); (bank) check **cheque** *m.* (16)
bar **bar** *m.* (9)
bargain **ganga** (3); **regatear** (3)
baseball **béisbol** *m.* (9)
basketball **basquetbol** *m.* (9)
bath: to take a bath **bañarse** (4)
bathing suit **traje** (*m.*) **de baño** (3)
bathroom **baño** (4); bathroom sink **lavabo** (4)
bathtub **bañera** (4)
battery **batería** (14)
be **estar** (*irreg.*) (1); **ser** (*irreg.*) (2); **encontrarse (ue)** (10); to be able **poder** (*irreg.*) (3); to be (feel) warm, hot **tener** (*irreg.*) **calor** (5); to be (very) hungry **tener** (*irreg.*) **(mucha) hambre** (6); to be . . . years old **tener** (*irreg.*) **. . . años** (2); to be a fan (of) **ser** (*irreg.*) **aficionado/a (a)** (9); to be afraid (of) **tener** (*irreg.*) **miedo (de)** (3); to be boring **ser** (*irreg.*) **aburrido/a** (9); to be born **nacer (zc)** (15); to be cold **tener** (*irreg.*) **frío** (5); to be comfortable (*temperature*) **estar** (*irreg.*) **bien** (5);

to be flexible **ser** (*irreg.*) **flexible** (11); to be fun **ser** (*irreg.*) **divertido/a** (9); to be happy (about) **alegrarse (de)** (12); to be in a hurry **tener** (*irreg.*) **prisa** (3); to be late **estar** (*irreg.*) **atrasado/a** (7); to be left **quedar (se)** (11); to be (very) thirsty **tener** (*irreg.*) **(mucha) sed** (6); to take place in/at (*place*) **ser** (*irreg.*) **en** + *place* (8)
beach **playa** (5)
bean **frijol** *m.* (6)
beautiful **bello/a** (14)
because **porque** (2)
become + *adj.* **ponerse** (*irreg.*) + *adj.* (8)
bed: **cama** (4); to get up on the wrong side of the bed **levantarse con el pie izquierdo** (11); to go to bed **acostarse (ue)** (4); to make the bed **hacer** (*irreg.*) **la cama** (9); to stay in bed **guardar cama** (10)
bedroom **alcoba** (4)
beer **cerveza** (1)
before *conj.* **antes (de) que** (15); *prep.* **antes de** (4)
begin **empezar (ie) (c)** (4)
beginning: at the beginning of **al principio de** (16)
behave **portarse** (8)
behind **detrás de** *prep.* (5)
believe (in) **creer (y) (en)** (2)
bellhop **mozo, botones** *m. s., pl.* (18)
below **debajo de** *prep.* (5)
belt **cinturón** *m.* (3)
bend **doblar** (14)
beside **al lado (de)** *prep.* (5)
best **mejor** (5)
better **mejor** (5)
between **entre** *prep.* (5)
beverage **bebida** (6)
bicycle **bicicleta** (12); mountain bike **bicicleta de montaña** (12); to ride a bicycle **pasear en bicicleta** (9)
bicycling **ciclismo** (9)
big **gran, grande** (2)
bilingual **bilingüe** (11)
bill (*for service*) **cuenta** (6); **factura** (16)

bird **pájaro** (2)
birth **nacimiento** (15)
birthday **cumpleaños** *m. s., pl.* (5); birthday cake **pastel** (*m.*) **de cumpleaños** (8); to have a birthday **cumplir años** (8)
black **negro/a** (3)
blond(e) **rubio/a** *n., adj.* (2)
blood **sangre** *f.* (10)
blouse **blusa** (3)
blue **azul** (3)
boarding house **pensión** *f.* (18); room and full board **pensión completa** (18); room with breakfast and one other meal **media pensión** (18)
boat **barco** (7)
body **cuerpo** (10)
book **libro** (1)
bookshelf **estante** *m.* (4)
bookstore **librería** (1)
boot **bota** (3)
border **frontera** (18)
bore **aburrir** (13)
bored **aburrido/a** (5); to get bored **aburrirse** (9)
boring: to be boring **ser** (*irreg.*) **aburrido/a** (9)
born: to be born **nacer (zc)** (15)
borrow **pedir (i, i) prestado/a** (16)
boss **jefe/a** (12)
bother **molestar** (13); it bothers me (you, him, . . .) **me (te, le, . . .) molesta** (13)
boy **muchacho** (4); **niño** (2)
boyfriend **novio** (5)
brain **cerebro** (10)
brakes **frenos** (14)
branch (office) **sucursal** *f.* (16)
bread **pan** *m.* (6)
break **romper** (*p.p.* **roto/a**) (11); to break up (with) **romper (con)** (15)
breakfast **desayuno** (4); to have breakfast **desayunar** (6)
breathe **respirar** (10)
bring **traer** (*irreg.*) (4)
brother **hermano** (2)
brown **pardo/a** (3)
brunet(te) **moreno/a** *n., adj.* (2)

brush one's teeth **cepillarse los dientes** (4)

budget **presupuesto** (16)

build **construir (y)** (14)

building **edificio** *n.* (1); apartment building **casa/bloque** (*m.*) **de apartamentos** (12); building manager **portero/a** (12)

bump into **darse** (*irreg.*) **con** (11); **pegarse (gu) en/contra** (11)

bureau (*furniture*) **cómoda** (4)

bus **autobús** *m.* (7); bus station **estación** (*f.*) **de autobuses** (7); bus stop **parada del autobús** (18)

business **empresa** (16); business administration **administración** (*f.*) **de empresas** (1)

businessperson **hombre** (*m.*)/**mujer** (*f.*) **de negocios** (16)

busy **ocupado/a** (5)

but **pero** *conj.* (P)

butter **mantequilla** (6)

buy **comprar** (1)

by **por** *prep.* (4); in the morning (afternoon, evening) **por la mañana** (**tarde, noche**) (1); by check **con cheque** (16)

C

cabin **cabina** (*on a ship*) (7)

café **café** *m.* (18)

cafeteria **cafetería** (1)

cake **pastel** *m.* (6); birthday cake **pastel de cumpleaños** (8)

calculator **calculadora** (1)

calendar **calendario** (11)

call *v.* **llamar** (6); to be called **llamarse** (4)

calm **tranquilo/a** (10)

camera: video camera **cámara de vídeo** (12)

campground *camping* *m.* (7)

camping: to go camping **hacer** (*irreg.*) *camping* (7)

campus **campus** *m. s.* (12)

can **poder** *v. irreg.* (3)

candidate **aspirante** *m., f.* (16)

candy **dulces** *m. pl.* (6)

capital city **capital** *f.* (5)

car **coche** *m.* (2); car telephone **teléfono del coche** (12); convertible car **carro descapotable** (12)

card: credit card **tarjeta de crédito** (6); identification card **tarjeta de identificación** (11); to play cards **jugar (ue) (gu) a las cartas** (9); (post)card **tarjeta (postal)** (7)

cardinal directions **puntos** (*m. pl.*) **cardinales** (5)

care: take care of oneself **cuidarse** (10)

carrot **zanahoria** (6)

carry **llevar** (3)

case **caso**; in case **en caso de que** (15); just in case **por si acaso** (11)

cash (*a check*) **cobrar** (16); in cash **en efectivo** (16); to pay in cash **pagar (gu) al contado / en efectivo** (16)

cashier **cajero/a** (16)

cat **gato/a** (2)

catch a cold **resfriarse (me resfrío)** (10)

CD-ROM **CD-ROM** *m.* (12)

celebrate **celebrar** (5)

cellular telephone **teléfono celular** (12)

ceramics **cerámica** (13)

cereal **cereales** *m. pl.* (6)

certain **seguro/a** *adj.* (5); **cierto/a** (13)

chair **silla** (1); armchair **sillón** *m.* (4)

chalkboard **pizarra** (1)

change *v.* **cambiar (de)** (12)

channel **canal** *m.* (12)

charge (*to an account*) **cargar (gu)** (16); (*someone for an item or service*) **cobrar** (16)

cheap **barato/a** (3)

check (*bank*) **cheque** *m.* (16); (*restaurant*) **cuenta** (6); by check **con cheque** (16); traveler's check **cheque de viajero** (18); to check **revisar** (14); to check into (*a hospital*) **internarse en** (10); to check one's bags **facturar el equipaje** (7)

checkbook: to balance a checkbook **sacar (qu) el saldo** (16)

checking account **cuenta corriente** (16)

check-up **chequeo** (10)

cheese **queso** (6)

chef **cocinero/a** (16)

chemistry **química** (1)

chess **ajedrez** *m.* (4); to play chess **jugar (ue) (gu) al ajedrez** (9)

chicken **pollo** (6); roast chicken **pollo asado** (6)

chief **jefe/a** (12)

child **niño/a** (2); as a child **de niño** (9)

childhood **niñez** *f.* (9)

children **hijos** *m. pl.* (2)

chop **chuleta** (6) pork chop **chuleta de cerdo** (6)

chore: household chore **quehacer** *m.* **doméstico** (9)

Christmas **Navidad** *f.* (8)

Christmas Eve **Nochebuena** (8)

citizen **ciudadano/a** (17)

city **ciudad** *f.* (2); capital city **capital** *f.* (5)

civic **cívico/a** (17)

class **clase** *f.* (1); first class **primera clase** (7); tourist class **clase turística** (7)

classical **clásico/a** (13)

classmate **compañero/a de clase** (1)

clean *adj.* **limpio/a** (5)

clean **limpiar** (9); to clean the (whole) house **limpiar la casa (entera)** (9)

cleaner: vacuum cleaner **aspiradora** (9)

clear the table **quitar la mesa** (9)

clerk **dependiente/a** (1)

clever **listo/a** (2)

client **cliente** *m., f.* (1)

climate **clima** *m.* (5)

clock: alarm clock **despertador** *m.* (11)

close **cerrar (ie)** (4)

close to *prep.* **cerca de** (5)

closed **cerrado/a** (5)

closet **armario** (4)

clothes dryer **secadora** (9)

clothing **ropa** (3); to wear (*clothing*) **llevar, usar** (3)

cloudy: it's (very) cloudy, overcast **está (muy) nublado** (5) clumsy **torpe** (11)

coat **abrigo** (3)

coffee **café** *m.* (1)

coffee pot **cafetera** (9)

cognate **cognado** (6)

cold (*illness*) **resfriado** (10); to be cold **tener** (*irreg.*) **frío** *n.* (5); to catch a cold **resfriarse** (10); it's cold (*weather*) **hace frío** (5); very cold **congelado/a** (5)

collect **recoger (j)** (11)

collide (with) **chocar (qu) (con)** (14)

collision **choque** *m.* (17)

color **color** *m.* (3)

comb one's hair **peinarse** (4)

come **venir** (*irreg.*) (3)

comfortable **cómodo/a** (4); to be comfortable (*temperature*) **estar** (*irreg.*) **bien** (5)

communicate (with) **comunicarse (qu) (con)** (17)

communication (*major*) **comunicación** *f.* (1); means of communication **medio de comunicación** (17)

community **comunidad** *f.* (12)

compact disc **disco compacto** (12)

comparison **comparación** *f.* (5)

complain (about) **quejarse (de)** (8)

composer **compositor(a)** (13)

computer **computadora** (*L.A.*) (12); **ordenador** *m.* (*Sp.*) (12); computer disk **disco de computadora** (12); computer file **archivo** (12); computer science **computación** *f.* (1); laptop computer **computadora/ ordenador portátil** (12)

concert **concierto** (9); to go to a concert **ir** (*irreg.*) **a un concierto** (9)

confirm **confirmar** (18)

congested **congestionado/a** (10)

congratulations **felicitaciones** *f. pl.* (8)

conjunction **conjunción** (*f.*) *gram.* (15)

conserve **conservar** (14)

contact lenses **lentes** (*m. pl.*) **de contacto** (10)

content *adj.* **contento/a** (5)

continue **seguir (i, i) (g)** (14); to continue straight ahead **seguir (i, i) derecho** (14)

control: remote control **control** (*m.*) **remoto** (12)

convertible (*car*) **descapotable** (12)

cook *v.* **cocinar** (6); *n.* cook **cocinero/a** (16)

cookie **galleta** (6)

cool: it's cool (*weather*) **hace fresco** (5)

copy **copia** (12); to copy **hacer** (*irreg.*) **copia** (12)

corn **maíz** *m.* (5)

corner (*street*) **esquina** (14)

corporation **empresa** (16)

cost: how much does it cost? **¿cuánto cuesta?** (3)

cotton **algodón** *m.* (3); it is made of cotton **es de algodón** (3)

cough **tos** *f.* (10); to cough **toser** (10); cough syrup **jarabe** *m.* (10)

count **contar (ue)** (17)

country **país** *m.* (2)

countryside **campo** (12)

couple (*married*) **matrimonio** (15), **pareja** (15)

course (*of a meal*) **plato** (6); of course **por supuesto** (11)

courtesy **cortesía** (P)

cousin **primo/a** (2)

cover **cubrir** (*pp.* **cubierto/a**) (14)

crafts: arts and crafts **artesanía** (13)

crash (*computer*) **fallar** (12)

crazy **loco/a** (5)

create **crear** (13)

credit card **tarjeta de crédito** (16)

crime **delito, crimen** *m.* (14)

cross **cruzar (c)** (18)

cry **llorar** (8)

custard: baked custard **flan** *m.* (6)

custom **costumbre** *f.* (9)

customs **aduana** *s.* (18); (customs) duty **derechos** (*m. pl.*) **(de aduana)** (18); (customs) inspector **inspector(a) (de aduanas)** (18)

D

dad **papá** *m.* (2)

daily routine **rutina diaria** (4)

dance **baile** *m.* (13); **danza** (13); to dance **bailar** (1)

dancer **bailarín, bailarina** (13)

date (*calendar*) **fecha** (5); (*social*) **cita** (15); what's today's date? **¿cuál es la fecha de hoy?** (5)

daughter **hija** (2)

day **día** *m.* (1); day after tomorrow **pasado mañana** (4); every day **todos los días** (1)

deadline **fecha límite** (11)

dear **querido/a** *n., adj.* (5)

death **muerte** *f.* (15)

December **diciembre** *m.* (5)

declare **declarar** (18)

delay *n.* **demora** (7)

delighted **encantado/a** (P)

deluxe **de lujo** (18)

demonstrative **demostrativo** (3)

dense **denso/a** (14)

dentist **dentista** *m., f.* (10)

deny **negar (ie) (gu)** (13)

department store **almacén** *m.* (3)

departure **salida** (7)

deposit **depositar** (16)

desk **escritorio** (1); front desk **recepción** *f.* (18)

dessert **postre** *m.* (6)

destroy **destruir (y)** (14)

detail **detalle** *m.* (6)

develop **desarrollar** (14)

dictator **dictador(a)** (17)

dictatorship **dictadura** (17)

dictionary **diccionario** (1)

die **morir (ue, u)** (*p.p.* **muerto/a**); to be dying **morir(se)** (8)

difficult **difícil** (5); **pesado/a** (9)

dining room **comedor** *m.* (4)

dinner **cena** (6); to have dinner **cenar** (6)

directions: cardinal directions **puntos** (*m. pl.*) **cardinales** (5)

director **director(a)** (13); personnel director **director(a) de personal** (16)

dirty **sucio/a** (5)

disadvantage **desventaja** (10)

disaster **desastre** *m.* (17)

disc: compact disc **disco compacto** (12)

discotheque, disco **discoteca** (9)

discover **descubrir** (*pp.* **descubierto**) (14)

discrimination **discriminación** *f.* (17)

dish (prepared) **plato** (4)

dishwasher **lavaplatos** *m. s., pl.* (9)

disk: computer disk **disco de computadora** (12)

divorce **divorcio** (15)

divorced: to get divorced (from) **divorciarse (de)** (15)

dizzy **mareado/a** (10)

do **hacer** (*irreg.*) (4); (*do something*) again **volver a** + *inf.* (4); to do aerobics **hacer** (*irreg.*) **ejercicios aeróbicos** (10); to do exercise **hacer** (*irreg.*) **ejercicio** (4)

doctor (*medical*) **médico/a** (2)

dog **perro/a** (2)

don't they (you, etc.)? **¿no?, ¿verdad?** (3)

door **puerta** (1)

doorman **portero/a** (12)

dormitory **residencia** (1)

double **doble** (18); double room **habitación** (*f.*) **doble** (18)

doubt **dudar** (12)

downtown **centro** (3)

drama **drama** *m.* (13)

draw **dibujar** (13)

dress **vestido** (3)

dressed: to get dressed **vestirse (i, i)** (4)

dresser (*furniture*) **cómoda** (4)

drink **bebida** (6); **copa, trago** (*alcoholic*) (18); *drink similar to a milkshake* **batido** (18); to drink **tomar** (1); **beber** (2); soft drink **refresco** (6)

drive (*a vehicle*) **conducir** (*irreg.*) (14); **manejar** (12); hard drive **disco duro** (12)

driver **conductor(a)** (14); driver's license **licencia de manejar/conducir** (14)

dryer: clothes dryer **secadora** (9)

during **durante** (4); **por** (4)

dust the furniture **sacudir los muebles** (9)

duty: (customs) duty **derechos** (*m. pl.*) **(de aduana)** (18)

E

each **cada** *inv.* (4)

ear (inner) **oído** (10); (outer) **oreja** (10)

early **temprano** *adv.* (1)

earn **ganar** (9)

earring **arete** *m.* (3)

east **este** *m.* (5)

Easter **Pascua (Florida)** (8)

easy **fácil** (5)

eat **comer** (2); eat breakfast **desayunar** (6); eat dinner **cenar** (6)

economics **economía** (1)

economize **economizar (c)** (16)

egg **huevo** (6)

eight **ocho** (P)

eight hundred **ochocientos/as** (3)

eighteen **dieciocho** (P)

eighth **octavo/a** *adj.* (13)

eighty **ochenta** (2)

either: not either **tampoco** (6)

electric **eléctrico/a** (14)

electrician **electricista** *m., f.* (16)

electricity **luz** *f.* (*pl.* **luces**) (11)

electronic mail **correo electrónico** (12)

electronics **electrónica** (12)

eleven **once** (P)

e-mail **correo electrónico** (12)

embarrassed **avergonzado/a** (8)

emergency room **sala de emergencias/urgencia** (10)

emotion **emoción** *f.* (8)

employment office **dirección** (*f.*) **de personal** (16)

end table **mesita** (4)

energy **energía** (14)

engagement **noviazgo** (15)

engineer **ingeniero/a** (16)

English (*language*) **inglés** *m.* (1); *n., adj.* **inglés, inglesa** (2)

enjoy oneself, have a good time **divertirse (ie, i)** (4)

enough **bastante** *adv.* (15); **lo suficiente** (10)

entertainment **diversión** *f.* (9)

entire **entero/a** (9)

envelope **sobre** *m.* (18)

environment **medio ambiente** *m.* (14)

equality **igualdad** *f.* (17)

equipment: stereo equipment **equipo estereofónico** (12); photography equipment **equipo fotográfico** (12)

era **época** (9)

evening **tarde** *f.* (1); good evening **buenas tardes** (P); in the afternoon, evening **de la tarde** (P); in the evening **por la tarde** (1)

event **acontecimiento** (17); **evento** (17); **hecho** (8)

every **cada** *inv.* (4); **todo(s)/a(s)** *adj.* (2); every day **todos los días** (1)

everything **de todo** (3)

everywhere **por todas partes** (11)

exactly, on the dot (*time*) **en punto** (P)

exam **examen** *m.* (3)

examine **examinar** (10); **registrar** (18)

example: for example **por exemplo** (11)

excuse me **con permiso, perdón** (P); **discúlpeme** (11)

exercise **ejercicio** (3); **hacer** (*irreg.*) **ejercicio** (4)

expect **esperar** (6)

expend **gastar** (8)

expense **gasto** (12)

expensive **caro/a** (3)

explain **explicar (qu)** (7)

expressions: greetings and expressions of courtesy **saludos** (*m. pl.*) **y expresiones** (*f. pl.*) **de cortesía** (P)

extract **sacar (qu)** (10); extract a tooth **sacar una muela** (10)

eye **ojo** (10)

eyeglasses **gafas** *f. pl.* (10)

F

fact **hecho** *n.* (8)

factory **fábrica** (14)

faithful **fiel** (2)

fall (*season*) **otoño** (5)

fall *v.* **caer** (*irreg.*) (11); to fall asleep **dormirse** (4); to fall down **caerse** (11); to fall in love (with) **enamorarse (de)** (15)

family **familia** (2)

fan **aficionado/a** (9); to be a fan (of) **ser** (*irreg.*) **aficionado/a (a)** (9)

far from **lejos de** *prep.* (5)

farm **finca** (14); farm worker **campesino/a** (14)

farmer **agricultor(a)** (14)

fashion **moda**; the latest fashion; style **de última moda** (3)

fast **rápido/a** *adj.* (6); **acelerado/a** (14)

fat **gordo/a** (2)

father **papá** *m.*, **padre** *m.* (2)

fax *fax m.* (12)

fear **miedo** (3); to fear **temer** (13)

February **febrero** (5)

feel **sentirse** (ie, i) (8); **encontrarse (ue)** (10); to feel like (*doing something*) **tener** (*irreg.*) **ganas de** + *inf.* (3); to feel sorry **sentir (ie, i)** (13)

female soldier **mujer soldado** (16)

fever **fiebre** *f.* (10)

fifteen **quince** (P); a quarter (fifteen minutes) to (the hour) **menos quince** (P); a quarter (fifteen minutes) past (the hour) **y quince** (P)

fifth **quinto/a** *adj.* (13)

fifty **cincuenta** (2)

fight **pelear** (9)

file: computer file **archivo** (12)

fill (up) **llenar** (14); to fill out (*a form*) **llenar** (16)

finally **por fin** (4)

find **encontrar (ue)** (8); to find out (about) **enterarse (de)** (17)

fine **muy bien** (P)

fine *n.* **multa** (18)

finger **dedo (de la mano)** (11)

finish **acabar** (11)

first **primer, primero/a** *adj.* (4); at first sight **a primera vista** (15); first of (month) **el primero de (mes)** (5); first class **primera clase** (7); for the first time **por primera vez** (11)

fish (*cooked*) **pescado** (6)

five **cinco** (P)

five hundred **quinientos/as** (3)

fix **arreglar** (12)

fixed price **precio fijo** (3)

flat (*tire*) **desinflado/a** (14)

flexibility **flexibilidad** *f.* (11)

flexible **flexible** (11)

flight **vuelo** (7); flight attendant **asistente** (*m., f.*) **de vuelo** (7)

floor (*of a building*) **planta, piso** (12); ground floor **planta baja** (12); to sweep the floor **barrer el piso** (9)

flower **flor** *f.* (7)

folkloric **folklórico/a** (13)

following *adj.* **siguiente** (5)

food **comida** (6)

foolish **tonto/a** (2)

foot **pie** *m.* (11)

football **fútbol** (*m.*) **americano** (9)

for (intended) **por** *prep.* (4); **para** *prep.* (2); for example **por ejemplo** (11); for God's sake **por Dios** (11); for the first/last time **por primera/última vez** (11)

forbid **prohibir (prohíbo)** (12)

foreign languages **lenguas** (*f. pl.*) **extranjeras** (1)

foreigner **extranjero/a** *n.* (1)

forest **bosque** *m.* (14)

forget (about) **olvidarse (de)** (8)

form **forma** (3); (*to fill out*) **formulario** (18)

forty **cuarenta** (2)

four **cuatro** (P)

four hundred **cuatrocientos/as** (3)

fourteen **catorce** (P)

fourth **cuarto/a** *adj.* (13)

free time **ratos** (*m. pl.*) **libres** (9)

freedom **libertad** *f.* (17)

freeway **autopista** (14)

freezer **congelador** *m.* (9)

French (*language*) **francés** *n. m.* (1); **francés, francesa** *n., adj.* (2); (French-fried) potato **patata (frita)** (6)

frequently **con frecuencia** (1)

fresh **fresco/a** (6)

Friday **viernes** *m. s., pl.* (4)

fried **frito/a** (6); **patata frita** French-fried potato (6)

friend **amigo/a** (1)

friendly **amable** (2); **amistoso/a** (15)

friendship **amistad** *f.* (15)

from **de** (P); from the **del** (*contraction of* **de** + **el**) (2); where are you from? **¿de dónde es Ud.?** (2)

front desk **recepción** *f.* (18)

front: in front of **delante de** *prep.* (5)

frozen **congelado/a** (5)

fruit **fruta** (6); **jugo de fruta** fruit juice (6)

full (*no vacancy*) **completo/a** (18)

full-time job **trabajo de tiempo completo** (11)

fun: to be fun **ser** (*irreg.*) **divertido/a** (9)

function **funcionar** (12)

furious **furioso/a** (5)

furniture **muebles** *m. pl.* (4); to dust the furniture **sacudir los muebles** (9)

G

garage **garaje** *m.* (4)

garden **jardín** *m.* (4)

gas **gas** *m.s.* (12)

gas station **estación** (*f.*) **de gasolina, gasolinera** (14)

gasoline **gasolina** (14)

generally **por lo general** (4)

German (*language*) **alemán** *m.* (1); **alemán, alemana** *n., adj.* (2)

get: to get **conseguir (i, i) (g)** (8); **obtener** (*like* tener) (12); **sacar (qu)** (11); to get + *adjective* **ponerse** (*irreg.*) + *adj.* (8); to get a cold **resfriarse** (10); to get along well/poorly (with) **llevarse bien/mal (con)** (15); to get angry (at) **enojarse (con)** (8); to get bored **aburrirse** (9); to get down (from) **bajar (de)** (7); to get good/bad grades **sacar (qu) buenas/malas notas** (11); to get off (of) **bajar (de)** (7); to get on/in (*a vehicle*) **subir** (7); to get sick **enfermarse** (8); to get together (with) **reunirse (me** reúno) (con) (8); to get up **levantarse** (4); to get up on the wrong side of the bed **levantarse con el pie izquierdo** (11)

gift **regalo** (2)

girl **niña** (2); **muchacha** (4); *girl's fifteenth birthday party* **quinceañera** (8)

girlfriend **novia** (5)

give **dar** (*irreg.*) (7); to give (*as a gift*) **regalar** (7); to give a party **dar** (*irreg.*) **una fiesta** (8); to give (someone) a shot, injection **poner(le)** (*irreg.*) **una inyección** (10)

glasses **gafas** *pl.* (10)

go **ir** (*irreg.*) (3); to be going to (*do something*) **ir a** + *inf.* (3); to go (to) (*a function*) **asistir (a)** (2); to go away, leave **irse**; to go abroad **ir al extranjero** (18); to go by (train/airplane/bus/boat) **ir en (tren/avión/autobús/barco)** (7); to go home **regresar a casa** (1); to go on vacation **ir** (*irreg.*) **de vacaciones** (7); to go out **salir** (*irreg.*) **(de)** (4); to go out with **salir** (*irreg.*) **con** (15); to go shopping **ir de compras** (3); to go to bed **acostarse (ue)** (4); to go to see a movie **ir** (*irreg.*) **a ver una película** (9); to go to the movies **ir** (*irreg.*) **al cine** (9); to go up **subir** (7)

God: for God's sake **por Dios** (11)

golf **golf** *m.* (9)

good **buen, bueno/a** *adj.* (2); good morning **buenos días** (P); good night **buenas noches** (P); it's good weather **hace buen tiempo** (5); the good thing, news **lo bueno** (10); to have a good time **divertirse** (ie) (4); **pasarlo bien** (8)

good-bye **adiós** (P); to say good-bye (to) **despedirse (i, i) (de)** (8)

good-looking **guapo/a** (2)

goods: woven goods **tejidos** (13)

govern **gobernar (ie)** (17)

government **gobierno** (14)

grade **calificación** *f.*, **nota** (11); **grado** (9)

graduate (from) **graduarse (me gradúo) (en)** (16)

grandchildren **nietos** *m. pl.* (2)

granddaughter **nieta** (2)

grandfather **abuelo** (2)

grandmother **abuela** (2)

grandparents **abuelos** *m. pl.* (2)

grandson **nieto** (2)

gray **gris** (3)

great **gran, grande** (2)

green **verde** (3)

green pea **arveja** (6)

greet each other **saludarse** (10)

greeting **saludo** (P); greetings and expressions of courtesy **saludos y expresiones de cortesía** (P)

ground floor **planta baja** (12)

grow **crecer (zc)** (15)

guest **invitado/a** *n.* (8); **huésped(a)** (18)

guide **guía** *m., f.* (13)

H

habit **costumbre** *f.* (9)

haggle **regatear** (3)

hair: to comb one's hair **peinarse** (4)

hairstylist **peluquero(a)** (16)

ham **jamón** *m.* (6)

hamburger **hamburguesa** (6)

hand in **entregar (gu)** (11)

hand **mano** *f.* (11)

handsome **guapo/a** (2)

happen **pasar** (5)

happening **acontecimiento** (17)

happy **alegre** (5); **feliz** (*pl.* **felices**) (8); **contento/a** (5); to be happy (about) **alegrarse (de)** (12)

hard **difícil** (5)

hard drive **disco duro** (12)

hardworking **trabajador(a)** (2)

hat **sombrero** (3)

hate **odiar** (7)

have **tener** (*irreg.*) (3); **haber** (*irreg.*) *auxiliary* (12); to have a birthday **cumplir años** (8); to have a good/bad time **pasarlo bien/mal** (8); to have a pain in **tener** (*irreg.*) **dolor de** (10); to have a party **dar** (*irreg.*) **hacer** (*irreg.*) **una fiesta** (8);

to have a picnic **hacer** (*irreg.*) **un picnic** (9); to have been (*doing something*) for (*a period of time*) **hace** + *time ago* (11); **hace** + *period of time* + **que** + *present tense* (11); to have just (*done something*) **acabar de** (+ *inf.*) (6); to have to (*do something*) **tener** (*irreg.*) **que** + *inf.* (3)

he **él** (1)

head **cabeza** (10)

headache **dolor** (*m.*) **de cabeza** (10)

health **salud** *f.* (10)

healthy **sano/a** (10)

hear **oír** (*irreg.*) (4)

heart **corazón** *m.* (10)

heat **calor** *m.* (5); **gas** *m.s.* (12)

heavy (*meal, food*) **fuerte** (6)

Hebrew (*language*) **hebreo** (15)

hello **hola** (P); **buenos días** (P)

help **ayudar** (6)

her *obj.* (*of prep.*) **ella**

her *poss.* **su(s)** (2)

here **aquí** (1)

highway **carretera** (14)

his *poss.* **su(s)** (2)

history **historia** (1)

hit **pegar (gu)** (9)

hobby **pasatiempo, afición** *f.* (9)

hockey **hockey** *m.* (9)

holiday **día** (*m.*) **festivo** (8)

home **casa** (2); at home **en casa** (1); home appliance **aparato doméstico** (9); to go home **regresar a casa** (1)

homework **tarea** (4)

honest **honesto/a** (15)

honeymoon **luna de miel** (15)

hope **esperanza** (17); to hope **esperar** (12); I hope, wish (that) **ojalá (que)** (13)

hors d'oeuvres **entremeses** *m. pl.* (8)

horseback: to ride horseback **montar a caballo** (9)

host **anfitrión** (8)

hostess **anfitriona** (8)

hot dog **salchicha** (6)

hot: to be (feel) hot **tener** (*irreg.*) **calor** (5); it's hot **hace calor** (5) hotel **hotel** *m.* (18); hotel guest **huésped(a)** (18)

hour **hora** (P)

house **casa** (2)

household chore **quehacer** (*m.*) **doméstico** (9)

housing **vivienda** (12)

how? what? **¿cómo?** (P); how are you (doing)? **¿qué tal?** (P); how are you? **¿cómo está(s)?** (P); how many? **¿cuántos/as?** (P); how much does it cost? **¿cuánto cuesta?** (3); how much is it? **¿cuánto es?** (3)

human **humano** (10)

humanities **humanidades** *f. pl.* (1)

hundred, one hundred **cien, ciento** (2)

hunger **hambre** *f.* (*but* el hambre)

hungry: to be (very) hungry **tener** (*irreg.*) **(mucha) hambre** (6)

hurry: to be in a hurry **tener** (*irreg.*) **prisa** (3)

hurt **doler (ue)** (10)

hurt oneself **hacerse** (*irreg.*) **daño** (11)

husband **esposo** (2); **marido** (15)

hydraulic **hidráulico/a** (14)

I

I **yo** (1); I am **soy** (P); I'm sorry **discúlpeme** (11), **lo siento** (11)

ice cream **helado** (6)

identification card **tarjeta de identificación** (11)

if **si** (2)

illness **enfermedad** *f.* (10)

immigration **inmigración** *f.* (18)

impression: to make a good/bad impression on someone **caerle bien/mal a alguien** (16)

in **en** (P); (*the morning, evening, etc.*) **por** *prep.* (1); in a balanced way **equilibradamente** (10); in case **en caso de que** (15); in cash **efectivo: en efectivo** (16); in order to **para** *prep.* (2)

incredible: it's incredible **es increíble** (13)

indefinite **indefinido** (6)

inequality **desigualdad** *f.* (17)

inexpensive **barato/a** (3)

infancy **infancia** (15)

inform **informar** (17)

injection **inyección** *f.* (10)

injure oneself **lastimarse** (11)

inner ear **oído** (10)

inspector (customs) **inspector(a) (de aduanas)** (18)

installment: to pay in installments **pagar (gu) a plazos** (16)

instead of **en vez de** (16)

intelligent **inteligente** (2)

intend **pensar (ie)** (4)

Internet **red** *f.* (12)

interrogative **interrogativo** (P)

interview **entrevistar** *v.* (16)

interviewer **entrevistador(a)** (16)

invite **invitar** (6)

invoice **factura** (16)

iron clothes **planchar la ropa** (9)

is (located) **está** (P)

island **isla** (5)

isolation **aislamiento** (14)

Italian (*language*) **italiano** (1)

item: news item **noticia** (8)

its *poss.* **su(s)** (2)

J

jacket **chaqueta** (3)

January **enero** (5)

jeans **jeans** *m. pl.* (3)

job **trabajo** (11); **puesto** (16); full-time/part-time job **trabajo de tiempo completo/parcial** (11)

jog **correr** (9)

joke **chiste** *m.* (8)

journalist **periodista** *m., f.* (16)

juice: (fruit) juice **jugo (de fruta)** (6)

July **julio** (5)

June **junio** (5)

just: to have just (*done something*) **acabar de** + *inf.* (6)

just in case **por si acaso** (11)

K

keep (*a place/documents*) **guardar** (7)

key **llave** *n. f.* (11)

kind **amable** (2)

king **rey** *m.* (17)

kiosk **quiosco** (18)

kitchen **cocina** (4)

know **conocer (zc)** (6); to know (how) **saber** (*irreg.*) (6)

L

laborer **obrero/a** (16)

lack **falta** (11); **escasez** *f.* (*pl.* escaseces) (14); lack of flexibility **falta de flexibilidad** (11)

lacking: to be lacking **faltar** (8)

lady **señora (Sra.)** (P)

lamp **lámpara** (4)

landlady **dueña** (12)

landlord **dueño** (12)

language: foreign languages **lenguas** (*f. pl.*) **extranjeras** (1)

laptop computer **computadora portátil** (12); **ordenador** (*m.*) **portátil** (12)

large **gran, grande** (2)

last **último/a** (7); to last **durar** (17); for the last time **por última vez** (11)

late **tarde** *adv.* (1); to be late **estar** (*irreg.*) **atrasado/a** (7); to arrive late **llegar (gu) tarde** (11)

later: see you later **hasta luego** (P)

latest: the latest style **de última moda** (3); latest news **últimas novedades** (17)

laugh (about) **reírse (i, i) (de)** (8)

law **ley** *f.* (17)

lawyer **abogado/a** (16)

layer: ozone layer **capa de ozono** (14)

lazy **perezoso/a** (2)

lead a healthy/calm life **llevar una vida sana/tranquila** (10)

learn **aprender** (2)

least **menos** (5); at least **por lo menos** (10)

leave **salir** (*irreg.*) **(de)** (4); (behind) (in, at) **dejar (en)** (9); to take leave (of) **despedirse (i, i) (de)** (8)

left: to the left (of) **a la izquierda (de)** (5); to be left **quedar(se)** (11)

leg **pierna** (11)
lend **prestar** (7)
lenses: contact lenses **lentes** (*m. pl.*) **de contacto** (10)
less **menos** (5); less . . . than **menos… que** (5)
letter **carta** (2)
lettuce **lechuga** (6)
level **nivel** *m.* (14)
liberty **libertad** *f.* (17)
librarian **bibliotecario/a** (1)
library **biblioteca** (1)
license **licencia** (14); driver's license **licencia de manejar/conducir** (14)
life **vida** (11); to lead a healthy/calm life **llevar una vida sana/tranquila** (10)
light **luz** *f.* (*pl.* **luces**) (11); *adj.* light, not heavy **ligero/a** (6)
like **gusto** (P); do you (*form.*) like . . . ? **¿le gusta… ?** (P); I (don't) like . . . **(no) me gusta(n)…** (P); I would like . . . **me gustaría…** (7); to like very much **encantar** (7)
likeable **simpático/a** (2)
likewise **igualmente** (P)
limit **límite** *m.* (14); speed limit **límite de velocidad** (*f.*) (14)
line: to stand in line **hacer** (*irreg.*) **cola** (7)
listen (to) **escuchar** (1)
literature **literatura** (1)
little, few **poco/a** *adj.* (3); little bit **un poco** (1)
live **vivir** (2); to live a healthy life **llevar una vida sana** (10)
living room **sala** (4)
loan **préstamo** (16)
lobster **langosta** (6)
lodging **alojamiento** (18)
long **largo/a** (2)
look at **mirar** (2); to look for **buscar** **(qu)** (1)
lose **perder (ie)** (4)
lot, a lot **mucho** (1)
love **amar** (15); **encantar** (7); **querer** (*irreg.*) (15); *n.* **amor** *m.* (15); to fall in love (with) **enamorarse (de)** (15)

luck: what bad luck **qué mala suerte** (11)
luggage **equipaje** *m.* (7)
lunch **almuerzo** (6); to have lunch **almorzar (ue) (c)** (4)
lung **pulmón** *m.* (10)
luxury *n.* **lujo** (12); luxury hotel **hotel** (*m.*) **de lujo** (18)

M

machine: answering machine **contestador** (*m.*) **automático** (12); automatic teller machine **cajero automático** (16); washing machine **lavadora** (9)
made: it is made of . . . **es de…** (3)
magazine **revista** (2)
maid **criada** (18)
mail **correo** (18); electronic mail **correo electrónico** (12)
make **hacer** (*irreg.*) (4); to make a good/bad impression on someone **caerle** (*irreg.*) **bien/mal a alguien** (16); to make a mistake **equivocarse (qu)** (11); to make plans to (*do something*) **hacer** (*irreg.*) **planes para +** *inf.* (9); to make stops **hacer** (*irreg.*) **escalas/paradas** (7); to make the bed **hacer** (*irreg.*) **la cama** (9)
mall: shopping mall **centro comercial** (3)
man **hombre** *m.* (1); **señor** **(Sr.)** *m.* (P)
manager: building manager **portero/a** (12)
many **muchos/as** (2); as many . . . as **tanto/a(s)… como** (5); how many? **¿cuántos/as?** (P)
March **marzo** (5)
market(place) **mercado** (3)
marriage **matrimonio** (15)
married **casado/a** (2); married couple **pareja** (15); **matrimonio** (15)
marry **casarse (con)** (15)
masterpiece **obra maestra** (13)
match **fósforo** (18)
material **material** *n. m.* (3)
mathematics **matemáticas** *f. pl.* (1)
May **mayo** (5)

me *d.o., i.o.* **me**; *obj.* (*of prep.*) **mí** (5)
meal **comida** (6)
means: that means **eso quiere decir** (10)
means of communication **medio de comunicación** (17); means of transportation **transporte** *m.* (14)
meat **carne** *f.* (6)
mechanic **mecánico/a** (14)
media: news media **prensa** (17)
medical **médico/a** (10); medical office **consultorio** (10)
medicine **medicina** (10)
meet (*someone somewhere*) **encontrarse (con)** (10)
memory **memoria** (12)
menu **menú** *m.* (6)
merchant **comerciante** *m., f.* (16)
messy **desordenado/a** (5)
metro stop **estación** (*f.*) **del metro** (18)
Mexican **mexicano/a** *n., adj.* (2)
microwave oven **horno de microondas** *f. pl.* (9)
middle age **madurez** *f.* (15)
midnight **medianoche** *f.* (8)
military service **servicio militar** (17)
milk **leche** *f.* (6)
milkshake **batido** (18)
million **millón** *m.* (3)
mineral water **agua** *f.* (*but* **el agua**) **mineral** (6)
minus **menos** (5)
miss (*a function, bus, plane, etc.*) **perder (ie)** (4)
Miss **señorita (Srta.)** (P)
mistake: to make a mistake **equivocarse (qu)** (11)
modem **módem** *m.* (12)
modern **moderno/a** (13)
molar **muela** (10)
mom **mamá** (2)
Monday **lunes** *m. s., pl.* (4)
money **dinero** (1)
month **mes** *m.* (5)
moped **moto(cicleta)** *f.* (12)
more **más** *adv.* (1); **más… que** more . . . than (5)

morning **mañana** *n.* (P); in the morning **de la mañana** (P); during the morning **por la mañana** (1); good morning **buenos días** (P)

mother **mamá, madre** *f.* (2)

motorcycle **moto(cicleta)** *f.* (12)

mountain **montaña** (7); mountain bike **bicicleta de montaña** (12)

mouse **ratón** (*m.*) (12)

mouth **boca** (10)

move (*residence*) **mudarse** (16)

movie **película** (4); **cine** *m.* (4); movie theater **cine** *m.* (4); to go to the movies **ir** (*irreg.*) **al cine** (9)

Mr. **señor (Sr.)** *m.* (P)

Mrs. **señora (Sra.)** (P)

Ms. **señorita (Srta.)** (P)

much **mucho** *adv.* (1); as much … as **tanto como** (5); **tanto/a(s) … como** (5); how much does it cost? **¿cuánto cuesta?** (3); how much is it? **¿cuánto es?** (3)

museum **museo** (9); to visit a museum **visitar un museo** (9)

mushroom **champiñón** *m.* (6)

music **música** (13)

musician **músico/a** *n. m., f.* (13)

must (*do something*) **deber** (+ *inf.*) (2)

my *poss.* **mi(s)** (2)

N

named: to be named **llamarse** (4); what's your name? **¿cómo se llama usted?** (*form.*) (P); what's your name? **¿cómo te llamas?** *fam.* (P); my name is . . . **me llamo...** (P)

nap: to take a nap **dormir (ue, u) la siesta** (4)

nationality **nacionalidad** *f.* (2)

natural resources **recursos** (*m. pl.*) **naturales** (14)

nature **naturaleza** (14)

nauseated **mareado/a** (10)

neat **ordenado/a** (5)

necessary **necesario/a** (2); it is necessary to (*do something*) **hay que** + *inf.* (13)

need *v.* **necesitar** (1)

negative **negativo** (6)

neighbor **vecino/a** (12)

neighborhood **barrio, vecindad** *f.* (12)

neither, not either **tampoco** (6)

nephew **sobrino** (2)

nervous **nervioso/a** (5)

net: to surf the net **navegar (gu) la red** (12)

never **nunca** (2); **jamás** (6); almost never **casi nunca** (2)

new **nuevo/a** (2); New Year's Eve **Noche** (*f.*) **Vieja** (8)

news **noticias** *f. pl.* (8); the good (bad) news **lo bueno (malo)** (10); news item **noticia** (8); news media **prensa** (17); **novedades** (*f. pl.*) (17)

newscast **noticiero** (17)

newspaper **periódico** (2)

next **próximo/a** *adj.* (4); next to **al lado de** *prep.* (5); next (Tuesday) **el próximo (martes)** (4); next week **la semana que viene** (4)

nice **simpático/a** (2), **amable** (2)

niece **sobrina** (2)

night **noche** *f.*; good evening/night **buenas noches** (P); in the evening/at night **de la noche** (P); in the night **por la noche** (1); tonight **esta noche** (5)

nine **nueve** (P)

nine hundred **novecientos/as** (3)

nineteen **diecinueve** (P)

ninety **noventa** (2)

ninth **noveno/a** (13)

no **no** (P); **ningún (ninguno/a)** (6); no one **nadie** (6)

nobody **nadie** (6)

noise **ruido** (4)

none **ningún, ninguno/a** (6)

nonsmoking section **sección** (*f.*) **de no fumar** (7)

north **norte** *m.* (5)

North American **norteamericano/a** *n., adj.* (2)

nose **nariz** *f.* (*pl.* **narices**) (10)

not **nada** (6); **no** (P); not any **ningún (ninguno/a)** (6); not

anybody **nadie** (6); not anything **nadie** (6); not either **tampoco** (6); not ever **jamás** (6)

note **nota** (11)

notebook **cuaderno** (1)

nothing **nada** (6)

noun **sustantivo** *gram.* (1)

November **noviembre** *m.* (5)

now **ahora** (1)

nuclear **nuclear** (14)

number **número** (P)

nurse **enfermero/a** (10)

O

obey **obedecer (zc)** (14)

obligation **deber** *m.* (17)

obtain **conseguir (i, i)** (8); **obtener** (*like* **tener**) (12)

ocean **océano** (7)

October **octubre** *m.* (5)

of **de** *prep.* (P); of the **del** (*contraction of* **de** + **el**) (2); of course **por supuesto** (11)

offer **ofrecer (zc)** (7)

office **oficina** (1); medical office **consultorio** (10); post office **oficina de correos** (18) personnel office **dirección** (*f.*) **de personal** (16)

officer: police officer **policía** *m. f.* (14)

oil **aceite** *m.* (14)

OK **regular** *adj.* (P)

old **viejo/a** *adj.* (2); old age **vejez** *f.* (15); to be . . . years old **tener... años** (2)

older **mayor** (5)

on **en** (P); on top of **encima de** *prep.* (5)

once **una vez** (10); once a week **una vez a la semana** (2)

one **un, uno/a** (P); no one **nadie** (6)

one hundred **cien, ciento** (2)

one thousand **mil** (3)

one-way (*ticket*) **de ida** (7)

only **sólo** *adv.* (1)

open **abierto/a** (5); to open **abrir** (*p.p.* **abierto/a**) (2)

opera **ópera** (13)

operate (*a machine*) **manejar** (12)

or **o** (P)

oral **oral** (11); oral report **informe** (*m.*) **oral** (11)

orange (*color*) **anaranjado/a** *adj.* (3); orange (*fruit*) **naranja** (6)

order (*in a restaurant*) **pedir (i, i)** (4); in order to **para** (2); (*someone to do something*) **mandar** (12)

ordinal numbers **números ordinales** (13)

other **otro/a** (1); others **los/las demás** (12)

ought to (*do something*) **deber** (+ *inf.*) (2)

our *poss.* **nuestro/a(s)** (2)

outdoors **afuera** *adv.* (5)

outskirts **afueras** *n. pl.* (12)

oven: microwave oven **horno de microondas** (9)

over there **allí** (3)

overcast: it's overcast **está nublado** (5)

overcoat **abrigo** (3)

overseas **extranjero** (18)

own **propio/a** *adj.* (15)

owner **dueño/a** (6)

ozone layer **capa de ozono** (14)

P

pace **ritmo** (14)

pack one's suitcases **hacer** (*irreg.*) **las maletas** (7)

package **paquete** *m.* (18)

pain **dolor** *m.* (10); to have a pain (in) **tener** (*irreg.*) **dolor (de)** (10)

paint (the walls) **pintar (las paredes)** (9)

painter **pintor(a)** (13)

painting **cuadro, pintura** (13)

pair **par** *m.* (3)

pants **pantalón, pantalones** *m.* (3)

paper **papel** *m.* (1)

pardon me **(con) permiso, perdón** (P); **discúlpeme** (11); **lo siento mucho** (11)

parents **padres** *m. pl.* (2)

park **parque** *m.* (5); to park **estacionar** (11)

part **parte** *f.* (4)

part-time job **trabajo de tiempo parcial** (11)

participate (*in a sport*) **practicar (qu)** (1)

partner **pareja** (15)

party **fiesta** (1); to give/have a party **dar/hacer** (*irreg.*) **una fiesta** (8)

passage **pasaje** *m.* (7)

passenger **pasajero/a** *n.* (7)

passport **pasaporte** *m.* (18)

pastime **pasatiempo** (9)

pastry (small) **pastelito** (18); pastry shop **pastelería** (18)

patient **paciente** *n., adj. m., f.* (10)

patio **patio** (4)

pay **pagar (gu)** (1); to pay cash **pagar al contado / en efectivo** (16); to pay in installments **pagar a plazos** (16)

pea: green pea **arveja** (6)

peace **paz** *f.* (*pl.* **paces**) (17)

peasant **campesino/a** (14)

pen **bolígrafo** (1)

penalty **multa** (18)

pencil **lápiz** *m.* (*pl.* **lápices**) (1)

people **gente** *f. s.* (15)

perform (*a part*) **desempeñar** (13)

permit **permitir** (12)

person **persona** (1)

personnel director **director(a) de personal** (16); personnel office **dirección** (*f.*) **de personal** (16)

pet **mascota** (2)

pharmacist **farmacéutico/a** (10)

pharmacy **farmacia** (10)

philosophy **filosofía** (1)

phone: car phone **teléfono de coche** (12); cellular phone **teléfono celular** (12); to talk on the phone **hablar por teléfono** (1)

photo(graph) **foto(grafía)** *f.* (7)

photographer **fotógrafo/a** (15)

photos: to take photos **sacar (qu) fotos** *f. pl.* (7)

physics **física** (1)

pick up **recoger (j)** (11)

picnic: to have a picnic **hacer** (*irreg.*) **un** *picnic* (9)

pie **pastel** *m.* (6)

piece: piece of news **noticia** (8); piece of work **trabajo** (11)

pill **pastilla** (10)

pink **rosado/a** (3)

place (*in line, etc.*) **puesto** (7); **lugar** (1); to place **poner** (*irreg.*) (4); to take place **ser** (*irreg.*) **en** + *place* (8)

plaid **de cuadros** (3)

plans: to make plans to (*do something*) **hacer** (*irreg.*) **planes para** + *inf.* (9)

plate **plato** (4)

play (*a game, sport*) **jugar (ue) (gu) (a)** (4); to play cards **jugar (ue) (gu) a las cartas** (9); to play chess **jugar (ue) (gu) al ajedrez** (9); to play (*a musical instrument*) **tocar (qu)** (1); to play music **tocar (qu) música** (1); to play (*a part*) **desempeñar** (13)

player **jugador(a)** (9); tape player **grabadora** (12)

playwright **dramaturgo/a** (13)

please **por favor** (P); to please **agradar** (13)

pleased to meet you **encantado/a** (P); **mucho gusto** (P)

pleasing: to be pleasing **gustar** (7)

plumber **plomero/a** (16)

poet **poeta** *m., f.* (13)

point **punto** (5)

police officer **policía** *m., f.* (14)

politician **político/a** (17)

politics **política** *s.* (17)

polka-dotted **de lunares** *m. pl.* (3)

pollute **contaminar** (14)

pollution: there's (lots of) pollution **hay (mucha) contaminación** *f.* (5)

pool: swimming pool **piscina** (4)

poor **pobre** (2)

poorly **mal** *adv.* (1)

population **población** *f.* (14)

pork chop **chuleta de cerdo** (6)

port **puerto** (7)

portable *adj.* **portátil** (12)

porter **maletero** (7)

possessive **posesivo** *gram.* (2)

possible **posible** (2)

post office **correo; oficina de correos** (18)

postcard **tarjeta postal** (7)

potato **patata** (*Sp.*) (6); French fried potato **patata frita** (*Sp.*) (6)

pottery **cerámica** (13)

practical **práctico/a** (2)

practice **practicar (qu)** (1); **entrenar** (9)

prefer **preferir (ie, i)** (3)

preferable **preferible** (13)

preference **gusto, preferencia** (P)

prepare **preparar** (6)

preposition **preposición** *f. gram.* (4)

prescription **receta** (10)

present (*gift*) **regalo** *n.* (2)

press *n.* **prensa** (17)

pressure: to be under pressure **sufrir presiones** *f. pl.* (11)

pretty **bonito/a** (2)

price **precio** (3); fixed price **precio fijo** (3)

print **imprimir** (12)

printer **impresora** (12)

profession **profesión** *f.* (16)

professor **profesor(a)** (1)

programmer **programador(a)** (16)

prohibit **prohibir (prohíbo)** (12)

promise *v.* **prometer** (7)

pronoun **pronombre** *m. gram.* (1)

protect **proteger (j)** (14)

provided (that) **con tal (de) que** (15)

psychiatrist **siquiatra** *m., f.* (16)

psychologist **sicólogo/a** (16)

psychology **sicología** (1)

public **público/a** *adj.* (14)

punish **castigar (gu)** (17)

purchases **compras** (*f. pl.*) (3)

pure **puro/a** (14)

purple **morado/a** (3)

purse **bolsa** (3)

put **poner** (*irreg.*) (4); to put on (*clothing*) **ponerse** (*irreg.*) (4)

Q

quarter past (*with time*) **y cuarto** (P)

queen **reina** (17)

question: ask a question **hacer una pregunta** (4); **preguntar** (6); (*issue*) **cuestión** (16)

quit **dejar** (16); (*doing something*) **dejar de** + *inf.* (10)

quiz **prueba** (11)

R

radio **radio** *m.* (*set*); portable radio **radio portátil** (12); radio (*medium*) (12) **radio** *f.*

rain **llover (ue)** (5); it's raining **llueve** (5)

raincoat **impermeable** *m.* (3)

raise **aumento** (12); (in salary) **aumento de sueldo** (16)

rare **raro/a** (8)

rather **bastante** *adv.* (15)

react **reaccionar** (8)

read **leer (y)** (2)

reader **lector(a)** (13)

reason **razón** *f.* (3)

receive **recibir** (2)

recommend **recomendar (ie)** (7)

record **grabar** (12)

recorder: tape recorder **grabadora** (12); videocassette recorder (VCR) **videocasetera** (12)

recycle **reciclar** (14)

red **rojo/a** (3); red wine **vino tinto** (6)

reduction **rebaja** (3)

refreshment **refresco** (8)

reflexive **reflexivo** (4)

refrigerator **refrigerador** *m.* (9)

regret **sentir (ie, i)** (13)

relationship **relación** (*f.*) **sentimental** (15)

relative **pariente** *m., f.* (2)

remain (*in a place*) **quedar(se)** (5); to remain, stay (*as a guest*) **alojarse** (18)

remember **recordar (ue)** (8); **acordarse (ue) (de)** (11)

remote control **control** (*m.*) **remoto** (12)

rent **alquiler** *m.* (12); to rent *v.* **alquilar** (12)

renter **inquilino/a** (12)

repair **arreglar** (12); (repair) shop **taller** *m.* (14)

report **informe** *m.;* **trabajo** (11)

reporter **reportero/a** (17)

represent **representar** (13)

reservation **reserva, reservación** (*f.*) (18)

resign (from) **renunciar (a)** (16)

resolve **resolver (ue)** (*p.p.* **resuelto/a**) (14)

resource **recurso**; natural resources **recursos naturales** (14)

responsibility **responsabilidad** *f.;* **deber** *m.* (17)

rest **descansar** (4); the rest **los/las demás** (12)

restaurant **restaurante** *m.* (6)

résumé **currículum** *m.* (16)

retire **jubilarse** (16)

return (*to a place*) **regresar** (1); **volver (ue)** (*p.p.* **vuelto/a**) (4); (*something*) **devolver (ue)** (*pp.* **devuelto/a**) (16)

rhythm **ritmo** (14)

rice **arroz** *m.* (6)

rich **rico/a** (2)

ride a bicycle **pasear en bicicleta** (9); to ride horseback **montar a caballo** (9)

right (*legal*) **derecho** *n.* (17); (*direction*) **derecha** *n.* (5); right? **¿verdad?** (3); to be right **tener** (*irreg.*) **razón** (3); to the right (of) **a la derecha (de)** (5)

ring **sonar (ue)** (9)

road **camino** (14)

roast chicken **pollo asado** (6)

role **papel** *m.* (13)

roller skates **patines** *m. pl.* (12)

rollerblade *v.* **patinar en línea** (9)

room **cuarto** (1); room (*in a hotel*) **habitación** *f.* (18); dining room **comedor** *m.* (4); double room **habitación** (*f.*) **doble** (18); emergency room **sala de emergencias/ urgencia** (10); living room **sala** (4); room and full board (all meals) **pensión** (*f.*) **completa** (18); room with(out) bath/shower **habitación** (*f.*) **con/sin baño/ducha** (18); single room **habitación** (*f.*) **individual**

(18); waiting room **sala de espera** (7)

roommate **compañero/a de cuarto** (1)

round-trip ticket **billete** (*m.*)**/boleto de ida y vuelta** (7)

routine: daily routine **rutina diaria** (4)

rug **alfombra** (4)

ruin *n.* **ruina** (13)

rule **gobernar (ie)** (17)

run **correr** (9); (*machines*) **funcionar** (12); to run into **darse** (*irreg.*) **con, pegarse (gu) en/contra** (11); **chocar (qu) (con)** (14); to run out of **acabar(se)** (11)

S

sad **triste** (5)

sake: for God's sake **por Dios** (12)

salad **ensalada** (6)

salary **sueldo** (12); **salario** (16); raise in salary **aumento de sueldo** (16)

sale **rebaja** (3)

salesperson **dependiente/a** (1); **vendedor(a)** (16)

salmon **salmón** *m.* (6)

same **mismo/a** (10); same here **igualmente** (P)

sandal **sandalia** (3)

sandwich **sándwich** *m.* (6)

Saturday **sábado** (4)

sausage **salchicha** (6)

save (*a place/documents*) **guardar** (7); **conservar** (14); (*money*) **ahorrar** (16)

savings **ahorros** *m. pl.*; savings account **cuenta de ahorros** (16)

say **decir** (*irreg.*) (7); to say good-bye (to) **despedirse (i, i) (de)** (8)

schedule **horario** (11)

school **escuela** (9)

schoolteacher **maestro/a** (16)

science **ciencia** (1); computer science **computación** *f.* (1)

script **guión** *m.* (13)

sculpt **esculpir** (13)

sculptor **escultor(a)** (13)

sculpture **escultura** (13)

sea **mar** *m., f.* (7)

seaport **puerto** (7)

search **registrar** (18); in search of **en busca de** (16)

season **estación** *f.* (5)

seat *n.* **asiento** (7)

second **segundo/a** *adj.* (13)

secretary **secretario/a** (1)

section: (non)smoking section **sección** (*f.*) **de (no) fumar** (7)

see **ver** (*irreg.*) (4); see you around **nos vemos** (P); see you later **hasta luego** (P); see you tomorrow **hasta mañana** (P)

seem **parecer (zc)** (13)

self **mismo/a** (10)

sell **vender** (2)

send **mandar** (7)

separate (from) *v.* **separarse (de)** (15)

September **septiembre** *m.* (5)

servant **criado/a** (16)

serve **servir (i, i)** (4)

service **servicio** (14); military service **servicio militar** (17)

set: television set **televisor** *m.* (4); set the table **poner** (*irreg.*) **la mesa** (9)

seven **siete** (P)

seven hundred **setecientos/as** (3)

seventeen **diecisiete** (P)

seventh **séptimo/a** *adj.* (13)

seventy **setenta** (2)

shame **lástima** (13); it is a shame **es lástima** (13); what a shame! **¡qué lástima!** (13)

shampoo **champú** *m.* (18)

shave oneself **afeitarse** (4)

she **ella** (1)

shellfish **marisco** (6)

ship **barco** (7)

shirt **camisa** (3)

shoe **zapato** (3); tennis shoe **zapato de tenis** (3)

shop **tienda** (3); (repair) **taller** *m.* (14); pastry shop **pastelería** (18); tobacco shop **estanco** (18)

shopkeeper **comerciante** *m., f.* (16)

shopping **de compras** (3); shopping mall **centro comercial** (3); to go shopping **ir** (*irreg.*) **de compras** (3)

short (*in height*) **bajo/a** (2); (*in length*) **corto/a** (2)

shortage **escasez** *f.* (*pl.* **escaseces**) (14)

shot **inyección** *f.* (10)

should (*do something*) **deber** (+ *inf.*) (2)

show **mostrar (ue)** (7)

shower **ducha** (18); to take a shower **ducharse** (4)

shrimp **camarón** *m.* (6)

sick **enfermo/a** *adj.* (5); to get sick **enfermarse** (8)

sickness **enfermedad** *f.* (10)

side: to get up on the wrong side of the bed **levantarse con el pie izquierdo** (11)

sight: at first sight **a primera vista** (15)

signal: traffic signal **semáforo** (14)

silk **seda** (3); it is made of silk **es de seda** (3)

silly **tonto/a** (2)

since: it's been (*time*) since… **hace** + *time* + **que…** + *present* (11)

sing **cantar** (1)

singer **cantante** *m., f.* (13)

single (*not married*) **soltero/a** (2); single room **habitación** (*f.*) **individual** (18)

sink (bathroom) **lavabo** (4)

sir **señor (Sr.)** *m.* (P)

sister **hermana** (2)

sit down **sentarse (ie)** (4)

six **seis** (P)

six hundred **seiscientos/as** (3)

sixteen **dieciséis** (P)

sixth **sexto/a** *adj.* (13)

sixty **sesenta** (2)

skate *v.* **patinar** (9)

skateboard **monopatín** *m.* (12)

skates: roller skates **patines** *m. pl.* (12)

ski **esquiar (esquío)** (9)

skirt **falda** (3)

skyscraper **rascacielos** *m. s.* (14)

sleep **dormir (ue, u)** (4)

sleepy: to be sleepy **tener** (*irreg.*) **sueño** (3)

slender **delgado/a** (2)
small **pequeño/a** (2)
smart **listo/a** (2)
smile **sonreír(se) (i, i)** (8)
smoke **fumar** (7)
smoking (nonsmoking) section
  sección (*f.*) **de (no) fumar** (7)
snow **nevar (ie)** (5); it's snowing
  nieva (5)
so that **para que** (15)
soap **jabón** *m.* (18)
soccer **fútbol** *m.* (9)
social worker **trabajador(a)
  social** (16)
sociology **sociología** (1)
sock **calcetín, calcetines** *m.* (3)
sofa **sofá** *m.* (4)
soft drink **refresco** (6)
solar **solar** (14)
soldier **soldado**; female soldier
  mujer (*f.*) **soldado** (16)
solve **resolver (ue)** (*p.p.* **resuelto/a**)
  (14)
some **algún, alguno/a** (6)
someone **alguien** (6)
something **algo** (3)
sometimes **a veces** (2)
son **hijo** (2)
song **canción** *f.* (13)
soon **pronto**; *conj.* as soon as **tan
  pronto como** (16); **en cuanto** (16)
sorry: I'm sorry **discúlpeme** (11); **lo
  siento mucho** (11); to feel sorry
  sentir (ie, i) (13)
sound *v.* **sonar (ue)** (9)
soup **sopa** (6)
south **sur** *m.* (5)
Spanish (*language*) **español** *m.* (1);
  español(a) *n., adj.* (2)
spare time **ratos libres** (9)
speak **hablar** (1)
speed **velocidad** *f.* (14); speed limit
  límite (*m.*) **de velocidad** (14)
spend (*money*) **gastar** (8); (*time*)
  pasar (5)
sport **deporte** *m.* (9)
sports-loving **deportivo/a** *adj.* (9)
spouse **esposo/a** (2)
spring **primavera** (5)

stage **escenario** (13); (*of life*)
  etapa (15)
stamp **sello** (*postage*) (18)
stand in line **hacer** (*irreg.*) **cola** (7); to
  stand up **levantarse** (4); tobacco
  stand **estanco** (18)
start (*a motor*) **arrancar (qu)** (12)
state **estado** (2)
station **estación** *f.* (7); bus station
  estación de autobuses (7); gas
  station **estación** (*f.*) **de gasolina,
  gasolinera** (14); train station
  estación del tren (7); station wagon
  camioneta (7)
stationery **papel** (*m.*) **para cartas**
  (18); stationery store **papelería** (18)
stay *n.* (*in a hotel*) **estancia** (18); to
  stay (*in a place*) **quedar(se)** (5);
  alojarse (18); to stay in bed
  guardar cama (10)
steak **bistec** *m.* (6)
stereo equipment **equipo estereofónico** (12)
stick out one's tongue **sacar (qu) la
  lengua** (10)
still **todavía** (5)
stockings **medias** *f. pl.* (3)
stomach **estómago** (10)
stop **parar** (14); (*doing something*)
  dejar de + *inf.* (10); to make stops
  hacer (*irreg.*) **escalas/paradas** (7);
  bus stop **parada del autobús** (18);
  subway stop **estación** (*f.*) **del
  metro** (18)
store **tienda** (3); department store
  almacén (*m.*); stationery store
  papelería (18)
stove **estufa** (9)
straight ahead **todo derecho** (14)
straighten (up) **arreglar** (12)
strange **raro/a** (8); **extraño/a** (13);
  how strange **qué extraño** (13); it's
  strange **es extraño** (13)
street **calle** *f.* (12); **camino** (14); street
  corner **esquina** (14)
stress **estrés** *m.* (11)
strike (*labor*) **huelga** (17)
striped **de rayas** (3)
strong **fuerte** (6)

student **estudiante** *m., f.* (1);
  estudiantil *adj.* (11)
study **estudiar** (1)
style: latest style **de última moda** (3)
subject (*school*) **materia** (1)
suburb **afueras** *n. f. pl.* (12)
subway station **estación** (*f.*) **del
  metro** (18)
succeed in (*doing something*) **conseguir (i, i) (g)** + *inf.* (8)
suddenly **de repente** (10)
suffer **sufrir** (11)
sufficiently **bastante** *adv.* (15)
suggest **sugerir (ie, i)** (8)
suit **traje** *m.* (3); bathing suit **traje
  de baño** (3)
suitcase **maleta** (7); to pack one's
  suitcases **hacer** (*irreg.*)
  las maletas (7)
summer **verano** (5)
sunbathe **tomar el sol** (7)
Sunday **domingo** (4)
sunny: it's sunny **hace sol** (5)
supper **cena** (6)
support **apoyar** (17)
sure **seguro/a** *adj.* (5); it's a sure
  thing **es seguro** (13)
surf the net **navegar (gu) la red** (12)
surprise **sorpresa** (8); to surprise
  sorprender; it surprises me (you,
  him, . . .) **me (te, le, ...)
  sorprende** (13)
sweater **suéter** *m.* (3)
sweep (the floor) **barrer (el piso)** (9)
sweets **dulces** *m. pl.* (6)
swim **nadar** (7)
swimming **natación** *f.* (9); swimming
  pool **piscina** (4)
swimsuit **traje** (*m.*) **de baño** (3)
symptom **síntoma** *m.* (10)
syrup: cough syrup **jarabe** (10)
systems analyst **analista** (*m., f.*) **de
  sistemas** (16)

T

T-shirt **camiseta** (3)
table **mesa** (1); table (end) **mesita** (4)
take **tomar** (1); to take (*a class*)
  llevar (3); to take (photos) **sacar**

(qu) (7); to take a bath **bañarse** (4); to take a nap **dormir la siesta** (4); to take a shower **ducharse** (4); to take a trip **hacer** (*irreg.*) **un viaje** (4); to take a walk **dar** (*irreg.*) **un paseo** (9); to take care of oneself **cuidar(se)** (10); to take leave (of) **despedirse (i, i) (de)** (8); to take off (*clothing*) **quitarse** (4); to take out **sacar (qu)** (11); to take out the trash **sacar (qu) la basura** (9); to take place in/at (*place*) **ser** (*irreg.*) **en** + *place* (8); to take someone's temperature **tomarle la temperatura** (10)

talk **hablar** (1); to talk on the phone **hablar por teléfono** (1)

tall **alto/a** (2)

tank **tanque** *m.* (14)

tape **cinta** (3); to tape **grabar** (12); tape recorder/player **grabadora** (12)

task **tarea** (4)

taste **gusto** (P)

tea **té** *m.* (6)

teach **enseñar** (1)

teacher **maestro/a** (16)

technician **técnico/a** *n.* (16)

teeth: to brush one's teeth **cepillarse los dientes** (4)

telephone: cellular/car phone **teléfono celular / de coche** (12)

television set **televisor** *m.* (4); to watch television **mirar la televisión** (2)

tell **decir** (*irreg.*) (7); **contar (ue)** (7); to tell jokes **contar chistes** *m. pl.* (8)

teller **cajero/a** (16); automatic teller machine **cajero automático** (16)

temperature **temperatura** (10); to take someone's temperature **tomarle la temperatura** (10)

ten **diez** (P)

tenant **inquilino/a** (12)

tennis **tenis** *m. s.* (9); tennis shoe **zapato de tenis** (3)

tent **tienda de campaña** (7)

tenth **décimo/a** (13)

terrorist **terrorista** *m., f.* (17)

test **examen** *m.* (3); **prueba** (11)

text **texto** (1); textbook **libro de texto** (1)

thank you **gracias** (P); thank you very much **muchas gracias** (P)

that *adj.,* that one *pron.* **ese, esa** (3); that *adj.,* that one *pron.* (*over there*) **aquel, aquella** (3); that *pron.* **eso** (3); that *pron.* (*over there*) **aquello** (3); *conj.* **que** (2); so that **para que** (15); that which **lo que** (7)

theater **teatro** (9); movie theater **cine** *m.* (4)

their *poss.* **sus** (2)

there: (over) there **allí** (3); **allá** (4)

there is (not), there are (not) **(no) hay** (P)

therefore **por eso** (1)

these *adj.,* these (ones) *pron.* **estos/as** (2)

they **ellos/as** (1)

thin **delgado/a** (2)

thing **cosa** (1); the good (bad) thing **lo bueno (malo)** (10)

think **creer (y) (en)** (2); **pensar (ie)** (4)

third **tercer, tercero/a** *adj.* (13)

thirst **sed** *f.*

thirsty: to be thirsty **tener** (*irreg.*) **sed** (6)

thirteen **trece** (P)

thirty **treinta** (P); thirty, half past (*with time*) **y treinta** (P)

this *adj.* this one *pron.* **este, esta** (2); this *pron.* **esto** (3)

those *adj.* those (ones) *pron.* **esos/as** (3); those *adj.* (*over there*) those (ones) *pron.* (*over there*) **aquellos/as** (3)

thousand, one thousand **mil** (3)

three **tres** (P); (three) thirty, half past (three) (*with time*) **media: (las tres) y media** (P)

three hundred **trescientos/as** (3)

throat **garganta** (10)

through **por** *prep.* (4)

Thursday **jueves** *m. s., pl.* (4)

ticket **boleto, billete** *m.* (7); **pasaje** *m.* (7); one-way ticket **billete**

(*m.*)/**boleto de ida** (7); round trip ticket **billete** (*m.*)/**boleto de ida y vuelta** (7)

tie **corbata** (3)

time **tiempo** (5); time (*period*) **época** (9); ahead of time **con anticipación** (18); at times **a veces** (2); for the first/last time **por primera/última vez** (11); on time **a tiempo** (7); spare time **ratos** (*m. pl.*) **libres** (9); to arrive on time **llegar (gu) a tiempo** (11); to have a bad time **pasarlo mal** (8); to have a good time **divertirse (ie)** (4); **pasarlo bien** (8); to spend time (with) **pasar tiempo (con)** (15); full-time (part-time) job **trabajo a tiempo completo (parcial)** (11); what time is it? **¿qué hora es?** (P)

tip (*to an employee*) **propina** (18)

tire *n.* **llanta** (14); flat tire **llanta desinflada** (14)

tired **cansado/a** (5); to be tired **estar** (*irreg.*) **cansado/a** (5)

to **a** (P); to the **al** (*contraction of* **a** + **el**) (3)

toast **pan** (*m.*) **tostado** (6)

toasted **tostado/a** (6)

toaster **tostadora** (9)

tobacco stand/shop **estanco** (18)

today **hoy** (P); **¿cuál es la fecha de hoy?** what's today's date? (5)

toe **dedo del pie** (11)

together **juntos/as** (15); to get together (with) **reunirse (me reúno) (con)** (8)

tomato **tomate** *m.* (6)

tomorrow **mañana** *adv.* (P); day after tomorrow **pasado mañana** (4); see you tomorrow **hasta mañana** (P)

tongue: to stick out one's tongue **sacar (qu) la lengua** (10)

tonight **esta noche** (5)

too **también** (P)

tooth **diente** *m.* (10)

toothpaste **pasta dental** (18)

top: on top of **encima de** (5)

tourist **turístico/a** *adj.*; tourist class **clase** (*f.*) **turística** (7)
trade (*job*) **oficio** (16)
tradition **tradición** *f.* (13)
traffic **tránsito; circulación** *f.* (14); traffic signal **semáforo** (14)
train **tren** *m.* (7); train station **estación** (*f.*) **de trenes** (7); to go by train **ir** (*irreg.*) **en tren** (7); to train **entrenar** (9)
translator **traductor(a)** (16)
transportation (means of) transportation **transporte** *m.* (14)
trash: to take out the trash **sacar (qu) la basura** (9)
travel **viajar** (7); travel agency **agencia de viajes** (7); travel agent **agente** (*m. f.*) **de viajes** (7)
traveler **viajero/a** (18); traveler's check **cheque** (*m.*) **de viajero** (18)
treatment **tratamiento** (10)
tree **árbol** *m.* (14)
trip **viaje** *m.* (7); have a good trip **buen viaje** (7); on a trip **de viaje** (7); round-trip ticket **billete** (*m.*)**/boleto de ida y vuelta** (7); to go on a trip **ir** (*irreg.*) **de viaje** (10); to take a trip **hacer** (*irreg.*) **un viaje** (4)
try **intentar** (13); try to (*do something*) **tratar de** + *inf.* (13)
Tuesday **martes** *m. s., pl.* (4)
tuition **matrícula** (1)
tuna **atún** *m.* (6)
turkey **pavo** (6)
turn **doblar** (14); to turn in **entregar (gu)** (11); to be someone's turn **tocarle (qu) a uno** (9)
twelve **doce** (P)
twenty **veinte** (P)
twice **dos veces** (10)
two **dos** (P)
two hundred **doscientos/as** (3)
type **escribir** (*pp.* **escrito/a**) **a máquina** (16)

U

ugly **feo/a** (2)
unbelievable **increíble** (13)

uncle **tío** (2)
under: to be under pressure **sufrir presiones** (11)
understand **comprender** (2); **entender (ie)** (4)
underwear **ropa interior** (3)
unintentional: it was unintentional **fue sin querer** (11)
university **universidad** *f.* (1); (of the) university **universitario/a** (11); university campus **campus** *m. s.* (12)
unless **a menos que** (15)
unoccupied **desocupado/a** (18)
unpleasant **antipático/a** (2)
until **hasta** *prep.* (4); **hasta que** *conj.* (16); until tomorrow **hasta mañana** (P)
urgent **urgente** (13)
us **nos** *d.o.; i.o.* to/for us; *refl. pron.* ourselves; see you around **nos vemos** (P)
use **usar** (3); **gastar** (8); to use up completely **acabar (se)** (14)
useful **útil** (15)

V

vacancy: no vacancy **completo/a** (18)
vacant **desocupado/a** (18)
vacation **vacación** *f.* (7); to be on vacation **estar** (*irreg.*) **de vacaciones** (7); to go on vacation **ir** (*irreg.*) **de vacaciones** (7)
vacuum cleaner **aspiradora** (9); to vacuum **pasar la aspiradora** (9)
vegetable **verdura** (6)
vehicle **vehículo** (12)
verb **verbo** *gram.* (1)
very **muy** (1); very well **muy bien** (P)
veterinarian **veterinario/a** (16)
video camera **cámara de video** (12)
videocassette recorder (VCR) **videocasetera** (12)
view **vista** (12)
violence **violencia** (14)
visit a museum **visitar un museo** (9)
volleyball **vólibol** *m.* (9)
vote **votar** (17)

W

wagon: station wagon **camioneta** (7)
wait (for) **esperar** (6)
waiter **camarero** (6)
waiting room **sala de espera** (7)
waitress **camarera** (6)
wake up **despertarse (ie)** (4)
walk **caminar** (10); to take a walk **dar** (*irreg.*) **un paseo** (9); to walk (go on foot) **ir** (*irreg.*) **a pie** (10)
walkman *walkman* (12)
wall **pared** *f.* (4)
wallet **cartera** (3)
want **desear** (1); **querer** (*irreg.*) (3)
war **guerra** (17)
warm: to be (feel) warm, hot **tener** (*irreg.*) **calor** (5)
wash **lavar** (9); to wash (the windows, the dishes, clothes) **lavar (las ventanas, los platos, la ropa)** (9); to wash (oneself) **lavar(se)**
washing machine **lavadora** (9)
waste **desperdiciar** (14)
watch **reloj** *m.* (3); to watch **mirar** (2); to watch television **mirar la televisión** (2)
water **agua** *f.* (*but* **el agua**); mineral water **agua** *f.* (*but* **el agua**) **mineral** (6); waterbed **cama de agua** (4)
way: one-way ticket **billete/boleto de ida** (7)
we **nosotros/as** (1)
wear (clothing) **llevar, usar** (3)
weather **tiempo** (5); it's good/bad weather **hace buen/mal tiempo** (5); what's the weather like? **¿qué tiempo hace?** (5)
weave **tejer** (13)
wedding **boda** (15)
Wednesday **miércoles** *m. s., pl.* (4)
week **semana** (4); next week **la semana que viene** (4); once a week **una vez a la semana** (2)
weekend **fin** (*m.*) **de semana** (1)
welcome: you're welcome **de nada, no hay de qué** (P)

well **bien** *adv.* (P); well . . . *interj.*
  bueno... (2)
well-being **bienestar** *m.* (10)
west **oeste** *m.* (5)
what **lo que** (7)
what . . . ! **¡qué... !**; what a shame!
  ¡qué lástima! (13)
what? which? **¿qué? ¿cuál(es)?** (P);
  what are you like? **¿cómo es usted?**
  (P); what is the date today? **¿cuál
  es la fecha de hoy?** (5); what time is
  it? **¿qué hora es?** (P); what's your
  name? **¿cómo te llamas? / ¿cómo
  se llama usted?** (P)
when? **¿cuándo?** (P)
where (to)? **¿adónde?** (3)
where? **¿dónde?** (P); where are you
  from? **¿de dónde es Ud.?** (2)
which **que** (2); **¿cuál (es)?** (P); that
  which **lo que** (7)
while **mientras** (9); **rato** *n.* (9)
white **blanco/a** (3); white wine
  vino blanco (6)
who **que** (2)
who? whom? **¿quién(es)?** (P)
whole **entero/a** (9)
whose? **¿de quién?** (2)
why? **¿por qué?** (2)
wife **esposa** (2); **mujer** *f.* (15)
win **ganar** (9)
wind *n.* **viento** (5); *adj.* **eólico/a** (14)
window **ventana** (1)
windshield **parabrisas** *m. s.* (14)
windy: it's windy **hace viento** (5)
wine (white, red) **vino (blanco,
  tinto)** (6)

winter **invierno** (5)
wish **deseo** (8); **esperanza** (17); I
  wish **ojalá (que)** (13)
with **con** (1)
withdraw (*money*) **sacar (qu)** (16)
without **sin** (4)
witness **testigo** *m., f.* (17)
woman **señora (Sra.)** (P);
  mujer *f.* (1)
wool **lana** (3); it is made of wool **es
  de lana** (3)
word **palabra** (P)
work (of art) **obra (de arte)** (13); *n.*
  trabajo (11); to work **trabajar** (1);
  (*machine*) **funcionar** (12)
worker **obrero/a** (16); social worker
  trabajador(a) social (16)
world **mundo** (7)
worried **preocupado/a** (5)
worse **peor** (5)
woven goods **tejidos** *m. pl.* (13)
write **escribir** (*p.p.* **escrito/a**) (2)
writer **escritor(a)** (13)
written **escrito/a** *p.p.* (11); written
  report **informe** (*m.*) **escrito** (11)
wrong: to be wrong **no tener** (*irreg.*)
  razón (3); **equivocarse (qu)** (11);
  to get up on the wrong side of the
  bed **levantarse con el pie
  izquierdo** (11)

Y

yard, **patio** (4); **jardín** *m.* (4)
year **año** (5); (*in school*) **grado** (9); to
  be . . . years old **tener** (*irreg.*)...
  años (2)

yellow **amarillo/a** (3)
yes **sí** (P); yes, I like . . . **sí, me
  gusta...** (P)
yesterday **ayer** (4); yesterday was
  (Wednesday) **ayer fue
  (miércoles)** (4)
yet **todavía** (5)
yogurt **yogur** *m.* (6)
you *sub. pron.* **tú** (*fam. s.*) (P); **usted
  (Ud., Vd.)** (*form. s.*) (P);
  vosotros/as (*fam. pl., Sp.*); **ustedes
  (Uds., Vds.)** (*pl.*); *d.o.* **te, os, lo/la,
  los, las**; to/for you *i.o.* **te, os, le,
  les**; *obj.* (*of prep.*) **ti, Ud., Uds., voso-
  tros/as** (5)
you're welcome **de nada, no hay de
  qué** (P)
young **joven** (2)
young woman **señorita (Srta.)** (P)
younger **menor** (5)
your *poss.* **tu** (*fam. s.*) (2); **su(s)**
  (*form.*) (2); **vuestro/a(s)** (*fam. pl.,
  Sp.*) (2)
youth **joven** *n. m., f.* (2); *adj.* young
  (2); as a youth **de joven** (9); (*young
  adulthood*) **juventud** *f.* (15)

Z

zero **cero** (P)

In this Index, cultural notes, reading strategies, and vocabulary topic groups are listed by individual topic as well as under those headings.

CREDITS

Grateful acknowledgment is made for use of the following:

Photographs: *Page iii and 1* © Wartenberg/Picture Press/Corbis; *2* Marty Granger; *7 (from left)* Stephanie Cardinale/Corbis Sygma, AP/Wide World Photos, Mitchell Gerber/Corbis, Gregory Pace/Corbis Sygma; *10* © Stuart Cohen; *16* SuperStock; *24 (left)* Pictor/Uniphoto, *(right)* © Antonio Mendoza/Stock Boston; *25 (clockwise from left)* SuperStock, © Ulrike Welsch, © Peter Menzel; *27* Marty Granger; *iv and 29* Peter Vandermark/Stock Boston; *31* Steve Vidler/SuperStock; *32* A.G.E. Fotostock; *39* © Bettman/Corbis; *40* Susan Casarin; *44* AP/Wide World Photos; *49* © Ulrike Welsch; *iv and 53* © Vince Dewitt/D. Donne Bryant Stock; *64* © Museo del Prado, Madrid, Spain/Giraudon, Paris/SuperStock; *66* Commissioned by the Trustees of Dartmouth College; *67* © Llewellyn/Uniphoto; *71* Susan Casarin; *75* © Trapper Frank/Corbis Sygma; *v and 80* © Larry Luxner 2000; *83 (top)* © Reuters NewMedia Inc./Corbis, *(bottom)* © Gonzalo Endara Crow; *89* Marty Granger; *93* © Corbis-Bettman; *96* © Topham/The Image Works; *97* Marty Granger; *v and 102* Martin Rogers/Corbis; *106* © Ric Ergenbright; *113* © Bill Gentile/Corbis; *117* Vincente Wolf Associates, Inc.; *119* Marty Granger; *128* © Vince Streano/Corbis; *131 (top and bottom) A logo for America* by Alfredo Jaar; *137* © Rob Crandall/The Image Works; *138 (top)* Uniphoto, *(bottom)* © Ulrike Welsch; *144* Marty Granger; *146* © Frans Lating/Getty Images/Stone; *vi and 149* Richard Lord/PhotoEdit; *152 (left)* © FoodPix, *(right)* © Peter Guttman/Corbis; *154* Marty Granger; *161* Courtesy of Oswaldo & Alice Arana; *162* SuperStock; *168* Marty Granger; *vii and 173* © Suzanne Murphy-Larronde/D. Donne Bryant Stock; *175* © Alfred Buellesbach/Plus 49/The Image Works; *176* © Stuart Cohen; *185* © Stephen and Donna O'Meara/Photo Researchers, Inc.; *186* Marty Granger; *189* © Corbis; *192* Marty Granger; *194* SuperStock; *vii and 197* © AFP/Corbis; *200* © Jack Kurtz/The Image Works; *208* © Prensa Latina/Getty Images; *211* © Bob Riha/Getty Images; *213* Marty Granger; *viii and 217* © Robert Frerck/Odyssey/Chicago; *219 (top)* Corbis-Bettmann, *(bottom)* AP/Wide World Photos; *226 (left)* © Stephanie Cardinale/Corbis Sygma, *(right)* Associated Press; *228* © George Holton/Photo Researchers, Inc.; *231* © Monica Graff/The Image Works; *232* Marty Granger; *234* Joe Viesti/Viesti Collection; *viii and 237* © D. Donne Bryant Stock; *242* Marty Granger; *248* © Ken Fisher/Getty Images/Stone; *250* AP/Wide World Photos; *253* Marty Granger; *ix and 257* © Suzanne Murphy-Larronde/D. Donne Bryant Stock; *265* © Dalle Luche/Sestini/Grazia Neri/Corbis Sygma; *268* © Ulrike Welsch; *273* Marty Granger; *275* Pictor/Uniphoto; *ix and 279* © Corbis; *288* Marty Granger; *292* David Young-Wolfe/PhotoEdit; *293* © Robert Frerck/Odyssey/Chicago; *298* Marty Granger; *xi and 302* © Craig Duncan/D. Donne Bryant Stock; *305* © Charles Kennard/Stock Boston; *307* © Joe Sohm/The Image Works; *311 Madre y niño* by Oswaldo Guayasamín, Oleo sobre tela 80 x 80 cm, Fundacion Guayasamín, Quito, Ecuador; *312* Collection of the Art Museum of the Americas, Organization of American States, Gift of IBM; *315* © Susana Gonzalez/Getty Images; *316* The Granger Collection; *317* Marty Granger; *xi and 322* © Terry Whittaker/Photo Researchers, Inc.; *325* © David Simpson/Stock, Boston; *331* © Robert Frerck/Odyssey; *336* AP/Wide World Photos; *338* Marty Granger; *xi and 342* © D. Donne Bryant Stock; *350* © Mathias Opperdorff/Photo Researchers, Inc.; *353* © AP/Wide World Photos; *355* Marty Granger; *xi and 360* © Matthew Bryant/D. Donne Bryant Stock; *363* Marty Granger; *371* © Chip and Rosa Maria Peterson; *378* Marty Granger; *xii and 383* © John Mitchel/D. Donne Bryant Stock; *392* © Getty Images; *395* Courtesy of Algonquin Books; *397* Marty Granger; *xii and 401* © George Holton/Photo Researchers, Inc.; *403* © Stuart Cohen; *411* © Stuart Cohen; *412* © Peter Menzel/Stock Boston; *414* Marty Granger

Realia: *Page 11* © Joaquín S. Lavado, Quino, Toda Mafalda, Ediciones de la Flor, 1997; *13* Ansa International; *85 Quo*, HF Revistas; *166* © Goya Foods, Inc.; *209* © Joaquín S. Lavado, Quino, Toda Mafalda, Ediciones de la Flor, 1997; *219 Cambio 16*; *249* © Green Comics; *318 Diario EL PAÍS*; Architect Eduardo Scheck, President of MUVA, *Museo Virtual de Artes EL PAÍS*; Professor Alicia Haber, Director of *Museo Virtual de Artes EL PAÍS*; Guillermo Pérez Rosell, General Coordinator, Digital Department of *Diario EL PAÍS*; *335 (left)* © Joaquín S. Lavado, Quino, Toda Mafalda, Ediciones de la Flor, 1997, *(right)* © ALI, Brussels; *346* © Joaquín S. Lavado, Quino, Toda Mafalda, Ediciones de la Flor, 1997; *356* Consejo General del Poder Judicial, Instituto Nacional de Estadística e Instituto de la Mujer, from *EL PAÍS*; *361* © Joaquín S. Lavado, Quino, Toda Mafalda, Ediciones de la Flor, 1997; *366* © Joaquín S. Lavado, Quino, Toda Mafalda, Ediciones de la Flor, 1997; *375 People en español*, September 1998. Used by permission of Time Inc.; *385* © Joaquín S. Lavado, Quino, Toda Mafalda, Ediciones de la Flor, 1997; *394* Antonio Mingote; *406* © Joaquín S. Lavado, Quino, Toda Mafalda, Ediciones de la Flor, 1997.

Readings: *Page 98 Quo*, no. 31, April 1998; *145* Courtesy of *Muy Interesante*; *193 GeoMundo*; *208 Poema con niños* by Nicolás Guillén. Used by permission of the heirs of Nicolás Guillén and the Agencia Literaria Latinoamericana; *233 Quo*, 1997; *275 GeoMundo*; *318 Museo Virtual de Artes*. Courtesy of *GeoMundo*; *356* El País; *350* Reprinted with permission of Provincia Franciscana de la Santisima Trinidad, Santiago de Chile; *399 Cubanita descubanizada*, in *Bilingual Blues* by Gustavo Pérez Firmat, *Bilingual Review Press*, Arizona State University, Tempe, AZ, 1995.

Thalia Dorwick is Editor-in-Chief of Humanities, Social Sciences, and Languages for McGraw-Hill. She is in charge of the World Languages college list in Spanish, French, Italian, German, Japanese, and Russian. She has taught at Allegheny College, California State University (Sacramento), and Case Western Reserve University, where she received her Ph.D. in Spanish in 1973. Dr. Dorwick is the coauthor of several textbooks and the author of several articles on language teaching issues. She was recognized as an Outstanding Foreign Language Teacher by the California Foreign Language Teachers Association in 1978.

Ana María Pérez-Gironés is an Adjunct Assistant Professor of Spanish at Wesleyan University, Middletown, Connecticut, where she teaches and coordinates Spanish language courses. She received a Licenciatura en Filología Anglogermánica from the Universidad de Sevilla in 1985, and her M.A. in General Linguistics from Cornell University in 1988. She is a coauthor of *¿Qué tal?*, Fourth Edition.

Marty Knorre was formerly Associate Professor of Romance Languages and Coordinator of basic Spanish courses at the University of Cincinnati, where she taught undergraduate and graduate courses in language, linguistics, and methodology. She received her Ph.D. in foreign language education from The Ohio State University in 1975. Dr. Knorre is coauthor of *Cara a cara* and *Reflejos* and has taught at several NEH Institutes for Language Instructors. She received a Master of Divinity at McCormick Theological Seminary in 1991.

William R. Glass is the Publisher for World Languages at McGraw-Hill. He was formerly an Assistant Professor of Spanish at The Pennsylvania State University, where he taught both undergraduate and graduate courses in language and applied linguistics. He received his Ph.D. from the University of Illinois at Urbana-Champaign in Spanish Applied Linguistics with a concentration in Second Language Acquisition and Teacher Education (SLATE). Dr. Glass' research interests include second language reading theory and second language acquisition in tutored contexts. He is also a coauthor of *Puntos de partida*, Sixth Edition and the *Manual que acompaña ¿Sabías que... ?*, both by McGraw-Hill.

Hildebrando Villarreal is Professor of Spanish at California State University, Los Angeles, where he teaches undergraduate and graduate courses in language and linguistics. He received his Ph.D. in Spanish with an emphasis in Applied Linguistics from UCLA in 1976. Professor Villarreal is the author of several reviews and articles on language, language teaching, and Spanish for Native Speakers of Spanish. He is the author of *¡A leer! Un paso más*, an intermediate textbook that focuses on reading skills.

Los hispanos en los Estados Unidos	1500–1600	1700–1776	1835–1836	1846–1848
	Exploraciones españolas	Establecimiento de misiones en Arizona y California	Guerra de la independencia tejana	Guerra entre México y los Estados Unidos

México y Centroamérica	a.C.ª 800–400	d.C.ᵇ 300–900	1200–1521	1821
	Civilización olmeca	Civilización maya	Civilización azteca florece hasta la conquista de Tenochtitlán por Hernán Cortés	Independencia de México y Centroamérica

ªantes de Cristo ᵇdespués de Cristo

Las naciones caribeñas	d.C. 25–600	1492–1498	1500–1512	1821
	Civilización igneri y fundación del pueblo de Tibes en Puerto Rico	Viajes de Cristóbal Colón al Caribe y a Venezuela	Colonización española de Venezuela, Puerto Rico y Cuba	Independencia de Venezuela y Colombia

Las naciones andinas	1000–1500	1200–1532	1532	1821
	Civilización nasca en el Perú	Imperio incaico	Francisco Pizarro conquista a los incas	Independencia del Perú

Las naciones del Cono Sur	1536	1724	1816	1818
	Primera fundación de Buenos Aires	Expulsión de los portugueses del Uruguay	Independencia de la Argentina, el Paraguay, el Uruguay	Independencia de Chile

España	a.C. 200	711–1492	1492	1500–1700
	Llegada de los romanos a la Península	Establecimiento del imperio moro en la Península	Reconquista de Granada; expulsión de los judíos de España; primer viaje de Cristóbal Colón	El Siglo de Oro

Los Estados Unidos y el Canadá	a.C. 800–d.C. 1600	1534	1600–1750	1776–1789
	Varias culturas indígenas	Jacques Cartier reclama el Canadá en nombre de Francia	Fundación de las colonias británicas	Guerra de la Independencia en los Estados Unidos